THE CAMBRIDGE WORLD HISTORY

*

VOLUME I

Volume I of *The Cambridge World History* is an introduction to both the discipline of world history and the earliest phases of world history up to 10,000 BCE. In Part I leading scholars outline the approaches, methods, and themes that have shaped and defined world history scholarship across the world and right up to the present day. Chapters examine the historiographical development of the field globally, periodization, divergence and convergence, belief and knowledge, technology and innovation, family, gender, anthropology, migration, and fire. Part II surveys the vast Paleolithic era, which laid the foundations for human history, and concentrates on the most recent phases of hominin evolution, the rise of *Homo sapiens* and the very earliest human societies through to the end of the last ice age. Anthropologists, archaeologists, historical linguists, and historians examine climate and tools, language, and culture, as well as offering regional perspectives from across the world.

DAVID CHRISTIAN is Professor of History at Macquarie University in Sydney. He is the author of *Maps of Time: An Introduction to Big History*, and co-founder with Bill Gates of the Big History Project.

The Cambridge World History is an authoritative new overview of the dynamic field of world history. It covers the whole of human history, not simply history since the development of written records, in an expanded time frame that represents the latest thinking in world and global history. With over two hundred essays, it is the most comprehensive account yet of the human past, and it draws on a broad international pool of leading academics from a wide range of scholarly disciplines. Reflecting the increasing awareness that world history can be examined through many different approaches and at varying geographic and chronological scales, each volume offers regional, topical, and comparative essays alongside case studies that provide depth of coverage to go with the breadth of vision that is the distinguishing characteristic of world history.

Editor-in-chief

MERRY E. WIESNER-HANKS, *Department of History, University of Wisconsin-Milwaukee*

Editorial Board

GRAEME BARKER, *Department of Archaeology, Cambridge University*
CRAIG BENJAMIN, *Department of History, Grand Valley State University*
JERRY BENTLEY, *Department of History, University of Hawaii*
DAVID CHRISTIAN, *Department of Modern History, Macquarie University*
ROSS DUNN, *Department of History, San Diego State University*
CANDICE GOUCHER, *Department of History, Washington State University*
MARNIE HUGHES-WARRINGTON, *Department of Modern History, Monash University*
ALAN KARRAS, *International and Area Studies Program, University of California, Berkeley*
BENJAMIN Z. KEDAR, *Department of History, Hebrew University*

THE CAMBRIDGE WORLD HISTORY

*

VOLUME I

Introducing World History,
to 10,000 BCE

*

Edited by

DAVID CHRISTIAN

Macquarie University

CAMBRIDGE
UNIVERSITY PRESS

CAMBRIDGE
UNIVERSITY PRESS

University Printing House, Cambridge CB2 8BS, United Kingdom

Cambridge University Press is part of the University of Cambridge.

It furthers the University's mission by disseminating knowledge in the pursuit of
education, learning and research at the highest international levels of excellence.

www.cambridge.org
Information on this title: www.cambridge.org/9780521763332

© Cambridge University Press 2015

First published 2015
Paperback edition first published 2017

Printed in the United Kingdom by TJ International Ltd., Padstow, Cornwall

A catalogue record for this publication is available from the British Library

Library of Congress Cataloguing in Publication data
The Cambridge world history.
volumes cm
Includes bibliographical references and index.
Contents: v. 1. Introducing world history (to 10,000 BCE) / edited by David Christian, Macquarie
University – v. 2. A world with agriculture, 12,000 BCE-400 CE – v. 3. Early cities and comparative history, 4000 BCE-1200 CE / edited by Norman Yoffee, University of Michigan – v. 4. A world
with states, empires, and networks, 1200 BCE-900 CE / edited by Craig Benjamin, Grand Valley State
University – v. 5. Expanding webs of exchange and conquest, 500 CE-1500 CE – v. 6, pt. 1. The
construction of a global world, 1400–1800 CE: Foundations – v. 6, pt. 2. The construction of a global
world, 1400–1800 CE: Patterns of change – v. 7, pt. 1. Production, destruction, and connection, 1750-
present : Structures, spaces, and boundary making – v. 7, pt. 2. Production, destruction, and
connection, 1750-present: Shared transformations.
ISBN 978-0-521-76333-2 (v. 1: Hardback : alk. Paper) – ISBN 978-0-521-19008-4 (v. 3: Hardback : alk.
paper) – ISBN 978-1-107-01572-2 (v. 4: Hardback : alk. paper) 1. World history.
D20.C195 2014
909–dc23 2014026364

ISBN 978-0-521-76333-2 Hardback
ISBN 978-1-108-40642-0 Paperback

Contents

Contents

Figures

Maps

Table

Contributors

DAVID CHRISTIAN, Macquarie University

LUKE CLOSSEY, Simon Fraser University

ROBIN DENNELL, University of Exeter

CHRISTOPHER EHRET, University of California, Los Angeles

FELIPE FERNÁNDEZ-ARMESTO, University of Notre Dame

JACK GOODY, University of Cambridge

JOHAN GOUDSBLOM, University of Amsterdam

DANIEL R. HEADRICK, Roosevelt University

PETER HISCOCK, University of Sydney

JOHN F. HOFFECKER, University of Colorado

MARNIE HUGHES-WARRINGTON, Australian National University, Canberra

MICHAEL LANG, University of Maine

PATRICK MANNING, Pittsburgh University

MARY JO MAYNES, University of Minnesota

DAVID R. NORTHRUP, Boston College

DOMINIC SACHSENMAIER, Jacobs University Bremen

NICOLE M. WAGUESPACK, University of Wyoming

ANN WALTNER, University of Minnesota

MERRY E. WIESNER-HANKS, University of Wisconsin-Milwaukee

Preface

The Cambridge Histories have long presented authoritative multi-volume overviews of historical topics, with chapters written by specialists. The first of these, the *Cambridge Modern History*, planned by Lord Acton, and appearing after his death, from 1902 to 1912, had fourteen volumes and served as the model for those that followed, which included the seven-volume *Cambridge Medieval History* (1911–1936), the twelve-volume *Cambridge Ancient History* (1924–1939), the thirteen-volume *Cambridge History of China* (1978–2009), and more specialized multi-volume works on countries, religions, regions, events, themes, and genres. These works are designed, as the *Cambridge History of China* puts it, to be the "largest and most comprehensive" history in the English language of their topic, and, as the *Cambridge History of Political Thought* asserts, to cover "every major theme."

The Cambridge World History both follows and breaks with the model set by its august predecessors. Presenting the "largest and most comprehensive" history of the world would take at least three hundred volumes – and a hundred years – as would covering "every major theme." Instead the series provides an overview of the dynamic field of world history in seven volumes over nine books. It covers all of human history, not simply that since the development of written records, in an expanded time frame that represents the newest thinking in world history. This broad time frame blurs the line between archaeology and history, and presents both as complementary approaches to the human past. The volume editors include archaeologists as well as historians, and have positions at universities in the United States, Britain, France, Australia, and Israel. The essays similarly draw on a broad author pool of historians, art historians, anthropologists, classicists, archaeologists, economists, linguists, sociologists, biologists, geographers, and area studies specialists, who come from universities in Australia, Britain, Canada, China, Estonia, France, Germany, India, Israel, Italy, Japan, the Netherlands, New Zealand, Poland, Portugal, Sweden, Switzerland,

Singapore, and the United States. They include very senior scholars whose works have helped to form the field, and also mid-career and younger scholars whose research will continue to shape it in the future. Some of the authors are closely associated with the rise of world history as a distinct research and teaching field, while others describe what they do primarily as global history, transnational history, international history, or comparative history. (Several of the essays in Volume I trace the development of these overlapping, entangled, and at times competing fields.) Many authors are simply specialists on their topic who the editors thought could best explain this to a broader audience or reach beyond their comfort zones into territory that was new.

Reflecting the increasing awareness that world history can be examined through many different approaches and at varying geographic and chronological scales, each volume offers several types of essays, including regional, topical, and comparative ones, along with case studies that provide depth to go with the breadth of vision that is the distinguishing characteristic of world history. Volume I introduces key frames of analysis that shape the making of world history across time periods, with essays on overarching approaches, methods, and themes. It then includes a group of essays on the Paleolithic, covering the 95 percent of human history up to 10,000 BCE. From that point on, each volume covers a shorter time period than its predecessor, with slightly overlapping chronologies volume to volume to reflect the complex periodization of a truly global history. The editors chose the overlapping chronologies, and stayed away from traditional period titles (for example, "classical" or "early modern") intentionally to challenge standard periodization to some degree. The overlapping chronologies also allow each volume to highlight geographic disjunctures and imbalances, and the ways in which various areas influenced one another. Each of the volumes centers on a key theme or cluster of themes that the editors view as central to the period covered in the volume and also as essential to an understanding of world history as a whole.

Volume II (*A World with Agriculture, 12,000 BCE–500 CE*) begins with the Neolithic, but continues into later periods to explore the origins of agriculture and agricultural communities in various regions of the world, as well as to discuss issues associated with pastoralism and hunter-fisher-gatherer economies. It traces common developments in the more complex social structures and cultural forms that agriculture enabled, and then presents a series of regional overviews accompanied by detailed case studies from many different parts of the world.

Volume III (*Early Cities and Comparative History, 4000 BCE–1200 CE*) focuses on early cities as motors of change in human society. Through case studies of cities and comparative chapters that address common issues, it traces the creation and transmission of administrative and information technologies, the performance of rituals, the distribution of power, and the relationship of cities with their hinterlands. It has a broad and flexible chronology to capture the development of cities in various regions of the world and the transformation of some cities into imperial capitals.

Volume IV (*A World with States, Empires and Networks, 1200 BCE–900 CE*) continues the analysis of processes associated with the creation of larger-scale political entities and networks of exchange, including those generally featured in accounts of the rise of "classical civilizations," but with an expanded time frame that allows the inclusion of more areas of the world. It analyzes common social, economic, cultural, political, and technological developments, and includes chapters on slavery, religion, science, art, and gender. It then presents a series of regional overviews, each accompanied by a case study or two examining one smaller geographic area or topic within that region in greater depth.

Volume V (*Expanding Webs of Exchange and Conquest, 500 CE–1500 CE*) highlights the growing networks of trade and cross-cultural interaction that were a hallmark of the millennium covered in the volume, including the expansion of text-based religions and the transmission of science, philosophy, and technology. It explores social structures, cultural institutions, and significant themes such as the environment, warfare, education, the family, and courtly cultures on both a global and Eurasian scale, and continues the examination of state formation begun in Volume 4 with chapters on polities and empires in Asia, Africa, Europe, and the Americas.

The first five volumes each appear in a single book, but the last two are double volumes covering the periods conventionally known as the early modern and modern, an organization signaling the increasing complexity of an ever more globalized world in the last half millennium, as well as the expanding base of source materials and existing historical analyses for these more recent eras. Volume VI (*The Construction of a Global World, 1400–1800 CE*) traces the increasing biological, commercial, and cultural exchanges of the period, and explores regional and transregional political, cultural, and intellectual developments. The first book within this volume, "Foundations," focuses on global matrices that allowed this increasingly interdependent world to be created, including the environment, technology, and disease; crossroads and macro-regions such as the Caribbean, the Indian Ocean, and

Southeast Asia in which connections were especially intense; and large-scale political formations, particularly maritime and land-based empires such as Russia, the Islamic Empires, and the Iberian Empires that stretched across continents and seas. The second book within this volume, "Patterns of Change," examines global and regional migrations and encounters, and the economic, social, cultural, and institutional structures that both shaped and were shaped by these, including trade networks, law, commodity flows, production processes, and religious systems.

Volume VII (*Production, Destruction, and Connection, 1750–Present*) examines the uneven transition to a world with fossil fuels and an exploding human population that has grown ever more interactive through processes of globalization. The first book within this double volume, "Structures, Spaces, and Boundary Making," discusses the material situations within which our crowded world has developed, including the environment, agriculture, technology, energy, and disease; the political movements that have shaped it, such as nationalism, imperialism, decolonization, and communism; and some of its key regions. The second book, "Shared Transformations?" explores topics that have been considered in earlier volumes, including the family, urbanization, migration, religion, and science, along with some that only emerge as global phenomena in this era, such as sports, music, and the automobile, as well as specific moments of transition, including the Cold War and 1989.

Taken together, the volumes contain about two hundred essays, which means *The Cambridge World History* is comprehensive, but certainly not exhaustive. Each volume editor has made difficult choices about what to include and what to leave out, a problem for all world histories since those of Herodotus and Sima Qian more than two millennia ago. Each volume is arranged in the way that the volume editor or editors decided is most appropriate for the period, so that organizational schema differ slightly from volume to volume. Given the overlapping chronologies, certain topics are covered in several different volumes because they are important for understanding the historical processes at the heart of each of these, and because we as editors decided that viewing key developments from multiple perspectives is particularly appropriate for world history. As with other Cambridge Histories, the essays are relatively lightly footnoted, and include a short list of further readings, the first step for readers who want to delve deeper into the field. In contrast to other Cambridge Histories, all volumes are being published at the same time, for the leisurely pace of the print world that allowed publication over several decades does not fit with twenty-first-century digital demands.

In other ways as well, *The Cambridge World History* reflects the time in which it has been conceptualized and produced, just as *The Cambridge Modern History* did. Lord Acton envisioned his work, and Cambridge University Press described it, as "a history of the world," although in only a handful of chapters out of several hundred were the principal actors individuals, groups, or polities outside of Europe and North America. This is not surprising, although the identical self-description of the *New Cambridge Modern History* (1957–1979), with a similar balance of topics, might be a bit more so. The fact that in 1957 – and even in 1979, when the last volume of the series appeared – Europe would be understood as "the world" and as the source of all that was modern highlights the power and longevity of the perspective we have since come to call "Eurocentric." (In other languages, there are perspectives on world history that are similarly centered on the regions in which they have been produced.) The continued focus on Europe in the mid-twentieth century also highlights the youth of the fields of world and global history, in which the conferences, professional societies, journals, and other markers of an up-and-coming field have primarily emerged since the 1980s, and some only within the last decade. The *Journal of World History*, for example, was first published in 1990, the *Journal of Global History* in 2005, and *New Global Studies* in 2007.

World and global history have developed in an era of intense self-reflection in all academic disciplines, when no term can be used unself-consciously and every category must be complicated. Worries about inclusion and exclusion, about diversity and multivocality are standard practice in sub-fields of history and related disciplines that have grown up in this atmosphere. Thus as we editors sought topics that would give us a balance between the traditional focus in world history on large-scale political and economic processes carried out by governments and commercial elites and newer concerns with cultural forms, representation, and meaning, we also sought to include topics that have been important in different national historiographies. We also attempted to find authors who would provide geographic balance along with a balance between older and younger voices. Although the author pool is decidedly broader geographically – and more balanced in terms of gender – than it was in either of the Cambridge Modern Histories, it is not as global as we had hoped. Contemporary world and global history is overwhelmingly Anglophone, and, given the scholarly diaspora, disproportionately institutionally situated in the United States and the United Kingdom. Along with other disparities in our contemporary world, this disproportion is, of course, the result of the developments traced in this series, though the authors might disagree about which volume holds the key to its origins, or whether one should spend much time searching for origins at all.

My hopes for the series are not as sweeping as Lord Acton's were for his, but fit with those of Tapan Raychaudhuri and Irfan Habib, the editors of the two-volume *Cambridge Economic History of India* (1982). In the preface to their work, they comment: "We only dare to hope that our collaborative effort will stimulate discussion and help create new knowledge which may replace before many years the information and analysis offered in this volume." In a field as vibrant as world and global history, I have no doubts that such new transformative knowledge will emerge quickly, but hope this series will provide an entrée to the field, and a useful overview of its state in the early twenty-first century.

MERRY E. WIESNER-HANKS

Acknowledgments

I have received a lot of help in editing this volume. First, I would like to thank Merry Wiesner-Hanks, who played a huge role in putting this volume together, as she did with all the volumes in this series. Second, I would like to thank Marnie Hughes-Warrington, who worked with me as we planned the basic structure of this volume. I would like to thank all the authors for their efficiency in getting papers to me and handling queries, and for their patience as this volume came together over several years. Finally, I would like to thank the editorial staff at CUP, in particular Michael Watson and the Copy-editor Julene Knox.

Introduction and overview

DAVID CHRISTIAN

As Merry Wiesner-Hanks writes in her series preface, the *Cambridge World History* is authoritative and comprehensive, but not exhaustive. World history must limit its ambitions precisely because its scope is so vast, so an exhaustive history of humanity, like a map the same size as the landscape it charts, would be of little use because it would have avoided the hard work of distillation. This is why world historians have to be good at selecting. The chapters in Volume I are indeed authoritative; they cover a great deal of territory (literally and metaphorically); but they are not exhaustive. Like all the best scholarship in world history, they try to convey both the detailed texture of human history and its major themes and trajectories.

Volume I is introductory in two distinct senses. Part I is about world history as a sub-discipline of history, while Part II is about the earliest phases of world history.

Part I introduces approaches, methods, and themes that have shaped and defined scholarship in world history. It ranges over world history as a whole, but does not visit every village and province. For readers new to the field, these chapters can illustrate the diversity of approaches that historians have brought to the project of world history. For world historians, they will offer recapitulations of important themes and approaches, and introductions to some less familiar aspects of world history. Many of the themes and topics introduced here are taken up with greater chronological and geographic specificity in the chapters in the second part, and also in later volumes in the series.

I have received a lot of help in editing this volume. First, I would like to thank Merry Wiesner-Hanks, who played a huge role in putting this volume together, as she did with all the volumes in this series. Second, I would like to thank Marnie Hughes-Warrington, who worked with me as we planned the basic structure of this volume. The overall shape of the volume owes much to Marnie I would like to thank all the authors for their efficiency in getting papers to me and handling queries, and for their patience as this volume came together over several years. Finally, I would like to thank the editorial staff at CUP and in particular Michael Watson and Julene Knox.

Part ii surveys the earliest phases of human history during the Paleolithic era: the vast period extending back hundreds of thousands of years, in which our human and hominin ancestors laid the foundations for human history. As is appropriate in a volume intended mainly for those interested in the human past, it concentrates on the most recent phases of hominin evolution, the rise of our own strange species, *Homo sapiens*, and the very earliest human societies. Part ii closes at the end of the last ice age, just over 10,000 years ago, when in some parts of the world some of our ancestors took up agriculture. Agriculture allowed human communities to divert more and more of the biosphere's energy income to their own support, and is explored in depth in Volume 2 of this series, *A World with Agriculture*. The resulting energy bonanza would drive human history into utterly new pathways, transforming human communities and accelerating the pace of change throughout the world, developments examined in Volumes 3 through 7 of this series.

This Introduction summarizes the chapters in the two parts of Volume 1. It describes some of the main themes of each chapter and makes comparisons among them, but inevitably skips most of the evidential detail and interpretative nuance. Like world history itself, it is a distillation, in this case a distillation of distillations, but some readers may want to use it as an extended table of contents before going on to the chapters themselves.

Part 1: Historiography, methods, and themes

As a sub-discipline of the modern history discipline, world history is surprisingly new. In the words of the late Jerry Bentley: 'As it has developed since the 1960s and particularly since the 1980s, the new world history has focused attention on comparisons, connections, networks, and systems rather than the experiences of individual communities or discrete societies'.[1] Most modern world historians have been trained as historians, so they accept the discipline's ground rules. But they also try to move beyond the national frames and evidential ground rules that shaped and limited historical scholarship in the nineteenth and twentieth centuries. As many chapters in this volume show, world historians have worked particularly hard (though with qualified success) to escape the Eurocentrism of so much earlier historical scholarship: the sometimes unquestioned assumption that if it

---

1 Jerry H. Bentley, 'The Task of World History', in Jerry H. Bentley (ed.), *The Oxford Handbook of World History*, Oxford: Oxford University Press, 2011, p. 2.

didn't happen in Europe or the West, it probably wasn't original or significant or influential.

The impulse to a more global understanding of the past has been driven in part by globalization and decolonization. Shifts in the global balance of economic, military, and even intellectual power and increasing global connections between scholars have exposed the severe conceptual and empirical limitations of the nationalistic and Eurocentric attitudes to the past that dominated historical scholarship in earlier centuries. The same pressures have encouraged more and more historians to explore the past as part of a shared human heritage. Paradoxically, that move has also taught us that world history is not as new as it may seem at first sight. Indeed, some form of world history can be found in most human cultures.

As Marnie Hughes-Warrington points out in her brief history of world history in **Chapter 2**, we find many different labels for the same core project. They include 'universal history', 'global history', 'transnational history', 'macrohistory', 'comparative history', 'big history', and more. She also points out that, whatever we call it, the world history project is ancient. All attempts to make sense of the past depend on imagining a coherent and meaningful 'world' of some kind, though they vary in the extent to which 'the purpose of world construction is explicit'. But as this suggests, constructing a world that is *ours* also encourages an interest in the worlds of *others*. Over 2,000 years ago, Herodotus in Greece and Sima Qian in Han China drew sharp lines between their own world of civilization and the barbarous realms beyond the borders. For some writers, gender divided the barbarian from the non-barbarian: witness the contrast between Christine de Pizan's *The Book of the City of Ladies* (1405), a 'universal history of female warriors, good wives and saintly women', and Joseph Swetnam's *The Arraignment of Lewd, Idle and Forward Women* (1615), which insisted that women, being fashioned from Adam's rib, are 'crooked by nature'.

Printing, the 'philosophical turn' of the Enlightenment, and the professionalization of scholarship in the nineteenth century might have helped erase these lines, but in practice, they redrew them. Historians became entranced by the nation state and the challenge of constructing national histories; and world history fell into disfavour. Much world history continued to be written, often outside the formal structures of the history profession, but from the late nineteenth century, professional historians began to frown on the practice. From the middle of the twentieth century, new themes for historical research, including modernization, world-systems, area studies, and post-colonial studies encouraged new ways of framing historical problems.

So, too, did new approaches to history in general, including gender history (Chapter 10), environmental history, and the rapid increase in research on inherently worldish themes such as migration (Chapter 12). This broadening of the scope of historical research, along with increasing global integration, helps explain the modern revival of world history within the institutional structures and conventions of modern historical scholarship.

Dominic Sachsenmaier's **Chapter 3** also surveys the history of world history. But while Hughes-Warrington notes the importance of world history scholarship outside the academy, Sachsenmaier focuses on secular academic writing in world history. He agrees that in some sense all history is world history, because every community and every historian understands the past as the past of a particular 'world'.

> In any culture and time period, the history of the world could only possibly mean the history of one's own world, that is, the world one was exposed to through lived experiences, personal travels and the accounts of others. In that sense, the worlds of a fourteenth-century Maya, a Northern European, a Japanese or a Polynesian were certainly unlike each other. Yet at the same time they had a decisive element in common: they all reached far beyond single political realms or cultural habitats.

Of course, such world histories always had to take notice of 'others', so that Sachsenmaier, like Hughes-Warrington, notes a fault line in all early world histories (and perhaps within the very nature of world history) between our world and the world of others, a tension visible at least from the time of Herodotus and Sima Qian and apparent also in Muslim historiography. Indeed, the very idea of world history seems to imply an interest in what lies beyond 'our' world.

From the sixteenth century, the number of possible 'other worlds' multiplied. Connections with worlds never imagined before helped detach world histories from their traditional roots, particularly in Europe. The creation of the first global networks of exchange prompted the earliest attempts to write history on planetary scales, such as George Sale's 65-volume *Universal History*, published between 1747 and 1768. But globalization also sharpened the familiar dichotomies of world histories, now re-cast as contrasts between Europe and the rest of the world. European writers as influential as G. W. F. Hegel, Karl Marx, and Max Weber put Europe at the centre of their global vision, and pushed other regions to the margins: 'Generally speaking, the rest of the world was seen as too far behind the Western engine to be seriously studied as a guide or reference'. Eurocentric world histories became less Universal and less 'worldish'.

4

Globalization also shaped historiographical traditions outside of Europe, but in different ways. Outside the emerging 'West', national historiographical traditions emerged in tension with or opposition to the history of the West, which was often re-classified as 'world history'. Here, therefore, 'world history' gained in importance because it meant the study of 'the West'. Professionalization of the history discipline, often on European models, heightened the sense of European exceptionalism. Even Jawaharlal Nehru's *Glimpses of World History*, though critical of the West, treated the West as paradigmatic of historical processes in general. So, too, did the historiography of most Communist societies, which retained the vision and spirit of Marx's Eurocentric accounts of world history.

In the twentieth century, several historians tried to break with overly Eurocentric approaches to the past. They include Oswald Spengler, who offered a vision of a declining West; Arnold Toynbee, who described a world of multiple distinct 'civilizations'; William McNeill, who stressed the importance of connections between civilizations; and other historiographical traditions such as world-systems historiography and the Négritude Movement. But their impact on historiography was limited until after the collapse of Communism in the last decade of the twentieth century. The breakdown of Cold War divisions gave a powerful new impetus to research on global processes and global connections, which is why world history can seem like a new historiographical project. But even today, and even in work produced by world historians, there remains a complex but powerful tension between traditional ways of framing the past around regions or nations (traditions still supported by the educational policies of most governments), and attempts at more global accounts of the past, 'bordercrossing scholarship', as Sachsenmaier calls it. We should not expect a homogeneous global historical scholarship to emerge from these efforts, but what we can expect is increasing dialogue between different traditions of world history scholarship.

In **Chapter 4**, Michael Lang tackles the problem of periodization. Though fundamental to all historical writing, periodization takes distinctive forms and raises distinctive problems within world history. 'To use the language of Kracauer and Adorno, the historiographical period is a "force field." It is pulled between poles of chronology and immanence, perpetually in tension, and without resolution'. By its very nature, the idea of a period hints at 'the universal of time, and therefore indicates, even when unexpressed, the history of the world'. Lang describes a series of attempts within modern historiography to manage the tension between the particular, and what Leopold von Ranke called the 'great whole' of universal history.

When Ranke wrote, periodizations based on national histories were already shaping much historical scholarship. But most historians retained a sense of multiple times, from those of evolution or geology ('nature's epochs' in Comte de Buffon's phrase), to the 'innumerable times, all at one time' of Johann Gottfried Herder. Ranke saw the nation itself as a partial resolution of the tensions between universality and particularity. The state itself was a sort of universal, integrating many within a larger unity; but of course each state was also its own specific universal. At times, though, even Ranke found the tensions insoluble, at least for humans: 'God alone knows world history. We perceive the contradictions'.

Other nineteenth-century historians were equally sceptical of universals, and equally captivated by the strange universal of the nation state. William Stubbs wrote that history showed endless differentiation rather than 'elemental unity'; yet he wrote, too, of a larger English national identity. At a more practical level, of course, the state provided a sort of methodological universal in the nineteenth century because it shaped not just the thinking of historians, but also the institutions they worked in and the conventions that shaped their careers and scholarship. And, as if to illustrate the tensions that frustrated Ranke, each state shaped historical scholarship in its own distinctive way.

In the twentieth century, the national conflicts that helped generate two World Wars undermined the assumption that the nation state offered a natural frame for historical periodization. But what could replace it? Toynbee offered civilizations. McNeill offered the world as a whole and the history of humanity as an evolutionary process. Was there a 'meaningful past' shared by humanity as a whole? McNeill found periodizations for such a past in processes of cultural diffusion (or even epidemiological diffusion) that linked large areas through evolutionary patterns of change. McNeill was not alone in seeking new universals. But is there a danger that, as Lang puts it, world history merely 'shifts the spiritual unity of the nation onto the world as a whole'? Many modern historians and historiographers have been deeply suspicious of such apparently universalizing projects. Martin Heidegger, Michel Foucault, and Jacques Derrida insisted on the selectiveness of universalist histories and the roles they played as ideologies and as forms of power. But what was the alternative? Was it perhaps to move back towards the specific and the contingent, towards the world of lived experience? In 1956, Roland Barthes wrote: 'It seems that this is a difficulty of our epoch . . . either posit a reality which is entirely permeable by history and ideologize; or else, inversely, posit a reality ultimately impenetrable, irreducible, and in this case, poeticize'. So, while attempts at world history moved towards universality, postmodern or post-colonial history moved towards particularity. 'Between these poles – chronology and immanence, evolution and rupture, universality and meaning – historiography employs the period'.

While Lang's chapter sees no easy resolution to the problem of periodization in world history, in **Chapter 5** David Northrup defends a powerful but extraordinarily simple periodization of human history. For most of human history we see divergence and diversification. But then, during the last thousand years, we begin to see convergence everywhere. 'At some point, centrifugal forces for global divergence began to be overtaken by centripetal forces for convergence. Despite some interruptions, that trend continued and gradually gained momentum. This was the Great Convergence'.

As Northrup points out, the most influential historical periodizations have cut across the very project of world history. Some, such as the traditional European partitioning of the past into Ancient, Medieval, and Modern periods, work best for particular regions; while some periodizations ignore everything before Sumer; and others ban the historical study of today's world. Yet world history cannot ignore the problem of periodization without turning into a random collection of local histories. The simple periodization Northrup proposes really is global; it embraces the whole of human history; and it encourages discussion of future trajectories.

For most of human history long-distance exchanges were limited, and each community constructed its own distinctive history. Genomes diverged, so did languages, lifeways, and religious beliefs and rituals. Early modern Papua New Guinea illustrates the spectacular possibilities for linguistic divergence. Here, 1 million people spoke 500 distinct languages from 33 different language families. Similarly, a single proto-Bantu language split into 250 different languages in less than 3,000 years. In retrospect, historians can see the commonality between these languages; contemporaries were surely more aware of the differences.

Today, though, the commonalities are more apparent. English and Spanish have spread not as language families, but as single languages, while many local languages are dying out so that the total number of languages is declining fast. Meanwhile, diseases, technologies, and conflicts (or news of conflicts) hurtle around the globe, creating what V. S. Naipaul called 'universal civilization'. When did convergence become the dominant trend? Regular contacts between all parts of the world began only in the sixteenth century, but Northrup argues that convergence has deeper roots. We find important exchanges of people, goods, ideas, and ritual objects deep in the Paleolithic. In the last 5,000 years, empires and trading diasporas multiplied exchanges of goods, ideas, fashions, and religions. When did the balance tip? Northrup inspects several possible dates before opting for 1,000 CE, when, as John Man argued, one can for the first time imagine a message being transmitted right around the inhabited world. Perhaps, as Northrup argues, the problem of periodization in world history is not quite as intractable as some historians imagine.

In Chapter 6, Luke Clossey explores the world history of ideas and thought. Can there be a world history of belief, knowledge, and language? This chapter, too, is shaped by the problem of Eurocentrism. It tracks the evolution of the idea that European science and secularism have colonized the world of thought, and it asks if a world history of ideas should or can yield a more ecumenical history of human thought.

In fact, as Clossey points out, there has been little 'world history' of ideas. 'Most of our books about knowledge are in fact about Euro-knowledge, rather than about the Wider World's ethno-knowledges'. Even the idea of 'ethno-knowledges' implicitly distinguishes them from 'knowledge' pure and simple, which is assumed to work everywhere, while ethno-knowledges are assumed to work only on their home grounds. Can we (particularly if 'we' are historians based in the 'West') possibly study ideas or beliefs free of such assumptions?

Some of the earliest attempts at a worldish understanding of religion and language were European, the products of some of the earliest global empires. But they launched a tradition of comparative scholarship that, in retrospect, seems surprisingly un-Eurocentric. That tradition begins with the work of William Jones, an English judge in British Bengal who lived in the eighteenth century and initiated the comparative study of languages and religions. The tradition he began was continued in the work of the philologist, Max Müller, and in that of George Sarton, who founded a journal on the history of science, called *Isis*, in 1927. Sarton came to appreciate the crucial role of Muslim science and duly learnt Arabic to pursue this insight.

Eventually, though, historians of thought became dissatisfied with the broad generalizations of the pioneers, and began to narrow the scope of their work, focusing increasingly on regional traditions, which they often portrayed as foils to modern European science. Seeing European thought itself as a local tradition is not easy, though there have been some remarkable attempts, such as Eric Wolf's *Europe and the People Without History*, and Dipesh Chakrabarty's *Provincializing Europe*. But even these help us do little more than nibble at the edges of Eurocentrism in the world history of thought.

The rest of Clossey's chapter assesses the nature and extent of Eurocentrism in debates over four worldish topics: hominization (the processes by which our ancestors became human), the idea of the Axial Age, the study of the European Scientific Revolution, and the idea that religion is in decline in the modern world. In all four discussions, he finds that Eurocentrism survives in subtle and not-so-subtle forms, despite growing awareness of its limitations. For example, it might seem that the study of hominization has to be 'worldish'; yet even here it is possible to identify subtle forms of Eurocentrism, if only because so many of those who study the subject are European or Western. (Some of the consequences will be discussed in Chapter 16.)

And this may lead to the heart of the problem of Eurocentrism; so much world history is the work of 'Western' scholars. So it is hardly surprising if a casual survey of courses and textbooks used in the University of Cambridge yields a list of 'knowledge makers' that is overwhelmingly European. Similarly, a quick survey of modern world history textbooks shows that science looms large in accounts of Western societies, while religion looms larger in accounts of non-Western societies. Is it surprising if a world history dominated by Western scholars is Eurocentric? And even if we can imagine a non-Eurocentric world history of thought, will it simply be from the perspective of another 'centrism', like the delightful *Beijing History of the World*, published in the year 2174, with which Clossey ends his chapter?

In Chapter 7, Dan Headrick explores a specific but critical aspect of intellectual history: the history of technology and innovation. Headrick defines technology as: 'the use of materials, energy, and living beings for practical purposes'. Of course, we can identify technologies in many non-human species. But humans are so good at dreaming up new technologies, and technological innovation has given our species such power over our surroundings (and over each other), that technological innovation counts as a defining feature of humanity, and a fundamental driver of human history. Despite this, the history of technology is a relatively new field of historical research; it is hard to trace it back much further than the Enlightenment and the *Encyclopédie* (1751–72). The first serious scholarly treatment of the history of technology is Johann Heinrich Moritz von Poppe's *Geschichte aller Erfindungen und Entdeckungen im Bereiche der Gewerbe, Künste und Wissenschaften von der frühesten Zeit bis auf unsere Tage* (History of all the Inventions and Discoveries in the Trades, Arts, and Sciences from Earliest Times to Our Day), first published in 1837. In the decades that followed, many scholars and thinkers, including Marx, took up the idea that technological innovation might be a fundamental driver of historical change. As Marx famously wrote in 1847, in his critique of Pierre-Joseph Proudhon, *The Poverty of Philosophy*: 'The windmill gives you society with the feudal lord; the steam-mill, society with the industrial capitalist'. Such claims raised a fundamental question for historians: if technological innovation is a powerful driver, what drives technological innovation?

Rapid technological change stimulated popular interest in technology in the nineteenth century. That interest was evident in the great exhibitions, beginning with the French industrial exposition of 1844; in the building of museums of science and technology, and museums dedicated to particular technologies, such as the railways; as well as in exhibitions such as Sturbridge Village in Massachusetts, which recreated displays of traditional technologies such as blacksmithing. *Scientific American*, a journal dedicated to disseminating information about science and technology, was founded in 1845. Popular interest in technology was normally, as Headrick puts it, 'Whiggish'. It assumed that technological and scientific change represented progress; and it assumed technological determinism – the belief that technological innovation drove historical change. Like many other historical sub-disciplines, the history of technology also fell into the force field of nationalistic historiography, as historians defended national claims for technological leadership. Was it a Briton, William Fox Talbot, who invented photography, or a Frenchman, Louis Daguerre? Was it a Frenchman, Clément Ader, who pioneered heavier-than-air flight, or the American brothers, Orville and Wilbur Wright?

Modern scholarship in the history of technology really begins in the twentieth century. George Sarton's multi-volume history of science was exceptionally broad in its approach and particularly in its willingness to highlight the achievements of Islamic science. Classic studies, such as those of Lewis Mumford and Abbott Payson Usher, also approached the history of technology with unusual sophistication. But much scholarship remained nationalistic and individualistic, focusing largely on the work of individual inventors.

The history of technology matured as a field after the Second World War, with the emergence of new journals and scholarly societies (such as the Society for the History of Technology, SHOT). The field became less Whiggish, more interested in technological failures, and less interested in the national origins of particular technologies. The International Committee for the History of Technology, founded in 1968, encouraged a more global approach; while scholarship by Joseph Needham and Vaclav Smil helped undermine the field's Eurocentric traditions. Needham's work, possibly the most important scholarship in the field in the twentieth century, raised the possibility that China was the world's technological leader until the fifteenth century. Global studies of particular technologies, such as firearms, demonstrated the extent to which innovation depended on (or in some cases was limited by) cultural diffusion. The work of Leslie White helped encourage interest in ancient technologies and the archaeology and anthropology of technology. Social historians and gender historians began to explore the social contexts and social consequences of innovation; Ruth Schwartz showed, for example, how labour-saving technologies could increase the burden of domestic labour.

As the field becomes both more mature and more global, we see increasing research into the social roots of innovation within international networks of commercial and informational exchange. Are we at last approaching a genuinely worldish history of technology, an update, perhaps, of von Poppe or Sarton for the twenty-first century?

In Chapter 8, Johan Goudsblom explores a particular cluster of technologies: those associated with fire. All human societies control fire, but no other species does. So fire management counts as a 'species monopoly', a defining feature of our species and our history. The ability to manage fire is also a clear product of cultural accumulation or 'collective learning'. So, we can say that the human relationship to fire is 'unique, universal, and cultural'. Though the early history of fire management remains unclear, there is a case for counting it as the first technological threshold in human history.

Fire is a form of energy and, like all forms of energy it can be used to manipulate matter. But to manage fire you need information, so to understand how humans have managed fire, we need the conceptual triad of energy, matter, and information. Fires need oxygen, so they must have been rare and short-lived before the appearance of an oxygen-rich atmosphere 2–3 billion years ago. They also require fuel, which probably means they were rare before the spread of plants on land in the last 400 million years. Finally, fires need temperatures high enough for ignition, but these can be supplied by many natural forces including lightning. So our hominin ancestors must surely have been familiar with fire, like all living organisms today.

There must have been a long period of increasing familiarity with fire, which is discussed in recent work by Frances Burton. Then, at some point in the last 2 million years, our ancestors became the first species capable of managing fire, creating it at will, and harnessing it to their own purposes, using accumulating cultural information to do so. The earliest firm dates for controlled use of fire by hominins date from 250,000 years ago, though some archaeologists have argued that there is good evidence of fire management from Israel and South Africa as early as 800,000 years ago.

As the great sociologist Norbert Elias would have insisted, controlling fire also surely meant increasing control by humans over their own behaviour. One of these behaviours may have been cooking. Richard Wrangham has argued that fire was critical in human evolution because it allowed our ancestors to cook (in other words to 'pre-digest') high-value foods such as meat, or foods that were toxic or could not be digested raw. The technology of cooking represented an energy revolution for our ancestors, as it provided high-energy foods in easily digestible forms that used little metabolic energy. A shortening of the human gut within the last 2 million years may be an indirect sign of the importance of cooking and therefore of fire management. Fire also offered an important defensive weapon, as well as a focus for increasing sociability. In the form of what is known in Australia as 'fire-stick farming', fire also provided a foretaste of agricultural intensification, as it was used to increase the productivity of the land.

Fire played a vital role in the second great technological revolution of human history: agrarianization. Farmers increased the production of favoured species of plants and animals by re-arranging the environments they inhabited. By doing so, they increased the resources and energy available to human beings. Fire was used to clear land (in slash and burn farming), so it was responsible for much of the deforestation of the Neolithic era. New and more specialized uses of fire also encouraged an emerging division of labour in occupations from blacksmithing to soldiering. On the other hand, fire brought new forms of danger, especially in towns and cities, whose closely clustered houses and workshops, each with its own fireplaces, provided the fuel and ignition for many a conflagration. Fire was both necessary and terrible. Not surprisingly, it looms large in myths and religions, as a godlike force, or as a power to be seized and used, as in the Prometheus legend.

Fire technologies also drove the third great technological revolution, that of industrialization, which depended on vast new supplies of fuel from coal, oil, and natural gas. Unlike traditional fuels such as wood, which released energy accumulated over just a few decades of photosynthesis, fossil fuels stored energy accumulated over hundreds of millions of years. The 'subterranean forest' of fossil fuels (as Rolf Peter Sieferle described it) drove new and vastly more powerful technologies of manufacturing and transportation. Concentrated forms of fire also became important as weapons of war; even most victims of nuclear weapons died from fire. Eventually, electrification allowed the indirect consumption of the energy of fire because the fires that supply electricity do their work far from the point of consumption. That may be why, today, it is so easy to ignore the role of fire in our lives. And that, in turn, may explain why today we talk of 'energy' rather than using the more vivid, even animistic images of fire present in most earlier societies. But fire itself is still omnipresent, both as a source of energy and as a source of danger, even if it prefers to work behind the scenes. Eventually, though, if we keep using the energy of fire on today's scales, we may have to acquire it in new forms, perhaps by finding new ways of tapping its energy directly from the largest source of fire in our solar system, the sun.

From technologies to social institutions. Chapter 9, by Mary Jo Maynes and Ann Waltner, discusses the family and household as central themes within world history. They suggest using the concepts of 'domestication' and 'biopolitics' to link family history and global history. Many archaeologists have used the term, 'domestication', to refer not just to the Neolithic era domestication of plants and animals, but also to the self-domestication of humans, and the emergence of new forms of family with 'the cultural invention of *human* domestic life'. Indeed, the Neolithic family and household were vital to human self-domestication. Clive Gamble argues that the earliest Neolithic communities may have been the first 'to develop fully modern minds and a fully symbolic culture'. Such approaches point to a powerful dialectic between the family and the state. They have encouraged research into families as objects of legislation and control, as key structures in the exercise of both political and commercial power, and as managers of labour and consumption. The notion of 'biopolitics' stresses the importance of political control over human bodies including attempts to count and measure them, and to regulate fertility and family structures. Michel Foucault famously described spectacular examples of biopolitical regulation in the modern world, but biopolitics, like domestication, can be traced back at least to the early Neolithic.

Of course, family relations of some kind pre-date the Neolithic both in the real world and in the world of scholarship. Until the 1970s, the widely accepted notion of 'Man the Hunter' implied a Paleolithic world of acquisition and production driven by the activities of males and a reproductive world of females shaped by biology rather than by culture. Feminist revisions of these models, and new interpretations of the scattered archaeological evidence, have highlighted the central role of females in production, the constructed nature even of Paleolithic families and their reproductive behaviour, and the importance of households in demographic behaviour, and in the education and socialization of children.

Given the importance of women as gatherers in many foraging societies, it is likely that women played a significant role in the transition to agriculture. Indeed, genetic evidence suggests that marriages between communities of farmers and foragers may have helped spread agricultural technologies and lifeways. Clive Gamble has argued that the Neolithic Revolution transformed patterns of child rearing and socialization, creating entirely new 'childscapes', new environments that transformed childhood experiences. Ian Hodder argues that the family and household were critical agents of socialization. For example, environments such as the cheek-by-jowl residences of the famous Turkish site of Çatalhöyük created childscapes that taught children how society and social networks were organized: 'important elements of social organization – cooperative production following a division of labor, settlement building, and kinship rules – all emerged without any form of the state. Social complexity here too focused on the local and the household'. The household could teach even deeper rules. In Çatalhöyük, internal burials connected the past to the future through distinct generations, creating a powerful sense of the movement of time. Such structures even carried cosmological information. For example, Egyptian cosmologies tell of gods linked by family ties, within which each god had its own distinctive role within a larger family network. Thus, in one telling, 'Isis discovered seeds and Osiris taught the Egyptian people how to plant them'. The monotheistic religions, on the other hand, offered cosmologies that implied clear gender hierarchies, and it is tempting to associate them with the emergence of new forms of patriarchy. However, religious cosmologies could also seem at odds with family structures, for example when they idealized celibacy, as Buddhism did in some forms.

Families provided idealized templates for states and political structures. Male rulers often represented themselves as members of ancient descent lineages through the male line, while Chinese philosophers described a well-ordered state on the analogy of a well-ordered family. The metaphors cut both ways: 'likening the power of the king to that of the father naturalized both masculine political power and masculine authority in the household'. The result was a sort of naturalization of political power, making its rules and authority seem as self-evident as those of the family. And that, perhaps, explains why from the very earliest states, rulers tried to regulate family structures. Fully a third of Hammurabi's law code of the eighteenth century BCE was concerned with the family. Less metaphorically, family structures often provided the sinews of political power and determined political rights such as citizenship.

Precisely because family structures seemed so self-evident, those who encountered new rules about marriage, kinship, and sexuality often found them peculiarly shocking. Such encounters multiplied from the sixteenth century. In Southeast Asia, traders from Europe and China were horrified by marriage practices that simplified divorce and allowed women to engage actively and publicly in commerce. Such reactions help explain why colonial rulers, such as those of New Spain, worked so hard to impose their own ideas and laws about how families should function. On the other hand, slave owners made and re-made the family structures of their slaves according to commercial calculations. In these ways, early forms of globalization began to transform kinship structures and ideas in many parts of the world.

As families changed so, too, did the metaphors they provided for the organization of social and political life. Lynn Hunt showed how, during the French Revolution, the idea of fraternity challenged older metaphors of paternal authority. As modern states extended their administrative reach, they began to measure and regulate domestic life in greater detail and with greater success than ever before, until in the twentieth century, biopolitics, 'the routine state surveillance, measurement, and management of human life', became a normal function of governments throughout the world. The most brutal forms of family regulation were associated with colonial regimes, or with the family and racial politics of fascism and the ideas of eugenics. But in more modest forms, the rules of family life – who can marry whom, what the ideal family should look like, and how big it should be – have become routine objects for government regulation, bringing the two domains of government and the family, and the two historiographies of politics and the family, 'ever closer together'. Families, it seems, have structured the worlds of every human, in every part of the world; but they have also structured many aspects of social and political life at larger scales.

In Chapter 10, Merry Wiesner-Hanks takes up the 'oldest category of difference in human history', that of gender. Gender, like the family, has structured human lives at such a deep level that it must loom large in any serious world history.

The category of gender looms large in recent historiography, along with other categories of difference and identity, as the nation has lost its centrality in historical thinking and research. World history, too, represents an attempt to find new ways of framing our understanding of the past, but, curiously, world history and gender history moved for several decades along parallel paths before eventually intersecting.

Most human communities have assumed the existence of dual gender roles. These roles have often been projected symbolically onto the world and the cosmos, as male and female principles, as yin and yang, as private and public. Gender dichotomies have shaped not just the roles of individual men and women, but also how men and women have understood their roles within the family and society. So intimate and pervasive are gender dichotomies that, like the kinship networks in which they are embedded, they have usually been experienced as natural, as intrinsic to the way the world is. This is despite the fact that, biologically speaking, gender is more complex than conventional dualities imply. Indeed, some societies do find room for third or in-between genders. Modern scholarship on gender is sensitive to these complexities, and careful to distinguish between cultural and biological aspects of gender. This means that: 'gender is generally understood to be a culturally constructed system of differences based on physical, morphological, and anatomical differences between the sexes, what are often called "biological differences"'.

Gender differences imply more than difference. In all societies that have left records, gender dualities have been interpreted as hierarchies, with the male side being interpreted as stronger or more positive. So, as Joan Scott put it in 1986: 'Gender is a constitutive element of social relationships based on perceived differences between the sexes, and gender is a primary way of signifying relationships of power.'

Traditionally, assumptions about gender seemed so fundamental that most historians overlooked them. Most historians were male, they took existing gender roles for granted, and they saw the past through male eyes and male preoccupations. Only since the rise of a women's movement in the nineteenth century have historians begun to see gender roles more clearly and to take them more seriously. And not until the second wave feminism of the mid twentieth century did feminist historians begin to show the extent to which 'history' was in fact 'male history', or history through male eyes. But attempts to write a distinctive 'women's history' often fell into the trap of writing it within pre-existing categories, such as those of class or nation. By the 1980s, increasing numbers of historians particularly in the English-speaking world began to study both male and female history through the category of gender, because it raised deep questions about how the roles of both women and men have been constructed and negotiated over time.

Partly under the pressure of gay rights movements, beginning in the English-speaking world, traditional gender categories began to be questioned at even deeper levels, generating renewed interest in the history of sexuality in general. Just as women's history had begun to explore men's history and then gender history, so, too, the history of homosexuality turned to the study of heterosexuality, and then to sexuality in general, and, particularly within 'queer theory', to forms of sexuality that did not fit comfortably within established or dominant dichotomies. Such studies showed how gender and sexual categories normalized and ab-normalized specific roles and behaviours. A particularly important theme in the emerging historiography of sexuality was the question of whether there were distinctively modern attitudes to gender and sexuality, or whether, perhaps, the categories themselves were products of modernity. Were these categories constructed by some of the same pressures and processes that lay behind modernity more generally?

Increasing interest in how historians constructed the categories they used to understand the past may help explain why historians of gender and sexuality were attracted to the broader historiographical movement often known as 'the cultural turn'. This fundamental shift in perspective moved historians from study of evidence about the past as it 'actually happened', in the words of Ranke, to study of how historians used evidence to construct accounts of the past. That move encouraged the idea that historians can never really study an unmediated past; at best, they can study the images historians and others have constructed of the past. Michel Foucault showed the extent to which those images, and even the language in which they were described, supported and reproduced existing power relations. His insight lent a critical edge to the study of historical discourses, including those of gender and sexuality. It also suggested the extent to which domination depended on collusion from below, an idea developed in Gramsci's notion of 'hegemony', another concept that proved attractive to historians of gender and sexuality. Extreme forms of 'social constructivism' ran the risk of depriving historians of any intellectual leverage, because they lacked anchors in a real world. But in more modest forms, the cultural turn sensitized historians in many different fields, including gender history, to the cultural filters through which historians view, describe, and explain the past, and to the many ways in which those filters also shape the present.

Eventually, the parallel tracks of gender history and world history began to overlap. Like gender history, world history attempted to break from established historiographical categories such as the nation state. But different historiographical breakouts led in different directions. While gender history worked with differences, world history looked for connections; and while gender history veered towards cultural history, world history usually stayed closer to the materialist traditions of earlier historical scholarship.

There are, nevertheless, many natural points of contact between gender history and world history, and they will be emphasized at many points in various volumes of the *Cambridge World History*. They include studies of early human societies, of marriage across cultural lines, of the construction of national identity, of migration, and of colonialism. Interest in the earliest eras of human history has encouraged both world historians and gender historians to re-interpret social and gender relations in Paleolithic societies. Modern accounts of Paleolithic societies emphasize the role of women as much as (and sometimes more than) the role of males (see Chapter 9). Gender and world historians have also found common ground in studies of how gender has shaped national identities and symbols. Was homosexuality compatible with full citizenship even in relatively liberal societies such as the USA? 'Often not' is the answer of historians such as Margot Canaday and Jasbir Puar. Gender roles also shaped migration, but the intersection of gender relations and global power relations has been particularly striking in studies of colonialism, where strongly held notions of gender and the family shaped many of the cultural and legal structures of domination.

Both world history and gender history have been forced to question and destabilize established dichotomies of domination and of gender. Research linking these once distinct historiographical traditions has added depth to both fields. It has shown the extent to which world history is itself gendered in content and construction, as well as the global reach of the themes explored by gender history.

In Chapter 11, Jack Goody describes the long, complex, and fraught relationship between world history and anthropology: another discipline that has attempted to understand humanity at large scales and has wrestled long and hard with Eurocentrism.

Goody has played an active role in the complex relationship between these two disciplines, and he argues that they have much to offer each other. Both world history and anthropology (and the closely related discipline of comparative sociology) aspired to an ecumenical understanding of humanity. But while history favoured written sources, anthropology preferred oral sources. For much of the twentieth century, these methodological differences drove the two fields apart. This was particularly true after the work of Bronislaw Malinowski and his followers encouraged anthropologists to engage in detailed field work in non-literate societies, and to focus on the distinctiveness and specificity of each culture. The broader theoretical perspectives of earlier anthropologists, such as Edward Tylor or James Frazer or Émile Durkheim were increasingly taken up within a different field, that of comparative sociology.

One odd consequence of this division of labour was that many anthropologists continued to study even complex societies such as India and China using the methods and assumptions they applied to small-scale societies. Often, that meant ignoring written sources. The result was to preserve nineteenth-century distinctions between a modern West and an archaic East. However, such approaches were undermined in the twentieth century by the work of Joseph Needham on Chinese science. As Goody writes: 'I myself was much struck by the fact that until the Italian Renaissance, as Needham claimed, science was more advanced in the east than in the west'. China's economic weight, too, was long underestimated within a Eurocentric world history despite the discovery that it was: 'the greatest exporter of manufactured products until the end of the eighteenth century'.

Though they have long travelled on different trajectories, anthropology and world history have much to offer each other. Anthropology has helped world history find new types of sources, beyond the books and records, and also to become less Eurocentric and avoid some traditional assumptions about Western exceptionalism. For example, anthropology can show that democracy as a form of government is not uniquely modern or Western, but that consultative forms of government are ancient and global. It can demonstrate how pervasive were early forms of capitalism. Anthropology can also demonstrate how ancient world history itself is: 'Thales may have been the first Phoenician philosopher to leave a written record; he was certainly not the first to try and conceptualize the world in a general moral and intellectual framework; the precursors of Ogotemmêli, the Dogon sage, did that'. In fact, Goody argues, 'All societies "placed" themselves in relation to their neighbours and sometimes others too. World history, then, is nothing new. All societies had some concept of how they themselves fitted into the wider picture'. (Here, Goody extends the arguments in Chapters 2 and 3 about the universality of world history.) But of course modern world history is very different from the world history of earlier cultures. Above all, it is secular in its approach and (at least in aspiration) less firmly anchored in local cultural or religious traditions.

Both anthropology and world history have attempted to escape from narrowly ethnocentric perspectives. But while world history tended to focus on complex societies, anthropology focused more on small-scale and simpler societies, and, particularly earlier in the twentieth century, it therefore tended to question the more Eurocentric narratives of some forms of world history, and also the related narratives of increasing complexity. Eric Wolf's *Europe and the People Without History* shows what can be done by systematically incorporating scholarship on the non-literate world into a global account of modern history. So, despite its limitations, anthropology has been a powerful force nudging world history away from the ethnocentric narratives of the nineteenth century or the even earlier narratives of civilizational superiority that go back at least to the time of Herodotus.

The theme of migration is as central within world history as that of gender relations. In Chapter 12, Patrick Manning argues that migration is not merely important; it is a natural, even inevitable theme for world history, because world history is, by definition, about connections. It discourages the study of communities as discrete units. Instead, world history stresses the permeability of communities, and the many differences that encourage migratory flows. World history also encourages historical study at multiple scales, an approach that is particularly appropriate for a theme as universal as migration. And world history works with an exceptionally wide range of sources, from those of archaeology, linguistics, and genetics to the more conventional written evidence of books and documents; all are powerful tools for understanding the history of migration. Finally, it's not just people that migrate, but also other species, as well as ideas, religions, diseases, and technologies, so that the study of migration touches on many sub-fields of world history.

While many species migrate, most human migrations are cross-community migrations, taking people (generally young people) from one already existing human community to another. The earliest human migrations were probably driven by environmental changes and by social evolution. Paleolithic migrations took our ancestors around the world, into environments where their technologies changed and even, eventually, their body types and skin colours. But even in the Paleolithic, most migrations were not into unoccupied regions, but from one community to another. Agriculturalists migrated in new ways and with different motivations and purposes. Their communities were also larger, which means that scholars can use genetic evidence with increasing precision to track migrations. Horse-based societies in Eurasia engaged in new long-distance migrations as well as new types of annual migrations. Larger networks created new types of communities, including linguistic, religious, and eventually national communities, and often people migrated within the containers provided by these networks. The great migratory movements of Austronesian or Bantu speakers are a reminder of how shared language and culture could shape migratory patterns. Cities also encouraged migrations from villages or small towns in search of work or opportunity; and trade networks by land and sea encouraged the evolution and spread of diaspora communities.

The first global migrations began from the end of the fifteenth century. Some modern migrations, such as the slave trade, were coercive, but most were voluntary, even if driven by economic pressures. In the nineteenth century, steam ships and railways encouraged larger numbers to migrate faster and further than ever before. 'Where ten million had crossed the Atlantic as slaves from 1550 to 1850, nearly fifty million Europeans crossed the Atlantic from 1840 to 1940, and another eighty million migrants moved from India and China. Two regions of sparse population – North America and Southeast Asia – each absorbed over thirty million immigrants'. These migrations created entirely new communities and diasporas, and increased the salience of racial and ethnic identities within large communities. Many modern migrants were peasants heading to cities in their own or other countries, so it is hardly surprising that by the early twenty-first century, most humans lived in urban areas.

But despite these distinctively modern patterns, we still see ancient patterns of migration. Today's cross-community educational migrations are a reminder of the importance throughout human history of migrations by the young away from their home community.

Part ii: The Paleolithic and the beginnings of human history

Part ii of this volume surveys the vast period of human history before the appearance of agricultural societies.

There is plenty of room for argument about when the Paleolithic era begins, and different chapters will take different positions. There are really two problems: when the Paleolithic itself begins, and when our own species first appeared. For most paleontologists, the Paleolithic era or the 'Old Stone Age', begins with the appearance of the first stone tools, over 2 million years ago. Those were made by our *Homo habilis* ancestors and are generally known as Olduvan because Louis Leakey first identified them in the 1930s in the Olduvai Gorge in Tanzania. However, for historians it may make sense to opt for a narrower definition of the Paleolithic era as that part of the Paleolithic era in which our own species, *Homo sapiens*, was present. Under that definition, the Paleolithic era really means the Paleolithic era of human history. But this definition raises the second problem of when our species evolved and, as we will see, the answer to that question is disputed. In the chapters that follow, dates for the evolution of modern humans range from about 200,000 years ago to about 70,000 years ago. But whatever date we adopt for the appearance of our own species, or for the beginning of the Paleolithic era, it is clear that the Paleolithic era embraces most of human history.

The Paleolithic era is therefore foundational, however we define it. This is when human history begins. It is in the Paleolithic era that we first find evidence of the behaviours that make our species so distinctive: above all, our cultural and ecological creativity. Ecological creativity meant increasing power over the environment, over landscapes, plants, and animals, and also over other humans. In the Paleolithic era, human ecological power can be measured in the development of new knowledge and technologies that allowed particular communities to occupy new niches until, eventually, our ancestors had spread to every continent apart from Antarctica.

Paleolithic lifeways laid the foundations for the rest of human history, so it is important to know how our ancestors lived. Unfortunately, we lack the fine detail that is available for more recent periods. Nevertheless, there are some important generalizations we can make about the lives our Paleolithic ancestors lived. Most Paleolithic communities were small by later standards. Until the end of the last ice age, most people probably lived in groups of no more than about fifty, with occasional gatherings of larger groups with perhaps several hundred people. Most Paleolithic communities lived by foraging, nomadizing over familiar territories. At the level of the community, we see little change in population densities or in the capacity to mobilize resources. Most communities probably mobilized little more energy and resources than they needed to survive, with a slight surplus for insurance. This means that at the level of the community we do not see evidence of increasing ecological power; we do not see what today we might call 'intensification'. And that may help explain why it is so tempting to think of the Paleolithic era as technologically and socially stagnant, particularly in contrast to the eras that followed. But as humans entered new niches, the ecological power of humanity as a whole was slowly increasing, and we can measure that increase in human occupation of new environments, as well as in plausible estimates pointing to a slow increase in human populations, particularly after about 70,000 years ago.

As some of the chapters in Part I remind us, Paleolithic lifeways shaped us psychologically, physiologically, and genetically. In some sense, we are still Paleolithic humans today. But of course we should not exaggerate the importance of the Paleolithic. Populations were so small that, of the 80 billion humans who may have lived since our species first appeared (according to the very rough estimates adopted by Massimo Livi-Bacci), fewer than 10 billion, or 12 per cent, lived in the Paleolithic era.[2] Even if the Paleolithic era is foundational, most human lives (80 per cent according to these same estimates) were lived in the period between the end of the Paleolithic era and 1750. It is appropriate that the allocation of volumes in the *Cambridge World History* should roughly match these proportions, with one volume out of seven (strictly half a volume) allocated to the Paleolithic era, and one to the era after 1750 (though that volume is a double one).

Though we should not underestimate the technological, cultural, and artistic creativity of Paleolithic communities, nevertheless, human ecological and technological creativity remained fragile and precarious, and was surely accompanied by many periods of retrogression and retreat. It was all too easy for small communities to vanish, along with the knowledge they had used to survive in their home territories. And this is one reason for thinking that forces such as climate change or natural disasters may have played a critical role in human history during the Paleolithic era. Most of the chapters that follow will touch at some point on the importance of climate change in the Paleolithic era.

In Chapter 13, Felipe Fernández-Armesto offers a broad general survey of the complex relationship between human lifeways and climate change during the Paleolithic era.

Driven partly by debates about global warming, research on ancient climates has been transformed in recent decades, so that it is now possible to explore such questions with a precision unthinkable just two or three decades ago.[3] As Fernández-Armesto points out, modern humans emerged during an ice age: 'We are creatures of cold'. When our species first appeared, the differences between humans and other communities of primates in East Africa would not have been particularly striking. By the end of the last ice age humans already stood out for their range, diversity, adaptability, and the size of their social networks. What were the major changes between these two eras and to what extent were they shaped by climatic changes?

Fernández-Armesto argues that the most distinctive features of human culture are: 'relative flexibility in adapting to a variety of environments and

---

2 Rough estimates from Massimo Livi-Bacci, *A Concise History of World Population*, Oxford: Blackwell, 1992, pp. 32–3.
3 A pioneering recent attempt to make use of this research is John L. Brooke, *Climate Change and the Course of Global History: A Rough Journey*, Cambridge: Cambridge University Press, 2014.

relative mutability'. Mutability leaves little room for climatic or environmental determinism; indeed we see over and over again that different groups could react in very different ways to similar environmental conditions. Our unique capacity for imagination must be part of the explanation for these differing reactions.

Nevertheless, climate and ecology clearly framed human history throughout the Paleolithic era. At large scales, global climates depend on the Milankovic cycles: changes in the earth's orbit, in the shape of its orbit, and the tilt of the earth's own axis of rotation. In the last million years, these variables have combined to generate a pattern of long cold, dry periods (so-called ice ages) lasting at least 100,000 years, interspersed with shorter warmer 'interglacials' lasting for approximately 10,000–20,000 years. Other factors, including changes in ocean currents, ensure that within these larger patterns there were many smaller and more erratic changes.

Skeletal remains and genetic evidence both suggest that our species evolved somewhere in East Africa during an ice age, some time between 150,000 and 200,000 years ago. In contrast, the history of recent millennia has been shaped by a period of rapid but erratic warming, from the low point of the last ice age, about 20,000 years ago, until the end of the Paleolithic era, some 10,000 years ago. Between the time of our appearance and the end of the last ice age, our ancestors spread around the world. Why and how?

Modern genetic techniques offer new (if imperfect) ways of tracing these migrations. There were modern humans in the Middle East 100,000 years ago; then a new wave entered the region from about 60,000 years ago. By then there were probably already humans in China and, more remarkably because it implies sophisticated sea-going technologies, by 50,000 years ago humans lived in Australia and Papua New Guinea. Humans entered the colder northern regions of Europe and perhaps even Siberia by perhaps 30,000 years ago and from there, eventually, they reached the Americas, crossing by the ice age land bridge of Beringia, or around its coasts. In the Americas, humans of the Clovis culture hunted to extinction several species of large mammals unfamiliar with humans and therefore not sufficiently wary of them. By 10,000 years ago, our ancestors had colonized the planet, and human populations had grown from a few tens of thousands to a few million.

It is a reasonable guess (and at present it can be little more than a guess) that warmer periods encouraged migration because they allowed our ancestors to occupy regions that had once been uninhabitable. Colder spells surely discouraged or reversed such migrations. Environmental calamities or even warfare may also have encouraged movements into new territories. There has been much debate about the antiquity of warfare, but Jane Goodall's demonstration of something like warfare among groups of chimps makes it difficult to rule out the possibility of violent conflicts. Still, in the absence of hard evidence, most hypotheses about the causes of these migrations remain speculative.

Migrations into new environments surely changed social and gender relationships and cultural ideas. They certainly changed foraging strategies. Despite the difficulties of migrating into the tundra lands of ice age northern Eurasia, hunters living along their southern edges found large, huntable animals whose meat and fat were a rich source of food. Skeletal remains suggest that many ice age hunters were well nourished. Perhaps this explains the aesthetic of the plump female figurines, such as the 30,000-year-old Venus of Willendorf, that are common in late Paleolithic Eurasia. Cave paintings, carvings, and sculptures from late in the Paleolithic era can be found in many parts of the world from Europe to Australia to South Africa. Similarities in late ice age art and technologies suggest the counter-intuitive hypothesis that, despite cultural variations, many aspects of ice age lifeways may have varied surprisingly little as our ancestors spread around the world. Prestige burials, such as the Sunghir burial of 28,000 years ago, from a site near Moscow, also suggest the emergence of embryonic social and economic hierarchies, as some individuals accumulated significant wealth by Paleolithic standards, and even managed to pass it on to their heirs.

At the end of the last ice age, climatic changes were sometimes so erratic that they could trap migrants in new environments and force them to try new ways of exploiting their environments. Some, such as the Natufians of the Fertile Crescent, or the Jomon communities of Japan, became sedentary and built villages. What may have seemed small changes at the time were harbingers of a revolutionary transformation in human lifeways.

In Chapter 14, the first of two linked chapters on the Paleolithic era in Africa, Chris Ehret takes up the thorny issue of when modern humans first appeared. Ehret, a specialist in the history of languages as well as in the archaeology of Africa, has modern humans appearing later than some other authors in this volume. 'Before about 48,000 years ago', he writes, 'human history was African history'. True, there are signs of modern-looking humans in the Levant from about 100,000 years ago, during a relatively warm period. But their disappearance and replacement by Neanderthal populations as climates deteriorated over the next few millennia suggest that they lacked the creativity of later human groups, some of which would leave Africa 50,000 years later. The distinction Ehret draws between archaic modern humans and fully modern humans provides the basic periodization for Chapters 14 and 15.

Not until about 70,000 years ago, Ehret argues, did fully modern humans evolve, and they evolved somewhere in East Africa: 'the full package of modern human capacities took shape between about 70,000 and 48,000 BCE [that is, 50,000 years ago]'. By 50,000 years ago, groups of modern humans began to migrate into other parts of Africa, and also into Eurasia and beyond. Everywhere, they encountered, and eventually displaced, groups of more archaic hominins. The groups they displaced still had technologies typical of the 'Middle Stone Age' (or 'Middle Paleolithic' in the terminology used in the archaeology of Eurasia), and probably lacked modern human linguistic abilities. In Africa, though, the differences between archaic and modern humans were probably less marked than in Eurasia, which may be why we find evidence of different groups coexisting for long periods of time.

Sudden technological changes provide one form of evidence for Ehret's periodization. In Africa, archaeologists have found relatively sudden transitions from the prepared-core stone technologies typical of the Middle Stone Age to more modern technologies characterized by carefully made small blades and tools made from small flakes and often associated with bone tools and art. Where skeletal remains survive, we find fully modern remains associated with modern technologies, and archaic skeletal remains with Middle Stone Age technologies. Skeletal remains also suggest that the modern form of the human pharynx, which is necessary to articulate the full range of sounds used by modern human language, only appeared after about 70,000 years ago.

The period about 70,000 years ago is particularly significant because genetic evidence suggests that human populations shrank to perhaps just 10,000 individuals. The cause may have been a sudden climatic deterioration caused by the eruption of Mt Toba in modern Indonesia about 72,000 years ago. But it is also possible that the impression of a demographic bottleneck actually arises from rapid growth in the populations among which modern human languages first appeared. Linguistic evidence provides some support for this idea. Modern linguistic studies show a clear linguistic trend away from complex consonantal systems as one moves outward from eastern and southern Africa; this suggests that all modern languages may derive from an original language that appeared about 70,000 years ago in East Africa, and was characterized by exceptional consonantal complexity. Genetic evidence also points to the importance of East Africa, for here and only here do we find all three of the major genetic groupings into which all contemporary humans fall. Here, too, we find evidence for new types of stone points that may have been used for projectile weapons, perhaps even for early bows and arrows. In addition, rock art suggests the presence of new forms of religious beliefs similar, perhaps, to some forms of shamanism. Modern forms of language may also have allowed the emergence of larger communities and networks, held together by more complex kinship systems.

Taken together, this evidence suggests a late evolution of fully modern humans with modern forms of language, followed by a slow accumulation of new skills, new social relationships, and new cultural forms. The consolidation of these new communities was slow and fitful. In the Howiesons Poort culture, for example, which dates from about 63,000 years ago, we find evidence of fully modern industries lying between layers of more archaic technologies. This suggests a slow ebbing and flowing of different cultural traditions. It also suggests that the advantages did not always lie with fully modern humans. But by 50,000 years ago, there is evidence of fully modern human communities from southern parts of East Africa all the way up to the Red Sea. From here, some modern humans would eventually enter Eurasia, where their appearance created the impression of a sudden transition to modernity. Others would move to other parts of Africa where they would slowly displace communities of archaic hominins.

In Chapter 15, Chris Ehret takes the story of human evolution in Africa up to the end of the Paleolithic era. From about 50,000 years ago, he writes: 'a new era in human history began'. Modern humans began to spread from East Africa through the Levant and north into Europe and Eurasia or eastwards through South Asia and to Australia. They also spread to the south, west, and north within Africa. Over more than 30,000 years, fully modern humans slowly displaced more archaic groups still characterized by Middle Stone Age cultures. However, in some parts of West Africa, Middle Stone Age cultures survived until the end of the last ice age.

From about 50,000 years ago we find evidence of fully modern technologies spreading southwards from East Africa into Botswana and parts of modern South Africa. But instead of a rapid displacement, the evidence suggests that modern and archaic cultures coexisted here for as long as 20,000 years. Modern cultural traditions also spread westwards; by 30,000 BCE Later Stone Age technologies have reached western Cameroon, but they seem not to have reached West Africa. Moving northwards, some groups of fully modern humans seem to have reached the Levant by 50,000 years ago, presumably through Egypt. So, by the Late Glacial Maximum, modern humans could be found in much of eastern, northeastern, and southern and Central Africa, but not yet in West Africa. Humans using Middle Stone Age industries survived alongside them in parts of southern and Central Africa 'although probably in declining numbers'.

The Late Glacial Maximum dates from approximately 22,000 BCE and lasted several thousand years. It brought cooler and drier climates and periods of rapid climatic change that accelerated change throughout Africa. From this time on, linguistic evidence based on the comparative study of modern languages begins to offer intriguing hints about lifeways, kinship structures, and even religious traditions.

Surviving Middle Stone Age populations vanished in the south, centre, and northwest of the continent at about the Glacial Maximum. In East Africa, a new Later Stone Age culture appeared soon after the Glacial Maximum. This may have been associated with early speakers of Khoesan languages. Two distantly related Khoesan languages are still spoken in the region, while the earliest Khoesan languages seem to have included words for bows and arrows and for arrow poisons, evidence that aligns well with the culture's archaeology. Rock art from the region also fits with what is known of ancient Khoesan religious traditions. In the Congo Basin, distinctive traditions emerged in the 'Batwa' cultural complex associated both with rock art and new stone industries. These traditions may well have been ancestral to peoples of the modern 'Batwa' tradition.

The northeast of Africa is the homeland of three of Africa's major language families: Nilo-Saharan, Afrasian (or 'Afroasiatic'), and Niger-Kordofanian. Such cultural fecundity suggests the presence of large populations near the headwaters of the Nile at and after the Late Glacial Maximum. From about 13,000 BCE, evidence begins to appear, particularly along the Nile, of semi-sedentary communities harvesting and grinding wild grains. These cultures may reflect the arrival of Afrasian-speaking peoples, some of whom would eventually bring the ancestors of the Semitic languages into the Levant region.

In West Africa, Middle Stone Age industries survived as late as 13,000 BCE. Then they vanished, to be replaced by Later Stone Age technologies brought, in all probability (the archaeological record is thin), by speakers of Niger-Kordofanian languages from the region of modern Sudan. Here, probably during the cold Younger Dryas, we begin to see early evidence for the cultivation of wild grains and even for early forms of pottery, apparently for cooking. Meanwhile, in the eastern Sahara evidence begins to appear in the ninth and eighth millennia BCE for the earliest forms of cattle herding in world history, as well as the cultivation of gourds and grains. As Ehret concludes: 'Africa at the beginning of the Holocene was not a place apart. The same trajectories of human change were emerging in Africa as in several other parts of the world – toward agricultural ways of life and, much farther off in time, toward more complex and more unequal societies'.

In Chapter 16, John Hoffecker discusses the Paleolithic era of Europe. Like Fernández-Armesto and Ehret, he insists that the challenge is not just to find human-like remains, but also to find evidence of distinctively human behaviours. Hoffecker's epigraph cites V. Gordon Childe, who argued that archaeologists study 'the fossilized results of human behavior'. As Hoffecker argues: 'It is the origin of the mind . . . that is the central issue in human evolution. It is not only the immense quantity of non-genetic information that modern humans collect and store, but it is their capacity for creating novel structures or arrangements of that information that render them unique among living organisms'.

Europe's role in the Paleolithic era is distinctive in several ways. First, the region is geographically distinct. It is separated from Africa and the Near East by the Mediterranean, the Black Sea, and the Caucasus Mountains, while its western regions are warmed by Atlantic Ocean currents that gave it a benign climate and a richer mix of species than lands to its east. Second, European archaeology is distinctive, so distinctive that for a long time its traditions warped our understanding of the Paleolithic era. Europe was the home of modern forms of science, and it was here that some of the earliest studies of human evolution were conducted. By the late nineteenth century, enough fossil remains and stone artefacts had been found for Sir John Lubbock to announce the existence of a distinctive 'Palaeolithic' era in human history. His period would eventually be divided into an Upper Paleolithic, associated with modern humans, a Middle Paleolithic, associated with Neanderthals, and a pre-Neanderthal Lower Paleolithic. European scholars so dominated early attempts to describe human evolution, and the Paleolithic evidence from Europe was so rich and so diverse that it seemed natural to assume that our species evolved in Europe. Only in the twentieth century has it become clear that the ancestral home of our species was really in Africa.

Before 2.5 million years ago, our ancestors were 'small-brained "bipedal apes"' living in Africa. The larger-brained *Homo* genus appeared about 2.5 million years ago. By 2 million years ago, some members of the genus had become the first human-like creatures to enter parts of Eurasia, though none of these early migrants travelled further north than *c.* 40°. These early migrations were temporary and occasional, and depended on stone tool technologies similar to those of the African Lower Paleolithic. Simple stone tools make it possible to butcher large animals, which increased the consumption of meat, and that may be why these early forays into cooler regions were possible. The earliest evidence of migrations into western Europe are the *Homo* remains from Atapuerca in northern Spain dated to just over 1 million years ago.

From about 600,000 years ago, we find a new species, *Homo heidelbergensis*, migrating from Africa into Europe, probably around the eastern Mediterranean and across the Bosporus. *Heidelbergensis* was the ancestor of both Neanderthals and modern humans. Their brain size overlapped with that of modern humans, they clearly controlled fire, and they made more complex and more sophisticated stone tools than their *erectus* predecessors. By 500,000 years ago, they could be found in England at the important site of Boxgrove. The important German site of Schöningen dates to *c.* 400,000 years ago and is one of the first Paleolithic sites to contain wooden artefacts including spears.

Conventionally, the Middle Paleolithic in Europe begins with the appearance of Neanderthals. Neanderthals evolved in Europe from *heidelbergensis* ancestors at least by *c.* 250,000 years ago. They were apparently well adapted to glacial conditions because, unlike other hominins, they were able to remain in Europe even in periods of extreme glacial climates. Analysis of Neanderthal bones shows that they depended largely on meat from large herbivores such as mammoth. Surprisingly, though, there is no evidence of sewn clothing or of the ability to make fire, though there is plenty of evidence that they could maintain fires. Their stone tools, however, were sophisticated, and have long been used as a marker for the beginning of the Middle Paleolithic, from about 300,000 years ago. It has recently been shown that Neanderthals could also make composite tools with multiple parts that were joined using sophisticated adhesives. Unfortunately, we have little understanding of the Neanderthal mind. They probably buried some of their dead, though that in itself is not necessarily proof of belief in an afterlife. Though they possess the FOXP2 gene, which seems to be important for human speech, the objects they made changed little over 200,000 years, which suggests that they lacked the rich creativity associated with modern human languages.

The Upper Paleolithic in Europe is conventionally (if somewhat anachronistically) associated with the appearance of our own species, *Homo sapiens*. The evidence is now overwhelming that modern humans evolved in Africa. Some members of our own species appeared in Europe about 50,000 years ago and Neanderthals may have vanished within 10,000 years of that date. There is now clear evidence of some interbreeding between the species, probably about 100,000 years ago when modern humans and Neanderthals lived near each other in the Near East. But the differences between the remains left behind by modern humans and Neanderthals are immense and significant, and they almost certainly arise from the appearance of modern human language: 'a fully syntactic language with phrase structure grammar and potentially infinite variety of sentences and narratives'. This change, Hoffecker argues, marks the 'advent of the modern mind'.

Modern humans reached Europe from the Near East, through the Caucasus or across the Bosporus and probably during a warm period. From 42,000 years ago we find evidence for proto-Aurignacian industries, showing the sort of diversity clearly characteristic of modern humans. Remains include eyed needles and hare traps, as well as rich artistic products, including an ivory carving, the Löwenmensch from Germany, which seems to depict a semi-human figure of myth. Some of these cultures are associated with an extremely cold spell, suggesting that modern humans rapidly developed technologies appropriate for glacial conditions.

Evidence for technological innovation multiplies between 30,000 and 25,000 years ago, in the Gravettian period. Large settlements in Central and Eastern Europe suggest improved food-producing technologies, and some sites contain ovens hot enough to make ceramics. The extreme cold of the Late Glacial Maximum forced the abandonment of many more northerly sites, as ice sheets spread over large parts of northern Europe for several thousand years. Then, after 20,000 years ago, more northerly sites were re-occupied by representatives of the Magdalenian and EpiGravettian cultures. By 12,000 there is evidence of large partly permanent settlements, some with houses made of mammoth bones. Here, as in the Near East, China, and parts of North Africa, we see cultural and technological changes that hint at the early stages of a shift towards agriculture.

In Chapter 17, Robin Dennell describes Paleolithic migrations into Asia, which also began in Africa and passed through the Near Eastern bottleneck. Like Hoffecker, Dennell stresses the importance of climate change in shaping the history of the Paleolithic era. Dennell's chapter tells a story of two major hominin dispersals: Out of Africa 1 (the most ancient hominin dispersal, from almost 2 million years ago); and Out of Africa 2 (the dispersal of *Homo sapiens* within the last 100,000 years).

The earliest evidence of hominins living outside of Africa has been found at Dmanisi, Georgia, where the remains of early forms of *Homo erectus* have been found, and dated to 1.77 million years ago. Though their brains were about half the size of those of modern humans, their use of stone tools suggests increasing dependence on meat and marrow in their diets. Indeed, these technologies, which presumably gave access to more food energy, may explain the first dispersals outside of Africa. Other early finds in Asia include skeletal remains in Sangiran, Java, from *c.* 1.5 million years ago; and hominin artefacts from north China, dated to about 1.66 million years ago. Coupled with evidence from Atapuerca in northern Spain, from *c.* 1.3 million years ago, these show that hominins could be found throughout Eurasia to a latitude of about 40° North by about 1.5 million years ago. But, as Dennell points out, the evidence is so thin that a single find, or a slight improvement in the precision of dating techniques, could easily force us to re-think both the geography and the timing of these early dispersals. It is also clear that the existing evidence provides a tiny sample of multiple dispersals and retreats, including perhaps reverse dispersals back into Africa.

The story of Out of Africa 2 is the story of our own species, *Homo sapiens*, and its dispersals from Africa. There is a broad consensus that remains dated to 190,000 years ago from the Awash Valley in Ethiopia belong to *Homo sapiens*. Modern human remains are first found outside of Africa in modern Israel, where they date to about 125,000–70,000 years ago; but this population seems to have been displaced by Neanderthals some time before 70,000 years ago, presumably as a result of climatic deteriorioration. Between 40,000 and 60,000 years ago there were new dispersals of modern humans from Africa. These took our ancestors to Southeast Asia, New Guinea, and Australia. The earliest evidence of these dispersals is associated with Middle Stone Age technologies similar to those of Neanderthals, and based on the removal of flakes from specially prepared cores. Like the Out of Africa 1 story, this story also rests on limited evidence, and could easily be transformed. For example, the discovery of new skeletal remains in the Levant and Southeast Asia before 125,000 years ago would suggest (as Peter Hiscock will argue in Chapter 18) that there may have been a successful earlier dispersal of modern humans from the Levant to South and Southeast Asia.

As evidence of ancient climate changes improves, it is tempting to link what we know of early human dispersals to the erratic climate changes of the ice ages. There were large cycles of change driven by the Milankovic cycles, but also shorter, more erratic, and more abrupt changes such as the 'Heinrich' events: cold snaps that could last for centuries or even millennia. In warmer and more humid periods, human populations could settle further north, while in colder and drier periods, populations probably contracted south and some groups may have been isolated from other populations for long periods. This means that there must in practice have been many different periods of advance and retreat, few of which have left behind direct evidence. In Tajikistan in Central Asia, we have direct evidence that modern humans arrived only in warmer periods, and evidence from China and Britain hints at similar patterns.

Changing technologies also shaped early hominin dispersals. Stone tools, which gave humans access to a meat-rich diet, probably enabled the earliest migrations into colder regions. As Chapter 8 argues, a meat-rich diet combined with a shrinking of the human gut may also help explain the rapid increase in brain size in the last few million years. And, as brain size correlates closely with group size in most primates, larger brains may imply larger social groups, more sharing of information, and the evolution of a 'social brain' that 'would have widened the potential scope for hominins to disperse into new types of environments, or to utilise them more effectively'.

In Asia, the impact of new technologies is most apparent in the last 50,000 years. We see little evidence for any widening of the hominin range over a million years; then, within the last 50,000 years, the range widens fast. Siberia was probably colonized from 40,000 to 50,000 years ago, bringing humans to the ice age land bridge of Beringia from which some would eventually cross into the Americas. Australia was colonized at least by 50,000–60,000 years ago (Peter Hiscock will give evidence for even earlier dates in Chapter 18), and Japan by 40,000 years ago. Both these dispersals required significant navigational skills. Rainforests of Southeast Asia were also occupied by 40,000–50,000 years ago. Finally, the Tibetan Plateau was occupied right at the end of the last ice age. The evidence from Asia, then, points to a very significant inflection in the human history of Asia from about 50,000 years ago, with the arrival of modern humans.

In Chapter 18, Peter Hiscock surveys recent evidence on the history of Australia in the Paleolithic era. During cooler periods of the ice ages, sea levels were low enough for Australia, New Guinea, and Tasmania to be linked within a single Paleo-continent, known as Sahul, that was separated from the ice age peninsula of Sunda/Indonesia by deep water.

Debates about the earliest colonization of Australia affect how we interpret the earlier migrations of modern humans out of Africa. The dominant model has modern humans leaving Africa as late as 60,000–65,000 years ago, and assumes that finds of modern humans in the Near East before 90,000 years represent a 'false start' (an interpretation we have encountered already in Chapters 14, 16, and 17). This model requires rapid migrations through

South Asia to Australia if it is to fit with the best dates for the colonization of Australia. For example, it has been suggested that we should imagine a migration of peoples who stayed close to the coasts, exploiting coastal resources and developing their sea-going skills en route to Australia. The late dispersion model also encouraged scepticism about any dates for Australian settlement earlier than about 45,000 years ago.

Hiscock argues that recent evidence undermines the late dispersal model. Genetic research suggests that human mutation rates may have been slower than has often been assumed, which is consistent with alternative models in which Australian populations diverged from African populations as early as 120,000 years ago. Perhaps early migrations from Africa were not false starts, but the beginnings of successful dispersals that have left little trace. Recent genetic evidence also points to genetic exchanges (analogous to those in Europe with Neanderthals) between modern humans from an early dispersal, and populations of other hominin species, including the Denisovan populations just identified in 2010 from remains in a Siberian cave whose ancestors had left Africa over half a million years ago. This allows the possibility that, instead of racing from the Near East to Australia, the populations whose descendants eventually colonized Australia may have ranged widely within Eurasia in a more leisurely dispersal before reaching Australia. The absence of Denisovan genes from modern East Asian populations also suggests that Australia was colonized by an earlier wave of modern humans, and East Asia by a later wave that displaced Denisovan populations. Finally, the presence of similar genetic lineages in both modern and ancient Australian populations suggests that most modern indigenous Australians are descended from a single early wave of colonization.

An early dispersal model aligns well with archaeological evidence suggesting that humans had arrived in Australia at least by 50,000–60,000 years ago. Rock shelters in Arnhem Land in northernmost Australia contain artefacts that have been dated (by thermoluminescence) to as early as 67,000 years ago. Though such early dates have been questioned, there is firm evidence that humans were present in many parts of Sahul by 50,000 years ago, and to have spread so widely they must have arrived well before that date.

The earliest human skeletal remains in Australia come from Lake Mungo in southern Australia and date to about 43,000 years ago. Mitochondrial DNA extracted from a Lake Mungo skeleton is similar enough to modern Australian Aboriginal DNA to show that they belong to the same lineage, which suggests that there were no major colonizations after the founding wave. By 45,000 to 55,000 years ago, humans already occupied a great variety of environments, including sandy and rocky deserts, semi-arid grasslands and savannahs, as well as uplands, tropical regions, and woodlands, and there is plenty of evidence for distinctive regional cultures. The disappearance of many large-bodied species at about the time of the arrival of humans may have been a result of human over-hunting; though the absence of kill sites (in contrast to the Americas, where they are abundant) weakens such interpretations. A period of cooler, drier climates may also have played a role in these extinctions. Whatever the cause, the removal of many large herbivores must have transformed the environment. For example, it would have allowed the accumulation of large amounts of fuel and increased the likelihood of natural firing of the land.

From about 45,000 years ago, until the Late Glacial Maximum, Sahul underwent a 'great drying'. Sea levels dropped, exposing new exploitable regions along the continent's shorelines, while the interior became drier and many lakes vanished. Changing conditions generated new technologies, some adapted to dry conditions, some making use of ground seeds. Evidence of long-distance exchanges, over many hundreds of kilometres, suggests the importance of extensive networks in drier environments.

Between 25,000 and 18,000 years ago, during the Late Glacial Maximum, oceans dropped to 125 metres below their current level and climates became exceptionally dry and cold. Glaciers formed in some upland regions and the land area of Sahul reached its largest extent. Many older archaeological sites were abandoned, and even bodies adapted, becoming larger and more robust than the bodies of later populations.

From about 19,000 to 10,000 years ago, climates began to warm erratically and sea levels began to rise, from 125 metres below today's sea levels to just 20 metres below 10,000 years ago. Australia's land area shrank by a third. Along Australia's northern borders, shorelines retreated as much as 1,000 kilometres as once occupied lands were drowned, forcing groups to migrate and re-arrange their territories. Tasmania was separated from the mainland, as was New Guinea. The changes of this period were so erratic that ecologies seem not to have stabilized until the Holocene; and not until the last 3,000–4,000 years were climates stable enough to allow more specialized and intensive systems of exploitation to emerge, systems that may parallel developments in the Near East before the first appearance of agriculture.

In Chapter 19, Nicole Waguespack describes the Paleolithic colonization of the Americas: a landmass even larger and more varied than that of Australia. Humans reached the Americas through the harsh environments of northeastern Eurasia, which explains why the Americas were occupied after the Late Glacial Maximum. Even if Siberia was colonized temporarily from as early as 40,000–50,000 years ago (Chapter 17), more permanent Siberian settlements appear only c. 18,000 years ago. At the Late Glacial Maximum, North America's major ice sheets may have merged, blocking movements from Beringia southwards. But after the coldest period a corridor opened between major ice sheets, which may have allowed travel along the Yukon and McKenzie River Valleys into the Americas. Colonists may also have moved through Beringia and around the Pacific coastline.

There is little doubt that humans entered the Americas from northeastern Siberia, or that some had arrived by 14,500 years ago. However, evidence on the founder populations is thin enough to generate heated debates about the exact chronology and geography of their arrival. Many forms of evidence show that the first human communities in the Americas were highly nomadic and dispersed over large areas, and this itself may explain the scanty archaeological record they left behind. It also makes it likely that many groups left no trace at all; sporadic traces of such groups may help explain the large number of claims for earlier arrivals. Sites that might eventually provide evidence for occupation before 15,000 years ago include Monte Verde in Chile, Pedra Furada in Brazil, and Meadowcroft in Pennsylvania and Buttermilk Creek in Texas in the USA.

Before the 1920s, it was still possible to argue either that the Americas were occupied very recently, or that human occupation was as ancient as in the Old World. The discovery of Paleolithic sites in the western United States, beginning with the Folsom site in 1927, provided the first clear evidence of early human arrivals. From the middle of the twentieth century, radiometric dating helped clarify the chronology of American sites. The earliest period of human occupation of the Americas is now described as Paleoindian. Cultural, social, and technological continuities explain why that period extends into the Holocene, ending with the appearance of new tool kits, and signs of sedentism during the period known as the Archaic, which conventionally begins from about 8,000 BCE.

American Paleoindian cultures were highly mobile and produced distinctive stone tools. The best known Paleoindian cultural tradition is the Clovis tradition, named after a distinctive type of projectile point first found near Clovis, New Mexico. Up to 4,000 similar points have been found in an area reaching from Canada to Mexico, often in association with the remains of large herbivores such as mammoth. Most date from within about 600 years of 13,500 years ago. These and the later Folsom stone points are the only known stone tool traditions with fluted points. Most Clovis sites are kill sites, sometimes associated with camp sites. Many signs point to the mobility of Clovis foragers; they include the absence of large grindstones and the presence of tools made from stone quarried hundreds of kilometres from where they were found. High mobility may help explain why the first populations in the Americas rapidly colonized large areas.

As in Australia, the arrival of efficient hunters in a continent whose megafauna had no experience of humans may help explain the disappearance of many of their species from about 13,000 years ago. We know that Clovis peoples hunted megafauna, and we also know that large species are vulnerable to over-hunting because they reproduce slowly. But, as in Australia, it is also possible that rapid climate change played a role in the disappearance of many species of megafauna. The sudden cold snap of the Younger Dryas coincided quite closely with America's megafaunal extinctions.

The hypothesis of a rapid spread of highly mobile Clovis peoples throughout the Americas, which dominated thinking from the 1930s to the 1960s, has recently been questioned. Some archaeologists see Clovis cultures as an inland development, quite distinct from other colonizing groups that specialized in shoreline resources and moved along coastal routes that we no longer see because they were drowned as sea levels rose at the end of the ice age. The paucity of skeletal remains from this period adds to the difficulty of clarifying such issues; at present early Paleoindian cultures are represented by the remains of fewer than ten individuals. As with much of the archaeology of the Paleolithic era, the available evidence is sparse enough that a single discovery could transform our understanding of the early colonization of the Americas.

As the chapters in Part II of this volume demonstrate, the Paleolithic history of our species is coming into sharper focus, and that makes it more important to integrate Paleolithic history more fully within modern world history scholarship, teaching, and research. New techniques, including radiometric dating, genetic comparisons, and increasingly precise ways of tracking climate change, have allowed the construction of a clearer account of the vast periods of time between the evolution of our species and the emergence of agricultural societies early in the Holocene Epoch. As we have seen, dates for the evolution of fully modern humans are still contested; the dates adopted in this volume range from almost 200,000 years ago to as late as 70,000 years ago. The chapters in this volume also differ on the significance of early human dispersals from Africa. Modern humans seem to have been present in the Levant 100,000 years ago, but precisely how modern were they? And was that dispersal a false start, or the first step in migrations that eventually led our ancestors into much of Europe, Asia, and eventually Australia? But if the precise chronologies are contested, the main lines of the story are now much clearer than they were a generation ago. We are an African species; but our ancestors displayed such ecological and technological creativity that they were able to occupy lands in all the continents apart from Antarctica by the end of the Paleolithic era. The remarkable and distinctive history of our species begins deep in the Paleolithic era. But we can also see that the migrations themselves came in pulses, only some of which are visible in the archaeological record. Those pulses were shaped, in part, by climate change. During colder, drier phases, deteriorating climates checked and even reversed migrations, and inhabited regions were abandoned, often to be re-occupied, sometimes with new technologies, once conditions improved. The migratory pulses were also shaped by our ancestors' technological creativity and by the slow accumulation of new techniques and new ecological and social understanding, so that, despite the checks and reversals, our ancestors eventually occupied environments ranging from tropical forests to the tundras of Siberia and North America. These Paleolithic movements laid the foundations for everything that would follow in the Holocene history of our species.

PART I

★

HISTORIOGRAPHY, METHOD, AND THEMES

2

Writing world history

MARNIE HUGHES-WARRINGTON

The term 'world history' describes one of the oldest, most persistent and most pliable forms of history writing.[1] No simple definition is possible, for world histories vary widely in narrative style, structure and spatio-temporal scope. Furthermore, a wide assortment of labels have been used to describe them, including 'universal history', 'ecumenical history', 'regional history', 'comparative history', 'world systems history', 'macrohistory', 'transnational history', 'big history' and the 'new world' and 'new global' histories. Despite terminological differences, however, world histories share the purpose of offering a construction of and thus a guide to a meaningful 'world' or 'realm or domain *taken for* an entire meaningful system of existence or activity' by historians or people in the past.[2] Thus *all* histories are world histories. Where histories differ is in the degree to which the purpose of world construction is explicit.

Indigenous universal histories

Surveys of history making typically begin with ancient Greece, but there are strong grounds for giving consideration to the narratives constructed by Indigenous communities around the world to make sense of the past, present and future. Far from being fanciful constructions, they are better described in the sense coined by Mircea Eliade, as 'sacred history'.[3] Eliade used this terminology to capture the idea of the past as being the source of rules or

---

1 This chapter was adapted from 'World history, writing of' by Marnie Hughes-Warrington in William H. McNeill, *et al.* (ed.), *Encyclopedia of World History* (2nd edn.), pp. 2847–56. Copyright © 2010 Berkshire. Reproduced with permission of Berkshire Publishing Group, Great Barrington, Mass.
2 Marnie Hughes-Warrington (ed.), *World Histories* (London: Palgrave Macmillan, 2004).
3 Mircea Eliade, 'Cosmogonic myth and "sacred history"', *Religious Studies* 2/2 (1967), 171–83.

mores that not only explain the present, but also help people living in the present to create a better future. This is akin to universal histories of the Judaeo-Christian tradition, but the format of these works can be a challenge to anyone who assumes that histories are chronologically ordered written accounts. Indigenous universal histories are painted, sung, danced and traced across landscapes. Deborah Bird Rose's work on Australian Indigenous histories, for example, highlights the importance of events *taking place* rather than being in time.[4] Geography is the primary organising principle of meaning in Australian Indigenous histories, meaning that it is quite possible for figures from different times to connect with one another as if they were contemporaries. The moral import of these stories also becomes clear when we consider the common figure of the 'trickster' in Native American tales. As Richard Erdoes has shown, bodily transformations and transgressive actions by figures such as the Raven of the Northwest peoples remind audiences about the permeability of boundaries between the human and the other, and between proper and improper action.[5] The continuation of these traditions today highlights the deep history of world history making.

Ancient universal histories

Herodotus (*c.* 484–20 BCE) is commonly described as the 'father of Western history' and he is also credited for having recognised that history can be a means for understanding the world. In his *Histories*, Herodotus delimited the military and political history of the Greeks in part by discrimination from barbarian 'others', and thus established the link between world history writing and actual and desired world order. Studies of the field, however, typically begin at a later point, with the emergence of the genre of 'universal history'. 'Universal history' has at least four meanings. First, it denotes a comprehensive and perhaps also unified history of the known world or universe; second, a history that illuminates truths, ideals or principles that are thought to belong to the whole world; third, a history of the world unified by the workings of a single mind; and fourth, a history of the world that has passed down through an unbroken line of transmission.[6]

---

4 Deborah Bird Rose, *Dingo Makes Us Human* (Cambridge: Cambridge University Press, 2000).
5 Richard Erdoes and Alfonso Ortiz, *American Indian Trickster Tales* (Harmondsworth: Penguin, 1999).
6 For a series of essays on universal history, see Peter Liddel and Andrew Fear (eds.), *Historiae Mundi: Studies in Universal History* (London: Duckworth, 2010).

Universal history is thought to have emerged with the Greek writer Ephorus (405–330 BCE) and the climate of cosmopolitanism engendered by the conquests of Alexander of Macedon. Raoul Mortley has also tried to demonstrate the influence of Aristotelian philosophy on the emergence of the genre, but the survival of less than 5 per cent of Hellenistic literature makes the formulation of general explanations difficult.[7] Additionally, it is not always clear whether extant histories might have been parts of universal histories: for example, commentators have argued that the Roman historian Arrian's (c. 92–c. 180 CE) *Anabasis Alexandri* and *Indica* were originally united. Even José Miguel Alonso-Núñez's more inclusive description of the first universal historians as those who dealt 'with the history of humankind from the earliest times, and in all parts of the world known to them' is problematic, because it masks the contribution of those – particularly women – who composed biographical catalogues.[8] While not spatio-temporally exhaustive, biographical catalogues were designed to illuminate universal social, moral or political principles.

Any history of the field must also take into account the rich traditions of Chinese and Islamic universal history writing, which date from at least the third century BCE and the ninth century CE respectively. In China, Han historian Sima Qian (c. 145–90 BCE) synthesised historical processes into an organic whole in his presentation of events, activities and biographies of emperors, officials and other important people, beginning with the semi-mythical first sage rulers of China. The Muslim historian Abu Ja'far al-Tabari (c. 839–923) began before the creation of Adam, and used Biblical, Greek, Roman, Persian and Byzantine sources to present history as a long and unbroken process of cultural transmission.

Ancient universal history writing flourished after campaigns of political expansion, the advent of standardised systems of chronology and the spread of monotheistic religions such as Christianity and Islam. Writers followed no single template, and, as a result, their works varied widely in scope, structure and world vision. In simple terms, there is no template for universal history. The adoption of a particular view of universal history could depend on a host of reasons, both intellectual and pragmatic. Polybius (c. 203–120 BCE) and

---

7 Raoul Mortley, *The Idea of Universal History from Hellenistic Philosophy to Early Christian Historiography* (Lewiston: Edwin Mellen, 1996).
8 J. M. Alonso-Núñez, 'The emergence of universal historiography from the 4th to the 2nd Centuries B.C.', in H. Verdins, G. Schepens and E. de Keyser (eds.), *Purposes of History: Proceedings of the International Colloquium – Leuven, 24–26 May 1988* (Leuven: Peeters Publishers, 1990), p. 197.

Diodorus of Sicily (*c.* 90–21 BCE), for instance, agreed that the truth of history was to be gleaned by treating it as a connected whole, but whereas Polybius' decision was based on an observation of the spread of Roman power, Diodorus assumed the existence of a universal human nature.

Variations were also evident across cultural and religious groups. For example, as viewed by Eusebius of Caesarea (*c.* 263–339 CE), St Augustine of Hippo (354–430), Paulus Orosius (fl. 414–17) and Bishop Otto of Freising (*c.* 1111–58), God's work in the world and the victory of Christianity was to be narrated through a seven-age framework that had been adapted from Jewish works like Josephus ben Matthias' *Jewish Antiquities* (93 CE). Islamic writers like Abu Ja'far al-Tabari also saw universal history as structured through successive ages and infused their accounts of events with predictions of future judgement. The number of ages in their works, however, was more often three than seven. Furthermore, they derived their status as universal histories in part because of their construction out of *isnads*: unbroken chains of transmission. For many Islamic writers of the Abbasid dynasty (749/750–1258), universal history thus entailed both chronological and historiographical continuity. Exceptions, like Abu Al-husayn 'ali ibn Al-husayn Al Ma'sudi's (*c.* 888–957) chronologically, philosophically and geographically arranged *Muruj adh-dhahab wa ma'adin al-jawahir* (The Meadows of Gold and Mines of Gems), were given a highly critical reception. Later writers eschewed *isnads* as a narrative and methodological intrusion and built upon Al Ma'sudi's approach. Ibn Khaldun (1332–1406), for instance, combined philosophy, geography and social theory in his *Kitab al-'Ibar.*

Chronologically arranged universal histories were also produced in China, as Sima Guang's (1019–86) *Zi Zhi Tong Jian* (Comprehensive Mirror to Aid in Government) attests. However, it is the synchronic, encyclopaedic structure of official Chinese histories that most sets them apart from other historiographical traditions. The first four official histories – the *Shiji* (Records of the Grand Historian) begun by Sima Tan (d. *c.* 110 BCE) and completed by Sima Qian, the *Hanshu* (History of the Former Han Dynasty) by Ban Gu (32–92 CE), the *Sanguozhi* (History of the Three Kingdoms) by Chen Shou (d. 297 CE) and the *Hou Hanshu* (History of the Later Han) by Fan Ye (398–445 CE) – established a four-part division of histories into imperial annals (*benji*), tables (*biao*), treatises (*shu*) and biographies or memoirs (*juan* or *liezhaun*). The first part documented major events in imperial families, the second month-to-month events for government offices, the third knowledge of an enormous range of activities and the fourth accounts of virtuous and infamous individuals and collective biographies. Though modified, this

44

structure was employed in official histories right up to *Qingshi gao* (Draft History of the Qing Dynasty, 1928).[9]

Global exchanges and unity

The growth of intellectual, economic and socio-political networks of exchange in the paleolithic and agrarian eras prompted the defence, augmentation and revision of universal and later world historical views. Labels and typologies were used to bestow respect upon, to accommodate or to subjugate newly encountered peoples. In many European universal histories, for instance, race and gender typologies coalesced in narratives of the stagnation of the effeminate East and the progressive perfection of the masculine West. Some writers used other cultures to make criticisms about their own: to take one example, Voltaire (1694–1778) used the history of China in *Essai sur les Moeurs et l'Espirit des Nations* to highlight the savagery, superstition and irrationality of Christian Europe. Corresponding examples from outside of Europe may also be found, like Wei Yuan (1794–1856), who compared the historical paths of Europe and China in *Haiguo Tuzhi* (Illustrated Treatise on the Sea Kingdom), or the argument that learning the superior technology of the Europeans could be a means to control them. Universal histories were also used to promote the interests and ideals of particular social groups: for example, Philip Melancthon (1497–1560) and Bishop Jacques Bénigne Bossuet (1627–1704) saw universal history as an excellent means to defend Christian beliefs. Promoting a different cause, in *The Book of the City of Ladies* (1405) Christine de Pizan narrated a hierarchically arranged universal history of female warriors, good wives and saintly women to empower female readers to aspire to the city of womanly virtue. Joseph Swetnam, on the other hand, argued in his pamphlet *The Arraignment of Lewd, Idle and Forward women* (1615) that women are, like the rib that they were fashioned from in the Judaeo-Christian creation story, 'crooked by nature'.

Universal histories proliferated after the aggregration of printing technologies in fifteenth-century Europe. This made decisions on the proper means of

---

9 For comparisons of universal history in China and Greece, see Siep Stuurman, 'Herodotus and Sima Qian: History and the anthropological turn in ancient Greece and Han China', *Journal of World History* (2008), 1–40; Thomas R. Martin, *Herodotus and Sima Qian. The First Great Historians of Greece and China. A Brief History with Documents* (Boston and New York: Bedford/St. Martins, 2010); Craig Benjamin, 'But from this time forth history becomes a connected whole: state expansion and the origins of universal history', *Journal of Global History* 9/3 (2014), 357–78.

researching, writing and reading them increasingly urgent to many writers. In *Method for the Easy Comprehension of History*, for example, Jean Bodin (1530–96) advanced that the logical order of universal history was chronological, from the general to the specific and from Europe outwards to the rest of the known world. Misorder, in his view, could weaken the powers of the mind. Conversely, Christopher Cellarius (1638–1707) argued for the tripartite division of history into 'ancient', 'medieval' and 'new' periods.

The philosophical turn and the rise of mass literacy

Over the course of the seventeenth century more universal historians endeavoured to establish a proper 'scientific' or 'philosophical' foundation for history. What these terms meant varied from place to place. In Scotland, for instance, 'conjectural historians' such as Francis Hutcheson (1694–1746), Adam Smith (1723–90), Adam Ferguson (1723–1816), John Millar (1735–1801), William Robertson (1721–93), Dugald Stewart (1753–1828) and David Hume (1711–76) worked to explain the origins of human sociability, a 'moral sense' that would account not only for human community, but also for human progress. The Italian scholar Giambattista Vico (1688–1744), on the other hand, saw the Latin language, Roman law and the Homeric poems as a point of entry into the 'scientific' study of the course and recourse of nations' histories. French historians like Fontenelle (1657–1757), Étienne Bonnot de Condillac (1715–80), the Marquis de Condorcet (1743–94), Anne Robert Jacques Turgot (1727–81) and Jean Étienne Montucla (1725–99) tracked the history of the 'human spirit' or mind from barbaric beginnings to the height of enlightened, mannered 'civilisation'. In Germany, G. W. F. Hegel (1770–1831) noted, the Enlightenment was not against religious belief, as he believed it was in France. Johann Gottfried Herder (1744–1803) adopted an organic view, outlining the unique features of cultures in childhood, infancy, manhood and old age. Immanuel Kant (1724–1804) detected reason in the long history of humanity's 'unsocial sociability', Leopold von Ranke (1795–1886) sought the 'holy hieroglyph' or mark of God and meaning in world cultures and Hegel detected 'progress of the consciousness of freedom' in the movement of world history from the East to the West.[10] Later in the nineteenth century, Karl Marx (1818–83) inverted Hegel's philosophical programme, suggesting that the material conditions of life shape human

---

10 G. W. F. Hegel, *Philosophy of History* (New York: Dover, 1956 [1899]), p. 19.

freedom, not the other way round. Chinese historians, too, including Guo Songtao (1818–91), Xue Fucheng (1838–94), Wang Tao (1828–90), Yan Fu (1854–1921) and Liang Qichao (1873–1929) increasingly urged the recognition of world history as a narrative of struggle for technological supremacy.

Universal histories designed for mass consumption were also produced. Reader, reviewer and publisher demands for morally edifying works favoured the production of overtly didactic texts, often in the form of biographical catalogues. This type of writing proved particularly popular with middle-class women, who were given access to works designed to describe a world order in which women were the domestic companions of men. Notable examples include Mary Hay's *Female Biography, or Memoirs of Illustrious and Celebrated Women, of all Ages and Countries* (1803), Lucy Aikin's *Epistles on Women, Exemplifying their Character and Condition in Various Ages and Nations with Miscellaneous Poems* (1810), Anna Jameson's *Memoirs of Celebrated Female Sovereigns* (1832), Laure Junot's *Memoirs of Celebrated Women* (1834), Mary Elizabeth Hewitt's *Heroines of History* (1852), Sarah Josepha Hale's *Woman's Record* (1853), Mary Cowden Clarke's *World-Noted Women* (1858), Sarah Strickley Ellis' *The Mothers of Great Men* (1859) and Clara Balfour's *Women Worth Emulating* (1877). While often dismissed as methodologically impoverished, many of these works acted as conduits for womanist and reformist thought. Lydia Maria Child's *The History of the Condition of Women, in Various Ages and Nations* (1835), for example, is underpinned by arguments against slavery and for female suffrage. Hester Piozzi's *Retrospection* (1801) is also an important example, revealing how history written on the largest scales could serve one person's desire to achieve social acceptance.

Universal history as primitive world history?

From the eighteenth century, existing ideas about universal history came to be seen as increasingly out of step with the specialised national research that accompanied the professionalisation of history teaching, research and writing. Some accommodation was achieved through the production of multi-author, multi-volume universal history compendia or encyclopaedias, and some single-authored world histories continued. For example, right after the devastation of the First World War, and in part as a response to the slaughter, H. G. Wells (1866–1946) wrote *The Outline of History*, which readers could buy in cheap bi-weekly instalments, just as they had Wells' earlier novel *The War of the Worlds*, and millions did. In this, he explained that true universal history was defined in part by the 'unity of presentation attainable only when the whole subject has been passed through one single mind'.[11] It is assumed by many historiographical commentators that Wells' efforts were akin to Canute's attempt to defy the tide. In their view, universal history was a proto-world history that was ushered aside in the twentieth century as speculation was replaced by rigorous forms of analysis and a greater respect for primary evidence. Universal history, however, survives in many forms, such as philosophies of history (for example, Aron, *The Dawn of Universal History*, 1961; and Dennett, *Freedom Evolves*, 2002), compendia (UNESCO, *History of Humankind*, 1963), the fusion of science and history in the sub-field of 'big' history (Spier, *The Structure of Big History*, 1996; and Christian, *Maps of Time*, 2004) and of course multi-volume overviews such as this.

Universal history did not disappear in the twentieth century: it simply became one of a number of approaches to the writing of what was increasingly called 'world history'. Roughly contemporary with Wells' *Outline of History* were Oswald Spengler's *The Decline of the West* (1918–22), Sigmund Freud's *Civilization and its Discontents* (1930), Arnold J. Toynbee's *A Study of History* (1932–61), Jawaharlal Nehru's *Glimpses of World History* (1934), Lewis Mumford's *Technics and Civilization* (1934), V. Gordon Childe's *Man Makes Himself* (1936), Pitirim A. Sorokin's *Social and Cultural Dynamics* (1937), Norbert Elias' *The Civilizing Process* (1939), José Karl Polanyi's *The Great Transformation* (1944), Mary Ritter Beard's *Woman as Force in History* (1946), Karl Jaspers' *The Origin and Goal of History* (1947), Ortega y Gasset's *An Interpretation of Universal History* (1949) and Christopher Dawson's *The Dynamics of World History* (1956). Though presenting a wide range of foci – psychological, religious, political, philosophical, sociological, cultural, archaeological and technological – an interest in the trajectories of civilisations spans these works. In Spengler's view, for example, Western civilisation was 'Faustian' because the limitless ambition of its people was likely to be its downfall; similarly, when Toynbee began *A Study of History*, he detected a number of suicidal tendencies in Western civilisation. During the composition of volume six of twelve, however, he modified his view and concluded that the future would bring an age of universal churches or states of selflessness or compassion. It is worth wondering whether Niall Ferguson's most recent works such as *The Great Degeneration: How Institutions Decay and Economies Die* (2013) are a continuation of the dystopic vision of the world promoted by Spengler.

11 H. G. Wells, *The Outline of History: Being a Plain History of Life and Mankind* (New York: Macmillan, 1920), p. 2.

Modernisation, dependency and world system analyses

A more optimistic assessment of 'modern' or 'Western' civilisation was also offered in the works of modernisation scholars. Of interest to them were the historical paths of development in the West that might be used to study and foster development in the 'developing' world. Key contributions to modernisation analysis included W. W. Rostow's *How it all Began: Origins of the Modern Economy* (1975), Cyril Black's *The Dynamics of Modernization: A Study in Comparative History* (1966), Reinhard Bendix's *Nation-Building and Citizenship* (1977) and E. L. Jones' *The European Miracle: Environments, Economies, and Geopolitics in the History of Europe and Asia* (1986).

A disparate group of neo-Marxist scholars disagreed, noting the inability of modernisation scholars to explain Latin American economic development, and suggested an alternative in the form of dependency and, later, world system theory. While modernisation scholars looked to the internal characteristics of particular civilisations, dependency and world system theorists stressed the need to study networks of economic and political exchange and more particularly inequalities in the distribution of roles, functions and power that fostered states of dependency. Dependency theory was advanced first in the writings of Latin American scholars like Paul Baran (*The Political Economy of Growth*, 1957) and then taken to a global audience in Andre Gunder Frank's *World Accumulation, 1492–1789* (1978) and *Dependent Accumulation and Underdevelopment* (1979). Frank's work, in turn, influenced Immanuel Wallerstein, who went on to elaborate world system theory in a series of works including *The Modern World System* (three volumes, 1974–89) and *Historical Capitalism* (1983). In *The Modern World System*, he argued that the system of the title originated in fifteenth-century Europe and that it was composed of a 'core' (advanced industrial states), a 'periphery' (weak states engaged in raw materials production) and a 'semi-periphery' (intermediate states).

World system analysis was combined with a range of methodologies, including anthropology (Eric Wolf, *Europe and the People without History*, 1982), archaeology (N. Kardulias (ed.), *World-Systems Theory in Practice: Leadership, Production, and Exchange*, 1999), geography (Paul Knox and Peter Taylor, *World Cities in a World-System*, 1995) and cultural history (John Obert Voll, 'Islam as a Special World-System', *Journal of World History*, 1994). The spatio-temporal scope of world system studies also increased, with Leften Stavrianos (*Global Rift*, 1981), Janet Abu-Lughod (*After European*

Hegemony, 1989), Andre Gunder Frank (*ReOrient*, 1997), Frank and Barry Gills (*The World System: Five Hundred Years or Five Thousand?*, 1993) and Christopher Chase-Dunn and Thomas Hall (*Core/Periphery Relations in Precapitalist Worlds*, 1991) exploring Afro-Eurasian systems of exchange up to 7,000 years ago.

The relational shift: postcolonial, transnational, new imperial, comparative and new world histories

Postcolonial scholars also adapted dependency and world system theory. First brought to the attention of world historians with the publication of Edward Said's *Orientalism* (1978), postcolonial theorists enhanced political and economic criticisms of colonialism with cultural analyses. Representation and language are crucial for the construction of an 'Other': for example, Marshall Hodgson (*Rethinking World History*, 1993), Dipesh Chakrabarty (*Provincializing Europe*, 2000), Ranajit Guha (*History at the Limit of World-History*, 2002) and Samir Amin (*Global History: A View from the South*, 2010) argued that the language, concepts, periodisation and structure of world histories can minimise and even mask the historical activities of those 'outside' the West. Guha's work advances an alternative, asking us to consider whether the work of the Indian poet Tagore might serve as the foundation for a new approach to history. World historians with an interest in postcolonial themes such as Michael Adas (*Islamic and European Expansion*, 1993) and Margaret Strobel (*Gender, Sex, and Empire*, 1993) sought to balance the demands of aligning the experiences of colonised subjects and recognising the specificities of race, class, nationality, religion, sexuality, and epistemic, social, political and economic hierarchies and gender relations.

Dependency, world system and postcolonial world histories formed part of the wider shift in the twentieth century towards the study of relations between peoples across the globe. This shift is clearly discernible over the long career of William H. McNeill, who is often taken as a central or 'father' figure in twentieth-century world historical studies. While the theme of diffusion shaped his first major world historical work – *The Rise of the West* (1963) – the depth and breadth of his interest in world historical webs of interaction emerged more fully in *Plagues and Peoples* (1976), *The Pursuit of Power* (1982), *Keeping Together in Time* (1990) and *The Human Web* (2003, with J. R. McNeill). Human interaction on the largest scale – over the globe – was also the subject of new global historical studies. New global historians like Bruce Mazlish and Ralph Buultjens (*Conceptualizing Global History*, 1993),

Anthony Hopkins (*Globalization in World History*, 2001), Roland Robertson (*Globalization*, 1992), Manuel Castells (*The Information Age*, 1996–98) and Arjun Appadurai (*Modernity at Large*, 1996) looked to economic, anthropological, political and cultural evidence to track the phenomenon of globalisation – the emergence of an integrated anthropogenic globe – over the course of the twentieth century.

Transnational, comparative, new imperial and new world historians were also interested in human interaction, but their works were smaller in spatio-temporal focus than those of other world historians. This contraction may be explained by reference to, among other things, the perception that the recent explosion in evidence made large-scale synthesis too demanding, and postmodern and postcolonial claims that large-scale narratives were instruments of intellectual imperialism. Of particular interest to these writers were phenomena such as intergovernmental organisations, internationalist movements, technological exchange and diffusion, migration and diasporas, cultural hybridity and transnational corporations. For example, Fernand Braudel (*The Mediterranean and the Mediterranean World in the Era of Philip II*, 1949), Philip Curtin (*The Atlantic Slave Trade*, 1969; *The Rise and Fall of the Plantation Complex*, 1990; *Cross-Cultural Trade in World History*, 1984), Niels Steensgaard (*The Asian Trade Revolution of the Seventeenth Century*, 1974), K. N. Chaudhuri (*Trade and Civilisation in the Indian Ocean*, 1985; *Asia before Europe*, 1990), Eric Jones, Lionel Frost and Colin White (*Coming Full Circle*, 1993), John Thornton (*Africa and Africans in the Making of the Atlantic World, 1400–1680*, 1992; *A Cultural History of the Atlantic World, 1250–1820*, 2012), Adam McKeown (*Chinese Migrant Networks*, 2001; *Melancholy Order: Asian Migration and the Globalization of Borders*, 2011) and Matt Masuda (*Pacific Worlds: A History of Seas, Peoples, and Cultures*, 2012) analysed trade and cultural diasporas centred on the Mediterranean, Indian, Atlantic and Pacific Oceans.

A widening view: gender and world history and world environmental histories

Relations of power between persons were also of central concern to women's and gender world historians. Gender history is not women's history, but rather the study of varying relations between constructed gender categories. For example, Michel Foucault noted the shifting shape of 'sexuality' across ancient and modern history (*The History of Sexuality*, 1976–84) and Ida Blom has demonstrated how varying gender systems shaped understandings of the nation-state.[12] More recently, Merry Wiesner-Hanks and Judith Zinsser have drawn attention to gender in world history writing, and argued that favoured concepts, narrative forms and even periodisation frameworks have served to render the experiences of many women and men invisible.[13]

In the second half of the twentieth century, world histories took an increasing interest in the ways in which the organic and inorganic environment have both shaped and been shaped by human activities. Jared Diamond, for instance, looked at the role of environmental factors in the emergence of the 'developing' and 'developed' world divide (*Guns, Germs and Steel*, 1998) and John Richards at the environment in the age of exploration and conquest (*The Unending Frontier*, 2006). Brian Fagan considered the role of climatic phenomena like El Niño in shaping historical events (*Floods, Famines and Emperors*, 2001), while, in contrast, Mike Davis stressed the opportunistic use of El Niño by colonial powers to create a world market economy (*Late Victorian Holocausts*, 2001). John R. McNeill outlined growing awareness of the impact of human activities on the earth from the pedosphere to the stratosphere (*Something New Under the Sun*, 2000). Other writers have drawn upon conceptual models and theories from the natural sciences to explain historical changes: for example, in *Nonzero* (2000), Robert Wright looked to game theory, Stephen J. Gould (*Wonderful Life*, 1989) and Murray Gell Mann (*The Quark and the Jaguar*, 1994) disagreed about whether evolution implied increasing complexity, and Eric Chaisson tracked increasing energy flows from the big bang to the evolution of humans (*Cosmic Evolution*, 2000). More radically, too, writers like Dorion Sagan and Lynn Margulis (*Microcosmos*, 1986) questioned the privileging of human actions and argued for a world history centred on cells.

World history: professional and popular

While the twentieth century saw the emergence of organisations, journals, conferences, internet discussion forums and syllabuses focused on world history, the field was not – and likely will never be – of interest to trained specialists alone. Following in the tradition of H. G. Wells, Mark Kurlansky

12 M. Morris, 'Sexing the survey: The issue of sexuality in world history since 1500', *World History Bulletin* 14/2 (1998), 11, accessed 13 September 2014, www.thewha.org/bulletins/fall_1998.pdf; and I. Blom, 'World history as gender history', in R. Dunn (ed.), *The New World History: A Teacher's Companion* (New York: Bedford, 2000).

13 M. Weisner-Hanks (ed.), *Gender in History: Global Perspectives*, 2nd edn. (Oxford: Wiley-Blackwell, 2010); and J. Zinsser, 'Gender', in Wiesner-Hanks, *Gender in History*.

(*Salt: A World History*, 2002), Charles C. Mann (*1493: Uncovering the World Columbus Created*, 2012) and Lincoln Paine (*The Sea and Civilization: A Maritime History of the World*, 2013) are just three of the many writers who have produced world historical works for the benefit of non-specialist readers around the world. David Christian's web-based Big History project highlights the power of digital platforms for rewriting approaches to world history education, as does *World History Connected*, an e-journal published through editorial offices at Hawaii Pacific University. World history is, and probably will continue to be, characterised by multiplicity: first, in the use of data from different times and places; second, in the blending of many methods from a broad range of disciplines; third, in the diverse backgrounds and purposes of authors; and finally, in the mixture of narrative styles and organisational concepts. For this reason, it makes sense to speak of 'world histories' rather than of 'world history'.

FURTHER READING

Alonso-Núñez, J. M., *The Idea of Universal History in Greece: From Herodotus to the Age of Augustus*, Amsterdam: J. C. Gieben, 2001.

'The emergence of universal historiography from the 4th to the 2nd centuries BC', in H. Verdin, G. Schepens and E. de Keyser (eds.), *Purposes of History: Proceedings of the International Colloquium – Leuven, 24–26 May 1988*, Leuven: Peeters Publishers, 1990.

Bentley, J., *Shapes of World History in Twentieth-Century Scholarship*, Washington, D.C.: American Historical Association, 1996.

Breisach, E., *Historiography: Ancient, Medieval and Modern*, 3rd edn. Chicago, IL: University of Chicago Press, 2008.

Burke, P., 'European views of world history from Giovo to Voltaire', *History of European Ideas* 6/3 (1985): 237–51.

Chakrabarty, D., *Provincializing Europe: Postcolonial Thought and Historical Difference*, Princeton, NJ: Princeton University Press, 2000.

Christian, D., 'Big History Project', www.bighistoryproject.com

'The return of universal history', *History and Theory*, Theme Issue, 49 (December 2010): 5–26.

Clarke, K., *Between Geography and History: Hellenistic Constructions of the Roman World*, Oxford: Oxford University Press, 1999.

Costello, P., *World Historians and their Goals: Twentieth Century Answers to Modernism*, DeKalb, IL: Northern Illinois University Press, 1994.

Curtis K. R., and J. H. Bentley (eds.), *Architects of World History: Researching the Global Past*, Oxford: Wiley-Blackwell, 2014.

Dirlik, A., V. Bahl and P. Gran (eds.), *History after the Three Worlds: Post-Eurocentric Historiography*, Lanham, MD: Rowman & Littlefield, 2000.

Dumont, G.-H., UNESCO History of Humanity: Description of the project, accessed 13 September 2014, www.unesco.org/culture/humanity/html_eng/projet.htm.

Dunn, R. (ed.), *The New World History: A Teacher's Companion*, New York: Bedford, 2000.

Duara, P., V. Murthy and A. Sartori (eds.), *A Companion to Global Historical Thought*, Oxford: Wiley-Blackwell, 2014.

Eliade, M., *The Myth of the Eternal Return*, Princeton, NJ: Princeton University Press, 2005 [1954].

Erdoes, R., and A. Ortiz, *American Indian Trickster Tales*, Harmondsworth: Penguin, 1999.

Geyer, M., and C. Bright, 'World history in a global age', *American Historical Review* 100 (1987): 1034–60.

Guha, R., *History at the Limit of World-History*, New York: Columbia University Press, 2002.

Hodgson, M., *Rethinking World History: Essays on Europe, Islam and World History*, Edmund Burke III (ed.), Cambridge: Cambridge University Press, 1993.

Hughes, J. D., 'Bibliographic essay: Writing on global environmental history', in *An Environmental History of the World*, London: Routledge, 2002, pp. 242–8.

Hughes-Warrington, M., 'Big History', *Historically Speaking* 4/2 (2002): 16–17, 20.

(ed.), *World Histories*, London: Palgrave Macmillan, 2004.

'World history', in M. Spongberg, B. Caine and A. Curthoys (eds.), *The Palgrave Companion to Women's Historical Writing*, London: Palgrave Macmillan, 2005.

H-World (internet discussion) www.h-net.msu.edu/~world/

Iriye, A., and P.-Y. Saunier (eds.), *The Palgrave Dictionary of Transnational History: From the Mid-19th century to the Present Day*, New York: Palgrave Macmillan, 2009.

The Journal of Global History 1, 2006–.

The Journal of World History 1, 1990–.

Manning, P., *Navigating World History: Historians Create a Global Past*, New York: Palgrave, 2003.

Mazlish, B., and R. Buultjens (eds.), *Conceptualizing Global History*, Boulder, CO: Westview, 1993.

McNeill, J. R., and E. S. Mauldin (eds.), *A Companion to Global Environmental History*, Oxford: Wiley-Blackwell, 2012.

Meade T. A., and M. E. Wiesner-Hanks (eds.), *A Companion to Gender History*, Oxford: Wiley-Blackwell, 2004.

Momigliano, A., 'Greek historiography', *History and Theory* 17/1 (1978): 1–28.

Morris, M., 'Sexing the survey: The issue of sexuality in world history since 1500', *World History Bulletin* 14/2 (1998), 11, accessed 13 September 2014, www.thewha.org/bulletins/fall_1998.pdf.

Mortley, R., *The Idea of Universal History from Hellenistic Philosophy to Early Christian Historiography*, Lewiston: Edwin Mellon, 1996.

Northrop, D. (ed.), *A Companion to World History*, Oxford: Wiley-Blackwell, 2012.

Pomper, P., R. Elphick and R. Vann (eds.), *World History: Ideologies, Structures, Identities*, Malden, MA: Blackwell, 1998.

Robinson, C., *Islamic Historiography*, Cambridge: Cambridge University Press, 2003.

Rose, D. B., *Dingo Makes Us Human*, Cambridge: Cambridge University Press, 2000.

Schneide, A., and S. W. Schwierdrzik (eds.), 'Chinese historiography in comparative perspective', *History and Theory* 35/4 (1996).

Sogner, S. (ed.), *Making Sense of Global History: The 19th International Congress of the Historical Sciences*, Oslo: Universitetsforlaget, 2001.

Steensgaard, N., 'Universal history for our times', *Journal of Modern History* 45 (1973): 72–82.

Stuchtey, B., and E. Fuchs (eds.), *Across Cultural Borders: Historiography in Global Perspective*, Lanham, MD: Rowman & Littlefield, 2002.

Writing World History 1800–2000, Oxford: Oxford University Press, 2003.

Weisner-Hanks, M., *Gender in History: Global Perspectives*, 2nd edn., Oxford: Wiley-Blackwell, 2010.

World History Connected: The EJournal of Learning and Teaching, www.worldhistoryconnected.org

Zeitschrift fuer Weltgeschichte 1, 2000–.

3

The evolution of world histories

DOMINIC SACHSENMAIER

Trajectories outside of academia

Reflecting upon the evolution of world history leads us to some foundational questions about historiography at large.[1] After all, we need to leave the international landscapes of modern-day universities behind and consider multifarious ways of dealing with the past, throughout the world. Particularly if we are regarding a wide variety of cultural contexts, history and historiography are rather hard to define. Quite a lot of scholars have debated the demarcation lines between history and other genres such as literature. For example, there is the question whether to include oral traditions such as legends, myths or even songs into the picture. The same is the case with religious texts, which played an important role in the genesis of historical scholarship.[2]

In recent years, academic historians have become somewhat more reluctant to use modern Western definitions as the universal standard from which "historiography" can be understood. This growing willingness to pay more attention to other genres and cultural possibilities also impacts the ways in which we conceptualize the trajectories of "world history." When we have to be more flexible with the meaning of "history," it will be impossible to define the "world" in "world history" as a space of clear-cut, universal dimensions. In any culture and time period, the history of the world could only possibly mean the history of one's own world, that is, the world one was exposed to through lived experiences, personal travels and the accounts of others. In that sense, the worlds of a fourteenth-century Maya, a Northern European, a

1 Research for this chapter has been supported by an Academy of Korean Studies Grant funded by the Korean government (AKS-2010-DZZ-3103).
2 Peter Burke, "History, myth and fiction: Doubts and debates," in José Rabasa, Masayuki Sato, Edoardo Tortarolo, and Daniel Woolf (eds.), *The Oxford History of Historical Writing* (New York: Oxford University Press, 2012), vol. III, pp. 261–81.

Japanese or a Polynesian were certainly unlike each other. Yet at the same time they had a decisive element in common: they all reached far beyond single political realms or cultural habitats.

Seen from this perspective, world history differed from other forms of history in the very basic sense that it not only focused on one's own heritage but also sought to include "others" into the picture. If we define world history along those very basic lines, we certainly find important examples for it all over the globe. This is even the case with societies that did not transmit historical information through writing but rather orally, often using special mnemonic techniques.[3] For instance, in Australia Aboriginal legends and songs dealt with the history of the known world and its peoples.[4] An African example are the Arokin, a professional group in the Yoruba kingdom in present-day Nigeria, Togo and Benin, whose task has been to remember experiences and recount them orally.[5] Already at a rather early stage, the accounts of Arabic travelers and traders impacted this tradition by providing information about other parts of the world. In return, Sub-Saharan oral traditions were an important source for written Muslim reports, which found their ways into Arabic "world historical" scholarship. As this example suggests, already at an early stage there was no categorical divide between oral and written forms of world history.[6]

It would be flawed to treat such oral – mythological and other – traditions merely as the precursors to today's world historical scholarship. This would assume that these earlier traditions of world history have ceased to exist and university-based approaches largely came to replace them. Yet up until the present day oral accounts and legends play a strong role around the world, and so do decidedly religious visions of world history. For the latter, one only needs to think of the pluriverse of today's religious schools, a large number of which disseminate their own interpretations of the world and its history. Examples range from history education at many Islamic madrasas to the wealth of Christian world history textbooks in the United States. Particularly in fundamentalist circles, many of these texts are written from

---

3 Jan Vansina, *Oral Tradition as History* (Madison: University of Wisconsin Press, 1985).
4 Paul Faulstich, "Mapping the mythological landscape: An Aboriginal way of being in the world," *Philosophy & Geography* 1 (1998), 197–221; and Margaret C. Ross, "Australian Aboriginal oral traditions," *Oral Tradition* 1 (1986), 231–71.
5 Falola Toyin, "History in Sub-Saharan Africa," in Stuart Macintyre, Juan Maiguashca, and Attila Pók (eds.), *The Oxford History of Historical Writing*, vol. IV, pp. 597–618.
6 For example about Isidore O. Benin, *Once Upon a Kingdom: Myth, Hegemony and Identity* (Bloomington: Indiana University Press, 1998).

unambiguously Islamic or biblical perspectives, sometimes even demonizing other societies and cultures.[7]

Hence there is little reason to render religious traditions of world history to a distant past, and the same is the case with oral traditions. Both are vibrant genres, and as such they continue to influence the world historical interpretations of countless people around the world. Given the state of the art of scholarship dealing with the evolution of world history, this chapter will not be able to systematically cross the divide between religious and secular forms of world history; neither will it be able to provide a balanced perspective between elite and other interpretations of the global past.[8] I will chiefly concentrate on educated circles and highbrow texts, and for my discussion of the nineteenth and twentieth centuries this means that I primarily focus on academic literature.

Early written traditions

Already more than two thousand years ago, there were quite a number of scholars – some of whom we may duly call "historians" – who paid much attention to cultural experiences outside their own societies and traditions. In European antiquity, one of the most prominent examples is Herodotus of Halicarnassus who lived between *c.* 484 and 425 BCE and has often been labeled as the "Father of History."[9] His masterpiece, the *Histories*, an account of the Greco-Persian War, is often praised for trying to depict different conditions and traditions from a neutral perspective. This might be an exaggeration since the work's narrative is structured around a somewhat problematic juxtaposition of the Greek polis as the harbor of freedom and the Persian Empire as a stronghold of tyranny.[10] In many regards, the *Histories* display a great cultural and political self-confidence against which other civilizations are measured.

7 See for instance Jerry H. Bentley, "Myths, wagers, and some moral implications of world history," *Journal of World History* 16 (2005), 51–82; and R. Scott Appleby, "History in the fundamentalist imagination," *Journal of American History* 89 (2002), 498–511.

8 For such movements in the field of intellectual history see Anthony Grafton, "The history of ideas: Precepts and practice, 1950–2000 and beyond," *Journal of the History of Ideas* 67 (2006), 1–32.

9 See for example Patrick Manning, *Navigating World History: Historians Create a Global Past* (New York: Palgrave Macmillan, 2003); and David Christian, "Scales," in Marnie Hughes-Warrington (ed.), *Palgrave Advances in World History* (London: Palgrave, 2006), pp. 64–89.

10 For more details see François Hartog, *The Mirror of Herodotus: The Representation of the Other in the Writing of History* (Berkeley: University of California Press, 1998).

Similar statements could be made about the massive, 130-chapter-long work *Historical Records* (*Shiji*) by the Chinese historian Sima Qian (d. 86 BCE). While the great Han-scholar also included China's neighboring peoples in his historical portraits, his depictions were nevertheless based on the idea of China's elevated civilizational and political status.[11] While Sima's work covers topics ranging from music to politics,[12] his main narrative strings moved chiefly through the Middle Kingdom and adjacent areas. Even though at his time some information on places such as India or the Central Asian kingdoms was available, Sima's work did not seek to cover their history. Still, in his work Sima Qian professed to be as accurate as possible: analogous to the (albeit unproven) claims of Herodotus to have traveled through much of his world, he undertook extensive journeys while working on his *Historical Records*.

The works of scholars like Herodotus or Sima Qian were certainly exceptional in scope and depth but one should avoid portraying them as the sole representatives of "world historical" thought within their respective cultures and epochs. For instance, in ancient Greece also scholars like Ephoros (d. 330 BCE), Polybius (d. *c.* 118 BCE) and Diodorus (d. 21 BCE) were making efforts to consider at least some outside experiences when writing about history. Similar statements could be made about quite a number of Chinese historians during the Han period such as Ban Gu (d. 92 CE).[13] The same is the case with the subsequent dynasties – an important scholar to be mentioned in this context is Cheng Hao (d. 1085), one of the most important thinkers during the Song period who famously emphasized that the histories of different countries follow specific timelines.[14]

A particular combination of "universal" historical scopes, geographic depictions and ethnographic accounts was flourishing in parts of the Islamic World. Already starting from the seventh and eighth centuries, many learned travelers published accounts of the world that they had either seen themselves or had been informed of, for example by trusted couriers.[15] Such texts

---

11 See for example Stephen W. Durrant, *The Cloudy Mirror: Tension and Conflict in the Writings of Sima Qian* (Albany: State University of New York, 1995).

12 Interesting reflections on Sima Qian's methodology: Grant, Hardy, "Can an ancient Chinese historian contribute to modern Western theory? The multiple narratives of Ssu-ma Ch'ien," *History and Theory* 33 (1994), 20–38.

13 See Q. Edward Wang, "History, space, and ethnicity: The Chinese worldview," *Journal of World History* 10 (1999), 285–305.

14 For more details see Masayuki Sato, "Comparative ideas and chronology," *History and Theory* 30 (1991), 275–301.

15 S. Akbar Muhammad, "The image of Africans in Arabic literature: Some unpublished manuscripts," in John R. Wills (ed.), *Islam and the Ideology of Slavery* (London: F. Cass, 1985), pp. 47–74.

could contain quite a lot of historical information, as in the case of the Baghdad-born traveler Ali ibn al-Husayn al-Masudi (d. 956), who in one of his works dealt with both pre-Islamic or non-Islamic world regions.[16] Other writings were based more on ethnographic descriptions but also contained important historical references – an example is the Spanish Muslim Ibn Jubayar's (d. 1217) account of his pilgrimage to Mecca.[17]

Among a wealth of learned Islamic accounts of other world regions, it is particularly the work of Ibn Khaldun (1332–1406) that deserves special mention.[18] Unsurpassed during its own time and long after, the work of the Tunisian-born thinker offered historical interpretations of areas ranging from Sub-Saharan Africa to Persia. He went far beyond mere descriptive accounts, for example by developing some cyclical theories of the rise and fall of great powers. He furthermore reflected on patterns of society and trade, and did so in ways that today are often interpreted as precursors to modern sociological and economist traditions. While Ibn Khaldun developed theories of general historical patterns, his work was still based on the idea that the Muslim World was exemplary and unique.

Compared to such Islamic accounts of the world, the Christian genre of universal histories was typically framed around even more immediate religious worldviews. Christian universal histories were repeatedly written in a spirit that sought to divide divine truth from heretical viewpoints. They had their origins in the later Roman Empire where they were famously represented by such scholars as Eusebius (d. 340) or Orosius (d. 417). However, they also blossomed during the European Middle Ages when they had such renowned representatives as Otto the Bishop of Freising (d. 1158).[19] They remained important until the eighteenth century and even after. Like many ancient Greek texts, Christian universal histories often contained ethnographical descriptions of distant peoples. Yet they typically followed biblical timelines with events such as the creation, the deluge or the incarnation of Christ as the main modes of periodization.

---

16 Tarif Khalidi, *Islamic Historiography: The Histories of Mas'udi* (Albany: State University of New York Press, 1975).

17 Ian R. Netton, "Basic structures and signs of alienation in the 'Rihla' of Ibn Jubayr," *Journal of Arabic Literature* 22 (1991), 21–37.

18 Allen Fromherz, *Ibn Khaldun: Life and Times* (Edinburgh: Edinburgh University Press, 2010).

19 Otto, Bishop of Freysing, *The Two Cities: A Chronicle of Universal History to the Year 1146 AD* (New York: Octagon, 1996).

World historiography during the
early modern period

Starting from the late fifteenth century, the European conquests began having massive impacts on entire world regions, particularly the Americas and the coastal regions of Sub-Saharan Africa. This also heavily influenced conceptions of history and "world" in societies that were being colonized by European powers. By contrast, in regions such as China or the Arabic World, European influences on historical thinking remained far more limited, and they did so until the late eighteenth or nineteenth centuries. Yet European expansionism was not the only transformation of power systems that proved to have a strong influence on "world historical thought" in important regions. For instance, Indian conceptions of the world were affected by the Moghul conquests and the ensuing influx of Islamic literature.[20]

The growing information about an increasingly interdependent world characterized by trans-continental flows of silver, spices and other commodities was chiefly gathered by European agents. But it also left its mark outside of Europe.[21] For example, Jesuit annotated world maps, which contained historical information, met such a degree of interest in early seventeenth-century China that there were multiple editions within a year of their first publication.[22] A telling example are also the annals by the Franciscan-educated Meso-American nobleman Chimalpahin who in his native Nahuatl language recorded both local history as well as events from Europe to Japan.[23] In addition, important Ottoman schools, which emerged during the expansion of the empire in the sixteenth and seventeenth centuries, incorporated some newly obtainable facts about other parts of the world. For instance, already during the 1500s some historically oriented works dealt with the Americas.[24]

In Europe, travelogues and learned accounts about distant lands and peoples appeared and dramatically widened the amount of information available on different parts of the world. An important example is Gonzalo

20 Daniel Woolf, *A Global History of History: The Making of Clio's Empire from Antiquity to the Present* (Cambridge: Cambridge University Press, 2011), pp. 178–229.
21 See for example Donald F. Lach, *Asia in the Making of Europe* (Chicago: University of Chicago Press, 1993), vol. IV.
22 See for example Joanna Waley-Cohen, *The Sextants of Beijing: Global Currents in Chinese History* (New York: W. W. Norton & Company, 1999); and D. E. Mungello, *The Great Encounter of China and the West, 1500–1800* (Lanham, MD: Rowman & Littlefield, 1999).
23 Serge Gruzinski, *Les Quatre Parties du Monde: Histoire d'une Mondialisation* (Paris: Martinière, 2004).
24 Thomas D. Goodrich, *The Ottoman Turks and the New World: A Study of Tarih-i-Hind-i Garbi and Sixteenth-Century Ottoman Americana* (Wiesbaden: Harrassowitz, 1990).

Fernández de Oviedo y Valdés' *Historia General y Natural de las Indias*, which was first published in 1535. Additional works include a history of China written fifty years later by the Augustinian Juan Gonzáles de Mendoza,[25] as well as the writings of Richard Hakluyt (d. 1616) and his students who portrayed British explorations in different parts of the globe.[26] These reports were often highly constructed and written through decidedly Christian or other European lenses. Yet at the same time they provided information about other world regions and their cultural heritage that could hardly be ignored by "world historical" scholarship.

The growing knowledge about different world regions fed into the epistemological crises of European historiography.[27] During the early modern period, many societies experienced their own "culture wars" or "history wars," for example between religious and proto-secular narratives. In this context, newly accessible non-European chronologies and historical records gave the debates on the nature and purpose of historiography a very peculiar spin. Especially Europe's universal historical traditions were being challenged through them: for instance, translations of Chinese, Japanese and Indian chronologies ran counter to biblical modes of historical periodization.[28] After all, Chinese timelines, of which proven records seemed to exist, preceded the assumed dates of events such as the deluge. This was obviously incompatible with the idea that such events had affected the entire world at the same time. Still, many later universal historians did not abandon the idea of global biblical timelines but instead chose to re-compute them. An important example for a work of this kind is Jacques-Bénigne Bossuet's *Discourse of Universal History* (1681).

As part of a more general trend, however, the connotation of "universal history"[29] became more disentangled from its biblical meanings. Now the

---

25 Juan González de Mendoza, *Historia des las Cosas Mas Notables, Ritos y Costumbres, del Gran Reyno de la China* (History of the Most Notable Things, Rites and Uses of the Great Kingdom of China) (Rome: Grassi, 1585).

26 See Diogo R. Curto, "European historiography of the East," in Rabasa, Sato, Tortarolo, and Woolf (eds.), *Oxford History of Historical Writing*, vol. III, pp. 536–55; and Kira von Ostenfeld-Suske, "A new history for a 'New World': The first one hundred years of Spanish historical writing," in Rabasa, Sato, Tortarolo, and Woolf (eds.), *Oxford History of Historical Writing*, vol. III, pp. 556–74.

27 Sanjay Subrahmanyam, "On world historians in the sixteenth century," *Representations* 91 (2005), 26–57.

28 See Edwin J. van Kley, "Europe's 'discovery' of China and the writing of world history," *American Historical Review* 76 (1971), 358–85.

29 Like "world history," the term "universal history" also dates back to premodern times, and both concepts never categorically differed from one another. "Universal history" is

term increasingly referred to works that covered most, if not all, parts of the known world – no matter whether these works were based on Christian timelines or not.[30] Partially reflecting the growing specialization of area expertise among scholars in most branches of historiography,[31] the eighteenth century witnessed the publication of some prominent multi-authored erudite universal histories. An example is the 65-volume *Universal History* that was mainly edited by the Arabist George Sale between 1747 and 1768.

It was particularly during the Enlightenment period when world historical reflections enjoyed an elevated standing among Europe's intellectual circles. Some of the most renowned thinkers of the time chose to engage in cultural or civilizational comparisons in order to accentuate their own ideas. For instance, Jean-Marie de Voltaire (d. 1778) or Christian Wolff (d. 1754) referred to Jesuit and other reports from China in order to espouse their ideal of political order without legal privileges for aristocrats and clergymen. An interesting development during this period is the growing number of cultural or civilizational comparisons. An example, which continues to be renowned up until the present day, is Charles de Montesquieu's (d. 1755) *Spirit of the Laws*. The work is centered on the idea that climate has a strong influence on forms of political, social and legal order.[32] Other scholars focused on different topics, for example Joseph de Guignes (d. 1800), who even compared historiographical methods and traditions across cultural boundaries.

The rising presence of comparative scholarship should not lead us to hurriedly celebrate Enlightenment cosmopolitanism, however. Thinkers like Voltaire may have referred to outside cultures in order to accentuate their critique of conditions at home. Yet at the same time they regarded European culture as a uniquely enabling framework for human reason – and it was reason that they appreciated more than any other human quality or talent. Scottish Enlightenment thinkers such as Lord Kames (d. 1782), William Robertson (d. 1793) or Adam Ferguson (d. 1816) tended to operate with even more clearly defined conceptions of civilizational maturity when theorizing about changes in political, social and economic systems. In most works, the main narrative put European regions ahead of other civilizations, at least in respects considered to be crucial for the progress of societies. At the same

---

no longer widely used in Anglophone publications but the expression remains rather common in some other languages, including French.

30 Tamara Griggs, "Universal history from Counter-Reformation to Enlightenment," *Modern Intellectual History* 4 (2007), 219–47.

31 For the following see particularly Woolf, *A Global History of History*, pp. 281–343.

32 Charles de Montesquieu, *De l'Esprit des Loix* (Geneva: Barrillot & fils, 1748).

time, both Scottish Enlightenment thinkers and their counterparts in the rest of Europe still regarded "civilization" chiefly as a pluralistic category. The idea that every epoch and people was characterized by distinct principles and hence could not be evaluated by universal criteria was particularly enunciated by thinkers such as Johann Gottfried Herder (d. 1803).

During the 1600s and 1700s, European world historical scholarship certainly had no parallels in China, India or elsewhere in terms of the amount and quality of information available about other world regions. Yet at the same time, it would be erroneous to celebrate historical scholarship during the European Enlightenment as the global cradle of critical inquiry and multi-perspectivity. As discussed, most world historical works coming out of the European Enlightenment carried more belief in European exceptionalism than is often assumed. Furthermore, around the same time other parts of the world also experienced intellectual movements that criticized homemade notions of cultural superiority. For instance, during the late Ming dynasty some Buddhist texts argued that India ought to be understood as the "Middle Kingdom" rather than China.[33]

The professionalization of historical scholarship and world historical ideas

World historical narratives depicting Europe as a self-enveloping culture of rationality became even more pronounced and widely shared during the nineteenth century. Moreover, they now started gaining more ground outside of the West. Eurocentric interpretations of the world's past were conditioned by the present: the global frameworks of a century in which much of the planet's landmass was subjugated under European rule. During the 1800s and early 1900s it was particularly the spread of history education systems and university-based departments that helped to translate Eurocentric world orders into commonly accepted ways of world historical thinking. In an intricate and drawn-out process, history departments with professors employed as civil officials were being established, first in parts of Europe and North America and subsequently in other world regions.[34]

---

33 See for example Marsha Smith Weidner (ed.), *Cultural Intersections in Later Chinese Buddhism* (Honolulu: University of Hawaii Press, 2001).

34 See for example Gabriele Lingelbach, "The institutionalization and professionalization of historiography in Europe and the United States," in Macintyre, Maiguashca, and Pók (eds.), *Oxford History of Historical Writing*, vol. IV, pp. 78–96.

Modern historical scholarship around the world came to be characterized by similar criteria for obtaining degrees such as the doctorate, and it cultivated identical tools such as the use of the footnote. Furthermore, societies with highly divergent epistemological traditions developed similar definitions of what was acceptable into the canon of academic historiography.[35] There was a growing demand for Western-style scholarship that, however, did not lead to a complete homogenization of historical thinking across the globe. Rather, locally specific traditions continued to season patterns and paradigms even within new forms of university-based historical scholarship.

Also in the field of historiography, the emerging global academic system did not operate on the logics of a flat world. Rather, the power patterns of a colonial or imperialist world order left a deep imprint on the professional milieu of academic historians, which was nationally divided but at the same time transnationally entangled.[36] In other words, from its very beginnings the global system of academic historiography, the single national units were not horizontally aligned. As a global network of knowledge, academic historiography was characterized by significant hierarchies that reflected nineteenth- and twentieth-century Western dominance. In this pattern, the position of central societies and peripheral ones became clearly visible in daily academic practice. For example, historians in societies such as Germany, France, Great Britain or the United States only needed to be familiar with scholarship in some supposedly "advanced" key societies in the West. By contrast, their colleagues in other parts of the world, ranging from Chile to Japan, could hardly build a career as historians without even considering (either through translations or through reading relevant texts in English) the most relevant literature produced in the West.[37]

These hierarchical sociologies of knowledge also impacted the ways in which world historical narratives developed in different societies around the globe. In Europe, the tendency to narrate the history of the world while assuming the privileged position of a higher civilization got even more accentuated during the 1800s. Moreover, the notion that European learning was equipped with unique amounts of information about other cultures

35 Anthony Grafton, *The Footnote: A Curious History* (Cambridge, MA: Harvard University Press, 1997).
36 Walter D. Mignolo, *Local Histories/Global Designs: Coloniality, Subaltern Knowledges, and Border Thinking* (Princeton, NJ: Princeton University Press, 2000).
37 For more details see Dominic Sachsenmaier, *Global Perspectives on Global History: Theories and Approaches in a Connected World* (Cambridge: Cambridge University Press, 2011), Chapter 1.

added further stimulus to the idea that as a global powerhouse, the continent was uniquely equipped with the potential to develop master narratives for the rest of the world. Whereas many Enlightenment thinkers had at least professed the ideals of civilizational learning, the most influential world historical works of the nineteenth century were written from the posture of a higher civilization. The readiness to accept alternative cultural perspectives as viable options decisively declined.

There was also a shrinking interest in scholarship that was trying to relate Western history to other cultural experiences in a rather equal manner. Many of Europe's most influential thinkers now envisioned history ultimately as a progressive force that was no longer driven by providence but by civilizational achievements. An important example is the positivism of Auguste Comte (d. 1857), who regarded evolvement toward higher forms of sociopolitical order as one of the main principles of history. His positivism was based on the idea that scientific knowledge, which was seen as universal and basically without cultural attributes, was a key to achieving progress.[38] Needless to say, he regarded parts of Europe as the cradle of scientism, which seemed to elevate their history above any other cultural experience.

In addition, historical interpretations by representatives of German idealism, most notably Georg Wilhelm Friedrich Hegel (d. 1831), were committed to the idea of human progress but operated on different assumptions. Hegel doubted the existence of absolute truths and rather assumed that all ideas were closely interconnected with their own historical contexts. According to him, historical interpretations progressed with the self-realization of human kind at large. For Hegel this meant that only at the end of human progress, which he understood as a self-enveloping process of individual and collective freedom, would it be possible to gain a holistic perspective of the meaning of history. In Hegel's eyes, it was European societies, most notably Prussia, which had come close to establishing the societal and political conditions of human freedom. His verdict on other civilizations was that they were either, like Africa, without any kind of historical progress or, as in the case of China, stuck in rather early stages of it.

Such crude Eurocentrism was by no means limited to positivism and German idealism but also dominated many other nineteenth-century

---

38 For the rise of scientism and the nation state paradigm in Western and East Asian historiography see for example George G. Iggers, Q. Edward Wang, and Supriya Mukherjee, *A Global History of Modern Historiography* (Harlow: Pearson Longman, 2008), pp. 117–56.

philosophical schools, including Marxism.[39] Even Max Weber's civilizational comparisons, which stemmed from very different academic traditions, were chiefly based on the hypothesis that in contrast to all other cultures, Europe had given birth to a civilization with uniquely rational and hence universalizable character traits.[40] While Weber certainly was not a blind advocate of progress, his famous introduction to *The Sociology of World Religions* is centered on a cascade of questions about what character traits of European civilization were lacking elsewhere in the world.[41]

Certainly, also in the West there were counter-currents to this Eurocentric mainstream. Yet at the same time, nineteenth-century European cultural identities and visions of world order not only manifested themselves through changing world historical narratives. They also grew visible through the changing position of world history within the guildhalls of historians. Universal history or world history as a genre itself became far more marginalized in Europe than it had been before. As an overall trend, knowledge about world regions outside of the West was less and less regarded as belonging to the standard portfolio of modern education. Generally speaking, the rest of the world was seen as too far behind the Western engine to be seriously studied as a guide or reference. Around the same time, the study of world regions such as China or India was segregated into special fields like sinology or indology, which were largely philologically oriented and primarily focused on the premodern period.[42]

In the newly established history departments it was the new national histories that were commonly regarded as defining the rhythm of the field. In addition to other intellectual transformations this meant that macroscopic cultural and social comparisons declined both in number and impact. Within this changing intellectual climate, world historical accounts continued being written but were often regarded as emerging from a fading genre. Moreover, many world histories now tended to brush over territories where national states had not yet been established. This neglect of large swaths of Africa, Central Asia and other parts of the world reflected the now common idea that the nation state constituted the highest form of political order.

---

39 Dipesh Chakrabarty, *Provincializing Europe: Postcolonial Thought and Historical Difference* (Princeton, NJ: Princeton University Press, 2000).

40 See W. Schluchter, *The Rise of Western Rationalism: Max Weber's Developmental History* (Berkeley: University of California Press, 1981).

41 M. R. Naffrisi, "Reframing Orientalism: Weber and Islam," *Economy and Society* 27 (1998), 97–118.

42 Immanuel Wallerstein, *et al.* (eds.), *Open the Social Sciences: Report of the Gulbenkian Commission on the Restructuring of the Social Sciences* (Stanford, CA: Stanford University Press, 1996).

While (or after) this was happening in Europe, a related trend took place in a growing number of societies elsewhere. The outcome of this transformation did, however, often point in a very different direction. In many societies, ranging from the Ottoman Empire to China and from India to Japan, "world history" started gaining a more prominent standing rather than declining in importance. It did so in conjunction with the growing appeal of national historiography and new, scientific methodologies. The new importance of world history in a good number of countries outside of the West reflected an important intellectual transformation spreading across several influential opinion camps: Western powers were often not only regarded as almost worldwide hegemons but also as the source of ideas that were central for modernization efforts. As part of the same trend, a large number of historical works written on all continents did either explicitly or implicitly endorse the idea that Europe was a uniquely dynamic civilization whose rationalism, dynamism and opportunities for freedom carried a high potential for the other parts of the world.[43] Through studying the example of advanced societies many historians between Latin America and Southeast Asia hoped to gain knowledge that they regarded as immediately relevant for their own societies' modernization drives.[44]

As a consequence, the history of Europe received much attention at both the levels of research universities and the general education system. In numerous states history education developed a dual concentration, focusing on national or regional history on the one side, and Western history on the other side. The latter was often institutionalized as "world history." For instance, historiography under the Tanzimat reforms in the late Ottoman Empire, treated "Europe" as an important reference space.[45] Also the efforts toward gaining new conceptions of history in Japan were heading in similar directions, even though in this case Rankean influence was more accentuated than in Turkey.[46] At the same time, the Japanese education system put great emphasis on Western history or "world history" in addition to national history. Likewise, in China after the revolution of 1911 Western history became part of the middle school and, a little later, of university

---

43 For more details see Sachsenmaier, *Global Perspectives on Global History*, Chapter 1.
44 See for example Woolf, *A Global History of History*, pp. 399–454.
45 Ercüment Kuran, "Ottoman historiography of the Tanzimat period," in Bernard Lewis and P. M. Holt (eds.), *Historians of the Middle East* (London: Oxford University Press, 1962), pp. 422–9.
46 See Masayuki Sato, "Historiographical encounters: The Chinese and Western traditions in turn-of-the-century Japan," *Storia della Storiografia* 19 (1991), 13–21.

curricula[47] – which reflected a common tendency to conceptualize the pathways of Western Europe and the Atlantic as the epicenter of a global transformation.[48]

Outside of the West, this triumph of Western-oriented national history could occur in both independent countries and under colonial conditions. In both types of situations, parts of the local elites displayed a strong interest in historiographical concepts and methodologies of Western provenance.[49] They played a strong role in nation-building programs of independent or newly decolonized societies ranging from Japan to Egypt. But also under colonial rule the cultures of historiography could acquire a dual character of this kind. Here historical thinking was often forced onto the binary lines of national/local history on the one side and the history of the colonizer or Europe at large on the other side. An illustrative critique of a colonial history education system was articulated by the Caribbean historian and first prime minister of Trinidad and Tobago, Eric Williams (d. 1981).[50]

Rivaling schools during the twentieth century

The Eurocentric orientation of historiographical cultures in general and world history in particular continued during much of the twentieth century. Within a global constellation that clearly differentiated between "advanced" and "backward" societies, it is small wonder that rather Eurocentric master narratives of world history remained strong in different societies and languages. In many history education systems, "world historical" scholarship often boiled down to the study of advanced societies, most notably Western powers. No matter whether in Africa, in South Asia, East Asia or elsewhere: voluminous works narrated the history of the world chiefly as the rise of the West.

The important position of Western history, which was often labeled as "world history," is evidenced by the very fact that some of the most influential minds behind nation formation efforts published their own reflections on Western and world history. Examples across various generations range from

47 See Q. Edward Wang, "Between myth and history: The construction of a national past in modern East Asia," in Stefan Berger (ed.), *Writing the Nation: A Global Perspective* (New York: Palgrave Macmillan, 2007), pp. 126–54.
48 See Prasenjit Duara, *Rescuing History from the Nation: Questioning Narratives of Modern China* (Chicago: University of Chicago Press, 1995).
49 Stefan Berger, "Introduction: Towards a global history of national historiographies," in Berger (ed.), *Writing the Nation*, pp. 1–29.
50 Eric Williams, *Education in the British West Indies* (Port of Spain: Guardian, 1946).

the Japanese reformer Fukuzawa Yukichi (d. 1901) to the Chinese scholar and public intellectual Liang Qichao (d. 1929) and the Indian scholar and statesman Jawaharlal Nehru (d. 1964). Nehru's famed *Glimpses of World History*, written in prison during the colonial period, was openly critical of Western imperialism and not driven by the concern that India needed to emulate Western experiences. Yet at the same time the text did not abandon the idea that as a civilization, Europe's rise carried great cultural, political and intellectual implications for societies in other parts of the world.[51]

Eurocentric conceptions of world history could (and still can) be observed within rather different political contexts. For instance, in line with Marxist traditions world history was granted a strong institutional presence in a rather wide spectrum of Communist countries. There were certainly significant differences between the cultures of historiography in single socialist societies, and yet among them the field of world history shared many elements in common. The field was typically dominated by nation-centered perspectives and teleological outlooks that ascribed European history a key role in international developments that would supposedly culminate in a global communism. At certain times, historians in countries like the Soviet Union or the People's Republic of China had quite some leeway to maneuver around the conceptual blocks of historical materialism. Yet as a general tendency, world historical works produced in Communist countries were framed around Marxist-Leninist theories and timelines that had been derived from the study of European history. For example, during the Mao period entire cohorts of Chinese historians were seeking to relate the Chinese and global past to concepts such as "bourgeoisie" and "feudalism" even though these had been derived from the European context.[52] Moreover, Chinese world historical works tended to focus on the history of the West and the Soviet Union, thereby marginalizing other parts of the world.

Certainly, local factors, ranging from institutional settings to political conditions and from intellectual traditions to funding structures, continued to season national and world history in different countries and world regions. Moreover, there were prominent counter-movements to this overarching

51 Jawaharlal Nehru, *Glimpses of World History: Being Further Letters to His Daughter, Written in Prison, and Containing a Rambling Account of History for Young People* (London: Lindsay Drummond Limited, 1939). Gandhi was one of the few Indian independence leaders who expressed great concern over the new conceptions of history.

52 See for example Q. Edward Wang, "Encountering the world: China and its other(s) in historical narratives, 1949–89," *Journal of World History* 14 (2003), 327–58.

trend.[53] For instance, during the interwar period several European societies witnessed the publication of very well-known works seeking to leave nation- and Europe-centered perspectives behind. An example is Oswald Spengler's (d. 1936) *Decline of the West*, which was first published in German between 1918 and 1922.[54] The work challenged the notion of universal science and, as an alternative, it was framed around the idea of rather independent civiliza- tional cycles. Within that structure, Spengler portrayed the trajectories of Western modernity as the forces of a civilizational downward movement – which gained him much fame in conservative circles across Europe.

Whereas Spengler had openly positioned himself against the historio- graphical establishment at universities, another famous world historian of the time, Arnold J. Toynbee (d. 1975), operated from the firm basis of various British institutions of higher learning. In his magnum opus, *A Study of History*, published in twelve volumes between 1934 and 1961, Toynbee sought to grasp the history of humankind and global interactions while carefully avoiding Western triumphalist narratives. Toynbee focused on cultural and spiritual factors (rather than political and materialist patterns) as the driving forces of history. Not convinced by national perspectives, civilizations were his preferred main containers when thinking about history on a worldwide scale.

Also in other parts of the world, there were numerous voices criticizing Eurocentric teleologies. For example, transnational groups such as the Négritude Movement openly articulated their doubts about the promises of materialism, scientism and other "white mythologies."[55] Moreover, quite a number of intellectuals in Asia at least partly directed their critique of Western epistemologies against interpretations of Europe as the cradle of worldwide progress.[56] Whereas some prominent historians like the aforementioned Eric Williams and the late Liang Qichao partook in intel- lectual movements of this kind, history departments in many countries remained hardly affected by such critical interventions.

53 See for example Jürgen Osterhammel, "World history," in Axel Schneider and Daniel Woolf (eds.), *The Oxford History of Historical Writing* (New York: Oxford University Press, 2012), vol. v, pp. 93–112.

54 The English edition was published in 1926. The original German title is *Der Untergang des Abendlandes*.

55 Robert J. C. Young, *White Mythologies: Writing History and the West* (New York: Routledge, 1990).

56 Cemil Aydin, *The Politics of Anti-Westernism in Asia: Visions of World Order in Pan-Islamic and Pan-Asian Thought* (New York: Columbia University Press, 2007).

Similarly, historians like Toynbee and Spengler found little resonance within the historians' guildhalls in Europe and the United States. Certainly, especially after the Second World War there were some important examples for world historical works seeking to explore new horizons. Some of them even gained considerable fame, for example *The Rise of the West* by William McNeill, who taught at the University of Chicago and had worked with Arnold Toynbee.[57] In this work, McNeill did not seek to provide a triumphant account of North Atlantic societies but rather sought to relativize the era of Western dominance by placing it into wider world historical contexts. He emphasized that prior to the sixteenth century, the continental nexus of Eurasia and Africa had been characterized by other large-scale power systems that had not been centered on Europe. McNeill actually left the question open whether other global power constellations beyond Western hegemony would emerge in the future.

Yet despite the rather enthusiastic reception of McNeill's work, world history in the United States long remained a field that had its institutional basis in small colleges. Likewise, it did not play a more pronounced role in Europe. Arguably the most active historical research field, which already at a rather early stage paid much attention to global connections and entanglements, was economic history. For example, Immanuel Wallerstein's *The Modern World System*, the first volume of which appeared in 1974,[58] was widely influential among economic historians. Departing from earlier theoretical schools, Wallerstein provided an elaborate study of what he saw as the emergence of a geographically expanding economic system based on unequal exchanges. Within this system, entire countries and world regions figured as centers while others took a peripheral or semiperipheral status. According to Wallerstein, the world system's patterns largely determined factors such as the global distribution of wealth and the topographies of free and unfree labor.[59]

As a general tendency, however, historiography in most parts of the world remained remarkably conservative in the sense that the vast majority of its practitioners stuck to national frameworks and in their own research did not

57 William H. McNeill, *The Rise of the West: A History of the Human Community* (Chicago: University of Chicago Press, 1963).
58 Immanuel Wallerstein, *The Modern World System*, 4 vols. (New York: Academic Press, 2011).
59 For a general overview of global economic history during the Cold War and after see Peer Vries, "Global economic history: A survey," in Schneider and Woolf (eds.), *The Oxford History of Historical Writing*, vol. v, pp. 113–35.

systematically seek to challenge Eurocentric paradigms. It was only around the end of the Cold War that one could observe a growing interest in themes like global connections and cross-regional entanglements. This was much later than the beginnings of similar developments in other academic fields like, for instance, sociology or anthropology. This movement within historiography arguably occurred decades after new global connections had become blatantly visible in economic, cultural and social life. For this reason, the historian Akira Iriye assumes that toward the end of the Cold War, one could actually observe "historians falling behind history."[60]

Developments since the 1990s

Since the late 1980s or 1990s there has been a sharp increase in scholarship seeking to explore cross-regional connections, flows and entanglements. As a consequence of recent developments, transnational and world historical scholarship is no longer regarded as a marginal exception to a nation-centered disciplinary reality. Quite to the contrary, bordercrossing studies are frequently seen as important centers of innovation. The underlying change in scholarly predilections took place as a diffuse process within most branches of historiography, ranging from cultural history to political history,[61] and no area of research figured as a clear epicenter. To put it in a different way, transnational and world historical research has flourished in many different branches of historiography, ranging from economic history to cultural history and from environmental history to labor history.

In contrast to the main body of world historical scholarship during the Cold War and before, much of the more recent literature emerges from primary source-based projects. Up until the 1980s, large-scale historical accounts, textbooks and trade books constituted the core of the field. Certainly, great works narrating the history of the world or the global history of entire centuries continue being written but in contrast to the Cold War period and before, these works can now draw on a rich body of research literature that explores single topics and themes from global and

---

60 Akira Iriye, *Global and Transnational History: The Past, Present and Future* (New York: Palgrave Macmillan, 2013), p. 19.
61 In addition to books mentioned above the following works provide accounts of this research trend, Jerry H. Bentley, *Shapes of World History in Twentieth-Century Scholarship* (Washington, D.C.: American Historical Association, 1996), vol. xiv; Sebastian Conrad, *Globalgeschichte: Eine Einführung (Global History: An Introduction)* (Munich: C. H. Beck, 2013); and Manning, *Navigating World History*.

transnational perspectives.[62] As a general trend, the narrative frameworks of such macroscopic works have become more complex, and an increasing number of authors now pay more attention to topics like non-Western forms of global agency.

In many regards, this development has come to challenge some of the disciplinary cultures and structures that had long supported the mental maps of historiography. An increasing number of scholars are now pursuing topics that had long been rather neglected due to the institutional set-ups of history departments. For example, more and more historians have grown interested in the historical relations between South Asia and East Asia, or between Latin American and African regions. For a long time, not much attention had been paid to connections of this kind. Certainly, fields like East Asian history or South Asian history had not been completely ignoring past interactions between their region and the rest of the world. But scholars chiefly concentrated on entanglements with the West, thereby marginalizing the multifarious historical interactions between East Asia, South Asia and other regions. For instance, modern historiography paid only comparatively scant attention to the partly dense interactions between societies such as China and India. One of the main reasons underlying this problematic pattern is that hardly any historian of East Asia (including scholars who were based in countries like China, Japan or Korea) had received significant training about an additional world region outside of the West. This situation has not changed dramatically but a growing number of historians now feel willing and able to bridge the gaps created by area-specific expertise.

The question has been raised whether this new research movement can still be called "world history" or whether other field designations need to be found.[63] After all, "world history" long primarily stood for grand perspectives that were often structured around Eurocentric master narratives. For this reason, quite a number of scholars prefer the term "global history" as a marker for the new research trends unfolding since the end of the Cold War. Also other concepts such as "transnational history" or "entangled histories" have appeared on the

---

62 Examples of the wealth of new macroscopic studies, published in various languages and commonly seeking to decenter world historical narratives, are C. A. Bayly, *The Birth of the Modern World, 1780–1914: Global Connections and Comparisons* (Malden, MA: Blackwell, 2004); Jürgen Osterhammel, *Die Verwandlung der Welt: Eine Geschichte des 19. Jahrhunderts* (Munich: C. H. Beck, 2009). The English translation is "The Transformation of the World: A History of the 19th Century." Shirong Qi and Yujin Wu (eds.), *Shijie shi* (World History), 3 vols. (Beijing: Gaodeng jiaoyu chubanshe, 1994).

63 For example Bruce Mazlish, "Terms," in Hughes-Warrington (ed.), *Palgrave Advances in World Histories*, pp. 18–43.

scene. However, the expression "world history" has also changed its connotations and now points to a rather vibrant and diverse community of approaches that have departed widely from the earlier contours of the field. Hence it is small wonder that many researchers have come to use terms such as "global history" and "world history" as interchangeable with one another. In essence, this means that a categorical distinction between them is no longer possible. A more special case is big history, which investigates structures, patterns and changes from the Big Bang up until the present day, thereby linking historical inquiry with themes studied primarily by the natural sciences.[64]

It is very important to note that neologisms like "transnational history" or "global history" have found their ways into many languages, ranging from Spanish to Japanese. In fact, the growth of new forms of bordercrossing scholarship can be observed among historians in many societies around the world.[65] It would certainly be misleading to assume that the new interest in historical connections and translocal themes originated in the West, and that from there it spread to the rest. The patterns and rhythms of this rather young academic trend are in fact far more complex than any model based on the idea of Western diffusionism could possibly grasp.[66] Certainly, the growing significance of global and world history has been related to events in global time, particularly the end of the Cold War divides and the emerging facets of globalization. Yet in every place it has also been impacted by transformations in local time, that is, political, societal, institutional and other transformations that impacted historiographical cultures as well.

Despite all intensifying academic exchanges, world historical scholarship has not become identical all over the world. Local, regional or national elements still continue to season the field because they have an effect on the narratives, methodologies and debates among scholars. For example, academic funding structures, the patterns of academic systems, opinion climates, intellectual traditions and modes of historical memory all have an influence on the field of world history. In that sense, current world historical research and teaching looks different in societies such as Japan, India, France or Canada. This is not to say that each of these academic communities operates primarily within

---

64 See for example David Christian, *Maps of Time: An Introduction to Big History* (Berkeley: University of California Press, 2004).

65 Examples can be found in Patrick Manning (ed.), *Global Practice in World History: Advances Worldwide* (Princeton, NJ: Markus Wiener Publishers, 2008); and Douglas Northrup (ed.), *A Companion to World History* (Hoboken: Wiley-Blackwell, 2012).

66 For more details (also of the following paragraphs) see Sachsenmaier, *Global Perspectives on Global History.*

isolated national communities; also one should not assume that there are monolithic national or cultural traditions of world historical scholarship. The local specificities of current world historical research are much more subtle, and they are enmeshed with an increasingly pluralistic and transnationally entangled landscape of bordercrossing historical studies.

In some contexts, important social changes and political transformations could decisively influence the cultures of academic histories in general and world history in particular. For example, in the United States the social revolutions, which brought an unprecedented ethnic diversity to university faculty and student bodies, had a strong impact on the ways in which the later waves of historiography would unfold.[67] Partly influenced by the aftershocks of the civil rights movement, academic history witnessed particularly strong challenges to concepts such as "Western civilization" and "progress" during the 1970s and 1980s. A growing number of scholars started seeing these and other terms as too loaded with power interests to be useful as analytical tools for the historian's workshop.

This concern about hegemonic discourses, which stemmed from America's internal "history wars," also had a bearing on the rather large community of scholars (due to Cold War funding for the area studies) specializing in world regions outside of the West. For example, many prominent historians came to problematize the Eurocentric categories with which different world regions such as China, India or the Middle East were being assessed and analyzed.[68] This opinion climate, which gave philosophical movements such as postmodernism or postcolonialism a comparatively strong stance in US historiography, also left some marks on the more recent literature in transnational and world history. For instance, the vast majority of scholars in these fields are now reluctant to use concepts such as "modernity" as methodological devices or descriptive terms.

In China, concepts of this kind play a much stronger role, even though there is also a debate about the problem of Eurocentric categories and concepts. Here the institutional contexts for the recent rise of bordercrossing research were rather different from those in the United States. After all, for many decades world history has already had a strong presence in most Chinese history departments as well as in the overall education system. Nevertheless, an increasing number of historians started actively searching for alternatives to

67 See for example Thomas Bender, "Politics, intellect, and the American university, 1945–1995," *Daedalus* 1261 (1997), 1–38.
68 See Joyce Applebee, Lynn Hunt, and Margaret Jacob, *Telling the Truth About History* (New York: W. W. Norton & Company, 1995).

well-established historiographical cultures and structures. Most notably, a wealth of transnational studies is now seeking to overcome the institutional divides between Chinese history and world history, which have existed for decades.[69] In a related step, there have been sustained efforts to move away from Europe-centered narratives – for instance by reflecting upon the possibility of specifically Chinese perspectives of world history. Nevertheless, compared to their US-American counterparts the majority of Chinese world and global historians are much more hesitant to deconstruct concepts such as "modernization" when describing more recent processes of change; neither is there a strong wave challenging the idea of the nation as a core container of the past. Academic works trying to find new ways of thinking about the world while at the same time leaving the idea of a national past rather intact are certainly endorsed by the Chinese state. Yet recent generational experiences also make numerous Chinese scholars more prone to regard global and national perspectives not as contradictory with one another. It would certainly be very problematic to suppose that Chinese scholarship is just "lagging behind" and will naturally gravitate toward the Western mainstream.

There are strong reasons to assume that such local differences in world historical scholarship are there to stay. Despite this rather obvious fact, they have not been sufficiently debated among world and global historians yet. Even further than that, theoretical debates within the field have not sufficiently focused on changing the global landscapes of academic life in general historiography in particular. However, doing so would be a decisive step in the direction of establishing the bases for more balanced scholarly exchanges between world historians from different parts of the globe.[70] Many of the divisions and power gaps, which characterized the global academic system since its inception during the nineteenth and early twentieth centuries, remain intact today. Needless to say, this hierarchical international pattern certainly is an obstacle to developing the field of world history into further, promising directions.

Given this situation, it should now be a primary task of this generation of global historians to put different scholarly traditions into more sustained dialogues with one another. This is particularly the case with scholarly communities from countries whose academic systems have, up until the present day, been rather detached from one another. Especially during the

---

69 See for example Luo Xu, "Reconstructing world history in the People's Republic of China since the 1980s," *Journal of World History* 18 (2007), 235–50.
70 Dominic Sachsenmaier, "World history as ecumenical history?," *Journal of World History* 18 (2007), 433–62.

past few decades, it was particularly Anglo-American universities that played the role of global academic transaction hubs. A more pluralistic landscape of such hubs and, by implication, more decentered networks of collaboration around the world still remain largely a project for the future, even though important steps heading in this direction have already been taken. Yet if scholarship fails to create new sociologies of knowledge in the age of the internet and comparatively cheap long-distance travel, it will also fall short of its potentials for academic innovation.

Increasing levels of communication among historians from various world regions can produce more than mere cross-fertilizations between different research approaches. They can trigger wider debates on key concepts, epistemological assumptions and world-views that necessarily frame any attempt at thinking about history on a global scale. Exchanges reaching to the very depths of our current historiographical cultures can bring some of the excitement back to a discipline whose intellectual fervor has somewhat suffered from the logics of academic over-professionalization. The field may even come to play important, albeit still ill-defined new public roles, particularly in dialogues with global institutions and other civil society agents.

Certainly, world historians cannot and should not be the manufacturers of new historical identities, be they global or regional. Unlike historians during the age of nation formation, world historians will not have a political might behind them rolling out historical ideas through education systems. But this lack of political structures throwing their full weight of support behind the study of world history is also a huge opportunity since it will grant more space to visions of the past that run counter to the logics of political establishments and economic power-holders. The precondition for such interventions, however, is that transnational dialogues and collaboration among world historians and like-minded scholars are being further intensified.

Certainly, as already mentioned in the introduction, academic historiography cannot hope to function as the figurehead of new forms of global concern and transnational consciousness. After all, historical visions are being disseminated to countless people through a wide spectrum of forums. Particularly the mass media, ranging from newspapers to movies and from internet clips to cartoons, have a strong effect on popular understandings of national as well as world historical events.[71] For instance, they influence the

---

71 Serap Özer and Gökçe Ergün, "Social representation of events in world history: Crosscultural consensus or Western discourse? How Turkish students view events in world history," *International Journal of Psychology* 48 (2012), 574–82.

main categories and concepts with which a large number of people think about world history, and they popularize ideas of which regions played a central role in the global past. The same is the case with religious institutions that often disseminate their own historical interpretations to their own followers.

Despite its limited impacts, university-based historical scholarship has a strong influence on general education systems as well as, to a certain extent, on the media. Yet in the future, world history and global history can only hope to affect these spheres if they further actualize the enormous potentials of historiography as a global professional field. The very fact that there are trained historians based in almost all countries of the world has not been translated into a significant worldwide community of letters because the current academic system is still widely based on the same national divisions and international hierarchies as before. Changing those can mean a decisive step ahead in the trajectories of world historical thinking, writing – and the deeper concerns that should be driving both.

FURTHER READING

Primary source materials

de Mendoza, Juan González, *Historia des las Cosas Mas Notables, Ritos y Costumbres, del Gran Reyno de la China* (History of the Most Notable Things, Rites and Uses of the Great Kingdom of China), Rome: Grassi, 1585.

de Montesquieu, Charles, *De l'Esprit des Loix*, Geneva: Barrillot & fils, 1748.

Nehru, Jawaharlal, *Glimpses of World History: Being Further Letters to His Daughter, Written in Prison, and Containing a Rambling Account of History for Young People*, London: Lindsay Drummond Limited, 1939.

Otto, Bishop of Freysing, *The Two Cities: A Chronicle of Universal History to the Year 1146 AD*, New York: Octagon, 1996.

Spengler, Oswald, *The Decline of the West*, 2 vols., London: Allen & Unwin, 1926.

Williams, Eric, *Education in the British West Indies*, Port of Spain: Guardian, 1946.

Secondary source materials

Applebee, Joyce, Lynn Hunt, and Margaret Jacob, *Telling the Truth About History*, New York: W. W. Norton & Company, 1995.

Appleby, R. Scott, "History in the fundamentalist imagination," *Journal of American History* 89 (2002), 498–511.

Aydin, Cemil, *The Politics of Anti-Westernism in Asia: Visions of World Order in Pan-Islamic and Pan-Asian Thought*, New York: Columbia University Press, 2007.

Bayly, C. A., *The Birth of the Modern World, 1780–1914: Global Connections and Comparisons*, Malden, MA: Blackwell, 2004.

Bender, Thomas, "Politics, intellect, and the American university, 1945–1995," *Daedalus* 126*I* (1997), 1–38.

Rethinking American History in a Global Age, Berkeley: University of California Press, 2002.

Benin, Isidore O., *Once Upon a Kingdom: Myth, Hegemony and Identity*, Bloomington: Indiana University Press, 1998.

Bentley, Jerry H., "Myths, wagers, and some moral implications of world history," *Journal of World History* 16 (2005), 51–82.

Shapes of World History in Twentieth-Century Scholarship, Washington, D.C.: American Historical Association, 1996, vol. XIV.

Berger, Stefan, "Introduction: Towards a global history of national historiographies," in Stefan Berger (ed.), *Writing the Nation: A Global Perspective*, Basingstoke: Palgrave Macmillan, 2007, pp. 1–29.

Burke, Peter, "History, myth and fiction: Doubts and debates," in José Rabasa, Masayuki Sato, Edoardo Tortarolo, and Daniel Woolf (eds.), *The Oxford History of Historical Writing*, New York: Oxford University Press, 2012, vol. III, pp. 261–81.

Chakrabarty, Dipesh, *Provincializing Europe: Postcolonial Thought and Historical Difference*, Princeton, NJ: Princeton University Press, 2000.

Christian, David, *Maps of Time: An Introduction to Big History*, Berkeley: University of California Press, 2004.

"Scales," in Marnie Hughes-Warrington (ed.), *Palgrave Advances in World History*, London: Palgrave, 2006, pp. 64–89.

Conrad, Sebastian, *Globalgeschichte: Eine Einführung* (Global History: An Introduction), Munich: C. H. Beck, 2013.

Conrad, Sebastian, and Dominic Sachsenmaier (eds.), *Conceptions of World Order: Global Moments and Movements, 1880s–1930s*, Basingstoke: Palgrave Macmillan, 2007.

Curto, Diogo R., "European historiography of the East," in José Rabasa, Masayuki Sato, Edoardo Tortarolo, and Daniel Woolf (eds.), *The Oxford History of Historical Writing*, New York: Oxford University Press, 2012, vol. III, pp. 536–55.

Duara, Prasenjit, *The Global and Regional in China's Nation Formation*, New York: Routledge, 2009.

Rescuing History from the Nation: Questioning Narratives of Modern China, Chicago: University of Chicago Press, 1995.

Durrant, Stephen W., *The Cloudy Mirror: Tension and Conflict in the Writings of Sima Qian*, Albany: State University of New York, 1995.

Faulstich, Paul, "Mapping the mythological landscape: An Aboriginal way of being in the world," *Philosophy & Geography* 1 (1998), 197–221.

Fromherz, Allen, *Ibn Khaldun: Life and Times*, Edinburgh: Edinburgh University Press, 2010.

Goodrich, Thomas D., *The Ottoman Turks and the New World: A Study of Tarih-i-Hind-i Garbi and Sixteenth-Century Ottoman Americana*, Wiesbaden: Harrassowitz, 1990.

Grafton, Anthony, *The Footnote: A Curious History*, Cambridge, MA: Harvard University Press, 1997.

"The history of ideas: Precepts and practice, 1950–2000 and beyond," *Journal of the History of Ideas* 67 (2006), 1–32.

Griggs, Tamara, "Universal history from Counter-Reformation to Enlightenment," *Modern Intellectual History* 4 (2007), 219–47.

Gruzinski, Serge, *Les Quatre Parties du Monde: Histoire d'une Mondialisation*, Paris: Martinière, 2004.

Hardy, Grant, "Can an ancient Chinese historian contribute to modern Western theory? The multiple narratives of Ssu-ma Ch'ien," *History and Theory* 33 (1994), 20–38.

Hartog, François, *The Mirror of Herodotus: The Representation of the Other in the Writing of History*, Berkeley: University of California Press, 1998.

Hoerder, Dirk, *Cultures in Contact: World Migrations in the Second Millennium*, Durham, NC: Duke University Press, 2002.

Iggers, George G., Q. Edward Wang, and Supriya Mukherjee, *A Global History of Modern Historiography*, Harlow: Pearson Longman, 2008.

Iriye, Akira, *Global and Transnational History: The Past, Present and Future*, New York: Palgrave, 2013.

  Global Community: The Role of International Organizations in the Making of the Contemporary World, Berkeley: University of California Press, 2002.

Khalidi, Tarif, *Islamic Historiography: The Histories of Mas'udi*, Albany: State University of New York Press, 1975.

Kuran, Ercüment, "Ottoman historiography of the Tanzimat period," in Bernard Lewis and P. M. Holt (eds.), *Historians of the Middle East*, London: Oxford University Press, 1965, pp. 422–9.

Lach, Donald F., *Asia in the Making of Europe*, Chicago: University of Chicago Press, 1993, vol. IV.

Lingelbach, Gabriele, "The institutionalization and professionalization of historiography in Europe and the United States," in Stuart Macintyre, Juan Maiguashca, and Attila Pók (eds.), *The Oxford History of Historical Writing*, New York: Oxford University Press, 2012, vol. IV, pp. 78–96.

Manning, Patrick (ed.), *Global Practice in World History: Advances Worldwide*, Princeton, NJ: Markus Wiener Publishers, 2008.

  Navigating World History: Historians Create a Global Past, New York: Palgrave Macmillan, 2003.

Mazlish, Bruce, "Terms," in Marnie Hughes-Warrington (ed.), *Palgrave Advances in World Histories*, London: Palgrave Macmillan, 2006, pp. 18–43.

McNeill, John R., *Something New Under the Sun: An Environmental History of the Twentieth-Century World*, New York: W. W. Norton & Company, 2000.

McNeill, William H., *The Rise of the West: A History of the Human Community*, Chicago: University of Chicago Press, 1963.

Mignolo, Walter D., *Local Histories/Global Designs: Coloniality, Subaltern Knowledges, and Border Thinking*, Princeton, NJ: Princeton University Press, 2000.

Moyn, Samuel, *The Last Utopia: Human Rights in History*, Cambridge, MA: Harvard University Press, 2010.

Muhammad, Akbar, "The image of Africans in Arabic literature: Some unpublished manuscripts," in John R. Wills (ed.), *Islam and the Ideology of Slavery*, London: F. Cass, 1985, pp. 47–74.

Mungello, D. E., *The Great Encounter of China and the West, 1500–1800*, Lanham, MD: Rowman & Littlefield, 1999.

Naffrisi, M. R., "Reframing Orientalism: Weber and Islam," *Economy and Society* 27 (1998), 97–118.

Netton, I. R., "Basic structures and signs of alienation in the 'Riḥla' of Ibn Jubayr," *Journal of Arabic Literature* 22 (1991), 21–37.

Northrup, Douglas (ed.), *A Companion to World History*, Hoboken: Wiley-Blackwell, 2012.

Osterhammel, Jürgen, *The Transformation of the World: A History of the 19th Century*, Princeton: Princeton University Press, 2014.

"World History," in Axel Schneider and Daniel Woolf (eds.), *The Oxford History of Historical Writing*, New York: Oxford University Press, 2012, vol. v, pp. 93–112.

Özer, Serap, and Gökçe Ergün, "Social representation of events in world history: Cross-cultural consensus or Western discourse? How Turkish students view events in world history," *International Journal of Psychology* 48 (2012), 574–82.

Pagden, Anthony, *The Fall of Natural Man: The American Indian and the Origins of Comparative Ethnology*, Cambridge: Cambridge University Press, 1982.

Pomeranz, Kenneth, *The Great Divergence: China, Europe, and the Making of the Modern World Economy*, Princeton, NJ: Princeton University Press, 2001.

Ross, Margaret C., "Australian Aboriginal oral traditions," *Oral Tradition* 1 (1986), 231–71.

Sachsenmaier, Dominic, *Global Perspectives on Global History: Theories and Approaches in a Connected World*, Cambridge: Cambridge University Press, 2011.

"World history as ecumenical history?", *Journal of World History* 18 (2007), 433–62.

Sato, Masayuki, "Comparative ideas and chronology," *History and Theory* 30 (1991), 275–301.

"Historiographical encounters: The Chinese and Western traditions in turn-of-the-century Japan," *Storia della Storiografia* 19 (1991), 13–21.

Schluchter, Wolfgang, *The Rise of Western Rationalism: Max Weber's Developmental History*, Berkeley: University of California Press, 1981.

Shirong, and Wu Yujin (eds.), *Shijie shi* (World History), 3 vols., Beijing: Gaodeng jiaoyu chubanshe, 1994.

Smith Weidner, Marsha (ed.), *Cultural Intersections in Later Chinese Buddhism*, Honolulu: University of Hawaii Press, 2001.

Subrahmanyam, Sanjay, "On world historians in the sixteenth century," *Representations* 91 (2005), 26–57.

Sydnor, Roy, "The constitutional debate: Herodotus' exploration of good government," *Histos* 6 (2012), 298–320.

Toyin, Falola, "History in Sub-Saharan Africa," in Stuart Macintyre, Juan Maiguashca, and Attila Pók (eds.), *The Oxford History of Historical Writing*, New York: Oxford University Press, 2012, vol. iv, pp. 597–618.

van der Linden, Marcel, *Workers of the World: Essays Towards a Global Labor History*, Leiden: Brill, 2008.

van Kley, Edwin J., "Europe's 'discovery' of China and the writing of world history," *American Historical Review* 76 (1971), 358–85.

Vansina, Jan, *Oral Tradition as History*, Madison: University of Wisconsin Press, 1985.

von Ostenfeld-Suske, Kira, "A new history for a 'New World': The first one hundred years of Spanish historical writing," in José Rabasa, Masayuki Sato, Edoardo Tortarolo, and Daniel Woolf (eds.), *The Oxford History of Historical Writing*, New York: Oxford University Press, 2012, vol. III, pp. 556–74.

Vries, Peer, "Global economic history: A survey," in Axel Schneider and Daniel Woolf (eds.), *The Oxford History of Historical Writing*, New York: Oxford University Press, 2012, vol. V, pp. 113–35.

Waley-Cohen, Joanna, *The Sextants of Beijing: Global Currents in Chinese History*, New York: W. W. Norton & Company, 1999.

Wallerstein, Immanuel, *The Modern World System*, 4 vols., New York: Academic Press, 2011.

et al. (eds.), *Open the Social Sciences: Report of the Gulbenkian Commission on the Restructuring of the Social Sciences*, Stanford, CA: Stanford University Press, 1996.

Wang, Wang, "Encountering the world: China and its other(s) in historical narratives, 1949–89," *Journal of World History* 14 (2003), 327–58.

"History, space, and ethnicity: The Chinese worldview," *Journal of World History* 10 (1999), 285–305.

Xu, Xu, "Reconstructing world history in the People's Republic of China since the 1980s," *Journal of World History* 18 (2007), 235–50.

4

Evolution, rupture, and periodization

MICHAEL LANG

The children were playing by the sea – then came a wave and swept their toy into the deep; now they cry. But the same wave shall bring them new toys and spill before them new shells of many colors!

Friedrich Nietzsche, *Thus Spoke Zarathustra*[1]

Periodization is the methodological foundation of modern historical study. A period gives past events intelligibility through context, and periods normally designate the scope of any historical argument. In 1932, Michael Oakeshott wrote, "To Lord Acton's advice – 'Study problems in preference to periods' – we must reply first, that there is no difference."[2] Historians today would surely agree, especially those working in world history. The subfield has challenged and transformed the discipline through geographical reorganization, methodological innovation, and the revision of many periodization schemes. Across historical studies, however, the conceptual apparatus of periodization remains largely unexplored. At its notional core, periodization entails the universal of time, and therefore indicates, even when unexpressed, the history of the world.

This chapter sets world historical study within a larger history of periodization, showing the relation between its methodological difficulties and its immense historiographical significance. It starts with the systemization of disciplinary practice in Ranke, who inherited from the eighteenth century a paradox concerning global time. For him, chronology and the individual period could never be fully reconciled. Much notable historiography that followed him dispensed with this problem thanks to the identity it posed

---

1 Friedrich Nietzsche, *Sämtliche Werke: Kritische Studienausgabe*, Giorgio Colli and Mazzino Montinari (eds.), 11 vols. (Munich: Deutscher Taschenbuch Verlag, 1988), vol. IV, p. 123.

2 Michael Oakeshott, *Experience and Its Modes* (Cambridge: Cambridge University Press, 1933), p. 143, n. 1.

between the spiritual nation and the worldly state. Darwinian evolution might have threatened this identity, but was inverted instead to strengthen the bond. Still, nationalist historiography could not easily meet the global complexities of the twentieth century, and two major alternatives emerged. They each drew a contrasting half from Ranke's dyad. Starting with Toynbee through McNeill and to the present, world history has sought a basis in evolution, and therefore chronology. Starting with Heidegger through post-modernism and to the present, the critique of historical thought has sought a basis in distinct horizons of meaning, and therefore rupture. The limits of both return to us today the antinomy of history.

Ranke and nationalist historiography

The codification of historical methodology in the early nineteenth century drew from a very diverse array of sources, including the natural sciences, political theory, philology, and, of course, earlier histories. Recent world historical study has further complicated this picture by pointing to the non-European circumstances that influenced many such sources and the non-European intellectual traditions from which they often borrowed and distinguished themselves. Pooling several hundred years of global inputs, "the nineteenth century is the great reservoir in the modern history of history."[3] Concerning periodization in particular, Enlightenment era studies in geology and epistemology significantly impacted the subsequent approach. Taken together, they contributed to the "paradoxical character" of eighteenth-century thought.[4] First, the European engagement with the wider world spurred a revival of integrative, universal histories. Among the different influences on its methodology, geology was perhaps the most significant. Specifically, fossils – previously used to help examine the *human* past – were for the first time recognized as indicators of pre-human times and geo-history, what Buffon called "nature's epochs." Naturalists and others increasingly replaced static and theocentric views of creation with developmental accounts of ever deepening timescales. Out of this "critical arena," Fontenelle, followed by Voltaire, Montesquieu, and others, formulated sequential causality as the basis for historical explanation. The universal scope of

---

3 Daniel R. Woolf, *A Global History of History* (Cambridge: Cambridge University Press, 2011), p. 345.
4 Donald R. Kelly, *Fortunes of History: Historical Inquiry from Herder to Huizinga* (New Haven, CT: Yale University Press, 2002), p. 9.

Enlightenment historiography was thus mirrored by the universal chronology of earthly time.[5] Second, the sheer flood of global information and scientific discovery outpaced the "convertibility of time and space" employed by historical writers of the earlier tradition.[6] Historical truth now became subject to historical conditions, and self-reflecting expressions like "viewpoint," "position," and "standpoint" entered regularly into the scholarship.[7] Thomas Abbt, in his 1766 History of the Human Race, noted that the narrative would have been quite "different" if written from Asia, rather than Europe.[8] Herder famously turned this perspectival epistemology against Voltaire and others, whose naturalist chronologies, he argued, illegitimately judged the past by the present, and then relegated present-day non-Europeans into that past. "In the universe," he wrote, "there are innumerable times, all at one time."[9] Here, the global differentiation facing historical thought was mirrored by differences in the experience of time. The European nineteenth century opened with an intense interest in and knowledge about the world as a whole, and with that came an ambivalent sense of history as a universal disjointed from itself.

Pulling together many strands of the eighteenth century, Ranke set out to formalize the proper conditions of historical knowledge. He endeavored to find for the field its own methodological autonomy and rejected any simple derivation from natural science or idealism. This distinguished him from previous writers, and transformed the discipline profoundly.[10] Regarding the central problem of time, Ranke sought an intermediate space between the two previous tendencies. In his formulation, a period delineated a self-contained logic, yet it was also chronologically chained to its neighboring configurations. After the facts, Ranke wrote, "comes the unity and progression of events." This brief phrase encapsulated the axiomatic temporality of

5 Martin J. S. Rudwick, *Bursting the Limits of Time: The Reconstruction of Geohistory in the Age of Revolution* (Chicago: University of Chicago Press, 2005), p. 195; and Jonathan Israel, *Enlightenment Contested: Philosophy, Modernity, and the Emancipation of Man, 1670–1752* (Oxford: Oxford University Press, 2006), pp. 496–504 and 733–50, 744.
6 Anthony Grafton, *What Was History? The Art of History in Early Modern Europe* (Cambridge: Cambridge University Press, 2007), p. 121.
7 Reinhart Koselleck, *Futures Past* (Cambridge: The MIT Press, 1985), pp. 140–1.
8 Koselleck, *Futures Past*, pp. 140–90
9 Johann Gottfried von Herder, *Philosophical Writings*, Michael N. Forster (ed.) (Cambridge: Cambridge University Press, 2002), pp. 276–80; and Johann G. von Herder, *Verstand und Erfahrung: Eine Metakritik zur Kritik der reinen Vernunft* (Leipzig: Johann Friedrich Hartknoch, 1799), pp. 120–1.
10 Frederick C. Beiser, *The German Historicist Tradition* (Oxford: Oxford University Press, 2011).

subsequent historical methodology: a period was both an immanent meaning and a moving force within universal chronological time. On the one hand, a period possessed its own internal coherence. Its significance for historical study relied on neither its preconditions, nor its consequences, but rather "on its existence itself, on its ownness itself [*in ihrem Eigenen selbst*]." As Ranke famously proclaimed, "every epoch is immediate to God." On the other hand, every period also partook in the world's overall course of development. "All these epochs themselves belong to the great whole, what we call universal history ... the sequence of centuries, each in its original essence, all linked to one another ... from the very beginning to the present day."[11] An epoch was entirely present unto itself as well as mediated by others along the chain of time. This enigmatic joining of the intrinsic and the developmental helps explain some of the unusual contrasts in Ranke's reception. Pieter Geyl, for example, valued the temporal interiority and differentiation, while Hans-Georg Gadamer faulted the chronology of power. More astutely than both, Friedrich Meinecke called it "an irreconcilable dualism."[12]

Ranke himself acknowledged the dilemma. To grasp the event both in its singularity and human universality, "one attempts, one strives, but in the end, one does not achieve it." He made the opposition manageable by condensing it into his principal object of study, the state. As in his conception of time, Ranke characterized the state as a selfsame spiritual unity and as an interacting material force. It possessed "together, a godly trace and a human impetus." A state was a noumenal essence, a divine immanence irreducible to any external relations or historical fluctuations, in Ranke's phrase, "identical only with itself." Conversely, every state derived from a natural, "common necessity," each one conditioned by its context within the universal struggle for "independence" and "position in the world." Like a period, a state exhibited "not only historical roots," but also its own meaning, a particular and unifying "spirit which binds past and present, and which must also give life to the future." For Ranke, these "earthly-spiritual communities" furnished an actual form to the antinomy between unity and progression, immediacy and interrelation. Historical intelligibility thus centered on the

11 Leopold von Ranke, *Geschichten der romanischen und germanischen Völker von 1494 bis 1514* (Leipzig: G. Reimer, 1824), p. vii; Leopold von Ranke, *Aus Werke und Nachlass*, Walter Peter Fuchs and Theodor Schieder (eds.), 4 vols. (Munich: R. Oldenbourg, 1971), vol. II, pp. 59–60; and von Ranke, *Aus Werke*, vol. IV, pp. 296–7.

12 Pieter Geyl, *Debates with Historians* (London: B. T. Batsford, 1955), p. 8; Hans-Georg Gadamer, *Truth and Method*, 2nd edn. (New York: Crossroad, 1989), pp. 204–8; and Friedrich Meinecke, *Werke*, Hans Herzfeld et al. (eds.), 10 vols. (Munich: R. Oldenbourg, 1963), vol. I, p. 445.

state, even as the contradiction remained insoluble: "God alone knows world history. We perceive the contradictions."[13]

In his final years, Ranke altered a key element in this formula. He began to designate the state's spiritual realm as its "nationality." Previously, he had opposed any equivalence between state and nation. Now, following the Prussian unification of Germany, his analysis highlighted their uniformity. In Leonard Krieger's reading, this synthesis finally resolved for Ranke the contradiction between the selfsame and the continuous. Ranke, defying his own earlier warning, could now embrace a universal "science of world history."[14] It appears, though, that Krieger somewhat overweighted the dialectics of conciliation, for the *temporal* antinomy in Ranke indeed continued.[15] Still, Ranke's *Weltgeschichte*, among other late works, did largely parallel the nationalist and Hegelian turn of mid-century historians. "Man was both in nature and outside it," Hayden White observed of the era's historiography.[16] Yet, this duality was camouflaged – or, if one prefers, reconciled – by the transubstantiations of liberal-nationalist history.

The nineteenth-century institutionalization of historical thought included as a matter of course Ranke's critique of philosophical generalization. History demanded the archival source and the concrete detail, what Johann Droysen called the method of "individualization." This principle applied fundamentally to the historical period, whose unique demarcation enabled the requisite contextualization of every other particular. To focus only on development, Droysen stressed, "sacrifices the truth." George Bancroft declared similarly, "truth itself knows nothing of the succession of ages." William Stubbs argued that historical knowledge showed endless differentiation, not "elemental unity." Even Jules Michelet, in his early *Introduction à l'Histoire Universelle*, separated from the short narrative a considerably larger section of "clarifications" that contextualized particulars into their own era.[17] In all such cases

---

13 Von Ranke, *Geschichten der romanischen*, p. viii; Leopold von Ranke, *Zur Geschichte Deutschlands und Frankreichs im 19. Jahrhundert*, Alfred Dove (ed.) (Leipzig: Dunder und Humblot, 1887), pp. 338, 329, 328, 322, 329; and Ranke, *Aus Werke*, vol. IV, p. 83.

14 Leonard Krieger, *Ranke: The Meaning of History* (Chicago: University of Chicago Press, 1977), pp. 332–4, and Leopold von Ranke, *Weltgeschichte*, 9 vols. (Leipzig: Dunder und Humblot, 1880), vol. I, p. v.

15 Von Ranke, *Weltgeschichte*, vol. I, p. vi.

16 Hayden White, *The Historical Imagination in Nineteenth-Century Europe* (Baltimore, MA: The Johns Hopkins University Press, 1973), p. 45.

17 Johann Gustav Droysen, *Historik: Historische-Kritische Ausgabe* (Stuttgart: Frommann-Holzboog, 1977), p. 19 quoted in Robert Southard, *Droysen and the Prussian School* (Lexington: University Press of Kentucky, 1995), p. 28; George Bancroft, *The Necessity, the Reality, and the Promise of the Progress of the Human Race* (New York: New York

though, the immanent meaning of every period appeared to contradict the universal progressivity that nationalist historians credited to the actions of their own states. The harmonization of these temporalities invariably derived from the nation-state itself. As John Burrows skillfully showed, Victorian historians such as Stubbs fashioned a spiritual-political English national "identity" to mediate synchronic local details and diachronic causal connections. Droysen bridged his irreducible epochs to the "uninterrupted stream" of time by giving German unification a peerless world historical significance, namely, as resolution to the ancient problem of freedom. Michelet likewise fused his single chronology and assortment of times by interweaving through both the all-encompassing force of France, the "pilot of the ship of humanity." And for Bancroft, the United States now brought to "consummation" every age of the civilized human past. "Our country holds the noblest rank," he wrote, bestowing to western Europeans "the renewal of their youth," while "the hoary civilization of the farthest antiquity leans forward from Asia to receive the glad tidings of the messenger of freedom."[18]

These temporal reconciliations relied specifically upon the categorical correspondence between nation and state, what Droysen described as an "essential mutuality, like body and soul." The nation-state, he wrote, uniquely integrated the many and the one, moral freedom and willful action, and its history expressed the greatest synthesis of all: "that which for humans is godly." With this embrace of Hegel, numerous historians of the nineteenth century voided the methodological antinomy that otherwise bisected the concept of the period. Transported by the equivalence of nation and state, spirit now fully entered into the course of history, and in this way the *nunc stans* of every period, the immediacy of each before God, was now also discernible across the succession of time. As events "pass away," Bancroft argued, "God is visible in History." Michelet, with characteristic bombast, claimed to have finally discovered the true purpose of historical scholarship, "Thierry called it *narration*, and M. Guizot *analysis*. I have named it *resurrection*." More modest by a tad, Droysen defined it as "consecration," likening historical study to John the Baptist, a "witness to the light." Through the

---

Historical Society, 1854), p. 9; William Stubbs, *Lectures on Early English History* (London: Longmans, Green, and Co., 1906), p. 195; and Jules Michelet, *Introduction à l'Histoire Universelle* (Paris: L. Hachette, 1834).

18 J. W. Burrows, *A Liberal Descent: Victorian Historians and the English Past* (Cambridge: Cambridge University Press, 1981), pp. 108 and 146–7; Southard, *Droysen*, pp. 10, 37–8, and 47–8 (translation modified); Michelet, *Introduction*, p. vi; and Bancroft, *Necessity*, pp. 28–9.

metaphysical unity of the nation-state, meaning and chronology were reconciled without remainder.[19]

Nineteenth-century historiography, it is often noted, served the political interests of the nation-state. Yet the reverse was also true. Nationalism gave to historical thought an invaluable connecting passage between its two conflicting treatments of time. Occasionally, historians figured the sequential half of this formulation by using the developmental language of the latest geological and biological findings. The final distillation of Darwin's theory of evolution, however, threatened their synthesis, for within the universal drift of change, *post hoc* period markers could index descriptions, but they could offer nothing of spirit or meaning. In subsequent decades, many historians did more fully absorb what Henry Adams dubbed Darwin's "violent impulse," but only by inverting its relativism. Frederick Jackson Turner, for example, portrayed the periodization of American history as a "record of social evolution." The buffalo trail, Indian society, the fur-trader, the intensifying phases of agriculture, the industrialization of cities: each expressed a "higher stage" in the "single file ... procession of civilization." At the same time, the westward expansion that propelled these changes also occasioned an ever new encounter with the wilderness frontier. For Turner, a historical period thus marked a stage of American evolutionary development as well as the "perennial rebirth" of its nationality. "The land with no history," he wrote, quoting Achille Loria, "reveals luminously the course of universal history."[20]

Turner's evolutionism was not just the dress of "Darwinian metaphors."[21] It found historical determination in natural processes and natural settings. Beyond the chronology of "adaptation," however, the American national "spirit" gave to each period its meaning and then to their sequence a world historical direction.[22] During these same years, Karl Lamprecht's philosophy

---

19 Southard, *Droysen*, pp. 47–8 (translation modified); Bancroft, *Necessity*, p. 16; Jules Michelet, *Le Peuple* (Paris: Hachette, 1846), p. 37; and Droysen, *Historik*, p. 411.

20 Henry Adams, "The tendency of history," in *Annual Report of the American Historical Association for the Year 1894* (Washington, D.C.: Government Printing Office, 1895), p. 19; Frederick Jackson Turner, *The Frontier in American History* (New York: Henry Holt, 1921), pp. 2 and 11–12; Loria, an evolutionary economist, in turn credited Hegel, *Analisi della proprietà capitalista*, 2 vols. (Turin: Fratelli Bocca, 1889), vol. II, p. 15.

21 William Cronon, "Revisiting the vanishing frontier: The legacy of Frederick Jackson Turner," *Western Historical Quarterly* 18 (1987), p. 206; on spirit, see the focused discussions, Turner, *Frontier in American History*, pp. 166 and 176, and Frederick Jackson Turner, *Frontier and Section: Selected Essays of Frederick Jackson Turner* (Englewood Cliffs: Prentice Hall, 1961), pp. 152–3.

of history likewise concentrated on stages of natural development and expansion. A nation, he wrote, was "the highest social organization in nature." An "element of universal lawfulness inhered" within the "evolutionary progression" of a nation, and Lambrecht linked such laws to his advocacy for German territorial annexations.[23] Yet historical analysis required more than Darwin's "one-sided mechanical explanation." A nation, like an individual, also possessed a unique and undivided "soul." On the one hand then, "everywhere on earth" nations evolved through a "common" sequence of stages. On the other hand, a national period could be grasped "in itself . . . without needing to consider either chronology or terrestrial localization." For Lamprecht, the contradiction resolved through the "world-historical context" itself, the great timeless totality of evolution-history, which provided both "connection" and "coherency." With this naturalistic synthesis of development and immanence, Lamprecht dispensed with God as its guarantor. The reconciliation still hinged, however, upon the singularity of the nation-state.[24]

The chronology of the world

From the start, Ranke acknowledged the "great whole" of "universal history." Yet he never stopped contrasting it to the insurmountable meaning of the specific period. By hiding this antinomy inside the black box of national identity, Hegelian historiography appeared to resolve the problem. And as nineteenth-century national consolidations helped propel territorial and overseas projections of state power, the universal chronology of national history modulated into an empirical possibility for nation-centric global history. Lamprecht claimed, as did Turner, that "world history remains the final goal of all historical science."[25] By the first decades of the twentieth century, however, historiography's embedded national framework began to strain under the pressure of events. The unprecedented global theater of interlocking forces threatened the international and imperial designs of the most powerful nation-states, while new border-crossing lines of social

---

23 Karl Lamprecht, *Moderne Geschichtswissenschaft* (Freiburg im Breisgau: H. Heyfelder, 1905), p. 129; K. Lamprecht, "Was ist Kulturgeschichte? Beitrag zur einer empirischen Historik," *Deutsche Zeitschrift für Geschichtewissenschaft Neue Folge* 1 (1896–1897), 99; Lamprecht, *Moderne*, p. 90; and Karl Lamprecht, *Deutsche Geschichte, Zur jüngsten deutschen Vergangenheit* (Freiburg im Breisgau: H. Heyfelder, 1904), pp. 626–7 and 736–7.
24 Lamprecht, *Moderne*, pp. 97, 27, 3, 92–3, 97, 115, and 119.
25 Lamprecht, *Moderne*, p. 125, and Turner, *Frontier and Section*, pp. 11–27.

reproduction increasingly fragmented political and personal identities. Territory and culture, Arnold J. Toynbee wrote in 1915, were becoming "less and less identical."[26] What then could replace the nation-state as the unitary subject of history?

Toynbee ventured "civilization," a hemispheric framework that satisfied the demands of the global scale, while structuring into single, underlying units the otherwise dispersive trajectories of the present day. He maintained the familiar pattern, whereby his key term signified both a natural existence and an immanent meaning. Civilizations were "higher organisms," each one a "living creature" with cycles of growth and death dictated by "nature herself." A civilization was also an undivided "spirit," a "law unto itself." Each of these manifestations, in turn, inhabited a distinct temporal dimension. The "life-history" of a civilization involved "movement in Time" and the "universality" of developmental stages. Alternatively, a civilization was "something permanent," each of them, even dead ones, "contemporaneous" with all the others. Toynbee thus drew from the liberal commonplace of social evolution, but without its hierarchy of progress. Endeavoring to write world history free of Eurocentrism, he replaced temporal advancement with the spatialization of difference. Despite this, the spiritual side of civilization, unlike nationality in the earlier historiography, lacked the purposive agency of a corresponding state. The historical identity of civilization remained split, and hence unable to hyphenate chronology and immediacy. Throughout his career, Toynbee shuttled endlessly between determinism and mysticism: between tracing a "manifestly inevitable ... 'law'" across the "the history of Life on this planet" and witnessing for each "temporal abode" the "unchanging ... inner light" of God.[27]

Like Ranke, Toynbee acknowledged that his conceptions of spirit and history faced an "apparent contradiction." And like Ranke, Toynbee's reception normally bifurcated onto one side or other.[28] By contrast, historians in the years between them proclaimed a confident reconciliation through the

---

26 Arnold J. Toynbee, *Nationality and the War* (London: J. M. Dent and Sons, 1915), p. 19.

27 Arnold J. Toynbee, *The Western Question in Greece and Turkey, A Study in the Contact of Civilizations* (London: Constable and Co., 1922), pp. 363, 337, and 345; Arnold J. Toynbee, *Greek Civilization and Character: The Self-Revelation of Ancient Greek Society* (London: J. M. Dent and Sons, 1924), p. xi; Arnold J. Toynbee, *Greek Historical Thought: From Homer to the Age of Heraclitus* (London: J. M. Dent and Sons, Ltd., 1924), p. xiii; and Arnold J. Toynbee, *A Study of History*, 12 vols. (London: Oxford University Press, 1939), vol. IV, pp. 423 and 648.

28 Toynbee, *A Study of History*, vol. IV, p. 157; Michael Lang, "Globalization and global history in Toynbee," *Journal of World History* 22 (2011), 747–83.

nation-state, and, in Toynbee's own time, events themselves helped to recenter historiography in the nation. As Toynbee began publishing *A Study of History* in the 1930s, various anti-Western struggles sharpened their nationalist historiographies, while rising intra-European violence helped to reassert the primacy of nationalist historiography there. These commitments remained well entrenched for decades, but the intensity and complexity of postwar global politics generated a fresh demand for world-scale historical writing. A long and large historical framework, William H. McNeill explained in 1954, provided "correction" to the confusing rush of daily events and could thus help build "a better and more stable world society." The impulse toward thematic integration was additionally boosted by the high-modernism of what Carl Hempel, among others, called the "methodological unity of empirical science." In anthropology, for instance, the idiographic culturalism dominant since Franz Boas now confronted the influential updating of evolutionary explanations.[29] Within historical studies, McNeill was surely the most prominent and influential exponent of these tendencies.

In his earliest works, McNeill concentrated on several present-day global challenges, including militarization, pressures on state sovereignty, enormous wealth disparities, and large-scale cultural and racial divisions. All of these rested, though, on an even more basic problem – "moral and religious uncertainty." Technological modernization and the attendant worldwide mixing of ideas now corroded every long-standing system of belief. Western industrial rationality unleashed a global scale of human power, but left unanswered the question of human purpose. The intellectual foundations of social stability were everywhere fragmenting under this "infinitely varying strain."[30] This split between universal instrumentality and disaggregated meaning constituted the dominant concern of McNeill's entire career. In *The Rise of the West*, he called it the "angry uncertainty of the twentieth century" and in the 1990s, "the radical instability that prevails worldwide." Responding to this global crisis, world history – "generalizations and formulas ... large numbers of men over long periods of time" – aided the

---

29 William H. McNeill, *Past and Future* (Chicago: University of Chicago Press, 1954), p. 212; Carl G. Hempel, "The function of general laws in history," *The Journal of Philosophy* 39 (1942), 48; and Leslie A. White, "Evolutionary stages, progress, and the evaluation of cultures," *Southwestern Journal of Anthropology* 3 (1947), 165–82.

30 McNeill, *Past and Future*, p. 114, and William Hardy McNeill, *America, Britain, and Russia: Their Co-operation and Conflict, 1941–1946* (London: Oxford University Press, 1953), p. 768; McNeill, *Past and Future*, p. 111.

moral restoration now needed for the human community as a whole. McNeill described *The Rise of the West* as "a secular substitute for the Christian worldview." Expanding "the meaningful past" to the whole of humanity was a "moral duty," a "holy calling." In this sense, history functioned as a myth, "the most potent of all methods of political leadership." McNeill regarded myths as accepted truths that "direct attention to what is common amidst diversity." The "reality of world society" now required a single, unifying world history, "the grandest mythical plane of which we are capable."[31]

McNeill's program encountered the obvious dilemma that disciplinary history was itself just one of the many competing strands in the worldwide tangle of messages, doctrines, and religions. On what basis could he assert meaning and morality for the globe given the predicament itself, the overlapping proliferation of other conceptions and beliefs? Here, McNeill swapped registers, grounding his "mythistory" on the universality of "evolution," arguing that in the "long-run test for survival," an "ever-evolving" world history would flourish over other, more rigid "faiths." Flip side to the global crisis of belief, such evolutionary thought spanned McNeill's entire career. Above all, he focused famously on cultural diffusion as a struggle of adaptation and survival, what he called the "mainspring" of "social evolution." His world historical periodizations thus traced the major intervals of this process. In *Past and Future*, he periodized four great epochs of human transportation and communication: walking, horse-riding, sailing, and mechanical power. In *The Rise of the West*, he periodized the human adaptation process itself: the ancient era of transformative diffusions, the medieval era of interregional balance, and the tumultuous modern era of Western take off and global unification. In *Plagues and Peoples*, he downshifted the eras of adaptation directly into biology: early human struggles with parasites, coalescence into regional disease pools, Eurasian interactions, transoceanic interactions, and modern efforts of control. Across his many such books, McNeill labeled each

31 William H. McNeill, *The Rise of the West: A History of the Human Community* (Chicago: University of Chicago Press, 1991), p. 752; William H. McNeill, "Fundamentalism and the world of the 1990s," in R. Scott Appleby and Martin E. Marty (eds.), *Fundamentalisms and Society: Reclaiming the Sciences, the Family, and Education* (Chicago: University of Chicago Press, 1993), p. 573; McNeill, *Past and Future*, p. 2; William H. McNeill, *The Pursuit of Truth: A Historian's Memoir* (Lexington: University Press of Kentucky, 2005), p. 75; William H. McNeill, *Mythistory and Other Essays* (Chicago: University of Chicago Press, 1986), pp. 16 and 226; McNeill, *America, Britain, and Russia*, p. 763; William H. McNeill, "Make mine myth," *New York Times*, December 28, 1981, A19; McNeill, *Mythistory*, p. 42.

of these periods an "equilibrium," a more or less stable pattern of activity within which "revolutionary changes" provoked "transformations" that concluded one period and started another. With this concept, McNeill thus merged global periodization and evolutionary time. As systems of equilibria, he declared, historical and biological "patterns of change . . . are exactly parallel phenomena."[32]

In 1966, Marshall Hodgson identified *The Rise of the West* as "the first genuine world history ever written." Since that time, McNeill's research and advocacy have influenced the discipline profoundly. In the era of "globalization," his broad scope has moved to the center of historical studies. Network dynamics has largely replaced his attention to diffusion, but McNeill's two underpinning principles remain paradigmatic among today's generation of world historians. First, they commonly warrant their scholarship with an ethical import of global proportions, in Patrick O'Brien's words, to advance "moral purposes, connected to the needs of a globalizing world." Jerry Bentley and David Christian, among many others, likewise endorse world history in this way. More sensitive than O'Brien, however, they acknowledge the global jumble of competing conceptions, and so they also label world history a "myth."[33] Second, many world historians employ naturalist and evolutionary models to explain change. Christian's chronology, for example, is driven by increasing cosmological complexity, and he ventures that a process of selection may inform both inorganic and cultural developments. Dan Flores calls for a "deep time" study of world "bioregions," a "sequential" history that treats political borders as "mostly useless" and cultural heritage as a type of "natural selection." The historical study of world systems likewise tends toward evolutionary accounts. And while most contemporary world historians continue to draw from traditional subdisciplinary models for interpreting change, even here, as in Bentley or A. G. Hopkins, global

---

32 McNeill, *Mythistory*, pp. 19–20; and McNeill, *Past and Future*, p. 13; William H. McNeill, *Plagues and Peoples* (Garden City, NY: Anchor Books 1997); William H. McNeill, "Humankind in the balance of nature," in Robert P. Bareikis (ed.), *Science and the Public Interest: Recombinant DNA Research* (Bloomington: Poynter Center, Indiana University, 1978), p. 237.

33 Marshall G. S. Hodgson, *Rethinking World History: Essays on Europe, Islam, and World History* (Cambridge: Cambridge University Press, 1993), p. 92; Patrick O'Brien, "Historiographical traditions and modern imperatives for the restoration of global history," *Journal of Global History* 1 (2006), 38; Jerry H. Bentley, "Myths, wagers, and some moral implications of world history," *Journal of World History* 16 (2005), 79 and 82; and David Christian, *Maps of Time: An Introduction to Big History* (Berkeley: University of California Press, 2004), p. 8.

periodizations take from evolution its uniformity of time, what Christian in a related context calls, "absolute dates."[34]

Following McNeill, the study of world history has contributed substantially to the reframing of disciplinary scope, topics, and approach. Above all, it has insisted on relational and dynamic methods that historicize identities rather than presuming them. In its naturalist and evolutionary variants, world history has extended this transactional orientation to human beings themselves, who are then decentered – and opened – into ecological and cosmological contexts. In *Maps of Time*, Christian adds to this a wonderment and aesthetic joy that is otherwise totally missing from professional historical studies. The potential political and scholarly importance of such a stance is rich for disciplinary self-reflection. Yet the question remains, how does world history combine its descriptive chronology with historical meaning? How does evolution reconcile with moral purpose? Already in 1942, Hempel distinguished the homogeneous time of world history by limiting "meaning" to the "relevant connections" between events, whether "as 'causes' or as 'effects.'" Sixty years later, McNeill likewise displaced meaning entirely into sequence, professing that "conscious purposes . . . largely cancel one another out, thereby sustaining an evolutionary process that no one intended."[35] This subordination to chronology comes at obvious cost to understanding any past imaginings, beliefs, or desires. Causal sequences can condense and homogenize these meanings into factors, but only partially. Strongly functionalist endeavors, like Daniel Lord Smail's *On Deep History and the Brain*, are thus forced into large conjectures and teleological connections. As Wilfrid Sellars maintained, to rehearse an "intention" should not be confused with explaining it. A "way of life" can be "joined" to the "scientific image of man," but not "reconciled" with it. For the writing of world history, a sentiment akin to this lies beneath Patrick Manning's sanguine call for "multiple dimensions" and "multiple perspectives." It lies beneath Michael Bentley's conversely doubtful reproach that "one cannot pile up 'monographs' from all over the globe and treat them as though they were scientific

---

34 Christian, *Maps of Time*, pp. 46, 147, and 510; Dan Flores, "Place: An argument for bioregional history," *Environmental History Review* 18 (1994), 14, 6, and 11; George Modelski, "World system evolution," in Robert A. Denemark *et al.* (eds.), *World System History: The Science of Long-Term Change* (London: Routledge, 2000); Jerry H. Bentley, "Cross-cultural interaction and periodization in world history," *American Historical Review* 101 (1996); and A. G. Hopkins (ed.), *Globalization in World History* (New York: W. W. Norton & Company, 2002); Christian, *Maps of Time*, p. 65.

35 Hempel, "The function of general laws," p. 45, and William H. McNeill, "One world: Divisible or indivisible?," *Journal of Contemporary History* 37 (2002), 492.

reports." And it lay beneath Ranke's declaration that every period was immediate to God.[36]

Related to this, the self-proclaimed morality of world history cannot rest on chronological sequence alone, and adding complexity or evolution will still not secure the link. Increasing levels of complexity could just as easily connote amorality, as in Nietzsche's idea of "greatness," the uppermost incorporation of "multiplicity" and difference, and therefore "beyond good and evil." In evolutionary science, various studies do find cooperation to be an adaptation, though generally as a structure, with locally contingent and indeterminate contents. As Michael Ruse notes in what is otherwise a statement of support, natural selection for cooperation provides "no foundations to normative ethics."[37] Evolution may no longer be able to countersign for imperialism, but nor can it do so for some posited opposite. Smail, for example, seeks to replace the normal disciplinary "rupture" from the Paleolithic – what he derides as today's "sacred history" – with "a seamless narrative" of evolutionary "chronology." He states, "I believe we are morally compelled to examine the hidden legacies that continue to prevent us from teaching a history that begins in Africa."[38] One could easily agree, but also ask, who are "we" and from whence comes our moral obligation?

In the "seamless" recountings of world history, time is but a container, filled sequentially by causes and effects. Periodization thus appears like a typology, like a series of natural historical "ages." Herder's differential temporality is gone. In homogenous time, periods are drained of immanent individuality, bonded instead to a universal imperative purportedly revealed by the globalization process itself. Here, world history shifts the spiritual unity of the nation onto the world as a whole. The field advances a moral claim, not merely as the civic application of its scholarship, but, by necessity, as its own foundation. Otherwise, the chronology of world history would become, like evolution, a description without meaning. As it stands, the insistent coupling of past events and universal historical significance is

---

36 Daniel Lord Smail, *On Deep History and the Brain* (Berkeley: University of California Press, 2008), and a potent criticism, William Reddy, "Neuroscience and the fallacies of functionalism," *History and Theory* 49 (2010), 412–25; Wilfrid Sellars, *Science, Perception and Reality* (New York: Humanities Press, 1962), pp. 39–40; Patrick Manning, "Epistemology," in Jerry H. Bentley (ed.), *The Oxford Handbook of World History* (Oxford: Oxford University Press, 2011), p. 118; Michael Bentley, "The singularities of British world history," in Benedikt Stuchtey and Eckhardt Fuchs (eds.), *Writing World History, 1800–2000* (Oxford: Oxford University Press, 2003), p. 193.

37 Nietzsche, *Sämtliche Werke*, vol. v, pp. 145–7, and Michael Ruse, *Evolutionary Naturalism: Selected Essays* (London: Routledge, 1995), p. 248.

38 Smail, *On Deep History*, pp. 3 and 10.

troubled by the convoluted global dynamic itself. The discipline's more self-reflective practitioners thus authorize world history as an integrative "myth." Nonetheless, the causal chronology remains untouched, displaying in its scientism the irony of the modern "social myth," described by Hans Blumenberg as "the residue left by a 'demythologizing' process."[39] The wedge in world history between sequential connections and meaningful purpose reproduces the global disjunction from which it starts. World history faces limits not because of its disciplinary roots in nationalism – the genetic fallacy of Heather Sutherland, among others[40] – but because it finds no political or cultural replacement for the synthesis of nation-state time.

The site of meaning

For nearly a century, world history has commonly examined its topics with methods derived from evolutionary theory. Throughout the same time, a separate tradition of historical thought, also concerned with the global scale, has empathically resisted it. Explicitly opposed to Darwinian naturalism, the early twentieth-century revival of idealism stressed the irreducible conditionality of perspectives and values. A scientific "object," neo-Kantians argued, was itself derived from the intersubjective, pre-theoretic background of what Edmund Husserl called the human "life-world." The mind, Wilhelm Dilthey conceded, "represents the highest evolutionary stage on earth," and science could indeed explain it as the "physical phenomena" behind it. But the mind was also "woven" into a "common sphere," the shared meanings of language, custom, style, family, society, the state, and law. And within all of these, inextricable historical legacies lived on: "the past is a permanently enduring present." Separate then from the study of physical systems, the knowledge of mind required assessing the "experience" of human interactions, and, with that, the "comprehension of communities as the subject of historical activity."[41] A student of Husserl and deeply impacted by Dilthey, Martin Heidegger extended these ideas into his complex philosophy of historical time, a position of continuing influence, witnessed most recently in postcolonial historiography.

---

39 Hans Blumenberg, *Work on Myth* (Cambridge: The MIT Press, 1985), p. 224.
40 Heather Sutherland, "The problematic authority of (world) history," *Journal of World History* 18 (2007), 491–522.
41 Edmund Husserl, *The Crisis of European Sciences and Transcendental Phenomenology* (Evanston: Northwestern University Press, 1970), pp. 121–48; and Wilhelm Dilthey, *W. Dilthey: Selected Writings*, H. P. Rickman (ed.) (Cambridge: Cambridge University Press, 1976), pp. 211, 191, 194, 221.

Heidegger, like many others after the First World War, characterized the era in the language of crisis. Similar to the young Toynbee, he focused his attention on contemporary changes to the spatial parameters of identity, what he described as the "de-distancing of the 'world' . . . the overcoming of distance." In his first major volume *Being and Time*, he countered this placeless global dimension with the authenticity of the life-world. For Heidegger, the life-world evidenced both temporality and "being with others," and taken together, these conditions made the reckoning of time a necessity. Communal time, for those sharing it, "reveals" meaning and significance; it "constitutes the worldliness of the world."[42] Heidegger contrasted this initially solar and astronomical time-reckoning to its commonplace derivative – the quantification and measurement of clocks. Temporal numeration, he stated, obscured the underlying stretch of existential time. It made duration appear like a "multiplicity of nows . . . a pure succession." Replacing the shared meanings of an actual "location," this "vulgar interpretation of time" produced only the placelessness of "segment and number." Communal time mutated into an abstract universal, belonging to "everyone, and that means no one."[43]

Heidegger characterized these two public temporalities as "authentic" and "inauthentic," or "of its own" and "not of its own" (*eigentlich*/*uneigentlich*). Modern historiography bolstered the latter, because it treated existence in time, rather than as time. Like mechanical clocks, historiography concealed the temporal span of the life-world when it altered a past event into a "time point." Temporal existence "does not fill up an objectively present track," but "rather stretches *itself* along." This "historicity" could never appear in the work of historians, whose universalism instead "inverted" the stretch of time into "a supratemporal pattern." "Historiography," he lectured elsewhere, "is a narcotic averting us from history." By contrast, an authentic retrieval of history responded to past possibilities for the sake of future ones, what Heidegger called "heritage." Historical thinking, in this sense, enabled "the community, the people" to "choose its heroes." Only through this authentic retrieval could the community itself become "authentic" and "complete." No antinomy divided it or its historical time.[44]

Despite the "Heil Hitler" he brought to this "community," Heidegger's attack on universalist historiography – in behalf of local temporality – deeply

---

42 Martin Heidegger, *Sein und Zeit* (Halle: Max Niemeyer, 1927), pp. 105, 410, 411, and 414.
43 Heidegger, *Sein und Zeit*, pp. 417, 425, 417, 422, 418, 425.
44 Heidegger, *Sein und Zeit*, pp. 424 and 376, 374, 395; Martin Heidegger, *Basic Questions of Philosophy: Selected "Problems" of "Logic"* (Bloomington: Indiana University Press, 1994), p. 108, Heidegger, *Sein und Zeit*, pp. 383–5.

influenced later postmodern theory and critique. Key writers differed in important ways, but they shared an exacting focus on textual production and power, oftentimes correlating the ideological authority of historical writing to the great scale of European violence. In general, postmodern authors emphasized temporal discontinuity and dissimilarity, and challenged historiographical presumptions of dialectical progression, chronological identity, and teleology. In a canonical essay of 1971, Michel Foucault argued that "the historical sense" should "free itself from suprahistorical history." Jacques Derrida sought in a similar vein to "fissure structure and history." From "the interior of every epoch," he wrote, "an irreducible rupture and excess can always be shown." Neither denied that linkages of force and concept could arc across durations of various length, but both insisted that such continuities always rested on disconnection, contest, and disjuncture. Underneath the sequential, Foucault asserted, it was "rupture" that secured for historical study its "object."[45]

Postmodern thought emerged in France from a complex combination of historical elements. The Holocaust, the embarrassment of collaboration, and the brutal failures of communism were all important. So too was decolonization, what Derrida described as the political and economic "decentering" of Europe. Already in his qualifying *mémoire* of 1954, Derrida pointed to "Europe" as a crucial though empty concept in the philosophy of Husserl. Later, he explored the "growing and threatening pressure" on Eurocentrism, arguing that Western concepts of human "universality" aimed to "interiorize this difference," a domesticating endeavor he aligned with the US war on Vietnam. Another influential voice in this current, Jean-François Lyotard, defined postmodernity as the split between global heterogeneity and the Western system of scientific and ethical legitimation. Foucault, in his first major volume, described his project as a study of the "confrontation" line between "European culture" and "what it is not." In the prime instance of this, he wrote, Western "colonizing reason" delineated "the Orient" as both its origin and its externality, an "original division" that gave the West its identity, at once universal and unique. Soon after, in his methodological manifesto *The Archeology of Knowledge*, Foucault situated the general critique of historiographical continuity precisely within this theme. Posing an ironic query to the disciplinary historian, he concluded the book: "What, therefore,

---

45 Michel Foucault, "Nietzsche, la généalogie, l'histoire," in Suzanne Bachelard, *et al.* (eds.), *Hommage à Jean Hyppolite* (Paris: Presses Universitaires de France, 1971), p. 167; Jacques Derrida, *Marges de Philosophie* (Paris: Minuit, 1972), p. 206, n. 14; and Michel Foucault, "Réponse au cercle d'épistémologie," *Cahiers pour L'Analyse* (1968), 11.

is this fear which makes you seek, beyond all limits, ruptures, jolts, and separations, the great historical-transcendental destiny of the West?"[46] The geopolitical eclipse of Europe, these authors argued, signaled as well the displacement of its historiographical thought.

By the 1980s, the postmodern critique of history entered the discipline itself. Depending on the subfield, this occurred in assorted ways and to differing degrees. In the context of world history, subaltern and postcolonial studies advanced a substantial disciplinary challenge and secured a lasting impact. The authors of these influential works often distanced themselves in some manner from postmodernism, at times criticizing its own colonialist reinscriptions and "ethnocentric limitations." Whatever the strengths of such claims, much of postcolonial historiography drew sharp-edged techniques and strategies from the previous generation's anti-foundationalism. Gyan Prakash dates the emergence of subaltern studies from the corrosion of national authority and its crisis of popular representation in 1970s India. From there, researchers probed intensely at the colonial and postcolonial construction of the nation. Ranajit Guha, in the opening pages of *Subaltern Studies 1*, declared the Indian nation a "failure," the study of which now "constitutes the central problematic" of Indian historiography. The nation, Antoinette Burton later argued along these lines, was not a "sovereign ontological" identity, but "an unstable subject-in-the-making."[47] Such authors contested the historiographical nation by pulling it apart into contradictory halves. They attacked historiographical universalism as a discursive mode of national and national-imperial power, while empirically foregrounding the social fragments otherwise obscured. To undermine the nation, they dissevered chronology from meaning.

"The practice of subaltern history," explained Dipesh Chakrabarty, "would aim to take history to a point where its unworking becomes visible." In an

---

46 Jacques Derrida, *L'Écriture et la Différence* (Paris: Éditions de Seuil, 1967), p. 414; Jacques Derrida, *The Problem of Genesis in Husserl's Philosophy* (Chicago: University of Chicago Press, 2003), pp. 153–60; Derrida, *Marges*, 133; Jean-François Lyotard, *The Postmodern Condition: A Report on Knowledge* (Minneapolis: University of Minnesota Press, 1984), p. 8; Michel Foucault, *Folie et Déraison: Histoire de la Folie à l'Âge Classique* (Paris: Plon, 1961), pp. iii–iv; Michel Foucault, *L'Archéologie du Savoir* (Paris: Gallimard, 1969), p. 273.

47 Homi K. Bhabha, *The Location of Culture* (London: Routledge, 1994), p. 244; Gyan Prakash, "Postcolonial criticism and history: Subaltern studies," in Axel Schneider and Daniel Woolf (eds.), *The Oxford History of Historical Writing* (Oxford: Oxford University Press, 2011), vol. v, pp. 74–5; Ranajit Guha, "On some aspects of the historiography of colonial India," in Ranajit Guha (ed.), *Subaltern Studies 1: Writings on South Asian History and Society* (Delhi: Oxford University Press, 1982), p. 7; and Antoinette Burton (ed.), *After the Imperial Turn: Thinking With and Through the Nation* (Durham, NC: Duke University Press, 2003), p. 5.

extraordinary evaluation that bridged imperial and national historiography, Guha traced the function of "continuum" and "causality" in evacuating the Santal Uprising of its peasant consciousness and agency, an operation he incisively called the "counter-insurgency" of "assimilative thinking." Stefan Tanaka likewise described disciplinary "chronology" as an "alibi" for the Japanese nation-state, an orchestration of divergent, contradictory, and non-national pasts into a reflection of itself. "Linear History," according to Prasenjit Duara, was "the sublation of the other into the self," an inoculation against "a rupture in the body of the nation." To some advocates then, this strategy signaled the "dissolution of world history," the "end of universal narratives."[48]

On the other side of the methodological fissure were the local and embedded horizons of community and belonging, what Chakrabarty called "very particular ways of being-in-the world." Throughout his scholarship, Guha insisted on the human habitation of myths, spirits, stories, rituals, and practices – the "primordial relations" of everyday community life and the "sovereignty" of subaltern consciousness. As they depicted these sites of meaning and intention, postcolonial historians sought to shelter them against the abstraction of disciplinary equivalency, presenting instead a complex array of irreducible singularities, multiple narratives, and "different orders of temporality." Historicity of the life-world thus represented a "radical heterogeneity" with the ruling powers of its time as well as with historical knowledge itself. By replacing national "evolution" with "multiplicity," Duara explained, critical history offered a glimpse at those "meanings" once and still "repressed."[49]

Postcolonial history jolted powerfully at the discipline's nationalist, Eurocentric, and teleological defaults. Like world history, it responded to fracture lines emerging from changing global circumstances, and by necessity it too engaged its topics with a transnational and multi-archival scope. Moreover, it intensified the democratizing impulse of social history in a manner and to a degree previously unseen. Yet its reception among world historians was

---

48 Dipesh Chakrabarty, *Provincializing Europe: Postcolonial Thought and Historical Difference* (Princeton, NJ: Princeton University Press, 2000), p. 96; Ranajit Guha, "The prose of counter-insurgency," in Ranajit Guha (ed.), *Subaltern Studies 2: Writings on South Asian History and Society* (Delhi: Oxford University Press, 1983), pp. 30 and 32; Stefan Tanaka, *New Times in Modern Japan* (Princeton, NJ: Princeton University Press, 2004), pp. 118–26; Prasenjit Duara, *Rescuing History from the Nation: Questioning Narratives of Modern China* (Chicago: University of Chicago Press, 1995), p. 33; Steven Feierman, "Africa in history: The end of universal narratives," in Gyan Prakash (ed.), *After Colonialism* (Princeton, NJ: Princeton University Press, 1994), p. 60.

49 Chakrabarty, *Provincializing Europe*, p. 255; Guha, "The prose of counter-insurgency," pp. 3 and 40; Chakrabarty, *Provincializing Europe*, p. 92; Prakash, "Postcolonial criticism," p. 82; and Duara, *Rescuing History*, pp. 233–6.

oftentimes lukewarm. Misunderstanding accounted for a substantial part of this, as when O'Brien attempted to dispel the subaltern polemic with a promise of greater historiographical "inclusion," regarding the disquiet as a matter of addition, rather than relation. Historians might have looked elsewhere though: at the strategy's deep reliance on Heidegger and his overwrought dismissal of historiographical thought. In a targeted and very beautiful discussion of his own methodological position, Guha coupled Heidegger with Rabindranath Tagore, both of whom, he said, twined every-dayness to a communal sense of time.

> Such a way to be implies being with others in a social time based on a mutually subscribed notion of the past. Without the latter there can be no agreed codes of conduct or rules of comportment to enable people to form anything like a public, nor can there be a tradition or history for such a society to call its own.

How did this mutuality sustain itself through time? The past "comes alive again," Guha explained, when "grasped in a creative manner." Otherwise, the past would be reduced into the "dull uniformity" of mere traditionalism. In that case though, how could one determine whether the creative act recovered the previous subscription or founded something else? One would need to have already identified a public, a tradition, or a history. Gayatri Chakravorty Spivak attempted to deflect this kind of problem by tossing it back onto historiography; she labeled it "a strategic use of positivist essentialism." But the general form behind every specific "being with others" did not derive from historical facts or methods. It was rather an ontology of unalloyed community, what Theodor Adorno in a bitter attack on Heidegger called "the jargon of authenticity."[50]

As universal chronology, historiography dislodges this idealization of "primordial" community. Contrary to Heidegger's characterization, however, historiography also simultaneously localizes and differentiates. In their meticulous study of early modern clock time, Paul Glennie and Nigel Thrift show that mechanical clocks did not segment and destroy existential time, but extended it. The authors characterize clock time as a "web of practices,"

---

50 O'Brien, "Historiographical traditions," p. 38; Ranajit Guha, *History at the Limits of World-History* (New York: Columbia University Press, 2002), p. 93; Gayatri Chakravorty Spivak, "Subaltern studies: Deconstructing historiography," in Ranajit Guha and Gayatri Chakravorty Spivak, *Selected Subaltern Studies* (New York: Oxford University Press, 1988), p. 13; Theodor W. Adorno, *The Jargon of Authenticity* (Evanston, IL: Northwestern University Press, 1973).

proliferating multiple possibilities that varied enormously by circumstance and temporal context. "Not everyone occupies the same now, because both the one and the now are plural events." In microhistory generally, historio-graphical localization is stressed, and context analyzed as a multi-scalar "space of possibilities" for divergent manifestations of social life. This principle of differentiation aligns with the critical side of the subaltern strategy, which saw in all modern historiography only the dominance of temporal homogeneity and teleological direction. In an eloquent passage, Chakrabarty explained that for a historian to make past peoples intelligible, they must illuminate some aspect of life in the present. Modern historical understanding depended upon an "unstated . . . premise of identification" with these other ways of being. The historian's present thus contained within it "a plurality of times," though in historiographical practice, heterogeneity was ironed out and "disavowed" by universal chronology. As Chakrabarty wrote elsewhere, "old Hegel has the last laugh." This insight into the discipline's disjunctive temporality was a striking and much-needed elaboration. It echoed, however, Ranke's own antinomy and its limitation on universality. History, Ranke wrote, "does not conform to a concept." The historian thus needed a "real appreciation for the varied forms of life that constitute the human race, an entity of which we are a part, forever continuous and always other."[51]

Conclusion

In 1956, Roland Barthes closed his lengthy evaluation of "Myth Today" with a single, distilled contradiction: "It seems that this is a difficulty of our epoch . . . either posit a reality which is entirely permeable by history and ideologize; or else, inversely, posit a reality ultimately impenetrable, irredu-cible, and in this case, poeticize." The latter approach, he explained, searched "for the inalienable meaning of things." As in the sway of his own essay, between its poetical language and its epochal delineations, Barthes' antinomy obtained as a paradox of modern time. A few years later, Siegfried Kracauer targeted this theme in the enigmatic subtitle of

51 Paul Glennie and Nigel Thrift, *Shaping the Day: A History of Timekeeping in England and Wales 1300–1800* (Oxford: Oxford University Press, 2009), pp. 235, 97; Jacques Revel, "Microanalysis and the construction of the social," in Jacques Revel and Lynn Hunt (eds.), *Histories: French Constructions of the Past* (New York: New Press, 1995), p. 500; Chakrabarty, *Provincializing Europe*, pp. 109–13; Dipesh Chakrabarty, "In defense of Provincializing Europe: A response to Carola Dietze," *History and Theory* 47 (2008), 90; Ranke, *Aus Werke*, vol. IV, pp. 88–9.

his neglected masterpiece *History: The Last Things Before the Last*. The time of last things is – as an ending – absolute. Yet here, it is also linked to the next time, itself an ending, and so another absolute. Kracauer named his chapter on periodization after "Ahasuerus," the Wandering Jew. He imagined him in frightening terms, "restlessly" trapped between his "many faces, each reflecting one of the periods which he traversed" and "the one time he is doomed to incarnate."[52]

To use the language of Kracauer and Adorno, the historiographical period is a "force field."[53] It is pulled between poles of chronology and immanence, perpetually in tension, and without resolution. This unique temporal disjuncture emerged out of the European imagination of the globe. In the eighteenth century, the unity of historical time reflected the natural unity of the earth; the disunity of particular times reflected the different and immeasurable pasts also present in the global space. The antipathy between world history and life-world is hardly "dated."[54] It endures as a foundation of modern historical thought. For a long while, the gap was patched by historiographical nationalism. Throughout the twentieth century, however, it became increasingly clear that the nation was an insufficient framework for understanding how the past became present. From the intense and violent reconfigurations of global power, world history and postcolonial history each essayed an alternative by moving toward one of the poles, and each generally backed away from the full implications of either chronology or incommensurability.

Perhaps today, the position of the poles is again changing. In his current, remarkable research, Chakrabarty seeks to align them anew. Planetary climate change, he says, requires a history for which his previous methodologies are insufficient. This dire aggregate of human actions points to "a human collectivity, an us." It reveals in a tangible and unprecedented way the human as a "species." At the same time though, the species offers no experience of itself and shares no self-identity. Despite its cognitive validity, it "cannot subsume particularities." He calls his response, in a phrase from Adorno, "negative universal history." Benjamin Lazier, in his outstanding history of planetary and life-world conceptions, likewise describes "the combination, and also the clash,

52 Roland Barthes, *Mythologies* (Paris: Éditions de Seuil, 1957), pp. 267–8, and Siegfried Kracauer, *History: The Last Things Before the Last* (New York: Oxford University Press, 1967), p. 157.

53 Theodor Adorno, *Notes on Literature*, 2 vols. (New York: Columbia University Press, 1992), vol. II, p. 59.

54 O'Brien, "Historiographical traditions," p. 33.

of the earthly with the Earthly that now conditions human experience."[55]
Between these poles – chronology and immanence, evolution and rupture,
universality and meaning – historiography employs the period.

FURTHER READING

Adams, Henry, "The tendency of history," in *Annual Report of the American Historical Association for the Year 1894*, Washington, D.C.: Government Printing Office, 1895.

Adorno, Theodor W., *The Jargon of Authenticity*, Evanston, IL: Northwestern University Press, 1973.

Notes on Literature, 2 vols., New York: Columbia University Press, 1992.

Bancroft, George, *The Necessity, the Reality, and the Promise of the Progress of the Human Race*, New York: New York Historical Society, 1854.

Barthes, Roland, *Mythologies*, Paris: Éditions de Seuil, 1957.

Beiser, Frederick C., *The German Historicist Tradition*, Oxford: Oxford University Press, 2011.

Bentley, Jerry H., "Cross-cultural interaction and periodization in world history," *American Historical Review* 101 (1996), 749–70.

"Myths, wagers, and some moral implications of world history," *Journal of World History* 16 (2005), 51–82.

Bentley, Michael, "The singularities of British world history," in Benedikt Stuchtey and Eckhardt Fuchs (eds.), *Writing World History, 1800–2000*, Oxford: Oxford University Press, 2003.

Bhabha, Homi K., *The Location of Culture*, London: Routledge, 1994.

Blumenberg, Hans, *Work on Myth*, Cambridge: The MIT Press, 1985.

Burrows, J. W., *A Liberal Descent: Victorian Historians and the English Past*, Cambridge: Cambridge University Press, 1981.

Burton, Antoinette (ed.), *After the Imperial Turn: Thinking With and Through the Nation*, Durham, NC: Duke University Press, 2003.

Chakrabarty, Dipesh, "The climate of history: Four theses," *Critical Inquiry* 35 (2009), 197–222.

"In defense of *Provincializing Europe*: A response to Carola Dietze," *History and Theory* 47 (2008), 85–96.

Provincializing Europe: Postcolonial Thought and Historical Difference, Princeton, NJ: Princeton University Press, 2000.

Christian, David, *Maps of Time: An Introduction to Big History*, Berkeley: University of California Press, 2004.

Cronon, William, "Revisiting the vanishing frontier: The legacy of Frederick Jackson Turner", *Western Historical Quarterly* 18 (1987), 157–76.

Derrida, Jacques, *L'Écriture et la Différence*, Paris: Éditions de Seuil, 1967.

Marges de Philosophie, Paris: Minuit, 1972.

The Problem of Genesis in Husserl's Philosophy, Chicago: University of Chicago Press, 2003.

---

55 Dipesh Chakrabarty, "The climate of history: Four theses," *Critical Inquiry* 35 (2009), 199 and 222, and Benjamin Lazier, "Earthrise; or, the globalization of the world picture," *American Historical Review* 116 (2011), 630.

Dilthey, Wilhelm, *W. Dilthey: Selected Writings*, H.P. Rickman (ed.), Cambridge: Cambridge University Press, 1976.

Droysen, Johann Gustav, *Historik: Historische-Kritische Ausgabe*, Stuttgart: Frommann-Holzboog, 1977.

Duara, Prasenjit, *Rescuing History from the Nation: Questioning Narratives of Modern China*, Chicago: University of Chicago Press, 1995.

Feierman, Steven, "Africa in history: The end of universal narratives," in Gyan Prakash (ed.), *After Colonialism*, Princeton: Princeton University Press, 1994.

Flores, Dan, "Place: An argument for bioregional history," *Environmental History Review* 18 (1994), 1–18.

Foucault, Michel, *L'Archéologie du Savoir*, Paris: Gallimard, 1969.

Folie et Déraison: Histoire de la Folie à l'Âge Classique, Paris: Plon, 1961.

"Nietzsche, la généalogie, l'histoire," in Suzanne Bachelard, *et al.* (eds.), *Hommage à Jean Hyppolite*, Paris: Presses Universitaires de France, 1971.

"Réponse au cercle d'épistémologie," *Cahiers pour L'Analyse* (1968), 9–40.

Gadamer, Hans-Georg, *Truth and Method*, 2nd edn., New York: Crossroad, 1989.

Geyl, Pieter, *Debates with Historians*, London: B. T. Batsford, 1955.

Glennie, Paul, and Nigel Thrift, *Shaping the Day: A History of Timekeeping in England and Wales 1300–1800*, Oxford: Oxford University Press, 2009.

Grafton, Anthony, *What Was History? The Art of History in Early Modern Europe*, Cambridge: Cambridge University Press, 2007.

Guha, Ranajit, *History at the Limits of World-History*, New York: Columbia University Press, 2002.

"On some aspects of the historiography of colonial India," in Ranajit Guha (ed.), *Subaltern Studies 1: Writings on South Asian History and Society*, Delhi: Oxford University Press, 1982.

"The prose of counter-insurgency," in Ranajit Guha (ed.), *Subaltern Studies 2: Writings on South Asian History and Society*, Delhi: Oxford University Press, 1983.

Heidegger, Martin, *Basic Questions of Philosophy: Selected "Problems" of "Logic,"* Bloomington: Indiana University Press, 1994.

Sein und Zeit, Halle: Max Niemeyer, 1927.

Hempel, Carl G., "The function of general laws in history," *The Journal of Philosophy* 39 (1942), 35–48.

von Herder, Johann Gottfried, *Philosophical Writings*, Michael N. Forster (ed.), Cambridge: Cambridge University Press, 2002.

Verstand und Erfahrung: Eine Metakritik zur Kritik der reinen Vernunft, Leipzig: Johann Friedrich Hartknoch, 1799.

Hodgson, Marshall G. S., *Rethinking World History: Essays on Europe, Islam, and World History*, Cambridge: Cambridge University Press, 1993.

Hopkins, A. G. (ed.), *Globalization in World History*, New York: W. W. Norton & Company, 2002.

Husserl, Edmund, *The Crisis of European Sciences and Transcendental Phenomenology*, Evanston, IL: Northwestern University Press, 1970.

Israel, Jonathan, *Enlightenment Contested: Philosophy, Modernity, and the Emancipation of Man, 1670–1752*, Oxford: Oxford University Press, 2006.

Kelly, Donald R., *Fortunes of History: Historical Inquiry from Herder to Huizinga*, New Haven, CT: Yale University Press, 2002.

Koselleck, Reinhart, *Futures Past*, Cambridge: The MIT Press, 1985.

Kracauer, Siegfried, *History: The Last Things Before the Last*, New York: Oxford University Press, 1967.

Krieger, Leonard, *Ranke: The Meaning of History*, Chicago: University of Chicago Press, 1977.

Lamprecht, Karl, *Deutsche Geschichte, Zur jüngsten deutschen Vergangenheit*, Freiburg im Breisgau: H. Heyfelder, 1904.

    Moderne Geschichtswissenschaft, Freiburg im Breisgau: H. Heyfelder, 1905.

    "Was ist Kulturgeschichte? Beitrag zur einer empirischen Historik," *Deutsche Zeitschrift für Geschichtewissenschaft Neue Folge* 1 (1896–7), 75–150.

Lang, Michael, "Globalization and global history in Toynbee," *Journal of World History* 22 (2011), 747–83.

Lazier, Benjamin, "Earthrise; or, the globalization of the world picture," *American Historical Review* 116 (2011), 602–30.

Loria, Achille, *Analisi della proprietà capitalista*, 2 vols., Turin: Fratelli Bocca, 1889.

Lyotard, Jean-François, *The Postmodern Condition: A Report on Knowledge*, Minneapolis: University of Minnesota Press, 1984.

McNeill, William Hardy, *America, Britain, and Russia: Their Co-operation and Conflict, 1941–1946*, London: Oxford University Press, 1953.

    "Fundamentalism and the world of the 1990s," in Martin E. Marty and R. Scott Appleby (eds.), *Fundamentalisms and Society: Reclaiming the Sciences, the Family, and Education*, Chicago: University of Chicago Press, 1993.

    "Humankind in the balance of nature," in Robert P. Bareikis (ed.), *Science and the Public Interest: Recombinant DNA Research*, Bloomington: Poynter Center, Indiana University, 1978.

    "Make mine myth," *New York Times*, December 28, 1981, A19.

    Mythistory and Other Essays, Chicago: University of Chicago Press, 1986.

    "One world: Divisible or indivisible?", *Journal of Contemporary History* 37 (2002), 489–95.

    Past and Future, Chicago: University of Chicago Press, 1954.

    Plagues and Peoples, Garden City, NY: Anchor Books 1997.

    The Pursuit of Truth: A Historian's Memoir, Lexington: University Press of Kentucky, 2005.

    The Rise of the West: A History of the Human Community, Chicago: University of Chicago Press, 1991.

Manning, Patrick, "Epistemology," in Jerry H. Bentley (ed.), *The Oxford Handbook of World History*, Oxford: Oxford University Press, 2011.

Meinecke, Friedrich, *Werke*, Hans Herzfeld *et al.* (eds.), 10 vols., Munich: R. Oldenbourg, 1963.

Michelet, Jules, *Introduction à l'Histoire Universelle*, Paris: L. Hachette, 1834.

    Le Peuple, Paris: L. Hachette, 1846.

Modelski, George, "World system evolution," in Robert A. Denemark *et al.* (eds.), *World System History: The Science of Long-Term Change*, London: Routledge, 2000.

Nietzsche, Friedrich, *Sämtliche Werke: Kritische Studienausgabe*, Giorgio Colli and Mazzino Montinari (eds.), 11 vols., Munich: Deutscher Taschenbuch Verlag, 1988.

Oakeshott, Michael, *Experience and Its Modes*, Cambridge: Cambridge University Press, 1933.

O'Brien, Patrick, "Historiographical traditions and modern imperatives for the restoration of global history," *Journal of Global History* 1 (2006), 3–39.

Prakash, Gyan, "Postcolonial criticism and history: Subaltern studies," in Axel Schneider and Daniel Woolf (eds.), *The Oxford History of Historical Writing*, Oxford: Oxford University Press, 2011, vol. v.

von Ranke, Leopold, *Aus Werke und Nachlass*, Walter Peter Fuchs and Theodor Schieder (eds.), 4 vols., Munich: R. Oldenbourg, 1971.

Geschichten der romanischen und germanischen Völker von 1494 bis 1514, Leipzig: G. Reimer, 1824.

Weltgeschichte, 9 vols., Leipzig: Dunder und Humblot, 1880.

Zur Geschichte Deutschlands und Frankreichs im 19. Jahrhundert, Alfred Dove (ed.), Leipzig: Dunder und Humblot, 1887.

Reddy, William, "Neuroscience and the fallacies of functionalism," *History and Theory* 49 (2010), 412–25.

Revel, Jacques, "Microanalysis and the construction of the social," in Jacques Revel and Lynn Hunt (eds.), *Histories: French Constructions of the Past*, New York: New Press, 1995.

Rudwick, Martin J. S., *Bursting the Limits of Time: The Reconstruction of Geohistory in the Age of Revolution*, Chicago: University of Chicago Press, 2005.

Ruse, Michael, *Evolutionary Naturalism: Selected Essays*, London: Routledge, 1995.

Sellars, Wilfrid, *Science, Perception and Reality*, New York: Humanities Press, 1962.

Smail, Daniel Lord, *On Deep History and the Brain*, Berkeley: University of California Press, 2008.

Southard, Robert, *Droysen and the Prussian School*, Lexington: University Press of Kentucky, 1995.

Spivak, Gayatri Chakravorty, "Subaltern studies: Deconstructing historiography," in Ranajit Guha and Gayatri Chakravorty Spivak, *Selected Subaltern Studies*, New York: Oxford University Press, 1988.

Stubbs, William, *Lectures on Early English History*, London: Longmans, Green, and Co., 1906.

Sutherland, Heather, "The problematic authority of (world) history," *Journal of World History* 18 (2007), 491–522.

Tanaka, Stefan, *New Times in Modern Japan*, Princeton, NJ: Princeton University Press, 2004.

Greek Civilization and Character: The Self-Revelation of Ancient Greek Society, London: J. M. Dent and Sons, 1924.

Greek Historical Thought: From Homer to the Age of Heraclitus, London: J. M. Dent and Sons, Ltd., 1924.

Nationality and the War, London: J. M. Dent and Sons, Ltd., 1915.

A Study of History, 12 vols., London: Oxford University Press, 1939.

The Western Question in Greece and Turkey, A Study in the Contact of Civilizations, London: Constable and Co., 1922.

Turner, Frederick Jackson, *Frontier and Section: Selected Essays of Frederick Jackson Turner*, Englewood Cliffs: Prentice Hall, 1961.

The Frontier in American History, New York: Henry Holt, 1921.

White, Hayden, *The Historical Imagination in Nineteenth-Century Europe*, Baltimore, MA: Johns Hopkins University Press, 1973.

White, Leslie A., "Evolutionary stages, progress, and the evaluation of cultures," *Southwestern Journal of Anthropology* 3 (1947), 165–92.

Woolf, Daniel R., *A Global History of History*, Cambridge: Cambridge University Press, 2011.

5

From divergence to convergence: centrifugal and centripetal forces in history

DAVID R. NORTHRUP

Dividing the great sweep of history into discrete eras is inevitably a subjective exercise. For example, once their religions had achieved success, Christians and Muslims pivoted history around their founders' lives, much as the Jews before them had calculated time from the supposed date of the creation of the Earth. Some Romans (and many of their later admirers) employed a system of dating based on the supposed founding of their capital city (*ab urbe condita*). Renaissance Europeans saw their era as the end of the Dark Ages and the beginning of a Modern period characterized by a revival of classical standards. That division of history into Ancient, Medieval, and Modern eras is still in use. Fortunately, the impulse to devise new schemas is rare. In proposing to split the human past into two unequal periods, this chapter does not intend to launch a new calendar or mandate new names for historical eras. Rather, it is a meditation on the global past from the perspective of our own times.

Projected beyond the Mediterranean world where it evolved, the division of history into Ancient, Medieval, and Modern can be a clumsy fit. In places like China and India, for example, the distinction between Ancient and Medieval is not so clear as in the Latin West, and the beginning of Modern history is usually placed well after 1500. In parts of Africa below the Sahara, one can identify an era of medieval empires, such as Ghana, Mali, and Songhay in the Western Sudan, Solomonic Ethiopia, and the Zimbabwe empire. Outside the Nile Valley, however, there is no readily apparent era of classical antiquity, despite the continent's uniquely long human history.[1]

---

1 Using a different definition of classical, Christopher Ehret, *An African Classical Age: Eastern and Southern Africa in World History, 1000* B.C. *to* A.D. *400* (Charlottesville: University of Virginia Press, 1998) argues that the cultural and economic foundations for Bantu-speaking Africa were created in the absence of writing, empires, and monumental architecture.

Since the Americas also lack an age of classical antiquity (except for the Maya), historians commonly divide their history into pre-Columbian, colonial, and independent eras. World historians mostly evade the problems of a one-size-fits-all schema by just ignoring it, though it is harder to evade the tripartite schema's implicit assumptions about the development of high culture ("civilization") and aristocratic society, which do not accord well with present-day views of class, gender, and cultural diversity. In addition, having no common periodization can reduce world history to a series of regional narratives, which some have argued was in fact the case until the world began to globalize.[2]

A more fundamental problem is that the conventional periodization omits most of human history. Initially this was done out of simple ignorance, which is evident in the Jewish calculation that human creation occurred in 3760 BCE or the more refined calculation by Archbishop James Ussher (1581–1656) that the world began on a day in late October 4004 BCE, a calculation that remained popular in some circles well into the nineteenth century. Since the advances in science by Darwin and other biologists undercut the assumption of an actual creation event and archaeologists uncovered evidence of human life much further back in time, historians have been willing to concede the existence of something called "prehistory" that might be worthy of study by other disciplines, while steadfastly persisting in beginning "history" at about the same date that the Jews and Ussher said marked Creation. In effect they agree with Samuel Noah Kramer's famous proposal a half-century ago that history begins at Sumer in Mesopotamia some 6,000 years ago.[3] Some historians may be willing to push the date back another 2,000 years or so to the beginning of agriculture. Yet that definition of history still excludes 95 percent of human existence, if one restricts one's definition of "human" to modern humans (*Homo sapiens sapiens*) who appeared some 200,000 years ago. The omission grows to 99.6 percent if one includes earlier forms of humankind existing from about 2.5 million years ago.

The argument for beginning history about 6,000 years ago is often based on the fact that that is when writing appeared. While written records do make the reconstruction of the past easier, they are not so crucial or so reliable as was once assumed. As will be discussed below, we have learned a

2 Bruce Mazlish and Ralph Buultjens (eds.), *Conceptualizing Global History* (Boulder, CO: Westview Press, 1993).
3 Samuel Noah Kramer, *History Begins at Sumer* (Philadelphia: University of Pennsylvania Press, 1956).

great deal about "prehistoric" times in the past half-century, and that knowledge tells us more about daily life than the legal texts, proclamations, and religious and philosophical speculations that dominate ancient writing. In addition, tying history closely to written texts excludes the majority of humans, who, until recent times, were illiterate. It was once quite common to argue that non-elites, most non-Western people, and most women essentially had no history, although few will openly defend that proposition now.

A second remarkable omission from most historians' conception of "history" is what some would term "current events," often whatever has occurred since they earned their degrees. While safeguarding historical objectivity from contamination by "presentist" norms, such an omission largely abandons the idea that historical study should give a perspective on the present. That may be a better trade-off than mining the historical record primarily for things that support contemporary notions, but neither position achieves a balance between history for its own sake and history as a dialogue between past and present. Contemporary events are not simply more of the same; they are essential to understanding our past.

Like it or not, we live in a new age, the age of globalization. Global interactions – economic, cultural, and political – have shifted into high gear and the pace of change continues to accelerate. Yet few historians include globalization in their teaching and writing; even fewer seek to explain how globalization came about. As historian Tony Hopkins has pointed out, "the analysis of the origins, nature, and consequences of globalization ... is currently the most important single debate in the social sciences," a debate, he notes, that most historians ignore.[4] By leaving the explanation of the current trajectory of events to other disciplines, historians are truncating their professional duty in a way that may be even more irresponsible than the omission of humanity's first 200,000 years. Far from being a passing phase, the bundle of changes called globalization is a crucial aid in making sense of history.

For these reasons, world historians recognize the need for a framework that encompasses the full range of human history, embraces all types of people, and acknowledges that globalization is not a passing fad but a significant outcome of deep historical forces. In aid of that enterprise this chapter looks at history in terms of two dominant historical trends: divergence and convergence. From the beginning most of history was a story of

---

4 A. G. Hopkins, "Globalization – An agenda for historians," in A. G. Hopkins (ed.), *Globalization in World History* (New York: W. W. Norton, 2002), p. 2.

divergence: humans' biological and cultural differentiation as they evolved and dispersed across the planet. For the past millennium, history has been dominated by convergent forces, of which globalization is the latest phase. During this era that I call the Great Convergence, human interaction, trade, and intercommunication have increased at a rapid rate.

The long Age of Divergence

As the number of modern humans slowly increased, differences developed among populations both within Africa and then among those who spread out of Africa to the distant corners of the planet. Some changes were biological, but over time cultural differences became far more profound. The long millennia during which biological and cultural diversification were dominant can be called the Age of Divergence.

In part, divergence was nature's way for species to adapt to new circumstances and for new species to evolve. Modern humans (*Homo sapiens sapiens*) evolved from earlier primates and hominids through such an evolutionary process. The physical differences that continued to evolve among modern humans are both obvious and subtle. Thus, visible differences in hair and skin pigmentation are obvious, while the existence of multiple blood types and two types of human earwax is largely of interest to specialists. During the past quarter century, tremendous advances in genetics have revolutionized our understanding of human variation and simultaneously undermined unscientific prejudices. The mapping of the human genome, for example, has brought to light evidence that supports a coherent narrative of early human dispersal across the planet. DNA evidence confirms archaeological evidence that modern humans evolved in tropical Africa about 200,000 years ago, and from about 70,000 years ago began moving into the other continents. Distinguishable genetic lineages transmitted through females, known as mitochondrial DNA haplogroups, show that the earliest migrations were across southern Asia and into Australia, followed by later movements into the colder regions of Europe and northern Asia, from where people moved on into the Americas (see Map 5.1).[5] Along the way, each branch of humanity's family tree developed distinctive traits.

5 Corinna Herrnstadt, et al., "Reduced-median-network analysis of complete mitochondrial DNA coding-region sequences for the major African, Asian, and European haplogroups," *American Journal of Human Genetics* 70 (2002), 1,152–71; "Human mitochondrial DNA haplogroups," *Wikipedia, The Free Encyclopedia*, accessed October 23, 2012, http://en.wikipedia.org/wiki/Human_mitochondrial_DNA_haplogroup.

African: L, L1, L2, L3
Near Eastern: J, N
Southern European: J, K
General European: H, V
Northern European: T, U, X
Asian: A, B, C, D, E, F, G (*M is composed of C, D, E, and G*)
Native American: A, B, C, D, and sometimes X

Map 5.1 DNA evidence of global human migration since about 170,000 years ago. The map traces human dispersal out of Africa of mitochondrial DNA haplogroups (populations genetically related through the female line) and the subsequent development of new mtDNA haplogroups. The capital letters on the map locate common groups. Source: Wikipedia Commons, licensed under the Creative Commons Attribution-Share Alike 3.0 Unported license.

Genetic variations had a number of causes. Since Darwin, the importance of natural selection in shaping evolution has been widely recognized. Even before humans moved out of Africa, other major differences had developed, such as the small body size among Pygmies that enhanced their movement through tropical rainforests. As the human species colonized the full range of the planet's climate zones and geographical regions, one obvious example of natural selection was the variation in skin color. Human populations that had gained pigmentation to reduce the harmful effects of the tropical sun lost pigmentation to enhance the beneficial effects of sunlight in more northern climes. Other variations in the human genome resulted from genetic drift, that is, random alterations in genes that occur naturally. Some isolated populations also changed as a result of assortative mating, that is, mating within a local gene pool, which had the effect of reducing the population's genetic variety and increasing the distance between them and other groups. In the early process of expansion out of Africa there is also evidence of interbreeding with other varieties of humanity, such as Neanderthals in the Mediterranean region and similar populations in Melanesia.

Two other circumstances affected human biological diversity. The first is that humans in Africa had long millennia to develop significant genetic variations. Second, DNA evidence suggests that the number of individuals who left Africa about 70,000 years ago was very small and thus represented a tiny part of the genetic diversity within the mother continent. All of the populations of Eurasia, Australasia, and the Americas developed from this restricted gene pool. For these reasons, genetic variation outside of Africa is actually less than within Africa. Overall, the biological diversity among humans is of modest proportions.

Unlike other species, modern humans have an enormous capacity for cultural change, which has been a far more important force for differentiation than biological change. Cultural changes came slowly during most of human existence, but they were inexorable because human communities were small and had limited contacts with others. Cultural differences would have occurred in a variety of contexts, including technologies, beliefs, food prefer-ences, and forms of adornment. Because direct evidence for many forms of cultural variation is quite uneven (or absent) in early times, language multi-plication is a useful surrogate for discussing the broader cultural changes that were taking place.

Although direct records of spoken languages date only from the invention of writing, linguistics can provide striking indications of ancestral speech and of how, over time, a single language could fragment into dozens, even hundreds, of mutually unintelligible languages. By 1000 CE some 10,000 to 18,000 languages were in use, and great numbers of older languages had passed out of existence. Today humans are more than one hundred times as numerous as a millennium ago, yet we speak far fewer languages. Why did so few people once have so many languages and why has the number of living languages declined?

Distinct languages evolved among populations that experienced prolonged isolation from each other, a circumstance that was common when human numbers were few. Such isolation could occur even on a single island, as was the case on New Guinea, whose highlands became home to the greatest concentration of distinct languages in the world. The island's population of less than a million in 1500 developed 500 languages divided among 33 language families. Evidently people who settled in the island's deep inland valleys had so little contact with those in the neighboring valleys that each community developed a distinctive language and other cultural traits.

Other populations became even more isolated by vast expanses of ocean, as was the case of island communities in the Pacific. Similarly, isolated communities in the larger continents of Australia and the Americas developed great linguistic diversity as they dispersed over vast territories with abundant wild game. At the time outsiders opened sustained contacts with Australia in the late eighteenth century, the aboriginal inhabitants numbered about a quarter of a million and were divided into between 360 and 750 distinct social groups, each speaking a distinct language. The size of the populations of the Americas at the time of sustained outside contacts began in 1492 was much larger, though estimates vary widely. Based on evidence recorded much later, the number of languages spoken in the Americas 2,000 years ago is conservatively estimated at about 500. Estimates of the number of indigenous languages still spoken in the Americas range from around 150 into the thousands.[6]

New Guinea, Australia, and the Americas are extreme examples of places where the average language before the end of isolation had only a few hundred or a few thousand speakers, but analogous linguistic situations existed in much of the rest of the world for most of history. Communities that survived through hunting and gathering had to be small and spread very thinly on the ground. Pastoralists also needed vast grazing lands to survive. In 10,000 BCE there were perhaps 4 million people in the world and some 7,000 spoken languages. In striking contrast to more recent times, none of the languages had more than a few thousand speakers, and the average was fewer than 600 per language.[7]

---

6 M. Paul Lewis (ed.), *Ethnologue: Languages of the World*, 16th edn. (Dallas, TX: SIL International, 2009), accessed September 10, 2013, www.ethnologue.com; "Languages of Papua New Guinea," *Wikipedia, The Free Encyclopedia*, accessed September 10, 2013, http://en.wikipedia.org/wiki/Languages_of_Papua_New_Guinea; "Australian Aboriginal languages," *Wikipedia, The Free Encyclopedia*, accessed September 10, 2013, http://en.wikipedia.org/wiki/Australian_Aboriginal_languages; and "Indigenous languages of the Americas," *Wikipedia, The Free Encyclopedia*, accessed September 10, 2013, http://en.wikipedia.org/wiki/Indigenous_languages_of_the_Americas.
7 Frances Karttunen and Alfred W. Crosby, "Language death, language genesis, and world history," *Journal of World History* 8 (1995), 159, and Tore Janson, *The History of Languages: An Introduction* (New York: Oxford University Press, 2012), pp. 22–3.

It appears that new languages may have emerged at an even faster rate after the development of agriculture, since farmers were tied to smaller terrains than pastoralists and hunter-gatherers. One example of language fragmentation during early agriculture is the development of the Bantu language family in the vast southern cone of Africa. Over the course of the past 2,500–3,000 years a single ancestral language ("proto-Bantu") branched into approximately 250 separate languages. The growth of the family was associated with the spread of people possessing agriculture and other technological advantages that enabled their numbers to multiply much more rapidly than those of the hunter-gather populations they displaced or absorbed. Even though some historians cite the spread of the Bantu-speaking peoples as a unifying trend, the actual outcome was the creation of hundreds of distinct languages and ethnicities. Bantu expansion was not a "migration" (as it has often been called) or even several "migrations," but appears to have been a very slow, gradual drift of populations across an extensive area. As food-rich agricultural communities increased in numbers, some among the younger generation had to move out to new farm and pasture lands beyond the periphery of the ancestral community. Over dozens of generations, such short movements eventually frayed or broke the ties to ancestral communities and led to the formation of new identities, languages, and cultural complexes (see Map 5.2).

Archaeologist Colin Renfrew has used the model of Bantu expansion to interpret the expansion of the older and larger Indo-European language family. Renfrew starts with the hypothesis that, like the spread of Bantu-speaking peoples, the giant Indo-European family was not the product of a migration or an invasion but resulted from a long, slow drift of people outward from an agriculture center. He also believes that the fruits of their agricultural labors enabled these populations to multiply faster than the pastoralists or hunter-gatherers they were displacing or absorbing. The farmers' superior numbers also led to the dominance of their languages. Even though linguistic evidence did not then support the proposition, he posited an origin of the process in central Turkey because it was an area of early agricultural innovation. New linguistic evidence has recently been marshaled in support of this thesis. Not all specialists agree that Turkey was the starting point nor that agriculture (along with nomadic pastoralism in the steppes) was the mechanism for Indo-European language spread over Europe, the Middle East, Central Asia, and South Asia. Nevertheless, a peaceful outward movement of a growing population could account for

Map 5.2 African language map, showing Bantu language area (Niger-Congo B).
Source: Wikipedia Commons, licensed under the Creative Commons Attribution-Share
Alike 3.0 Unported license; created by Mark Dingemanse.

the process that over six millennia led to the formation of nine Indo-European sub-families consisting of some 450 languages.[8]

The formation of thousands of distinct languages and the other cultural differences bundled with them was a formidable achievement. So was the

---

8 Colin Renfrew, *Archaeology and Language: The Puzzle of Indo-European Origins* (New York: Cambridge University Press, 1987); Heather Pringle, "New method puts elusive Indo-European homeland in Anatolia," *Science* 24 (2012), 902.

spread of humans across the planet, mastering of new environments, domesticating plants and animals, and developing new technologies. But over millennia the process of cultural differentiation also created formidable barriers to understanding and laid the basis for animosities and conflicts that are still being played out.

Despite their differences, communities also shared many cultural features, such as the much-studied Indo-European religious traditions. Many commonalities seem to have arisen from ideas and aims that were widely shared. For example, formal burials with grave goods were widespread from early times, implying belief in an afterlife. In addition, aesthetic expression was a common human impulse. An entrenched belief that artistic expression could not have existed among "cavemen" had made the dating of the cave paintings at Altamira and Lascaux to between 15,000 to 20,000 years ago highly controversial. Newer evidence of finely made, decorated stone tools from Blombos Cave in South Africa show that such sensibilities existed fifty millennia earlier. Despite the lack of physical evidence, other arts, including dance, music, and rituals, also must have had a similarly long history.

Although present-day scholars can assign languages into families and detect broad cultural commonalities (such as, African art or "primitive" art), such connections would not have been meaningful enough to support ties among those who lived at those times. Similarly, while world historians might categorize technologies such as agriculture and iron smelting as commonalities for large numbers of humans in the last few millennia, it is unlikely that the diverse populations using such technologies would have perceived them as significant enough to overcome entrenched cultural differences. Indeed, it now seems that such technologies, once thought to have had a single origin, were in fact the product of separate inventions in different places. The evidence for agriculture is the most compelling, with separate inventions occurring not just in the Middle East and the Americas, but also in East Asia and at least three separate places in sub-Saharan Africa.[9] Even the borrowing of technologies and ideas by different groups did not form meaningful ties. Those who borrowed food plants, for example, might prepare them for consumption in their own distinctive ways. There is no evidence of people bonding on the basis of eating the

---

9 Ehret, *African Classical Age*, pp. 5–16, discusses the linguistic evidence for African agriculture and iron making.

same grain, root, or fruit. Differences, not commonalities, were (and are) the basis of cherished identities.

The Great Convergence

Our present age seems the polar opposite of the long, slow age of divergence. Interaction, integration, and innovation occur with breathtaking speed. Fast, quick communication and transportation blur cultural boundaries. Trade and travel, infrastructure integration, and alliances diminish the significance of political and economic boundaries. Although conflicts still erupt, the level of violence in the world appears to be declining.[10] The number of spoken languages has also declined, as national and regional languages have gained importance. For the first time in history, one language, English, has emerged as the global language.[11] The age of globalization is both awesome and terrifying. On the positive side, globalizing forces have raised living standards, spread powerful new technologies, and promoted international and transnational cooperation. On the negative side, people fear the loss of traditional customs, global competition for resources and markets risks promoting global conflict, and rising consumption is causing such severe threats to the global environment that, in the worst scenarios, human progress and humanity itself may be at risk. For better and/or worse, globalization seems here to stay.

Historians aren't able to predict where globalization will take the planet, but we can provide useful perspectives on its origins, even though a consensus about when globalization began seems elusive. Many social scientists describe globalization as a new phenomenon that came into existence toward the end of the twentieth century, but most will concede that it has roots going back to the period after 1945 that saw the formation of the United Nations, the expansion of international trade, and the emergence of what V. S. Naipaul in 1990 called "universal civilization." Other scholars see a longer trajectory. Many economists are inclined to place the origins of globalization in the Industrial Revolution.[12] Not surprisingly, world

---

10 Stephen Pinker, *The Better Angels of Our Nature: Why Violence Has Declined* (New York: Penguin Books, 2012); and Joshua Goldstein, *Winning the War on War: The Decline of Armed Conflict Worldwide* (New York: Plume, 2012).

11 David Northrup, *How English Became the Global Language* (New York: Palgrave Macmillan, 2013).

12 For example, Jeffrey G. Williamson, *Globalization and the Poor Periphery before 1945* (Cambridge, MA: The MIT Press, 2006); and Martin Wolf, *Why Globalization Works* (New Haven, CT: Yale University Press, 2004), Chapter 8.

historians who have bothered to look are inclined to place the beginnings earlier. Tony Hopkins has usefully identified several periods of globalization: "archaic" (encompassing trends in the Old World continents up to about 1600), "proto" (associated with the expansion of political, financial, and commercial systems between 1600 and 1800), and "modern" (beginning with industrialization). Others give greater attention to European maritime expansion or consolidation in Asia.[13]

One can sidestep some of these issues by not extending the term globalization too far back and using global "convergence" instead, as this chapter does. Convergence includes many of the same phenomena as globalization (political integration and cooperation, economic and cultural integration, movement of people and ideas, etc.), but allows the term "globalization" to be used just for the intense integration of recent times. Convergent forces seem to be as old as divergent ones. Historian William H. McNeill writes, "human societies [have] always exchanged messages with strangers and altered their behavior every so often when something new and attractive came along."[14] Gregarious by nature, humans belong to groups based on kinship, community, and other social and economic associations. People within groups share and borrow. Borrowing among groups also occurs whether freely or through raids, theft, and kidnapping. The most common type of exchanges has been through trade, the earliest forms of which reflected different environments and lifeways. Pastoralists exchanged milk and hides for grain with farmers. Salt is the earliest item known to have been traded over long distances, because all humans need salt for health.[15]

Historians have long identified the political centralization in the Nile and Indus Valleys, China, and Mesopotamia during the first millennium BCE as a break with the past, which indeed it was. Empires united people on a new scale, promoted trade in luxury goods for the royal courts and elite classes, and fostered cultural uniformity. For example, records from ancient Egypt

13 Hopkins, "Globalization – An agenda for historians"; Fernand Braudel, *Civilization and Capitalism, 15th–18th Century*, Sian Reynolds (trans.), 3 vols. (New York: Harper & Row, 1984); Immanuel Wallerstein, *The Modern World System*, 3 vols. (New York: Academic Press, 1974–89). For a fuller discussion of this historiography see David Northrup, "Globalization in historical perspective," in George Modelski (ed.), *World System History*, in the online *Encyclopedia of Life Support Systems (EOLSS)*, UNESCO, Eolss Publishers, accessed September 10, 2013, www.eolss.net.

14 William H. McNeill, "Afterward: World history and globalization," in A. G. Hopkins (ed.), *Global History: Interactions Between the Universal and the Local* (New York: Palgrave, 2006), p. 285.

15 Harlan W. Gilmore, "Cultural diffusion via salt," *American Anthropologist* 57 (1955), 1,010–5; and Mark Kurlansky, *Salt: A World History* (New York: Penguin, 2003).

and ancient Israel tell of trading expeditions south into Africa to get animal pelts, rare woods, spices and aromatics, and, of course, gold. Over time, long-distance trade expanded its markets. A shipwreck off Java dated to about 1000 CE contained tons of Malay tin, glass beads from the Southeast Asian mainland, Chinese silver and iron ingots, and ceramics from China and Persia. It had probably also carried Indian cotton textiles and Chinese silks that did not survive under water.[16] This complex cargo documents the existence of communities mining and manufacturing for export as well as professional trading communities.

Long-distance trade was connected to two other convergent cultural trends. The first was the spread of trading languages. Ancient sources tell of people who had to trade through silent barter, piling up goods on each side until both traders agreed to the exchange. However, verbally bargaining was more expeditious. In antiquity, for example, Koine Greek was used widely as a trading language. In the thirteenth century Marco Polo was able to converse in Persian as he crossed the vastness of Central Asia on his way to China. Arabic also spread across the western Indian Ocean as an important language of trade, turning that body of water into an Arabian Sea. In the eastern Indian Ocean, about 1500, the trading state of Malacca had official linguists to deal with the dozens of languages spoken by foreign merchants who came there. Generally, trading languages were acquired as second languages and did not displace local vernaculars. Over time, however, they became some people's first language, as is the case with Arabic in much of the Middle East.

The development of trans-regional religions was another form of cultural convergence often spread along trade routes. Jewish traders dispersed to Persia, western India, and along the Silk Road to the Far East. Indian traders introduced Hinduism into Southeast Asia. Even earlier, Buddhism had spread from India into South Asia, along the maritime trade routes of the Indian Ocean and overland into the Middle East, and along the Silk Road. Judaism and Hinduism largely kept their ethnic base, while Buddhism transcended its origins. After some initial hesitation, Christianity and Islam also embraced universalism. Christianity spread within the Roman empire and outward along trade routes, a notable example being the Nestorian Christian communities along the Silk Road. Islam was spread by conquest and Arab settlement in the Middle East, North Africa, and Iberia and through

---

16 Described in Stewart Gordon, *When Asia Was the World* (Philadelphia, PA: Da Capo, 2008), Chapter 4.

trading connections in the Indian Ocean, across the Sahara, and in Central Asia. By about 1000, for example, gold and slaves flowed out of sub-Saharan Africa into the Muslim world, while horses and other goods, along with Islam and the Arabic language moved into lands south of the Sahara and along the Swahili Coast.

At some point, centrifugal forces for global divergence began to be overtaken by centripetal forces for convergence. Despite some interruptions, that trend continued and gradually gained momentum. This was the Great Convergence. The tipping point need not have been sudden or associated with any dramatic event and people living at the time need not have been aware of the transition. Only with the value of hindsight might people notice that a shift had taken place. Even if dating when this shift occurred is possible, doing so may seem to be of purely academic interest. Yet working out when and how the convergent forces became dominant is of great significance to those who seek to make sense of human history.

One place to start the quest for that tipping point is with the big surveys. Most world history textbooks come in two volumes, the first of which almost invariably ends in 1500, the conventional round number for dividing medieval and modern history. However, textbook authors often hedge their bets (and broaden their appeal) by beginning the second volume a few centuries earlier. For example, the second volume of Felipe Fernández-Armesto's *The World: A History* (2007) ostensibly starts in 1300, but the first chapter in that volume actually begins nearly a century earlier with the Mongol conquests and the great expansion of trade overland along the Silk Road. David Christian starts his *Maps of Time: An Introduction to Big History* much earlier in time, devoting the first five chapters to the origins of the universe and the evolution of life with a sixth chapter to the evolution of human life. The next eight chapters recount human history from the Agricultural Revolution to the end of the twentieth century, the "Modern Era" being the subject of the last four chapters. While preserving a conventional division at 1500, Christian expresses some doubt about that periodization. The first of the Modern chapters begins with the statement, "in the past thousand years, and particularly in the past two or three hundred years, a transformation more rapid and more fundamental than any other in human history has taken place."[17] For Christian a historical divide around 1000 CE allows him to place the rise of the Mongol empire in the context of the splendors of the Sung Dynasty that

---

17 David Christian, *Maps of Time: An Introduction to Big History* (Berkeley: University of California Press, 2004), p. 335.

attracted Genghis Khan's invaders. As Christian also makes clear in the sentence just quoted and elsewhere, the key changes of the Modern era were slow in coming and only picked up speed from about 1750.

The global watershed: 1500?

Christian and Fernández-Armesto are not alone in identifying accelerating change as the dominant characteristic of the Modern era and in suggesting that the dramatic changes around 1500 are best understood as the culmination of several centuries of global changes.[18] The size and splendors of Asian empires are not the only reason for moving the narrative earlier. World historians have also commonly emphasized several other contexts more closely connected with the Iberian voyages, as do some European historians.[19] One such context is the dependence of the Iberian voyages on borrowings from the East. Not only was the printing press that diffused knowledge of the voyages and discoveries originally a Chinese invention, but the numerals used to record locations at sea were also based on those developed by Indian mathematicians that had spread west through the Arabian world. More fundamentally, the Iberian ships navigated with magnetic compasses (first developed in China) and used the astrolabe (an Arab or Greek invention) to determine their locations at sea. Lateen sails were probably copied from those on Arab ships. Even the infectious diseases inadvertently introduced to the Americas with such devastating consequences had a historical precedent with the similarly calamitous epidemic known as the Black Death that spread rapidly along trade routes from South Asia to Western Europe.

Though dramatically important, the Iberian voyages were not unique. In the Atlantic, Vikings and perhaps Irish had made earlier crossings to North America.[20] It has also become common for world historians to preface the Iberian voyages of exploration with the once forgotten Ming voyages across the Indian Ocean in the first third of the 1400s under Admiral Zheng He. The Chinese fleets were much larger than those of Columbus and da Gama, as were the largest vessels in them. The Ming vessels followed Indian Ocean

---

18 For others see David Northrup, "Globalization and the Great Convergence: Rethinking world history in the long term," *Journal of World History* 16 (2005), 249–67.
19 J. R. S. Phillips, *The Medieval Expansion of Europe* (Oxford: Clarendon Press, 1988).
20 Benjamin Hudson, *Viking Pirates and Christian Princes: Dynasty, Religion, and Empire in North America* (Oxford: Oxford University Press, 2005), and Tim Severin, *The Brendan Voyage* (New York: Modern Library, 2000).

routes that southern Asians had been sailing since antiquity, and the spread of Islamic trading turned the western half of that ocean into an Arabian Sea. In the 1300s, the Moroccan Muslim Ibn Battuta had undertaken arduous journeys throughout the Muslim world, traveling with merchant caravans and on merchant ships. It may well be, as scholars have argued, that his accounts of travel to China are so lacking in detail as to cast doubt on his claim to have gone so far, but he did cross the Sahara and described the empire of Mali, visited Mecca and the Swahili Coast, and crossed to India. Ottoman explorers continued this tradition.[21] Two large fleets that the Sultan of Mali reportedly sent out across the Atlantic in the 1400s may not have reached the Americas, but several delegations of Ethiopian Christians are known to have visited Mediterranean Europe in the fourteenth and fifteenth centuries in search of Christian allies. Tales of these visitors helped feed the legend of Prester John and inspired Prince Henry the Navigator to seek out Christian allies beyond the lands of Islam.[22]

Besides emphasizing that the Iberian voyages relied on borrowed technologies and historical precedents, world historians also pay much more attention to the lure of Eastern riches in motivating the Iberian maritime expansion than do some Eurocentric and Americentric accounts. They emphasize that, while Columbus' voyages across the Atlantic led to the unexpected discovery of the Americas, they failed in their intention to find a new route to the East, whereas Vasco da Gama's successful voyage to India in 1497–8 was the culmination of nearly a century of Portuguese efforts. Globally minded historians are also aware that the resulting new maritime trade with Asia and sub-Saharan Africa was more valuable for Europeans during the next two and a half centuries than the trade with the Americas.

There is no need to belabor the point of Asian riches. *When Asia Was the World* (2008) is the trenchant title historian Stewart Gordon uses for his studies of Asian commercial and cultural supremacy in the period between 500 and 1500 CE. Most recently Philippe Beaujard has made a similar point in

---

21 George F. Hanouri, *Arab Seafaring in the Indian Ocean in Ancient and Medieval Times* (Princeton, NJ: Princeton University Press, 1995); and Giancarlo Casale, *The Ottoman Age of Exploration* (New York: Oxford University Press, 2010).

22 Al Umari says that when the sultan Mansa Musa of Mali made his famous pilgrimage he told the Sultan of Egypt that his predecessor had sent out 400 ships on the first expedition and 2,000 on the second; in J. F. P. Hopkins and Nehemia Levtzion (eds.), *Corpus of Early Arabic Sources for West African History* (Princeton, NJ: Markus Wiener, 2000), pp. 268–9. The Ethiopian travels are summarized in David Northrup, *Africa's Discovery of Europe, 1450–1850*, 3rd edn. (New York: Oxford University Press, 2013), pp. 2–6.

greater depth in his study of the Indian Ocean.[23] Gordon and Beaujard do not use Marco Polo as a source, but the Venetian's account of the great size and wealth of the markets and cities of thirteenth-century China leaves no doubt of Asia's advanced position, even if his European contemporaries found Polo's descriptions hard to believe. For example, Polo says the markets surrounding Kublai Khan's capital city were so enormous that 20,000 prostitutes made their livings servicing the foreign merchants who passed through them. He describes the city of Hangzhou in southeast China as "noble and magnificent," a city whose grandeur and beauty were superior to all others.[24] Polo knew the city well, but perhaps his most telling detail is his description of Hangzhou's many canals, which he notes were traversed by 12,000 bridges. At that time Polo's none-too-shabby hometown, Venice, had only one bridge over the Grand Canal, a wooden structure near the Rialto market, much more modest than the magnificent stone bridge that would replace it in the sixteenth century. The traders of Venice and Genoa were also aware of the tantalizing wealth of the markets of South and Southeast Asia through their contacts with their Muslim counterparts who plied them. It is revealing that upon reaching Calicut in 1498, the Portuguese were rudely greeted in Castilian by a visiting Muslim trader. The Iberian mariners deserve enormous credit for their search for a new route to the East, but their goal was to gain better access to a giant economy far older than the 1400s.

Portugal's pioneering explorations down the African coast and into the Indian Ocean were also rooted in a much older religious conflict: the centuries-old struggle between Christians and Muslims. Since world historians often underestimate the importance of this connection, it is worth exploring at length. One need only think of the red Crusader crosses emblazoned on the sails of Vasco da Gama's fleet that sailed for India in 1497 to realize how much the Portuguese saw that venture as a continuation of centuries of bitter conflict with the expanding Islamic world. The Muslim conquest of the Iberian Peninsula, begun in 711, had not been undone easily. The struggle to wrest back control of Iberia gradually merged with the idea of a larger Holy War against Islam during the eleventh century. From this perspective the traditional First Crusade (1096–9) to liberate the Holy Land from the Muslims was the second front of the ongoing struggle for Christian

---

23 Philippe Beaujard, *Les Mondes de l'Océan Indien*, 2 vols. (Paris: Armand Colin, 1913), vol. II.
24 Thomas Wright (ed.), *The Travels of Marco Polo, the Venetian*, W. Marsden (trans.) (London: Henry G. Bohn, 1854), pp. 313–14.

Iberia, as papal leaders recognized in asking the knights involved in the *reconquista* not to be lured away to the liberation of the Holy Land.[25]

The successful conquest of Palestine by the First Crusade was temporary. Writing a century later, Archbishop William of Tyre pointed to a key change that had taken place in the region since then: "In former times almost every city had its own ruler . . . they were not dependent on one another; they were rarely actuated by the same motives, but, in fact, very often by those directly opposite." Unfortunately for the Latin Christians, their conquest of the Holy Land had spurred Muslim unity, so that, when William wrote from Tyre, "all the kingdoms adjacent to us have been brought under the power of one man [Saladin] . . . they do the will of one man, and at his command alone, however reluctantly, they are ready, as a unit, to take up arms for our injury."[26]

The city of Tyre remained in Christian hands until it was incorporated into Egypt's Mamluk Sultanate in 1291, but that was not the end of the conflict between expanding Islamic and Christian forces. Tyre and a great many other places were then incorporated into the resurgent Ottoman empire, which in 1453 seized the city of Constantinople, the last remnant of the Christian Byzantine empire. In a letter the next year, Aeneas Sylvius Piccolomini assessed the political divisions in Europe in terms reminiscent of William of Tyre's assessment of Middle Eastern fragmentation at the time of the First Crusade: "Christendom has no head whom all will obey – neither the pope nor the emperor receives his due," lamented the man who would soon become Pope Pius II. "Every city has its own king, and there are as many princes as there are households."[27] As it turned out, a series of narrow Christian victories over the next two centuries proved wrong Piccolomini's fears that European Christians could not withstand the Ottoman onslaught, although that outcome does not diminish the significance of the centuries-long struggle between Christians and Muslims.

The fifteenth-century voyages of the Portuguese cannot be properly understood apart from the Latin Christian struggle against Muslim expansion, a point emphasized by papal encyclicals of the 1450s. As Henry the Navigator's biographer explained, the young prince's participation in the Portuguese conquest of Ceuta in Morocco in 1415 had been an extension of

---

25 Glenn Ames, *Vasco da Gama: Renaissance Crusader* (New York: Pearson Longman, 2005).

26 William of Tyre, in Mary Martin McLaughlin and James Bruce Ross (eds.), *The Portable Medieval Reader* (New York: Penguin Books, 1977), pp. 456–7.

27 Aeneas Sylvius Piccolomini to Leonardo di Bentivoglio, 1454, in James Bruce Ross and Mary Martin McLaughlin (eds.), *The Portable Renaissance Reader* (New York: Penguin Books, 1977), p. 75.

the crusades that had pushed into Muslim North Africa following Portugal's successful reconquest. Writing well before the prince's death, Gomes de Azurara enumerated Henry's motives for exploring south along the Atlantic coast of Africa, listing intellectual curiosity first, followed by reasons having to do with religion: finding Christian trading partners beyond the Muslim-controlled lands, learning the extent of Muslim power, making alliances with other Christians against them, and spreading the Christian faith. Is this a pious gloss on the prince's life? Perhaps a bit, since Azurara fails to mention the quest for gold from below the Sahara that was traded to Ceuta and other North African ports. Even if Azurara understates the importance of secular motives, Henry's actions and those of later Portuguese are incomprehensible without also giving great credence to the enduring crusading motives that lay behind Prince Henry's navigation efforts.[28]

A broader historical context may make European expansion seem less exceptional, but does a less Eurocentric perspective diminish the significance of these voyages? Opinions may differ, but this writer is inclined to think a comparative context actually enhances them. The key persons may have been motivated by a mixture of bellicose feudalism, religious fanaticism, and treasure seeking, but they got results. Europeans deserve no criticism for making use of technologies developed elsewhere; they deserve high praise for making better use of them. Not only did little Portugal sponsor exceptionally long voyages through uncharted waters with far fewer resources than the Ming, but the new connections to the East were also sustained and enhanced over time, as those of Zheng He were not. Although many of the connections to sub-Saharan Africa and Asia were built upon older Muslim connections, Europeans introduced new economic forces of lasting impact.

The discovery of the Americas invites fewer comparisons, although some have claimed that, besides the Vikings, Ming ships and Mali canoes also reached the Americas before Columbus.[29] Again, the salient point seems to be that only Columbus' voyages led to sustained and expanding contacts sufficient to change the course of history. Those changes produced different results for different people, falling heaviest on the native inhabitants of the Americas. Hardships were also substantial for enslaved Africans, indentured European immigrants, and even free immigrants relocated far from their

---

28 Gomes de Azurara, 1434, in McLaughlin and Ross (eds.), *Portable Medieval Reader*, pp. 491–3.
29 Gavin Menzies, *1421: The Year China Discovered America* (New York: William Morrow, 2003); and Ivan van Sertima, *They Came before Columbus: The African Presence in Ancient America* (New York: Random House, 1976).

homes. Even so, the historic importance of the Iberian voyages for Europeans and for the course of world history is beyond dispute.

The monumental convergences in the Atlantic are not only obvious in hindsight but were also apparent to contemporary observers. In 1588, the French essayist Michel de Montaigne wrote, "Our world of late has discovered another, no less large, fully peopled, yielding in all things, and mightier in strength than ours." Yet, in phrases that echo those uttered about present-day globalization, the essayist worried that, however good the outcome of the encounter had been for Europeans, the outcome for the indigenous peoples of the Americas had been unfortunate: "I fear that by our contagion we shall directly have furthered his decline and hastened his ruin, and that we shall too dearly have sold him our opinions, our new fangles and our arts."[30] Yet, for all their genuine importance, the extraordinary discovery of a "new" world and the eventual rise of powerful new nations there should not be allowed to exaggerate the periodization of history. Like the new ties between Europe and the East, the new connections to the Americas came out of a much larger process with deep roots in earlier centuries.

A subtler watershed

If, then, the events around 1500 were as much the culmination of other convergent forces as the beginning of a new phase of history, the larger watershed out of which the Iberian voyages emerged needs to be placed several centuries earlier. Is the quest for antecedents never-ending? After all, as the ancients said, history does not make leaps. Each event is connected to others in long historical strings. Andre Gunder Frank has provocatively argued that world systems can be traced back 5,000 years.[31] Beginnings, however, are different from watersheds. Geographic watersheds may be dramatic mountain ranges, but often they are barely perceptible rises in the landscape. The historical watershed between the age dominated by divergent forces and the new age in which convergent forces moved to the fore is of the latter sort. It would not have been obvious to those living at the time, and only slowly did it dawn on some that they were living in a new age.

---

30 Michel de Montaigne, "On coaches," in Ross and McLaughlin (eds.), *Portable Renaissance Reader*, pp. 158–9.
31 Andre Gunder Frank, "A theoretical introduction to 5,000 years of world-system history," *Review* 13 (1990), 155–248, and Andre Gunder Frank, *ReOrient: Global Economy in the Asian Age* (Berkeley: University of California Press, 1998).

Even though nothing dramatic happened that year, 1000 CE seems about the point when the forces for divergence were overtaken by ones promoting convergence. Historian John Man suggests a salient fact about that year: "it was possible for the first time . . . to pass an object, or a message, right around the world." The Pacific was still a formidable barrier, but the Vikings' trans-Atlantic link reconnected the Americas to the three Old World continents. That link stayed open until about a century before Columbus' voyages, but, as Man admits, the potential was unrealized: no object, idea, or individual did indeed make a global circuit.[32] If 1000 was a watershed, the more visible steps to the present came somewhat later as the Great Convergence gained speed.

Underlying this intensification of contacts (and conflicts) was a growing human population, which had risen from an estimated 5 million in 5000 BCE to 50 million in 1000 BCE and to some 265 million in 1000 CE. Despite the devastation caused by the Black Death, world population doubled by the late 1500s. After a pause, the number of humans doubled and redoubled at ever-shorter intervals, recently passing 6,000 million.[33] Whatever the causes of this growth, the effect was to promote human contact and interaction. Language again provides a convenient shorthand for tracing the power of convergence. As the result of political consolidation some languages gained in importance, whether as first or second languages, while others became marginalized or disappeared. From an estimated 10,000 or 18,000 in use in 1000 CE, the number of spoken languages fell to half that by the late twentieth century. Globalization is expected to cut the number in half again before 2100, but envisioning a world in which everyone speaks a single language seems far-fetched. The 500 to 600 languages that are now the mother tongues of 96 percent of the world's people seem destined to survive.[34] In language, creed, and custom the products of millennia of divergence persist as a powerful subtext in the age of convergence.

There are a number of advantages to conceptualizing the past as two great eras: one dominated by divergence, the other dominated by convergence. In the first place, these eras include the entire human past and provide insight into unfolding future events. Prehistory ceases to be a meaningless prelude to "real" history. The dramatic changes of the present day cease to be novelties and become meaningful lenses through which to understand major

---

32 John Man, *Atlas of the Year 1000* (Cambridge, MA: Harvard University Press, 1999), pp. 8–9.

33 Colin McEvedy and Richard Jones, *Atlas of World Population History* (New York: Penguin, 1978), pp. 342–5.

34 Lewis (ed.), *Ethnologue*; and Kartturen and Crosby, "Language death," pp. 157–74.

historical trends. Secondly, divergence and convergence are neutral concepts compared to the value-laden "classical antiquity" and "modern." Divergence is not a story of disintegration or failure any more than convergence is a story of providence or progress. The age of divergence produced successful adaptations to different environments and the development of a wealth of ideas, technologies, and forms of artistic expression that could be borrowed, exchanged, or discarded as contacts increased. Divergence also laid the basis for violent conflicts based in identity, many of which still smolder. Convergence has promoted cooperation and understanding, but has also increased the size and destructiveness of global clashes. As Tom Friedman suggested in his first major meditation on globalization, the internationally produced technological perfection of the Lexus and the passionately defended, local olive tree reflect human values, values that may be equally prized, even if they may not be equally relevant to the present stage of history.[35] Pairing divergence and convergence as coequal themes makes it easier to talk about diversity as a norm, not an exception. Finally, it should be stressed that convergence is more complex than homogenization, just as divergence is more complex than disintegration. Elements of divergence and convergence are evident in both eras, even if they are not dominant. For all their importance as centrifugal forces, empires need to be understood as operating within a rich cultural heritage rather than as the beginning of history.

FURTHER READING

Frank, Andre Gunder, *ReOrient: Global Economy in the Asian Age*, Berkeley: University of California Press, 1998.

Hopkins, A. G. (ed.), *Globalization and World History*, New York: W. W. Norton, 2002.

Northrup, David, "Globalization and the Great Convergence: Rethinking world history in the long term," in George Modelski (ed.), *World System History*, in the online *Encyclopedia of Life Support Systems (EOLSS)*, UNESCO, Eolss Publishers, accessed September 10, 2013, www.eolss.net.

Phillips, J. R. S., *The Medieval Expansion of Europe*, Oxford: Clarendon Press, 1988.

Renfrew, Colin, *Archaeology and Language: The Puzzle of Indo-European Origins*, New York: Cambridge University Press, 1987.

Wallerstein, Immanuel, *The Modern World System*, 3 vols., New York: Academic Press, 1974–89.

35 Thomas L. Friedman, *The Lexus and the Olive Tree: Understanding Globalization* (New York: Anchor Books 1999).

6

Belief, knowledge, and language

LUKE CLOSSEY

How do I know that what I call knowing is not ignorance? How do I know that what I call ignorance is not knowing?

庸知吾所謂知之非不知邪？庸知吾所謂不知之非知邪？

Zhuangzi 莊子

We ought not to be ashamed of appreciating the truth and of acquiring it wherever it comes from, even if it comes from races distant and nations different from us.

و ينبغي لنل الا نستحيي من استحسان ألحق ، اقتناء ألحق، من أين أتى. وان أتى من ألاجناس القاصية عنا، و الأمن المباينة.

al-Kindī, On First Philosophy[1]

The publication of this *Cambridge World History* signals that the new world history has reached a certain maturity, and this chapter takes advantage of the moment to take stock of the vast scholarship on the history of ideas and the meagre scholarship on the global history of ideas by responding to a single question: what role has the *entire* world played in how we write and understand the history of belief, knowledge, and language?

Historians have approached language, belief, and knowledge in many ways, and these differences are reflected in large measure by the confidence we have in various aspects of language, belief, and knowledge, and by the extent we consider language, belief, and knowledge to be universal. Generally speaking, a pound of doubt added to knowledge creates belief; add a pound of confidence to belief and you have knowledge. We are still knee-deep in a sociological and cultural morass that sees a clean break between a traditional and irrational religion and a modern and rational science. Picturing the likely author and likely audience of an academic essay

---

1 *Al-Kindi's Metaphysics*, Alfred L. Ivry (trans.)(Albany: State University of New York Press, 1974), p. 58.

written today, we might associate science with confidence and religion with doubt; "scientific knowledge" and "religious belief" roll off the tongue, while "scientific belief" hesitates, and "religious knowledge" feels qualified, or patronizing. In the plural, "beliefs" sounds natural, but "knowledges" annoys the word processor's spellcheck, which seems to doubt there can be multiples of a universal.

Because this chapter describes historiography rather than history, we will decline to define terms that historians themselves rarely and inconsistently define. As with "belief" and "knowledge" above, we mainly describe how these terms are used, their behaviours in the historiographical wild. "Europe" refers to the continent, itself with fuzzy boundaries, but when appearing in the world history of knowledge "European" usually refers also to the places most colonized by Europeans in the last two centuries, and to those places' peoples and their ideas. For practical purposes, we will refer to the "West"; for its complement, we'll use the name "Wider World", hopefully without reification. Each term has its silliness: a round rotating world can have an absolute north and south, but not an absolute "West", and referring to the larger part of the planet in terms of its not being the smaller part is certainly backwards. Travelling peoples and travelling ideas burst through such divisions in both directions, and historians are increasingly aware of and interested in these trespassers, even as the fundamental geographical division endures in most minds.

With both "West" and "science" amorphous, we have exactly twice as much wiggle room as we need to define each in terms of the other, and historians implicitly do this. Science is the knowledge developed in the West, which consists of those places with science, which is the knowledge developed in the West. . . Even those who deny the monopoly of the West on science usually admit that Western science is unique for its raw kind of power to save lives and blow things up. This sense of science being an objective thing that we have achieved may, of course, be illusory. The medicine of comedian Steve Martin's medieval Theodoric of York is perfectly modern in its confidence if not in its explanations: "Why, just fifty years ago, they thought a disease like your daughter's was caused by demonic possession or witchcraft. But nowadays we know that Isabelle is suffering from an imbalance of bodily humors, perhaps caused by a toad or a small dwarf living in her stomach."[2]

Religion is no less problematic. It emerges as a category largely as an involuntary and unintentional collaboration between Christian missionaries

2 "Theodoric of York", *Saturday Night Live*, season 3, episode 18, aired 22 April 1978.

and their targets, shaping local beliefs and practices into a mould resembling something like Christianity. The first British missionaries to Sri Lanka, for example, reported that the local Buddhist monks did not seem to be very religious – with some accuracy, as Buddhist practices had not yet become a Western-style "Buddhist religion".[3]

In the eyes of the academy, religion may do things, too, but if it once resurrected the dead its focus has shifted to moral subtleties, psychological reassurance, societal duct tape, and dubious miracles sometimes involving images on tortillas. Frustrated in his prayers for a bicycle, Emo Philips finally stole one and prayed for forgiveness, one of the few things modern religion can still dispense.[4]

This idea that European science "won", in some crude sense, exists perhaps because it is objectively true and capitalizes on an empiricism that the Wider World found less compelling, perhaps because we (and anyone who touches a Cambridge History may join this "we" to some degree) are ourselves in a European tradition and must stretch to value what is outside it, and perhaps because European empires once claimed dominance over much of the world. Most of our books about knowledge are in fact about Euro-knowledge, rather than about the Wider World's ethno-knowledges. We so implicitly understand knowledge to be the stuff of Kant and Newton that we forget to qualify it explicitly with a "Euro-" prefix, and often we forget that it needs to be qualified at all.

The division between Euro-knowledge and ethno-knowledges works differently in various cases, depending on the kind of knowledge under discussion, its perceived universality, and the confidence with which we know it. At one end of the continuum is mathematics. Most of us know that $2 + 2 = 4$, in Cambridge as well as in Timbuktu, and we have deductions (surprisingly complex) from axioms (surprisingly arbitrary) to give us tremendous confidence in this our universal knowledge. Outside of this Euro-mathematics we have several traditions of ethno-mathematics, most of which care little for deductions and axioms; their knowledges typically consist of different methods, and different objectives, but the results are compatible with Euro-mathematics

---

3 Richard Gombrich, *Theravada Buddhism: A Social History from Ancient Benares to Modern Colombo* (London: Routledge and Kegan Paul, 1988). See also Talal Asad, *Genealogies of Religion: Discipline and Reasons of Power in Christianity and Islam* (Baltimore, MD: The Johns Hopkins University Press, 1993); and Peter van der Veer, *Imperial Encounters: Religion and Modernity in India and Britain* (Princeton, NJ: Princeton University Press, 2001).

4 Cinemax Comedy Experiment, 17 November 1985.

and indeed can be legitimized by Euro-mathematicians using their own methods. Consider the process of the Tamil mathematician Ramanujan (1887–1920): after the goddess Lakshmi had put the seeds of ideas in his head, Ramanujan grew them out on his writing slate, and recorded his results on paper for posterity, but the path he took to them (along with any hint of proofs) vanished as he wiped clean his slate.[5] In Asian mathematics, the articulation of convincing explanations was traditionally, on pedagogical grounds, the responsibility of the mathematician's students; in Ramanujan's case distinguished Euro-mathematicians have since his death played this role, with these efforts teaching them as much as Ramanujan's results themselves. The distinction between Euro- and ethno- works much the same ways in many of the natural sciences. We think universal laws of physics are no less universal in Timbuktu, and the odd term "ethno-physics" exists mostly as a heuristic foil, as it does here. The case of philosophy is still in flux, with the mainstream academy perhaps seeing in Europe a logical, systematic philosophy made by individuals, while Africa has an ethno-philosophy or folk philosophy, more intuitive than logical, more communal than built by individual genius.[6]

Extending the Euro / ethno-distinction into religion requires great care. It may be tempting to equate ethno-religions with the primitive or primal religions, or with religions that are not Christian. For our purposes, however, we can continue the thrust of the previous paragraphs by describing all religions as ethno-religions, and leaving the category of Euro-religion as empty, though we might perhaps mention the temptation to include there Euro-science itself. Such is the secularism of the contemporary academy that no religion enjoys the same confidence we have in chemistry, and religion only survives under the protection of the same wilful suspension of disbelief we might apply to ethno-knowledges – although in this case without a real Euro-religion there are no reliable Euro-religionists to check Muhammad's maths, so to speak, after the fact, as Euro-mathematicians have done for Ramanujan.

---

5 Robert Kanigel, *The Man Who Knew Infinity: A Life of the Genius Ramanujan* (New York: Charles Scribner's Sons, 1991), p. 36.
6 For a survey of attitudes on the existence of an "African philosophy", see Paulin J. Hountondji, *African Philosophy: Myth and Reality*, Henri Evans (trans.) (London: Hutchinson University Library for Africa, 1983); and H. Odera Oruka (ed.), *Sage Philosophy: Indigenous Thinkers and the Modern Debate on African Philosophy* (Leiden: Brill, 1990). See also R. T. Ames and D. L. Hall, *Thinking Through Confucius* (Albany: State University of New York, 1987), which seeks to clear away Euro-normative assumptions about ancient Chinese philosophy before putting it to work sorting out current issues.

The upshot is that the ethno-prefix allows non-European knowledges to be included and excluded simultaneously, to be included but only conditionally, as at the children's table of a wedding dinner. This "xkcd" cartoon[7] (Figure 6.1) points at the key issues: whether science works, and the effects of cultural circumstances ("you're so cute when you get into something") on that science. If the second figure's hat were a Buddhist monk's robes (some Buddhist *siddha* adepts have been known to levitate and to zap things), we would have an image that works out the tension between scientific knowledge and religious belief, in favour of the latter – yet this cartoon is humorous only because science does seem to "work". I will stipulate that I am not advocating for this division between science/knowledge/West and religion/belief/Wider World, but merely am attempting to distill the consensus sense of the intellectual West. The extent to which this preliminary discussion holds for the academy will become clear below.

The state of scholarship

Let's look at the origins of the modern, Western study of language, belief, and knowledge. A case might be made for early Jesuits as pioneers here,[8] but most historiographers find a sea change in the early nineteenth century, which saw major advances in both scholarship (cuneiform, hieroglyphics, Sanskrit) and public interest. DNA tests serve us poorly in the polyamorous world of scholars' ideas, where paternity is arbitrary and disputed, but foremost among the claimants, the most frequently named fathers of the modern study of language, belief, and knowledge – called in their early days comparative linguistics, the scientific study of religion, and the history of science – are William Jones (1746–94), Max Müller (1823–1900), and George Sarton (1884–1956).

William Jones was a puisne judge in British Bengal, and his practical approach to the administration of empire encouraged his scholarship. His linguistic and epistemological horizons globalized step by step: enthusiasm for the Hebrew Psalms encouraged the study of Arabic, which took him to Persian, whence he became a student of "Peruvian" (less seriously), Chinese (more), and Sanskrit, where he made his most famous conclusion, essentially

---

7 Randall Munroe, "Tesla Coil", accessed 23 August 2013, http://xkcd.com/298.

8 Claudio M. Burgaleta, *José de Acosta, S.J., 1540–1600: His Life and Thought* (Chicago: Jesuit Way, 1999); Luke Clossey, *Salvation and Globalization in the Early Jesuit Missions* (New York: Cambridge University Press, 2008); and Paula Findlen (ed.), *Athanasius Kircher: The Last Man Who Knew Everything* (London: Routledge, 2004).

Figure 6.1 Tesla coil XKCD cartoon (www.xkcd.com).

that "bhartr" and "frater" (and "brother") are brothers, descendants from a common ancestral Indo-Aryan word. His motivations ranged from the practical – Sanskrit gave him access to the Law of Manu, to improve Indian jurisprudence by incorporating local law where it complemented British law – to the ideal – Persian poetry might inject vitality into the moribund English literature of his era.[9]

Comparative philology begat comparative theology. Jones' idea to group languages into families soon extended to the idea to group religions into families, a strategy central to the new "science of religion". That term, rendering the German *Religionswissenschaft*, was promoted especially by Max Müller, professor of comparative philology at Oxford. "There is no science of single things", Müller proclaims, "and all progress in human knowledge is achieved through comparison, leading on to the discovery of what different objects share in common, till we reach the widest generalisations and the highest ideas that are within the ken of human knowledge."[10] He can thus apply Goethe's dictum "He who knows one language, knows none" to religion, and so implicate "thousands of people whose faith is such that it could move mountains, and who yet, if they were asked what religion really is, would remain silent."[11] This comparative approach occasioned a relativism of religious revelation. Müller affirms that "we share in the same truth, and we are exposed to the same errors, whether we are Aryan or Semitic or Egyptian in language and thought".[12] Christian contemporaries disagreed, and managed to have the Bible excluded from Müller's series of sacred world literature, lest their Bible become merely one among the bibles of humanity.

Our third pioneer, George Sarton, was founder of the history-of-science journal *Isis* (1912) and its associated History of Science Society (1924), and author of the five-volume, but still hugely incomplete, *Introduction to the History of Science* (1927–47). Sarton's internationalism was explicitly opposed to the nationalism to which he as a Belgian may have been particularly

---

9 Garland Cannon, *The Life and Mind of Oriental Jones: Sir William Jones, the Father of Modern Linguistics* (Cambridge: Cambridge University Press, 2006); R. K. Kaul, *Studies in William Jones: An Interpreter of Oriental Literature* (Shimla: Indian Institute of Advanced Study, 1995); and S. N. Mukherjee, *Sir William Jones: A Study in Eighteenth-century British Attitudes to India* (Hyderabad: Orient Longman, 1987).

10 F. Max Müller, *Natural Religion: The Gifford Lectures Delivered before the University of Glasgow in 1888* (London: Longmans, 1892), pp. 417–19.

11 F. Max Müller, *Lectures on the Science of Religion, with a Paper on Buddhist Nihilism, and a Translation of the Dhammapada or "Path of Virtue"* (New York: Scribner, 1872), p. 11.

12 F. Max Müller, *Physical Religion: The Gifford Lectures Delivered before the University of Glasgow in 1890* (London: Longmans, 1891), p. 274.

sensitive. He understood his history of science as an internationalist movement of a "new Humanism" leading towards universal truth. "I can reject
Islam or Buddhism without making myself ridiculous", Sarton testifies,
"but I cannot deny the sphericity of the earth without ruling myself out
of the community of rational beings, irrespective of race, nationality
or religion."[13] His practice was as ecumenical as his theory. Naming his
journal after an Egyptian goddess augured his future. When he came to
appreciate the importance of Muslim thinkers for the history of science,
Sarton moved mid-career in his mid-forties to the Middle East to study
Arabic, a professional courage today few could safely emulate. He also
studied Chinese, and became a member of the Da'irat al-Ma'arif al-'Uth-
maniyya in Hyderabad.[14]

None of our three fathers set out to establish a particularly *world* history
of his subject, yet, unexpectedly, much of what made their studies revolutionary was their global range. Our pioneers were sometimes animated by
nationalism (Müller sought in the Vedas an Aryan replacement for the
Hebrew Old Testament, and Jones could rush a Persian translation to race a
French competitor), but the first "modern" histories of language, belief, and
knowledge were also global, and not uncontroversially so. Müller had to
confess that

> the very title of the Science of Religion jars on the ears of many persons,
> and a comparison of all the religions of the world, in which none can claim a
> privileged position, must seem to many reprehensible in itself, because
> ignoring that peculiar reverence which everybody, down to the mere fetish
> worshipper, feels for his *own* religion and his *own* God. Let me say then at
> once that I myself have shared these misgivings ... I do not say that the
> Science of Religion is all gain. No; it entails losses, and losses of many things
> which we hold dear.[15]

Similarly, Jones' own pitch for the study of other religions is instructive, both
for what it says of him, and his times, and for its pragmatic rhetoric that we

---

13 George Sarton, *The History of Science and the New Humanism* (New York: Holt, 1931),
   p. 47.
14 I. Bernard Cohen, "George Alfred Leon Sarton (1884–1956)", *American Philosophical
   Society Year Book* (1956), 126–7. See George Sarton, "Remarks on the study and teaching
   of Arabic", in David B. MacDonald (ed.), *The Macdonald Presentation Volume, a Tribute
   to Duncan Black Macdonald, Consisting of Articles by Former Students, Presented to him on
   his Seventieth Birthday, April 9, 1933* (Princeton, NJ: Princeton University Press, 1933),
   pp. 341–7.
15 F. Max Müller, *Introduction to the Science of Religion: Four Lectures Delivered at the Royal
   Institution in 1870* (London: Spottiswoode, 1870), pp. 2–3.

globalistas today might do well to emulate. In the introduction to his "A Hymn to Lacshmí" (1788), Jones writes,

> We may be inclined perhaps to think, that the wild fables of idolaters are not worth knowing, and that we may be satisfied with misspending our time in learning the Pagan Theology of old *Greece* and *Rome*; but we must consider, that the allegories contained in the Hymn to LACSHMÍ constitute at this moment the prevailing religion of a most extensive and celebrated Empire, and are devoutly believed by many millions, whose industry adds to the revenue of *Britain*, and whose manners, which are interwoven with their religious opinions, nearly affect all *Europeans*, who reside among them.[16]

Jones assumes a parochial attitude ("wild fables of idolaters"), maintains this critical attitude while switching to his own position ("misspending our time"), and then justifies an extra-European scholarship by the demographic strength of those non-Europeans, and finally by the cultural and economic impact it will have on the British, abroad and at home, themselves.

Two centuries passed between William Jones and the emergence of the "new world history" in the 1980s. This is not a simple story of ever-increasing global scope. Instead we have an ecumenical and optimistic first act, followed by a retreat and break-up into the steadier ground of neatly circumscribed regional and sub-regional studies of thick description – in the case of science, this is compounded with a more narrow conceptual sense of the subject and its geography. As historians of language, religion, and science improved their knowledge their pioneers' broad outlook became unwieldy, and less attractive. Even the new world historians were slow to take up these questions, and their early triumphs were in fields less ethereal, primarily in economic history. In *Europe and the People Without History* (1982) Eric Wolf shamed both the historians who ignored non-European peoples, and the anthropologists who ignored their histories. Having brought history to the "people without history", could historians after Wolf go on to discover the history of these people's knowledge?

The most high-profile recent meditation on the place of Euro-centric thought in history is Dipesh Chakrabarty's *Provincializing Europe*. The density of the work, which the author has frankly described as "cryptic", makes summary dangerous. Broadly speaking, the book argues that we should question the universality of European ideas, categories, and assumptions, a

---

16 "A hymn to Lacshmí", in Frances Gladwin (eds.), *The New Asiatic Miscellany: Consisting of Original Essays, Translations, and Fugitive Pieces* (Calcutta: Joseph Cooper, 1789), vol. 1, pp. 1–12.

universality often and dangerously unacknowledged, and instead establish their origins in a particular time, place, and tradition. Chakrabarty, however, does not advocate abandoning the Euro-centric, for "European thought is a gift to us all now"; rather, he seeks to renew the Euro-centric "by and from the margins". The core values of the European Enlightenment endure. For example, today not even "radical" historians defy the Enlightenment's disavowal of undomesticated deities; local claims pointing to the local god Thakur as the instigator of the 1855 Santhal rebellion, we are told, must be "anthropologized" until compatible with core Euro-centric thought (paralleling the inconvenient scriptural passages "allegorized" by the faithful). We are left with a Euro-centre reinforced by troops called up from the Wider World with their "subaltern pasts, pasts that cannot ever enter academic history as belonging to the historian's own position".[17]

How does this work in practice? We look now at how historians and others have treated four key moments in the history of knowledge and belief, and specifically at what role the Wider World plays in their scholarship. The four inflection points are familiar: hominization (the prehistoric process of becoming human), the Axial Age of religious development, the European Scientific Revolution, and recent and continuing secularization. Because we are using our language, knowledge, and beliefs to study language, knowledge, and belief, we are in a bit of a self-referential intellectual swamp, and so will work in reverse chronological order, much as a nurse secures a fracture by working from the point of maximum relative stability. As we look back a century, a half millennium, two millennia, and hundreds of thousands of years, we see these four joints bearing the greatest explanatory burden.

Secularization

The most recent of the four moments is secularization, and this is particularly important as it motivates what was described in the opening paragraphs of

---

17 Dipesh Chakrabarty, *Provincializing Europe: Postcolonial Thought and Historical Difference* (Princeton, NJ: Princeton University Press, 2000), pp. xiii, 5, 16, 101–4, and 255; Dipesh Chakrabarty, "In defense of *Provincializing Europe*: A response to Carola Dietze", *History and Theory* 47 (2008), 85–6. For an example of a (Canadian) historian attempting history from a non-Eurocentric perspective, which Chakrabarty would, presumably, expel out beyond the radical, see Luke Clossey, "Asia-centred approaches to the history of the early-modern world", in David Porter (ed.), *Comparative Early Modernities: 1100–1800* (Basingstoke: Palgrave Macmillan, 2012), pp. 73–96. Perhaps the ridiculousness of Clossey's romp proves Chakrabarty's point; alternatively, perhaps a light touch is necessary to sneak past the guards sworn to defend the Enlightenment.

this chapter as the distinction reigning in the academy between knowledge and belief. The Latin *saeculum* originally meant "era" but extended to include "world", not in terms of global geography but in the sense of the world beyond the monastery walls, as for example "secular clergy". Formulations vary, but the general sense of the secularization thesis is that as modernity (or wealth or science or rationalism) increases, religiosity declines. Scholars have imagined such a decline in religion would find expression in fewer people identifying as religious, less frequent participation in religious activities such as churchgoing, less religious influence in public or government or academic life, an increased neutrality towards religion in those same spheres, and in religion becoming compartmentalized, declawed, and domesticated. When Christian Scientist parents refuse medical treatment for their children, on the grounds that "material medicine" second-guesses God and thus dilutes the efficacy of prayer, the state intervenes, making clear the place of religion in modern Western society, and showing that it cannot be realized or appealed to exclusively.

In the eighteenth, nineteenth, twentieth, and twenty-first centuries scholars have predicted that secularization would happen "very soon now". It has been "very soon" for a very long time, always the heaven or hell – depending on your perspective – lurking just around the corner. Consistency over so many centuries creates an unavoidable vagueness and uncertainty. As scholars actually look for data, in vain, there is increasingly a consensus that the thesis itself is false. The sociologist Peter Berger has since retracted his 1968 prophecy that "by the twenty-first century, religious believers are likely to be found only in small sects, huddled together to resist a worldwide secular culture".[18]

What role has the Wider World played in the construction and destruction of the secularization thesis? The thesis was, of course, formed in a European scholarly milieu, based on ideas about contemporary and past Christianity, and only then subsequently expanded to the Wider World. Indeed, Charles Taylor finds one root of secularism anchored in Christianity itself: "What is peculiar to Latin Christendom is a growing concern for Reform, a drive to make over the whole society of higher standards."[19] Subtle Euro-centric assumptions remain in some versions of the secularization thesis. For example, the idea that contradictory religions brought together by pluralizing globalization are a recipe for secularism depends on a concept of religion

18 Peter Berger, "A bleak outlook is seen for religion", *New York Times*, 25 April 1968, p. 3.
19 Charles Taylor, *A Secular Age* (Cambridge, MA: Harvard University Press, 2007), p. 63.

with enough coherence and hard boundaries to cause crashes rather than syncretisms, a concept of religion particularly Western before recent times. Mischievously reapplying a term normally used to describe Germany's atypical-for-Europe history, Hartmut Lehmann writes of secularization itself as a *Sonderweg* (particular/peculiar path) for Europe, thus forcing the thesis back to its homeland.[20]

Sometimes the Wider World is used to confirm the secularization thesis. The expansion of the thesis beyond Europe moved rather smoothly; at first glance the Wider World confirms it (especially when scholars considered the new evidence no more closely than they had their Western data), for the Wider World in our imagination and in reality remains relatively unmodern and relatively religious. For sociologist Talcott Parsons, the Wider World fills in for history: contemporary Australian aboriginals (or Durkheim's presentations of them) play the role of an early stage of his evolutionary scheme, which was a development of Durkheim's own semi-explicit evolutionary scheme.[21] A 2008 study by the Pew Institute does indeed show an inverse correlation between religiosity (measuring belief in the necessity of God for morality, respondents' claimed importance of religion, and daily prayer – admittedly Western criteria) and GDP per capita. (Only a handful of odd places contradict the secularization thesis: Kuwait and the United States, each astonishingly religious given its wealth, and some ex-Communist countries astonishingly irreligious given their poverty. See Figure 6.2.) Most countries in the Wider World prove the obversion of the thesis by being poor and religious, while Israel, Canada, and Japan all confirm the rich-and-irreligious correlation – and indeed values for Japan more precisely match the Western Europe average scores than do any of the countries' in Western Europe.[22]

In other cases, however, the Wider World has not been so predictable. In recent years, years presumed to be more modern, powerful examples of religiosity flare up, contradicting the thesis: Islamic enthusiasm (especially when government limits the "free market" of religious ideas), Evangelicalism in Africa and Latin America, and the religious underpinnings of the terror wars. Indeed, modernization has been seen as a cause of Islamism. Norris and Inglehart use the demography of the Wider World to qualify their

---

20 Hartmut Lehmann, *Säkularisierung: Der europäische Sonderweg in Sachen Religion* (Göttingen: Wallstein, 2004).
21 Talcott Parsons, *The Evolution of Societies* (Englewood Cliffs, NJ: Prentice Hall, 1977).
22 Pew Global Attitudes Project, accessed 23 August 2013, www.pewglobal.org/2007/10/04/world-publics-welcome-global-trade-but-not-immigration/.

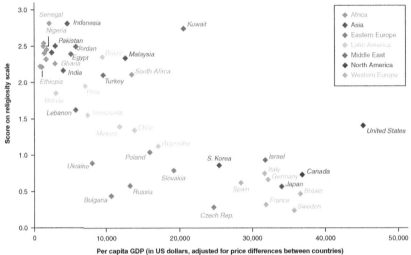

Figure 6.2 Graph of wealth and religiosity (www.pewglobal.org/2007/10/04/world-publics-welcome-global-trade-but-not-immigration).

version of the secularization thesis that links greater security (rather than modernity per se) to greater secularism: that the more religious Wider World has avoided the secular collapse of birth rates means that their populations grow more rapidly, and so the world as a whole is moving towards more religion.[23] The Wider World thus plays a limited role in the fight against the thesis. Perhaps it is more the situation in Europe, where religion survives modernity, that drives the thesis' decline, just as it was once the situation in Europe – modernity seemingly eroding religion – that motivated the thesis in the first place.

Scientific Revolution

In the 1930s Sarton highlighted the seventeenth-century changes in science, which were collectively named "Scientific Revolution" by Alexandre Koyré,

---

23 Pippa Norris and Ronald Inglehart, *Sacred and Secular: Religion and Politics Worldwide* (Cambridge: Cambridge University Press, 2004). See also Talal Asad, *Formations of the Secular: Christianity, Islam, Modernity* (Stanford, CA: Stanford University Press, 2003).

in the years he was teaching in Cairo. In 1543 Nicholas Copernicus' *De Revolutionibus* had put the sun in the centre of the universe; in subsequent centuries historians put Europe in the centre of science. Copernicus and the historians together share motivations sometimes rational, sometimes arbitrary, and come up with results in part rooted in reality and in part distortions of that reality. As an icon, the mere fact of moving the sun to the centre may herald the dawn of modernity, but a scientist today would find little to embrace in *De Revolutionibus* except for the results, and perhaps the impressive trigonometry and the use of zero, the only two features distinguishing it from ancient Greek science. Without modern methods motivating it, Copernicus' breakthrough could have just as well come from luck, and European exceptionalism might then reduce to a genius for guessing. In fact, *De Revolutionibus* was both "the cradle and the coffin"[24] for Copernicus' system, but it caused problems whose solutions by later proto-scientists developed fundamental components of the Scientific Revolution: empiricism, the mathematicization of nature, the mechanical universe, and institutional supports for science, among others.

This emergent science is a complex of technological, methodological, and social changes, so lacking an agreed-upon core that Steven Shapin can write "there was no such thing as the Scientific Revolution, and this is a book about it".[25] When the debates' dust dies down, however, most undisputed is that science is European. Indeed, the early-modern volume of the Cambridge History of Science only pretends to step outside of Europe in its final chapter, "European Expansion and Self-definition", but even here remains Euro-centric and introverted in its formulation. McClellan and Doris' *Science and Technology in World History*, which won the World History Association's book prize, fulfils the obligations of its title by devoting seventy-seven pages to the "world's people", but after a show-and-tell in which Ulugh Beg has presented his observatory, Montezuma I his zoo, Akbar his canal department, and the Ming their 1609 encyclopaedia, the book surrenders to the West, and science shines only on Europe and its colonial extensions. Institutionally, some historians of non-Western science have been forced out of history-of-science programs.[26]

---

24 Joseph T. Clark, "'Something old, something new, something borrowed, something blue' in Copernicus, Galileo, and Newton", in Everett Mendelsohn (ed.), *Transformation and Tradition in the Sciences* (Cambridge: Cambridge University Press, 2003), p. 70.
25 Steven Shapin, *The Scientific Revolution* (Chicago: University of Chicago Press, 1996), p. 1.
26 Sujit Sivasundaram, "Sciences and the global: On methods, questions and theory", *Isis* 101 (2010), 146–58.

Despite and because of historians' focus on Europe, historians of science in the Wider World have found themselves unable to escape it. In the last century, the world has entered the historiography of science primarily through the "grand question" of Joseph Needham (and earlier, of Max Weber): why did China, despite an apparent early advantage in technology, not develop modern science?[27] Replace technology with theory, and the same question could be asked for the medieval Islamicate world.

Some historians have sportingly taken up this question. We have sweeping works in comparison or synthesis, much in the old cosmopolitan spirit.[28] Such comparative work tends to accept a European scientific revolution, but explains it in terms of indirect accidental and contingent factors (inheritance of other traditions, educational institutions, commercial and geographical expansion) rather than in some essential European superiority. The list of answers and explanations for European exceptionalism has swelled, reflecting a lack of consensus on the very definition of modern science: the handiness of an alphabet, the concept of the corporation, the end of feudalism, greater curiosity, institutional support, the shock of Chinese technologies arriving in rapid succession, Islamic iconoclasm, the discovery of the Americas, neutral spaces of free enquiry, a moderate amount of scepticism, strong nation-states, and more.

Other responses to Needham involved denying the answerability and reasonableness of the question, or denying the coherence of China and the "West," or the existence of any vast distance between them.[29] Instead, the more innovative if less explicitly ambitious scholarship looks deeply *into* (construction) or *between* (circulation) the more traditional places, categories,

---

27 The most accessible treatment is Joseph Needham, *The Great Titration: Science and Society in East and West* (London: George Allen & Unwin, 1969).

28 See Geoffrey E. R. Lloyd, *Adversaries and Authorities: Investigations into Ancient Greek and Chinese Science* (New York: Cambridge University Press, 1996); Geoffrey E. R. Lloyd, *Ancient Worlds, Modern Reflections: Philosophical Perspectives on Greek and Chinese Science and Culture* (New York: Oxford University Press, 2004); Toby E. Huff, *The Rise of Early Modern Science: Islam, China and the West* (Cambridge: Cambridge University Press, 1993); and Toby E. Huff, *Intellectual Curiosity and the Scientific Revolution: A Global Perspective* (Cambridge: Cambridge University Press, 2011).

29 Nathan Sivin, "Why the Scientific Revolution did not take place in China – or didn't it?", in Nathan Sivin, *Science in Ancient China* (Aldershot: Variorum, 1995), and at: http://ccat.sas.upenn.edu/~nsivin/scirev.pdf. See also Roger Hart, "Beyond science and civilization: A post-Needham critique", in *East Asian Science, Technology, and Medicine* 16 (1999), 88–114. One of the most encouraging variations on this is the attempt to push the scientific revolution into the nineteenth century; in global perspective the revolution happens when the new physics conquers knowledge, just as Europe conquers the world. For more on the "Cunningham thesis", see Iwan Rhys Morus, *When Physics Became King* (Chicago: University of Chicago Press, 2005).

and objects.[30] Not least among the latter's insights is how the concept of "Western science" was developed, often outside the "West", as a product of globalizing imperialism.[31] Recent attention to the global roots and branches of Euro-science has shifted the story from European revolution to global evolution. Proponents of the roots of Western science in the Wider World tend to yell shrilly into the Euro-centricists' deaf ears, and the shrillness and deafness encourage each other. Still, the roots of modern science clearly run via Arabic-language texts that intermediate between Europe and south Asia even while introducing their own innovations. The zero and trigonometry that makes Copernicus something more than ancient Greek science have these extra-European origins, and Copernicus' aversion to the equant may also be inherited from Nasir al-Din al-Tusi. Bala offers a recent synthesis of research on the extra-European roots of Western science, as does Joseph's *The Crest of the Peacock* for mathematics. Many such assertions of influence entail only compounded possibilities: some minority view in China may have travelled to Europe where it may have been inhaled by some proto-scientist who may have incorporated it into some writing or device that may have played a role that may have been crucial in the Scientific Revolution. Joseph includes a chart (Figure 6.3), which shows possible and known lines of transmission of mathematical ideas. Scientific ideas followed similar paths, and the underlying idea here goes back to Sarton, who testified that "experimental science is a child not only of the West but also of the East; the East was its mother, the West was its father".[32] Recent scholarship has suggested how Western knowledge is, potentially, anticipated (Copernicus by the thirteenth-century al-Tusi), informed (Locke by the twelfth-century Ibn Tufail's *tabula rasa*), and inspired (the formal rules of Saussure and Chomsky by the fourth-century BCE Pāṇini) by non-Western knowledge.[33] The reverse

---

30 See Fa-ti Fan, *British Naturalists in Qing China: Science, Empire, and Cultural Encounter* (Cambridge, MA: Harvard University Press, 2004); Sujit Sivasundaram, *Nature and the Godly Empire: Science and Evangelical Mission in the Pacific, 1795–1850* (Cambridge: Cambridge University Press, 2005); Kapil Raj, *Relocating Modern Science: Circulation and the Construction of Knowledge in South Asia and Europe, 1650–1900* (Basingstoke: Palgrave Macmillan, 2010); Neil Safier, *Measuring the New World: Enlightenment Science and South America* (Chicago: University of Chicago Press, 2008); Carla Nappi, *The Monkey and the Inkpot: Natural History and its Transformations in Early Modern China* (Cambridge, MA: Harvard University Press, 2009); and special focus issue on "Global histories of science", in *Isis* 101 (2010).
31 Marwa Elshahkry, "When science became Western: Historiographical reflections", *Isis* 101 (2010), 98–109.
32 Sarton, *History of Science and the New Humanism*, pp. 94 and 119.
33 G. A. Russell, "The impact of the Philosophus autodidactus: Pocockes, John Locke and the Society of Friends", in G. A. Russell (ed.), *The 'Arabick' Interest of the Natural*

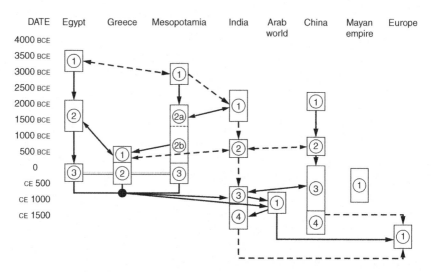

Figure 6.3 Chart of the spread of mathematical ideas (Figure 1.4, pp. 14–15, George Gheverghese Joseph, *The Crest of the Peacock: Non-European Roots of Mathematics*, 2nd edn. (London: Penguin Books, 2000).

story can be told of science's branches, how modern science moved out of Europe into the Wider World. The classic case is astronomy in China, but scholars are increasingly drawn to how European science uses data from the Wider World as it propagates globally, often in imbalanced power situations associated with colonialism and imperialism.[34]

Axial Age

In his 1949 *Vom Ursprung und Ziel der Geschichte* (The Origin and Goal of History) philosopher Karl Jaspers popularized the Axial Age, the three centuries before and after 500 BCE, in which regions across Eurasia witnessed revolutionary developments, parallel but independent, in religion and science.[35] In part motivated by the Holocaust, he pointedly avoided a focus on

Philosophers in Seventeenth-Century England (Leiden: Brill, 1994), pp. 224–62; Frits Staal, "The science of language", in Gavin D. Flood (ed.), *The Blackwell Companion to Hinduism* (Oxford: Blackwell Publishing, 2003), pp. 357–8.

34 For example, Richard H. Grove, *Green Imperialism: Tropical Island Edens and the Origins of Environmentalism, 1600–1860* (Cambridge: Cambridge University Press, 1996); and Lissa Roberts, "Situating science in global history: Local exchanges and networks of circulation", *Itinerario* 33 (2009), 9–30.

35 Karl Jaspers, *Vom Ursprung und Ziel der Geschichte* (The Origin and Goal of History), Michael Bullock (trans.) (London: Routledge and Keegan Paul, 1953).

Europe alone.[36] These were the centuries of Confucius, the Buddha, Socrates and other Greek philosophers, Daoism's shadowy Laozi, and a dozen Hebrew prophets. As any concept so grand and vast might, the Axial Age met sharp criticisms, especially charges of a lack of specificity or empiricism, or that it secularized salvation.

In some ways, the Axial Age appears to be to religion what the Scientific Revolution is to science, and through the Greeks science enters the Age too. Its historiographical effects, however, tend to work in the opposite direction to those of the Scientific Revolution. While the Scientific Revolution is important for creating and privileging one tradition, the Axial Age dazzles precisely for the plurality of traditions it produces. The sociologically inclined might see in this plurality only a superficial cover over an essential unity, but G. K. Chesterton held rather that the only common ground between religions, fundamentally different, was precisely that superficial cover, those "same external methods".[37] It is very difficult to compare religions without constructing a highly artificial common ground that could almost be described as secular, and a neo-orthodox theologian like Karl Barth might object even to desecrating what he considers truth by calling it "religion" at all, for "religion is unbelief".[38] Cross-cultural connections tend to be less relevant in the Axial Age than in the Scientific Revolution, in part because there were fewer, and in part because this is a plurality not about to become the single, universal Euro-religion. In many ways the Axial Age is less important for what happened in it than for the story we tell about it. Few of these figures probably intended to found a religious tradition in our modern sense; it is subsequent generations in a line from them to us who look backward to award these thinkers special status.

Scholars of the Axial Age revel in the Wider World; at its very soul the concept has a Wider World significance. Some scholars see in this geographical universalism a concrete certainty somewhat analogous to that of modern science. Karen Armstrong, for example, imagines a real religious truth – broadly speaking, compassion – that humanity essentially discovered in this period ("we have never surpassed the insights of the Axial Age"). In her writings, the sense of this objective religious truth is clear enough to her that

---

36 Karl Jaspers, *The Question of German Guilt*, E. B. Ashton (trans.) (New York: Fordham University Press, 2000), p. 17.

37 G. K. Chesterton, *Orthodoxy* (Rockville, MD: Arc Manor, 2008), p. 111.

38 Karl Barth, "Gottes Offenbarung als Aufhebung der Religion", in Karl Barth, *Die kirchliche Dogmatik* (Zurich: Theologischer Verlag, 1932), vol. 1, p. 327.

she can spot flaws in earlier manifestations of religion: "The Axial Age was not perfect", she writes, "a major failing was its indifference to women."[39] By implication, Jesus' "Do not think that I came to bring peace on the earth; I did not come to bring peace, but a sword" (Matthew 10:34) would presumably show that he never really "got" Christianity. Although this bias is not explicitly Euro-centric, it is teleological in that "our" modern religious sensibility is the yardstick by which others could be judged, and it inherits the Euro-centrism in which this modernism emerged. This may be the Euro-religion conjectured in the beginning of this chapter. My informal survey of bookstores in India reveals that the Armstrong corpus commands more shelf space than do the ancient Indian religious texts.

Rodney Stark's *Discovering God* attempts to get around Euro-centrism, and indeed around the Euro-centric de-privileging of religion. Here BC becomes BCE, but Christ becoming "Common Era" turns a particular birthday that happens to be in common use into a "common" chronological marker normative for the planet. Then the usual "God" becomes "Gods", an attempt to get around the monotheism of the West, but notice the capital letter: he has created a pantheon stocked by multiples (almost in a Warholian sense) of the monotheistic Judaeo-Christian-Islamic God, a pantheon alien to religious eyes, alien if not blasphemous.[40] At places Stark appeals to God's revelations as historical explanations, but as this fails to make his overall narrative unusual, the role of God appears to be only a rhetorical flourish. His brave sortie out of Euro-centrism fails.[41]

Hominization

The obstacles inherent in the study of language, knowledge, and belief are compounded by a daunting paucity of evidence – and total lack of written sources – to make the study of their births tremendously difficult. Much of the evidence for prehistoric humans is extrapolated from observable groups today. When not looking at Western university-student psychology-experiment

---

39 Karen Armstrong, *The Great Transformation: The Beginning of Our Religious Traditions* (Toronto: Random House, 2007), pp. xvii and xxi.

40 Rodney Stark, *Discovering God: The Origins of the Great Religions and the Evolution of Belief* (New York: HarperOne, 2007).

41 For discussions of the evolution of the study of religion see Tomoko Masuza, *The Invention of World Religions: Or, How European Universalism was Preserved in the Language of Pluralism* (Chicago: University of Chicago Press, 2005); Hans Kippenberg, *Discovering Religious History in the Modern Age* (Princeton, NJ: Princeton University Press, 2002); and Asad, *Genealogies of Religion*.

volunteers, scholars try to approximate the first humans by looking at apes, or children (assuming the cognitive development of an individual parallels that of the species), or hunter-gatherers (a tactic reliable exactly to the extent that hunter-gatherers "have no history", have not changed over the centuries). The uncertainty of this reconstructed evidence is then compounded as it is interpreted through assumed answers to a variety of philosophical questions: Is language instinctive or learned? Is the Sapir–Whorf hypothesis true? Do nonhumans have language? Is the "mind" in the brain? How do symbols work? What is the ultimate goal of the species? Typical results are ingenuous causal chains; one goes from a newly upright posture to hands now free to make tools and gestures, which causes brain asymmetry, which gives us linguistic and cognitive super powers.[42] Unfortunately, scholars may be more confident in our conclusions than they have any right to be. If alien anthropologists came to a post-apocalyptic earth, they could use our own anthropologists' methods to find in a precious artefact such as the "Girls With Guns Calendar 2009" a magical device for promoting fertility (note the enlarged breasts), success in the hunt (note the high-calibre firearms), and measuring time (not so bad a conjecture, but surely missing the calendar's primary appeal).

Some recent studies have looked at the meta-history of hominization, to analyze the various ways we have explained this process. Wiktor Stoczkowski has demonstrated that almost every scholar's "recipe for making a human being" can be reduced to one of two variations, depending on assumptions about human nature: "Take an ape who could be incited to act only by necessity, remove it from the protective shell of environment A and put it on the grill of a hostile nature for a few million years (environment of period B). If your ape is more orientated towards optimization of profit, surround it with a host of savoury ingredients of Period A in order to obtain the same end result": the creation of a proper human. Despite apparent advances in anthropology and biology, he argues, the story scholars tell of our species' origins is a rehashing of ideas – assumptions, really – from the ancient Greeks, no later than the fourth century BCE.[43] Glynn Isaac points to the function of these accounts ("As replacement material for Genesis . . . they have allegorical content, and they convey values, ethics and attitudes"), while Misia Landau, looking at the classics in the field, reports that "you see

---

42 Michael C. Corballis, *The Lopsided Ape: Evolution of the Generative Mind* (New York: Oxford University Press, 1991).

43 Wiktor Stoczkowski, *Explaining Human Origins: Myth, Imagination and Conjecture* (Cambridge: Cambridge University Press, 2002), pp. 67 and 125.

clearly a narrative structure, but they are more than just stories. They conform to the structure of the hero folk tale."[44] Heroic apes struggle to achieve their destiny: us.

Although individual scholars argue with vigour in contradiction to each other, works that take an ecumenical approach can synthesize something like a consensus. Rather than a one-way causal process, they speak of "feedback loops" that allow influences to go either way.[45] A recent emphasis on the importance of sociability now complements an earlier focus on the importance of tools. Thus connecting multiple factors with multiple pathways gives a picture of multiple possibilities and complexities that few could reject. One textbook, for example, includes a chart that causally links an increase in intelligence to better communication, technology, and social skills, which in turn cause rising social complexity (either directly or indirectly via more complex subsistence patterns), which in turn causes an increase in intelligence.[46] Still, religious beliefs are mostly ignored or dismissed as fictions, perhaps playing some role in natural selection, perhaps caused by changes in our ancestors' neurological make-up.

How global are these histories? Typically scholarship focuses on Africa as the place of origin, or avoids grounding its subjects geographically entirely. Of course, all kinds of Euro-centricisms can enter into the more philosophical speculations. One cognitive scientist argues for humans' "ultimate goal" by listing bite-sized plot summaries of the classics of Western literature.[47] At times, as our focus moves beyond and before Europe, the Euro-centric narrow-mindedness we have been seeing broadens into an anthropocentric narrow-mindedness, a kind of human exceptionalism. Humans have distinct language (specifically a lower larynx permitting greater vowel range) and social skills (including manipulation and deceit) that facilitate longer survival and greater reproductive opportunities – suggesting that soap operas and reality television are not the worst of humanity, but its soul.[48] Those prehistorians arguing that thinking cannot occur without language necessarily take other species' inability to communicate with us verbally as indicative

---

44 Glynn L. Isaac, "Aspects of human evolution", in D. S. Bendall (ed.), *Evolution from Molecules to Men* (Cambridge: Cambridge University Press, 1983), pp. 509–43; and M. Landau, "Human evolution as narrative", *American Scientist* 72 (1984), 262–8.

45 For example, David Christian, *Maps of Time: An Introduction to Big History* (Berkeley: University of California Press, 2004), p. 166.

46 Roger Lewin, *Human Evolution: An Illustrated Introduction* (Malden, MA: Blackwell, 2005), p. 221.

47 Steven Pinker, *How the Mind Works* (New York: Norton, 1997), pp. 541–2.

48 See Terrence Deacon, *The Symbolic Species: The Co-Evolution of Language and the Human Brain* (London: Penguin, 1998).

of their lack of intelligence, an intellectual assumption that echoes conclusions made about indigenous people at first contact with Europeans and their scholarship. More encouragingly, some scholars assign an important role to the early long-distance migration processes as one important landmark in humans' cognitive development, indicating a flexibility or a capacity for planning so advanced that it must depend on language.[49] More subtly, fundamental to world history is a decentring of the self, a curiosity, and an appreciation of difference, and we see that increasingly in the newest scholarship on hominization. When not tending towards tautology (for example, social products reflect the society that produces them), new theory tends towards diversity, an appreciation of the diversity of data, and an acceptance of a diversity of interpretation.[50]

The state of the classroom

In our cursory survey of historians' treatment of knowledge and belief, we have seen a quite consistent Euro-centrism, but a great diversity in what that means, in what its consequences are. The Wider World mostly reinforces the secularization thesis, begs questions of the Scientific Revolution, and delights in the level playing field of the Axial Age. In every case that involves a "Europe", Euro-centrism plays important roles. How does the state of this historiography translate into our classrooms? To get a manageable panorama of the field, I did two small experiments, neither reliable by Euro-scientific standards nor multicultural by ethno-scientific standards. Both, I hope, help us see the underlying structural patterns in how historians approach belief and knowledge.

For the first experiment, I surfed through dozens of websites of the University of Cambridge with a net trawling for names of the key producers of knowledge. Because Cambridge does not aggregate course descriptions in the style of the North American academic catalogue, and because not all webpages are open to external eyes, I ended up working through a diversity of tripos descriptions, lecture titles, undergraduate prospectuses, and staff research interests. Ignoring textbook authors, my trawl caught the names of

---

49 Christian, *Maps of Time*, p. 164; William Noble and Iain Davidson, *Human Evolution, Language and Mind: A Psychological and Archaeological Inquiry* (Cambridge: Cambridge University Press, 1996). See also Clive Gamble, *Timewalkers: The Prehistory of Global Colonization* (Cambridge, MA: Harvard University Press, 1994).

50 For recent essays by the most influential writers in the field, see Maggie Tallerman and Kathleen R. Gibson (eds.), *The Oxford Handbook of Language Evolution* (Oxford: Oxford University Press, 2012); and David R. Begun (ed.), *A Companion to Paleoanthropology* (Oxford: Wiley-Blackwell, 2013).

people whose selves or thoughts or schools had been deemed worthy of study. Putting aside the Faculty of Divinity, to which we turn below, I looked at all the faculties and departments of the university, although only about half gave up these sorts of names. Much depends on the vicissitudes of webpage design, or indeed on the more explicit interest a sociologist professes in Weber than a scientist in Newton, but I believe the resulting lists are telling, and give us a sense of the Cambridge pantheon of knowledge makers.

Putting a dot on each knowledge maker's birthplace gives us a visual representation of the geography of knowledge at Cambridge (see Map 6.1). The vast majority are Europeans, with Plato, Kant, and Wittgenstein in the first row, as most frequently appearing. There is a small contingent of Americans, such as Nozick and Rawls, Quine, the trumpeter Miles Davis, and T. S. Eliot – who would become legally British and intellectually very British. The entire rest of the planet, the entire non-Western world, is represented by four dots: Italo Calvino in Cuba, Marguerite Duras in French Indochina, Jacques Derrida in French Algeria, and J. G. Ballard, by virtue of his birth in the Shanghai International Settlement. Calvino returned to Europe as a baby, and the other three as teenagers. A full eighty-eight members of this group of ninety-seven men and four women were born within 1,000 miles of Konstanz, Germany, which indeed might serve us as a kind of absolute "West Pole", around which our intellectual world revolves. These results – the peoples with knowledge and those without – visually echo the century-old map distinguishing between the colourful places of the "people with history" and the inky blackness of the land of the people merely with tradition (see Figure 6.4).

Names from the Faculty of Divinity's website were treated separately, in part because of our sense of difference between religious belief and scientific knowledge, and in part because they ran opposite to the grain of the overall pattern. Here, if we deny Jesus and Augustine honorary status as Europeans, we are left with only three Europeans' names: Maimonides (1137/8–1204) and Ibn Juzay (1321–57), both of Andalusia, and the Sicilian Thomas Aquinas (1225–74) – one Jew, one Muslim, and one Christian. The list is dominated by non-European Muslims and Jews, and bucks the overall trend yet again by being populated mostly by medievals. Here religion saves the non-European intellectual world from complete obscurity. Because of the relative decline in theology's prestige as it has been crowded out in modern times by new secular fields of study,[51] these names make only a small broadening in the overall pattern.

51 See Thomas A. Howard, *Religion and the Rise of Historicism: W. M. L. de Wette, Jacob Burckhardt, and the Theological Origins of the Nineteenth-Century Historical Consciousness* (Cambridge: Cambridge University, 2000), pp. 18–19.

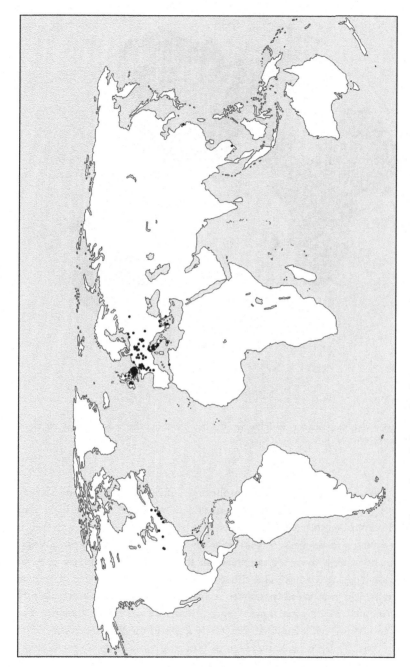

Map 6.1 "Knowledge makers" in courses taught at the University of Cambridge.

Figure 6.4 1890 map of areas with history and those without (from *Synchronological Chart of Universal History*, Edward Hull, 1890).

My point is not to pick on Cambridge University, and indeed deeper digging reveals a layer of more recent and more global reading lists. This experiment suggests its excellence is as a regional university, and that it might avoid the dangers of parochialism by reaching out to the Wider World, or at least by being cognizant of the narrow geographical basis of the knowledge it teaches. The situation is not better elsewhere. The best universities in non-Western countries have a similar curriculum, slightly supplemented by regional knowledge; an African university looks to the West and Africa, while an Asian university looks to the West and Asia, or its part of Asia. There is no knowledge of universal authorship. In our universities, knowledge was created by Europeans.

Our second experiment shifts its focus from space to time. Here I have chosen three popular and reliable world history textbooks (Bentley and Ziegler's *Traditions and Encounters*, Fernández-Armesto's *The World: A Global History*, and the Princeton historians' *Worlds Together Worlds Apart*), worked through their over 1,500 subsections and 3,000 pages, and noted when knowledge or belief shows up in the narrative. Of course, both appear well integrated throughout these texts, so to bring some precision to an impossible task, I counted subsections in which most paragraphs were mostly about science or about religion. I found some 200 such subsections, and classified these into Western versus Wider World, and religion versus science. The division was crude and bloody. Science became defined as the sort of thing that would be found in a history of science book. Religion became everything else, including "bad science", fields that might have been science except for our disbelief in them today, such as divination. Religion also included religious beliefs no one holds anymore; those classified as science held up better over time.

The shape of this story appears in (Figure 6.5). Religion dominates, with a great peak during an extended, and slightly delayed, Axial Age before beginning a long decline that gains speed in the wake of the Scientific Revolution. Less dramatic in its movements, science has a lower baseline it rises from twice, once to partake modestly in the Axial Age, and then for the Scientific Revolution (a peak no greater than that for the Axial Age) – after which it dips and begins a slower rise. Only for the twentieth century do our textbooks pay more attention to science than to religion.

When we look at the geography of this data, we get a sense of how the West-versus-Wider-World question resolves itself in our textbooks. Figure 6.6 plots, for each era but the first, the percentage of discussion that focuses on the West, for both science and for religion. (I offer no data for the earliest period, as what little coherence the Western/Wider World division has in later centuries completely disappears here.) For every era, the science line is higher than the religion line; that is, discussions of science are more focused on the West than are discussions of religion. For the most part, science stays above the 50-per-cent boundary, and religion below it; that is, discussions of science are almost always more Western while discussions of religion are almost always more Wider World. Religion trespasses only once, is only once more Western than Eastern, from 1400 to 1600, during the Christian reformations. These are also the early years of the Scientific Revolution, and so even here science moves ever further West as if to accommodate religion's brief intrusion into Europe. Science trespasses twice, is only twice more Eastern than Western: the first millennium BCE, when so

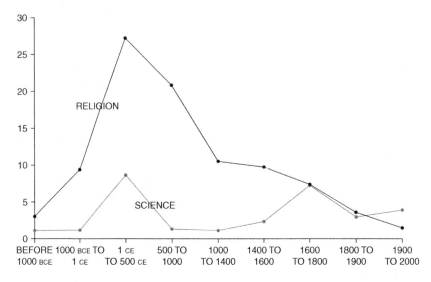

Figure 6.5 Percentage of world history textbook content about science or religion, by era.

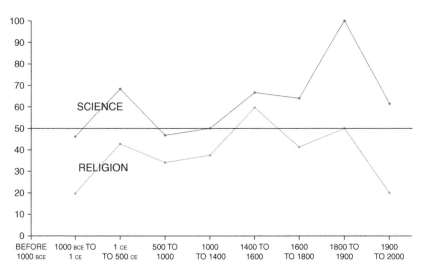

Figure 6.6 Percentage of world history textbook content centred on "the West" for science and religion.

158

little science is discussed that even brief consideration of the Maya calendar drags it outside of the West, and the five centuries from 500 to 1000 CE, the so-called European "dark ages". Comparing both charts (Figures 6.5 and 6.6) indicates that when science is most important, it is also most Western.

For most of human history, neither science nor religion was a distinctive category, so this search is historically anachronistic, but historiographically revealing. Because the number of atheists – despite their greater propensity than, say, Australian aboriginals to advertise their views on the sides of buses – has been so small, we might think the amount of religion in the world has essentially been constant. If the coverage in textbooks is not constant, we then have here an opportunity to understand how belief and knowledge fit into our artifices of world history periodization. This reflects not only the historiography as a whole (reflecting the current "further readings" bibliographies), but also the story we tell our university students, the story that those students – including most future world historians – are told in their formative years.

Outlooks

Is this Euro-centrism a problem? On the one hand, we – in this chapter and in the academy more broadly – have spent so much time looking at it that other issues get short shrift. Many of these may be more interesting than the West-versus-rest problem, which after all is fundamentally a question of organizing knowledge. Other issues are related to the Euro-centrism: For example, Edward Said's much criticized *Orientalism* is surely not completely wrong in linking Western scholarship on the Wider World to Western imperial dominance over the Wider World. It is, moreover, not easy to avoid carrying one's cultural presuppositions into studies of other cultures: so, because writings of the third-century Buddhist philosophy Nagarjuna became accessible to the West during or after the ascendancy of Wittgenstein, there was a tendency to see Nagarjuna as Wittgensteinian, seventeen centuries in advance.[52] Cultural incommensurability is one of the more fashionable of a long list of reasons why comparative study is impossible, though much of the list had been anticipated by the ancient wise. If you had told Zhuangzi that he could not know what a Hindu thought, he would have asked how *you* could then know what he could or could not know – intercultural incommensurability reduces to interpersonal incommensurability, which then ends all our

---

52 See Andrew P. Tuck, *Comparative Philosophy and the Philosophy of Scholarship: On the Western Interpretation of Nagarjuna* (Oxford: Oxford University Press, 1990).

scholarly conversations. Foregrounding these geographical divisions in our knowledge may also reinforce an unwanted gap between West and rest that is at least partly historiographical.

The greatest obstacle is Western scholars' relative disinterest in the histories of belief and knowledge in the Wider World. From that disinterest follows not only a relative ignorance, but also some sense that Wider World peoples, their beliefs, and their knowledges are less deserving of our notice. The geographical interests of historians in the top history departments of the United Kingdom, Canada, and the United States are proportionate not to population numbers, but to gross domestic product per capita; our collective professional specialization is the history of the very wealthy. History departments in the West are dominated by historians of Western history, and those in Britain seem to be shifting even more towards Western history, after a brief, slight, but evidently unsatisfying flirtation with the Wider World. Some historians of the Wider World are somewhat hidden from view in the various area-studies academic units, but this does nothing to ameliorate the reality that half of history departments skip Africa.[53]

We are furthermore relatively uninterested in the Wider World's languages. In the United States' universities, only some one-seventh of foreign-language enrolments are in non-Western languages, a proportion steadily growing over the last five decades, a growth fuelled before the 1990s slowdown by enthusiasm for Japanese, and now mostly by jumps in Chinese and Arabic enrolments. This should not make us optimistic, as the total number of students studying language has largely remained steady in the last half-century, despite the undergraduate population in the United States more than doubling.[54] In the United Kingdom, only some tenth of undergraduate students whose subjects of study are language work in non-European languages. (Typically in the United Kingdom language students are twice as likely to be female, but this gender imbalance disappears when only students of non-Western languages are considered.[55]) Note that three-quarters of the earth's population are native speakers of a non-Western language. Even looking at the rates of change based on the

---

53 Luke Clossey and Nicholas Guyatt, "It's a small world after all: The Wider World in historians' peripheral vision", *Perspectives on History* 51 (2013), 24–7.

54 I base my calculations on data from Nelly Furman, David Goldberg, and Natalia Lusin, "Enrollments in languages other than English in United States institutions of higher learning, Fall 2006", *Modern Language Association*, tables 4, 5, 6, and 8, accessed 23 August 2013, www.mla.org/2006_flenrollmentsurvey.

55 I base my calculations on data from the Higher Education Statistics Agency, accessed 23 August 2013, www.hesa.ac.uk/index.php/component/option,com_datatables/Itemid,121/task,show_category/catdex,3/#subject.

less discouraging American data, we do not expect enrolments to reach this level until, perhaps, the twenty-third century.[56]

Problems with language compound and are compounded by problems with accessibility of sources. Key treatises from Muslim scientists working before the European Scientific Revolution have not yet been translated into a Western language.[57] Sometimes even whole collections of the originals of non-Western sources are endangered. Soon some 30,000 of the historical manuscripts in Timbuktu will have been evacuated into the Ahmed Baba Institute's new building (where, ironically, the first document-refugees became easy targets for Islamist rebels). The fate of the hundreds of thousands re-evacuated or remaining precarious in private institutions is an open question. If we ignore these sources, their histories will go away.

Of course we cannot discount the possibility that there will be a future historiography of language, belief, and knowledge that introduces wholly new issues and changes the variables that seem most meaningful. In this digital age we record per person each year some 800 megabytes of information, which may prove intellectually overwhelming even if it is not in media solid enough to suffocate us physically.[58] Perhaps a Silencepeace movement will arise to save us from information pollution, or monasteries of apophatic monks will prune bonsai libraries. David Macaulay's masterful *Motel of the Mysteries* (1979) – perhaps the greatest meditation on historians' ability to know past knowledge and understand past belief – deals with the apocryphal apocalyptic junk-mail tsunami of 1985. Perhaps future attention will swivel from language, belief, and knowledge to silence, doubt, and ignorance.

It may be helpful to consider, through the magic of imagination and extrapolation, the next century's *Beijing History of the World* (Beijing UP: forthcoming, 2174). Historians of the future will have remembered the early-twenty-second-century shift of the core of the academy from West to East, following not long after the Asian dominance of the world economy.[59]

---

56 A silver lining here is that world histories of language tend to be exceptionally balanced in their coverage and approach to non-European languages. See, for example, Nicholas Ostler, *Empires of the Word: A Language History of the World* (New York: HarperCollins, 2005).

57 Arun Bala, *The Dialogue of Civilizations in the Birth of Modern Science* (New York: Palgrave Macmillan, 2006).

58 Peter Lyman and Hal R. Varian, "How much information? 2003", accessed 23 August 2013, www2.sims.berkeley.edu/research/projects/how-much-info-2003/.

59 Between 2007 and 2011 China had 11 per cent of world scientific research output, in terms of papers written; at current growth rates that will double by the time of this volume's publication. Jonathan Adams, David Pendlebury, and Bob Stembridge, *Building Bricks: Exploring the Global Research and Innovation Impact of Brazil, Russia, India, China and South Korea* (New York: Thomson Reuters, 2013), pp. 10–13.

Chinese and Indian scientists accumulated Nobel prizes for finding the Higgs particle (had it been hiding in Urumchi all along?), resolving the proton-spin crisis, equating P and NP, and much else. If you turn to the *History*'s chapters on the history of science, you will see a great many Chinese names, even from much earlier centuries. The section on physics, for example, traces modern (that is, twenty-second-century) physics back to its roots in the atomism of the ancient school of Mozi 墨子. A special boxed text section on ethno-science, inserted at the eleventh hour by an editor keen on multiculturalism, mentions the probable additional influence of 笛卡儿 and 波义耳. Their names are helpfully romanized in the index (volume 14) as Descartes and Boyle, although Chinese has become the academy's default language, and even scholars primarily anglophone might drop in a classical allusion with no translation and with minimal pretension; after all, 人不知而不愠、不亦君子乎 (论语 1).

Although the Beijing History helps us see our own blind spots, it does little more than replace one centrism with another. Perhaps our imagination has not drifted quite far enough into the future. Looking down the bookshelf, we can just make out the cover of the twenty-fifth-century *Lunar History of the Earth*. This may promise the objectivity born of great distance, but we notice the publisher is Copernicus Crater University Press, the name reminding us of the iconic yet ironic place of Copernicus in all of these discussions. Who knows what perspectives the lunar inhabitants will have? A great deal depends on what beliefs and knowledges the CCU history department's colonist ancestors will have brought with them – and whether they are packed in boxes labelled "religion" or "science" – and a great deal depends on whether they will have been lifted to the moon by nuclear thermal rockets, or by devas and angels.

FURTHER READING

Asad, Talal, *Formations of the Secular: Christianity, Islam, Modernity*, Stanford, CA: Stanford University Press, 2003.

    Genealogies of Religion: Discipline and Reasons of Power in Christianity and Islam, Baltimore, MD: The Johns Hopkins University Press, 1993.

Bala, Arun, *The Dialogue of Civilizations in the Birth of Modern Science*, New York: Palgrave Macmillan, 2006.

Begun, David R. (ed.), *A Companion to Paleoanthropology*, Oxford: Wiley-Blackwell, 2013.

Cannon, Garland, *The Life and Mind of Oriental Jones: Sir William Jones, the Father of Modern Linguistics*, Cambridge: Cambridge University Press, 2006.

Chakrabarty, Dipesh, *Provincializing Europe: Postcolonial Thought and Historical Difference*, Princeton, NJ: Princeton University Press, 2000.

Christian, David, *Maps of Time: An Introduction to Big History*, Berkeley: University of California Press, 2004.

Clossey, Luke, "Asia-centred approaches to the history of the early-modern world", in David Porter (ed.), *Comparative Early Modernities: 1100–1800*, Basingstoke: Palgrave Macmillan, 2012.

Clossey, Luke, and Nicholas Guyatt, "It's a small world after all: The Wider World in historians' peripheral vision", *Perspectives on History* 51 (2013), 24–7.

Elshahkry, Marwa, "When science became Western: Historiographical reflections", *Isis* 101 (2010), 98–109.

Fan, Fa-ti, *British Naturalists in Qing China: Science, Empire, and Cultural Encounter*, Cambridge, MA: Harvard University Press, 2004.

Gamble, Clive, *Timewalkers: The Prehistory of Global Colonization*, Cambridge, MA: Harvard University Press, 1994.

Gombrich, Richard, *Theravada Buddhism: A Social History from Ancient Benares to Modern Colombo*, London: Routledge and Kegan Paul, 1988.

Grove, Richard H., *Green Imperialism: Tropical Island Edens and the Origins of Environmentalism, 1600–1860*, Cambridge: Cambridge University Press, 1996.

Hall, D. L., and R. T. Ames, *Thinking Through Confucius*, Albany: State University of New York Press, 1987.

Hart, Roger, "Beyond science and civilization: A post-Needham critique", *East Asian Science, Technology, and Medicine* 16 (1999), 88–114.

Hountondji, Paulin J., *African Philosophy: Myth and Reality*, Henri Evans (trans.), London: Hutchinson University Library for Africa, 1983.

Howard, Thomas A., *Religion and the Rise of Historicism: W. M. L. de Wette, Jacob Burckhardt, and the Theological Origins of the Nineteenth-Century Historical Consciousness*, Cambridge: Cambridge University Press, 2000.

Huff, Toby, *Intellectual Curiosity and the Scientific Revolution: A Global Perspective*, Cambridge: Cambridge University Press, 2011.

  The Rise of Early Modern Science: Islam, China and the West, New York: Cambridge University Press, 1993.

Isaac, Glynn Lloyd, "Aspects of Human Evolution", in D. S. Bendall (ed.), *Evolution from Molecules to Men*, Cambridge: Cambridge University Press, 1983, pp. 509–43.

Joseph, George Gheverghese, *The Crest of the Peacock: Non-European Roots of Mathematics*, 2nd edn., London: Penguin Books, 2000.

Kippenberg, Hans, *Discovering Religious History in the Modern Age*, Princeton, NJ: Princeton University Press, 2002.

Landau, M., "Human evolution as narrative", *American Scientist* 72 (1984), 262–8.

Lloyd, Geoffrey E. R., *Adversaries and Authorities: Investigations into Ancient Greek and Chinese Science*, New York: Cambridge University Press, 1996.

  Ancient Worlds, Modern Reflections: Philosophical Perspectives on Greek and Chinese Science and Culture, New York: Oxford University Press, 2004.

Macaulay, David, *Motel of the Mysteries*, Boston: Houghton Mifflin, 1979.

Masuza, Tomoko, *The Invention of World Religions: Or, How European Universalism was Preserved in the Language of Pluralism*, Chicago: University of Chicago Press, 2005.

Morus, Iwan Rhys, *When Physics Became King*, Chicago: University of Chicago Press, 2005.

Nappi, Carla, *The Monkey and the Inkpot: Natural History and its Transformations in Early Modern China*, Cambridge, MA: Harvard University Press, 2009.

Needham, Joseph, *The Grand Titration: Science and Society East and West*, London: Allen & Unwin, 1969.

Noble, William, and Iain Davidson, *Human Evolution, Language and Mind: A Psychological and Archaeological Inquiry*, Cambridge: Cambridge University Press, 1996.

Norris, Pipa, and Ronald Inglehart, *Sacred and Secular: Religion and Politics Worldwide*, Cambridge: Cambridge University Press, 2004.

Odera Oruka, H. (ed.), *Sage Philosophy: Indigenous Thinkers and the Modern Debate on African Philosophy*, Leiden: Brill, 1990.

Ostler, Nicholas, *Empires of the Word: A Language History of the World*, New York: HarperCollins, 2005.

Raj, Kapil, *Relocating Modern Science: Circulation and the Construction of Knowledge in South Asia and Europe, 1650–1900*, Basingstoke: Palgrave Macmillan, 2010.

Roberts, Lissa, "Situating science in global history: Local exchanges and networks of circulation", *Itinerario* 33 (2009), 9–30.

Safier, Neil, *Measuring the New World: Enlightenment Science and South America*, Chicago: University of Chicago Press, 2008.

Scharfstein, Ben-Ami, *A Comparative History of World Philosophy: From the Upanishads to Kant*, Albany: State University of New York Press, 1998.

Shapin, Steven, *The Scientific Revolution*, Chicago: University of Chicago Press, 1996.

Sivasundaram, Sujit, *Nature and the Godly Empire: Science and Evangelical Mission in the Pacific, 1795–1850*, Cambridge: Cambridge University Press, 2005.

Sivin, Nathan, "Why the Scientific Revolution did not take place in China – or didn't it?", in Nathan Sivin, *Science in Ancient China*, Aldershot: Variorum, 1995.

"Sciences and the global: On methods, questions and theory", *Isis* 101 (2010), 146–58.

Stoczkowski, Wiktor, *Explaining Human Origins: Myth, Imagination, and Conjecture*, Cambridge: Cambridge University Press, 2002.

Tallerman, Maggie, and Kathleen R. Gibson (eds.), *The Oxford Handbook of Language Evolution*, Oxford: Oxford University Press, 2012.

Tuck, Andrew P., *Comparative Philosophy and the Philosophy of Scholarship: On the Western Interpretation of Nagarjuna*, Oxford: Oxford University Press, 1990.

van der Veer, Peter, *Imperial Encounters: Religion and Modernity in India and Britain*, Princeton, NJ: Princeton University Press, 2001.

Wolf, Eric R., *Europe and the People without History*, Berkeley: University of California Press, 1982.

7

Historiography of technology and innovation

DANIEL R. HEADRICK

Technology – the use of materials, energy, and living beings for practical purposes – is a defining feature of the human species. Though it has played a role throughout history, its recognition by the historical profession has been a long time coming. Only recently have works on the history of technology entered the mainstream of scholarship and aroused the interest of literate elites.

In the Western world, Denis Diderot and Jean d'Alembert's *Encyclopédie* (1751–72) was among the first works of literate culture to feature articles and images of everyday crafts and techniques. This encyclopedia, though quite elaborate, was soon rendered obsolete by the many changes taking place in the sciences and technologies in the late eighteenth century. Its publisher therefore proposed to issue a new and more up-to-date encyclopedia called *Encyclopédie Méthodique, ou par Ordre de Matières* (Methodical Encyclopedia in Thematic Order). This work, begun in 1782, was intended to become a sixty-volume work, but ended up many years later with 200 volumes and few readers. Though a general, not a technical, encyclopedia, it contained many volumes devoted to the technology of the day, making it a valuable source for later historians. Meanwhile, in 1794 the French revolutionaries founded the first institution for the collection and study of technological artifacts, the Conservatoire National des Arts et Métiers (National Conservatory of Arts and Crafts).

While an interest in technology dates back to the eighteenth century, the *history* of technology and technological innovation is a nineteenth-century phenomenon. The first book to treat the history of technology as a scholarly subject is Johann Heinrich Moritz von Poppe's *Geschichte aller Erfindungen und Entdeckungen im Bereiche der Gewerbe, Künste und Wissenschaften von der frühesten Zeit bis auf unsere Tage* (History of all the Inventions and Discoveries in the Trades, Arts, and Sciences from Earliest Times to Our Day).[1] Karl

---

1 Johann Heinrich Moritz von Poppe, *Geschichte aller Erfindungen und Entdeckungen im Bereiche der Gewerbe, Künste und Wissenschaften von der frühesten Zeit bis auf unsere Tage*

Marx based his theory of historical materialism on changes in technology as the causative factors in social evolution; in his pithy phrase, "The windmill gives you society with the feudal lord; the steam-mill, society with the industrial capitalist."[2] They and their successors have wrestled with the major questions in the history of technology: How do technological innovations arise? Why are some societies more open to innovation than others? In a given society, why do some innovations succeed and others fail? What roles do individuals, organizations, and societies play in encouraging or obstructing innovations? What are the relations between science and technology? And how do technological innovations impact society?

Popular history of technology

While historians and philosophers were debating these issues, popular culture was also attracted by new technologies. In the mid-nineteenth century, along with the first stirrings of interest in the history of technology among the literate elite, a phenomenon appeared that was to have a far greater impact upon the general population: national exhibitions of industrial and crafts products, beginning with the French Industrial Exposition of 1844. This exhibition was overshadowed by the Great Exhibition of the Works of Industry of All Nations that opened in London in 1851, popularly known as the "Crystal Palace Exhibition" because it was housed in a gigantic greenhouse (see Figure 7.1). In it were displayed, as the title indicates, industrial products and machinery (fields in which Great Britain enjoyed a substantial lead over all other nations), but also agricultural and crafts products from around the world. The Crystal Palace Exhibition was the model for many subsequent expositions and world's fairs, such as those in Paris in 1889 and 1900, Chicago in 1893, and New York in 1939–40, the most recent being the one in Shanghai in 2010.

World's fairs and other technological exhibitions privileged the most recent innovations rather than historical ones. But another phenomenon closely related to temporary exhibitions was the museums of science and technology that appeared two centuries ago and which have proliferated since. The Conservatoire National des Arts et Métiers had several rooms where the public could view machinery, the origin of the Musée National des

(History of all the Inventions and Discoveries in the Trades, Arts, and Sciences from Earliest Times to Our Day) (Stuttgart: Hoffman'sche Verlags-Buchhandlung, 1837).

2 Karl Marx, *The Poverty of Philosophy* (Chicago: Charles H. Kerr, 1920), p. 119.

Figure 7.1 "The Opening of the Great Exhibition by Queen Victoria on 1 May 1851" by Henry Courtney Selous, 1851–2 (oil on canvas) (reproduced by kind permission of the Trustees of the Victoria & Albert Museum).

Arts et Métiers. Since then it has been quite overshadowed by the Cité des Sciences et de l'Industrie at La Villette, founded in 1986 on the northeastern edge of Paris, the largest science museum in Europe. Among its rivals we might cite the Science Museum in London, the Museum of Science and Industry in Chicago, the Science Museum in Boston, the Deutsches Museum in Munich, and the Smithsonian Institution's Museum of American History in Washington, D.C., a repository of historic American artifacts. Though several of these institutions call themselves "science" museums, the scientific phenomena and artifacts they feature are almost all from the applied sciences and are commercial products that the public can easily relate to.

In addition to museums of technology in general, there are numerous museums devoted to particular technologies. Railway museums have sprouted up wherever there are old locomotives and rolling stock to be preserved. Of the several hundred such museums in the world, the United States has fifty-two, Germany thirty-four, and Great Britain twenty-six. Many of these are in private or municipal hands and feature not only static exhibitions but also working trains pulled by steam locomotives, to the delight of rail-buffs and children alike. In the same vein (without the live performance, however) are the museums of airplanes and rockets, the most elaborate of which is the Smithsonian Institution's Museum of Air and Space. Almost all nations that have produced aircraft or space-related artifacts have created museums to display their achievements. Likewise, there are museums of automobiles, ships and boats, clocks and watches, computers, and other artifacts.

Nor must we forget "villages" with old buildings (much cleaned up and prettified, of course) in which re-enactors demonstrate how old-time artisans spun yarn, forged horseshoes, built boats, and the like; Sturbridge Village in Massachusetts and Colonial Williamsburg in Virginia are but two examples of this phenomenon. Evidently, the more technology advances into the post-industrial information age, the more popular are places where tourists can relive an idealized past and parents can show their children what life was like in the "good old days."

Popular interest in matters technological was also evidenced by the appearance of magazines aimed at the general public. In the United States, *Scientific American* was among the earliest, starting in 1845; despite its name, it always featured as many articles on inventions and devices, such as railroads, steam engines, and electric lights, as on scientific matters. It was followed by *Popular Science Monthly* in 1872 and *Popular Mechanics* in 1902, and similar magazines in other countries.

Whiggish and nationalist history of technology

It may seem odd to list exhibitions, museums, and magazines in a chapter on the historiography of technology, but popular perceptions and enthusiasms for various technologies form a presence around which historians of technology carry out their scholarly pursuits, for popular ideas on technology and its history are imbued with a philosophy historians call Whiggism.

There are two aspects to the Whiggish interpretation of history. The first is a belief in progress. Exhibitions, museum displays, and popular magazines stress the instrumental progress of technology, that is, the improvements in speed, power, convenience, safety, and so on brought about by the latest inventions. Associated with the idea of progress are two other ideas enshrined in the popular discourse on technology. One is that it is autonomous and beyond the control of ordinary people, therefore inevitable. The other is that its ultimate cause is science, which is by definition beyond the comprehension of ordinary citizens; hence the use of the word "science" in periodicals like *Scientific American* and *Popular Science* and in institutions like the Chicago Museum of Science and Industry. Epitomizing the ideas of scientific supremacy and technological determinism or inevitability is the motto of the Hall of Science at the Century of Progress Exposition in Chicago in 1933 and 1934: "Science Finds, Industry Applies, Man Conforms."

Historic displays and articles are featured in museums and magazines partly out of nostalgia (like steam trains for tourists), but also to showcase the *evolution* of a technology from primitive to contemporary to futuristic. What the public likes and wants to hear about the history of technology is the good news. Who, upon seeing a replica of the Zuse Z3 (1941) in the Deutsches Museum or parts of an ENIAC (1946) in the Smithsonian's National Museum of American History, is not awed by the size and complexity of these machines, but even more so by learning that even the smart phones in visitors' pockets are much faster and more powerful than these room-size behemoths? Who, upon seeing the Wright brothers' *Flyer* or Charles Lindbergh's *Spirit of Saint Louis*, does not compare them to the big jets that bring tourists to Washington to visit the Air and Space Museum where they hang on display? And when there have been attempts to show the dark side of technology, such as explaining the role of the B-29 bomber *Enola Gay* in dropping the first atomic bomb on Hiroshima in 1945, there was an immediate outcry from patriotic politicians (see Figure 7.2).

Which brings us to the second side of the popular history of technology: patriotism. Most of the displays in the larger museums of science and technology feature national inventions and artifacts. In the United States that means privileging the achievements of Samuel Morse, Thomas Edison, Henry Ford, Orville and Wilbur Wright, and other notable Americans; in Great Britain, James Watt, William Henry Fox Talbot (one of the inventors of photography), and Charles Wheatstone and William Fothergill Cooke (the inventors of the telegraph); in France, Louis Daguerre (one of the inventors of photography), the Montgolfier brothers (inventors of lighter-than-air balloons), Louis Pasteur, and Clément Ader (inventor of the first heavier-than-air flying machine); in Germany, Rudolf Diesel and Ferdinand von Zeppelin. As is evident, there were sometimes several inventors for each advance, such as Wheatstone and Cooke and Morse for the telegraph, Talbot and Daguerre for photography, and Ader and the Wright brothers for flight. Thus, several nations can vie for the title of first. And occasionally, an inventor can be claimed by several nations – such is the case of Guglielmo Marconi, son of an Irish mother and an Italian father who did most of his work on wireless radio transmissions in Britain. Where professional historians of

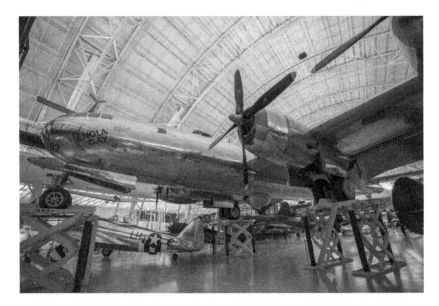

Figure 7.2 The *Enola Gay*, the Boeing B-29 Super Fortress bomber, which dropped the first atomic bomb over Japan in the Second World War (© Richard T. Nowitz/Corbis).

technology might see multiple inventors and complex social forces at work, popularizers stress the national element. In museum exhibitions, popular magazines, and textbooks for children, the history of technology serves a purpose similar to that of political, military, and literary history: inculcating national pride in children, reinforcing patriotism in a nation's citizens, and associating national pride with belief in progress (see Figure 7.3).

In addition to periodicals and museum exhibits, we might add another kind of popular – and generally Whiggish and nationalistic – history of technology: lavishly illustrated "coffee-table" books about airplanes, locomotives, guns, ships, and other technologies that fill the shelves in the history sections of bookstores. Some of these, despite their biases and narrow focus on hardware, contain information of value for the broader history of technology.

Prewar scholarship

It is in the presence of nationalism and the belief in progress – the two elephants in the room – that historians have been seeking to understand the evolution of technology and its role in society in an unbiased and scholarly manner.

Figure 7.3 James Watt's (1736–1819) prototype steam engine 'Old Bess' *c.* 1778 (World History Archive/Alamy).

Historians of science had established a beachhead in academia before there was a scholarly society in the history of technology. This was the achievement of George Sarton, a Belgian chemist and mathematician who emigrated to the United States and began writing a universal history of science, including medieval Islamic science, the first three volumes of which were published before his death in 1956. In 1912 he founded the journal *Isis*; in 1924 he helped found the History of Science Society; and in 1936 he founded the journal *Osiris*: all of them devoted to the history of science. Sarton's journals and the History of Science Society were only peripherally interested in technology, however.

Also interested in the history of technology, albeit in a secondary way, was the French journal *Annales d'Histoire Économique et Sociale*, founded by Marc Bloch and Lucien Fèbvre in 1929. While concentrating on economic and social questions, the editors were keenly interested in the material aspect of life, especially rural life and agriculture.

The history of technology lagged behind social and economic history and the history of science. The first scholarly societies and journals devoted to the history of technology were the creation of engineers with an interest in the history of their fields or historians with an engineering background. Such was the Newcomen Society for the Study of the History of Engineering and Technology, founded in 1920 and based at the Science Museum of London. It was named after Thomas Newcomen, inventor of the first working steam engine. Its journal, *Transactions*, concentrates on the history of engineering in Britain, Europe, and North America. Starting in 1923, it had an American affiliate, the Newcomen Society of the United States, which was directed by business leaders and concentrated on the history of American businesses; more political than scholarly, it ceased its activities in 2007.

There was also considerable scholarly interest in the subject in Germany, which saw the publication of scholarly books by Ludwig Darmstaedter, Edmund O. von Lippman, and Georg Neudeck, along with one in Belgium by Arthur Vierendeel.[3] Like von Poppe's work of 1837 mentioned earlier, these works were encyclopedic and heavily internalist, that is to say they privileged inventors of important and successful inventions (the "great men" of history), and largely ignored the social and economic environments in which they arose. Germany also had two scholarly journals, *Archiv für die Geschichte der Naturwissenschaften und der Technik*, published in Leipzig from 1909 on and mainly devoted to the sciences, and *Beiträge zur Geschichte der Technik und Industrie: Jahrbuch des Vereins deutscher Ingenieure*, published in Berlin from 1909 on and renamed *Technikgeschichte* in 1933, with a heavy emphasis on industrial engineering.

Two exceptions to this general trend and the only prewar works on the history of technology that have withstood the test of time appeared in the United States. Though Abbott Payson Usher's *History of Mechanical Inventions* was, as the title indicates, largely internalist and devoted to the history of important machines, the first four chapters introduced a general theory that placed innovations in their social and cultural context.[4] Even more significant and still influential almost a century later is Lewis Mumford's *Technics and Civilization*,

3 Ludwig Darmstaedter, *Handbuch zur Geschichte der Naturwissenschaften und der Technik* (Berlin: Julius Springer, 1908); Edmund O. von Lippman, *Beiträge zur Geschichte der Naturwissenschaften und der Technik* (Berlin: Julius Springer, 1923); Georg Neudeck, *Geschichte der Technik* (Stuttgart: W. Seifert, 1923); and Arthur Vierendeel, *Esquisse d'une histoire de la technique* (Brussels: Vromant, 1921).
4 Abbott Payson Usher, *History of Mechanical Inventions* (New York: McGraw Hill, 1929).

published in 1934.[5] Mumford was one of the leading American intellectuals of the mid-twentieth century, a noted social critic of modernity and American civilization. *Technics and Civilization* is basically a work of philosophy that situated technology in the broader context of "technics," a term Mumford uses to describe not only technological devices and processes, but also the culture in which they are embedded. His overview of technological history is very broad and sweeping, dividing the history of the world since 1000 CE into three phases: the Eotechnic from 1000 to 1800 in which the clock was the most important innovation because it divided time into small parts, laying the basis for the dominance of capitalist enterprises; the Paleotechnic from 1800 to 1900, the age of industry, huge cities, and dehumanizing labor; and the Neotechnic, after 1900, an age in which electricity, information devices, and communication networks promised to liberate humanity from the dangers of Paleotechnic industrialization, but also spawned mass automobility and advertising. Mumford therefore presents a powerful antidote to the mechanistic and internalist position that dominated the field before the Second World War.

Postwar enthusiasm and the Society for the History of Technology

Not until after the Second World War did the history of technology become a well-established branch of scholarship. Paralleling the explosion of scholarship was a continued popular interest in technology. Many of the world's fairs, museum exhibitions, and magazines mentioned earlier continued and expanded in the postwar era. In addition to the popular interest in machines of all sorts came a surge of excitement about postwar technologies. The media extolled every new development in computers and telecommunications, and many individuals personally experienced the ongoing evolution (or "progress") of PCs, laptops, cell phones, PDAs, smart phones, GPS devices, not to mention such innovations in software as word processing, spreadsheets, email, the World Wide Web, Facebook, Twitter, etc. Every innovation elicited a flurry of media and advertising hype, some of which compared the newest thing with its now-obsolete antecedents, a form of day-by-day history of technology. In addition to these personal technologies, there were the national or global technologies spawned by the Cold War, especially rockets and satellites. Interest reached a climax in July 1969 with

5 Lewis Mumford, *Technics and Civilization* (New York: Harcourt Brace, 1934).

the landing of men on the Moon, and resulted in numerous exhibitions and publications about rocketry and space.

It is in this atmosphere of techno-enthusiasm that scholarship in the history of technology emerged. The emergence of the field was marked by the founding of a new scholarly society. In 1957, four American academics with an interest in technology, Melvin Kranzberg of Case Western Reserve University, Thomas P. Hughes of the University of Pennsylvania, Carl Condit of Northwestern University, and John B. Rae of MIT, approached the History of Science Society to discuss widening that society's focus to include technology. Rebuffed, they founded a new organization, the Society for the History of Technology, or SHOT, in 1958. The next year, the society began publishing a journal called *Technology and Culture* under the editorship of Melvin Kranzberg until 1981, then of Robert Post (1982–95), John Staudenmaier (1995–2010), and Suzanne Moon (since 2010). It has also collaborated with the American Historical Association in the publication of a series of booklets entitled Historical Perspectives on Technology, Society, and Culture. From the beginning, the driving force behind these new initiatives was Melvin Kranzberg. Originally a scholar of European political and social history, he became interested in the history of technology as a result of teaching at Case Western Reserve, an engineering school. Besides founding SHOT and *Technology and Culture*, he wrote many articles (some under pseudonyms) and edited and co-authored several important books in the field.[6]

Since their inception, SHOT and *Technology and Culture* have adopted a broad focus, seeking to understand technology in its social and cultural contexts. As the home page of its website explains:

> An interdisciplinary organization, SHOT is concerned not only with the history of technological devices and processes but also with technology in history – that is, the relationship of technology to politics, economics, science, the arts, and the organization of production, and with the role it plays in the differentiation of individuals in society. Not least, it is concerned with interpretive flexibility, the conception that beliefs about whether a technology "works" are contingent on the expectations, needs, and ideologies of those who interact with it.[7]

In carrying out the mission of SHOT, *Technology and Culture* has featured articles on three kinds of themes: the context of technology, meaning how

---

6 See, for example, *Technology in Western Civilization* (Oxford: Oxford University Press, 1967) and *Energy and the Way We Live* (Boston: Heinle and Heinle, 1980).

7 The Society for the History of Technology, accessed October 3, 2013, www.historyof-technology.org.

society and culture shaped the emergence and success of various technologies; the impact of technologies on societies and cultures; and the relations between technology and science. By including articles about failures as well as successes, it helped undermine the popular perception of technology as an autonomous force and its history as the story of progress toward the future, in other words the Whiggish interpretation of technological history.[8] Its contributors have included not only historians and other social scientists with an interest in technology, but also engineers, scientists, and other technologists with an interest in history. In its early years, the journal stressed the economic history of technology, the mutual influences of science and technology, and the history of engineering. More recently, it has broadened its scope to include gender issues and the role of women in technology; the impact of industrialization on the environment; and the business and labor aspects of technological change. While *Technology and Culture* has gone far toward distancing the field from its Whiggish origins, many of its articles are still slanted toward the best-known – hence most successful – technologies. In short, the purpose of the journal has been partially fulfilled.

SHOT has been more successful in divorcing the history of technology from its national-chauvinist origins. In an effort to reach out beyond the confines of the United States, Melvin Kranzberg collaborated with three European historians of technology – Maurice Daumas of France, Eugeniusz Olszewski of Poland, and S. J. Schuchardine of the USSR – to found the International Committee for the History of Technology, or ICOHTEC in 1968. This organization was founded not only to give European scholars an opportunity to meet closer to home and give papers in their own languages (though English still predominates), but also to form links across the Iron Curtain, thereby demonstrating that technology was not a capitalist or communist phenomenon, but a human endeavor. ICOHTEC publishes in its journal *ICON* many of the papers given at its annual conferences.

In addition to collaborating with ICOHTEC, the Society for the History of Technology has also subsidized the travel expenses of foreign scholars to its annual meetings through its International Scholars Program. In recent years it has held one annual meeting overseas every four years, in London, Munich, Uppsala, Amsterdam, and Lisbon.

8 The story of technology and culture from its founding to 1985 is the theme of John M. Staudenmaier, *Technology's Storytellers: Reweaving the Human Fabric* (Cambridge, MA: The MIT Press, 1985).

Beyond SHOT

Although the Society for the History of Technology has been successful in broadening its purview in many directions, its conference papers and journal articles still concentrate predominantly on modern Western technology, that is, developments in Europe and North America since the Industrial Revolution. In addition to *Technology and Culture*, journals devoted to the history of technology have appeared in other countries, such as the German journal *Technikgeschichte* mentioned earlier, and the French journal *Techniques et Cultures*, published by the social science institute Maison des Sciences de l'Homme, and the British *History of Technology*, published since 1976.

The postwar era also saw a proliferation of scholarly books on the history of technology, of which we can only name a few. Foremost among them were the encyclopedic works covering all of Western technology. The most prominent of these was *A History of Technology*, edited by Charles Singer, E. J. Holmyard, and A. R. Hall, a seven-volume work published in Oxford from 1954 to 1978. While encyclopedic, it is a very internalist work that concentrates on "how things are done and made" and "what things are done and made," ignoring why things are done and made and what impact they have had on society.

A similar endeavor in French is *Histoire générale des techniques*, a five-volume work edited by Maurice Daumas and published in Paris from 1962 to 1979. The title of its English translation, *History of Technology and Invention: Progress Through the Ages* (1969–79), reveals the internalist and Whiggish perspective from which it was written.[9] Broader in scope, but from a doctrinaire Marxist perspective, is the work of Anatolii Alekseevich Zvorykin, translated into German as *Geschichte der Technik* and published in Leipzig in 1967.[10] The American work *Technology in Western Civilization*, in two volumes edited by Melvin Kranzberg and Carroll Pursell (1967), is of the same generation as these other works, but with a much broader perspective, as befitted the editor of *Technology and Culture*.[11]

Methodology

Historians of technology use many of the same research methods as other historians: reading books, visiting archives, perusing personal papers

---

9 Maurice Daumas, *Histoire générale des techniques* (Paris: Presses Universitaires de France, 1979); and Maurice Daumas, *History of Technology and Invention: Progress Through the Ages* (New York: Crown Publishers, 1970).

10 Anatolii Alekseevich Zvorykin, *Geschichte der Technik* (Leipzig: Fachbuchverlag, 1967).

11 Melvin Kranzberg and Carroll W. Purcell, Jr. (eds.), *Technology in Western Civilization* (New York: Oxford University Press, 1967).

whenever possible. But they also study artifacts, sometimes in museum or "historical village" settings, but also *in situ*, as in the case of industrial archaeologists who reconstruct the operations of abandoned mills, quarries, and machinery. There are even re-enactors who build replicas of trebuchets or triremes from ancient (often vague) descriptions in order to understand how they worked. In facilitating such "hands-on" research, museums and exhibitions do more than cater to a public eager to learn about material progress; they also contribute to serious scholarship.

Science, technology, and academia

Academia, a conservative institution, is always slow to open its doors (and minds) to new fields, and this has certainly been the case for the history of technology. In the half-century since the founding of SHOT, the history of technology in the United States has found its niche in schools of engineering including MIT, Case Western Reserve, and Georgia Tech, often as a humanities elective for engineering students, to ensure that their education is more than just preparation for a technical trade. But it has yet to be admitted into the more prestigious research universities. Part of the reason is an intellectual bias among academics against "manual labor," a prejudice that goes back to the ancient Greeks, if not long before. But part is also the important place taken by the history of science in the more prestigious institutions of higher learning since the First World War. A close ally of philosophy and of the natural sciences, it has enjoyed a privileged position as a purely intellectual field and, furthermore, as one that could more justifiably claim to illustrate the upward progress of humankind than did technology.

The history of technology *stricto sensu* may appear in the curricula of only a limited number of institutions, but in a broader sense, it is part of several other disciplines. Military history is replete with references to weapons and tactics. The history of medicine, often part of medical school curricula, is also closely allied to technology, as is the history of architecture as taught in schools of art and architecture as well as in art history departments in many universities. Also very similar to the history of technology, but in different cultures and eras, are archaeology and anthropology. These disciplines, which do not have written documents to rely on as evidence, perforce pay careful attention to the artifacts and material cultures of ancient or non-literate peoples. We may cite Leslie White (1900–75) as an example of an anthropologist whose ideas overlapped those of historians of technology.

In *The Science of Culture* (1949) and *The Evolution of Culture* (1959),[12] White equated the socio-cultural evolution of human societies with the level of their technology – "Social systems are determined by technological systems,"[13] he claimed – and the stage of cultural evolution achieved by a society correlated with the amount of energy per capita used by its inhabitants, from hunter-gatherers who used mainly human muscles, to herdsmen and farmers who used animals, to industrial societies that relied on fossil fuels, to the nuclear age. In short, White was a hard-nosed technological determinist.

Technology in its social context

Along with the proliferation of encyclopedic but often internalist works on the history of technology, the postwar era also saw the appearance of works that sought to place technological changes in their social contexts. One of the earliest of this new generation of historians who contributed to the trend to contextualize technology was Louis C. Hunter, whose book *Steamboats on the Western Rivers: An Economic and Technological History* (1949) blended, as the subtitle indicates, the economic history of steamboat transportation with the technological history of boats and navigation.[14]

Another and often cited work taking this new approach was Lynn White Jr.'s *Medieval Technology and Social Change*, published in 1962.[15] White (1907–87) was a medieval historian who taught at Princeton, Stanford, and the University of California at Los Angeles and was for a time the president of Mills College in Oakland, California. In this book, he demonstrated that early medieval Europe, far from being the "Dark Ages" so often described by cultural historians, was actually an age of intense technological change, producing such innovations as the windmill and water mill, the horse collar and stirrup, and the three-field system of agriculture, among others. In a very famous article entitled "The Historical Roots of Our Ecologic Crisis" and published in *Science* in 1967, White traced the origin of Western technological

---

12 Leslie White, *The Science of Culture: A Study of Man and Civilization* (New York: Farrar, Straus and Company, 1949); and Leslie White, *The Evolution of Culture: The Development of Civilization to the Fall of Rome* (New York: McGraw-Hill, 1959).

13 Leslie White, "Energy and the evolution of culture," in Henrietta L. Moore and Todd Sanders (eds.), *Anthropology in Theory: Issues in Epistemology* (Oxford: Blackwell, 2006), p. 108.

14 Louis C. Hunter, *Steamboats on the Western Rivers: An Economic and Technological History* (Cambridge, MA: Harvard University Press, 1949).

15 Lynn White, Jr., *Medieval Technology and Social Change* (Oxford: Clarendon Press, 1962).

success to the Middle Ages and to the religious beliefs that medieval Europeans derived from their reading of the Bible, especially their domineering attitude toward the natural world, considering nature to be a stockpile of resources provided by God for human use.[16]

Hunter and White were followed by several historians who were not as bold in finding connections between technology and society, but more subtle in tracing these links, especially in modern American and European society. Outstanding among the members of the generation that followed Lynn White, Jr. was Thomas P. Hughes, one of the co-founders of the Society for the History of Technology and for many years a professor at the University of Pennsylvania. Hughes is best known for his magisterial work *Networks of Power: Electrification in Western Society, 1880–1930,* in which he compares the growth of electrical networks in the United States, Great Britain, and Germany.[17] In so doing, he moved the field from innovative ideas, designs, and machines to complex networks and systems. A systems theorist, he also introduced the concepts of technological momentum and the social construction of technology (about which more below). Hughes is also known for more wide-angle views of technology, as in his *American Genesis* (1989) and *The Human-Built World* (2004).[18]

Another historian who advanced the field by contextualizing innovation was Merritt Roe Smith, a professor of history at MIT and past president of the Society for the History of Technology. When his book *Harper's Ferry Armory and the New Technology: The Challenge of Change* appeared in 1977, it was hailed as a breakthrough in the field, for it situated the evolution of the Harper's Ferry Armory (1794–1861) in the context of American society and politics and emphasized the cultural conditions in which the technology of arms manufacture took place.[19] To honor his work, Smith was awarded the Leonardo da Vinci Prize by SHOT as well as the Frederick Jackson Turner Prize by the Organization of American Historians, a recognition of the legitimacy of the history of technology by generalist historians.

---

16 Lynn White, "The historical roots of our ecologic crisis," *Science* 155 (10 March 1967), 1,203–7.
17 Thomas P. Hughes, *Networks of Power: Electrification in Western Society, 1880–1930* (Baltimore, MD: The Johns Hopkins University Press, 1983).
18 Thomas P. Hughes, *American Genesis: A Century of Innovation and Technological Enthusiasm, 1870–1970* (New York: Viking, 1989); and Thomas P. Hughes, *The Human-Built World: How to Think about Technology and Culture* (Chicago: University of Chicago Press, 2004).
19 Merritt Roe Smith, *Harper's Ferry Armory and the New Technology: The Challenge of Change* (Ithaca, NY: Cornell University Press, 1977).

In recent years, SHOT and the field of technological history have broadened their perspective in several directions. One of the most striking is the new interest in the role of women in technology, not only as creators but also as consumers of technology. Ruth Schwartz Cowan exemplifies this trend. After teaching for many years at the State University of New York at Stony Brook, she moved to the University of Pennsylvania in 2002. Like Merritt Roe Smith, she is a past president of SHOT and a recipient of its Leonardo da Vinci Prize. Her most famous contribution to the history of technology is *More Work for Mother: The Ironies of Household Technology from the Open Hearth to the Microwave* (1983), which traces the unexpected increase in women's household chores that resulted from "advances" in domestic appliances and other household technologies.[20]

Nor must we forget histories that are not specifically technological, but cover topics and periods in which technological innovations are so important that no general socio-economic history can avoid them. A classic case is the history of the Industrial Revolution in Great Britain and the European continent. Among the many works that deal with this important theme, we can mention only two: T. S. Ashton's classic *The Industrial Revolution, 1760–1830* first published in 1948 and reprinted several times since,[21] and David Landes' magisterial *Unbound Prometheus: Technological Change and Economic Development in Western Europe from 1750 to the Present*.[22] Both books, by well-known economic historians, take technology very seriously and devote considerable space to the innovations that made the Industrial Revolution so dramatic a turning point in Western history.

Beyond the West

While varied and innovative, much of the history of technology that appears in the aforementioned books and journals deals with Europe and North America. Yet much fine scholarship takes place outside the field as currently defined, for scholars interested in the history of technology in earlier times and in other civilizations have audiences in their own fields to whom they can address their work in journals such as *Modern Asian Studies*, *African*

20 Ruth Schwartz Cowan, *More Work for Mother: The Ironies of Household Technology from the Open Hearth to the Microwave* (New York: Basic Books, 1983).
21 T. S. Ashton, *The Industrial Revolution, 1760–1830* (London: Oxford University Press, 1948).
22 David Landes, *Unbound Prometheus: Technological Change and Economic Development in Western Europe from 1750 to the Present* (Cambridge: Cambridge University Press, 1969).

Studies Review, Hispanic American Historical Review, the *Journal of African Studies,* and countless other journals in foreign languages as well as English. As noted earlier, scholarly fields such as archaeology and anthropology that deal largely with material culture are heavily oriented toward the history of the technology of their time and place.

In recent years, historians have developed an interest in world history, including global histories of technology that would encompass all cultures and civilizations. Vaclav Smil's *Energy in World History* (1994) takes the same approach as Leslie White did a generation before, offering energy sources and uses as keys to understanding the evolution of civilization. A more balanced view, albeit in too brief a form, is presented by Arnold Pacey in *Technology in World Civilization* (1990) and by Daniel Headrick in *Technology: A World History* (2009).[23]

While the history of technology outside the West still lags behind, there is one remarkable exception to this rule: Joseph Needham's multi-volume *Science and Civilisation in China.*[24] Joseph Needham (1900–95) was trained as an embryologist and his *Chemical Embryology* (1931) became a classic in his field. While teaching at Cambridge University, he came under the influence of three Chinese scientists – Lu Guizhen, Wang Yinglai, and Chen Shizhang, who inspired him to learn Chinese and become interested in Chinese science and technology. During the Second World War, as a liaison officer between the British and the Nationalist Chinese governments, he traveled around China acquiring old books and manuscripts on these subjects. Upon his return to Cambridge, he collaborated with historian Wang Ling to begin a multi-volume work based on their research, the first volume of which appeared in 1954. Needham wrote the first fifteen volumes with the help of several collaborators. Since his death, the work has continued and has currently reached twenty-four volumes. It is arguably the most important work on the history of technology produced in the twentieth century.

Although the word "technology" does not appear in the title of his *magnum opus,* many volumes are devoted to such technical subjects as mechanical engineering, shipbuilding and navigation, paper and printing, gunpowder and missiles, metallurgy, ceramics, and agriculture. In this enormous work, Needham and his collaborators demonstrated that China was

23 Vaclav Smil, *Energy in World History* (Boulder, CO: Westview Press, 1994); Arnold Pacey, *Technology in World Civilization: A Thousand-Year History* (Oxford: Basil Blackwell, 1990); and Daniel R. Headrick, *Technology: A World History* (New York: Oxford University Press, 2009).
24 Joseph Needham (ed.), *Science and Civilisation in China* (Cambridge: Cambridge University Press, 1954).

well ahead of the rest of the world in most technological fields until the fifteenth century, and contributed several key inventions to the West, such as the compass, gunpowder, paper, and printing. In the process, he raised the so-called "Needham Question," one that has intrigued scholars even beyond the narrow confines of sinology: Why did Chinese innovation cease just as Europe was becoming more innovative? This question has recently attracted public attention as China has risen to the forefront of economic development and cutting-edge technologies.

Overall, the history of technology in other civilizations has lagged behind that of the West and China. Nonetheless, there have been a few remarkable exceptions to this generalization – among them we might cite Richard Bulliet's *The Camel and the Wheel* (1975), which explains why wheeled vehicles, which originated in ancient Mesopotamia and spread throughout the Middle East, Europe, and Asia, were eclipsed by camels during and after the Roman empire.[25]

Besides the history of technology in non-Western cultures, a few historians have found technology as a useful lens through which to understand the relations between civilizations. Among them we might cite the work of Geoffrey Parker, whose *Military Revolution: Military Innovation and the Rise of the West, 1500–1800* examines the changes in weapons, tactics, and strategy that transformed warfare not only among Europeans, but also between Europeans and non-Western states in the Middle East, Asia, and the Americas.[26] Another very important contribution to comparative military history is *Firearms: A Global History to 1700* (2003) by Kenneth Chase, which seeks to explain why explosives and firearms, though invented in China, had a much greater impact in Europe and the Middle East, and were deliberately banned for centuries in Japan.[27]

In a similar vein, the Italian historian Carlo Cipolla looked at the technological dimension of the encounter between West and non-West in two remarkable books. In *Guns, Sails and Empires* (1965), he demonstrated the importance of technological innovations in explaining European imperialism in the early modern period, and in *Clocks and Culture*, he focused on clocks as a means of understanding the different attitudes toward time and timekeeping in Europe and in China.[28]

---

25 Richard Bulliet, *The Camel and the Wheel* (Cambridge, MA: Harvard University Press, 1975).
26 Geoffrey Parker, *Military Revolution: Military Innovation and the Rise of the West, 1500–1800* (Cambridge: Cambridge University Press, 1988).
27 Kenneth Chase, *Firearms: A Global History to 1700* (New York: Cambridge University Press, 2003).
28 Carlo Cipolla, *Guns, Sails and Empires in the Early Phases of European Expansion, 1400–1700* (New York: Minerva Press, 1965); and Carlo Cipolla, *Clocks and Culture, 1300–1700* (London: Collins, 1967).

Following in the footsteps of Cipolla and Parker, Daniel Headrick has investigated the importance of technological factors in Western imperialism in three books: *The Tools of Empire: Technology and Imperialism in the Nineteenth Century* (1981), *The Tentacles of Progress: Technology Transfer in the Age of Imperialism, 1850–1940* (1988), and *Power over Peoples: Technology, Environments, and Western Imperialism, 1400 to the Present* (2010).[29]

Future trends

Historians are naturally disinclined to discuss the future, and all the more so in their own field. Yet some portents regarding the history of technology are already visible. One trend, the social construction of technology, has come to historians from the sociology of science and the study of large-scale technological systems pioneered by Thomas Hughes and others. Social constructivism argues that technologies do not come full-blown from the brains of great inventors, but result from the collaboration and conflicts among innovators, entrepreneurs, marketers, manufacturers, consumers, the media, governments, and other social groups. In effect, social constructivism represents a reaction to the technological determinism of the Whiggish school of technological history that dominated the field for so long. In its extreme form, its practitioners argue that technologies are entirely dictated by social conventions and powerful interests, without regard to the laws of physics. A more nuanced approach to this perspective can be found in *The Social Construction of Technological Systems: New Directions in the Sociology and History of Technology* (1987), edited by Wiebe E. Bijker, Thomas P. Hughes, and Trevor Pinch.[30]

And finally, we might cite a book that argues that the emphasis on *innovation* in technological history is misplaced, for most of the technologies in use today date back centuries; this is David Edgerton's *The Shock of the Old: Technology and Global History Since 1900* (2007).[31] Will a new appreciation for

---

29 Daniel R. Headrick, *The Tools of Empire: Technology and Imperialism in the Nineteenth Century* (New York: Oxford University Press, 1981); Daniel R. Headrick, *The Tentacles of Progress: Technology Transfer in the Age of Imperialism, 1850–1940* (New York: Oxford University Press, 1988); and Daniel R. Headrick, *Power Over Peoples: Technology, Environments, and Western Imperialism, 1400 to the Present* (Princeton, NJ: Princeton University Press, 2010).

30 Wiebe E. Bijker, Thomas P. Hughes, and Trevor Pinch (eds.), *The Social Construction of Technological Systems: New Directions in the Sociology and History of Technology* (Cambridge, MA: The MIT Press, 1987).

31 David Edgerton, *The Shock of the Old: Technology and Global History Since 1900* (New York: Oxford University Press, 2007).

old technologies become the norm in the field of the history of technology? As Zhou Enlai famously said of the impact of the French Revolution: "It is too soon to tell."

FURTHER READING

Arthur, W. Brian, *The Nature of Technology: What It Is and How It Evolves*, New York: Free Press, 2009.

Ashton, T. S., *The Industrial Revolution, 1760–1830*, London: Oxford University Press, 1948.

Bulliet, Richard, *The Camel and the Wheel*, Cambridge: Cambridge University Press, 1975.

Chase, Kenneth, *Firearms: A Global History to 1700*, New York: Cambridge University Press, 2003.

Cipolla, Carlo, *Clocks and Culture, 1300–1700*, London: Collins, 1967.

Cowan, Ruth Schwartz, *More Work for Mother: The Ironies of Household Technologies from the Open Hearth to the Microwave*, New York: Basic Books, 1983.

Derry, T. K., and Trevor I. Williams, *A Short History of Technology from Earliest Times to A.D. 1900*, Oxford: Clarendon Press, 1960.

Edgerton, David, *The Shock of the Old: Technology and Global History Since 1900*, Oxford: Oxford University Press, 2007.

Ferguson, Eugene S., *Bibliography of the History of Technology*, Cambridge, MA: Society for the History of Technology, 1968.

Headrick, Daniel, *Power Over Peoples: Technology, Environments, and Western Imperialism, 1400 to the Present*, Princeton, NJ: Princeton University Press, 2010.

   Technology: A World History, New York: Oxford University Press, 2009.

Hughes, Thomas P., *Networks of Power: Electrification in Western Society, 1880–1930*, Baltimore, MD: The Johns Hopkins University Press, 1983.

Mokyr, Joel, *The Lever of Riches: Technological Creativity and Economic Progress*, New York: Oxford University Press, 2009.

Mumford, Lewis, *Technics and Civilization*, New York: Harcourt Brace, 1934.

Needham, Joseph (ed.), *Science and Civilisation in China*, 7 vols., Cambridge: Cambridge University Press, 1954–2004.

Pacey, Arnold, *Technology in World Civilization: A Thousand-Year History*, Oxford: Basil Blackwell, 1990.

Parker, Geoffrey, *The Military Revolution: Military Innovation and the Rise of the West, 1500–1800*, Cambridge: Cambridge University Press, 1988.

Singer, Charles, A. R. Hall, E. J. Holmyard, and Trevor I. Williams (eds.), *The History of Technology*, 5 vols., Oxford: Clarendon Press, 1958.

Smith, Merritt Roe, *Harper's Ferry Armory and the New Technology*, Ithaca, NY: Cornell University Press, 1977.

Usher, Abbott Payson, *A History of Mechanical Inventions*, New York: McGraw Hill, 1929.

White, Lynn, Jr., *Medieval Technology and Social Change*, London: Oxford University Press, 1962.

8

Fire and fuel in human history

JOHAN GOUDSBLOM

This chapter deals with the peculiar bond between humans and fire: what, in the course of history, have we humans done with fire, and what has fire done to us?[1]

All animal species except one derive their own physical energy mainly from one single source: food. We humans are the only exception: we derive most of our physical energy from two sources: food and fuel.

The dependence on fuel reflects our strong and intimate bond with fire. This bond is unique: no other animal species has acquired the capacity to control fire and exploit the energy released by it. Control over fire is a human 'species monopoly'.

In addition to being unique, the human bond with fire is also universal. There are no known cases of human societies in recorded times that lacked the capacity to handle fire. Stories that sometimes appeared in the anthropological literature about peoples who had never learned to master the art of tending a fire have all been proved spurious.

Many unique and universal human features are, of course, directly related to our biological nature. The capacity to handle fire, however, is not a naturally inborn ability. It is acquired, it is a cultural asset, the result of collective learning.

These, then, are three general characteristics of the human bond with fire: it is unique, universal, and cultural – a remarkable combination.

1 I wish to thank the following persons for reading an earlier version of this text and giving their comments. In alphabetical order: Frances Burton, Frans Saris, Abram de Swaan, Peter Westbroek, Esther Wils, Nico Wilterdink, Cas Wouters, Richard Wrangham. I am particularly grateful to Frans Saris for drawing my attention to the ideas of Richard Buckminster Fuller (1982) about a global electricity grid.

Stories, phases, and concepts

Origins: from tales to scenarios

The realization that the bond with fire is a peculiar and exclusively human phenomenon has clearly puzzled people in many different cultures and led to the creation of a great variety of myths. In 1930, Sir James George Frazer published a collection from all over the world in *Myths of the Origins of Fire* (1930) – a collection that remains valuable even though the title is slightly misleading, for the tales are not really about 'the origins of fire' but the origins of exclusive human possession of fire.

Most myths represent the domestication of fire (as we now call it) as a single adventurous event, with one main character (a god or an animal or both in the same incarnation) who brought this precious gift to humankind. Such stories were no longer included in the sacred books of the three major monotheistic religions. Their disappearance was probably due to the fact that these religions emerged in advanced agrarian or pastoral societies in which fire played a less prominent part than in earlier phases of human history, when gathering and hunting were the main means of subsistence, and the communal fire was the centre of group life.

Still, in some advanced agrarian societies a sense of the importance of control over fire apparently persisted, and continued to find expression in myths. Well-known examples include the myths connected with the Zoroaster cult in Iran and, in Europe, the Prometheus myth, which has been recorded in several different versions in ancient Greek and Roman texts.

In Greek and Roman antiquity, some authors tried to go 'beyond mythology' and to describe and explain the origins of the human bond with fire in a more detached, philosophical manner, without attributing the art of controlling fire to the intervention of a semi-divine hero such as Prometheus. The writings of Lucretius in particular reflect a sophisticated theoretical mind, bent on a 'naturalistic' explanation of how humans came to control fire, but lacking the support of empirical findings.

It was not until the eighteenth and nineteenth centuries that more solid evidence became available in the emerging fields of palaeontology, archaeology, and anthropology which seemed to offer the promise of fitting the early history of the human bond with fire into a grand evolutionary theory.[2]

2 Marvin Harris, *The Rise of Anthropological Theory: A History of Theories of Culture* (New York: Harper & Row, 1968).

At the same time the physical sciences provided more realistic insight into the nature of fire and fuel.

The current chapter joins this tradition. Written by a sociologist, it aims at a synthesis of empirical knowledge and theoretical reasoning. While, especially with regard to the earliest stages, we have to rely on scenarios and hypotheses, we can still try to keep these as realistic as possible. Rather than viewing the domestication of fire as a single heroic event, I shall regard it as a process of 'collective learning'.[3] This approach encompasses and addresses a broad range of academic disciplines. The scope of the subject is truly world historical.

Phases: an overview

There must have been a time when *no* hominin or human group exercised any control over fire. Then, a time came when *some* hominin or human groups exercised at least some control over fire. This period of simultaneous co-existence came to an end when ultimately *all* human groups possessed the ability to control fire.

This sequence of phases or stages may appear trivial and self-evident. But that is only because it is so obviously valid. It can serve as the exemplary model of a far wider range of sequential series. If instead of 'control over fire' we speak of 'x', we can make 'x' stand for, for example, 'agrarian production' or 'industrial production'. Again, the same formulations apply: first, there were no human groups with agrarian production, then there were some, and nowadays all human groups at least share in the products of agrarian production – the process of agrarianization has reached the entire world population. The same can be said about the more recent and more rapid process of industrialization that has also passed through the phases of first affecting 'none', to affecting 'some', to affecting 'all' human societies.

The beginning of each new phase marked a transition in human history. A new socio-ecological regime emerged that made human groups more productive and, in confrontations with enemies, more formidable. The formation of these regimes contributed to an ongoing process of differentiation in both behaviour and power between humans and all other large animals.

After the first successful attempts at domestication had resulted in the establishment of a lasting fire regime controlled by humans, the world would never be the same again. The balance of power between hominin or human groups armed with fire and all other animals shifted in favour of those

3 David Christian, *Maps of Time: An Introduction to Big History* (Berkeley: University of California Press, 2004).

equipped with fire. The same applied to the mutual balance of power among proto-human or human groups themselves: those with fire prevailed in the long run over those without fire. Much later, the same pattern was repeated in the long-term processes of agrarianization and industrialization: eventually, even peoples who lived far away from the original centres were, after many generations, faced with the relentless expansion of the stronger agrarian and then industrial societies.

As they grew in productivity and power, human groups also became more destructive and more vulnerable. Since fire continued to be a destructive force, increasing control over fire and fuel endowed these groups with a greater potential for destruction – not only intentional destruction directed at enemy groups but also depletion of resources by over-exploitation.

In his fictional film *Quest for Fire* (1982), Jean-Jacques Annaud dramatically showed how a group of primeval foragers was threatened with death and extinction when it was deprived of its fire and unable to make a new fire. Control over a source of energy makes people more dependent on that which is being controlled and vulnerable to its loss. It seems only logical to assume that when – in the course of agrarianization and industrialization – the networks of control over various sources of energy grew in size and complexity, vulnerability to damage or even collapse of these networks would also increase.

Bearing these general observations in mind, and focusing our attention on the human bond with fire and fuel, we can distinguish four (and, including present trends, perhaps five) successive phases in human history:

1. The phase *before domestication*, spanning several million years, in the course of which numerous small steps may have been made towards closer 'association with fire', gradually leading to greater familiarity with burning matter and a commensurate recognition of the value of fuel.[4]
2. The phase of *domestication* of fire, beginning perhaps as early as 1.8 million years ago, marked by slowly increasing dependence on fire and appreciation of fuel.[5] The actual domestication of fire constituted a unique feat of collective learning that resulted in control over fire and fuel becoming not just an *exclusive* but also a *universal* feature of human group life, shared by all surviving human groups.

---

4 Frances D. Burton, *Fire: The Spark that Ignited Human Evolution* (Tucson: University of Arizona Press, 2009).
5 Richard Wrangham, *Catching Fire: How Cooking Made Us Human* (New York: Basic Books, 2009).

3. The phase that in analogy with the subsequent phase of 'industrialization' may be called *agrarianization*.[6] During this phase, starting somewhere between 15,000 and 10,000 years ago, dependence upon fire and fuel continued to be strong, and even continued to increase, but the major changes in human societies were related to the production and distribution of *food* rather than to innovations in the use of fire and fuel.[7]

4. *Industrialization*: the trend that became dominant in the middle of the nineteenth century, as a cascade of innovations in the exploitation of the fossil fuels coal, oil, and natural gas brought about rapid changes in virtually every aspect of social life all over the world.[8]

5. We are now perhaps witnessing the dawn of a new phase, in which fire and fuel will play a very different role than in the still current phase of industrialization. We do not seem yet to have reached the point at which we can identify the nature of the transition and give it a satisfactory label. I shall briefly return to this problem at the end of the chapter.

Leading concepts: matter, energy, information

The history of the human bond with fire and fuel has aspects that relate to practically all academic disciplines, in the humanities, the social sciences, and the natural sciences. In order to keep my account as coherent and consistent as possible I shall use three related concepts, each only vaguely definable, but together forming what I hope to be a comprehensible and enlightening conceptual triangle: Matter, Energy, and Information (MEI).

'Matter' refers to the general category of all objects, large and small, in the material world that are visible and tangible or otherwise observable – from sand and rocks to animals and artefacts. Many material objects appear at first sight to be static, unmoving, unchangeable, but at closer inspection the static impression will turn out to be misleading: as Heraclitus already noted, everything that 'is', is in movement, is not immutable but changing. Nothing in the whole world has always been in the same shape, at the same spot, forever.

---

6 Johan Goudsblom, *Fire and Civilization* (London: Allen Lane, 1992).

7 Valcav Smil, *Harvesting the Biosphere: What We Have Taken from Nature* (Cambridge: The MIT Press, 2012).

8 Rolf Peter Sieferle, *The Subterranean Forest: Energy Systems and the Industrial Revolution* (Cambridge: The White Horse Press, 2001); Manfred Weissenbacher, *Sources of Power: How Energy Forges Human History*, 2 vols. (Santa Barbara, CA: Praeger, 2009); and Daniel Yergin, *The Quest: Energy, Security, and the Remaking of the Modern World* (New York: Penguin Press, 2011).

'Energy', as noted by the physical scientist Frank Niele, is the general term indicating the forces that cause change.[9] Fire is a manifestation of energy, fuel is a source of energy. Another familiar form of energy is wind – a force that causes movement in objects that appear otherwise motionless, as the branches of a tree when the wind is still.

But even on a windless day, there is movement in trees. Other organisms are leading busy lives on the bark; and the trees themselves are continuously undergoing processes of growth and decay of cells, losing leaves and growing new ones. These processes are not, like the wind, 'dead' – they are expressions of life.

According to current scientific insight, wind as well as life derive their driving force, their energy, from the same source – sunlight. Both wind and life are transformations of solar activity into earthly *energy* that causes movement and change in *matter*.

'Information', the third angle in our conceptual triangle, is the general term we can use to deal with the problem of what it is that gives direction and shape to the multiple processes occurring in the combinations of matter and energy. Neither wind nor life occur haphazardly. The general heading of 'information' draws attention to the particular direction the wind takes, and to the seemingly endless variation of forms in which life manifests itself.

Applying the concept of information to fire may seem puzzling. It seems to flout common sense to imagine that fire, when it first began to ravage forests between 400 and 500 million years ago, was guided by 'information'. Fire seems almost prototypical of a wild natural force, blind and undirected. Nevertheless, it is not unreasonable to assume that, from the very start, there were patterns in burning, as there are patterns in life, no matter how bizarre. And the idea that fire is structured by information has become more plausible in the history of the past 1 million years, when the frequency and variety of fires have become more directed by humans, and thus submitted to ever higher degrees of control, which would have been impossible without being informed by collective learning.

In other words, as long as we are unaware of any specific patterns that might possibly explain the occurrences of ignition, we are inclined to speak of 'wild' or 'blind' natural forces. But when ignition is largely controlled and predictable, it makes perfect sense to say that it is subject to 'information'.

---

9 Frank Niele, *Energy: Engine of Evolution* (Amsterdam: Elsevier, 2005).

The domestication of fire

Fire and hominins before domestication

Fire is a process of combustion of organic matter. A momentary conjunction of three conditions is needed for it to occur: there has to be sufficient fuel, a sufficient supply of oxygen, and heat that is of a sufficiently high temperature so that it can ignite the fuel. Usually only the first two conditions are present on the land surface of our planet, providing a ubiquitous potential for fire that, in the absence of ignition, does not break out.

Ignition, the most ephemeral of the three conditions, is also the most ancient. Its most frequent cause, lightning, must have struck at land and water alike ever since the planet was formed. Volcanic eruptions and perhaps falling rocks may also have caused spells and moments of great heat. As long, however, as the other two conditions were lacking, no fire ensued.

Oxygen became a substantive part of the planetary atmosphere when, some 2.5 billion years ago, living organisms began producing it in processes of photosynthesis and emitting it into the air.[10] When, between 500 and 400 million years ago, large parts of the land surface had become covered with plants and trees, the proportion of oxygen in the air stabilized at a rate of about 21 per cent. At the same time, and by the same token, fuel became available in the form of abundant vegetation, and the world was ready for fire.[11]

By the time our earliest hominin forebears appeared, some 8 to 10 million years ago, fire was a regularly occurring feature in their habitats. It is, therefore, misleading to say, as is often done, that humans 'discovered', let alone 'invented' fire. Every hominin that reached adulthood was likely to have come across a fire at least once in his or her lifetime.

In a recent monograph the primatologist Frances Burton addresses on the basis of a wide range of current scientific knowledge the problem of how the unique relationship between humans and fire emerged.[12] She postulates a long and protracted phase of 'association' with fire, during which hominin groups gradually familiarized themselves with fire, spending the nights around it together, adjusting themselves to its presence, enjoying both the heat and the light as well as the protection it might offer from predators, and eventually learning to 'nourish' it with fuel and to transport it to cave entrances where it was sheltered against the rain.

---

10 Peter Westbroek, *Life as a Geological Force* (Berkeley: University of California Press, 1991).
11 Stephen J. Pyne, *Fire: A Brief History* (Seattle: University of Washington Press, 2001).
12 Burton, *Fire*.

This is a likely scenario, supported by evidence from many divergent sources. In the overall process preceding the actual domestication of fire, biogenetic evolution seamlessly coalesced with sociogenetic, or cultural, evolution (or development). Clearly, in the process of collectively learning to handle fire and fuel, the evolution of a larger and more complex brain played a part, and so did the evolution of walking on two legs, with the hands free for carrying objects – from branches that could serve as fuel, to burning sticks with which fire could be transported to another site or used as a weapon to ward off bears or lions. The very same physical features that were first preconditions for mastering fire may well have become mechanisms of selection in human evolution once the domestication of fire was underway.

Odd though it may sound, in order to form an image of what happened in the very early phase preceding domestication, it may be helpful to describe it in terms in which our early ancestors themselves may have experienced it: as a struggle to change the balance of power between themselves and fire – a struggle that was often lost, until in the long run the balance was tilted definitely towards increasing human control, in circumstances created according to their own ideas about the conditions for burning.

The domestication of fire meant a shift in the balance of control: the course taken by a fire was no longer solely determined by 'natural' forces, but it was determined, at least in part, by human direction. Our early ancestors may not have been aware of all the implications of what they were doing, but they did have a sense of how the fire would behave and, most importantly, how they wished it to behave. They applied their own information in order to conduct the combustion of matter.

There was, of course, another side to it: in order to submit the fire to their intentions, they had to adjust their own behaviour to the requirements of the fire.

From mere association to incipient control

The history of the human bond with fire is about *human* control over a *non-human* or *extra-human* force – fire, including, as a necessary precondition for fire, some control over fuel. As indicated by the sociologist Norbert Elias, control over non-human processes always implies a measure of control over social (*inter-human*) relations and individual (*intra-human*) impulses as well.[13] Neither of these three forms of control can ever be complete; in the last

---

13 Norbert Elias, *What Is Sociology?* (Dublin: University College Dublin Press, 2006), vol. v.

resort, it is a matter of balances, or ratios, between the controlling agencies and the forces that are being controlled.

Such a balance must also have existed from the start between the biogenetic and the sociogenetic aspects of the human attitudes towards fire. Biogenetic information warns us, as well as our early ancestors, to stay away from fire, to avoid contact with it. Sociogenetic information, acquired by collective learning, has added the insight that it is possible to manipulate fire (and thus exploit fuel) without touching it.

The capacity to acquire this information and to pass it on to future generations must have developed along with the evolution of a large and differentiated brain, 'expensive tissue' as some archaeoneurologists call it, hinting at the disproportionately great amount of energy this organ consumes. Another precondition, equally evident, was the upright position, making it possible to walk and run on two feet, with the hands free for carrying objects, if necessary even burning matter as long as it was kept isolated from the carrier's skin. Both 'preconditions' probably co-evolved with the changes in behaviour towards fire.

Just as the brain was 'expensive tissue', a human-controlled fire (a 'campfire') was an 'expensive' social institution. It demanded foresight and care: foresight already with regard to its location: preferably at a cave entrance, where it would not be quenched by rain, and still receive sufficient oxygen-saturated air. In order to be sure of having a fire available in wet seasons too, was useful to keep it burning continuously, with a stock of dry fuel at hand. Care was also required in order not to hurt oneself or other group members; and social co-ordination was needed to make sure that the fire was tended and protected against possible invaders.

The immediate effect of fire was always, put in the most neutral words, a re-arrangement of matter – a rapid re-arrangement that not only totally destroyed the combusted fuel, but also did so in a way that was irreversible. This destructive effect was turned into what from a human point of view was its very opposite: production. That began with cooking, the activity that in Richard Wrangham's appealing phrase 'made us human'. Cooking in the most elementary sense amounted to exposure of organic matter to great heat, thus making a whole range of nutritious ingredients digestible that would have remained very difficult or even impossible to digest without prior heating.

A very different use of fire was to employ it as a weapon, exploiting the pain it would cause when inflicted upon living skin. This made hominins and humans far more formidable and fearsome to any opponents in inter-species contests. By virtue of their familiarity with fire they could afford to spend the night sleeping on the ground, without fear of predators. The new behaviour towards fire led to a shift in the balance of power between hominins or humans and all other large animals. The ensuing differentiation of behaviour and power reinforced the commitment of hominins and humans to fire and fuel. From its very start, the species monopoly was a precious and costly privilege.

Phaseology and chronology

The previous section is written from the perspective of phaseology rather than chronology. Chronology has the great advantage of providing us with a fixed grid of years and centuries marked by regular intervals. As such it is an excellent instrument for locating events in time. But strictly speaking it only allows us to arrange those events in a scheme of what came earlier or later, in the 'one damned thing after another' mode. Thinking in terms of phases has the advantage of being based on a certain logic, the logic of sequences. As pointed out above in the section 'Phases', there is an irrefutable logic in the statement that a phase 3, when *all* human groups had fire was preceded by a phase 2, when *some* groups had fire, and that phase again was preceded by a phase 1, when there were *no* groups with fire.

According to her own estimate, Burton's scenario of phases covers a period from about 8 to 3 million years ago. Wrangham dates the origins of cooking on the basis of palaeo-anatomical finds at between 1.9 and 1.8 million years ago. Archaeologists, who generally prefer to use traces of human activity as the basis of their evidence, make more modest estimates. Until recently they were prepared to accept finds from 250,000 years ago as their oldest reliable evidence for active human fire use; all claims about more ancient evidence were rejected as unproven.

The tide is turning, however. There have been finds in Israel (at Gesher Benot Yaáqov) and in South Africa (at Wonderwerk Cave) pointing to active use of fire at least 800,000 years ago.[14] If it is possible to stretch the chronology so far, there is much to be said for assuming a far longer, and fuzzier, phase of transition when groups of hominins sometimes lived with fire for a while, until that was extinguished, and they had to return to living without fire, for we can only guess how long. Meanwhile, they also acquired greater dexterity in 'clearing land', by setting fire to the undergrowth of forests every so often, thus extending the territory they could safely use for hunting and gathering food. In these various

14 Chris Stringer, *The Origin of Our Species* (London: Allen Lane, 2011).

ways, the incipient human-controlled fire regime gave a wider scope to the human domain, the 'anthroposphere', in the overall biosphere.

Agrarianization: the formation and expansion of agrarian regimes

Fire in the agrarian regime: continuities

Human history over the past ten thousand years may be read as a series of events and trends accompanying agrarianization – a dominant socio-ecological process in the course of which humans extended the domain of agriculture and animal husbandry all over the inhabited world, and in so doing made themselves increasingly dependent upon their cultivated plants and domesticated animals as continuously available living energy sources.

Just as we can use the term 'fire regime' in both the singular and the plural forms, we can also refer to 'the agrarian regime' in the singular as well as to 'agrarian regimes' in the plural to indicate the particular forms this regime took in different parts of the world at different times. No two agrarian regimes were identical, and they were all subject to change; and yet they shared some typical features that justify also using 'agrarian regime' in the singular form as a generic concept encompassing them all.

The core of every agrarian regime was raising food; fire was an important means for this end, a link in the complex chain of activities that led to food production. It was widely used for 'clearing' pieces of land and turning them into fields where crops could grow or cattle graze. The existing vegetation, be it grass or bush or forest, would be burned down, and the ground, fertilized by the ashes, could then be used for growing selected species that would – as we now know – turn solar light into edible plant material.

Especially when the clearing job was done in a pristine forest, the removal of full-grown trees must have been a very laborious task that could only be carried out by first slashing off the branches with stone axes in order to kill the tree, and then, when it was dead and dry, burning the remaining trunk.

The technique of 'slash and burn', also known by other names such as 'shifting cultivation', was taken over from practices developed by foragers in order to make land more transparent and accessible to hunters. It was one of the clear continuities between the fire regime and the agrarian regime, and not the only one.

Agrarian regimes absorbed and elaborated several basic habits and skills that were engrained in human societies through their investments in learning to live with fire. It is hard to imagine how people could have begun cultivating plants and taming animals had the control over fire not already prepared them for a life in which conscious care for something non-human was taken for granted. The first crops grown on any large scale were cereals and tubers which, because of their nutritional value and their capacity to withstand storage for long periods, provided appropriate staple food for a human community; but to serve this purpose, they needed to be cooked. This in itself made fire and fuel indispensable for agrarian communities.

The same can be said about the human predominance over all other land mammals, initially secured with the aid of fire. By the time agrarianization began, the human monopoly over fire was so firmly established (and at present it is so easily taken for granted), that it is seldom given separate attention in this context. Yet it certainly was a necessary condition. Their hegemonic position in the animal kingdom enabled people not only to bring certain species, such as goats and sheep, under direct control, but also to keep most of the remaining 'wild' animals away from their crops and herds.

But no doubt the most spectacular use of fire in the agrarian economy was the practice of 'slash and burn', in which patches of abandoned cropland would be prepared for renewed cultivation by burning down the saplings and grasses that had meanwhile sprung up. The land was then sown with new crop seeds for one or more seasons, to be left fallow again when the harvest was no longer rewarding and the farmers turned to an adjacent lot. Eventually they would return to the first lot that by then was overgrown by bushes and trees, and start the entire cycle anew.

In modern times, the practice of 'slash and burn' was still common in large parts of the non-industrialized world. Urban visitors often frowned upon it as 'primitive', without realizing that in its initial stage 'slash and burn' repre-sented an important step in the collective learning of land management – a major breakthrough in which the destructive effects of fire were put to use in a longer-term ecological strategy. But it cannot be denied that this strategy sometimes caused serious air pollution and was always wasteful of fuel.

Beyond slash and burn

Agrarianization proceeded differently in different parts of the world. Yet, if we look at the world in its entirety, from a very long-term historical perspective, we can observe a clear dominant trend. In the preceding phase, human groups with fire had survived, whereas groups without fire had not. Now, for a period of at least the past 10,000 years, there was a similarly dominant tendency, not only for groups with agriculture to supersede groups without it, but later on also for groups with more intensive agriculture to supersede groups that stuck to more extensive agriculture.

This overall trend implied further differentiation. Just as the previous era had been marked by the increasing differentiation in behaviour and power between human groups and other animals, the agrarian era was marked likewise by increasing differentiation, again in both behaviour and power, not just vis-à-vis other animals, but also, and especially, among and within human societies.

In several parts of the world, where conditions turned out to be favourable for agrarian production, people began to cultivate the land more intensively, with newly invented methods such as irrigation and ploughing, so that, in a positive loop of economic and demographic changes, harvests became more plentiful and the population grew in numbers. This unleashed several other social processes. More and more people gave up their (semi-)nomadic existence and settled down in villages and towns. As these settlements grew in size, they offered opportunities for some people to specialize in other occupations than farming or herding. The ensuing differentiation of behaviour also led to differentiation of power, between and within occupational groups – a process of social stratification that often resulted in the formation of rigid hierarchies of classes or castes.[15]

Fire was so much a part of agrarian society that each of these trends also affected the ways it was used and appreciated. Being no longer the only non-human source of energy that had been brought under human control, fire also ceased to be the focus of group life it had been for thousands of generations; instead, it became increasingly dispersed over all sorts of separate hearths, braziers, ovens, and lamps, each with their own instrumental functions. Whereas, during the earlier phase, people were primarily concerned to keep the communal fire burning, now the very opposite issue became most pressing: how to prevent the many fires burning for various purposes from running out of control and causing a blaze.

The great majority of people in advanced agrarian societies continued to be peasants. They fulfilled a clear function: they grew the food. Almost paradoxically, this same self-evident function also kept most of them and their families in poverty, often not far above the level of starvation. They were tied to the land they had to till, and when the produce of land and labour had been harvested, they were tied to their harvests.

---

15 Johan Goudsblom, Eric Jones, and Stephen Mennell, *The Course of Human History. Economic Growth, Social Process, and Civilization* (Armonk, NY: M. E. Sharpe, 1996).

This state of dependency made them permanently vulnerable, to crop failure and to theft and robbery, and even to sheer destruction by fire. Their vulnerability to acts of human violence became increasingly troubling, when groups of bandits acquired weapons made of bronze and, later, iron, and learned to raise and command bands of men specializing in raiding. For a long time the only way peasants could protect themselves against irregular invasions by bands of warriors appeared to be by submitting themselves to a more regular relationship of authority and serfdom to other warriors.

This kind of arrangement was the crux of the military-agrarian societies that, at different moments in time, emerged on every continent. The central parts were always played by the peasants, the 'agrarians' who formed the vast majority, and by minorities of warriors, the 'military'. There were others partaking in this social configuration as well; a central function was performed by smiths – specialists in working with fire.

In agrarian societies ruled by warrior elites, the majority of peasants and the far fewer smiths found themselves in the same plight. In order to pursue the productive activities on which their social existence hinged both groups needed warriors – to protect them from other warriors. Just as the peasants supplied the rulers with food, the smiths, in addition to forging ploughs and other implements facilitating food production, supplied them with weapons. This simple statement brings out the importance of the social function of smiths as well as the structural weakness of their position. Their mastery over fire and metal was acknowledged and much needed; but they lacked mastery over people. They had to submit to the very social hierarchy that they sustained with their work.

Fire in cities

As cities in the agrarian world increased in number and size, more, and more diverse fires were kept burning within their walls, generating increasingly complex problems having to do with air pollution, the prevention and suppression of blazes, and fuel supply.

Air pollution was a regular source of complaints, expressed most vociferously by those who had the best chances of escaping from it, the privileged rich. As early as 1257 the foul-smelling smoke of coal fire, penetrating everywhere and spreading thick layers of soot, was said to have driven Eleanor, the Queen consort of England, out of London.

Prevention of conflagrations has been a concern of city dwellers, and city governments in particular, ever since towns or cities first emerged. One of the oldest recorded ordinances is from Hattusa, the capital of the Hittites from about 1650 to 1200 BCE. Temple servants were instructed to be very cautious with fire; negligence in this respect was considered a crime for which not just the culprit but also his descendants and his colleagues would be punished by death. 'So', the decree ended ominously, 'for your own good be very careful in the matter of fire'.[16] Caution with fire was thus presented as a social duty, an obligation to the community at large, with sanctions so severe that every person would accept it 'for his own good'.

Throughout antiquity and the Middle Ages big cities such as Rome and Constantinople were notorious for the blazes that every so often ravaged whole districts. Once a fire broke out, there was little the inhabitants could do to suppress it; water, sand, and prayer were said to be equally (in)effective. Usually water and sand were available only in very small quantities, which were carried to the blaze in buckets and then thrown onto it. The only way to protect neighbouring houses was by covering the roofs with wet cloth. If the conflagration was too great, the last remaining measure was to create a 'firebreak' by tearing down buildings that were standing in the fire's way.

Every city, large or small, was a concentration of people, combustible property, and fires. Since the means of fighting a fire once it was raging were so limited, strong emphasis was put on prevention. Town governments in medieval Europe regularly issued measures directed at all citizens but especially at craftsmen working with fire (as many of them did). The regulations about using fire in an urban setting were always local; but since the citizens in different towns learned from each other, the actual rules were remarkably similar. The general purport was to turn cities into 'fire-protected zones', where the use of fire was permitted only within specifically designated confines, and great restrictions were put on using fire after sunset, when 'curfew' time began. In all medieval cities, the gates were then closed, and night watches guarded against accidental fires and arson. From the sixteenth century onward, one city government after another prohibited using wood and thatch as construction material for exterior walls and roofs.

The plethora of preventive measures, especially those prescribing brick and stone as construction material, probably gave town dwellers better protection than country folk against blazes. In some rural regions, there were spells when threats of fire setting were uttered as a 'weapon of the weak', and were actually carried out against the houses of rich estate owners as well as in internecine feuds among peasants.[17]

---

16 For this and other unreferenced quotations, see Goudsblom, *Fire and Civilization*.
17 Cathy A. Frierson, *All Russia is Burning! A Cultural History of Fire and Arson in Late Imperial Russia* (Seattle: University of Washington Press, 2002).

The worst fate that could befall a city was when, during a war, the city had been under siege and had offered resistance. If it then had to capitulate, it ran the risk of being 'sacked and burned': all houses would be looted, and as a final act of triumph the conquerors would set the whole city on fire.

The many precautions normally surrounding the use of fire in cities inevitably reminded people that fire kept burning for domestic or commercial purposes was an 'expensive institution', risky and costly. The most immediately felt costs were those involving the purchase of fuel. Cities could not possibly be self-supporting in this respect; they needed a continuous import of wood, for both timber and fuel. This was an important reason for building urban settlements on the banks of a river, where wood could be brought in from upstream. As cities became larger, the demand for wood often led to deforestation in the surroundings. Complaints about depletion of woods were already recorded in ancient Greece and Rome, and even earlier in China. After the demise of the Western Roman empire, the trend in that part of the world was temporarily reversed: human numbers shrank and forests regained ground; but soon after the beginning of the second millennium, people began making inroads again in the rejuvenated forests. By the middle of the seventeenth century, in some of the most densely populated parts of Western Europe, especially Britain and Holland, hardly any forests survived, and most of the wood had to be imported from Scandinavia and the Baltics.

Fire and industrialization

The subterranean forest

Just as human history over the past 10,000 years has been the history of the agrarianization of the world, the history over the past 250 years has been the history of industrialization. In the process, the anthroposphere has become one global constellation extending all over the planet, and its impact on the biosphere has become increasingly intense.

The term 'industrialization' refers to the rise and spread of a new socioecological regime – the industrial regime, following the fire regime and the agrarian regime. It did not put an end to the older regimes. On the contrary, new applications of fire lay at the very core of industrialization: using fossil fuel to generate steam power and to smelt and refine iron. The smokestacks of the coal and iron industries and the red glow of furnaces at night became the icons of early industrialization.

There were also close connections with agriculture. Agrarian production had to provide a subsistence base for all workers employed in the mines and factories. Moreover, as soon as industrialization came to include the production of textiles and foodstuffs, the raw materials had to be supplied by farming. In return, factories started generating means of production for agriculture: first simple iron tools, then more complex new mechanized implements, and then, in the twentieth century, various types of combustion-driven machines and factory-made fertilizers and pesticides. By the end of that century, agriculture and industry in many parts of the world had become inseparable and often even barely distinguishable parts of an 'agro-industrial complex' that leaned heavily on the use of fossil fuels.

The primary effect of industrialization was to make immense supplies of fossil energy available that had lain virtually unused by any living species. In the eighteenth century, a series of inventions (in other words, innovations in the field of information) opened the possibility of tapping these supplies and using them to generate heat and mechanical motion. Similar to the way early humans had strengthened their position in the biosphere by learning to control the burning of wood and other organic material, their descendants now learned the art of using fire to exploit the energy contained in coal, oil, and gas.

Seen from a world historical perspective, these developments concerned humanity at large. But at closer quarters it was only a tiny section of humanity that took the lead and was the first to profit. A small entrepreneurial class in Britain had the advantage of being the pioneers of industrialization.

Industrialization started with single steam-powered factories – often called 'mills' like their predecessors which were driven by wind or water – standing apart in the agrarian landscape, and forming, as suggested by the environmental historian Rolf Peter Sieferle, 'industrial archipelagos'.[18] But from the very start, these 'islands' were enveloped in a much wider context. Industrialization was preceded by European overseas expansion, which gave a strong impetus to the process. British society in the eighteenth century was connected in many ways to a larger world: not just to the European continent but also to other continents. It had a strong navy and a large commercial fleet; trade with other continents (including the slave trade) brought in considerable wealth, while emigration across the Atlantic helped to relieve population pressures. The ensemble of these military, political, and economic relationships provided a robust infrastructure for the burgeoning

18 Sieferle, *Subterranean Forest.*

industries, guaranteeing protected access to a worldwide array of resources and markets.

The basis of industrialization was, literally, coal. As a fuel, coal had been used before, in ancient China and in medieval England, but that was always coal found at or near the surface of the earth, and its burning qualities were generally considered inferior to those of wood. Better coal was practically impossible to mine because it lay too deep, and the galleries dug to reach it were always in danger of being flooded by groundwater. In eighteenth-century Britain, a rapid succession of inventions improving the efficiency of steam engines made it possible to get rid of the water by pumping it up. While the steam engines made coal mines accessible, the coal thus gained served as fuel for the steam engines – a positive loop effect. Soon afterwards railways developed, and the trains, drawn by steam locomotives, joined the same configuration of mechanical forces by which coal could be extracted, distributed, and applied for the industrial production of goods, ranging from iron and steel instruments to textiles and canned food. In this configuration, the energy delivered by steam engines was not a single independent cause, but an essential link, just as fire had once been an essential link in the changing balance of power between humans and other animals in the early Stone Age.

When people began exploiting the enormous stores of solar energy contained in coal, they entered, in Sieferle's telling image, a 'subterranean forest' of huge dimensions that, in many decades to come, turned out to be even more abundant than originally expected. Compared to the somatic energy of humans and their domesticated animals, the amount of energy now available for manufacturing and traction, whether measured in units of horse power, kilowatts, calories, or megajoules, was tremendous (see Table 8.1).[19]

The 'energy bonanza' has resulted in unprecedented technological development and economic growth. Although these processes affect the entire world population, the benefits are not equally shared by all; thus, as Weissenbacher notes, some 2.5 billion people still depend on traditional biomass as their main fuel for cooking.[20] Fire also continues to show its Janus face: its destructive power is used for highly diverse productive applications, but also for deliberate destruction in war.

19 Ian Morris, *The Measure of Civilization: How Social Development Decides the Fate of Nations* (Princeton, NJ: Princeton University Press, 2013).
20 Morris, *Measure of Civilization*, and Weissenbacher, *Sources of Power*.

Table 8.1 *Global estimates of population (in millions) and energy use (GJ/capita)*

Year	Population (million)	Energy use (GJ/capita)
5000 BP	20	<3
0	200	<5
1000	300	<10
1800	900	23
1900	1,600	27
2000	6,100	75
2010	6,900	75

Note: Table from Smil, *Harvesting the Biosphere*, p. 222.

The worst carnages by fire in human history were brought about in interstate wars in the twentieth century. In the Second World War, the bombing of cities from the air resulted in the most fatal cases in firestorms killing tens of thousands of people at a time. Even in the attacks with atomic bombs on Hiroshima and Nagasaki in 1945, the greatest number of direct casualties and the most massive destruction of buildings were not caused by nuclear radiation but by the fires that immediately broke out.[21] In the second half of the century new techniques of incendiarism from the air were tried out in regional wars in Vietnam, Iraq, and elsewhere; widely published photos and films made the horrendous effects visible to worldwide audiences.

Maybe because of its impact on television screens, fire became an increasingly popular means for public display of discontent. Burning flags were often a first sign of political unrest, which could easily pass into burning tyres and more highly valued property, from cars to buildings. In protests against state authorities, collective arson served as a 'weapon of the weak'. As such it could take on big proportions, as in the devastating attacks on the World Trade Center in New York on 11 September 2001, with over 2,600 casualties – almost all of them victims of the fires that were ignited by the attacks.

Fire brigades were helpless against the largest conflagrations. But they too have benefited greatly from technological innovations. Moreover, in prosperous countries building regulations have resulted in a considerable reduction of urban blazes; the largest conflagrations occur on industrial premises. In residential areas there are far fewer open fires than in the initial stage of industrialization, and citizens can normally be assured of living in a highly fire-protected zone.

21 Lynn Eden, *Whole World on Fire: Organizations, Knowledge, and Nuclear Weapons Devastation* (Ithaca, NY: Cornell University Press, 2004).

Electrification and the eclipse of fire

Historians sometimes make a distinction between two major eras of industrialization. The first era was marked by the exploitation of coal, the second one by increasing reliance on oil and, as an indirect source of energy, electricity.

In contrast to coal and oil, the electricity that is now used almost everywhere (in many places only in the form of batteries) is not an autonomous source of energy. It is a carrier of energy that has been generated elsewhere, in power stations, some of which are driven by wind or water, but the vast majority of which operate by burning fuel – coal, oil, gas, or biomass. In the resulting energy all traces of fire have been eliminated; it arrives, ready for use, in a superbly 'clean' and 'cool' guise, noiseless and odour free, and ready for use in practically any application that human ingenuity has contrived, from the primeval functions of heating and lighting to such sophisticated purposes as refrigerating and computing. Some applications seem so far removed from the original energy source that people using them may not even realize that they are consuming energy. Thus, when surfing the Internet, they may be aware that their own computer is fuelled by electricity, but fail to acknowledge that the same is true of the servers sustaining the World Wide Web of Information.

Nor do they have to stop and think about the fact that most of the objects surrounding them in their daily lives have been produced with the aid of fire. Usually those objects do not show the slightest trace of any fire episode in either the production process or the necessary transport from factory to warehouse to the final destination in a 'fire-free' office or private house. Fire is rarely visible because it has been replaced at the consumers' end by electricity. The situation resembles a Cinderella effect: electricity is generated in a secluded place where visitors do not come, but is openly appreciated and welcomed at the receiving end.

The apparent eclipse of fire is reflected in its changing images in public life and in the sciences.

Changing images of fire and fuel

Looking back in time once again, we may reasonably assume that our early ancestors were prone to see fire as a living being, and to attribute good or evil intentions to it. When, in a far later phase, some people began leaving written records, they included pictograms of fire, in which we can recognize a clear distinction between 'good' (tamed) fire and 'bad' (wild) fire.

In a still later phase, philosophers began to formulate ideas about the elements out of which the world was composed. Some of those philosophers were prepared to regard the elements as 'given', without necessarily classifying them as good or bad. Thus Heraclitus declared that fire was the primeval element from which everything in the world had sprung, without passing judgement. Another doctrine, which eventually became dominant, postulated not one but four elements out of which the world was composed: earth, water, air, and fire. In ancient China and India similar systems of thought were developed and elaborated. With only minor modifications the worldview in which fire constituted one of the major elements remained generally accepted in natural philosophy and medicine well into the modern era.

In the eighteenth century, some leading European intellectuals rejected this scheme as incompatible with the outcome of scientific experiments and only giving rise to futile speculations. Chemists extended the number of elements to many dozens, but they no longer included fire. The invention of the steam engine temporarily aroused a revival of scientific interest in fire in the field of thermodynamics. But that interest waned, and thermodynamics lost its central place in the natural sciences.

Except for narrowly defined technological research directed at fire prevention and fire fighting, the very concept of fire disappeared from scientific discourse, to be replaced by the far more abstract concept of 'energy' – signifying a potential force that could not be directly seen, heard, smelled, or felt but could only be perceived in its effects.

The career of the subject of fire in science ran remarkably parallel to its virtual disappearance from both public and private view in everyday life. As noted in the previous section, while combustion continued to be used on an ever larger scale, it also became increasingly unwelcome. In the form in which people like to receive most of their extra-somatic energy, they prefer not to notice any traces of combustion.

Yet, while fire has indeed been eclipsed in scientific discourse and become hardly noticeable in daily life, it continues to be an essential ingredient of the human universe, the anthroposphere. It is omnipresent in industrialized society, even if the flames and smoke are hidden from view and smell. Fire and fuel continue to be indispensable in the production and distribution of almost all the food we eat and all the objects we handle, but we generally disregard this fact. Electricity has become the ubiquitous intermediary between fire as a source of energy and ourselves, as we use it for heating and cooling, for production and destruction, for transport and communication.

When thinking of fire, our associations tend to be mainly negative. Fire is dangerous, and fuel is dirty – this seems to be the prevailing sentiment, which is not easily reconciled with the fact that by far the greatest bulk of the electricity that is so highly valued is generated in power stations powered by fuel. Although the actual estimates vary, it is generally known that the remaining supplies of fossil fuels are finite and, moreover, that burning them in such huge quantities as we do may cause irreparable damage to the entire biosphere. Since we live on a planet that is regularly visited by lightning and dotted with volcanoes we shall never be able to abolish fire. But our present burning practices will have to come to an end.

If we wish the global trend to electrification to continue, we will have to sever our bondage to fire and fuel. Currently, the generation of electricity produces more greenhouse emissions than any other industry.[22] The actual energy yields are spent inefficiently: far more energy is spent in producing, transporting, and preparing our food than we actually take in by eating.[23] If these observations are correct (as I think they are), they imply that the present socio-ecological regime will have to be succeeded by a new regime, which will incorporate parts of the fire regime, the agrarian regime, and the industrial regime, but will also differ radically from its predecessors.

Coda

We humans are unable to predict the future, and we always will be. With an appeal to this observation that, like so many paradoxes, is only seemingly paradoxical, I shall end this chapter with a brief speculation. We have today a rapidly developing World Wide Web of Information, which was never planned as such, but is the unforeseen result of a multitude of planned human actions and interactions. Reflecting about a possible scenario for a next stage in the history of human use of fire and fuel, it seems reasonable to suppose that, unless very drastic changes happen, we will continue to need large supplies of extra-somatic energy, probably even a great deal larger than today. We shall have to restrain our habitual tendency to rely on fire and fuel; instead, we may turn our efforts to a more direct and efficient use of sunlight than we have been able to achieve until now. If technologists could succeed in meeting this challenge, they could help build a World Wide Web of Energy, connecting the Northern and Southern as well as the Eastern and

22 Weissenbacher, *Sources of Power*, p. 717. 23 See Smil, *Harvesting the Biosphere*.

Western hemispheres, creating a network in which it would always be summer and the sun would never set.

FURTHER READING

Bankoff, Greg, Uwe Lübken, and Jordan Sand (eds.), *Flammable Cities: Urban Conflagration and the Making of the Modern World*, Madison: University of Wisconsin Press, 2012.

Buckminster Fuller, R., *Critical Path*, New York: St. Martin's Press, 1982.

Burton, Frances D., *Fire: The Spark that Ignited Human Evolution*, Tucson: University of Arizona Press, 2009.

Christian, David, *Maps of Time: An Introduction to Big History*, Berkeley: University of California Press, 2004.

Davis, Mike, *Planet of Slums*, London: Verso, 2004.

Eden, Lynn, *Whole World on Fire: Organizations, Knowledge, and Nuclear Weapons Devastation*, Ithaca, NY: Cornell University Press, 2004.

Elias, Norbert, *The Process of Civilization: Sociogenetic and Psychogenetic Investigations*, Dublin: University College Dublin Press, 2012, vol. iii.

What Is Sociology?, Dublin: University College Dublin Press, 2006, vol. v.

Frazer, James George, *Myths of the Origin of Fire*, London: Macmillan, 1930.

Frierson, Cathy A., *All Russia is Burning! A Cultural History of Fire and Arson in Late Imperial Russia*, Seattle: University of Washington Press, 2002.

Goudsblom, Johan, *Fire and Civilization*, London: Allen Lane, 1992.

Goudsblom, Johan, and Bert de Vries (eds.), *Mappae Mundi: Humans and their Habitats in a Long-Term Socio-ecological Perspective*, Amsterdam: Amsterdam University Press, 2002.

Goudsblom, Johan, Eric L. Jones, and Stephen Mennell, *The Course of Human History: Economic Growth, Social Process, and Civilization*, Armonk, NY: M. E. Sharpe, 1996.

Harris, Marvin, *The Rise of Anthropological Theory: A History of Theories of Culture*, New York: Harper & Row, 1968.

Morris, Ian, *The Measure of Civilization: How Social Development Decides the Fate of Nations*, Princeton, NJ: Princeton University Press, 2013.

Niele, Frank, *Energy: Engine of Evolution*, Amsterdam: Elsevier, 2005.

Pyne, Stephen J., *Fire: A Brief History*, Seattle: University of Washington Press, 2001.

Sieferle, Rolf Peter, *The Subterranean Forest: Energy Systems and the Industrial Revolution*, Cambridge: The White Horse Press, 2001.

Smil, Vaclav, *Harvesting the Biosphere: What We Have Taken From Nature*, Cambridge: The MIT Press, 2012.

Stringer, Chris, *The Origin of Our Species*, London: Allen Lane, 2011.

Weissenbacher, Manfred, *Sources of Power: How Energy Forges Human History*, 2 vols., Santa Barbara, CA: Praeger, 2009.

Westbroek, Pieter, *Life as a Geological Force*, Berkeley: University of California Press, 1991.

Wrangham, Richard, *Catching Fire: How Cooking Made us Human*, New York: Basic Books, 2009.

Yergin, Daniel, *The Quest: Energy, Security, and the Remaking of the Modern World*, New York: Penguin Press, 2011.

9

Family history and world history:
from domestication to biopolitics

MARY JO MAYNES AND ANN WALTNER

Two concepts that are helpful in making connections between the history of the family and global history are "domestication" and "biopolitics." *Domestication* most often comes up in global histories as the process whereby humans asserted increasing control over the natural world in the era of the post-Ice Age "Neolithic Revolution," which began around 10,000 BCE. Control over animal species through herding and over plant species through agriculture assured a steadier, if not necessarily better, average diet; settlement and civilization followed. More recent work by feminist archaeologists and social archaeologists has broadened the notion of domestication to call attention to the "domus" – the cultural invention of *human* domestic life – that was essential to early human societies.

According to Ian Hodder, "interest in control over nature was not new in the Neolithic. But the focus of this interest was newly located in the 'domus'."[1] In this revision, human domestic life becomes a motor of early human history. Again according to Hodder: "the domus was not only the metaphor for change. It was also the mechanism of change, and it was through this dual role that what we normally talk about today as domestication and the origins of agriculture in the Middle East came about."[2] Clive Gamble argues that domestication was most significant in terms of its impact on human cognition and culture, which in turn grew from and with new patterns of child nurturance in the context of domestic group life. Indeed "the world's earliest village communities were also the first to develop fully modern minds and a fully symbolic culture."[3]

---

[1] Ian Hodder, *The Domestication of Europe: Structure and Contingency in Neolithic Societies* (Cambridge, MA: Blackwell, 1990), p. 41.
[2] Hodder, *Domestication of Europe*, p. 41.
[3] Trevor Watkins as cited in Clive Gamble, *Origins and Revolutions: Human Identity in Earliest Prehistory* (Cambridge: Cambridge University Press, 2007), pp. 30–1.

Expanding the concept of domestication to include not only the adoption of agriculture and animal husbandry, but also and more importantly the cognitive, social, and cultural processes that characterized early human settlement, has sparked exciting new research linking family history with the history of early human societies. The domestic realm has continued to be a site of history ever since the Neolithic, even as its nature has evolved historically. Reconsidering global history from this perspective highlights various and important connections between domestic and family-historical dynamics, on the one hand, and global-historical dynamics, on the other. The exercise and transmission of political power through dynastic inheritance, the creation of global business networks that relied on ties of intimacy and trust based in merchant "houses," the various forms of intimate domestic relations that were always a critical element of imperial control, the place of household labor organization in both agricultural and industrial economies, the use of laws and norms to regulate aspects of family in the name of the state or the cause – all of these are examples of close connections between family and global history.

The nature of *biopolitics* – the state exercise of control over the bodies of its population – has also shifted over time. When Michel Foucault defined bio-power, he indeed had modern Western states in mind:

> By [bio-power] I mean a number of phenomena that seem to me to be quite significant, namely, the set of mechanisms through which the basic biological features of the human species became the object of a political strategy, of a general strategy of power, or, in other words, how, starting from the eighteenth century, modern Western societies took on board the fundamental biological fact that human beings are a species.[4]

Techniques of rule thus expanded to include routine demographic measures and projections such as fertility rates or measurements of a population's health such as accident or STD rates.

Foucault argued that biopolitics in this sense is a modern invention, but it had its precedents. Although Foucault suggested that earlier state strategies focusing on the realm of the family and reproduction etc. relied on techniques of control over individuals rather than over "populations," thinking backwards from biopolitics also allows us to see important connections between the family and global history. A large proportion of the provisions

---

4 Michel Foucault, *Security, Territory, Population: Lectures at the Collège de France 1977–1978* (Lectures at the Collège de France), Graham Burchell (trans.) (New York: Picador, 2009), p. 1.

of the earliest known legal codes focused on family matters – who might marry whom, what sorts of transactions accompanied marriage, who could claim inheritance, and so forth. In imperial settings across time rulers paid careful attention to sexual relations and reproduction well ahead of specific notions of race or "population growth." And of course once we enter into the temporal regime of biopolitics proper, such interventions have multiplied. In the contemporary world, biopolitical programs have become standard techniques of rule.

Family, domestication, and human origins

Family relations have long played a role in accounts of human origins, but those accounts have been changing over the last several decades. Until the 1970s, most scholarly and popular accounts of early human society featured "Man the Hunter": according to this view, relationships among men – both cooperative and competitive – drove human development. Men organized the hunt and the production of the stone weapons it required; relationships around hunting and tool making contributed to the evolution of human social organization and culture. Men also competed – for territory and for mates. Heterosexual pair bonding was the basis of a tacit exchange: men supplied most of the food that allowed women to focus on bearing and nurturing children. According to this theory, the role of women was largely restricted to reproduction and reproduction was understood primarily in biological rather than cultural terms. Domestic life was not the focus of much scholarly concern since crucial evolutionary developments happened elsewhere.

Beginning in the 1970s, the feminist revision of the "Man the Hunter" thesis opened up new possibilities for thinking about family, gender relations, and the role of domestic life in human evolution. It has now become clear that archaeological evidence can support a very different view of human origins. Newer views agree that early human societies relied on gender divisions of labor but women were involved in production (especially foraging for food) as well as reproduction. Family or household dynamics figured into processes of transition from nomadic hunting and gathering to settled agrarian societies. Although the evidence is sketchy, it seems possible that a transition to agriculture may have been facilitated in some areas by intermarriages between groups who based their livelihoods on different ecologies. In Neolithic East Africa there is evidence of complementary cross-marriages between nomadic men and hunter-gatherer women, although other patterns of gender complementarity can also be found.[5] Similarly, Ruth Whitehouse argues that bone analysis of Bronze Age sites in Italy suggests gender-specific patterns of migration possibly related to intermarriage between "colonizing male farmers and indigenous hunter-gatherer women."[6] Moreover, apparently cooperative divisions of labor, often organized along gender lines and based around small co-residential groups, are reflected in evidence about diet at some early settlement sites. For example, the distribution of artifacts at sites in the valley of the Nile dating from around the ninth millennium BCE suggests that women in particular were involved with specific activities linked to agriculture and pottery making (useful for storage vessels at permanent domestic sites).[7] Specific family or kinship relations in co-resident groups can only be surmised on the basis of such evidence, but now DNA analysis promises to illuminate the role of kinship in early human settlement with somewhat more precision.

Moreover, recent investigations have been more attuned to the household and kin group as sites of human development and to women's domestic activities – including child socialization – as essential to human evolution. The manifestation of complex cognitive abilities is a hallmark of human evolution. Daniel Smail has argued that the human brain "did not evolve to solve the relatively simple problem associated with tool use, much less the problems posed by the hunt. Instead, the large human brain evolved over the past 1.7 million years to allow individuals to negotiate the escalating complexities posed by human social living."[8] However, archaeological evidence of this gradual evolution in the deep past is elusive; the traces that survive require new approaches to interpretation. Feminist archaeologist Diane Bolger points to "innovative research on the use of art and symbolism in the construction of early human social identities." Bolger identifies two quite different and widely separated periods when there is evidence of accelerated development of symbolic expression – the first beginning around 80,000 or more years ago – which saw what she terms a "creative explosion" among early sapient populations during the Upper Paleolithic

5 Diane Lyons, "A critical appraisal of gender research in African archaeology," in Sarah Milledge Nelson (ed.), *Worlds of Gender: The Archaeology of Women's Lives around the Globe* (Lanham, MD: AltaMira, 2007), pp. 12–13.
6 Ruth Whitehouse, "Gender archaeology in Europe," in Nelson (ed.), *Worlds of Gender*, p. 150.
7 Lyons, "Gender in African archaeology," pp. 12–13.
8 Daniel Lord Smail, *On Deep History and the Brain* (Berkeley: University of California Press, 2008), pp. 112–13.

period, and, the second, associated with post-Ice Age domestication, about 12,000 years ago.[9]

The focus of recent work by social archaeologists on early child nurturance is of special interest for making connections between family history and the development of early human societies. Evidence about the material, social, and cultural environment of the domestic setting can be read for its implications about cognitive abilities. These interpretations in turn are suggestive of the early childhood experiences that are key to the acquisition of cognitive skills and also to the construction of social relationships. In *Origins and Revolutions: Human Identity in Earliest Prehistory*, Clive Gamble tracks the gradual and long history during which hominid social and cognitive potentials were manifested. He begins his account in the remote hominid past, long before the invention of language. His tactics rely much on inferences around the concept of the "childscape" – "[t]he material project of growing children needs to be investigated at two interlocking scales, the locale and the landscape that together I refer to as the childscape: the environment for growth."[10] His focus is on the learning of social skills and cognitive maps by children. He calls for a way to make children "visible" that parallels the way that gender analysis made women visible to archaeologists.

Gamble argues that childscapes developed over a series of slow transformations of hominid spaces that structured the environment for growth. Very early on, around 100,000 BCE, *Homo sapien* societies show evidence of significant human cognitive developments rooted in early childhood nurturance and cultural transmission.[11] Child nurturance takes on a new prominence during the epoch of domestication (in Gamble's scheme *c.* 20,000 to 6,000 years ago). Gamble argues that domestication changed the world most significantly not in the usual sense of villages, crops, and gods and goddesses, but rather in terms of a new emphasis on the domestic nurturance of children.[12]

Ian Hodder uses the concept of "childscape" in his interpretation of evidence at Çatalhöyük, in Turkey, an unusually well-preserved early agricultural settlement that housed between 3,000 and 8,000 people around 7000 BCE. In Çatalhöyük kinship and household served as important organizing principles in the transition to agricultural settlement. Everyday life centered

9 Diane Bolger, "Gender and human evolution," in Sarah Milledge Nelson (ed.), *Handbook of Gender in Archaeology* (Lanham, MD: AltaMira, 2006), pp. 487–8.
10 Gamble, *Origins and Revolutions*, p. 228. 11 Gamble, *Origins and Revolutions*, p. 240.
12 Gamble, *Origins and Revolutions*, p. 206.

Figure 9.1 Reconstruction of a house at Çatalhöyük (© Mauricio Abreu/JAI/Corbis).

on the household. Residential buildings, which were filled in and rebuilt periodically, housed a domestic group of five to ten people. As Hodder explains:

> A child growing up in such a household would soon learn how the space was organized – where to bury the dead and where to make beads, where to find the obsidian cache and where to place offerings. Eventually, he or she would learn how to rebuild the house itself. Thus the rules of this complex urban society were transferred without centralized control, through the daily practices of the household. All those practices were carried out in the presence of dead ancestors and within a symbolic world immediately at hand, conveyed through rich artistic representation.[13]

Expanding domestication to include social and cultural processes that characterized early human societies has sparked exciting new research questions and findings. Going beyond what's "written in stone" has allowed feminist and social archaeologists to examine questions about the evolution of human skills, especially cognitive skills, beyond organizing the hunt. Early human

13 Ian Hodder, "This old house," *Natural History* (2006), accessed March 6, 2013, www.naturalhistorymag.com/htmlsite/0606/0606_feature.html.

settlement sites like Çatalhöyük are important for making visible the household dynamics and domestic activities critical for early agricultural societies. At Çatalhöyük the household was *the* unit of social organization; there is no evidence of a central government or higher political authority in the complex settlement.

To offer a second example of early domestication in the absence of larger political structures, the Yangshao culture (5000–3000 BCE) consisted of a series of small agricultural villages in river valleys in northern China. Yangshao farmers grew grains and domesticated animals such as pigs. The villages were built around a central plaza; residential buildings clustered around the plaza; and workspaces and burial grounds were located further from the center. Archaeologists deduce notions about kinship and social organization from the evidence of burial sites. Farm tools such as hoes or plow discs are normally not found in the same graves as grinding tools or spinning whorls. Although it is not always possible to determine the sex of grave occupants, the evidence does point to a gender division of labor that linked certain farm tasks to men and cooking and textile production to women.[14] Analysis of skeletal remains suggests that women in Yangshao villages married out; these marriages may have provided connections among these villages.[15] As in Çatalhöyük, important elements of social organization – cooperative production following a division of labor, settlement building, and kinship rules – all emerged without any form of the state. Social complexity here too focused on the locale and the household.

Families and cosmologies

Domestic life and family relations provided the setting in which individuals located themselves in time as well as space. Family life-cyclical practices such as burial produced material reminders of connections between ancestors and descendants, and thus past, present, and future, providing a link between family life and the production of cosmologies and eventually religious systems of thought.

The earliest known symbolic objects – flat pieces of ochre carved with geometric designs – date from about 75,000 years ago and were discovered in

---

14 Gideon Shelach, "Marxist and post-Marxist paradigms for the Neolithic," in Kathryn Linduff (ed.), *Gender and Chinese Archaeology* (Lanham, MD: AltaMira, 1999), p. 20.
15 Qiang Gao and Yun Kuen Lee, "A biological perspective on Yangshao kinship," *Journal of Anthropological Archaeology* 12 (1993), 293.

caves in southern Africa.[16] For more recent eras, burial sites suggest explicit connections between family and the emergence of religious practices. Çat-alhöyük offers pertinent evidence here as well; one interesting aspect of the Turkish site is that ritual objects and graves are found in special areas of domestic spaces. One domestic gravesite contained a reburied male skull that archaeologists believe might have belonged to a revered ancestor or relative of members of the household where it was found. It had been sculpted and painted; at some later point a woman died and the skull was buried along with her body. To offer just one additional example, Qiang Gao and Yun Kuen Lee argue that Yangshao burial sites also suggest that family relationships persisted beyond death in the form of an ancestral cult. They too find evidence of reburials, suggesting a ritual treatment of the dead, perhaps indicating the transformation of the dead into ancestors.[17]

Domestic life has played an important role in many of the world's cosmologies – in origin stories as well as in accounts of the lives of deities. Egyptian cosmologies feature the couple Isis and Osiris, deities who, among other things, introduced agriculture: in some version of the creation story Isis discovered seeds and Osiris taught the Egyptian people how to plant them. The origin stories of Judaism, Christianity, and Islam look quite different from those of Egypt. The biblical book of Genesis introduces a male monotheistic god, who alone creates Adam in his image, and, from that man, creates Eve to be his wife. Contrasting these stories with origin stories such as the Egyptian one with its multiple gods and goddesses and complex family dynamics, feminist historians have associated the emergence of major monotheistic religious traditions with the "origins of patriarchy" in ancient Mesopotamia.[18]

Religious traditions can also reflect anxieties about or tensions with family or domestic life. For example, divine births often seem to circumvent normal family relations. Christ, as the son of the Judeo-Christian God, had no human father. The Buddha was born from the side of his mother. He was thus spared from the pollution of ordinary birth, though the unusual birth resulted in the death of his mother. Rather than simply positing deities as living in families akin to those of humans, these extraordinary births place

16 Ian Tattersall, *The World from Beginnings to 4000 BCE* (New York: Oxford University Press, 2008), p. 100.
17 Gao and Lee, "A biological perspective," p. 293.
18 Barbara Watterson, *Women in Ancient Egypt* (Stroud: Sutton Publishing, Ltd., 1991), pp. 19–21 as well as Gerda Lerner, *The Creation of Patriarchy* (New York: Oxford University Press, 1987).

Figure 9.2 Coffins of children unearthed at a Yangshao burial site at Luoyang, in China's central Henan province (© Imaginechina/Corbis).

the gods beyond the realm of the ordinary mortal even where "birth" is still conceptually crucial.[19]

And there are other kinds of tensions between religious and domestic life apparent in the development of world religious traditions. Many early Christian theologians were suspicious of the family and sexual relations as a distraction from the spiritual life, if not downright sinful, and so posited celibacy as the best form of existence for the Christian. The Buddha, born into a princely household in north India, left home as a young father to investigate the nature of suffering. Monastic contemplation, away from

19 See *The Life of Buddha by Asvaghosa*, Patrick Olivelle (trans.) (New York: New York University Press, 2008); Gary Seaman, "The sexual politics of karmic retribution," in Emily Martin Ahern and Hill Gates (eds.), *The Anthropology of Taiwanese Society* (Stanford, CA: Stanford University Press, 1981), pp. 381–96; and Rita Gross, *Buddhism after Patriarchy: A Feminist History, Analysis and Reconstruction of Buddhism* (Albany: State University of New York Press, 1993).

family, was thus established as the highest form of devotion in Buddhist practice in many of the regions to which it spread. Buddhists developed important monastic institutions that usually demanded celibacy. Indeed, when Buddhism was first introduced into China, critics were concerned that celibate monks would cut off the line of descent stretching back generations and deprive that line of ancestors of the sacrifices that were essential to a happy afterlife. Advocates of Buddhism countered that conversion would benefit ancestors; to reconcile skeptics, Chinese ideas such as filial piety became an important part of Chinese Buddhism. The Chinese Buddhist story of Mulian, a man who goes through myriad hells to save his mother, is one example of how Buddhists reconciled Chinese beliefs about the duties a person owes his parents with the demands of the religious life.[20]

The family and the state

Early states presumed family life and kinship as models according to which political power was practiced and transmitted. Kingship, a common form of rule in early state societies, typically rested on the transmission of authority through kin lines, often from father to son. A Sumerian king list from the early second millennium BCE recounts the descent of kings from a mythical ancestor, Alulim, and serves to legitimate political power by mapping the genealogical connections from one ruler to the next across the millennia. To offer another example, even though Chinese dynastic histories begin with tales of several sage kings who did not have worthy sons, these tales nevertheless culminate in the legitimation of the principle of dynastic succession. When Yu passed the throne on to his son, he founded the Xia dynasty (traditionally dated as beginning in 2070 BCE); thereafter, the normative transmission of power within a Chinese dynasty, until the overthrow of the last dynasty in 1911, was from father to son (or other male relative). In certain exceptional cases, like that of pharaonic Egypt, women played an important role in dynastic transmission. According to Lana Troy, "[w]hile remaining a gendered domain, the political and cosmic power of the ancient Egyptian kingship required the interaction of male and female components, and could take feminine, as well as masculine, form and reflect the self-

---

20 A good introduction to this story is Stephen Teiser, *The Ghost Festival in Medieval China* (Princeton, NJ: Princeton University Press, 1988).

Figure 9.3 Stela depicting a woman presenting a jaguar mask to a priest, from Yaxchilan (stone), Maya (Museo Nacional de Antropologia, Mexico City, Mexico/Bridgeman Images).

generating dynamic of the organization of the universe."[21] In ancient Maya societies, too, queens could play an important role in the transmission of political power, as is evidenced by the lady Zac kuk, who crowned her son, the powerful king Pakal.[22] But even these deviations from patrilineal transmission of political authority underscore the importance of family ties to the transmission of power in ancient kingship.

The analogy between the power of the king in the realm of the state and the father in the family was mutually reinforcing; likening the power of the king to that of the father naturalized both masculine political power and masculine authority in the household. Presumptions about kinship were

21 Lana Troy, "She for whom all is said and done: The ancient Egyptian queen," in Sarah Milledge Nelson (ed.), Ancient Queens: Archaeological Explorations (Lanham, MD: Alta-Mira, 2003), p. 113.
22 Rosemary Joyce, Gender and Power in Prehispanic Mesoamerica (Austin: University of Texas Press, 2001), p. 85.

thus at the very root of beliefs about the exercise of political power. Chinese political thought provides a good example of one specific variant of how politics and kinship are intertwined. Chinese rulers and philosophers suggested that a well-regulated state began with a well-regulated family. Kinship metaphors abounded: the emperor was the son of heaven; local officials were known as father and mother officials. Family provided a key template for thinking about authority in a way which naturalized authority.[23]

Another significant connection between family history and the origins of the state lies in the realm of law. In early legal systems, such as the Code of Hammurabi (dating from about 1750 BCE), regulation of family is one of the key concerns of the code, occupying nearly one-third of its provisions. As Gerda Lerner notes, "what is remarkable about these laws is the increasing authority given to the state (king) in regard to the regulation of sexual matters."[24] Early Chinese ritual codes also demonstrate a concern with defining family relationships, for example through marriage; codes spelled out the rituals appropriate to marrying and also defined appropriate marriage partners. Those of the same surname are not appropriate spouses, no matter whether or not descent can be traced to a known common ancestor. So we can see that the domestic is, from the era of origins of state societies, never merely domestic. The intervention of state authorities in the regulation of sexual and family matters can be seen as at least partly reflecting a concern with reproduction – an interest on the part of the state in the creation of future generations, which might be seen as a precursor to modern biopolitics. Laws such as those found in the Code of Hammurabi are concerned with the transmission of property, but they are also concerned that sexual relations create appropriate offspring and families.

Early political communities were typically constructed through kin relations. Ancient Greek and Roman citizenship laws, for example, were built around family ties although not always in the same way; parentage was very important in determining citizenship. At the time of the legislation of Pericles (451–450 BCE), for example, it was necessary for both parents to be citizens in order for their child to claim Athenian citizenship. In other times, when there was concern about declining numbers of citizens, the children of Athenian

---

23 See the opening of the *Da Xue* (The Great Learning), one of the "Four Books" of Confucianism, a text traditionally attributed to Confucius. James Legge's translation is available in the *Chinese Text Project*, accessed February 27, 2013, http://ctext.org/liji/da-xue.

24 Lerner, *Creation of Patriarchy*, pp. 114–15.

fathers and foreign mothers could be citizens.[25] In the case of ancient Rome, the citizenship of the father was usually more important in determining the citizenship of the offspring than that of the mother.[26] While these rules may seem to be a far cry from modern biopolitics, they do suggest ways in which marriage and reproduction have long been at the core of many legal and political systems.

Family connections in early modern cross-cultural encounters

In the early modern era, marriage and kinship systems were organized in a variety of ways across the globe. Some marriage systems recognized only monogamous unions as legitimate, whereas others included polygamous families. In some regions, such as Europe and China, marriage was conceptualized as permanent, and divorce was difficult and rare. In other regions, including areas of Southeast Asia, marriages were easily terminated. In some settings, marriages needed to be formally registered; in others, they did not. For example, beginning in the sixteenth century, European Catholic marriages were supposed to be registered in the local parish; marriages in China, on the other hand, while highly ritualized, took place entirely within the domestic realm. No registration with either religious or state authorities was required, though this in no way implies that the state was not interested in marriage.

Other differences pertained to the very notions of what constituted kinship and how it was transmitted – notions often revealed in rules about who could marry whom.[27] Chinese kinship, for example, posited that your father's kin were more closely related to you than your mother's; therefore it was acceptable to marry your first cousins on your mother's side, but it was not permitted to marry persons of the same (patrilineally transmitted) surname. European marriage rules did not distinguish between the mother's and the father's lines; they prohibited marriages among close cousins bilaterally.[28]

---

25 Sarah B. Pomeroy, *Goddesses, Whores, Wives, and Slaves* (New York: Schocken Books, 1995), p. 66.

26 On Roman family law, see Suzanne Dixon, *The Roman Family* (Baltimore, MD: The Johns Hopkins University Press, 1992); and Judith Evans Grubbs, *Women and the Law in the Roman Empire: A Sourcebook on Marriage, Divorce and Widowhood* (New York: Routledge, 2002).

27 For comparative studies of ways of reckoning kinship in different world regions and time periods see Mary Jo Maynes, Ann Waltner, Birgitte Soland, and Ulrike Strasser (eds.), *Gender, Kinship and Power* (New York: Routledge, 1996).

28 For discussion of various aspects of marriage in Reformation era Europe, see Thomas Safley, *Let No Man Put Asunder: The Control of Marriage in the German Southwest,*

Variations across the globe in how kinship and family relations were conceptualized and practiced took on new significance in the context of cross-cultural encounters that multiplied in the era of early modern global travel and empire building. One of the first things voyagers noticed when they traveled to other parts of the world was the variety of marriage systems and gender relations they encountered. Kinship systems and domestic life were typically experienced as "natural." This naturalization was exposed and became problematic when cultures came into contact with one another. This is clear even in ancient travelers' accounts. When Herodotus visited Egypt in the fifth century BCE, for example, he noted that Egyptians seemed to have "reversed the ordinary practices of mankind. For instance, women attend to market and are employed in trade, while men stay at home and do the weaving."[29] Accounts like this convey a strong sense that proper domestic life is associated with a degree of civilization.

Trans-oceanic explorations of the fifteenth century widened the range of cross-cultural encounters. Sometimes this exposure caused moments of self-reflection, but more often it precipitated condemnations or attacks upon family systems perceived to be unnatural or barbaric.

For example, when the Omani traveler Ibn Majid (b. 1421) visited Melaka on the Malay Peninsula in the mid-fifteenth century he wrote of the residents: "They have no culture at all. The infidel marries Muslim women while the Muslim takes pagans to wife ... They drink wine in the market place and do not treat divorce as a religious act."[30] If the world that Ibn Majid encountered held some familiarity (Islam had been practiced in Melaka since the twelfth century), Europeans going to the New World later in the century encountered hitherto completely unknown peoples. In a letter written in 1493, Christopher Columbus noted the dress of the locals in the place he called Hispana (clothing of both sexes was minimal); he

1550–1620 (Kirksville: Northeast Missouri State University, 1984); Lucia Ferrante, "Marriage and women's subjectivity in a patrilineal system: The case of early modern Bologna," in Maynes, *et al.* (eds.), *Gender*, pp. 115–29; Merry E. Wiesner-Hanks, *Christianity and Sexuality in the Early Modern World: Regulating Desire, Reforming Practice* (London: Routledge, 2000); and John Witte, Jr., *From Sacrament to Contract: Marriage, Religion, and Law in the Western Tradition*, 2nd edn. (Louisville, KY: John Knox Press, 2012).

29 Herodotus, *The Histories: Second Book: An Account of Egypt*, G. C. Macaulay (trans.), accessed on Feb. 27, 2013, www.gutenberg.org/files/2131/2131-h/2131-h.htm.

30 Luis Filipe Ferrera Reiz Thomasz, "The Malay Sultinate of Melaka," in Anthony Reid (ed.), *Southeast Asia in the Early Modern Era* (Ithaca, NY: Cornell University Press, 1993), p. 79.

added that most marriages were monogamous (kings were excepted from this rule), and that "women appear to work more than the men."[31]

Early modern European projects of colonization and conversion involved relations in the intimate domestic sphere as well as in military, political, and ecclesiastical domains. New Spain provides a concrete example. The political and military elites of New Spain were comprised of men who had come from Spain, usually without wives and without landed property. They often married local women from among the landed indigenous elites; differences between the marriage systems quickly became apparent. Historical research suggests that marriage systems in much of Mesoamerica at the time of first contact with the Europeans in the sixteenth century did not demand monogamy; moreover, divorce was possible and cross-cousin marriages were common. Furthermore, there was no state or church entity that registered and formalized marriages.[32]

While some early marriage ceremonies uniting Spanish men and indigenous women combined both indigenous and Spanish customs, Christian missionaries to the Mesoamerican colony of New Spain regarded the reform of indigenous kinship systems and marriage practices as an integral part of their missionary work. Proper family life was essential to proper religious practice. The form of Catholic belief and practice that was introduced to New Spain reflected Reformation era debates and contests, including contests over marriage. Patricia Seed has shown ways in which this reformed Catholic vision of marriage was carried to New Spain. Her research shows that Catholic marriage made significant inroads among the colonial urban elite classes, even if older practices continued in rural and popular milieus.[33]

Marriages and other types of sexual unions between travelers and indigenous partners in the early modern era were of critical importance in the construction of colonial rule, the development of commercial networks, and the emergence of ideas about racial difference. Again, New Spain offers a case in point. By the eighteenth century, Mexicans produced paintings known as *casta* paintings that depicted in great detail the ways in which the mixed marriages of various combinations were seen as producing distinctive

---

31 "The first letter of Christopher Columbus to the Noble Lord Raphael Sanchez, 13," *Open Library*, accessed on Feb. 27, 2013, www.archive.org/stream/firstletterofchroocolu#page/n7/mode/2up.

32 Susan Kellog, *Law and Transformation of the Aztec Culture* (Norman: University of Oklahoma Press, 2005), pp. 202–3.

33 Patricia Seed, *To Love, Honor and Obey in Colonial Mexico: Conflicts over Marriage Choice, 1574–1821* (Stanford, CA: Stanford University Press, 1992).

Figure 9.4 "Black and Indian Produce a Wolf," *c.* 1715 (oil on canvas), Juarez, Juan Rodriguez (1675–1728). In the title of this *casta* painting, the term "wolf" refers to one of the fanciful names for a racial category (Breamore House, Hampshire, UK/Bridgeman Images).

categories of offspring each with its particular form of appearance, dress, and character traits. The casta paintings thus document the ideological role played by colonial marriage in emergent ideas about racial mixture, and the ways in which this ideology served to privilege Spanish ancestry over other lineages.[34] It was in this colonial domestic context that racial categories were first clearly expressed culturally. These ideological conceptualizations of difference were important even before modern scientific concepts of race emerged.

A different kind of colonial encounter occurred in Southeast Asia. Both Europeans and Chinese traders in early modern Southeast Asia were shocked by Southeast Asian marriage practices. As Barbara Andaya has shown, marriage in early modern Southeast Asia could be temporary; women were

34 See Ilona Katzew, *Casta Paintings: Images of Race in Eighteenth-century Mexico* (New Haven, CT: Yale University Press, 2005).

not restricted to the domestic sphere but freely occupied public spaces as traders, and exercised substantial economic agency.[35] In the early modern era, children born of mixed unions played an important role as brokers between the two cultures, but as time went on and outsiders' notions about family, kinship, and sexuality became more prevalent, there emerged an increasing suspicion of what were called "half-castes" in both colonial and indigenous courts.[36] In both the New World and Southeast Asia, then, offspring of the intimate encounters of colonialism played a pivotal role in the history of ideas about race and difference, anticipating the emergence of race as a critical category in modern biopolitical thinking.[37]

The early modern movement of peoples that redefined, disrupted, and reinscribed kinship relations was of course not always voluntary. The African slave trade had a profound impact on family structure and practices in both Africa and in the New World; the institution of slavery also served as a site for the further development of notions of racial difference and connections between ideas about race and family. Young men were disproportionately taken as slaves, which had a disruptive impact on West African family history. Reproduction of the labor force was a concern shared by plantation owners throughout the New World, but approaches varied in different regions. In the North American South, as Damian Pargas and others have argued, many plantation owners made the decision to allow slaves to form families, even if these were not legally recognized. Owners calculated that it was more economical to raise a slave child than to purchase a slave; moreover, slaves with families were often felt to be more tractable than isolates. But the decision to allow slaves to form families did not mean that slave holders guaranteed slave family stability, for family members were often separated for sale.[38] On the sugar plantations of the Caribbean and in

---

35 Barbara Andaya, "From temporary wife to prostitute: Sexuality and economic change in early modern Southeast Asia," *Journal of Women's History* 9 (1998), 11–34.

36 Andaya, "Temporary wife," p. 27.

37 For discussion of the intersections of domestic intimacy and race in the later imperial context see Ann Laura Stoler, *Carnal Knowledge and Imperial Power: Race and the Intimate in Colonial Rule* (Berkeley: University of California Press, 2002); Ann Laura Stoler, *Race and the Education of Desire: Foucault's History of Sexuality and the Colonial Order of Things* (Durham, NC: Duke University Press, 1995); Philippa Levine, *Prostitution, Race, and Politics: Policing Venereal Disease in the British Empire* (New York: Routledge, 2003); and Julia Clancy-Smith and Frances Gouda (eds.), *Domesticating the Empire: Race, Gender, and Family Life in French and Dutch Colonialism* (Charlottesville: University Press of Virginia, 1998).

38 Damian Alan Pargas, "Boundaries and opportunities: Comparing slave family formation in the Antebellum South," *Journal of Family History* 35 (2008), 316–45.

Latin America, where mortality rates among the enslaved African populations were even higher than in North America, slave holders made the
opposite calculation: they decided that it was cheaper for them to continually
buy enslaved Africans than to encourage reproduction through family formation.[39] Slave owners were quite calculating in their management of slave
populations; slaves throughout the New World encountered enormous
obstacles in their efforts to form and maintain family and kin ties.

Domestic intimacies and family reorganization resulted from and helped
to build early modern commercial networks and empires. Whether in the
form of voluntary sexual unions between foreign traders or colonizers and
indigenous people, or the coerced family formation (or prohibition thereof)
among the enslaved, early modern encounters restructured family life
around the globe and also brought family more explicitly into the realm of
global politics and emergent ideologies of difference and inequality.

Domesticity and biopolitics in the construction of the modern world

Family relations were intrinsic to ancient dynastic systems of rule; so too
were they at play in modernizing revolutions that brought dynastic rule to an
end in many regions of the world in modern times. And, with the intensification of communications that emerged in the first years of globalization,
political challenges in the household and the state could spread from one
world region to others.

The French Revolution is a clear illustration. During the Enlightenment
era, political critiques of absolute monarchy in France often involved family
metaphors and reimagined domestic relations. For example, Montesquieu's
Persian Letters (1721), a political treatise disguised as a novel, compared the
French monarchy to a Persian harem. The portrayal of gender oppression
within the harem was meant to stand for the political oppression suffered by
the French under the Bourbon dynasty. The French philosopher Jean-Jacques
Rousseau also saw a more "natural" domestic order as the basis for a new
social and political order. In his works and those of others, virtuous heroines
drew their moral superiority from their domesticity, in contrast with deca-
dent women of the aristocracy and royal court.

39 Elizabeth Anne Kuznezof, "Slavery and childhood in Brazil (1550–1888)," in Ondina E.
Gonzalez and Bianca Premo (eds.), *Raising an Empire: Children in Early Modern Iberia
and Colonial Latin America* (Albuquerque: University of New Mexico Press, 2007).

During the Revolution itself, the rebellion against and execution of the king raised urgent questions about citizenship in the new political system. As Lynn Hunt has argued, family metaphors had to be rethought – fraternity displaced paternal authority as the key metaphor, at least temporarily.[40] And new laws also undermined the long-established rule of the father (until many of the Revolutionary changes were undone by Napoleonic restoration of patriarchalism). For example, Revolutionary law codes eliminated primogeniture and gave daughters equal right to inherit; divorce was legalized on equal grounds for men and women.[41]

To offer a different example, the May Fourth Movement that followed in the wake of the overthrow of the Qing dynasty in 1911 – the last dynasty to rule in China – drew on critiques of the traditional Chinese family to further the cause of political modernization. Some of these critiques drew on an awareness of alternate political and family traditions in other parts of the world, even as they searched for appropriately Chinese models of modernization. Chen Duxiu, one of the leaders of the movement, saw the traditional Confucian elevation of the father as the core of China's problems: "When people are bound by the Confucian teachings of filial piety and obedience to the point of the son not deviating from the father's way even three years after his death and the woman obeying not only her husband and her father but her son, how can they form their own political party and make their own choice?"[42] Moreover, the May Fourth Movement was a young movement and the prominence of youth (young men *and* women, many of whom were students) embodied the overthrow of patriarchal authority.

Modern forms of governance have brought the realms of the domestic and the political ever closer together. State authorities of the modern era began to intervene more forcefully and directly in the household and in family matters as they increasingly conceived of the inhabitants of their realms as "populations" whose condition was their responsibility. An official government census taken every five or ten years that records details about every inhabitant at the level of the household is one example of the modern project of imagining and managing a population. Many state programs aimed at improving the condition of the state's population involved measures to

---

40 Lynn Hunt, *The Family Romance of the French Revolution* (Berkeley: University of California Press, 1993).
41 See Suzanne Desan, *The Family on Trial in Revolutionary France* (Berkeley: University of California Press, 2004).
42 Merry E. Wiesner-Hanks, *et al.*, *Discovering the Global Past*, 4th edn. (Independence, KY: Wadsworth Publishing, 2011), vol. II, p. 97.

improve health and well-being (as well as staving off political threats arising from grievances) – for example, health insurance programs launched in Germany in the 1880s or the infant milk programs that could be found in European and American cities by around 1900. Biopolitics – that is, the routine state surveillance, measurement, and management of human life – had by the twentieth century become a hallmark of governing throughout the world.

European empires were also sites of biopolitical interventions, often of a far less benign character. Some programs aimed to lure white settlers into the colonies with the aim of stabilizing political control in the colonies while addressing the perception of "surplus" populations in the metropole. Colonial laws also regulated who could marry whom, and outlined citizenship rules that hardened the lines both between racial groups and between European settlers and indigenous populations. Colonial population management practices often turned brutal, notoriously, for example, in the forced relocations of Herero and Nama people in German Southwest Africa, which resulted in the first genocide of the twentieth century.[43]

Biopolitics of the more brutal sort were also intrinsic features of fascist regimes in early twentieth-century Europe. Fascist movements exalted nation or race above all else and advocated a political program of economic, political and social regimentation on behalf of the race or nation – and were in Foucauldian terms, then, explicitly biopolitical. Fascist movements that came to power in Italy in the 1920s and in Germany in the 1930s sought to reconfigure family law and policy to encourage the reproduction and flourishing of those segments of the population deemed desirable and to discourage reproduction among those whom the state deemed undesirable.

Such policies were exemplified by a series of Racial Hygiene Laws passed by the Nazi regime between 1933 and 1939. The Law for the Encouragement of Marriage passed in 1933 granted racially appropriate newlywed couples a government loan of 1,000 marks; a portion of the loan was forgiven for each child born to the couple. In contrast, a sterilization program was begun in the same year to keep people deemed genetically inferior from reproducing. This early eugenic sterilization program was a precedent for the explicitly racist sterilization later carried out in concentration camps. Other laws were passed that prohibited marriages between Jews and Germans of "Aryan" racial stock.

43 See Jürgen Zimmerer, "Annihilation in Africa: The 'race war' in German Southwest Africa (1904–1908) and its significance for a global history of genocide," *Bulletin of the German Historical Institute* Issue 37 (2005), 51–7.

Figure 9.5 Advertisement for a German public information brochure titled "Healthy Parents – Healthy Children!", 1934 (color litho) (Deutsches Historisches Museum, Berlin, Germany/DHM/Bridgeman Images).

The Nazi regime was extreme in its pursuit of racist forms of biopolitics, but less extreme versions of these programs were put in place elsewhere in the first half of the twentieth century. Some American eugenicists had helped to pass state sterilization laws even before those of the Nazis; in his 1934 book *The Case for Sterilization*, American eugenicist Leon Whitney openly expressed his admiration for Nazi policies; he wrote "[m]any far-sighted men and women in both England and America have long been working earnestly toward something very like what Hitler has now made compulsory."[44]

During the Depression, sterilization gained support beyond eugenic circles in some American states, when it was seen as a means of reducing costs for institutional care and poor relief. US sterilization rates climbed during the Depression. New laws were also passed in Finland, Norway, and Sweden during the same period, although the numbers of persons sterilized never came close to the mass scale of the Nazi program. Shortly after the Second World War, in South Africa, the white supremacist Nationalist Party passed laws that codified the racist system of apartheid. The Prohibition of Mixed Marriages Act of 1949 prohibited marriages between white people and people of other races. The Immorality Amendment Act of 1950 outlawed sexual relations across racial lines. These laws remained in effect in South Africa until the overthrow of the apartheid regime in 1994.

The postwar era also saw the politicization of exemplary families, gender relations, and domestic life and their enshrinement as a tool of foreign policy during the Cold War. Efforts to "normalize" life in the United States after the war involved government programs designed to encourage marriage and home purchase. The promotion of the "male breadwinner" model reflected the concern that the "traditional" family order had been disrupted during the Depression and the Second World War.

The model was given a government stamp of approval through such programs as the GI Bill for veterans' education, which supported veterans – overwhelmingly men – to pursue higher education and professional careers. Meanwhile, the government supports for "Rosie the Riveter" – women who entered the labor force during the war – disappeared. These policies contrasted sharply with those followed in the USSR and Eastern Europe, where the emphasis was on creating institutional supports to allow women to

---

44 Cited in Stefan Kühl, *The Nazi Connection: Eugenics, American Racism, and German National Socialism* (New York: Oxford University Press, 2002), p. 36.

Figure 9.6 US advertisement showing a man returning from work to a suburban home, greeted by his family in the front yard, 1956 (© GraphicaArtis/Corbis).

combine labor force participation with housework and childrearing. These two dueling models were put on the world stage in the 1959 "kitchen debates" between then US vice president Richard Nixon and Soviet premier Nikita Khrushchev, which pitted the virtues of American full-time housewives against those of Soviet working women.[45]

Toward the turn of the twenty-first century, new biopolitical intersections between the state and the family/domestic realm are evident in the arenas of sexuality, reproductive technologies, the management of elder care, and global migration including international adoptions. For example, US states such as Illinois have passed legislation regulating contracts between surrogate mothers and adoptive parents, although in most of the United States and much of the world these relationships remain unregulated. The situation leaves bioethicists concerned that children so produced are reduced to commodities.

Not all biopolitical policies are racist or anti-democratic. As Edward Dickinson has argued, biopolitical measures are an accepted realm of governance

---

45 See Elaine May, *Homeward Bound: American Families in the Cold War Era* (New York: Basic Books, 1990).

in virtually all modern states, however democratic or authoritarian.[46] Democratic regimes can, arguably, engage in more democratic forms of biopolitics. For example, governments can establish clinics or school lunch programs in the interest of improving the health of the population. Or, for that matter, they can take actions such as the 1967 US Supreme Court decision to call on the federal government to protect the individual's right to marry a partner of choice regardless of race. The larger point here is that whatever their specific politics, biopolitical calculations are now routine aspects of governance in most regions of the world thus bringing family history and political history – at the household and the global scales – ever closer together.

FURTHER READING

Primary sources

Da Xue (The Great Learning), James Legge (trans.), *Chinese Text Project*, accessed Feb. 27, 2013, http://ctext.org/liji/da-xue.

"The first letter of Christopher Columbus to the Noble Lord Raphael Sanchez, 13," *Open Library*, accessed on Feb. 27, 2013, www.archive.org/stream/firstletterofchroocolu#-page/n7/mode/2up.

Herodotus, *The Histories: Second Book: An Account of Egypt*, G. C. Macaulay (trans.), accessed on Feb. 27, 2013, www.gutenberg.org/files/2131/2131-h/2131-h.htm.

The Life of Buddha by Asvaghosa, Patrick Olivelle (trans.), New York: New York University Press, 2008.

Secondary sources

Andaya, Barbara, "From temporary wife to prostitute: Sexuality and economic change in early modern Southeast Asia," *Journal of Women's History* 9 (1998), 11–34.

Bolger, Diane, "Gender and human evolution," in Sarah Milledge Nelson (ed.), *Handbook of Gender in Archaeology*, Lanham, MD: AltaMira, 2006.

Clancy-Smith, Julia, and Frances Gouda (eds.), *Domesticating the Empire: Race, Gender, and Family Life in French and Dutch Colonialism*, Charlottesville: University Press of Virginia, 1998.

Cook, Michael, *A Brief History of the Human Race*, New York: W. W. Norton, 2003.

Desan, Suzanne, *The Family on Trial in Revolutionary France*, Berkeley: University of California Press, 2004.

Dickinson, Edward Ross, "Biopolitics, fascism, democracy: Some reflections on our discourse about 'Modernity,'" *Central European History* 37 (2004), 1–48.

Dixon, Suzanne, *The Roman Family*, Baltimore, MD: The Johns Hopkins University Press, 1992.

---

46 Edward Ross Dickinson, "Biopolitics, fascism, democracy: Some reflections on our discourse about 'Modernity,'" *Central European History* 37 (2004), 1–48.

Ferrante, Lucia, "Marriage and women's subjectivity in a patrilineal system: The case of early modern Bologna," in Mary Jo Maynes, et al. (eds.), *Gender, Kinship and Power*, New York: Routledge, 1996.

Foucault, Michel, *Security, Territory, Population: Lectures at the Collège de France 1977–1978* (Lectures at the Collège de France), Graham Burchell (trans.), New York: Picador, 2009.

Gamble, Clive, *Origins and Revolutions: Human Identity in Earliest Prehistory*, Cambridge: Cambridge University Press, 2007.

Gao, Qiang, and Yun Kuen Lee, "A biological perspective on Yangshao kinship," *Journal of Anthropological Archaeology* 12 (1993), 266–98.

Gross, Rita, *Buddhism after Patriarchy: A Feminist History, Analysis and Reconstruction of Buddhism*, Albany: State University of New York Press, 1993.

Grubbs, Judith Evans, *Women and the Law in the Roman Empire: A Sourcebook on Marriage, Divorce and Widowhood*, New York: Routledge, 2002.

Hodder, Ian, *The Domestication of Europe: Structure and Contingency in Neolithic Societies*, Cambridge, MA: Blackwell, 1990.

"This old house," *Natural History*, June 2006, accessed March 6, 2013, www.naturalhistorymag.com/htmlsite/0606/0606_feature.html.

Hunt, Lynn, *The Family Romance of the French Revolution*, Berkeley: University of California Press, 1993.

Joyce, Rosemary, *Gender and Power in Prehispanic Mesoamerica*, Austin: University of Texas Press, 2001.

Katzew, Ilona, *Casta Paintings: Images of Race in Eighteenth-century Mexico*, New Haven, CT: Yale University Press, 2005.

Kellog, Susan, *Law and Transformation of the Aztec Culture*, Norman: University of Oklahoma Press, 2005.

Kühl, Stefan, *The Nazi Connection: Eugenics, American Racism, and German National Socialism*, New York: Oxford University Press, 2002.

Kuznezof, Elizabeth Anne, "Slavery and childhood in Brazil (1550–1888)," in Ondina E. Gonzalez and Bianca Premo (eds.), *Raising an Empire: Children in Early Modern Iberia and Colonial Latin America*, Albuquerque: University of New Mexico Press, 2007.

Lerner, Gerda, *The Creation of Patriarchy*, New York: Oxford University Press, 1987.

Levine, Philippa, *Prostitution, Race, and Politics: Policing Venereal Disease in the British Empire*, New York: Routledge, 2003.

Lyons, Diane, "A critical appraisal of gender research in African archaeology," in Sarah Milledge Nelson (ed.), *Worlds of Gender: The Archaeology of Women's Lives around the Globe*, Lanham, MD: AltaMira, 2007.

May, Elaine Tyler, *Homeward Bound: American Families in the Cold War Era*, New York: Basic Books, 1990.

Maynes, Mary Jo, and Ann Waltner, *The Family: A World History*, New York: Oxford University Press, 2012.

"Temporalities and periodization in deep history: Technology, gender, and benchmarks of 'human development,'" *Social Science History* 36 (2012), 59–83.

Maynes, Mary Jo, Ann Waltner, Birgitte Soland, and Ulrike Strasser (eds.), *Gender, Kinship and Power*, New York: Routledge, 1996.

Pargas, Damian Alan, "Boundaries and opportunities: Comparing slave family formation in the Antebellum South," *Journal of Family History* 35 (2008), 316–45.

Pomeroy, Sarah B., *Goddesses, Whores, Wives, and Slaves*, New York: Schocken Books, 1995.

Safley, Thomas, *Let No Man Put Asunder: The Control of Marriage in the German Southwest, 1550–1620*, Kirksville: Northeast Missouri State University Press, 1984.

Seaman, Gary, "The sexual politics of karmic retribution," in Emily Martin Ahern and Hill Gates (eds.), *The Anthropology of Taiwanese Society*, Stanford, CA: Stanford University Press, 1981.

Seed, Patricia, *To Love, Honor and Obey in Colonial Mexico: Conflicts over Marriage Choice, 1574–1821*, Stanford, CA: Stanford University Press, 1992.

Shelach, Gideon, "Marxist and post-Marxist paradigms for the Neolithic," in Kathryn Linduff (ed.), *Gender and Chinese Archaeology*, Lanham, MD: AltaMira, 1999.

Smail, Daniel Lord, *On Deep History and the Brain*, Berkeley: University of California Press, 2008.

Stoler, Ann Laura, *Carnal Knowledge and Imperial Power: Race and the Intimate in Colonial Rule*, Berkeley: University of California Press, 2002.

   Race and the Education of Desire: Foucault's History of Sexuality and the Colonial Order of Things, Durham, NC: Duke University Press, 1995.

Tattersall, Ian, *The World from Beginnings to 4000 BCE*, New York: Oxford University Press, 2008.

Teiser, Stephen, *The Ghost Festival in Medieval China*, Princeton, NJ: Princeton University Press, 1988.

Thomasz, Luis Filipe Ferrera Reiz, "The Malay Sultanate of Melaka," in Anthony Reid (ed.), *Southeast Asia in the Early Modern Era*, Ithaca, NY: Cornell University Press, 1993.

Troy, Lana, "She for whom all is said and done: The ancient Egyptian queen," in Sarah Milledge Nelson (ed.), *Ancient Queens: Archaeological Explorations*, Lanham, MD: AltaMira, 2003.

Watterson, Barbara, *Women in Ancient Egypt*, Stroud: Sutton Publishing, Ltd., 1991.

Whitehouse, Ruth, "Gender archaeology in Europe," in Sarah Milledge Nelson (ed.), *Worlds of Gender: The Archaeology of Women's Lives around the Globe*, Lanham, MD: AltaMira, 2007.

Wiesner-Hanks, Merry E., *Christianity and Sexuality in the Early Modern World: Regulating Desire, Reforming Practice*, London: Routledge, 2000.

   et al., *Discovering the Global Past*, 4th edn., Independence, KY: Wadsworth Publishing, 2011, vol. II.

Witte, John Jr., *From Sacrament to Contract: Marriage, Religion, and Law in the Western Tradition*, 2nd edn., Louisville, KY: John Knox Press, 2012.

Zimmerer, Jürgen, "Annihilation in Africa: The 'race war' in German Southwest Africa (1904–1908) and its significance for a global history of genocide," *Bulletin of the German Historical Institute* Issue 37 (2005), 51–7.

Gendered world history

MERRY E. WIESNER-HANKS

Gender is the oldest category of difference in human history, and the most enduring. Gender is thus one of the fundamental categories of world history, which seeks to embrace all of human history. It has become even more important in the last decades, as issues of difference and identity have become crucial in historical thought in general, and particularly in world history. The historiographical traditions of an earlier period were largely dominated by the idea of the nation as the key historiographical unit. Both world history and gender history have broken with this focus on the nation, but have faced difficulties and complexities in creating new categories of analysis to replace it. As movements to break out of the limitations of earlier ways of doing history, world history and gender history have developed along parallel trajectories, but are increasingly intersecting, with studies beginning to incorporate insights from both.

This chapter looks first at concepts of gender, noting contradictions and paradoxes in what might initially seem to be a neat dichotomy of male and female. It then examines the development of gender history, and the ways this was interwoven with political movements and with trends in history scholarship. The chapter discusses five key areas of gendered world history research: early human societies; intermarriage; national identity and citizenship; migration; colonialism and imperialism. It ends with some observations about ways in which the subject matter, theory, and methodology within world and global history and the history of gender and sexuality interconnect.

Concepts of gender

The vast majority of human groups have a system of two main genders in which there are enormous differences between what it means to be a man and what it means to be a woman. This dualistic gender system has often been associated with other dichotomies, such as body/spirit, public/private, nature/culture, light/dark, up/down, outside/inside, yin/yang, right/left, sun/moon. Some of these dichotomies, such as sun/moon and light/dark, are naturally occurring and in many places viewed as divinely created, which has enabled people to view the male/female dichotomy also as natural or divinely ordained. In contemporary scholarship, gender is generally understood to be a culturally constructed system of differences based on physical, morphological, and anatomical differences between the sexes, what are often called "biological differences."

Cultural norms about gender are more powerful than mere biology, however. In addition to the two primary genders, in some parts of the world a few individuals have been classified as a third or even fourth gender. Some of these individuals are born with ambiguous sexual and reproductive organs and occasionally they are eunuchs, but more commonly they are morphologically male or female but understood to be something else. Third genders include two-spirit people found among several Native American peoples, who combined – and in some cases still combine – the clothing, work, ceremonial roles, and other attributes of men and women. They also include the *bissu* of South Sulawesi, who carried out rituals thought to enhance and preserve the power and fertility of the rulers; the *hijra* of northern India, who perform blessings at marriages and the births of male children; the *xanith* in Oman and the *mahus* in Polynesia, who were morphologically male but performed women's rituals and women's work, and others in Alaska, the Amazon region, Australia, Siberia, and elsewhere.

Third gender categories suggest that gender is fluid and malleable, but other evidence points to the power of the male/female dichotomy. Children born with ambiguous external sexual and reproductive anatomy – now termed "intersexed" – have generally not been assigned to a third gender, but categorized "male" or "female" at birth, according to the sex they most closely resembled. Since the nineteenth century this gender assignment has sometimes been reinforced by surgical procedures modifying or removing the body parts that do not fit with the chosen gender, generally shortly after birth. Although very recently such surgery has become extremely controversial, the search for an infallible marker of sex differences has continued, now involving chromosomal and hormonal patterns. Thus dichotomous cultural norms about gender (that everyone *should* be a man or a woman) often determined (and continue to determine) "biological" sex, rather than the other way around.

The gender dichotomy, along with other dichotomies with which it was associated, has generally been viewed as a hierarchy, with the male linked with the stronger and more positive element in other pairs (public, culture, light, right, sun, etc.) and the female with the weaker and more negative one (private, nature, dark, left, moon, etc.). This gender hierarchy is highly variable in its intensity and manifestations, but it is found in every human group that left written records, and most that did not, including those in which there were and are individuals of third and fourth genders. It is found in every environmental condition, social structure, and political system. It has survived every change: every revolution, whether French, Haitian, Scientific, or Industrial, every war, religious transformation, technological development, and cultural encounter. Twentieth-century Russia provides a good example: whether under the czars or the Communists or the post-Soviet government, women still did the shopping and the housekeeping and most of the child care, adding an unpaid "second shift" to their jobs in the paid workforce; these tasks were necessary to keep society functioning, but left women no time for the things that were valued and rewarded, such as further education or political activities. This gender hierarchy has interlocked with other hierarchies based on qualities such as age, physical strength, wealth, family origin, and spiritual authority to create the most common form of human society: patriarchy, in which men have more power and access to resources than women, and some men have more power and access to resources than others.

People's notions of gender shaped not only the way they thought about men and women, but the way they thought about their society in general. As the historian Joan Scott put it in an extremely influential article first published in 1986: "Gender is a constitutive element of social relationships based on perceived differences between the sexes, and gender is a primary way of signifying relationships of power."[1] Thus hierarchies in other realms of life were often expressed in terms of gender, with dominant individuals or groups described in masculine terms and dependent ones in feminine. These ideas in turn affected the way people acted, though explicit and symbolic ideas of gender could also conflict with the way men and women chose or were forced to operate in the world.

The development of gender history

Despite, or perhaps because of, its ubiquity, gender is a relatively new conceptual framework for studying the human past. Until the middle of

---

1 Joan Scott, "Gender: A useful category of historical analysis," *American Historical Review* 91 (1986), 1,053–75.

Figure 10.1 Elderly women in Moscow wait in front of a counter on a food line to buy blocks of butter (© Shepard Sherbell/CORBIS SABA).

the twentieth century, most people who obtained a formal education or held positions as official recorders and transmitters of history and tradition were men. Women who were members of the elite did learn to read and write in many cultures, but this was a small group compared to the larger number of men who wrote professionally as scribes, copiers, and record-keepers, or who used writing in their work. For some cultures that have left many written works by men, such as ancient Rome, no complete written works by a female author have survived at all, and very few appear to have been written by female authors in the first place. Educated men also spent much of their time in all-male environments, whether the symposia of ancient Athens, the academies of Song China, the madrases of the early modern Muslim world, or the scientific and literary societies of eighteenth-century cities. Not surprisingly, the men who wrote history within these milieus viewed the male experience as universal; when women appear in their histories, they are exceptions that usually bring disaster. In the nineteenth century, scholars at universities first in Germany and then elsewhere created academic "disciplines" – divisions of learning through which knowledge was categorized and validated. History was one of these, and the scholars who developed it decided that the proper focus of real history was political and military. They also decided that professional history could only be done through years of intensive training accompanied by debate and discussion in university seminars, and that only men had the time or mental capacity to undergo the rigors of real historical research.

The women's movement changed this, as it changed so much else. The women's rights movement of the nineteenth and early twentieth centuries – later termed the "first wave" of feminism – led to a rise in interest in women's history. It also improved opportunities for women in the West to obtain higher education and teach in colleges and universities, giving them an institutional base in departments of history, classics, anthropology, and related fields from which to conduct scholarly studies of the past. Those women wrote histories, some of which focused on women. Similarly, the "second wave" feminist movement of the 1960s and 1970s led advocates of women's rights in the present to look more closely at what they had been taught about the past. Scholars and activists asserted that history as it had been studied and taught was really "men's history," though it had not been identified as such. This combined with a growing interest in the history of ordinary people rather than simply political or intellectual elites – what was termed the New Social History – and led to an explosive growth in women's history. Historians recognized that there is really no historical change that does not affect the lives of women in some way, though often very differently than it affects the lives of men of the same class or social group. They discovered rich sources that had been lost or neglected, and mined familiar sources in new ways, finding comments on women everywhere.

As historians began to investigate the history of women more extensively, they first fit them into familiar historical categories – nations, historical periods, social classes, religious allegiance – and then realized that this approach, sarcastically labeled "add women and stir," was unsatisfying. This disruption of well-known categories and paradigms ultimately included the topic that had long been considered the proper focus of all history – man. Viewing the male experience as universal had not only hidden women's history, but it had also prevented analysis of men's experiences as those of men. Historians familiar with studying women increasingly began to discuss the ways in which systems of sexual differentiation affected both women and men, and by the early 1980s to use the word "gender" to describe these culturally constructed, historically changing, and often unstable systems of difference. Most of the studies with "gender" in the title still focused on women – and women's history continued as its own field – but a few looked equally at both sexes or concentrated on the male experience, calling their work "men's history" or the "new men's studies."

Historians interested in this new perspective asserted that gender was an appropriate category of analysis when looking at *all* historical developments, not simply those involving women or the family. *Every* political, intellectual, religious, economic, social, and even military change had an impact on the actions and roles of men and women, and, conversely, a culture's gender structures influenced every other structure or development. Hundreds of courses in women's and gender history were added to the university curriculum, first in the United States and Canada, and then in other parts of the world. (The history done in any country is shaped by regional and world politics, and issues other than gender have often seemed more pressing to historians in Latin America, eastern Europe, and other parts of the world where political and economic struggles have been intense. Universities and researchers in developing countries also have far fewer resources, which has hampered all historical research and limited opportunities for any new direction.)

Along with focusing on gender, some historians turned their attention more fully in the 1980s to the history of sexuality. Just as interest in women's history was inspired by feminist political movements, interest in the history of sexuality was inspired by the gay rights movement, which encouraged both public discussion of sexual matters in general and the study of same-sex relations in the past and present. Historians and activists studied same-sex relations in many periods, initially focusing primarily on men – whose lives have everywhere left more sources than those of women – but then also on women. Some put emphasis on continuities and similarities in the experiences of individuals and groups across time, and supported efforts to discover physical bases for same-sex attraction in the brain or genetic code. Others emphasized differences across time.

The most significant of these differences, asserted many historians of sexuality, was the break between "modern" sexuality and what came before, what is sometimes described as the point at which sexuality itself was born, created, or constructed. As the argument is usually framed, at some point between the seventeenth and the nineteenth centuries people discovered that they had a "sexuality," a quality defined by sexual object choice. Those who desired those of the same sex were "homosexuals" – a word devised in 1869 by the Hungarian jurist K. M. Benkert – and those who desired those of the opposite sex were "heterosexuals," a word originally used to describe individuals of different sexes who regularly engaged in non-procreative sex simply for fun, but increasingly used for all those who were sexually attracted to the "opposite" sex. Before this point there were sexual acts, but after this point people came to understand that they had a sexual identity or sexual orientation as a permanent part of the self. This acts versus identities, modern versus premodern binary has been widely challenged as overly dichotomizing and ahistorical, but it has been extremely powerful. The concept of sexual orientation has been even more powerful, of course; it now shapes legal decisions and self-descriptions on Internet dating services as well as history and psychiatry.

Early studies in the history of sexuality focused primarily on same-sex relationships, but in the same way that the development of women's history led scholars to start exploring men's experiences in history *as men* (rather than simply as "the history of man" without noticing that their subjects were men), gay and lesbian studies has led a few scholars to explore the historical construction of heterosexuality. Recognizing the constructed nature of heterosexuality has been just as difficult for many historians as recognizing that most history was actually "men's history," however. The cultural analyst Eve Sedgwick wryly notes that "making heterosexuality historically visible is difficult because, under its institutional pseudonyms such as Inheritance, Marriage, Dynasty, Domesticity, and Population, heterosexuality has been permitted to masquerade so fully as History itself."[2]

The cultural turn

Just at the point that gender history and the history of sexuality were emerging as historical fields, many historians were changing their basic understanding of the methods and function of history. Historians have long recognized that documents and other types of evidence are produced by particular individuals with particular interests and perspectives that consciously and unconsciously shape their content. Most historians thus attempted to keep the limitations of their sources in mind as they reconstructed events and tried to determine causation, though sometimes these got lost in the narrative. During the 1980s, some historians began to assert that because historical sources always present a partial picture from a particular point of view, one can never fully determine what happened or why; to try to do so is foolish or misguided. What historians should do

2 Eve Kosofsky Sedgwick, "Gender criticism," in Giles B. Gunn and Stephen Greenblatt (eds.), *Redrawing the Boundaries* (New York: Modern Language Association, 1992), p. 293.

instead is to analyze the written and visual materials of the past – what is often termed "discourse" – to determine the way various things are "represented" in them and evaluate their possible meanings. Historians should not be preoccupied with searching for "reality," in this viewpoint, because to do so demonstrates a naive "positivism." (Both advocates and critics of positivism often quote the words of the nineteenth-century German historian Leopold von Ranke, who regarded the best history as that which retold events "as they actually happened.")

This heightened interest in discourse among historians, usually labeled the "linguistic turn" or the "cultural turn," drew on the ideas of literary and linguistic theory – often loosely termed "deconstruction" or "post-structuralism" – about the power of language. Language is so powerful, argued some theorists, that it determines, rather than simply describes, our understanding of the world; knowledge is passed down through language, and knowledge is power. This emphasis on the relationship of knowledge to power, and on the power of language, made post-structuralism attractive to feminist scholars in many disciplines, who themselves already emphasized the ways language and other structures of knowledge excluded women. The insight of the French philosopher Michel Foucault that power comes from everywhere fit with feminist recognition that misogyny and other forces that limited women's lives could be found in many places: in fashion magazines, fairy tales, and jokes told at work as well as overt job discrimination and domestic violence.

Historians of gender and sexuality were thus prominent exponents of the cultural turn, and many analyzed representations of women, men, the body, sexual actions, and related topics within different types of discourses. Some historians came to assert that everything regarding gender and sexuality is determined by culture, a position often labeled "social constructionist." For social constructionists, the idea that everyone had a fixed sexual identity based on something internal was wrong, and those who sought physical bases for sexual orientation were "essentialists." Gender, too, was a matter of social construction. Because the differences among women (and among men) based on class, race, nationality, ethnicity, religion, and other factors were and are so great, many wondered whether "woman" (or "man") is a valid category whose meaning is self-evident and unchanging over time, or whether assuming so was, again, naive essentialism. Gender and sexuality, some concluded, are "performative," that is, roles that can be taken on or changed at will.

The linguistic/cultural turn – which happened in other fields along with history – elicited harsh responses from other historians, however, including many who focused on women and gender. They asserted that it denied women the ability to shape their world – what is usually termed "agency" – in both past and present by positing unchangeable linguistic structures. They wondered whether the idea that gender and perhaps even "women" were simply historical constructs denied the very real oppression that many women in the past (and present) experienced. Extending this to other groups, they questioned whether one can work to end discrimination against homosexuals, African-Americans, people with disabilities, or any other group, if one denies that the group has an essential identity, something that makes its members clearly homosexual or African-American or disabled. For a period in the 1980s and 1990s this debate was intense, but by the 2000s the division became less sharp, as cultural historians increasingly broadened their focus beyond discourse and representation, and historians who were initially suspicious of the linguistic turn used its insights about the importance of meaning in their work.

New developments and new theoretical perspectives are adding additional complexity. The notion of sexual orientation initially created a dichotomized sexual schema of homosexual and heterosexual, but then other categories were added to more fully reflect the wide range of human desires. Sex-change operations have also become more widely available for people whose external genitalia and even chromosomal and hormonal patterns mark them as male or female, but who mentally understand themselves to be the other. Transsexual surgery can make the body fit more closely with the mind, but it has also led to challenging questions about gender and sexual identity: At what point in this process does a "man" become a "woman," or vice versa? If sexual identity is based on the sex of one's partner, did individuals who underwent sex-change operations also change from being homosexual to heterosexual or vice versa? In the 1990s such questions began to be made even more complex by individuals who described themselves as "transgendered," that is, as neither male nor female or both male and female. Sexual and gender identities grew into an ever-lengthening list of categories: the longest version I have seen of this in the United States is LGBTTQQI2S – lesbian, gay, bisexual, transexual, transgender, queer, questioning, intersexed, two-spirit. Studies of individuals who challenged sexual and gender categorizations in the past have accompanied the growth of the trans rights movement in the present. These studies are not simply broadening historical scholarship, but are also proving politically useful, as people within the gay rights and transgender movements in many parts of the world today use them to demonstrate the variety in indigenous understandings of gender and

Figure 10.2 *Hijras* at a Pride March organized by the LGBT community in Mumbai, February 2014, to protest Indian laws that criminalize sexual acts between consenting adults of the same sex (© Subhash Sharma/ZUMA Press/Corbis).

sexuality and to stress that demands for rights for homosexuals or transgender people are not simply a Western import.

Some activists and theorists have wondered, however, whether this growing list of categories has reified boundaries instead of blurring or bending them. This point of view has emerged especially in queer theory, which was developed in the early 1990s, a period of intense AIDS activism, and combined elements of gay and lesbian studies with other concepts originating in literary and feminist analysis. Queer theorists argued that sexual notions were central to all aspects of culture, and called for greater attention to sexuality that was at odds with whatever was defined as "normal." They asserted that the line between "normal" and "abnormal" was always socially constructed, however, and that, in fact, all gender and sexual categories were artificial and changing. Identity of any sort could easily become false and oppressive, and instead what should be celebrated are hybridity and performance. In the last decade, queer theory has been widely applied, as scholars have "queered" – that is, called into question the categories used to describe and analyze – the nation, race, religion, and other topics along with gender and sexuality. This broadening has led some – including a few of the founders of the field – to wonder whether queer theory loses its punch when everything is queer, but it continues to be an influential theoretical perspective.

Related questions about identity, subjectivity, and the cultural construction of difference have also emerged from postcolonial theory. Postcolonial history and theory were initially associated with South Asian scholars and the book series Subaltern Studies, and focused on people who have been subordinated by virtue of their race, class, culture, or language as part of the process of colonization and imperialism in the modern world. Historians of Europe and the United States are increasingly applying insights from postcolonial theory to their own work as they investigate subaltern groups such as racial and ethnic minorities, and world historians apply them to analyze relationships of power in all chronological periods, not just the era of imperialism.

The notion of hegemony, initially developed by the Italian political theorist Antonio Gramsci, has been an important concept in much postcolonial theory and the history that builds on it. Hegemony differs from domination because it involves convincing dominated groups to acquiesce to the desires and systems of the dominators through cultural as well as military and political means. Generally this was accomplished by granting special powers and privileges to some individuals and groups from among the subordinated population, or by convincing them through education or other forms of socialization that the new system was beneficial or preferable. The notion of hegemony explains why small groups of people have been able to maintain control over much larger populations without constant rebellion and protest, though some scholars have argued that the emphasis on hegemony downplays the ability of subjugated peoples to recognize the power realities in which they are enmeshed and to shape their own history. Many historians have used the concept of hegemony to examine the role of high-status women, who gained power over subordinate men and women through their relationships with high-status men. The sociologist R. W. Connell has also applied the idea of hegemony to studies of masculinity, noting that in every culture one form of masculinity is hegemonic, but men who are excluded from that particular form still benefit from male privilege.[3]

Queer theory and postcolonial theory have both been criticized for falling into the pattern set by traditional history, that is, regarding the male experience as normative and paying insufficient attention to gender differences. Scholars who have pointed this out have also noted that much feminist scholarship

---

3 R. W. Connell, *Gender and Power: Society, the Person and Sexual Politics* (Oxford: Polity, 1987).

suffered from the opposite problem, taking the experiences of heterosexual white women in Europe and North America as normative and paying too little attention to differences of race, class, nationality, ethnicity, or sexual orientation. They argue that the experiences of women of color must be recognized as distinctive, and that no one axis of difference (men/women, black/white, rich/poor, gay/straight) should be viewed as sufficient. These criticisms led, in the 1990s, to theoretical perspectives that attempted to recognize multiple lines of difference, such as postcolonial feminism. Such scholarship has begun to influence many areas of gender studies, even those that do not deal explicitly with race or ethnicity. It appears this cross-fertilization will continue, as issues of difference and identity are clearly key topics for historians in the ever more connected twenty-first-century world.

Gender history and world history

Gender history developed, in part, as a revisionist interpretation of the past, arguing that the standard story needs to be made broader and much more complex. World history developed, in part, along the same lines. Both have, as Judith Zinsser has commented, "had to write with the stories of men's lives in the United States and Europe paramount in their readers' memories."[4] Because these shifts of focus called into question what had been understood for so long to be the "natural" focus of history, both fields have been viewed by those hostile or uninterested as "having an agenda."

Despite these parallels, however, until recently there has been relatively little intersection between the two fields, for which I see three primary reasons. First, each of these fields has concentrated on its own line of revision, so has not paid much attention to what is going on in the other. Second, the primary revisionary paths in world and global history and the history of gender and sexuality have been in opposite directions. World history has emphasized connections, links, and the crossing of boundaries. In contrast, after an initial flurry of "sisterhood is global," gender history over the last decades has spent much more time on *divergence*, making categories of difference ever more complex. Gender historians have emphasized that every key aspect of gender relations – the relationship between the family and the state, the relationship between gender and sexuality – is historically, culturally, and class specific. Today historians of masculinity speak of their

---

4 Judith P. Zinsser, "Women's history, world history, and the construction of new narratives," *Journal of Women's History* 12 (2000), 197.

subject only in plurals, as "multiple masculinities" appear to have emerged everywhere, just as have multiple sexualities in the works by historians of sexuality. Third, there is a powerful materialist tradition in world and global history, which stands in sharp contrast to the largely cultural focus of the history of gender and sexuality as these have developed over the last several decades. Most world history has focused on political and economic processes carried out by governments and commercial elites. Women's history also initially had a strong materialist wing, with many studies of labor systems and political movements, but since the linguistic/cultural turn of the 1980s more attention has been paid to representation, meaning, and discourse, which has also characterized the history of sexuality.

Despite this lack of intersection in the past, however, a growing number of studies in certain research areas are beginning to incorporate insights from both gender history and world history. This will be evident in every volume of the Cambridge World History, so I would here like simply to highlight five areas in which I see especially interesting research emerging: early human societies; intermarriage; national identity and citizenship; migration; colonialism and imperialism.

Early human societies

World historians are increasingly dissolving the border between prehistory and history, so that human evolution has become part of history. Thus considerations of the role of gender in early human societies, most of which have been undertaken by anthropologists, archaeologists, and evolutionary scientists in other fields, have shaped world history. Until recently, most scholars have seen the origins of human society and of patriarchy in male–male cooperation in organized violence that started in the primate past. Among chimpanzees, such scholars argue, males form alliances, generally with the kin with whom they live, to gain status against other males and to gain greater access to females. Male–male alliances allow for cooperative attacks on females, which makes female resistance difficult. In the animal world, male–male alliances are often short-lived, as there is much fighting for status among the group. Among humans, sometime during the Paleolithic Era males developed the ability to control male–male competition within the group so that the group could be more successful in its hunt for prey and in its competition with other humans. They did this by talking with one another, and they developed rules, norms, rituals, and eventually laws and political structures. Scholars also concluded that men gained authority because they supplied the bulk of the food through the hunting of large animals, and termed these early human groups "hunter-gatherers." Pregnancy, lactation, and the extended care of infants kept women dependent on men for food and protection, and limited their ability to gain food for the group to the less important task of gathering. Women had difficulty resisting male violence because they left their initial kin groups to mate, joining the kin group of their male mate in what the anthropologist Claude Lévi-Strauss long ago termed "the exchange of women." (The blander term for this is "patrilocation.")

Beginning in the 1990s, however, some evolutionary scientists and anthropologists have challenged every aspect of this story about gender in human evolution. They note that evidence of animal killing and consumption – stones and bones – survives better than that of plant consumption, but the sophisticated chemical and physical analysis possible today indicates that the majority of hunter-gatherers' diet comes from plants. Much of the animal protein in their diet comes from foods gathered or scavenged rather than hunted directly, for it consists of insects, shellfish, small animals caught in traps, and animals killed by other predators. The flaked stones that had generally been viewed as club heads or spear points had actually been used for a wide variety of tasks such as chopping vegetables, peeling fruits, cracking open shells, grinding seeds, weighting digging sticks, and working leather. Thus instead of hunter-gatherers, early human societies might be more accurately termed gatherer-hunters or foragers. If gathering was a women's task, it was essential to survival, and the man the hunter/woman the gatherer dichotomy might not be accurate anyway; much hunting may have been net or communal in which women and children as well as men participated. The most important element of early human success was flexibility and adaptability, with gathering and hunting probably varying in their importance from year to year depending on environmental factors and the decisions of the group.

This more egalitarian evolutionary biology does not dispute that humans are born more helpless than practically any other animal, so the investment of time and energy in bearing, nursing, and caring for offspring is particularly great. But fathers assisted, and because patrilocation was not practiced everywhere, in many groups women relied on their female relatives, including their own mothers, in what the anthropologist Kristen Hawkes has termed the "grandmother hypothesis." Hawkes and others note that communal care of offspring in humans far exceeds that of any other primates.[5] Cooperative child-rearing, and

5 Kristen Hawkes and Richard R. Paine, *The Evolution of Human Life History* (Sante Fe, NM: School of American Research Press, 2006); and Sarah Bluffer Hrdy, *Mothers and Others: The Evolutionary Origins of Human Understanding* (Cambridge, MA: Harvard University Press, 2009).

the development of social skills and adaptability it encouraged, may have been a more important source of the development of human culture than organized group violence. Humans share organized violence with other species, but are unique in the duration and complexity of their care for children, and in the fairly common involvement of males in this. Thus studies of other primates may not apply well to early humans. (And in fact, newer studies of one species of chimpanzee, the bonobo, indicate that peaceful relations, including sex, may be more important than violence in assuring group survival and cohesion among some primates as well.) The first tool, they conclude, may have been a sling of some sort for carrying an infant – found in all of the world's cultures – rather than a club. In this line of thinking, the origins of patriarchy are not to be sought in the primate or Paleolithic past, but in developments that are part of "civilization": property ownership, plow agriculture, the bureaucratic state, writing, hereditary aristocracies, organized religion, and philosophy. Many anthropologists have also pointed out the problems in focusing on the "origins" of anything, which tends to overlook multiple causation and divergent lines of development.

Intermarriage

In both the male dominant and more egalitarian views of early human societies, pair bonding and heterosexual procreative sexual relations are at the center of the story, which is also the case with the second area in which gender history and world history are increasingly intersecting, research on intermarriage and other types of sexual relationships among individuals from different groups. These occurred especially in colonies or border regions that Kathleen Brown termed "gender frontiers," and were interwoven with developing notions of racial and ethnic difference and national identity.[6] As with many topics in gender history, the role of intermarriage in the creation of racial categories has been particularly well studied in the Americas. Scholars have examined the ways that Spanish, Portuguese, English, and French policies toward intermarriage between indigenous peoples and European conquerors and settlers changed depending on the interests of the colonizing power. In seventeenth-century New France, for example, Saliha Belmessous and Guillame Aubert have noted that officials seeking to expand the fur trade initially promoted a process they termed *Fransication*, in which Native Americans would be "made French" through conversion to

---

6 Kathleen Brown, *Good Wives, Nasty Wenches and Anxious Patriarchs: Gender, Race, and Power in Colonial Virginia* (Chapel Hill: University of North Carolina Press, 1996).

Christianity and intermarriage between French men and indigenous women.[7] When most mixed marriages instead had the opposite effect, and French men adopted "savage" customs, official opinion changed and intermarriage was prohibited. This did not stop sexual relations between European men and Native American women, of course, nor did it stop intermarriage, particularly in areas where this worked to the benefit of the local people. Similar examples of shifting policy toward intermarriage and great variation in levels of enforcement can be found throughout the colonial world.

Marriage created an economic unit as well as a sexual relationship, and historians have begun to examine the economic consequences of intermarriage and other encounters involving men and women from different groups in frontier and border areas. George Brooks, for example, traces the ways in which European and local notions about acceptable marriage partners combined in the colonies of West Africa to create distinctive economic and social patterns.[8] In the patrilineal societies of West Africa, such as the Mandinka and Wolof, Portuguese men and their mixed-race children were not allowed to marry local people of free standing, as this could give them claims to land use; their children could not inherit or join the kin and age-grade associations that shaped political power structures. Brooks has found that this meant mixed-race children generally went into trade, and in some places women became the major traders, with large households, extensive networks of trade, and many servants and slaves. Because these wealthy female traders, *nharas* in Crioulo and *signares* in French, had connections with both the African and European worlds, they were valued as both trade and marriage partners by the French and English traders who moved into this area in the eighteenth century. When they married African women, European men paid bridewealth to their new in-laws (instead of receiving a dowry as was the custom in Europe), provided a large feast, and were expected to be sexually faithful. If the husband returned to Europe, the *signare* was free to marry again. Thus intermarriage facilitated and was a key part of a pattern of cultural exchange in which European men adopted local customs far more

---

7 Saliha Belmessous, *Assimilation and Empire: Uniformity in French and British Colonies, 1541–1954* (Oxford: Oxford University Press, 2013); and Guillaume Aubert, "'The blood of France': Race and purity of the blood in the French Atlantic world," *William and Mary Quarterly* 61 (2004), 439–78.

8 George E. Brooks, *Eurafricans in Western Africa: Commerce, Social Status, Gender, and Religious Observance from the Sixteenth to the Eighteenth Century* (Athens: Ohio University Press, 2003).

than their indigenous wives adopted European, just as did French men in western North America.

"Gender frontiers" were not only found in the colonies, however. In early modern Europe, they could also be found along the borders of states and cities that had different official religions than their neighbors. Political leaders debated whether people should be allowed to marry someone of a different Christian denomination. Most thought no, and ordered sermons to be preached against religiously mixed marriage, warning of the dangers to the soul and body this might bring. But they also worried that unmarried women would be free to saunter about and spend their wages on frivolous things. So they generally decided that a religiously mixed marriage was acceptable if the man was of the approved denomination, but not if the woman was.[9] Thus a gender frontier became a gendered frontier, in which notions of male and female honor and sexuality shaped state policies about difference and intermarriage.

This did not end with the early modern era, of course. Marilyn Lake and Henry Reynolds trace restrictions on immigration and intermarriage in the transnational community of "white men's countries" in the early twentieth century. Similarly, Dagmar Herzog comments about contemporary Europe: "The entire complex of issues surrounding European identities and citizenships, with all the accompanying assumptions about appropriate inclusions and exclusions, now rests with remarkable frequency on sex-related concerns."[10]

National identity and citizenship

Lake and Reynolds' book and Herzog's comment point to a third area where there has been a significant amount of scholarship that brings together world history and gender history: studies of national identity and citizenship. Essays and books have noted the ways in which national symbols, rituals, and myths are gendered, and traced both women's contribution to nation building and their exclusion from it by the state and its institutions. Scholars have explored the ways in which gender shaped citizenship as a claims-making activity, and stressed the role of war in defining citizenship for women and men. For example, recruiting posters made use of images of helpless women to

---

9 Merry Wiesner-Hanks, *Christianity and Sexuality in the Early Modern World: Regulating Desire, Reforming Practice*, 2nd edn. (London: Routledge, 2010).
10 Marilyn Lake and Henry Reynolds, *Drawing the Global Colour Line: White Men's Countries and the International Challenge of Racial Equality* (Cambridge: Cambridge University Press, 2008); and Dagmar Herzog, "Syncopated sex: Transforming European sexual cultures," *American Historical Review* 114 (2009), 1,305.

encourage men to enlist, but also portrayed competent women whose labor was essential to the war effort. They similarly portrayed heroic men fighting alongside their comrades, and men whose masculinity was somehow suspect because they had not fought.

Some of the studies of gender and nationalism focus on one country, but those that examine former colonial areas tend to put their subjects to some degree within a global perspective. Elizabeth Thompson, for example, looks at how French rulers and elite nationalists in Syria and Lebanon tacitly agreed to marginalize women in public life, despite – or perhaps because of – their participation in mass anti-colonial movements.[11]

Sexuality, as well as gender, has shaped the making of nations, especially in the twentieth century. Margot Canaday, for example, examines ways in which the United States excluded homosexuals from full citizenship through restrictions on immigration, military service, and access to public welfare.[12] Jasbir Puar analyzes ways in which race and religion have inflected the relationship between homosexuality and nationalism in the post-9/11 United States, noting that increasingly certain homosexuals, those who are white and middle-class, are incorporated into understandings of who is an "American," while those who appear as if they are or could be Muslim are not.[13] In Europe, debates about the immigration and citizenship of Muslims often revolve around gendered practices such as the veil, and include discussion of Muslim attitudes toward homosexuality.

Migration

Nations are built through policies of inclusion and exclusion, and entered and exited through migration, a topic that has been a central theme in world history and a fourth area in which there are growing numbers of studies that integrate gender or sexuality. Approximately half of all long-distance migrants today are female, with women's migration patterns sometimes similar to those of men but sometimes quite different. Recent studies examine the transnational character of migrants' lives, in which women and men physically move back and forth and culturally and socially create and maintain links across borders. They also discuss ways in which gendered

11 Elizabeth Thompson, *Colonial Citizens: Republican Rights, Paternal Privilege, and Gender in French Syria and Lebanon* (New York: Columbia University Press, 2000).

12 Margot Canaday, *The Straight State: Sexuality and Citizenship in Twentieth-century America* (Princeton, NJ: Princeton University Press, 2009).

13 Jasbir Puar, *Terrorist Assemblages: Homonationalism in Queer Times* (Durham, NC: Duke University Press, 2007).

Figure 10.3 US Army enlistment poster by H. R. Hopps, 1917–18 (© Heritage Images / Corbis).

Figure 10.4 British Second World War poster recruiting female factory workers
(© Heritage Images/Corbis).

Figure 10.5 British First World War recruiting poster (© Corbis).

and sexualized migration shaped (and continue to shape) the economies, societies, and polities through and across which people moved. Tony Ballantyne and Antoinette Burton, for example, assess ways in which distance and movement shaped intimacy, and in which intimacy, or the prospect of intimacy, or the desire for intimacy, influenced the formation of imperial power. The intimate served "not merely as a domain of power but as one of the technologies available to colonizer and colonized alike in the struggle over colonial territory, imperial goods, and the meanings of global aspirations."[14] Much of the work on gender and sexuality in migration, like much of the more general study of migration, focuses on the "globalization" of the very recent past. In their analyses of contemporary South and Southeast Asians, for example, Sonita Sarker and Esha Niyogi De examine the ways in which ideologies of gender and sexuality within the dominant colonial powers prefigured those of the contemporary postcolonial states. They define both migrants and individuals affected by globalization who do not themselves move as "trans-status subjects," explicitly choosing that prefix for its double meaning of "across" and "beyond."[15]

Research on sexuality and migration has emphasized that just as the state produced national identities, so it also produced (and continues to produce) sexual and gender identities, often at its borders when it lets in, or does not let in, individuals that it identifies as a certain type. To those policing geographic borders, "homosexual" was not simply a discursive category, but an actual, and threatening, type of person. As Eithne Luibhéid has traced for the United States, many countries refused (and continue to refuse) to allow in those judged to be homosexual, to say nothing of those who challenge the "natural" gender order of male and female to present themselves as transsexual.[16] Despite such restrictions, however, those whose sexual and/or gender identity and presentation were in some way "queer" have migrated extensively, so much so that scholars have been able to trace "queer diasporas" in many parts of the world, including Martin Manalansan for the Philippines and Gayatri Gopinath for South Asia.[17] They examine

14 Tony Ballantyne and Antoinette Burton (eds.), *Moving Subjects: Gender, Mobility, and Intimacy in an Age of Global Empire* (Urbana: University of Illinois Press, 2009), p. 12.

15 Sonita Sarker and Esha Niyogi De (eds.), *Trans-status Subjects: Gender in the Globalization of South and Southeast Asia* (Durham, NC: Duke University Press, 2002).

16 Eithne Luibhéid, *Entry Denied: Controlling Sexuality at the Border* (Minneapolis: University of Minnesota Press, 2005).

17 Martin F. Manalansan IV, *Global Divas: Filipino Gay Men in the Diaspora* (Durham, NC: Duke University Press, 2003); and Gayatri Gopinath, *Impossible Desires: Queer Diasporas and South Asian Public Cultures* (Durham, NC: Duke University Press, 2005).

ways in which people in different places challenged, adapted, appropriated, and reworked the conceptualization of sexual acts or identities, what is often termed "localization."

Colonialism and imperialism

Gendered migration patterns were very much shaped by colonialism and imperialism, and are only one of the many threads in the broad array of recent studies of gender and sexuality in colonialism and imperialism, a fifth area of fruitful intersection. Both men and women were agents in imperial projects, and colonial powers shaped cultural constructions of masculinity and femininity. Many recent works demonstrate that imperial power is explicitly and implicitly linked with sexuality, and that images of colonial peoples were gendered and sexualized. As Giulia Calvi summarizes in her 2011 comparison of global gender history in Europe and the United States, "the gendered bodies of colonizers and colonized formed a contact zone where racialized notions of gender relations and difference were constructed through the exercise and representation of colonial power."[18] Research on gender and sexuality in the context of imperialism has emphasized links between colonized areas and the metropole, arguing that the process of colonization shaped gender ideologies and practices everywhere. Kathleen Wilson, for example, examines the ways in which English men's and women's perceptions of their English identity were shaped by colonial expansion.[19] Zine Magubane traces colonial images of blackness from South Africa to England and back again, noting the ways these influenced representations of marginalized groups such as women, the poor, and the Irish.[20]

Among colonized areas, South Asia has seen the most research. Feminist historians of India, including Tanika Sarkar, Mrinalini Sinha, and Durba Ghosh, have developed insightful analyses of the construction of gender and national identity in India during the colonial era, and the continued, often horrific and violent, repercussions of these constructions today.[21] They

---

18 Giulia Calvi, "Global trends: Gender studies in Europe and the US," *European History Quarterly* 40 (2010), 645.

19 Kathleen Wilson, *The Island Race: Englishness, Empire and Gender in the Eighteenth Century* (New York: Routledge, 2003).

20 Zine Magubane, *Bringing the Empire Home: Race, Class, and Gender in Britain and Colonial South Africa* (Chicago: University of Chicago Press, 2004).

21 Tanika Sarkar, *Hindu Wife, Hindu Nation: Community, Religion and Cultural Nationalism* (Bloomington: Indiana University Press, 2001); Mrinalini Sinha, *Specters of Mother India: The Global Restructuring of an Empire* (Durham, NC: Duke University Press, 2006); and Durba Ghosh, *Sex and the Family in Colonial India: The Making of Empire* (Cambridge: Cambridge University Press, 2006).

Figure 10.6 Indian nationalist BJP party officials, including Narendra Modi, who became Prime Minister in 2014, light a candle in front of an image of Mother India (© AMIT DAVE/Reuters/Corbis).

highlight the role of female figures – the expected devoted mother, sometimes conceptualized as Mother India, but also the loving and sacrificing wife – in nationalist iconography.

Though the theoretical framework in this scholarship is postcolonial, these scholars also take much of postcolonial scholarship to task for viewing actual women largely as a type of "eternal feminine," victimized and abject, an essentialism that denies women agency and turns gender into a historical constant, not a dynamic category. The large number of works on India has led some scholars of colonialism to argue that Indian history has become the master subaltern narrative, and that Indian women have somehow become iconic of "gendered postcolonialism." Clearly a subfield that has developed an iconic representation to be contested is healthy and growing.

Conclusions

Current research trends suggest ways in which the subject matter, theory, and methodology within world and global history and the history of gender and sexuality can intersect, and indeed are intersecting. First there is the emphasis on movement, interconnection, and interaction. World history is a study of interactions, encounters, interconnections, and intertwinings. These interconnections also shaped the experiences of people who did not move a meter, for any fixed location can be saturated with global relationships. Sexual behavior, in its most common forms, is, of course, just these things: physical, emotional, mental, and other interactions and intertwinings. Gendered social and political structures, including families, dynasties, and nations, build on these sexual relationships.

Second, though both world history and the history of gender and sexuality have created binaries – elite/subaltern, colony/metropole, East/West, homosexual/heterosexual, masculine/feminine – they have also called for their destabilization. Both early world history and early women's and gay and lesbian history often involved a grand narrative of domination and resistance, in which the subordinate subject was either a victim or resistor (or both). This dichotomous grand narrative has now been thoroughly critiqued. Increasingly all categories are complicated, and the emphasis instead is on intersectionality, entanglement, and mixture. All dichotomies are too limiting, runs this line of thought, particularly in a globalized world in which individuals can blend and build on elements from many cultures to create hybridized or fluid gender, sexual, national, racial, and other identities.

Third, both fields underscore the need for multiple perspectives. Both world history and gender history stress the importance of presenting a multiplicity of possible viewpoints, both in the sources that one uses and the approaches that one applies to them. Thus both often cross disciplinary boundaries to draw on the conceptualizations and analytical perspectives of many fields: linguistics, anthropology, genetics, archaeology, economics, literary studies, psychology, and even biology and chemistry. All of these fields have contributed to our understanding of the ways in which gender has shaped world history, and will no doubt continue to do so in an even fuller and more sophisticated way in the future.

The intersections between world and global history and the history of gender and sexuality both enhance and complicate our stories of the past. This is unsurprising, as these historical projects all began with the assertion that the history that we knew was incomplete and wanting. The best work in these fields retains this critical lens, and has included its own assumptions, perspectives, and limitations within that analytical scope. It has continued to stress that the story needs to include a wide range of actors of every possible category and identity – including identities we may not yet recognize.

Bringing the insights of these fields together makes our task as historians more difficult, but also allows us to portray the world's encounters, interconnections, entanglements, and mixtures in their full complexity.

FURTHER READING

Aldrich, Robert, *Colonialism and Homosexuality*, London: Routledge, 2002.
"*American Historical Review* forum: Revisiting 'Gender: A useful category of historical analysis', with articles by Joanne Meyerowitz, Heidi Tinsman, Maria Bucur, Dyan Elliott, Gail Hershatter and Wang Zheng, and a response by Joan Scott," *American Historical Review* 113 (2008), 1, 344–430.
Ballantyne, Tony, and Antoinette Burton (eds.), *Bodies in Contact: Rethinking Colonial Encounters in World History*, Durham, NC: Duke University Press, 2005.
 (eds.), *Moving Subjects: Gender, Mobility, and Intimacy in an Age of Global Empire*, Urbana: University of Illinois Press, 2009.
Basu, Amrita (ed.), *The Challenge of Local Feminisms: Women's Movements in Global Perspective*, Boulder, CO: Westview Press, 1995.
Blom, Ida, Karen Hagemann, and Catherine Hall (eds.), *Gendered Nations: Nationalisms and Gender Order in the Long Nineteenth Century*, Oxford: Oxford International Publishers Ltd., 2000.
Canaday, Margot, Marc Epprecht, Dagmar Herzog, Tamara Loos, Joanne Meyerowitz, Leslie Peirce, and Pete Sigal, "*American Historical Review* forum: Transnational sexualities," *American Historical Review* 114 (2009), 1, 250–353.
Canning, Kathleen, and Sonya O. Rose (eds.), *Gender, Citizenships and Subjectivities*, Malden, MA: Blackwell, 2002.
Clancy-Smith, Julia, and Frances Gouda (eds.), *Domesticating the Empire: Race, Gender and Family Life in French and Dutch Colonialism*, Charlottesville: University of Virginia Press, 1997.
Hagemann, Karen, and María Teresa Fernández-Aceves (eds.), "Gendering trans/national historiographies: Similarities and differences in comparison," *Journal of Women's History* 19 (2007), 151–213.
Hall, Catherine, and Sonya Rose (eds.), *At Home with the Empire: Metropolitan Culture and the Imperial World*, Cambridge: Cambridge University Press, 2006.
Herdt, Gilbert (ed.), *Third Sex, Third Gender: Beyond Sexual Dimorphism in Culture and History*, New York: Zone Books, 1994.
Hodes, Martha (ed.), *Sex, Love, Race: Crossing Boundaries in North American History*, New York: New York University Press, 1999.
Hrdy, Sarah Bluffer, *Mothers and Others: The Evolutionary Origins of Human Understanding*, Cambridge, MA: Harvard University Press, 2009.
Levine, Phillipa (ed.), *Gender and Empire*, Oxford: Oxford University Press, 2007.
Meade, Teresa, and Merry E. Wiesner-Hanks (eds.), *Blackwell Companion to Gender History*, London: Blackwell, 2004.
Patton, Cindy, and Benigno Sánchez-Eppler (eds.), *Queer Diasporas*, Durham, NC: Duke University Press, 2000.

Riley, Denise, *"Am I that name?" Feminism and the Category of "Women" in History*, Minneapolis: University of Minnesota Press, 1988.

Roach Pierson, Ruth, and Nupur Chaudhuri (eds.), *Nation, Empire, Colony: Historicizing Gender and Race*, Indianapolis: Indiana University Press, 1998.

Rupp, Leila, *Worlds of Women: The Making of an International Women's Movement*, Princeton, NJ: Princeton University Press, 1997.

Scott, Joan, *Gender and the Politics of History*, New York: Columbia University Press, 1988.

Sharpe, Pamela (ed.), *Women, Gender, and Labour Migrations: Historical and Global Perspectives*, New York: Routledge, 2001.

Smith, Bonnie, *The Gender of History: Men, Women, and Historical Practice*, New York: Oxford University Press, 1998.

   (ed.), *Global Feminisms since 1945: A Survey of Issues and Controversies*, New York: Routledge, 2000.

   (ed.), *Women's History in Global Perspective*, 3 vols., Urbana: University of Illinois Press, 2004.

Stoler, Ann Laura, *Carnal Knowledge and Imperial Power: Race and the Intimate in Colonial Rule*, 2nd edn., Berkeley: University of California Press, 2011.

Wiesner-Hanks, Merry E., *Christianity and Sexuality in the Early Modern World: Regulating Desire, Reforming Practice*, 2nd edn., London: Routledge, 2010.

   Gender in History: Global Perspectives, 2nd edn., London: Blackwell, 2010.

Woollacott, Angela, *Gender and Empire*, New York: Palgrave Macmillan, 2006.

What does anthropology contribute to world history?

JACK GOODY

In the beginning

Although its name indicates an interest in all humankind (*anthropos*), anthropology nevertheless confined itself to earlier and simpler cultures and steered away from the modern. But what were the boundaries? In the work of the pioneers, E. B. Tylor and Sir James Frazer, this was 'primitive man' including 'survivals' – in later times, king-killing in Europe as well as monarchy's role in supposedly curing scrofula, known as the 'King's Evil'.[1] This role of anthropology meant collecting data in non-literate societies from anywhere in the world, and it provided a kind of social and intellectual account of those societies. This would have fitted the requirements of a history of the world very well.

But it had no substantial successors. With Bronislaw Malinowski and his Revolution in Anthropology, the subject concentrated on the analysis of particular non-literate societies, essentially through fieldwork methods, that is, through observation in a detailed study of a single society. The belief was that aggregating the knowledge of such cultures served to distort them. Since every society was different, comparison was impossible, or possible only among close neighbours. On the face of it, the fields of anthropology and world history moved far apart.

Thus, for many the two fields of history and anthropology have had their place at opposite ends of the academic spectrum. World history involves the consideration of written societies – before, that is, of prehistory. Earlier anthropology concentrated on the study of society before writing, and, therefore, lacked such accounts or observation. It has largely confined comparison to these 'primitive' and simple societies; however, in the post-world war period it also took its students through the classical sociologists,

---

1 Edward B. Tylor, *Primitive Culture: Researches into the Development of Mythology, Philosophy, Religion, Art, and Custom*, 2 vols. (London: John Murray, 1871); and James George Frazer, *The Golden Bough: A Study in Magic and Religion*, 12 vols. (London: Macmillan, 1915).

mainly via the works of Durkheim who had himself included 'simple' societies in his well-known study of the first Australians in *The Elementary Forms of Religious Life*,[2] as well as touching upon the works of Weber (but hardly Marx). This had involved recent societies, as in Durkheim's work on suicide[3] and the division of labour,[4] and therefore the problem of modernization. Modernization obviously meant dealing with 'complex' societies that lay outside the acknowledged scope of the subject since this had focused on the 'simple', or those without an elaborate division of labour. This concentration had defined the subject from the outset; it was the story of earlier humankind, of the Stone and Bronze Ages in archaeology, life before writing, and, before that, the emergence of humans in biological terms. Complexity, however, was seen largely in relation to colonization and to elementary industrialization, and sometimes also to the advent of writing. In practice the presence of literacy was largely ignored in favour of a distinction between European and 'other cultures'. This division clearly meant that some literate societies like China and Japan were not only 'other' but in some respects were also considered 'primitive' (as in Durkheim and Mauss' *Primitive Classification*[5]). Both China and Japan were studied by students of Malinowski, even though this should have involved the use of written records. However, 'history' was formally excluded as an explanatory factor since anthropology was held to depend upon observation of what went on in the here and now, not on reports. However, not only traditional literate societies, but more and more others were also now keeping records, so some attention (usually sporadic) had to be given to the past, even in dominantly oral societies. Because, although the culture itself may have operated without writing, as was the case among the LoDagaa of Northern Ghana, they were written *about*, and with colonization there was the inevitable development of administrative records. That was a condition of the expansion of Europe.

One might have thought anthropology would have little to do with world history, especially since the functionalists and the structuralists effectively dismissed history as an explanatory factor in the social sciences, it being essential to explain the present by the present in a living organism, in a

2 Émile Durkheim, *The Elementary Forms of Religious Life*, Karen E. Fields (trans.) (London: Free Press, 1995).
3 Émile Durkheim, *Suicide: A Study in Sociology*, George Simpson and John A. Spaulding (trans.) (London: Routledge, 2002).
4 Émile Durkheim, *The Division of Labour in Society*, W. D. Halls (trans.) (New York: Free Press, 1997).
5 Émile Durkheim and Marcel Mauss, *Primitive Classification*, Rodney Needham (trans.) (Chicago: University of Chicago Press, 1967).

biological manner. That is how things have been since the Malinowskian revolution of the 1920s but it was not so beforehand.

Drawing the boundary between 'modern' and 'traditional' in this way singled out later European societies, as being different from the rest, for example in 'culture' such as in the development of cuisine and the use of cultivated flowers. However, a brief examination of Indian and Chinese cuisines and restaurant cultures, as well as the use of flowers in their cere-monies and for dress, immediately indicated the kind of complexity that put the cultures on roughly the same level and threw doubts on this division. This was equally the case with communication, with writing. The earlier assump-tions of the uniqueness of the Greek alphabet were questioned by an increas-ing understanding of the eastern varieties and the realization that syllabic and logographic scripts had their own advantages as instruments of communi-cation. They could permit extensive literacy and the development of an elaborate written culture, which in China's case included long 'realistic' novels and both a philosophical and scientific tradition.

But world history and anthropology are in fact not so distant as was once thought. Historians are trained to examine written documents; their work is in the library rather than the field, that is, with reports of what has happened rather than undertaking first-hand observation, although the category 'oral history' has rather blurred this issue, since history normally involves written records, not oral accounts. Unless recorded in some way, these oral accounts cannot be rechecked and are therefore evanescent. In both fields, however, there is some tension between the intensive library and archival examination of particular groups or between particular observational studies on the one hand and the wider 'com-parative' ones that take into account a number of societies, or even all (the 'world', or perhaps just the Old World, with its written tradition). In anthropol-ogy (of the social and cultural kind) that interest had led to comparative study of the sort earlier practised by Tylor or Frazer but now quite out of fashion. It has been partly replaced not only by intensive fieldwork of the Malinowskian kind but also, after the work of Émile Durkheim and his British followers, especially A. R. Radcliffe-Brown and, to a lesser extent, E. E. Evans-Pritchard and others of his generation, by a theoretical interest in 'comparative sociology'.

At that time, in the 1940s and 1950s, there were few anthropological studies of western societies such as Lloyd Warner's on Newburyport in Massachusetts in 1941 (he had originally worked with the Murngin of Australia),[6] for Europe

---

6 W. Lloyd Warner, *The Social Life of a Modern Community* (New Haven, CT: Yale University Press, 1941).

was basically out of bounds (except for witchcraft and other 'survivals'); we studied other cultures, and even societies such as India and China with strong written traditions were held to be in the same category as the 'primitive', most notably by Durkheim for primitive classification in relation to China,[7] as well as by Lévi-Strauss in relation to marriage,[8] and for India especially by Dumont in relation to this and to general development.[9] In drawing this supposed distinction they failed to see the basic similarities even of these other written cultures with Europe that were emphasized by Needham in his magisterial work on China, which he showed was more 'modern' than earlier Europe.[10] So they drew the line round modern in a thoroughly nineteenth-century way, which was the wrong line in the wrong place, failing to accord sufficient importance to literacy, which was common to all the major Eurasian societies. Indeed when students of anthropology did work in such 'other cultures', they tended to ignore the written tradition, even to the extent of not knowing how to read its script. They cut themselves off from that aspect of local life and treated it as an 'oral' culture. The situation has now changed, sociology and anthropology have grown larger or created new boundaries, leading to the conceptual intermingling or even confusion of each field with the other, except that the second has specialized in micro-observation, the first in macro-sociology.

In practice, however, 'comparative sociology' was a dream; anthropology became nothing of the kind – except with Durkheim's school in France. Indeed it was impossible to marry up intensive and extensive study, and even the tentative steps to considering that possibility led to a conflict between Evans-Pritchard (who had earlier studied history, as had many other early anthropologists) and other social anthropologists. However, he did think wider comparison was possible within the context of 'Primitive Societies' and 'Other Cultures' and his students went on to produce a number of general volumes of this kind.[11] Nevertheless, comparative volumes were valued very much less than reports on particular societies, which were seen

---

7 Durkheim and Mauss, *Primitive Classification*.
8 Claude Lévi-Strauss, *Elementary Structures of Kinship*, James Harle Bell, Rodney Needham, and John Richard von Sturmer (trans.) (Boston: Beacon Press, 1969).
9 Louis Dumont, *Homo Hierarchicus: The Caste System and Its Implications*, Mark Sainsbury (trans.) (London: Weidenfeld & Nicolson, 1970).
10 Joseph Needham, et al. (eds.), *Science and Civilisation in China* (Cambridge: Cambridge University Press, 1954).
11 Ronald Godfrey Lienhardt, *Social Anthropology* (London: Oxford University Press, 1964); John Beattie, *Other Cultures: Aims, Methods and Achievements in Social Anthropology* (London: Cohen & West, 1964); and David Francis Pocock, *Social Anthropology* (London: Sheed & Ward, 1961).

as presenting the actual data as distinct from aggregate material that fitted some societies but not others. Comparison could distort and there was much concern, for example, about interpreting Dinka concepts of the 'soul' in Nuer terms. Every culture was different. Yes, but...

How can the oral help the written?

If 'history' is concerned with written cultures and anthropology with oral ones, can there be much traffic between the two? Yes. First, anthropology can help to make history less ethnocentric, less European in the case of the west. It can do this in two ways, by bringing other societies into consideration and by leading people back to earlier ones, in both cases trying to redress the bias in favour of one's own culture. Second, it can emphasize the value of direct observational evidence to supplement the use of books. Books are the backbone of historical study, but not so for anthropology, for which the main source of knowledge is fieldwork.

But apart from lessening ethnocentrism and emphasizing observations in the field, what does the study of social anthropology do for the historian? First, the societies studied by anthropologists are considered by historians primarily in terms of the impact of the west, as the receivers of colonialism. Many of them were certainly this, the subjects of the European takeover. But they had their own story, or prehistory from the standpoint of writing, a life of their own, and this too is often misunderstood by historians. They tend to neglect or misinterpret evidence from earlier times. For example, some classicists see Greece as having invented 'democracy', whereas many earlier societies with simpler forms of organization consulted their members at frequent intervals. And even in the later, historic, period, local government in the Ancient Near East often insisted on such consultation while some Phoenician towns, including the colony at Carthage, had a yet more elaborate system involving the written vote. Neither Greece, Europe nor the Near East, however, were the only practitioners of consultation, though they did develop writing that was used for many purposes. Thales may have been the first Phoenician philosopher to leave a written record; he was certainly not the first to try and conceptualize the world in a general moral and intellectual framework; the precursors of Ogotemmêli, the Dogon sage,[12] did that.

12 Marcel Griaule, *Conversations with Ogotemmêli: An Introduction to Dogon Religious Ideas* (Oxford: Oxford University Press, 1965).

Anthropology can contribute to world history by saving us from some of these errors into which literates are only too liable to fall.

Anthropology can therefore help to modify the inevitable tendency to attribute uniqueness to the institutions of one's own society, or to the west, not only for democracy, but also for 'law', 'religion', 'monogamy' or even the 'family', which leads to a general tendency to see those earlier societies as 'savage', and thus to erecting the imaginary 'evolutionary' schemas of 'conjectural history'. Rejecting such schemas meant that the differences that did exist between 'us' and 'them' had then to be explained in more concrete terms, not by means of questionable developmental sequences.

Most societies had created accounts of the world in which they 'placed' themselves in relation to their neighbours and sometimes others too. World history, then, is nothing new. All societies had some concept of how they themselves fitted into the wider picture. But earlier world histories were sometimes tied to a particular religion or even to a country, one's own. However, contemporary world history has become largely secularized in the sense that it is not linked to the superiority of one creed nor indeed to the events controlled by any supernatural power. It can no longer credit the idea of a deity with supernatural intervention either at Milvian Bridge or at Dunkirk, although, once established, religious belief of this kind may well affect the course of events; the Cross was important in urging Christian soldiers onward, as was the Crescent under Saladin. But as far as is possible the world historian must remain neutral, indeed secular, which was especially problematic under monotheism; polytheism was more permissive, as in classical Europe. But the secular story emerged only later when history had acquired some kind of long-term developmental perspective, such as that of the Three Ages of Man, which helped classify archaeological material.

Oral cultures already had some ideas about their past, even if this hardly counted as 'history', just as they had such ideas about geographical space. They had, for example, 'drum histories' (histories of a kingdom beaten out on a 'talking drum', one that imitates the pattern of speech) that offered a version of the past of a particular kingdom. In any case, a consideration of the past as the present was always acceptable to anthropologists. The history that was excluded was not the study of this past, they could do that, but a study of the written past, which required documents and libraries. So the literate European cultures were excluded from fieldwork, although even there the oral (or rather the lecto-oral), the spoken interaction in contrast to the written, became a focus of some anthropological enquiry. But primarily it was only the primitive, or simple, or 'other' that fell into their scope.

The 'modern' was out of bounds but nevertheless this was included in works recommended for their students. Moreover the 'simple' comprised oral not only in aboriginal societies but, surprisingly, in India and China too, although they had a substantial written tradition and their own version of 'history'. They had writing but on the other hand they were not considered 'modern', they were 'oriental', dealt with not in a history faculty but in an oriental department.

The 'simple' and the 'complex'

Setting a boundary between 'simple' and 'complex' was complicated. In the nineteenth century, Europeans produced various schema based on different things: the Three Ages of Man concept used the dominant material (stone, bronze, iron); Marx used modes of production; Weber used intellectual orientation and the 'Protestant ethic'; and others family and marriage, or political systems. In all of these, the notion was that European institutions were always the most advanced of all, thus justifying colonialism. Neither the Weberian nor the Marxist theses stand up to the test of comparative history, though they both bring the whole of Eurasia into their account. They both see 'capitalism' or 'true capitalism' as a European development, neglecting in my view the growth of exchange, manufacture, and accounting in the east and the Near East, which had first seen the development of written societies.

After querying the implications of the Eurocentric argument about the uniqueness of the Greek alphabet, a uniqueness that had been essential to the earlier discussions of Watt and myself[13] about the transformative role of (western) writing and modes of communication more generally, the view of most historians and sociologists, I drew the line in a different place, not between the modern and the traditional so much as between the literate and the 'oral'. This recognized the concrete fact of differences, but the emphasis on communication set aside the simple/complex division that had turned around the nineteenth-century obsession about 'the invention of capitalism' ('modernity') in Europe and the whole concern with the 'Uniqueness of the West'. It also recognized that literacy was not simply an aspect of an inherited 'culture' but could be acquired by others, and that the mass introduction of schools, then taking place on a worldwide scale, thanks to UNESCO and to colonial and newly independent regimes, could revolution- ize the transmission of knowledge, as had happened in many parts of the

13 Jack Goody and Ian Watt, 'The Consequences of Literacy', *Comparative Studies in Society and History* 5 (1963), 304–45.

world in the second quarter of the twentieth century. Once that discussion had been set aside, the whole rationale for the special analytic category of 'simple' societies was fatally weakened, and Eurasia, with its written history, could then be considered as a whole analytically, making 'world history', or at least Eurasian history of the written variety, more manageable. 'History' now included the story of all the major societies with writing (leaving aside 'history' in the wider sense of a study of the past).

Regional comparison

The regional interest among anthropologists had led to collections such as *African Political Systems*[14] edited by Fortes and Evans-Pritchard and *African Systems of Kinship and Marriage*[15] edited by Radcliffe-Brown and Forde, which were not simply aggregates of individual accounts, unlike many historical anthologies, but which comprised a 'theoretical' introduction discussing some general features of the regional societies and therefore acting in a preliminary way as a tool towards the story of the whole world, even if denying that intention. This attempt at the unified treatment of Africa drew some scholars to broader questions as it called attention to their general features, and led to comparisons with areas outside of Africa, such as studies of the difference between (and implications of) bridewealth in Africa on the one hand, and dowry transactions in Eurasia on the other. This realization cut the cake in a different way. World history was not just a matter of taking into account the east, as Marx and Weber had in fact done, but re-evaluating the whole boundary drawn between the modern west and the more trad-itional (and primitive) east, *and* in re-equilibrating the supposed imbalance between the two. Taking the world into account was not itself enough, unless one balanced the assumed disparity, which world events were now contradicting every day.

The similarities within Eurasia and Africa themselves were important; anthropologists usually stress the particular features of the culture in which they worked, as do the people themselves, disregarding the many similarities between them and their neighbours. This realization of similar features led me to contrast the structures of Africa and Europe in terms of the

---

14 M. Fortes and E. E. Evans-Pritchard (eds.), *African Political Systems* (London: Oxford University Press, 1940).

15 A. R. Radcliffe-Brown and Daryll Forde (eds.), *African Systems of Kinship and Marriage* (London: Oxford University Press, 1950).

development of advanced Bronze Age societies (with their technologies of metal, urbanization, and cultures of a written kind) and to see them as related to the structures of family (or kinship for anthropologists). For example, in Eurasia there was much more similarity between the east and west in this sphere than most had argued for, especially Malthus and those many historians (and anthropologists) who followed him in relating Western European achievement in the eighteenth and nineteenth centuries to supposed differences in family structure, a difference that has been set aside not only by the work with Tambiah[16] but more importantly by that of Lee and Feng,[17] who rejected the arguments that had sprung out of the undoubted dominance of Western Europe in many spheres at the beginning of the Industrial Revolution. Our understanding was based on quite another interpretation of the history, if not of the world, at least on a new rebalancing of the Old World and its literate civilizations. That can be seen not only by a broader history than European scholars (or others) have normally undertaken, but by going back not to supposedly significant differences between east and west, accounting for what we can now see in some respects as a temporary state of affairs instead of appealing to 'essentialist' factors of a more permanent 'ethnic' kind, but by going back to common origins.

The attempts to explain 'capitalism' as a western phenomenon, by nineteenth-century westerners themselves, suffer from myopia, that is, not looking widely enough but also not going back deeply enough in time to see the many connections between the written cultures of Eurasia in the Bronze Age that derived from a common origin in the Ancient Near East – a common origin that produced great cultural differences but stressed the shared commonalities in this period of the written word and of the metal age. Only a reshaped world history can do this justice. Reshaped it has to be because most previous attempts in Eurasia were too strongly influenced by their origins as in the case of Rashid al-Din's Islamic attempt, in the more restricted version of Chinese scholars, or especially in the work of many westerners in the nineteenth century. Clearly these written cultures had to 'place' themselves in the known world, as did all those elsewhere. And each did so in an ethnocentric way that was often heavily influenced by the prevailing religion. But it is the job of scholarship to check or modify such

---

16 Jack Goody and S. J. Tambiah (eds.), *Bridewealth and Dowry* (Cambridge: Cambridge University Press, 1973).

17 James Z. Lee and Feng Wang, *One Quarter of Humanity: Malthusian Mythology and Chinese Realities, 1700–2000* (Cambridge, MA: Harvard University Press, 1999).

widespread distortion, not to build on it and to assume a quasi-permanent superiority, as Western Europe (and others) did in the nineteenth century, translating temporary advantage into a long-term 'ethnic' or even 'racial' superiority.

Taking a wider view, we can see such advantage or superiority as a matter of alternation, as part of *un histoire pendulaire*, but such a perspective comes up against egocentric prejudice, which is partly why 'world history' meets with much resistance. The egocentric or even national point of view is one taught in every school and is 'natural' to us all, but it is one that has to be eradicated or at least greatly modified if one is to understand the history of the world, or even that of one's own country in this mondial age.

The Bronze Age, writing, and the history of others

Many aspects of contemporary life clearly began in the Bronze Age. Writing, metals, urban society, 'civilization', the religions of conversion, especially the monotheistic ones, and all that they implied. But humankind had existed long before and it was both this long *durée* of oral cultures and the relatively rapid change with literacy that world history aims to emphasize. However, we do not see exchange, technology, or family life as beginning with our first records but in various ways as being developed at that time.

Usually history takes a very egocentric view, as 'We the people'. 'Primitive history' is inevitably centred on one's own community and this is how it is still often taught in today's schools. That teaches of course about one's neighbours too, and what we know of the rest of the world has expanded with literacy and communication, especially in Europe's case with the Renaissance. But that was not just a western phenomenon. Others visited different societies. The Chinese too travelled, both by sea and by land. So too did the Indians and many other citizens of Bronze Age societies. As people and goods travelled, so too did knowledge of the world increase, especially with writing. However, that knowledge was often interpreted in terms of a society's view of others as inferior, even barbarous. And this was especially the case when reinforced by a conviction of religious superiority of the monotheistic variety.

So the major challenge in world history is not simply one of extending the scope from the national to the world, or at least to Eurasia if one is confining 'history' to written cultures; pre-Columbian America had some writing but it was hardly a full written culture in the Near Eastern sense, after, say, 2000 BCE. This extension itself took several forms. In simple societies there was the acknowledgement of neighbours. But with writing there was an elementary 'comparative history' that included accounts of other written cultures; in Europe this might just include Egypt and Rome. Any such effort was greatly helped by comprehensive studies like that of Needham[18] on Chinese science and in a very different way (and for non-literate societies) in compilations by the west in Africa and elsewhere. These were continental or regional but collected together knowledge that could then be used more widely.

The most severe challenge to Eurocentrism came from the other fully literate societies of China and India, and to some extent from the Near East. Needham's magnificent series on Chinese science and civilization has made it inexcusable for any English-speaking scholar to ignore their contribution to that field. The contributions of India and the Near East are more piecemeal, less easy to discover, and even many of the best-intentioned Europeans still view these cultures as giving little to modernity.

World history, like anthropology, may serve to make us less ethnocentric, or at least Eurocentric. It is of course hardly surprising that students of literature, studying what has been written in their own language, should consider Shakespeare, Goethe, or Molière, as *sans pareil*, without compare. The same is often initially true of English, German, or French history, but there is less excuse for this. Comparative literature may be difficult for most to study, since it involves many languages. But world history can be done in one's own tongue, though many documents may have to be translated. But that process is less sensitive than with literature and the task of providing a comprehensive summary is less problematic, so a wider, or even world, perspective can be achieved without too much difficulty, modifying in some measure the ethnocentric bias resulting from our egocentric view of the world as well as from early instruction in schools and colleges in 'national' history, even more critical for every new nation. This is a perspective that both fields must undertake if they are to be considered in any way 'scientific' and not simply celebratory.

In world history it is not simply a matter of extending the range but of rebalancing the comparison so that it questions the view that no one except Western Europe could develop 'capitalism' or 'modernization'. Today such a confining idea is immediately refuted by developments in China and India, which are not just a matter of copying those of the west but of building on

18 Needham, *et al.* (eds.), *Science and Civilisation.*

what these societies had themselves produced by way of a written, exchange economy with elaborate forms of knowledge and a technology that included cast iron and high-fired porcelain in China, cotton cloth and crucible iron in India, quite apart from the purely tropical products, the citrus fruit in China and the spices in India. As in the west, development occurred not in one society but often by a process of alternation. I myself was much struck by the fact that until the Italian Renaissance, as Needham claimed, science was more advanced in the east than in the west, and that China, India, and the Near East were in many ways more advanced than the west until relatively recently, well after the adoption of Arabic (that is, Indian) numerals to replace the more cumbrous Roman kind. Of course, world history does not always avoid Eurocentrism but it is an essential preliminary. Both Marx and Weber in different ways included the whole of Eurasia in their sights. Nevertheless, their reconstruction of the past was essentially Eurocentric in that they gave Europe, and indeed England, the credit for having invented the modern world order, that of 'capitalism'.

One virtue of anthropology for world history is that it considers pre-literate societies not simply in a mass as 'primitive', waiting for the advent of civilization (usually from Europe) that they were unable to achieve themselves. Rather it considers oral culture not only in its own right but also as part of the journey to a more complex mode of existence. It is this journey that archaeology tries to trace and which has culminated in attempts such as that of Eric Wolf to write the story of *Europe and the People without History*,[19] the story, that is, of the rest of the world. Wolf and other more recent scholars have set aside the dependency model, which viewed all other societies as dependent on western capitalism, and instead see western primacy as essentially contextual and alternating. Take the Near East. In the fourth or third millennium BCE this area saw the birth of 'civilization', which included the metal age and the birth of written culture, with its complex forms of exchange and of accounts. Accounting certainly did not begin with the double-entry of Weber's Protestants nor even with Marx's capitalism, nor yet with the Italian Renaissance. It is of course the case that the Near East did not seem to develop a complex industrial economy in the manner of nineteenth-century Europe, to which it had earlier exported 'urban society'. But then it did not have the supply of metals, of wood and coal, and of water, nor did it have any longer such a central place in the growing system

19 Eric R. Wolf, *Europe and the People Without History* (Berkeley: University of California Press, 1982).

of international exchange. The ideology and the desire were there, the resources were not. While later differences, although not irrelevant, were marginal, the important factor is that from the perspective of the written cultures of Eurasia, all civilizations of the cultures of cities derive, as Childe and other archaeologists have maintained, from a common origin in the Bronze Age of the Ancient Near East.

Comparative history is not only about the history of these written societies, much less of 'modern' ones. If it dwells only on those, it will concentrate upon differences in the Industrial Age for example, without getting to grips with the commonalities in earlier societies, especially in written ones. That latter procedure would tend to emphasize the common factors, in those in the east and the west, instead of searching for differences, as Malthus and many others have done. They existed, of course, but not in the way that western history has maintained. Only a world historical approach enables us to see these later divergences in a proper context, and how these have proved temporary especially with the 'emergence' of China and India as great manufacturing powers. The usual western account sees this emergence as being the result of the migration of 'capitalism'. This account is to give a much too limited interpretation of that concept and to disregard the fact that China was the greatest exporter of manufactured products until the end of the eighteenth century, and that India too was an exporter of steel in the Roman period as well as of painted cottons over a long period. To dismiss these nations as 'peripheral' in relation to a western 'core' is a peculiarly ethnocentric view based on the strictly temporary superiority of the latter's methods in the late eighteenth century, a view that tends to regard that particular situation as permanent and as connected with ethnicity rather than circumstance. But it clearly was not, neither in production nor in 'knowledge'. Needham has demonstrated the great achievements of Chinese science before the Renaissance while Indian mathematicians used more convenient 'Arabic' numerals to produce complex questions and answers in the intellectual field. The situation was not improved by those who assumed that Europe was unique in evolving a shift either to financial capitalism or to a world system. It was clearly unique in the sense that all historical situations are and in the advances it made in the Industrial Revolution but not in the assumption that there was a unique change of system. That would be to ignore the alternation, or rather the 'spiralling', that took place in the history of all written societies. Those societies were metal-using and both this and the writing represented points on the road to modernization rather than a shift to a completely different 'mode of production' such as 'capitalism'.

That again was a particularly western conception that excluded a consideration of the achievements of the east in an unacceptable way. There were as many 'shoots of capitalism' there as in the west; and some aspects of that 'system' (which has been called that of 'petty capitalism') were first manifested in the exchange economy of the Near East involving the written transactions that eventually led to double-entry book-keeping. Of this Max Weber wanted to make a special case as representing a form of rationality that only the west possessed (or perhaps developed, though it seemed to imply we are born with this as an 'ethnic' characteristic).[20] Many of the arguments of both west and east have assumed this permanent character, and indeed the very concept of culture in an anthropological context has something about it of this kind. Culture in Ruth Benedict's sense is certainly something you learn but often it is seen in a static rather than a dynamic way to indicate what are considered to be permanent features of a group, so that the ethic is not simply Protestant in a historical sense but an attitude that we acquire at birth.[21] In fact the Chinese also developed that form of book-keeping as well as philosophical rationality.

History's contribution to anthropology

What does a historical perspective do for the anthropologist? For the field-worker, not much, especially since Malinowski tried to banish the historical dimension as a mode of explanation for social facts. However, today it is generally felt that this rejection should apply to what Radcliffe-Brown called 'pseudo-history', that is, dynamic sequences constructed from static data for which there is little or no evidence. It is apparent that in the explanation of much observational work historical data should take a subordinate place. But world history has its place if only to give a dynamic context to static observations. For example, when I saw a friend's arm being gravely damaged in West Africa because of an exploding barrel of a gun being fired at a funeral, it is helpful to note that the smelting technology could not produce enough heat for the welding of ordinary barrels, so people had to rely on patched up imports, possibly from Europe. It was also true of the porcelain fragments decorating the doorways of merchants' houses: oven heat was insufficient to make stoneware and only easily soluble

20 Max Weber, *The Protestant Ethic and the Spirit of Capitalism*, Talcott Parsons (trans.) (London: G. Allen & Unwin, 1930).
21 Ruth Benedict, *Patterns of Culture* (Boston: Houghton Mifflin, 1989).

earthenware was possible before the eighteenth century either in Europe or in Africa. So 'China', high-fired pottery, was a valued import that could not be made locally; even fragments were prized. Like cast iron this was a luxury product to be brought in from the outside. These material and spiritual differences in cultures have to be understood in world historical terms, as does the absence of literacy except where Abrahamistic religions had penetrated. The penetration of those religions, and their goods and their technologies, including those of the intellect, were part of a long-term process that was affecting Africa just as it had earlier in other parts of the world, including Europe.

There have of course been attempts at world history in the past. Most of the 'world states' or 'world religions' had some view of the other inhabitants, as with the Islamic history of Rashid al-Din, or the Chinese dynastic histories, but these were made very much from the point of view of the country or the religions and were the equivalent of the 'primitive' history of tribes such as the Nuer who adopted a 'we, the people' standpoint.

Today what draws the fieldworker to world history? In my case it was partly watching people at work. You can't help being struck by the relative paucity of those in African villages compared with Indian or Eurasian ones, paucity and the absence of some complexity. A town in Africa was a village in India. And this was clearly related to the process of production, to the absence of the horse and cart (because no wheel) as well as that of the plough and of any animal traction. This was not an individual or societal difference but one that affected whole regions, indeed continents, and demanded an explanation, and that effectively was not forthcoming within the Weberian or Marxist frame.

World history is human history, that is to say, it is the history of humanity. It involves the emergence of our species from other animals, which means taking account of stages of physical evolution and that includes not only going back to the beginning but also going wider into human development.

FURTHER READING

Beattie, John, *Other Cultures: Aims, Methods and Achievements in Social Anthropology*, London: Cohen & West, 1964.
Benedict, Ruth, *Patterns of Culture*, Boston: Houghton Mifflin, 1989.
Dumont, Louis, *Homo Hierarchicus: The Caste System and Its Implications*, Mark Sainsbury (trans.), London: Weidenfeld & Nicolson, 1970.
Durkheim, Émile, *The Division of Labour in Society*, W. D. Halls (trans.), New York: Free Press, 1997.

The Elementary Forms of Religious Life, Karen E. Fields (trans.), London: Free Press, 1995.

Suicide: A Study in Sociology, George Simpson and John A. Spaulding (trans.), London: Routledge, 2002.

Durkheim, Émile, and Marcel Mauss, *Primitive Classification*, Rodney Needham (trans.), Chicago: University of Chicago Press, 1967.

Fortes, M., and E. E. Evans-Pritchard (eds.), *African Political Systems*, London: Oxford University Press, 1940.

Frazer, James George, *The Golden Bough: A Study in Magic and Religion*, 12 vols., London: Macmillan, 1915.

Goody, Jack, and Ian Watt, 'The consequences of literacy', *Comparative Studies in Society and History* 5 (1963), 304–45.

Goody, Jack, and S. J. Tambiah (eds.), *Bridewealth and Dowry*, Cambridge: Cambridge University Press, 1973.

Griaule, Marcel, *Conversations with Ogotemmêli: An Introduction to Dogon Religious Ideas*, Oxford: Oxford University Press, 1965.

Lee, James Z., and Feng Wang, *One Quarter of Humanity: Malthusian Mythology and Chinese Realities, 1700–2000*, Cambridge, MA: Harvard University Press, 1999.

Lévi-Strauss, Claude, *Elementary Structures of Kinship*, James Harle Bell, Rodney Needham, and John Richard von Sturmer (trans.), Boston: Beacon Press, 1969.

Lienhardt, Ronald Godfrey, *Social Anthropology*, London: Oxford University Press, 1964.

Needham, Joseph, et al. (eds.), *Science and Civilisation in China*, Cambridge: Cambridge University Press, 1954.

Pocock, David Francis, *Social Anthropology*, London: Sheed & Ward, 1961.

Radcliffe-Brown, A. R., and Daryll Forde (eds.), *African Systems of Kinship and Marriage*, London: Oxford University Press, 1950.

Tylor, Edward B., *Primitive Culture: Researches into the Development of Mythology, Philosophy, Religion, Art, and Custom*, 2 vols., London: John Murray, 1871.

Warner, W. Lloyd, *The Social Life of a Modern Community*, New Haven, CT: Yale University Press, 1941.

Weber, Max, *The Protestant Ethic and the Spirit of Capitalism*, Talcott Parsons (trans.), London: G. Allen & Unwin, 1930.

Wolf, Eric R., *Europe and the People without History*, Berkeley: University of California Press, 1982.

12

Migration in human history

PATRICK MANNING

Migration, because it inherently links points of origin and destination through trajectories, draws attention to the connections that are central to understanding world history. Studies of migration, especially in recent years, have been effective both in documenting the evolving patterns of human migration and in illustrating the accompanying historical connections. Migration history is thus a subfield of world history, and holds a place alongside other subfields that have become organized areas of study within world history: these include environment, health, empires, economy, genetics, and maritime history.

The study of migration is especially helpful in advancing the understanding of communities. Language communities, ethnic communities, political communities, religious communities – all of these are best studied not simply as discrete social groupings with their own traditions, but as permeable groups that are linked to each other through the voluntary and involuntary movement of individuals and groups. A migration-oriented approach to communities draws attention to heterogeneity and processes of interaction within communities. Further, study of migration facilitates the understanding of the multiple levels and scales at which the human experience unfolds. Effective stories of migration range from the individual tales of merchants, warriors, students, and the enslaved – male and female – to the chronicles of ethnic groups on the move or in formation, and to narratives of the repopulation of whole continents. More generally, studies of migration illustrate several types of scale: in space, in time, in the specific populations migrating, and in the range of human affairs affected by migration.

The study of migration relies on a range of methodologies, and recent research is bringing advances in the articulation of these methods. Documentary research based on records of governments and business firms has provided much of the information on migration in recent times. Written narratives and oral traditions have provided further information on migrations, especially in times before the past five centuries. Archaeological research was long the core of research on migration for times before the written record began. It has now been supplemented by research in historical linguistics, comparative social anthropology, and chemical techniques. The most spectacular new results come from the expanding analysis of genetics, a field that has the potential (when linked to other data) to give detailed information on human movements and exchanges from earliest times until the very recent past. In addition, the field of demography provides the basic tools for analyzing the data on birth, death, and migration to give a fuller picture of changes in human population.

Studies of migration need not be limited to the movement of people: they can also trace movements of technology (from bows and arrows to telephones), of ideas (Buddhism, literacy), and of associated or commensal species (lice, dogs, and potatoes). Indeed, the relations of these different aspects of migration to each other form a growing portion of current studies in migration. The full range of these studies begins to make it possible to develop an assessment of the function of migration in human society. That is, at the most basic levels migration brings genetic diversity and allows exchange of innovations that have enabled humans to learn and spread in ways exceeding the range of any previous large animals. While migration-induced learning has brought dramatic and recurring change in human experience, migration also reveals a fundamental continuity in history. Social processes relying on cross-community migration have been at the core of the big changes from the early days of humanity, and give every indication of continuing in similar form far into the future.

Basic patterns in human migration

The basic patterns of human migration have doubtless changed somewhat over the years, but the underlying logic of human migration is remarkably consistent. The common pattern of human migration is for the migrants – dominantly young adult males and females though a minority of that age-group – to leave home and move away to a destination where the landscape, culture, and language are different. Some migrants move to sparsely settled frontiers and others to centers of population; some return home, while others remain at their destination or even move further. Migrations are initiated by human decision but also by natural disasters that can force whole communities to move. The motivations of migrants include adventure, escape, expulsion, commerce, war, and a search for resources to bring back to their home community. Such migration is a recurring yet fluctuating process: for instance, migration has sometimes been principally along water routes and at other times along land routes.

Comparisons among species help to clarify certain unique characteristics in human migration. The general meaning of migration is movement of an individual organism from one habitat to another, where a *habitat* is a contiguous environment with resources enabling the organism to thrive. There is thus a difference between local mobility and cross-habitat migration. Migration generally serves a function in the life cycle of the individual and the species. Seasonal migration, commonly of whole communities, is thus important in reproduction and food supply for many species. In addition, species commonly migrate by diffusion as they gradually expand or contract their range. Thus *Homo erectus* spread, beginning a million years ago, from East Africa to various parts of the Old World, and gave rise to successor species in Asia, Europe, and Africa.

Our own species, *Homo sapiens*, succeeded in settling the whole world. The process for this migratory expansion was that of cross-community migration, in which young adults moved from one habitat to another. *Habitat*, however, must be redefined for human purposes to depend on the social as well as natural environment: that is, an environment with a given language and culture. The ancestral African habitat of *Homo sapiens* centered on tropical savannas, including locations at water's edge, and also including highlands – it was best to have a variegated habitat, which reinforced omnivorous eating habits. Humans hunted and gathered, but also ate plants and animals from the waters, swam, and created watercraft. These elements – the ancient migratory practices of mammals, the new practice of cross-community migration, and the reliance of humans on movement across water – provided a basis for modern *Homo sapiens* to occupy all the territories of the earth.

Human migrants, in entering new ecologies, transformed them as well as accommodated to them, making each into a new habitat. With each human colonization of a new continent, a great die-off of megafauna followed – for Australia (giant kangaroos), then in temperate Eurasia (mammoths), and later in the Americas (sloths). This was destructive behavior at one level, but also showed the potential of human migration for bringing about change. The social function of cross-community migration was to create and spread innovations from habitat to habitat, so that it has been a significantly adaptive behavior. The function of creating innovations – added to the benefits brought by sharing of the genome, technology, and culture – is important in explaining how learning got to be passed from generation to generation.

The early days of human history brought two big changes in migratory patterns that have been with us ever since. The first was determined by environment and climate, the second by biological and social evolution. First is the rise of an expanded pattern of migration within the homeland of modern humanity. *Homo sapiens* first emerged on the East African savannas some 200,000 years ago. Then a long, cool, dry period in East Africa, from 190,000 to 130,000 years ago, encouraged human communities to move south across the equator to the similar lands of southeastern Africa, which were relatively warm and wet at that time. Indeed, the annual and longer-term shifts of the monsoons (bringing precipitation alternately to northeast Africa and southeast Africa) may well have built up a pattern of migration back and forth among those regions, along with social networks to facilitate these movements. The result was to favor the expansion of the human gene pool and to build in social habits encouraging migration. The results show up in studies of the early human genome. This process facilitated migration, specialization, and broad sharing among communities (see Map 12.1).

The second step was the rise of syntactic language. At some point, certainly before 70,000 years ago, our ancestors gained improved vocal articulation and with it the beginnings of fully articulated speech. At least four types of change overlapped to bring about the rise of syntactic language. Desire for communication put selective pressure on devices to facilitate it. Physical evolution of the larynx, selected by this demand, enabled more precise articulation of sound. Other genetic mutations created the logic to facilitate the syntactic conventions by which children form sentences. Then generations of practice with language turned it into a device for communicating, categorizing, and storing learning. This revolutionary transformation appears to have taken place within communities totaling several thousand people in Northeast Africa. Development of speech built language communities – groups of several hundred people sharing common speech practice. With the rise of language, individual human communities expanded in size, as they became united by language and no longer simply by co-residence. Further, various communities gained distinctive identities because of the gradual separation of their language and customs. Those who migrated from one community to another had to learn new languages and customs: this pattern emphasized learning in individuals, the exchange of customs and technologies among groups, and innovations in assembling old ideas and new. Consequently, migration facilitated an acceleration of social evolution that began to account for most of the change in human societies. Such "cross-community migration" remains the basic style of human migration. The same underlying logic of crossing community boundaries and generating social innovations continues to this day, but has transformed human society almost beyond recognition.

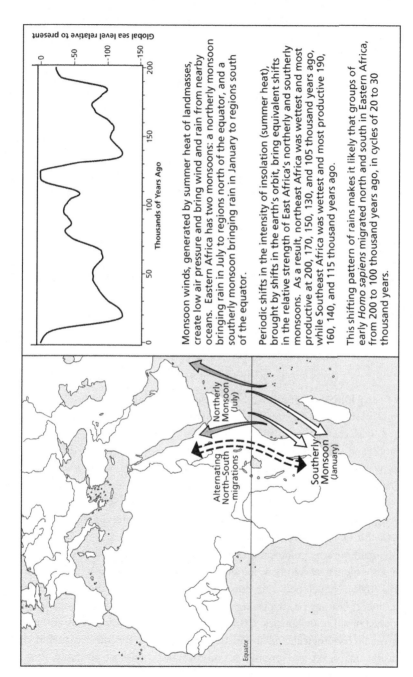

Global sea level relative to present

Thousands of Years Ago

Monsoon winds, generated by summer heat of landmasses, create low air pressure and bring wind and rain from nearby oceans. Eastern Africa has two monsoons: a northerly monsoon bringing rain in July to regions north of the equator, and a southerly monsoon bringing rain in January to regions south of the equator.

Periodic shifts in the intensity of insolation (summer heat), brought by shifts in the earth's orbit, bring equivalent shifts in the relative strength of East Africa's northerly and southerly monsoons. As a result, northeast Africa was wettest and most productive at 200, 170, 150, 130, and 105 thousand years ago, while Southeast Africa was wettest and most productive 190, 160, 140, and 115 thousand years ago.

This shifting pattern of rains makes it likely that groups of early *Homo sapiens* migrated north and south in Eastern Africa, from 200 to 100 thousand years ago, in cycles of 20 to 30 thousand years.

Northerly Monsoon (July)

Alternating North–South migrations

Southerly Monsoon (January)

Equator

Map 12.1 Shifting climate and migration in Africa, 200,000 to 100,000 years ago.

Migration patterns of today rely on the same social processes. Modern communications technology has allowed language communities to grow to many millions of members and to extend over immense geographic spaces, so that the meanings of "community," "cross-community migration," and "habitat" have changed greatly. In a world of literacy and schooling, learning now takes place through mechanisms other than migration – although migration remains important in learning, as any migrant can testify. The risks in migration are now much lower than before, and the number of migrants can expand without great cost in human life. With the passage of time, diaspora communities (migrants and their descendants who maintain a sense of common identity with their homeland) have been able to grow and play a distinctive historical role. In current research, we have learned to distinguish among individual migrants, their communities, gendered patterns in migration, recruiters, dispatchers, members of the networks facilitating migration, gatekeepers restricting migrants, methods of maintaining family contacts, and the shifts in identity accompanying migration. Because of the basic continuity in migration, the details we have learned about migration in contemporary society can be helpful in reconstructing parallel details in early times.

Occupying the planet: from 100,000 to 15,000 years ago

In very early human migrations, the principal movements were to territories ecologically similar to the grasslands and waterways of eastern Africa. Within Africa it was easiest for humans to occupy similar ecologies such as the grasslands and watersides of southern and western Africa. More difficult to occupy were the forested areas of Central and West Africa. Meanwhile, shifts in climate brought changes in vegetation and habitat. A warm and wet time from 110,000 years ago to 90,000 years ago made the Sahara inhabitable rather than desert, and it is known that populations of humans settled as far afield as the Qafzeh cave in Israel, dated at 100,000 years ago. But as the climate again became colder and drier, these settlements did not survive.

The emergence of syntactic language, some 70,000 years ago in northeastern Africa, developed the communities that spread throughout the planet, incorporating or displacing all other hominids and imposing their dominance on all other species. Christopher Ehret, elsewhere in this volume, draws on archaeological and linguistic evidence to trace the expansion of technically advanced and populous communities – almost certainly those with syntactic language – into region after region of the African continent from 70,000 to 20,000 years ago, progressively incorporating populations that were physically similar but had simpler technologies and may have lacked language. This was the early expansion of modern humanity by land.

At much the same time, modern humans who left Africa went primarily by watercraft across the mouth of the Red Sea to South Arabia and beyond. With early watercraft and newly polished languages, these adventurers were able to cross the few kilometers from Somalia to South Arabia and remain within a relatively constant environment. (Sea levels were then much lower than now.) Somewhere in the time between 70,000 years ago and 50,000 years ago, human populations worked their way eastward along the Indian Ocean coastline, presumably on both land and sea (see Map 12.2).

The migrants were able to find animal and vegetable resources, from land and water, similar to those known to their ancestors in Africa. Beyond the coastline they were able to explore and settle river valleys – the largest included the Indus, Godavari, Ganges, Irrawaddy, and Mekong. Moving upriver within these valleys, the migrants would eventually have come to mountainous areas – tropical and sub-tropical highlands parallel to those in East Africa, which held the advantage of being well-watered and sustaining a wide variety of plant and animal life at varying altitudes. The evidence of language groups suggests that some of these Asian highland areas – above the Irrawaddy, Brahmaputra, and Red River Valleys – developed concentrations of human population.

Along the coastline, the migrants continued their expansion through the tropics, settling on both mainland and islands. They settled the archipelago that is now Indonesia and was then the much larger continent of Sunda, as the low sea level revealed lands linking many of the islands. At the end of Sunda, the migrants found ways to reach still more distant lands: Australia (dated to 50,000 years ago), New Guinea (then joined to Australia as part of the continent of Sahul), and the Philippines. Each lay across a great oceanic strait, so that the migrants crossed open water of 100 kilometers, and did so on multiple occasions, as the genetic record attests. Similarly, humans followed the coast of the South China Sea, eventually reaching more northerly and even temperate zones.

Human migrants, having mastered the tropics, did not automatically move north to temperate zones, since the colder climate and the sharply different flora and fauna required new technology. Humans may have remained settled throughout the Old World tropics for as much as 20,000 years (that is, from 65,000 to 45,000 BP) before moving into the temperate zone. From well-dated European remains, we know that *Homo sapiens* (known locally as Cro-Magnon) reached Europe as early as 45,000 years ago and Central Asia and Mongolia at roughly the same time. What is not certain is the route by which

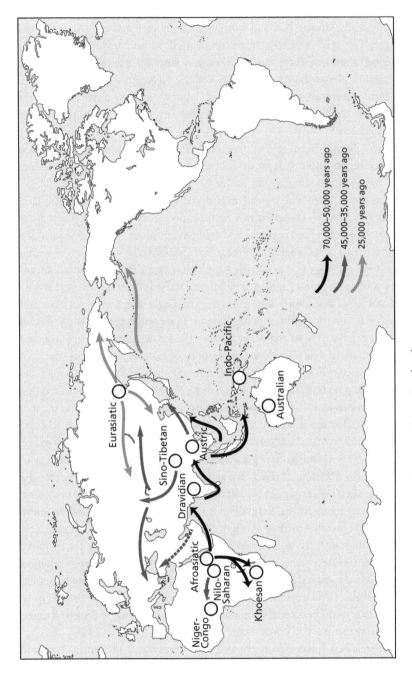

Map 12.2 Occupying the planet, 70,000 to 25,000 years ago.

70,000–50,000 years ago

45,000–35,000 years ago

25,000 years ago

Eurasiatic

Sino-Tibetan

Dravidian

Austric

Indo-Pacific

Australian

Afroasiatic

Nilo-Saharan

Niger-Congo

Khoesan

they moved from south to north. Potential routes include the Nile–Fertile Crescent corridor, the Persian Gulf–Caucasus corridor, routes north from India, and the Pacific coast of China. One route appears from present evidence to have had particular advantages – a corridor along the Ganges Valley and the slopes south and west of the Himalayas, to the grasslands in today's Kazakhstan. Along one or more of these routes, humans reached and learned to live with the sharply varying temperatures and rapidly running rivers of the temperate zone. With this achievement, they gained the ability to range east and west across the Eurasian grasslands along routes that have been used ever since.

While this narrative has focused on migratory occupation of new lands, there was much more to human history in this era than frontier expansion. At each stage, changes took place in social structure, technology, and even in human biology. Occupying each region required learning to live in its micro-ecologies and becoming acquainted with its flora and fauna – for instance, learning to take advantage of bamboo in eastern Asia. Changes in clothing accompanied new techniques in hunting and fishing. Meanwhile, entirely unconsciously, as communities occupied regions for thousands of years, their bodies underwent pressures that affected their stature, body type, skin, hair, and facial features. We can say, therefore, that these superficial physical differences that we use to identify "race" exist because of migration, and that they mostly emerged between 40,000 and 10,000 years ago.

Further, early human migration was not only and not principally to settle "empty" territories. According to the interpretation developed here, most migration was back and forth among existing human communities, rather than for the creation of new communities. Inter-communal migration in the era of human expansion may be characterized especially through the spread of the major language groups or phyla. For instance, the Afroasiatic and Nilo-Saharan language groups appear to have had their ancestry in the western half of Ethiopia. Yet members of the two groups have clearly undergone migrations at various times in their long histories, so that speakers of the two language groups have become widely dispersed.

Community change during the Glacial Maximum and Holocene Epoch

The era from 25,000 years ago to 5,000 years ago brought what was probably the most extreme set of climate changes that humans have ever experienced. Recent research shows that climate change, while regionally specific, has been chronologically united, so that no part of the earth escaped the sudden and repeated shifts in temperature and precipitation during these twenty millennia. First came the cold. From 25,000 to 15,000 years ago the Glacial Maximum brought a cold and dry time that reached its worst about 18,000 years ago, when the expansion of polar glaciers had lowered sea level, temperature, and humidity worldwide to the lowest levels of the preceding 100,000 years. Then came the warmth. The great fluctuations in climate continued with a warming period that melted glaciers, thus raising sea levels, temperatures, and precipitation. Within 4,000 years, the seas rose by nearly 100 meters, inundating coastlines everywhere. Even more remarkably, as of about 6,000 years ago this Holocene Epoch brought a suddenly stable climate, in contrast to the fluctuations that had long preceded. Geologists have drawn a line to specify the end of the Pleistocene Epoch and the beginning of the Holocene Epoch at about 12,000 years ago (see Map 12.3).

In this difficult time humans somehow accelerated a process of innovation that ultimately gave them increasing mastery over nature, even as nature provided the most severe of tests. Cross-community migration continued, and helped to provoke and disseminate the new ideas. The greatest attention in innovation has gone to the rise of agriculture during the first half of the Holocene Epoch. It is appropriate, however, to affirm a more general appreciation of human technological and social innovation over a somewhat longer era: the Glacial Maximum and the Holocene combined to bring the *era of production*. That is, in this era of turbulent environmental change, human innovation turned increasingly away from *collecting* and toward *producing* resources. While continuing to rely on hunting, gathering, and fishing, many types of community began to emphasize several new types of production – permanent homes, ceramics, new and increasingly precise sorts of tools, new forms of art, and experimentation with control of animals and plants. The new techniques appear in the record of the Glacial Maximum for Africa and Eurasia. Artisanal work persisted (as indicated by the art work, clothing, and watercraft on which humans had long relied), but the scope and skill of artisanal work expanded. Pottery began to appear, for instance in the Jomon ceramics of Japan beginning over 12,000 years ago. Archaeologists have long classified an aspect of this shift as the "Neolithic" era, referring to the "new" stone work that centered on very small and finely crafted stone implements. Social changes took place in this same era of innovation: for instance, unilineal descent systems appear to have arisen among African speakers of Nilo-Saharan and Afroasiatic languages.

The final great stage in occupying the continents was human settlement of the Americas. Migrants succeeded in moving further north and east in

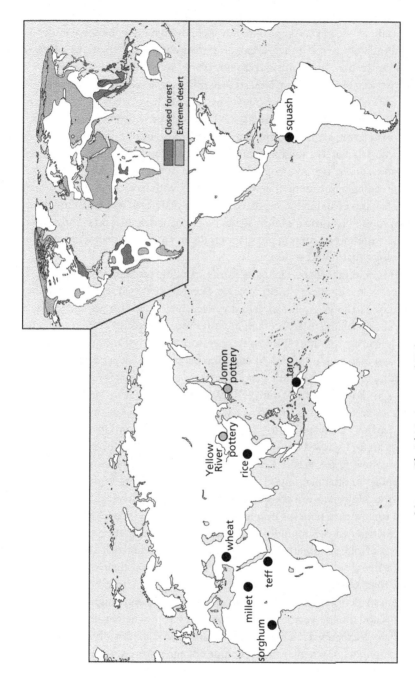

Map 12.3 Glacial Maximum and Holocene eras, 25,000 to 5,000 years ago.

Eurasia, into North America, at times estimated as early as 30,000 years ago and as late as 15,000 years ago. This advance, though not yet known in detail, may ultimately reveal much about the cross-community patterns of early human migration. Both land and sea migrations to North America are known to have taken place in later times, so that either mode of transportation could have worked for the first entry. Travel by sea may have been more feasible in this cool and ice-ridden era: the Pacific kelp beds provided offshore nourishment in a great arc along the coast from the South China Sea to South America. Ultimately, migrants entered Arctic tundra, temperate forests, grasslands, desert regions, tropical forests, and further ecologies, with migration spreading innovations. The Clovis culture, with its focus on finely honed points for knives and harpoons dated to 13,500 years ago, was long thought to represent the first arrival of humans in North America. It is now understood to reflect the spread, among populations already in place, of an innovation in technology that found wide use.

The agricultural chapter in the story of expanding production seems to have been provoked by sharp climatic change. Several privileged regions (including at least one in South America) shared variety in botanical species and physical relief, thus enabling experimentation with numerous plants. When temperatures began to rise after the low-temperature trough of the Ice Age 18,000 years ago, vegetation flourished and humans began to depend on gathering expanding food supplies. But a thousand-year cold snap starting some 12,000 years ago (known as the Younger Dryas) brought a severe decline in food supplies and an impetus to discover ways to produce rather than just gather food. Further, the response to climate change was most productive in mountainous areas: it played out over several thousand years to bring the production of wheat in the Fertile Crescent, taro in New Guinea, rice in Southeast Asia, millet in Ethiopia, squash in South America, and sorghum in the Sahara.

As the Holocene era took form, the developing system of production began to influence patterns of migration. In some ways, developing productive activities tied communities to particular places, restricting their nomadic patterns of old. In other ways, productive skills meant that humans could forge a living wherever they wished to go, relying on their own resources rather than simply on those available in nature. Agriculture brought higher population density, development of new diseases, and migration of both humans and disease vectors. Debate continues as to whether the agricultural populations expanded systematically in number and in territory in contrast to their neighbors or whether the techniques of agriculture spread more rapidly than the initial farming populations. While the full results are not yet in, the evidence is strong for a patchwork of particular cases. Rice may have spread through Southeast Asia through the expansion of farming communities, while wheat may have expanded through Western Asia through its adoption by different existing communities.

Growing populations tended both to concentrate and disperse. In concentrating, they created village communities, including several hundred or even more inhabitants. In a sense they can be seen as the initial stage of urban life. Equally important, villages established a style of life that thrives today throughout the world. With the greater concentration of labor power, it was possible for communities to undertake control of water flows and other public works: canals, dams, aqueducts, reservoirs, and ritual structures arose in many parts of the world.

In dispersing – and whether relying on agriculture, pastoralism, fishing, or hunting – populations entered and contested lands occupied by previous communities. Traces of recurrent or sustained migrations survive in the languages that are spoken today in regions far from where their ancestral languages can be shown to have originated. Thus, in times of the early Holocene before agriculture became well established, several important migrations left traces in the language groups of today (see Map 12.4). Migrants speaking Afroasiatic languages moved north along the Nile River as conditions became wetter, and formed four major language communities: the speakers of Ancient Egyptian languages in the lower Nile, the speakers of Semitic languages in what became the Fertile Crescent and the Arabian Peninsula, the speakers of Berber languages in Northwest Africa, and the speakers of Chadic languages in the region surrounding Lake Chad. At much the same time speakers of Indo-European languages moved westward to settle in the area north of the Black Sea; from this homeland they spread in multiple directions. Somewhat later, speakers of Pama-Nyungan languages in north-central Australia began to expand, and over several thousand years their languages became dominant in all the southern and central portions of Australia. It will take further research to establish the time frame and the sequence of these important movements of population and language, but the language patterns confirm that great migrations stopped and started periodically over the millennia.

Global patterns, Eurasian specificity:
3000 BCE–800 CE

The Holocene Epoch climatic processes continued, bringing dependable if somewhat drier climate during the past 5,000 years. Societies on every

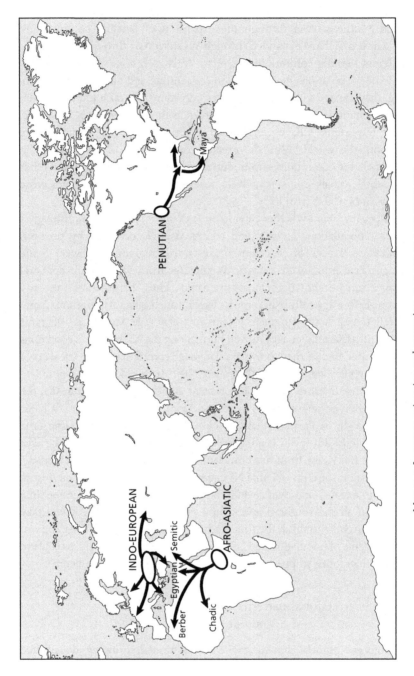

Map 12.4 Language migration and expansion, c. 10,000 to 5,000 years ago.

continent were able to expand the types of their productive activities, including domestication of new plants and animals, the expansion of villages and population centers, the development of new systems of social organization, and migration processes that carried innovations to new areas of settlement. For this time period it was the Eurasian continent that experienced the greatest social and technological change. Land that had previously been dry and unproductive now blossomed, and populations growing wheat, barley, rice, and yams – and caring for sheep, goats, cattle, and water buffalo – grew significantly. Early Holocene migrations, at much the same time as those mentioned just above, brought the expansion of substantial civilizations: Semitic languages, descended from Afroasiatic languages based in Africa, became predominant in the Fertile Crescent and Arabia. Indo-European languages, which spread both east and west from the Black Sea region, became predominant in Europe, in Iran, and in much of South Asia. Chinese languages, descended from Sino-Tibetan languages of the upper Yangzi Valley, spread north along the Pacific coast to the Yellow River Valley.

Interactions among these groups came with a late-arising domestication – that of horses, domesticated in the Central Asian steppes. The process took place through several stages requiring thousands of years, with breeding of horses for food as an early stage and harnessing of horses to pull chariots as a later stage. When harnessed to two-wheeled chariots, horses enabled peoples of the Caspian Sea region to raid and conquer in all directions. Surrounding states, at first suffering conquest, learned the new technology and later expanded their realms. Later, as saddles were developed, the cavalry formed to become an even more formidable tool of war. The military use of horses was sufficient to remake the political map of Eurasia from end to end, bringing migration both by conquerors and conquered. Horses became both the symbols and the motive force for hierarchical power – states and enslavement expanded from the Mediterranean to the Pacific. By 3,000 years ago horses had spread to almost every region of Eurasia and into northern Africa, bringing military, economic, political, social, and cultural change. In the wake of the restructuring of society around horses, new social structures evolved within the same Eurasian region: commerce, empires, and major religions (see Map 12.5). Camels came later, just 2,000 to 3,000 years ago, and brought a parallel but smaller effect.

In the terminology we use today, early civilizations gave rise to empires. In the rise of localized civilizations (initially along the Nile and Tigris–Euphrates Rivers), before the military use of horses, densely populated communities shared language and culture. Additional dense and coherent societies continued to emerge in various parts of the world. Empires, in contrast, were rather different structures, that could take form only through aggregation of distinctive societies. Imperial military force and prestige brought together numerous units differing in language, culture, and political system. From the first large-scale empire, that of Persia, to those that followed it in rapid succession – the Hellenistic, Mauryan, Roman, Qin, and Han – the powers of monarchies and bureaucracies now dispatched armies and navies in distant campaigns, brought artists and craftsmen to their capitals, and encouraged travel within their domains. The succeeding empires of the Gupta, the Umayyads, Abbasids, Tang, and Song similarly stimulated migration both within and beyond their borders. Empires thus caused migration through the movements of armies, refugees, officials, captives, and subject peoples required to move. But empires were not alone as causes of migration. Documents from this era show how migrations of small numbers of people, especially merchants and religious missionaries, could bring major social transformations.

The expansion of formal trade in the first millennium BCE – with the development of money, the beginnings of banking, construction of ports and caravanserai – enabled merchant families to travel and sustain long-distance connections necessary to the movement of commodities. Just as early politics laid the groundwork for empires, the ancient heritage of long-distance exchange laid the groundwork for formal commerce. In parallel, the formation at much the same time of large-scale religions – Zoroastrian, Judaic, Buddhist, Jain – and the subsequent rise of Christian, revived Hindu, Muslim, and other religions – brought migrations and connections among the faithful. Networks of family, faith, and commercial interest sustained the movement and connection of migrants over large areas: the Islamic *hajj* remains the largest, most persistent religious pilgrimage. Religion, in particular, may have expanded more through the preaching of individual missionaries than through the invasion and conquest of armies.

The rise of empire, commerce, and perhaps even religion also provided scope for the expansion of enslavement. For those captured, whether in war or by kidnapping, their movement and sale required a network of a different sort, including those who guarded them, fed them, and transported them to their destination. Forced migration, the expulsion of people by human or natural causes, led migrants into catastrophic departure from their home, movement through unfamiliar regions, and settlement in lands of destination. Forced migrations had most likely existed for all human time, but increased in this era. Enslavement, an outstanding form of forced migration, likewise expanded, especially at the fringes of states from the Mediterranean

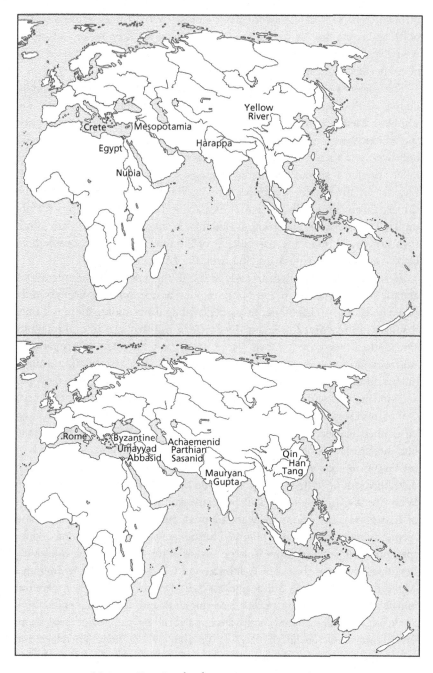

Map 12.5 Eurasian developments, 3000 BCE to 800 CE.

through Iran. This expansion of slavery drew captives from regions to the north and south and also within the core areas of Mediterranean and south-west Asian empires. Slavery in India developed less fully; in China slavery never became institutionalized as firmly.

The societies that absorbed the enslaved put them to work in building diasporas. Phoenician merchants spread west from the Levant along the southern Mediterranean; their Aramaic-speaking cousins, also merchants, spread eastward to the frontiers of India. A Greek-speaking diaspora spread both west and then east – all the way to Bactria under Alexander the Great. Later, migrants spread the Latin language throughout the huge Roman Empire. In these same centuries, the Buddhist religion spread from the Ganges throughout India to Central Asia and to China where it grew rapidly until a Tang dynasty repression of Buddhist monasteries in 845. Many more such stories add up to a remarkable set of Eurasian interconnections, linking lands from Britain to Vietnam, and from the Levant to Japan.

As striking as the growth of early cities, in this era, were the migrations and the social transformations of large regions, as documented through study of language and archaeology. In particular, linguistic studies show not only that agriculture thrived in major river valleys, but that agricultural migrants spread their ways of life over large areas (see Map 12.6). Rice-farming Austronesian speakers spread from Taiwan to the Philippines and through-out maritime Southeast Asia. As their outrigger canoes moved east, they met and intermarried with Papuan peoples of New Guinea and islands to the east. Out of this cross-cultural exchange emerged the Polynesians, now cultivating taro rather than rice, with a technology and social order enabling them to sail into the far reaches of the eastern Pacific, colonizing the remaining islands in the time from 1000 BCE to 1300 CE. At a similar time, Bantu languages, which developed out of a Niger-Congo subgroup that cultivated yams, spread from West Africa's Niger-Benue Valley far to the southeast. Once in the highlands of East Africa, the Bantu speakers adopted millet from local farmers, and spread its cultivation as they migrated further south and west. Overall, Bantu speakers occupied a territory as large as that of the Indo-European speakers. Penutian languages, based in California and Oregon, gave rise to migrants who moved east to the Caribbean coast (see Map 12.4). While they were not initially farmers, at some point these migrants adopted maize cultivation. Some of their descendants cultivated maize along the lower Mississippi River; others moved all the way to Yucatan, where their languages and ethnic groups became known as Maya. From the Maya archaeological record, we can estimate that these migrants must have reached the Maya

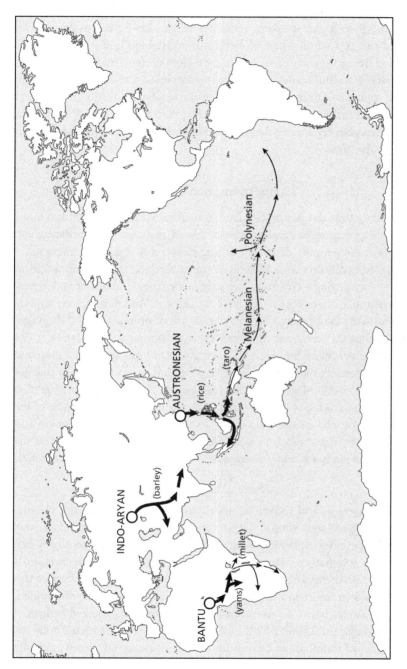

Map 12.6 Agricultural expansion, 3000 BCE to 800 CE.

region 3,000 or 4,000 years ago. Yet another group of migrating agriculturists were the Indo-Aryan speakers, members of an Indo-European group who moved east to Central Asia and then south to settle in Iran and South Asia. Some of the songs and poems retelling the lives of these migrants were long preserved – as the Vedas they were incorporated into what became the Hindu religion. Other groups, smaller in number but still of historical importance, included the Na-Dene speakers, who moved from Central Asia to the Canadian region of Athabasca; a portion of them later moved south to become the Navajo.

Connections, 800–1800 CE

Within just over the past millennium, four patterns of migration developed further importance: pastoral, maritime, forced migration, and urbanization. Each of these patterns depended on the basic rules of human migration – reliance especially on young adults as migrants, reaching across communities to learn by exchanging elements of language and culture, and reliance on improvised migratory networks to facilitate movement. Attention has commonly focused on the most spectacular breakthrough in communication – the voyages of Columbus, da Gama, and Magellan (the latter in 1519–22) (see Map 12.7). For overall interpretation, however, it is just as well to focus on the full thousand years of expanding movement and interconnection – the full range of changes that resonated with Magellan's circumnavigation. The four types of migration commonly interacted with each other as they influenced most corners of the world. By the end of this period, the expanded patterns of migration had brought three types of changes in identities: racial categorization and the formation of diasporas and nations as newly significant types of communities.

Pastoral migrations

Pastoral migrants had moved across Eurasia and Africa since the hunting and herding of large animals began, but an extraordinary period of such migrations continued from the eighth through the sixteenth centuries (see Map 12.7). In that era, numerous pastoral groups moved their animals across lands surrounding the great arid belt from Atlantic Africa to Manchuria: they grazed and marketed goats, sheep, cattle, camels, and horses. With the rise of Islam, armies from the Arabian Peninsula seized control of Mesopotamia, the Levant, Iran, and North Africa, and set up a capital for the Umayyad Caliphate in Damascus. Of those conquered, many gradually converted to Arab language and culture. Later, Arab pastoralists moved

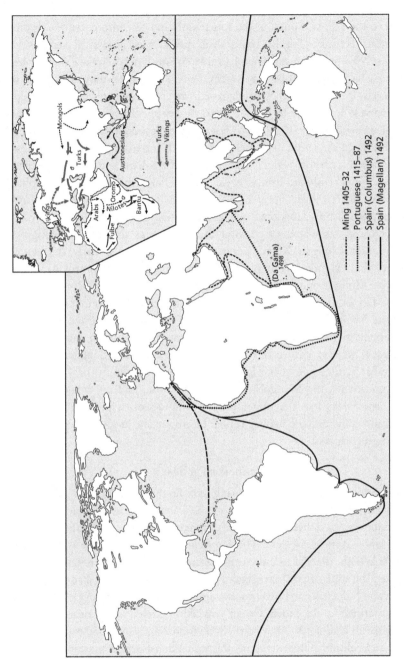

Map 12.7 Maritime and pastoral migration, 800–1500 CE.

Ming 1405–32
Portuguese 1415–87
Spain (Columbus) 1492
Spain (Magellan) 1492

(Da Gama) 1498

Mongols
Turks
Vikings
Turks
Austronesians
Oromo
Arabs
Nilotes
Fulbe
Bantu
Vikings

from Egypt west to the Maghrib in the tenth and eleventh centuries, and south to the Nilotic Sudan in the fourteenth and fifteenth centuries. From the eighth century, Turkish pastoralists spread west across the steppes to the Black Sea, into Iran and Anatolia, and into South Asia. To the east, peoples of the eastern steppes known as Khitan, Liao, and Jurchen moved southward both as families and as armies, gaining recurring influence in northern China up to the twelfth century. In the far west, Berber-speaking peoples known as Sanhaja expanded from the Sahara Desert in the eleventh century, establishing the Almoravid state with its capital at Marrakech and extending their conquest throughout North Africa and Iberia. South of the Sahara, cattle-keeping Fulbe families moved eastward from Senegal as far as Lake Chad, and cattle-keeping Nilotic speakers moved upriver from the middle Nile to Lake Victoria and beyond, establishing kingdoms including Rwanda.

The most extraordinary pastoral expansion was that of the Mongols, who, under Chinggis Khan, launched conquests in the early thirteenth century that extended the logistics of communication and control all across Eurasia. Mongol and other pastoral rulers moved to capital cities from which they dominated commerce, but new migratory movements arose to shift the balance of power. In sum, pastoral migration remained especially prominent in the Eastern Hemisphere from the eighth to the sixteenth century. The very nature of empire in this era depended significantly on pastoralist armies and social institutions, as seen through the Umayyads, the Almoravids, the Mongols, the Golden Horde, and the Manchu. Even after pastoralists lost the upper hand in interaction with settled polities, pastoralist alliances and armies remained important in global politics until the nineteenth century.

Maritime migrations

The world's best navigators, during the first millennium CE, were the Polynesian and Micronesian sailors of the Pacific, whose complex array of techniques enabled them to complete pinpoint navigation so that they reached tiny islands in immense seas. Their vessels and populations were small, but they linked the Pacific Islands to maritime Southeast Asia. Related groups founded the state of Sri Vijaya, based in Sumatra, which linked commerce of China and India from the seventh through the thirteenth century. Along with other mariners in the Indian Ocean – speaking Greek, Austronesian, Arabic, and Gujarati languages – they learned the monsoon system and expanded the range and volume of their shipping. In another dense area of maritime contact, Chinese, Korean, and Japanese mariners traded and warred with each other.

Their ships, built for the rough seas of the north Pacific, were able to make long voyages to Southeast Asia and into the Indian Ocean. The exchange among these competitors brought such technological advances as rudders, the compass, watertight compartments, and innovative configurations of sails and masts. The Mongols, in their conquest of China, learned from this naval tradition and led major expeditions against the Song, Japan, and Java.

Mariners from the Baltic Sea and North Sea suddenly expanded their range in roughly 800 CE, relying on light but seaworthy vessels for 300 years of prominence. To the west, these Viking warriors raided across open seas to the British Isles, along the north coast of Europe, across the Atlantic, and into the Mediterranean where they encountered dense waterborne traffic relying especially on galleys and their oarsmen. To the east, they raided along rivers to Slavic-speaking areas, leaving major imprints in Constantinople, on the Caspian shores of Persia, and among the Turkish-speaking rulers of the middle Volga. For other regions – the Americas and Africa – while the vessels rarely carried more than fifty oarsmen, mariners nevertheless traveled the coasts, the lakes, and great river systems. As a result, it can be said that, even before the voyages of Columbus, people all around the world were in maritime contact with one another.

It was European voyagers who achieved decisive advances in technology and social organization of long-distance seafaring. An earlier Chinese lead in long-distance voyaging was not sustained, so it was Portuguese, Spanish, Italian, and Dutch mariners who did the extraordinary work of mapping the coasts and charting the winds and currents of the open seas. The volume of trade and migration increased steadily across the Atlantic, the Indian Ocean, and the Western Pacific. By the late eighteenth century the volume of oceanic commerce and migration had increased several times over; with the mastery of longitude, the world became almost completely mapped.

Forced migrations

Forced migration also expanded during this millennium, especially as large states became established, and especially in the zone from the Mediterranean to the Indus, the historic center of slave societies. North of this zone, merchants dispatched captives from Slavic, Turkic, and Caucasian societies; from south of this zone, captives came from societies of the Nile Valley and West Africa. Still others came from South India and Southeast Asia. Enslavement became central to war and politics, as Slavic, Turkish, East African, and Caucasian slave soldiers became central to the military forces of the great powers.

Overlaying this terrestrial wave of enslavement was a steadily expanding maritime slave trade, especially across the Atlantic but also in the Indian Ocean (see Map 12.8). As the capitalistic economy developed, this trade in slaves focused on production of sugar and other commodities for sale. Over ten million enslaved Africans made the voyage to the Americas in the years up to 1850, far more than the number of European migrants to that time. (Other waves of slave trade – from the Eurasian steppeland, across the Sahara, and across the Indian Ocean – were also large but have yet to be estimated with precision.) Finally, expanded slave economies developed within Africa and Asia, reaching their peak in the late nineteenth century, after which slavery declined rapidly in the face of a worldwide anti-slavery movement. Yet racial categorization, reinforced by the centuries of enslavement, remained after slavery as an extreme form of social discrimination.

Urbanization

Urbanization, a fourth dimension of migration, developed gradually in this period. The leading cities included such imperial capitals as Constantinople, Baghdad, and later Beijing, and such commercial centers as Alexandria, Guangzhou, and the Silk Road center of Sarai on the lower Volga (though it prospered only in the thirteenth and fourteenth centuries). Cities maintained their size only through in-migration, as their death rates were high. After 1500 three great capital cities – London, Edo (later to be renamed Tokyo), and Constantinople (though now under Ottoman rule) – led in population for three centuries. As the global economy expanded, port cities grew in size and significance, including Lisbon, Nagasaki, Amsterdam, Batavia, Genoa, and Havana.

Diaspora, nation, and race

The various streams of migration, structured increasingly by empire, changed the character and complexity of identity, both for individuals and groups. Individuals could be defined specifically by gender, age, birthplace, color, marital status, language, religion, occupation, and slave/free/elite status – or more vaguely with group labels of race or ethnicity. During this millennium of expanded migration, the localized notion of ethnic group gave rise to expanded types of identity: the diaspora, the nation, and racial groupings. In diasporas, migrants and their descendants maintained a common identity and culture linking them to their homeland. (The term "diaspora" has only recently come to be used as a general term for a dispersed community held together by informal structures, but it is now

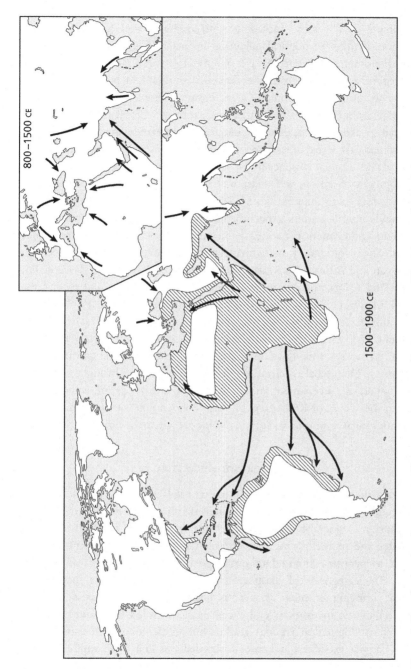

Map 12.8 Forced migration, 800–1900 CE. The arrows represent primary streams of forced migration, and the shaded areas regions in which forced migration had the most impact.

800–1500 CE

1500–1900 CE

recognized to reflect an important pattern in the modern world.) In nations, inhabitants of a region, including both migrants and locals, formed a common identity for political purposes. In racial categorization, one group labeled another in order to make a statement of social hierarchy.

Maritime migrations from the fifteenth century had built up diasporas around the Atlantic and Indian Ocean basins – people from many parts of Africa plus English, Irish, Scottish, Portuguese, Castilian, Dutch, Jews, German speakers, Arabs, Persians, Gujaratis, and Armenians. A Russian diaspora spread east across Siberia and a Chinese diaspora spread west and south, both within empires. Especially in the Americas, diasporas facilitated the development of nationhood: diaspora-based populations sought to redefine their identity in an imperial world. Thus, diasporas broke from their homelands and imperial centers to become nations in the cases of the United States and Haiti. Latin American nations defined themselves in wars of independence against Spain, ultimately recognizing national citizenship for members of European and African diasporas and for people of Amerindian descent. For Russia and China, the continental diasporas helped define and extend the nation. In Europe, national identities arose in France, briefly in Poland, and more fully in Germany. Racial categorizations, meanwhile, served to perpetuate hierarchies within empires and nations. In response the African diaspora, defined in racial terms, developed an increasingly influential common consciousness. The global reach of empires on land and sea brought about the interconnection, investment, and seizure of resources – primitive accumulation, in the words of Karl Marx, but also cooperation – that made possible dramatic global economic and demographic growth in the nineteenth century.

Capitalism since 1700

A series of great transformations intertwined with one another as the eighteenth century progressed. Capitalism, an economic system of new complexity, extended links in all directions, moving and transforming commodities and marketing them for profit. Globe-encompassing culture congealed as people continued to exchange foodstuffs, clothing, music, and sport. The categories of diaspora, race, and nation became increasingly explicit, bringing as much division as unity. War, made more destructive with capitalistic investment and racial passion, ended lives and expanded hierarchies. Population grew at gradual but accelerating rates, especially in cities. Languages shifted and spread, especially as linked to empires. Migration played a central role in linking these transformations; at the same time, the global interactions transformed the practices of migration. The remainder of this narrative is an effort at once to entangle and untangle this list of factors, and to show the central and sometimes causal role of migration in the social change of the past two centuries, when the absolute and perhaps relative numbers of migrants reached a new peak.

The emergence of capitalism became evident wherever commerce was intensive. Factory production and wage labor expanded in parts of Western Europe and North America. Mechanized plantations operated by slave labor along the West Atlantic. Shipping and marketing firms expanded their activities to all the large ports of the world. Combinations of wage labor and forced labor carried out tasks on the ships linking the ports, and among the port workers and workers who transported goods on land: the Dutch East India Company expanded such a combination beginning in 1602. Mines expanded along with demand for extracting iron, gold, silver, lead, copper, diamonds, and other minerals. Bankers and insurance firms, usually held by wealthy families, provided finance and collected profits. Competition brought conflict: the European continent was engulfed with warfare for over twenty years from 1792 – even more massive wars were to come.

Despite the divisions of war and race, the world had expanded its unities by the early nineteenth century. Remarkably, death rates were in decline in many parts of the world so that populations began to increase steadily. Centuries of global cultural exchange – of foods, clothing, customs, and diseases – crossed all the lines of race, religion, social class, language. The sum of these provided a basis for death rates to decline. In fact, increases in European, Asian, and American populations had already begun, the latter especially because of immigration. African populations remained in stagnation in this era, as a result of war and enslavement. In addition the Pacific Basin, which had been at the fringe of global interaction in previous centuries, was now incorporated with a vengeance into the imperial and capitalist order, with resulting high rates of mortality and migration throughout the region.

A sudden shift in about 1850 brought a wave of long-distance migration that lasted to 1940 (see Map 12.9). As Europeans gained the upper hand in the world economy, breakthroughs in factory production brought steam engines, railroads, textiles, plus mining and shipping of coal. The principal character of long-distance migration shifted from the forced migration of captives to voluntary migration (though many such migrants were semi-voluntary contract laborers). Sometimes it took a crisis to launch the flow of migrants, as with Ireland's 1845–9 potato famine. The outstanding change, however, was the development of new technology, especially steamships that traveled dependably and cheaply, but also telegraphs to convey information on conditions worldwide. The rise of industrial production expanded demand for minerals and agricultural produce.

Where ten million had crossed the Atlantic as slaves from 1550 to 1850, nearly fifty million Europeans crossed the Atlantic from 1840 to 1940, and another eighty million migrants moved from India and China. Two regions of sparse population – North America and Southeast Asia – each absorbed over thirty million immigrants. In addition, huge numbers of migrants traveled by land: North and Central Asia absorbed over twenty million immigrants in areas ruled by China and Russia. This great wave of migration transformed diasporas and formed nations. Diasporas, previously initiated by empires as much as by commerce, became more closely tied to capitalism. Diasporas sustained tradition and language among migrant communities; they also sought to influence affairs in their homeland. In Brazil and the United States, various diaspora communities joined each other to create nations by declaring independence; their westward-moving settlers became new diasporas that expanded the nation. Later diasporas coming to the United States and Brazil from Europe became part of each nation. The notion of nationhood was not necessarily inclusive, however: African diasporas of Brazil and the United States only became full citizens with the end of slavery; ultimately, many retained their African-diaspora identity too. The Chinese migrants north into Manchuria expanded the nation; the Chinese migrants to Southeast Asia remained a diaspora.

The nineteenth-century expansion of empires established imperial control from a few capitals over the great majority of the world's population. These empires accompanied – regardless of whether they caused – a huge expansion of intercontinental migration. In preceding centuries, as empires helped to mix populations to a new level, racial identities and antagonisms arose. Racial distinctions served to divide communities by color, physical type, even by dress and religious practice – and increasingly to place them in hierarchies. These factors of race, affirmed significantly in the eighteenth century, came to be reaffirmed even more forcefully in the expanding nations and empires of the late nineteenth century. Racial distinctions were to expand to a disastrous twentieth-century peak before declining. The African continent, which had been within the global system of interaction but beyond imperial control, succumbed to European conquest in the late nineteenth century and underwent most of a century of racially defined imperial rule. Much of Northeast Asia soon came under Japanese imperial rule. Empires, always eclectic collections of governing practices, now became reliant at once on racial divisions and on growing ties to industry.

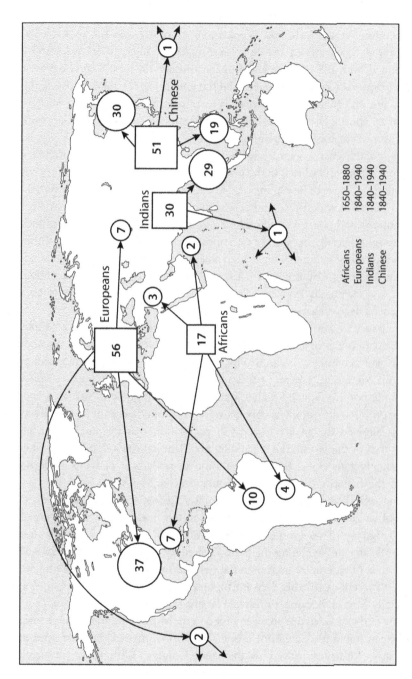

Map 12.9 Global migration after 1850. The numbers in the squares represent numbers of emigrants, in millions; the numbers in circles represent numbers of immigrants, in millions.

As expanding industry led to an arms race among imperial powers, the competition became ferocious. Wars among empires broke out sporadically: the United States seized the Spanish Empire in 1898; Japan successfully challenged both the Chinese and Russian Empires in 1905. The Great War raged from 1914 to 1918: by the end of it the empires of Germany, Austria, the Ottomans, and Russia had collapsed. The remaining empires, badly shaken, sought to consolidate their holdings, yet continued to use racial discrimination as a major tool for sustaining empire.

Imperial tensions soon arose again, and Nazi Germany especially used race as its principal political tool in the peak of racial discrimination, defining Jews and others as races to be eliminated. At the conclusion of the Second World War – the most widespread and destructive of wars – the expanded empires of Germany and Japan were dismantled, but so as well was the general idea of empire, especially because of its association with racial hierarchy. Within another thirty years empires had been abandoned – in response to independence movements – by Britain, France, the Netherlands, Belgium, the United States, and eventually Portugal. This appeared, at least for the time, to be a permanent decolonization.

The pause in war after 1945 brought the formation of the United Nations and the bare bones of a formal global community. Nevertheless, the threat of a great war continued for almost fifty years of Cold War, and decolonization brought continuing streams of casualties and refugees. A great postwar economic boom gradually fueled a new wave of migration. Increased economic productivity, while its benefits were distributed very unevenly, nevertheless allowed for an acceleration in population that eventually reached every area of the world; the expanding populations responded by crowding increasingly into cities. For the first time in millennia, peasants were no longer the majority of the human population (see Map 12.10).

Languages had shifted and moved for all of history, but expanded connections of language and diaspora developed in this era. Empires had imposed their language of government on small numbers of colonial officials, but migrants later moved along the paths created by imperial languages: people at far ends of an empire used imperial ties and imperial language to migrate in new directions. In this way Portuguese, Spanish, French, Russian, and especially English became worldwide languages.

New and expanded diasporas emerged in the wave of migration after 1950: Caribbean migrants settled in Europe and North America, Turks moved to Germany, Mexicans moved to the United States. With more advanced communications, people of the diaspora were better able to maintain contact with home, even after generations. Chinese, Irish, Filipino, and Palestinian diasporas each participated actively in affairs of their ancestral home; diaspora Jews participated in the affairs of a newly created homeland.

Urbanization took a new turn in the late twentieth century. For much of the period after 1850, migration was mainly from crowded regions to sparsely populated regions. From the second half of the twentieth century, however, the dominant pattern turned out to be the opposite – the movement of people from rural areas or small towns to centers of population expanded as never before. Urbanization in European and North American lands had seized the lead during the nineteenth century and reached, by the 1960s, rates near to 75 percent. For other parts of the world, urbanization picked up to a rapid rate that brought region after region to urban proportions even exceeding 75 percent. A dozen urban areas grew to include twenty million inhabitants or more, some on every continent. The urban settlers, in addition, came primarily from the immediate hinterland of the cities rather than from great distances. As a result, human society reached a tipping point at the beginning of the twenty-first century, in which a majority of the human population came to live in urban rather than rural areas.

Global popular culture developed in remarkable new directions as a result of multiple types of connections. While electronic communications were most obviously important, the expanded migration and multicultural atmosphere in many parts of the world encouraged the sharing of many aspects of popular culture: music, cuisine, dress, film, images. Remarkably, the African diaspora and the people of Africa – large groups that had suffered severe discrimination – played a disproportionate role in creating and spreading the new popular culture. In the twenty-first century, wherever one lived, it was no longer surprising to see a migrant from anywhere on the planet.

The future of migration

Migration remains a mix of old and new. With the expansion of higher education, one of the current migratory trends is that in which students leave home and even their country to attend university and prepare for their role in a high-tech world. Yet this same process includes much that is habitual. That is, young adults leave home, travel a distance, cross social boundaries, and learn new languages and customs (now those of the academic world); some of them will return home after the experience, while others will migrate further. The ancient human pattern of cross-community migration has now been put

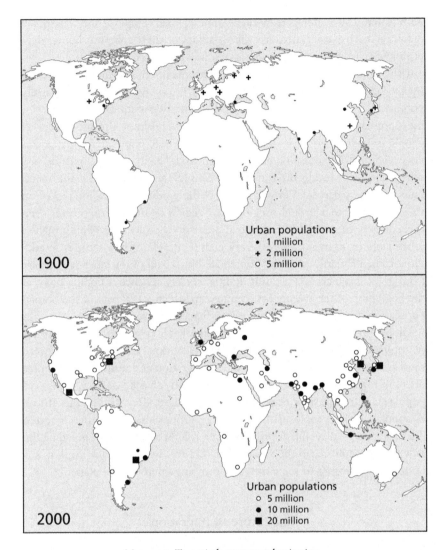

Map 12.10 Twentieth-century urbanization.

in the service of contemporary globalization, demonstrating the role of underlying human habits in even the most dramatic of changes.

The continuities in migration remain impressive. Land and sea both remain central to human movement. It is true that travel is increasingly by air for long distances and by automobile, bus, and train for shorter distances.

But if human travel by water has declined, a steadily growing proportion of commodities moves by water whenever possible. In a similar continuity, it seems that national units and national identities will continue and perhaps strengthen, even as migration expands. By the same token, the informal social organization of diasporas seems likely to continue, to expand, and to remain influential in human affairs. Meanwhile, urban, suburban, and rural areas will surely change as agriculture continues to mechanize and urban areas become increasingly dominant.

Where will future migrants settle? Our biggest cities grow at water's edge, even as the waters rise in response to climate change. People continue to leave rural areas for small and large urban areas. Perhaps future migration will be mostly from city to city. Will we move mostly to the tropics? What changes can we expect in languages – will people learn more or fewer languages? The dramatic spread of the English language in the last half-century has made some suggest that it will become a dominant or even unique language. The number of native speakers of English, some 350 million, is 5 percent of the human population (a somewhat larger number speak English as a second language); another 5 percent are native speakers of Spanish. Yet while the smallest languages are disappearing, others are growing. Most of the great cities are multilingual. So we will have a multilingual rather than an English-only future and the experience of learning new languages and cultures through migration will still continue for a long time.

The development of our globally multicultural society will bring new commonality but also new differentiation. Past migration has dependably brought connection in history, but the connections have included cultural differentiation and inequality as well as sharing of resources. Hopefully, our future will include not only more migration but also more careful study of the past of migration – at local and global levels – in order better to observe the current changes in migration.

FURTHER READING

Allsen, Thomas T., *Culture and Conquest in Mongol Eurasia*, Cambridge: Cambridge University Press, 2001.

Anthony, David W., *The Horse, the Wheel, and Language: How Bronze Age Riders from the Eurasian Steppes Shaped the Modern World*, Princeton and Oxford: Princeton University Press, 2007.

Aslanian, Sebouh David, *From the Indian Ocean to the Mediterranean: The Global Trade Networks of Armenian Merchants from New Julfa*, Berkeley: University of California Press, 2010.

Brooke, John L., *Climate Change and the Course of Global History: A Rough Journey*, New York: Cambridge University Press, 2014.

Cohen, Robin, *Global Diasporas: An Introduction*, Seattle: University of Washington Press, 1997.

Diamond, Jared, *Guns, Germs, and Steel: The Fates of Human Society*, New York: Norton, 1997.

Dingle, Hugh, *Migration: The Biology of Life on the Move*, Oxford: Oxford University Press, 1996.

Dufoix, Stéphane, *Diasporas*, William Rodarmor (trans.), Berkeley: University of California Press, 2008.

Ehret, Christopher, *An African Classical Age: Eastern and Southern Africa in World History, 1000 B.C. to A.D. 400*, Charlottesville: University Press of Virginia, 1998.

History and the Testimony of Language, Berkeley: University of California Press, 2010.

Gabaccia, Donna, *Italy's Many Diasporas*, Seattle: University of Washington Press, 2000.

Hoerder, Dirk, *Cultures in Contact: World Migrations in the Second Millennium*, Durham, NC: Duke University Press, 2002.

Lucassen, Jan and Leo Lucassen, "The mobility transition revisited, 1500–1900: What the case of Europe can offer to global history," *Journal of Global History* 4 (2009): 347–77.

(eds.), *Globalising Migration History: The Eurasian Experience (16th–21st Centuries)*, Leiden: Brill, 2014.

Lucassen Jan, Leo Lucassen, and Patrick Manning (eds.), *Migration History in World History: Multidisciplinary Approaches*, Leiden: Brill, 2010.

Manning, Patrick, *The African Diaspora: A History through Culture*, New York: Columbia University Press, 2009.

"Cross-community migration: A distinctive human pattern," *Social Evolution and History* 5,2 (2006): 24–54.

"*Homo sapiens* populates the Earth: A provisional synthesis, privileging linguistic data," *Journal of World History* 17,2 (2006): 115–58.

Slavery and African Life: Occidental, Oriental, and African Slave Trades, Cambridge: Cambridge University Press, 1990.

Manning, Patrick, with Tiffany Trimmer, *Migration in World History*, 2nd edn., London: Routledge, 2012.

McKeown, Adam, "Chinese migration in global context, 1850–1940," *Journal of Global History* 5 (2010): 95–124.

"Global migration, 1846–1940," *Journal of World History* 15 (2004), 155–89.

Melancholy Order: Asian Migration and the Globalization of Borders, New York: Columbia University Press, 2011.

Moch, Leslie Page, *Moving Europeans: Migration in Western Europe Since 1650*, 2nd edn., Bloomington, IN: Indiana University Press, 2003.

Perdue, Peter C., *China Marches West: The Qing Conquest of Central Asia*, Cambridge, MA: Belknap Press of Harvard University, 2005.

Peters, F. E., *The Hajj: The Muslim Pilgrimage to Mecca and the Holy Places*, Princeton, NJ: Princeton University Press, 1994.

Wilmshurst, Janet M., Terry L. Hunt, Carl P. Lipo, and Atholl J. Anderson, "High-precision radiocarbon dating shows recent and rapid initial human colonization of East Polynesia," *Proceedings of the National Academy of Sciences of the United States of America* 108,5 (February 1, 2011): 1,815–20.

PART II

THE PALEOLITHIC AND THE BEGINNINGS OF HUMAN HISTORY

13

Before the farmers: culture and climate, from the emergence of *Homo sapiens* to about ten thousand years ago

FELIPE FERNÁNDEZ-ARMESTO

We are creatures of cold. The changes that make the history of *Homo sapiens* distinctive began with a period of unprecedented cultural divergence during a spell of low temperatures (an 'Ice Age' in conventional parlance), about a hundred thousand years ago, or a little more. By the time global warming resumed, *Homo sapiens* had transformed from a small group in East Africa to a globally dispersed, relatively numerous species, living, by comparison with fellow-primates, in large communities, typically hundreds strong and sometimes larger, inhabiting environments more numerous and more diverse than those of any other known creature (apart from the bacteria we carry around in our bodies).

By comparison with other surviving great apes, all of whom occupy a relatively narrow ecological range and rarely migrate beyond contiguous zones, the reach of human dispersal seems astonishing. As they multiplied in numbers and embraced a widening variety of environmental challenges, groups of *Homo sapiens* lost touch with each other. A long history of mutual differentiation began, which is still going on in some respects, and which has equipped this single species with an incomparably bigger range of lifeways, and a faster (and, it seems, for still poorly understood reasons, generally accelerating) rate of cultural change than any other cultural animal.

This chapter represents an attempt at three objectives: first, to document the most conspicuous and widespread of the changes that occurred during the Ice Age, and others (equally spectacular in their way) that accompanied them and followed them during the next 10,000 years or so, when climate underwent considerable fluctuations and periodically reverted to prolonged cold spells; secondly, to relate the cultural changes to environmental conditions, as far as evidence permits; and finally to broach, at least, the problem of how far environment explains (or, in language some people prefer, 'determines') culture.

Initial assumptions

It must be acknowledged first that even before environment intervenes, intrinsic, genetically transmitted features condition the kinds of culture that cultural creatures can contrive. There is no agreement among students of the subject as to what those features are. By comparing humans with other cultural creatures, however, we can identify the traits that mark the distinctiveness (such as it is) of human culture: relative flexibility in adapting to a variety of environments and relative mutability. For two reasons, we can be sure that these traits are not simply the consequence of adjustments humans made to the diversity of the environments they colonized. First, the very impulse to traverse and occupy unfamiliar environments is itself a consequence of cultural mutability; secondly, the evidence is overwhelming that different human groups respond very differently to similar or identical environmental conditions.[1]

The archaeological record has not so far yielded evidence of rapid cultural divergence among human groups for the first hundred thousand years or so of the existence of *Homo sapiens*; so the pertinent characteristics may not be of any great antiquity in evolutionary terms. For the purposes of this chapter, I make assumptions that require justification at greater length than is available at present: that the pertinent characteristics did not necessarily evolve earlier than the foraging phase of our hominid ancestors' past; that they are connected with, and perhaps account for, mental faculties that, as far as we know, feature to an exceptional degree in human psyches; that the critical mental faculty of this kind in explaining human cultural diversity is imagination; that imagination is, in evolutionary jargon, a spandrel – an unpredictable and unnecessary consequence of evolutionary change; and that it is a by-product of evolutionarily determined characteristics of two other human mental faculties: anticipation and memory.[2] The power of imagination, according to my assumptions, freed human cultures to respond with extraordinary elasticity and diversity to the environments they confronted. It seems reasonable also to postulate language as a means of maintaining relatively large communities, compared with those of some other cultural creatures, and of doing innovative things with them – but we do not know when language became available, or even

---

1 Felipe Fernández-Armesto, *Civilizations: Culture, Ambition, and the Transformation of Nature* (New York: Free Press, 2003).
2 For detailed justification, see Felipe Fernández-Armesto, *A Foot in the River* (New York: Oxford University Press, forthcoming).

whether it is properly classified as a faculty, or whether it can be explained in evolutionary terms.[3]

The climatic setting

The strictly environmental influences on human cultures can be considered as comprising two elements: climate and ecology. Both, of course, over a period as long as this chapter covers, registered great differences from time to time as well as from place to place. In the case of climate, it is possible to make some valid assertions at a level of analysis that considers the whole world conspectually. Global climate depends, above all, on the relationship between Earth and the sun. At intervals, the planet tilts on its axis or wobbles in its orbit, increasing the intervening distance or the angle of incidence of the sun's rays.[4] Very roughly, however – on average, as far as evidence currently available shows, every hundred thousand years over the last million – the result is plain: an Ice Age, which may cool the entire planet, or, according to the extent of the tilt of the Earth, affect one hemisphere more than another. Apparently random variations, unexplained or unsatisfactorily explained (albeit not for want of effort), can buck the prevailing trends for periods of varying length, which, in fairly well documented cases, can extend for a couple of millennia or more. Even in the relatively warm interstices between cooling events, variations in sunspot activity can cause protracted reversions to intense cold. In well-documented periods, these have lasted for as long as a hundred years, interrupting longer spells of global warming.[5]

The changes in climate that form the framework of our story can be summarized at once. We can link the first emergence of *Homo sapiens* in the

---

3 Rudolf Botha, *Unraveling the Evolution of Language* (Bingley: Emerald, 2003); Daniel L. Everett, *Language: The Cultural Tool* (New York: Pantheon, 2012), pp. 290–8; and Christine Kenneally, *The First Word: The Search for the Origins of Language* (New York: Penguin, 2007), p. 263.

4 There is no agreement among climatologists about the relative importance of these two variables, though a strong body of opinion regards orbital variation as decisive. In any case, the reasons why some events are more pronounced than others are unknown. Robert F. Giegenback and Claudio Vita-Finzi, 'Climate change: Past, present and future', in A. Bruce Mainwaring, Robert F. Giegengack, and Claudio Vita-Finzi (eds.), *Climate Crises in Human History* (Philadelphia, PA: American Philosophical Society, 2010), pp. 7–24; Richard A. Muller and Gordon J. Macdonald, *Ice Ages and Astronomical Causes* (Dordrecht: Springer, 2000); and Wallace S. Broecker and Robert Kunzug, *Fixing Climate: The Story of Climate Science – and How to Stop Global Warming* (London: Profile, 2008), pp. 41–74.

5 Claudio Vita-Finzi, *Solar History: An Introduction* (Dordrecht: Springer, 2013), pp. 4–8 and 47–58; and Judit Brophy, *The Enigma of Sunspots: A Story of Discovery and Scientific Revolution* (Edinburgh: Floris, 2002), pp. 78–128.

archaeological record with a cool period at about 150,000–200,000 years ago. Dispersal over an unprecedented swathe of the globe, from about 100,000 years ago, with the accompanying cultural changes, coincided with an Ice Age that, at its most extensive, about 20,000 years ago, spread ice in the northern hemisphere as far south as the present lower courses of the Missouri and Ohio rivers in North America and deep into what are now the British Isles. Ice covered what is today Scandinavia. Most of the rest of what is now Europe was tundra or taiga. In central Eurasia, tundra reached almost to the present latitudes of the Black Sea. Steppe licked the shores of the Mediterranean. In the New World, tundra and taiga extended to where Virginia is today.

Not long after the resumption of warming, between about 18,000 and 15,000 years ago, an extended period of falling temperatures followed. Thereafter, the geological record shows enormous regional fluctuations in temperature. Melting ice meant cooling seas and temporary reversals of warming in affected latitudes. Further periods of perceptibly reduced temperatures worldwide, at intervals of about a millennium, with climaxes at about 13,000 and 12,000 years ago respectively, witnessed (and perhaps stimulated) new forms of cultural divergence, which multiplied when warming resumed and which, in some ways, have been going on ever since. The coincidences between climate change and cultural change do not warrant claims that climate determines culture. They do suggest that climate constitutes part of the framework in which cultural change unfolds and attains the limits of what may be possible from time to time.

Human dispersal

If climate is the context of our story, the experiences of Homo sapiens are its subject. The earliest available archaeological evidence of the existence and original habitat of our species emerged in 2003, in Herto, Ethiopia, where, near the remains of a butchered hippopotamus, three skulls turned up – a child's and two adults' – dated to about 154,000 to 160,000 years ago. They look similar to skulls of humans today, except that they are slightly larger than what is now average. The skulls had been stripped of flesh and polished after death, as if in the culture they belonged to people practised some death-linked ritual.[6]

---

6 Yonas Beyenne, 'Herto brains and minds: Behaviour of early Homo sapiens from Awash, Ethiopia', in Robin Dunbar, Clive Gamble, and John Gowlett (eds.), Social Brain, Distributed Mind (Oxford: Oxford University Press, 2010), pp. 43–55.

The date ascribed to the find roughly corresponds to inferences about the antiquity of *Homo sapiens* from genetic evidence. All humans today – as far as we can tell without actually testing everyone – have a component in our cells that a mother in East Africa passed on to her daughters about 150,000 years ago.[7] We nickname her Eve, but of course she was not our first ancestress nor the only woman of her day. By the best available estimates, there were perhaps 20,000 individuals of the species at the time, all living in the same region and presumably practising the same culture – eating the same food, prepared in the same way, with the same technology, sharing whatever might pass for notions of cosmology and transcendence, celebrating the same rites, and communicating by common means. Thanks to the hippopotamus bones and the cherished skulls, we can begin to picture not only the appearance of the African Eve – we can do that by looking in a mirror – but also something of her way of life or, at least, life at a time close to her own.

Eve's homeland of mixed grassland and sparse woodland was no Eden, but it was suitable for the creatures into whom our ancestor and her offspring had evolved. In this environment they could, like predecessor-species in the same circumstances, make up for their deficiency as climbers by standing erect to look out around them. Here, too, they could use techniques familiar to earlier hominids: they set fires to manage the grazing of the animals they hunted with fire-hardened spears, and sharpened stones to butcher the carcasses. They could exploit their modest physical advantages over competitor species. Humans are poorly equipped physically, with inferior senses of sight, smell, and hearing, slow movements, unthreatening teeth and nails, poor digestions, and weak bodies that confine us to the ground. But we can sweat profusely over our hairless skins to keep cool during long chases, and we can ward off rival predators with our relatively accurate throwing-arms and well-coordinated eye–arm movements.[8] In short, like most creatures, we are physically well equipped for a particular kind of habitat.

Nonetheless, from their beginnings in East Africa, Eve's descendants spread over the world.[9] Such dispersal had happened before – or something like it had. More than a million years before *Homo sapiens* set out, *Homo*

---

7 Bryan Sykes, *The Seven Daughters of Eve* (New York: Norton, 2001).
8 Alfred W. Crosby, *Throwing Fire: Projectile Technology throughout History* (Cambridge: Cambridge University Press, 2002).
9 Clive Gamble, *Timewalkers: The Prehistory of Global Colonization* (Cambridge, MA: Harvard University Press, 1994); and Stephen Oppenheimer, *Out of Eden: The Peopling of the World* (Bloomington: Indiana University Press, 2004).

erectus migrated from a similar region in East Africa and spread over most of what are now Africa and Eurasia, following numerous earlier, somewhat less far-reaching hominins.[10] But theirs was a much slower and more selective peopling of the Earth than *Homo sapiens* achieved, and as far as we know it did not lead to the startling cultural divergence that came to constitute the history of our own species.

At intervals *Homo sapiens* encountered other less widely dispersed, culturally homogeneous hominids, such as Neanderthals in Europe and southwest Asia, and perhaps the minute but technically well equipped *Homo floresiensis*.[11] Despite much speculation over the possible interactions that might have followed during various millennia of coexistence, the only incontestable fact about the interactions is that *Homo sapiens* survived while the other species became extinct.[12] The uniqueness of the experience of *Homo sapiens* overshadows everything else that we conventionally call history.

Nature and scope of the migrations

The first great problems early humans' dispersal poses for us are why they moved, and what made them so adaptable to different environments. These are big, perplexing problems because most species stay in the environments where they are best adapted. Even human populations rarely, if ever, seek new environments willingly, or adjust easily. Yet when groups of *Homo sapiens* migrated out of Africa to people the world, they often relocated in challengingly different places: deep forests, where grassland habits were of limited use; extremely cold climates, to which they were physically ill-suited; deserts and seas, which demanded technologies they had not yet developed. Some of these new habitats bred unfamiliar diseases. Still, people kept on moving, through them and into them. We are still struggling to understand how it happened. In these pages, I assume that 'migration' – rather than 'dispersion', a term that specialists in the movements of other species tend to prefer in disavowal of the implication of a conscious process – is the right term to designate human movements, even as long ago as 100,000 years. The

10 Christopher J. Norton and David R. Braun (eds.), *Asian Paleoanthropology: From Africa to China and Beyond* (Dordrecht: Springer, 2010); and John Fleagle, et al. (eds.), *Out of Africa: The First Hominin Colonization of Eurasia* (Dordrecht: Springer, 2010).
11 Dean Falk, *The Fossil Chronicles: How Two Controversial Discoveries Changed Our View of Human Evolution* (Berkeley: University of California Press, 2011), pp. 76–198.
12 Ian Tattersall, *The Last Neanderthal: The Rise, Success, and Mysterious Extinction of Our Last Human Relative* (New York: Macmillan, 1995).

equipage of migrants of that era contained artefacts associable with thoughts and sensibilities akin to our own: shell jewellery, incised slabs of ochre, and, in Blombos Cave in South Africa, in an area settled by migrants from East Africa about 100,000 years ago, shell-crucibles and spatulas for mixing pigments.[13] Investigators have perceived objects of art and the remains of musical instruments in stratigraphic layers up to 100,000 years old. That our ancestors then had 'a theory of mind' – consciousness of their own consciousness – is a proposition hard to resist in the presence of so much evidence of imaginations so creative and so constructive. They had the mental equipment necessary to be able to imagine themselves in changed circumstances and new environments, and to attempt to realize the changes.

To some extent, we can reconstruct where and when *Homo sapiens* travelled while peopling the Earth, even though the archaeological evidence is patchy, by measuring differences in blood type, genetic make-up, and language among populations in different parts of the world.[14] The greater the differences, the longer the ancestors of the people concerned are likely to have been out of touch with the rest of humankind. The science is inexact, because people are rarely isolated for long. Over most of Eurasia and Africa, populations have moved about tremendously in recorded history. Groups of people have frequently been mixed and restirred. There are, moreover, no agreed ways to measure the differences among languages. Readers should be aware that genetic and linguistic work has yielded few, if any, uncontested conclusions.

Still, for what it is worth, the best-informed research puts *Homo sapiens* in the Middle East by about 100,000 years ago. The colony failed, but newcomers reappeared about 60,000 years ago. Settlement then proceeded along the coasts of Africa and Asia, probably, at least in part, by sea.[15] The earliest agreed-upon archaeological evidence of *Homo sapiens* in China is about 67,000

13 Christopher Henshilwood, Francesco d'Errico, Karen L. van Niekerk, Yvan Coquinot, Zenobia Jacobs, Stein-Erik Lauritzen, Michel Menu, and Renata García-Moreno, 'A 100,000-year-old ochre-processing workshop at Blombos Cave, South Africa', *Science* 334 (2011), 219–22; and Lyn Wadley, 'Cemented ash as a receptacle or work surface for ochre powder production at Sibudu, South Africa, 58,000 years ago', *Journal of Archaeological Science* 37 (2010), 2, 397–406.

14 Luca Cavalli-Sforza and Flavio Cavalli-Sforza, *Chi siamo? La storia della diversità umana* (Milan: Mondadori, 1993); Luca Cavalli-Sforza, *Genes, Peoples, and Languages* (Berkeley: University of California Press, 2001); and Peter N. Peregrine, Ilia Peiros, and Marcus W. Feldman (eds.), *Ancient Human Migration: A Multidisciplinary Approach* (Salt Lake City: University of Utah Press, 2009), pp. 1–54.

15 Atholl Anderson, James H. Barrett, and Katherine V. Boyle (eds.), *The Global Origins and Development of Seafaring* (Cambridge: Cambridge University Press, 2010).

years old (although some digs have yielded puzzlingly earlier dates for remains that seem like those of *Homo sapiens*). It may seem surprising that humans developed nautical technology so early. Yet some evidence supports or, at least, invites inferences that even *Homo erectus* may have travelled short distances by sea, and the first colonizers of Australia arrived over 50,000 years ago and must have used boats, because at that time, water already separated what are now Australia and New Guinea from Asia.[16]

Homo sapiens reached Europe only a little later. Northern Asia – isolated by daunting screens of cold climate – was probably colonized about 30,000 years ago. The New World was settled from there in, for scholars, the most contested phase of the story. According to the formerly dominant theory, a gap opened between glaciers towards the end of the Ice Age. A race of hunters crossed the land link between Asia and North America, where the Bering Strait now flows, to enter a paradise where no human hunter had ever trod before. The abundance was so great and the animals so unwary that the invaders ate enormously and multiplied greatly. They spread rapidly over the hemisphere, hunting the great game to extinction as they went. The Clovis people, as these hunters were dubbed after an early archaeological site in New Mexico, seemed to resemble modern American pioneers. They exhibited quick-fire locomotion, hustle and bustle, technical prowess, big appetites, irrepressible strength, enormous cultural reach, and a talent for reforging the environment.

By comparison, the truth about the peopling of the hemisphere is disappointingly undramatic. These first great American superheroes – like most of their successors – did not really exist. Although archaeologists have excavated too few sites for a complete and reliable picture to emerge, a new theory dominates. We have evidence of early human settlement scattered from the Yukon to Uruguay and from near the Bering Strait to the edge of the Beagle Channel. This evidence is so widespread, over so long a period, in so many different geological layers, and with such a vast range of cultural diversity that one conclusion is inescapable – colonists came at different times, bringing different cultures with them.[17]

---

16 Peter Hiscock, *The Archaeology of Ancient Australia* (London: Routledge, 2008).
17 Nina G. Jablonski, *The First Americans: The Pleistocene Colonization of the New World* (San Francisco: California Academy of Sciences, 2002); C. Michael Barton, Geoffrey A. Clark, David R. Yesner, and Georges A. Pearson, *The Settlement of the American Continents: A Multidisciplinary Approach to Human Biogeography* (Tucson: University of Arizona Press, 2004); and Bradley T. Lepper and Robson Bonnichsen, *New Perspectives on the First Americans* (College Station: Texas A&M University Press, 2004).

Some came by sea and continued to come after the land bridge was submerged. Around 10,000 years ago, a catastrophic cluster of extinctions wiped out the mammoth, mastodon, horse, giant sloth, sabre-toothed tiger, and at least thirty-five other large species in the Americas. New hunting techniques and perhaps new hunting peoples were probably partly responsible. But we can only explain the events in the context of vast climatic changes that affected habitats and the whole ecology on which these animals depended.[18]

In any case, by the end of the era of climatic fluctuation, humans occupied almost all the habitats their descendants occupy today, with the exception of relatively remote parts of the Pacific, accessible only by high-seas navigation and unsettled, as far as we know, for many millennia more. A handful of Eve's children had multiplied to the point where they could colonize most of the habitable Old World in less than 100,000 years.

The expansion of *Homo sapiens* implies an astonishing rate of population growth. We have no idea – beyond guesswork – of the actual numbers that migrated, but we can estimate a figure in millions by the end of the process. As far as we know, everyone at the time lived by foraging and moved on foot. Because mothers cannot easily carry more than one or two infants, large numbers of children are unsuited to foraging life. Consequently, foragers usually limit their families, either by strictly regulating who can mate with whom or by practising other forms of population control. Their main contraceptive method is a long period of lactation. Breast-feeding mothers are relatively infertile. The demographic growth that peopled the Earth is surprising, therefore, because it breaks the normal pattern of population stability in foraging communities. How can we explain it? Was the increase in population cause or effect of the migrations? And how did it relate to the other changes migration brought? Migrating groups were doubly dynamic: not just mobile, but also subject to huge social changes.

Causes of the migrations

The only seemingly incontestable influence on the way people behaved in our period is climate – though it is so general in impact as to explain little or nothing in detail. Every episode of warming can be presumed to have

---

18 Stuart J. Fiedel, 'Did a bolide impact trigger the Younger Dryas and wipe out American Megafauna?', in Mainwaring, Giegengack, and Vita-Finzi (eds.), *Climate Crises*, pp. 85–111.

stimulated migration into cooler areas in search of climatic stability or of familiar ecological circumstances in pursuit of relocated food sources. Every episode of cooling must presumably have had an equal and opposite effect, sending migrants in search of warmth. The alternation of humid phases with periods of desiccation – both of which are impossible to date, in the present state of our knowledge, without margins of error of up to 10,000 years – and the periodic juxtaposition of drying and humidifying zones – can be presumed to account for some shifts of population.[19] Climatic instability generally may have habituated populations to a diversity of conditions and emboldened migrants to penetrate previously untried environments.

Perhaps new stresses drove the migrants on. Food shortages or ecological disasters might explain the necessity, but no evidence supports this or fits with the evidence of rising population. In every other case we know of, in all species, population falls when food sources shrink. This point is not decisive, as one can imagine a world in which survivors flee societies in crisis, and rapidly recover demographic buoyancy when they encounter new resources; but such a way of picturing the world of 100,000 years ago is speculative.

Warfare may be a more promising form of stress to consider for present purposes. Among the four horsemen of the Apocalypse – war, plague, famine, and natural disaster – war is the odd one out. The other three tend to inhibit human action, whereas war spurs us to new responses. One of the most fascinating problems of history is how and when war started. According to one school of thought, war is natural to humankind. Field Marshal Montgomery referred people who asked how he justified war to Maeterlinck's *The Life of the Ant*.[20] At the time, a number of distinguished anthropologists and zoologists agreed, arguing that evolution implanted aggressive and violent instincts in humans as it did in other animals.[21] Romantics defended the opposite point of view: that human nature is essentially peaceful until competition corrupts it. War, according to Margaret Mead, the great liberal anthropologist of the 1920s and 1930s, was an invention, not a biological necessity.[22]

---

19 Jennifer R. Smith, 'Pleistocene climate change and human occupation of eastern North Africa', in Mainwaring, Giegengack, and Vita-Finzi (eds.), *Climate Crises*, pp. 125–38.
20 Bernard Montgomery, *A History of Warfare* (New York: Morrow, 1983), p. 13.
21 Konrad Lorenz, *On Aggression* (New York: Harcourt, 1966); and Robert Ardrey, *The Territorial Imperative* (New York: Athenaeum, 1966), p. 5.
22 Margaret Mead, 'War is only an invention, not a biological necessity', in Douglas Hunt (ed.), *The Dolphin Reader* (Boston: Houghton, 1990), pp. 415–21.

At first, the evidence seemed divided. The earliest archaeological proof we have of large-scale warfare is a battle fought at Jebel Sahaba, near the modern border of Egypt and Sudan, about 11,000 years ago. The victims included women and children. Many were savaged by multiple wounds. One female was stabbed twenty-two times. At the time, agriculture was in its infancy. Today, peoples who practise the simplest agriculture as well as those who supposedly represent modernity and civilization massacre others. These facts have encouraged speculation that warfare began – or, at least, entered a new, more systematic phase – when settled communities started to fight one another to control land and resources.[23] Yet it seems that organized, collaborative violence must really be much older. In the 1970s, the primatologist Jane Goodall observed something like what we would now call gang warfare among chimpanzee communities.[24] When chimpanzee splinter groups secede from their societies, their former fellows try to kill them. Similar conflicts may have made early human splinter groups migrate to safety. It is an intriguing speculation, but, even if it were to prove correct, it poses other problems. What could have caused people to divide and fight each other a hundred thousand years ago? Rising population again? Competition for mates (which is a common reason for secessions from chimpanzee groups)? Or are we driven back to more speculation about increasing competition for supposedly diminishing food stocks, or even to assertions about innate animal aggression?

Whatever migrants' motives were, they needed sufficient technology to multiply and move. Cooking with fire probably helped to make population growth possible, because it made food easier to digest. Creatures like us, who have short guts, weak jaws, blunt teeth, and only one stomach each, can only chew and digest limited energy sources. As a result, anything that increased the range of foods available to early humans and encouraged and enabled them to eat a lot was a major evolutionary advantage. Still, the chronology of cooking does not seem to fit. The palaeoanthropologist Richard Wrangham has argued brilliantly for a starting date for cooking with fire more than 2 million years ago. His argument is based on inferences from physiology, such as the evolving shape of hominid teeth, which, apparently,

---

23 Fred Wendorf, 'Site 117: A Nubian final Paleolithic graveyard near Jebel Sahaba, Sudan', in Fred Wendorf, *The Prehistory of Nubia* (Dallas: Southern Methodist University Press, 1968), pp. 996–1,040; and Lawrence Keeley, *War Before Civilization* (New York: Oxford University Press, 1996).

24 Dale Paterson and Richard Wrangham, *Demonic Males: Apes and the Origins of Human Violence* (Boston: Houghton, 1996), p. 6.

got smaller and blunter at that time, presumably in response to food modified by flames; hominids' shortening gut, too, was probably a response to dietary changes in the same period.[25] There is no direct evidence of fire used for cooking at that time, and an increase in the consumption of meat prepared in other ways might explain the physiological evidence. Yet the domestication of fire still seems to have occurred too early to help explain the migrations. Fires that burned in caves between half a million and 1.5 million years ago look as if they were deliberately kindled. An almost irresistible case is that of Zhoukhoudian in China, where the great Jesuit scientist Pierre Teilhard de Chardin (1881–1955) excavated the evidence and the Abbé Henri Breuil (1877–1961), the leading archaeologist of the day, identified it. 'It's impossible', said the Jesuit, thinking the site was too early for the controlled use of fire, '[that] it comes from Zhoukhoudian'. 'I don't care where it comes from', the Abbé replied. 'It was made by a human, and that human knew the use of fire.'[26]

We are similarly uncertain about when other technologies started, such as drive lanes and corrals, which might have improved diet by enhancing hunting. But the earliest known examples of fire-hardened spears are only 150,000 years or so old, taking us back to a date near the start of the migrations. Presumably, the 'container revolution' – the beginnings of the technologies that transformed skins or fibres into easily transportable carriers – preceded or accompanied long-range human dispersals; the chronology of these developments cannot be satisfactorily established but they happened early enough to assist the first *Homo sapiens* migrating out of Africa.[27]

Consequences

If the causes of migration remain doubtful, some of its consequences are easier to specify. Migration changed people's relationships with each other, the size and organization of their groups, the way they saw the world, and

---

25 Richard Wrangham, *Catching Fire: How Cooking Made Us Human* (New York: Basic Books, 2009).
26 Alan Houghton Brodrick, *The Abbé Breuil, Historian: A Biography* (London: Hutchinson 1963), p. 11; and Johan Goudsblom, *Fire and Civilization* (New York: Penguin, 1994), pp. 16–34.
27 Clive Gamble, *Origins and Revolutions: Human Identity in Earliest Prehistory* (New York: Cambridge University Press, 2007).

the way they interacted with other species – including those they competed with, preyed on, and outlasted.

Sexual specialization is one of the most conspicuous consequences, and is consistent with the notion that migration and warfare may have been causally linked. In societies of increasing violence, men have enhanced roles, because, among all primates, including humans, greater competitiveness in mating makes males, on average, bigger and stronger than females. In consequence, alpha males rule, or at least boss, most ape societies. Human males usually seem to bond more closely with each other, or form more or stronger alliances, than females. This, too, is useful in competitive circumstances, such as those of war and politics. Yet women are, in at least one respect, more valuable in most societies than men. A society can dispense with most of its men – risking them, for instance, in war – and still reproduce. Women, moreover, are more easily mistaken as sacred because of the obvious correspondences between the cycles of their bodies and the rhythms of the heavens.

So how did male domination come to be normal in human societies? One theory ascribes it to a deliberate, collective power-seeking strategy by males, inspired by dislike of women or resentment or envy or a desire to get control of the most elementary of resources – the means of reproducing the species. By analogy with chimpanzees, a rival theory suggests that male dominance is a consequence of hunting, which, in the few chimpanzee groups known to practise it, is an almost exclusively male activity. Hunting increases male dominance in chimpanzee society because the hunters distribute the meat, in almost ritual fashion. Females line up and, in effect, beg for morsels. Female chimps often exchange sex for food, especially meat.[28] By contrast, among bonobos, despite some carnivorous behaviour, both sexes share foraging, and females tend to be socially equal or even dominant.[29] Hunting, in any case, seems to be a recent development in chimpanzee society and to have followed and strengthened male dominance – not caused it. Without evidence to the contrary, it is unwise to assume that early in the migration period either sex monopolized political power.

---

28 Paterson and Wrangham, *Demonic Males*; Craig B. Stanford, 'A comparison of social meat-foraging by chimpanzees and human foragers', in Craig B. Stanford and Henry T. Bunn (eds.), *Meat Eating and Human Evolution* (New York: Oxford University Press, 2001), p. 134; and Craig B. Stanford, *The Hunting Ape: Meat-eating and the Origins of Human Behavior* (Princeton, NJ: Princeton University Press, 1999).

29 Martin Surbeck and Gottfried Hohmann, 'Primate hunting by bonobo at LuiKotale, Salonga National Park', *Current Biology* 18 (2008), 906–7.

Still, migrating groups must have developed ways of liberating more women for childbirth, or increasing the fertile period of women's lives. Improved nutrition may have helped. Was there also some redistribution of economic activities, with men taking on more food-supplying roles? Some scholars have speculated that in the earliest kind of sexual economic specialization, men did most of the hunting, while women did most of the gathering.[30] But we do not know when this specialization started or how rigid or widespread it was. In any case, the balance between hunted and gathered foods in the diets of the migrants varied according to the environment. Gathering seems to have been more productive in terms of calorific value per unit of energy expended, for, in known cases, hunting supplied about a third of the nutrition. It is probably fair to assert that the migrations, and the accompanying demographic changes, would not have been possible without both hunting and gathering.

Within those broad categories, however, food-gathering strategies were also subject to change. The Ice Age suited some people, at least. For the hunters who inhabited the vast tundra that covered much of Eurasia, the edge of the ice was the best place to be, where a lot of mammals had adapted by efficiently storing their own body fat. Dietary fat has a bad reputation today, but for most of history, most people have eagerly sought it. Relatively speaking, animal fat is the world's most energy-abundant source of food, yielding on average three times as much reward, in calorific terms, as any other form of intake. In some parts of the tundra, concentrations of small animals could supply human populations: easily trapped arctic hare, or creatures vulnerable to the bows that appeared about 20,000 years ago could supply human populations. More commonly, however, hunters favoured species they could kill in large numbers by driving them over cliffs or into bogs or lakes.[31] For the killers, while stocks lasted, the result was a fat bonanza, achieved with a relatively modest expenditure of effort.

Abundant game guaranteed Ice-Age affluence. The remains of Ice-Age people encourage a proposition supported by anthropological data: on average, they were better nourished than most later populations.[32] Only modern

---

30 Rebecca Bird, 'Cooperation and conflict: The behavioral ecology of the sexual division of labor', *Evolutionary Anthropology* 8 (1999), 65–75; and Frank W. Marlowe, 'Hunting and gathering: The human sexual division of foraging labor', *Cross-Cultural Research* 41 (2007), 170–95.

31 Laura Niven, 'From carcass to cave: Large mammal exploitation during the Aurignacian at Vogelherd, Germany', *Journal of Human Evolution* 53 (2007), 362–82.

32 Marshall D. Sahlins, *Stone-age Economics* (London: Routledge, 1972); and S. Boyd Eaton, Loren Cordain, and Anthony Sebastiani, 'The ancestral biomedical environment', in

industrialized societies surpass their intake of perhaps 3,000 calories a day. In some Ice-Age communities, people ate about five pounds of food a day. The nature of the plant foods they gathered – few starchy grains, relatively large amounts of fruit and plants that grow underground – and the high ascorbic acid content of animal organ meats provided five times the average intake of vitamin C of an American today. High levels of nutrition and long days of leisure, unequalled in most subsequent societies, meant people had time to observe nature and think about what they saw.

Food preferences had consequences, or, at least, correspondences in aesthetic, emotional, and intellectual life. For Ice-Age artists, fat was beautiful. One of the oldest artworks in the world is the Venus of Willendorf – a plump little carving of a fat female, 30,000 years old and named for the place in Germany where she was found. Critics have interpreted her as a goddess, ruler, or, since she could be pregnant, a means of conjuring fertility. However, her slightly more recent lookalike, the Venus of Laussel, carved on a cave wall in France, evidently got fat the way most of us do: by enjoyment and indulgence. She raises a horn, which must surely contain food or drink.[33]

In the depths of the Ice Age, a stunningly resourceful way of life took shape. We know most about the period in Europe, where extensive art has survived because it was made in deep caves evidently chosen because they were inaccessible.[34] Only now are the effects of tourism – too many respiratory systems, too many camera flashes – damaging these works in their once-secret caverns. Most prehistoric art has been found in northern Spain and southwest France. About fifty cave complexes contain thousands of paintings, mostly of animals, and hundreds of smaller works. Examples of sculptures, carvings, and other art objects are also scattered across Europe, from Britain and the Atlantic in the west, to the Oder and Carpathians in the east, and, more sporadically, beyond to Ukraine and the Urals. Rarer finds have occurred all over the range of human habitats, suggesting that, in general terms, some conclusions valid for the places of greatest concentration of evidence are applicable over a wider area.

What was the art for? It surely told stories and had magical, ritual uses. Some animal images are slashed or punctured many times over, as if in

William C. Aird (ed.), *Endothelial Biomedicine* (Cambridge: Cambridge University Press, 2007), pp. 129–34.

33 Paul G. Bahn and Jean Vertut, *Journey through the Ice Age* (Berkeley: University of California Press, 1997).

34 Andrew J. Lawson, *Painted Caves: Palaeolithic Rock Art in Western Europe* (Oxford: Oxford University Press, 2012).

symbolic sacrifice. Where early artists used stencilling (tracing around a pattern), it seems believable that footprints and handprints inspired it. A good case has been made for seeing the cave paintings as aids to track prey. The shapes of hooves, the tracks, dung, seasonal habits, and favourite foods of the beasts are among the artists' standard stock of images. By analogy with the rock paintings of hunter-gatherers of later periods, Ice-Age art depicts an imagined world, full of the spirits of the animals people needed and admired: a magical world, accessed in mystical trances.[35]

The technology that made the cave art was simple: a palette mixed from three different colours of the mineral ochre – red, brown, yellow – and animal fat, applied with wood, bone, and animal hair. Even the earliest works appeal instantly to modern sensibilities. The looks and litheness of the animal portraits spring from the rock walls, products of practised, specialized hands and of learning accumulated over generations. Carvings from the same period exhibit similar elegance – ivory sculptures of 30,000-year-old arched-necked horses from Vogelherd in south Germany; female portraits from Brassempouy in France and Dolni Vestonice in Moravia, over 20,000 years old. Clay models of bears, dogs, and women were fired 27,000 years ago at Dolni Vestonice and at Maininskaya in what is now Russia.[36]

Outside Europe, what little we know of the peoples of the time suggests that they created equally skilful work.[37] Four painted rock slabs from Namibia in southwest Africa are about 26,000 years old, almost as old as any art in Europe, and bear similar animal images.[38] The earliest paintings that decorate the rocks of Arnhem Land in northernmost Australia show faint traces of long-extinct giant kangaroos and scary snakes. A clue to the very idea of representing life in art fades today from a rock face in Kenniff, Australia, where stencils of human hands and tools were made 20,000 years ago. But most of the evidence has been lost, weathered away on exposed

35 David Lewis-Williams, 'Harnessing the brain: Vision and shamanism in Upper Palaeolithic Western Europe', in Margaret W. Conkey, et al. (eds.), *Beyond Art: Pleistocene Image and Symbol* (Berkeley: University of California Press, 1996), pp. 321–42; and Jean Clottes and David Lewis-Williams, *The Shamans of Prehistory: Trance Magic and the Painted Caves* (New York: Abrams, 1998).

36 Richard G. Lesure, *Interpreting Ancient Figurines: Context, Comparison, and Prehistoric Art* (Cambridge: Cambridge University Press, 2011); and Henri Delporte (ed.), *La Dame de Brassempouy* (Brassempouy: Université de Liège Press, 1995).

37 Paul G. Bahn, *Cambridge Illustrated History of Prehistoric Art* (Cambridge: Cambridge University Press, 1998).

38 Alec Campbell, *African Rock Art: Paintings and Engravings on Stone* (New York: Abrams, 2001), pp. 105–12.

rock faces, perished with the bodies or hides on which it was painted, or scattered by wind from the earth where it was scratched.[39]

The discovery of so much comparable art, of comparable age, in such widely separated parts of the world suggests an important and often over-looked fact. The Ice Age was the last great era of what we would now call a kind of globalization. That is, key elements of culture were similar all over the inhabited world. Though languages and the structures of political and social life were probably already highly various, people practised hunter-gatherer economies with similar kinds of technology, ate similar kinds of food, enjoyed similar levels of material culture, and – as far as we can tell – had similar religious practices. Social change and intellectual shifts were challenging for people who experienced them, but they happened slowly by comparison with later periods. The earliest of the art-filled caves of southern France, at Chauvet, is 30,000 years old; that at Lascaux dates from 10,000 years later. Yet the subjects the artists painted, and the techniques and styles they used, hardly changed in all that time.

The material culture – concrete objects people create – that many arch-aeological digs yield offers clues to what goes on in the mind. A simple test establishes that fact. We can make informed inferences about people's religion, or politics, or their attitudes towards nature and society, or their values in general, by looking at what they eat, how they dress, and how they decorate their homes. For instance, the people who hunted mammoths to extinction 20,000 years ago on the Ice-Age steppes of what is now southern Russia built dome-shaped dwellings of mammoth bones on a circular plan twelve or fifteen feet in diameter that seem sublime triumphs of the imagin-ation.[40] They are reconstructions of mammoth nature, humanly reimagined, perhaps to acquire the beast's strength or to magically assume power over the species. Yet ordinary, everyday activities went on inside these extraordin-ary dwellings – sleeping, eating, and all the routines of family life – in communities, on average, of fewer than a hundred people. But no dwelling is purely practical. Your house reflects your ideas about your place in the world.

Thanks to the clues material culture yields, we can make some confident assertions about other aspects of Ice-Age people's lives: their symbolic

39 Robert Layton, *Australian Rock Art: A New Synthesis* (Cambridge: Cambridge University Press, 1992).
40 Ivan H. Pidoplichko, *Upper Palaeolithic Dwellings of Mammoth Bones in the Ukraine: Kiev-Kirillovskii, Gontsy, Dobranichevka, Mezin and Mezhirich* (Oxford: British Archaeological Reports, 1998).

systems, their magic, and the kind of social and political units they lived in. Although Ice-Age people had nothing we recognize as writing, they did have highly expressive symbols, which we can only struggle to translate. Realistic drawings made 20,000 to 30,000 years ago show recurring gestures and postures. Moreover, they often include what seem to be numbers, signified by dots and notches. Other marks, which we can no longer interpret, are undeniably systematic. One widely occurring mark that looks like a 'p' may be a symbol for female because it resembles the curves of a woman's body. What looks as if it might be a calendar was made 30,000 years ago in the Dordogne region in France. It is a flat bone inscribed with crescents and circles that may record phases of the moon.[41]

Clues to Ice-Age spiritual life appear in traces of red ochre, the earliest substance that seems to have had a role in ritual. At Blombos Cave in South Africa, ochre objects apparently engraved with patterns form part of an assemblage 75,000 years old. The oldest known ochre mine in the world, about 42,000 years old, is at Lion Cave in what is now Lesotho. The vivid, lurid colour was applied in burials, perhaps as a precious offering, perhaps to imitate blood and reinvest the dead with life. The speculation that people might also have used ochre to paint their living bodies is hard to resist.

Ice-Age people also used symbols and substances such as ochre in rites that conferred power. In paintings and carvings, we can glimpse the Ice-Age elite, people considered special and set apart from the group. In figures wearing animal masks – antlered or lionlike – the wearer is transformed. From anthropological studies of the recent past, we know such disguises are normally efforts to communicate with the dead or with the gods. The shaman may seek a state of ecstasy induced by drugs or dancing or drum-ming, to see and hear realms normally inaccessible to the senses. Shamanism can replace the strong with the seer and the sage. By choosing elites who had the gift of communicating with spirits, Ice-Age societies could escape the oppression of the physically powerful or those privileged by birth, effecting what might be called the first political revolutions.

Although we cannot be sure about the nature of the Ice-Age power class, we know it existed because of glaring inequalities in the way Ice-Age people were buried. In a cemetery at Sunghir, near Moscow, dated about 28,000 years ago, the highest-status person seems, at first glance, to have been an elderly man. His burial goods include a cap sewn with fox's teeth and about

---

41 Alexander Marshack, *The Roots of Civilization: The Cognitive Beginnings of Man's First Art, Symbol, and Notation* (New York: Moyer Bell, 1991).

twenty ivory bracelets. Nearby, however, two boys of about eight or ten years old have even more spectacular ornaments. As well as ivory bracelets and necklaces and fox-tooth buttons, the boys have animal carvings and beautifully wrought weapons, including spears of mammoth ivory, each over six feet long. About 3,500 finely worked ivory beads had been drizzled over the head, torso, and limbs of each boy.[42] Here was evidence of a further revolution – the inception of a society that marked leaders for greatness from boyhood and therefore, perhaps, from birth.

In our attempt to understand where power lay in Ice-Age societies, the final bits of evidence are crumbs from rich people's tables, fragments of feasts. Archaeologists have found ashes from large-scale cooking and the calcified debris of food at sites in northern Spain, perhaps from as long as 23,000 years ago. The tally sticks that survive from the same region in the same period may also have been records of expenditure on feasts. What were such feasts for? By analogy with modern hunting peoples, the most likely reason was alliance-making between communities. They were probably not male-bonding occasions, as some scholars think, because they are close to major dwelling sites where women and children would be present. Instead, from the moment of its emergence, the idea of the feast had practical consequences: to build and strengthen societies and enhance the power of those who organized the feasts and controlled the food.[43]

As the ice cap retreated and the great herds shifted with it, many human communities opted to follow them. Archaeology has unearthed traces of their routes. Along the way, in what is now northern Germany, about 12,000 years ago, people sacrificed reindeer by deliberately weighting them with stones sewn into their stomachs and drowning them in a lake. About 1,000 years later, hunters as far north as Yorkshire in England, who left a well-preserved camp at Star Carr, found an environment as abundant as the cave artists' had been. Not only was it filled with tundra-loving species such as red deer, elk, and aurochs but also with wild boar in surroundings that were becoming patchily wooded.

At Skateholm in Sweden, about 8,000 years ago, hunters founded the largest known settlement of the era. It was a winter camp in an area where roamed eighty-seven different animal species that the inhabitants ate:

42 'The Sunghir archaeological site', *Lab of Physical Anthropology of the Russian Academy of Sciences*, accessed 19 August 2013, http://soilinst.msu.ru/~ladygin/sungir/findings.

43 Martin Jones, *Feast: Why Humans Share Food* (Oxford: Oxford University Press, 2007); Michael Dietler and Bryan Hayden (eds.), *Feasts: Archaeological and Ethnographic Perspectives on Food, Politics, and Power* (Washington, D.C.: Smithsonian Press, 2001).

trapping river-fish, netting sea-birds, harpooning seals and dolphin, sticking pigs, and driving deer into pits or ponds. In summer, the people must have moved farther north. They lie today in graves decorated with beads and ochre and filled with the spoils of their careers, including antlers and boar's tusks. Their dogs are buried nearby. These burly, wolflike companions are sometimes interred with more signs of honour than humans were given. Dogs were full members of societies where hunting prowess and skill in war determined status. Many of the human dead bear wounds from man-made weapons. Here, too, is evidence of sexual specialization. Women have only a third as many wounds as the men.[44]

The beginnings of sedentary lifeways

Meanwhile, climate change trapped other foraging peoples in environments where they had to develop new ways of life. Some of these environments offered new kinds of abundance. Here were broad-leaved forests, rich in acorns (which make nutritious food for any humans who have enough time to fine-grind them), and lakes and rivers full of aquatic life. New World prairies held apparently inexhaustible stocks of bison (though the largest bison species was rapidly hunted to extinction or perished in challenging climatic conditions). Between the unstable periods of climate change around 12,000 years ago, foragers even colonized dense, tropical forests in southeast Asia and in the New World at Pedra Pintada in Brazil where the Amazon river now flows.[45] This is a region where foragers today have to struggle to find foods they can digest, but it seems to have been more environmentally diverse towards the end of the Ice Age.

Under some conditions, people can settle in one place without the trouble of farming. Archaeological evidence from the post-Ice-Age Middle East shows this. A frontier zone between forest and grassland stretched across the eastern shore of the Mediterranean and what are now Iran, eastern Turkey, and Iraq. The forests were full of acorns, pistachios, and almonds, which gatherers ground into flour and paste. The grasslands bred vast quantities of wild grass with edible seeds. These foods could all be

44 Lars Larsson, 'Dogs in fraction – Symbols in action', in P. M. Vermeersch and Phillip van Peer (eds.), *Contributions to the Mesolithic in Europe: Papers Presented at the Fourth International Symposium, 'Mesolithic in Europe'* (Leuven: Leuven University Press, 1990), pp. 153–60.

45 Cristiana Barreto, Colin McEwan, and Eduardo Neves (eds.), *Unknown Amazon* (London: British Museum Press, 2001).

warehoused between harvests and had the additional advantage of maturing at different times. Dense herds of gazelle in the grasslands provided more nutrition for hunters to bring home. Food was so plentiful that foragers did not have to move around much to find it.

By about 14,000 to 15,000 years ago, permanent settlements, known as Natufian from an example at Natuf in what is now Israel, arose across much of the region: clusters of dwellings with stone walls, or those made of wood on stone foundations, or cut from soft stone and roofed with reeds. The foragers who lived in these communities kept to themselves. Villages had distinctive identities and habits, which almost amounted to badges of identity. Some favoured gazelle toe bones for jewellery; some preferred fox teeth and partridge legs. The people married within their own communities, judging from the evidence of inherited physical characteristics. For example, in some villages, people were relatively short, while in others, they had distinctive dental patterns. These settlers cut what look like plans of their fields on limestone slabs, which suggests that they were territorial – that they had a sense of possession that tillers would recognize.[46]

In sum, the lives of pre-agricultural settlers were so much like the lives of the early farmers who succeeded them that when archaeologists first found the foragers' villages in the 1930s, they assumed the inhabitants were farmers and some recent scholarship has returned to something like the same notion.[47] Yet – though their means of life are the subject of debate – on the present balance of evidence the Natufians do not seem to have been farmers in the generally accepted sense of the term: they gathered food, rather than producing it themselves. Their settlements lasted only as long as the stands of wild grasses they harvested. But while their food stocks endured the settled foragers were actually better off than farmers. Their remains, on the whole, show better health and nourishment than the farming peoples who followed later in the same region. A diet rich in seeds and nuts had ground down their teeth, but – unlike the farmers – they have none of the streaked tooth-enamel common among people who suffer from food shortages.

Similar evidence of pre-agricultural settlements in overlapping periods exists in other places. The Jomon people of central Honshu Island in Japan lived in permanent villages 13,000 years ago, feeding themselves by fishing

46 Christophe Delage (ed.), *The Last Hunter-gatherers in the Near East* (Oxford: British Archaeological Reports, 2004).
47 Ofer Bar-Yosef, 'The Natufian culture in the Levant: Threshold to the origins of agriculture', *Evolutionary Anthropology* 6 (1998), 159–77.

and gathering acorns and chestnuts. They made pots for display, in elaborate shapes, modelled on flames and serpents and lacquered them with tree sap. Their potters were, in a sense, magicians, transforming clay into objects of prestige and ritual.[48] In the Egyptian Sahara, at Nabta Playa, about forty plant species, including sorghum, a type of cereal grass, grew alongside hearths and pit ovens, evidence of settled life from about 10,000 years ago. In other parts of central Sahara in the same period that had plenty of water and a cooler climate than now, foragers found sorghum and millet. At Göbekli Tepe, a hilltop site in southeast Turkey, contemporaries who lived mainly by gathering wild wheat hewed seven-ton pillars from limestone. They re-erected them in a sunken chamber in their village and decorated them with carvings of snakes, boar, gazelles, cranes, and symbols that look suspiciously like writing.[49]

What was life like in these earliest settlements? Small, permanent houses suggest that nuclear families – parents and children – predominated, though some sites clearly have communal work areas for grinding seeds and nuts. As for who did the work, the most stunning finding of recent archaeology in the Middle East suggests that work was probably shared between the sexes.[50] The way skeletons are muscled suggests that women did slightly more kneeling (and therefore slightly more grinding) than men, and men did more throwing (and therefore more hunting) than women. But both sexes did both activities. Male and female bodies began to reconverge after a long period during which they had evolved to look differently. As food production replaced hunting and gathering, war and child rearing became the main sex-specific jobs in society. The convergence between the physical features of men and women seems still to be in progress today. Indeed, it seems to be accelerating as men and women share more and more tasks, and the need for heavily muscled or big-framed bodies diminishes along with physically demanding jobs in much of the world.

Conclusions

In the post-Ice-Age world, little by little, over thousands of years, most societies abandoned foraging and adopted farming or herding as the way to

48 Junko Habu, *Ancient Jomon of Japan* (Cambridge: Cambridge University Press, 2004).
49 Klaus Schmidt, *Göbekli Tepe: A Stone-age Sanctuary in South-eastern Anatolia* (Berlin: Ex Oriente, 2012).
50 Jane Peterson, *Sexual Revolutions: Gender and Labor at the Dawn of Agriculture* (Walnut Creek: AltaMira Press, 2002), pp. 55–147.

get their food. The Ice-Age way of life, if not over, is drawing to a close. Hunting is now thought of as a primitive way to get food, long abandoned except as an aristocratic indulgence in some countries or as a supposedly manly sport in others. The story of the transition from gathering food to producing it is a subject for another chapter; on the basis of the foregoing pages, however, we can anticipate three conclusions.

First, the transition took a long time and included a long period in which tentative and selective planting, speciation, and hybridization coexisted with prevalent foraging techniques. Many foraging peoples practise the replanting of the roots or bulbs of some of the plants they gather, and have probably done so for many millennia. In times of stress on food sources it would be logically predictable, and consistent with such evidence as we have, for the settled foragers of the cool period that corresponds to the lifespan of the Natufian culture to attempt systematic selection, replanting, and nurturing of important plants. The evidence of remains of surprisingly large molluscs, especially snails, at deep stratigraphic levels of middens over 10,000 years old in various parts of the world suggests that the 'herding' of such creatures – their selection and collection for breeding – may have preceded other, more ambitious forms of pastoralism.[51] The management of wild pasture and the driving or corralling of wild animals blends imperceptibly into herding.

Secondly, the link between climate and culture seems inescapable: humans' huge range of occupancy of diverse environments, and the trans-formative multiplication of human numbers occurred during an Ice Age that seems to have suited humankind. The migrations that took *Homo sapiens* beyond the range explored by *Homo erectus* probably occurred, in part at least, as a result of the pursuit of fat-rich species across the frontiers of retreating cold as the ice of the Ice Age receded. The beginnings of agricul-ture are associable with warming phases that demanded critical responses from a species well adapted to the preceding ice age and to the intervening cold spells that punctuated the era of climatic instability that followed it. Yet the diversity of responses to changing climatic conditions shows that environ-mental influences alone are insufficient to explain the diversity of cultures that emerged in consequence.

Finally, though scholars no longer like to speak of the transition to agriculture as a 'revolution', it was a change without precedent and, in some

51 Felipe Fernández-Armesto, *Near a Thousand Tables: A History of Food* (New York: Free Press, 2004), pp. 55–8.

ways, without parallel. Not only did it ignite a period of rapidly accelerating cultural divergence; it also constituted a remarkable break in humankind's relationship to evolution, inaugurating a period, which continues to this day, when new species have appeared in the course of what we might call 'unnatural selection' – speciation and hybridization for human purposes, by human agency. The disappearance of foraging lifeways seems a remarkable turnaround for a predator-species such as *Homo sapiens*. There was a time before hunting and gathering, when our ancestors were scavengers, but for hundreds of thousands, perhaps millions, of years, foraging was reliable and rewarding. Its practitioners spread over the world and adapted successfully to every kind of habitat. As foragers, *Homo sapiens* dominated every ecosystem they became part of and competed successfully with most other species. They achieved startling increases in their numbers, which we struggle to explain. They founded more varied societies than any other species (though the differences among these societies were slight compared to later periods). They had art-rich cultures with traditions of learning and symbolic systems to record information. They had their own social elites, political customs, ambitious magic, and practical methods to exploit their environment, thriving through every change of climate.

FURTHER READING

Anderson, Atholl, James H. Barrett, and Katherine V. Boyle (eds.), *The Global Origins and Development of Seafaring*, Cambridge: Cambridge University Press, 2010.

Ardrey, Robert, *The Territorial Imperative: A Personal Inquiry Into the Animal Origins of Property and Nations*, New York: Athenaeum, 1966.

Bahn, Paul G., *Cambridge Illustrated History of Prehistoric Art*, Cambridge: Cambridge University Press, 1998.

Bahn, Paul G., and Jean Vertut, *Journey through the Ice Age*, Berkeley: University of California Press, 1997.

Barreto, Cristiana, Colin McEwan, and Eduardo Neves (eds.), *Unknown Amazon*, London: British Museum Press, 2001.

Barton, C. Michael, Geoffrey A. Clark, David R. Yesner, and Georges A. Pearson, *The Settlement of the American Continents: A Multidisciplinary Approach to Human Biogeography*, Tucson: University of Arizona Press, 2004.

Botha, Rudolf P., *Unravelling the Evolution of Language*, Bingley: Emerald, 2003.

Brophy, Judit, *The Enigma of Sunspots: A Story of Discovery and Scientific Revolution*, Edinburgh: Floris, 2002.

Campbell, Alan, *African Rock Art: Paintings and Engravings on Stone*, New York: Abrams, 2001.

Cavalli-Sforza, Luca, *Genes, Peoples, and Languages*, Berkeley: University of California Press, 2001.

Cavalli-Sforza, Luca, and Francesco Cavalli-Sforza, *Chi siamo? La storia della diversità umana*, Milan: Mondadori, 1993.

Clottes, Jean, and David Lewis-Williams, *The Shamans of Prehistory: Trance Magic and the Painted Caves*, New York: Abrams, 1998.

Crosby, Alfred W., *Throwing Fire: Projectile Technology throughout History*, Cambridge: Cambridge University Press, 2002.

Delage, Christophe (ed.), *The Last Hunter-gatherers in the Near East*, Oxford: British Archaeological Reports, 2004.

Delporte, Henri (ed.), *La Dame de Brassempouy*, Brassempouy: Université de Liège Press, 1995.

Dietler, Michael, and Bryan Hayden (eds.), *Feasts: Archaeological and Ethnographic Perspectives on Food, Politics, and Power*, Washington, D.C.: Smithsonian Press, 2001.

Everett, Daniel L., *Language: The Cultural Tool*, New York: Pantheon, 2012.

Falk, Dean, *The Fossil Chronicles: How Two Controversial Discoveries Changed Our View of Human Evolution*, Berkeley: University of California Press, 2011.

Fernández-Armesto, Felipe, *Civilizations: Culture, Ambition, and the Transformation of Nature*, New York: Free Press, 2003.

A Foot in the River, New York: Oxford University Press, forthcoming.

Near a Thousand Tables: A History of Food, New York: Free Press, 2004.

Fleagle, John, et al. (eds.), *Out of Africa: the First Hominin Colonization of Eurasia*, Dordrecht: Springer, 2010.

Gamble, Clive, *Origins and Revolutions: Human Identity in Earliest Prehistory*, New York: Cambridge University Press, 2007.

Timewalkers: The Prehistory of Global Colonization, Cambridge, MA: Harvard University Press, 1994.

Goudsblom, Johan, *Fire and Civilization*, New York: Penguin, 1994.

Habu, Junko, *Ancient Jomon of Japan*, Cambridge: Cambridge University Press, 2004.

Hiscock, Peter, *The Archaeology of Ancient Australia*, London: Routledge, 2008.

Jablonski, Nina G., *The First Americans: The Pleistocene Colonization of the New World*, San Francisco: California Academy of Sciences, 2002.

Jones, Martin, *Feast: Why Humans Share Food*, New York: Oxford University Press, 2007.

Keeley, Lawrence H., *War Before Civilization*, New York: Oxford University Press, 1996.

Kenneally, Christine, *The First Word: The Search for the Origins of Language*, New York: Penguin, 2007.

Kunzug, Robert, and Wallace Broecker, *Fixing Climate: The Story of Climate Science – and How to Stop Global Warming*, London: Profile, 2008.

Lawson, Andrew J., *Painted Caves: Palaeolithic Rock Art in Western Europe*, Oxford: Oxford University Press, 2012.

Layton, Robert, *Australian Rock Art: A New Synthesis*, Cambridge: Cambridge University Press, 1992.

Lepper, Bradley T., and Robson Bonnichsen, *New Perspectives on the First Americans*, College Station: Texas A&M University Press, 2004.

Lesure, Richard G., *Interpreting Ancient Figurines: Context, Comparison, and Prehistoric Art*, Cambridge: Cambridge University Press, 2011.

Lorenz, Konrad, *On Aggression*, New York: Harcourt, 1966.

Marshack, Alexander, *The Roots of Civilization: The Cognitive Beginnings of Man's First Art, Symbol, and Notation*, New York: Moyer Bell, 1991.

Muller, Richard A., and Gordon J. Macdonald, *Ice Ages and Astronomical Causes*, Dordrecht: Springer, 2000.

Norton, Christopher J., and David R. Braun (eds.), *Asian Paleoanthropology: From Africa to China and Beyond*, Dordrecht: Springer, 2010.

Oppenheimer, Stephen, *Out of Eden: The Peopling of the World*, Bloomington: Indiana University Press, 2004.

Paterson, Dale, and Richard Wrangham, *Demonic Males: Apes and the Origins of Human Violence*, Boston: Houghton, 1996.

Peregrine, Peter N., Ilia Peiros, and Marcus Feldman (eds.), *Ancient Human Migration: A Multidisciplinary Approach*, Salt Lake City: University of Utah Press, 2009.

Peterson, Jane, *Sexual Revolutions: Gender and Labor at the Dawn of Agriculture*, Walnut Creek: AltaMira Press, 2002.

Pidoplichko, Ivan H., *Upper Palaeolithic Dwellings of Mammoth Bones in the Ukraine: Kiev-Kirillovskii, Gontsy, Dobranichevka, Mezin and Mezhirich*, Oxford: British Archaeological Reports, 1998.

Sahlins, Marshall D., *Stone-age Economics*, London: Routledge, 1972.

Stanford, Craig B., *The Hunting Ape: Meat-eating and the Origins of Human Behavior*. Princeton, NJ: Princeton University Press, 1999.

Sykes, Bryan, *The Seven Daughters of Eve*, New York: Norton, 2001.

Tatersall, Ian, *The Last Neanderthal: The Rise, Success, and Mysterious Extinction of Our Last Human Relative*, New York: Macmillan, 1995.

Vita-Finzi, Claudio, *Solar History: An Introduction*, Dordrecht: Springer, 2013.

Wrangham, Richard, *Catching Fire: How Cooking Made Us Human*, New York: Basic Books, 2009.

14

Early humans: tools, language, and culture

CHRISTOPHER EHRET

Before about 48,000 BCE human history was African history. It was in the African continent that the evolution of the fully modern human ancestors of all of us alive today took place. Some of the technological and cultural features present among early fully modern humans had come by stages into being among more archaic humans in the eras preceding 70,000 BCE, but the full package of modern human capacities took shape between about 70,000 and 48,000 BCE. Then, from sometime around 48,000 BCE onward, armed with those capacities, fully modern humans spread outward from Africa, first into far southwestern Asia and from there into Europe and Asia and, much later, across the Bering Strait into the Americas.

Those of our fully modern ancestors who left Africa in those times moved into regions where other, more archaic hominin species had long lived – Neanderthals in the Middle East and Europe, and Denisovans and probably others in Asia. Those other hominins did not simply disappear; they persisted for thousands of years longer, only gradually losing out to our fully modern human ancestors in the competition for food and resources. Neanderthals survived in various refugia, such as the Iberian peninsula in the far west and Ural mountains in the north, for perhaps another 15,000 years before finally becoming extinct. Denisovans probably persisted as well for thousand of years before dying out. Other archaic hominins survived for thousands more years in East and Southeast Asia.[1]

Some few cases of interbreeding took place as well. A small Neanderthal component can be identified in the ancestry of all the modern human populations whose ancestors moved outward from Africa, reflecting the

---

1 P. Jeffrey Brantingham, Steven L. Kuhn, and Kristopher W. Kerry (eds.), *The Early Upper Palaeolithic Beyond Western Europe* (Berkeley: University of California Press, 2004), and Douglas D. Anderson, "Cave archaeology in southeast Asia," *Geoarchaeology: An International Journal* 12 (1997), 607–38.

presence of Neanderthals in the southwestern areas of Asia through which this initial dispersal passed. A similarly small Denisovan component occurs among the descendants of the first fully human settlers of island South Asia and Australia.[2] Those of our fully modern human ancestors who remained in our common African homeland passed through similar histories of encounter with more archaic hominins. The archaic African populations eventually died out also in the face of the spread of fully modern humans across the African continent, although, as in other parts of the world, small amounts of interbreeding took place in parts of Africa, too.[3]

But notable differences characterized the encounter in Africa. In particular, the archaic populations there were genetically closer related to fully modern humans. These archaic humans are often called "anatomically modern humans," as if they were no different from us today, but that label is misleading. Their skull shapes maintained features lost in all modern humans,[4] and in those cases where skeletal evidence of their throat structure exists, it seems that they also did not yet possess a fully modern vocal tract.[5] They were archaic in their tool-making capacities and apparently in their linguistic and social capacities, but they diverged out of the same ancestral archaic human stock as our own fully modern human ancestors. They belonged either to our own line of descent or to closely related sister lines of descent. In all likelihood they shared more capacities with us than the Neanderthals and Denisovans of Eurasia whose ancestors, in contrast, had diverged from our line of descent and moved out of Africa much earlier, as much as 500,000 years ago.

2 Richard E. Green, Johannes Krause, Adrian W. Briggs, Tomislav Maricic, Udo Stenzel *et al.*, "A draft sequence of the Neandertal genome," *Science* 328 (2010), 710–22; David Reich, Richard E. Green, Martin Kircher, Johannes Krause, Nick Patterson, *et al.*, "Genetic history of an archaic hominin group from Denisova Cave in Siberia," *Nature* 468 (2010), 1,053–60; and David Reich, Nick Patterson, Martin Kircher, Frederick Delfin, Madhusudan R. Nandineni, *et al.*, "Denisova admixture and the first modern human dispersals into Southeast Asia and Oceania," *American Journal of Human Genetics* 89 (2011), 516–28.

3 Michael F. Hammer, August E. Woerner, Fernando L. Mendez, Jeffrey C. Watkins, and Jeffrey D. Wall, "Genetic evidence for archaic admixture in Africa," *Proceedings of the National Academy of Sciences* 108 (2011), 15,123–8.

4 Katerina Harvati, Chris Stringer, Rainer Grün, Maxime Aubert, and Philip Allsworth-Jones, "The Later Stone Age calvaria from Iwo Eleru, Nigeria: Morphology and chronology" *PLOS ONE* www.plosone.org/article/info%3Adoi%2F10.1371%2Fjournal. pone.0024024.

5 Philip Lieberman and Robert McCarthy, "Tracking the evolution of Language and Speech," *Expedition* 49 (2007), 15–20.

That closer relationship between archaic and fully modern humans in Africa had consequences for how their encounters played in the long period from 70,000 to 12,500 BCE, as we shall see. In some areas separate archaic and fully modern human populations appear to have persisted for thousands of years after 48,000 BCE, utilizing different but nearby environments, or making different use of the same environments. In other regions the makers of Middle Stone Age cultures remained the predominant populations down nearly to the end of the last ice age. In some cases late-persisting Middle Stone Age populations may have sought to compete by imitating and adding features of Later Stone Age tool making to their existing toolkits. Scholars have often called these "transitional" industries, and they were transitional in the sense of having blended Later Stone Age features into an otherwise Middle Stone Age industry. But these phenomena belong to periods after 30,000 BCE, far too late in time to be part of the original evolutionary transition from the Middle to the Later Stone Age in Africa.

From the Middle to the Later Stone Age

To put history in Africa since 70,000 BCE into context, an understanding of the preceding long stage of hominin history is essential. That era, beginning before 200,000 years ago, has two archaeological names. Outside of Africa the common term for this age is the Middle Palaeolithic. In Africa it is called the Middle Stone Age. In Eurasia the Upper Palaeolithic succeeded the Middle Palaeolithic; in most of Africa the Later Stone Age followed or replaced the Middle Stone Age. These differing terms originally came into use because of uncertainties about the dating and the comparability of African archaeological cultures to the better-studied cultures outside the continent. But now that we have much better dating and know a great deal more about the African developments of these two ages, it turns out that there are good historical reasons for keeping these distinctive names. Archaic *Homo sapiens*, belonging to our own or to sister lines of descent, made the Middle Stone Age cultures; Middle Palaeolithic cultures were the work of hominins of more distant genetic relationship to us.

Prepared-core tool-making techniques, which first came into use in the later part of the preceding Lower Palaeolithic age, became the characteristic feature of Middle Palaeolithic and Middle Stone tool technologies. In this technology the toolmaker flaked off the edges all around a stone to form a prepared core with faceted platforms from which flakes could be struck off with a hammer stone. Because of the prior trimming and shaping of the core, the pieces that the knapper struck off in this manner would possess sharpened edges and, if not already of a fully utilitarian shape, could be retouched into blades, scrapers, or projectile points.

In the Later Stone Age of Africa and the Upper Palaeolithic of Eurasia, these industries were replaced by industries dominated by blade and small-flake tools, punched or struck from cores with plain platforms. Deliberately produced small blades and small backed blades and points became common. Ground stone tools also became a usual feature, and new social and cultural behaviors and practices appear in the archaeological record. The Upper Palaeolithic variant of the Later Stone Age originated, it appears, in north-eastern Africa. Its characteristic tools were small blades like those of other Later Stone Age industries, but with greater frequencies of burins and, initially, lacking in the types of microliths found relatively early in the Later Stone Age industries farther south in eastern Africa.[6]

Ancient stone tool finds occur almost everywhere, but findings of skeletal remains from earlier ages tend to be relatively few and widely scattered in time and place. One consistent relation holds, however, and provides a key interpretive principle: Wherever we do have skeletal materials in Later Stone Age contexts in Africa and in "Upper Palaeolithic" contexts (as these sites are termed outside the continent), they are those of fully modern humans like us. In contrast, wherever there exist skeletal materials associated with the Middle Palaeolithic or the Middle Stone Age, they are always the remains of more archaic hominins: Neanderthals in Europe and the Middle East; Denisovans in Central Asia; and archaic humans in Africa. It is possible that we may discover some day that this correlation does not always hold. But the evidence as it stands is without exception: archaic humans with the Middle Stone Age, and other archaic hominin species with the Middle Palaeolithic, versus fully modern humans like ourselves with the Later Stone Age and in its Upper Palaeolithic versions.

Outside of Africa the toolkit of the Later Stone Age/Upper Palaeolithic, with its accompanying suite of new cultural features, appears abruptly in the archaeological record, earliest in Sinai and the Negev from around 48,000

6 Ofer Bar-Yosef, "The dispersal of modern humans in Eurasia: A cultural interpretation," in Paul Mellars, Katie Boyle, Ofer Bar-Yosef, and Chris Stringer (eds.), *Rethinking the Human Revolution: New Behavioural and Biological Perspectives on the Origin and Dispersal of Modern Humans* (Cambridge: McDonald Institute, 2007), pp. 207–18, and Stanley H. Ambrose, "Small things remembered: Origins of early microlithic industries in sub-Saharan Africa," *Archaeological Papers of the American Anthropological Association* 12 (2002), 9–29.

BCE.[7] From there, the fully human bearers of the new kind of culture spread outward, reaching southeastern Europe by perhaps 45,000 BCE and moving farther west into parts of central and western Europe between 45,000 and 43,000 BCE. A second, contemporary line of spread of our fully human ancestors out of Africa seems likely to have emanated more directly from the Horn of Africa, passing eastward through tropical far southern Asia and reaching parts of island South Asia and Australia by around 44,000–42,000 BCE.[8] In Central and East Asia, interestingly, fully modern human populations with Upper Palaeolithic toolkits arrived later, from around 30,000 BCE onward, following more inland routes across Asia from the Middle East.[9]

But in Africa this story of cultural transformation began earlier. The fully modern ancestors of us all evolved in Africa. The blade-based toolkits of those fully modern ancestors and their associated features – such as bone tools and art – originated in Africa. The new cultural synthesis did not appear abruptly around 48,000 BCE, as it did outside the continent, but in stages between about 68,000 and 48,000 BCE. The fully modern human cultural package that took shape in that period built on and diverged out of an earlier Middle Stone Age heritage. It incorporated tool-making advances and features of personal expression and ornamentation, such as perforated shells, that originated in the Middle Stone Age in Africa, but were unknown previously outside the continent.[10]

Although the archaic human populations in most parts of Africa before around 70,000 BCE, in many aspects of their anatomies, appear almost modern, their cultural behaviors and their responses, for example to climatic challenge, reveal that they did not yet possess the full range of modern human capacities. The history of the first archaic humans to spread out of

---

7 Radiocarbon (^{14}C) dates are calibrated here in accord with P. J. Reimer, et al., "IntCal09 and Marine09 radiocarbon age calibration curves, 0–50,000 years cal BP," Radiocarbon 51 (2009), 1, 111–50. The calibrated dates before the present (BP) are then converted to calendar dates. An uncalibrated date of 45,000 BP reflects a calibrated date of approximately 48,500 BP or, in historians' reckoning, 46,500 BCE. The uncalibrated dating of the first Upper Palaeolithic in the southern Levant to 47,000/45,000 BP (Bar-Yosef, "Dispersal of modern humans") is equivalent to calendar dates clustering around 48,000 BCE.

8 Bar-Yosef, "Dispersal of modern humans"; James M. Bowler, Harvey Johnston, Jon M. Olley, et al., "New ages for human occupation and climatic change at Lake Mungo, Australia," Nature 421 (2003), 837–40; and Graeme Barker, Huw Barton, Michael Bird, et al., "'The human revolution' in lowland tropical Southeast Asia: The antiquity and behavior of anatomically modern humans at Niah Cave (Sarawak, Borneo)," Journal of Human Evolution 52 (2007), 243–61.

9 Bar-Yosef, "Dispersal of modern humans."

10 Alison Brooks and Sally McBrearty, "The revolution that wasn't: A new interpretation of the origin of modern human behavior," Journal of Human Evolution 39 (2000), 453–563.

Africa into the Levant and the Arabian peninsula, a bit before 100,000 years ago, is a case in point.[11] The archaeology of this population was Middle Stone Age; in the Arabian peninsula it has specific links to the contemporary Nubian complex of northeastern Africa.[12] The archaic humans advanced, it appears, into lands previously occupied solely by Neanderthals. But with the return of a colder climate sometime before 70,000 BCE, the archaic humans in the Levant disappeared from the record, and Neanderthals, better adapted by physique to cold climates, once again prevailed.

The contrast with the capacities displayed by our fully modern human ancestors from 48,000 BCE onward could hardly be sharper. Fully modern humans proved able to adapt to almost every terrestrial clime, and their expansions led to the eventual extinction of Neanderthals and other hominins. Clearly the archaic humans of 100,000 years ago did not yet have the capacities for adaptation to all manner of climates and the capabilities for outcompeting all other hominins. By 48,000 BCE, however, our common, fully human ancestors did possess those capacities.

Syntactic language and its consequences

One particularly notable anatomical difference distinguishes the fully modern humans of the past 50,000 years from both the archaic hominins, such as the Neanderthals, outside Africa and the archaic humans in Africa. In all early hominins, including the archaic humans in the Levant of 100,000 years ago, the pharynx extended downward at an oblique angle from the back of the tongue and was shorter than the oral cavity. In contrast, by 6–8 years of age in all fully modern human beings the pharynx descends at a right angle from the oral cavity, and the two segments of the vocal tract are of roughly equal length. All humans since 50,000 years ago possess this configuration.[13] This modern human configuration has a high biological cost, however – it makes fully modern human beings, unlike archaic humans, Neanderthals, and all other primates, susceptible to choking to death. But this configuration is also

---

11 Harvati, et al., "Later Stone Age calvaria." The skull shapes of the "anatomically modern" humans at Skhul and Qafzeh, as well as at other African locations, share archaic features that separate them off from all modern humans as well.

12 Jeffrey L. Rose, Vitaly I. Usik, Anthony E. Marks, Yamandu H. Hilbert, Christopher S. Galletti, Ash Parton, Jean Marie Geiling, Victor Cerny, Mike W. Morley, and Richard G. Roberts, "The Nubian complex of Dhofar, Oman: An African Middle Stone Age industry in southern Arabia", PLOS ONE, www.plosone.org/article/info%3Adoi% 2F10.1371%2Fjournal.pone.0028239.

13 Lieberman and McCarthy, "Tracking the evolution of language and speech."

the essential enabler of our human ability to pronounce the full range of speech sounds, especially the primary vowels, which make modern human language possible. Clearly its benefits – its enhancement of human communication – conferred survival benefits that outweighed its costs.

But the ability to make all manner of vocal sounds does not by itself transform communication. Syntactical capacity is the essential accompaniment. To confer an advantage that outweighed the increased danger of choking to death, the new vocal tract configuration must largely have coevolved with the cerebral hardwiring for full syntactic language. The evolution of that hardwiring would have selected for the survival and reproduction of those who could best exploit its communicative potential – those who were able to create and articulate the widest range of different meaning-bearing combinations of sounds – the vast number of words and other meaning units that have come to characterize human language.

From the physiological perspective, the precise timing of this evolutionary changeover in pronunciation capacities, and of the probable associated development of full syntactic language, remains uncertain. Diagnostic skeletal materials from the crucial period in Africa between 100,000 and 50,000 years ago are lacking thus far. But there are suggestive indications in the archaeological record that, in broad terms, this evolutionary change was underway by around 70,000 BCE.

Why is full syntactic language so crucial to the emergence of fully modern humans, the ancestors of us all? Acquiring the full capacities for syntactic language conferred on our common ancestors the ability to build abstract interpretive structures for dealing with other people and with the world around them and to conceive of things not physically experienced and not seen, and to imaginatively build structures of meaning for coming to terms with factors beyond human control.

This is not to say that there was no verbal communication among earlier hominins and among archaic humans. But there is a chasm of difference between the ability these groups might have possessed to make utterances – even a large range of distinct utterances – that communicated things seen or actions taken, and the ability of fully modern humans to put words and thus ideas together in the endless variety that the capacity for syntax allows. Syntax is essential to being able to abstract; to classify things and experiences; and to organize one's knowledge and, from the patterns or the lack of pattern, to conceive the possibility of other things not immediately present. Possessing syntactic language allowed humans to think about, and to talk with each other about, the surrounding conditions of their lives. Because fully syntactic language allows logical sorting, it allows for planning, for thinking ahead to consequences, for organizing and carrying out cooperative activities, for conceiving of novel things and novel relations among things, for categorizing, and for formulating ideas about the meaning of one's existence.

Possibly most important of all, the possession of full syntactic language engendered a new scale of social cooperative abilities. It allowed for the conceptualizing and formalizing of kinship relations as a basis for building up larger territorial social groupings of people and for structuring networks of cooperative relations among those groupings. The size of the local bands and the networks of reciprocal relations among bands in the Later Stone Age and the Upper Palaeolithic contrasts sharply with the very small size of residential groups, hardly more than nuclear families, among Neanderthals. Fully syntactic language gave fully modern humans the potential to form cooperative networks operating over distances not possible earlier. They could form larger-sized local groups as well as wider cooperative networks, which in turn allowed for more efficient exploitation of their environments. Once the full Later Stone package had emerged, these capacities, time and again, would have given the advantage to fully modern humans in their encounters with their archaic contemporaries.

One particular demographic event may be associated with the establishment of the capabilities for full syntactic language. Geneticists have found that the total population of the ancestors of all of us living today passed through a bottleneck, shrinking to under 10,000 individuals in all, and possibly as low as 1,000 breeding pairs, sometime in the millennia surrounding 70,000 BCE. The archaeologist Stanley H. Ambrose has proposed that a particular natural event, the great eruption around 72,000 BCE of the Toba volcano in Indonesia, may have caused this bottleneck.[14] This eruption, the most massive in millions of years, brought several years of volcanic winter to tropical climes in southern Asia and dumped volcanic ash as far west as Africa.

---

14 Stanley H. Ambrose, "Late Pleistocene human population bottlenecks, volcanic winter, and the differentiation of modern humans," *Journal of Human Evolution* 34 (1998), 623–51, and Stanley H. Ambrose, "Did the super-eruption of Toba cause a human population bottleneck? Reply to Gathorne-Hardy and Harcourt-Smith," *Journal of Human Evolution* 45 (2003), 231–7. For the date of the eruption, see Michael Storey, Richard G. Roberts, and M. Saidin, "Astronomically calibrated $^{40}Ar^{39}$ age for the Toba supereruption and global synchronization of late Quaternary records," *Proceedings of the National Academy of Sciences USA* 109, 46 (2013), 18,684–8.

But one can also view a population bottleneck as a contingent effect of the evolution of the capability for full syntactic language. From an evolutionary perspective, mutations with mutually reinforcing, positive effects – of the kinds that encoded the capacities for full syntactic language and for the full range of human pronunciation – propagate most quickly in a cohering and compact population. In such a context, mutations that confer natural and social selection advantages can become general within a period of generations. The acquisition of the capacity for full syntactic language would have set this population sharply off in its capabilities, interests, and outlooks from all other, contemporary, more archaic modern human groups and, over the longer term, would increasingly have reduced the potential for interbreeding with those more archaic humans.

From this perspective the population bottleneck through which the ancestors of all modern humans passed can be understood as a consequence rather than a cause of the acquisition of the new abilities. This solution does not rule out the possibility of climatic stress, such as volcanic winter, as a contributing factor in consolidating or accelerating those evolutionary processes. The archaeological transition to the Later Stone Age seems, after all, to have begun around 68,000 BCE, close in time to the Toba eruption.

The linguistic evidence that still remains to us from the formative eras of full syntactic language favors the conclusion that all present-day languages descend either from a single original language or, probably more correctly, from a cluster of mutually evolving, mutually interacting original dialects.[15] That kind of linguistic history has a particular demographic implication: It indicates that the transition from the oral communication systems of earlier, archaic humans to full syntactic language as we know it took place in a relatively compact, geographically contiguous cluster of interacting, related communities. A population for our common ancestors of under 10,000 individuals, and possibly as few as 1,000 breeding pairs, meets that condition.

The earliest human languages would have differed in some ways from most languages spoken today. It seems, for example, that the early fully modern humans, as they experimented and grew more and more aware of their capacities, created an elaborate consonant system, with possibly as many as a hundred or more consonants. The predominant, although not universal, trend in language history since then has been toward decreasing

---

15 Christopher Ehret, "Nostratic – or proto-human?", in Daniel Nettle and A. Colin Renfrew (eds.), *Nostratic: Examining a Linguistic Macrofamily* (Cambridge: The McDonald Institute, 1999), pp. 93–112.

the number of consonants. This trend appears in the phonological histories of many language families of the world. It also has an interesting long-term consequence: Although there are certainly exceptions, the overall historical tendency has been a decrease in the complexity of consonant systems the farther our human ancestors moved from our common African homeland.[16] The most complex consonant systems today tend to occur in the eastern and southern African regions, in which our fully modern human ancestors first emerged. One of the simplest systems of all, with eight consonants, occurs in Hawaiian, as far out in the Pacific as one can get from Africa.

The earliest human languages also probably put in use an elaborate set of demonstratives. Modern English has, basically, just two demonstratives, *this* and *that*.[17] But many languages today have much more complex systems. Some possess different demonstratives for up to four distances, distinguishing, for example, "this right here," "this nearby," "that," and "that far away," along with perhaps a separate demonstrative for "that spoken about." Other languages may use a variety of different demonstrative words, with the choice of demonstrative depending not just on where the thing referenced is located, but also on where the person addressed is located relative to the object and to the person who is speaking.[18] A goodly number of the same ancient demonstrative root words recur again and again across the languages of the world, many more than would be required by a simple system such as the English one. Their presence in languages from southern Africa to Asia to South America indicates that they go back to the original era of human language and that early human language most likely possessed a system of demonstratives similar to some of the complex systems that still exist today.[19]

The emergence of early modern human cultures, 70,000–48,000 BCE

We should not expect that advantage immediately accrued to our first fully modern ancestors with full syntactic language. Stanley Ambrose and Karl Lorenz have suggested computer similes for the cultural effects of the acquisition of the capacity for fully modern language. The mutations that

---

16 Quentin D. Atkinson, "Phonemic diversity supports serial founder effect model of language expansion from Africa," *Science* 332 (2011), 346–9.
17 Early modern English had a third demonstrative, *yon*, for an object still farther away.
18 Philip J. Jaggar and Malami Buba, "The space and time adverbials NAN/CAN in Hausa: Cracking the deictic code," *Language Sciences* 16 (1994), 387–421.
19 www.sscnet.ucla.edu/history/ehret/World_deictics.pdf.

enabled this capacity produced the necessary hard drive. But to use a hard drive one needs software. Our common human ancestors, now fully modern in their linguistic *potential*, still had to accumulate the body of knowledge and skills – the software – through long experience and experimentation, that would allow them to take advantage of their new capacities for communication, cooperation, planning, and reasoning.[20] We can expect, as a result, that the full suite of Later Stone Age technology and cultural behaviors came together only gradually over an extended period. That expectation is borne out in the archaeology.

Africa, our common homeland, was still entirely occupied by archaic humans with Middle Stone Age technology down to as late as 70,000 BCE (Map 14.1). Most of these industries had existed already for thousands of years, changing little in their techniques and tools over long spans of time. One complex, the Nubian, had outliers extending out of Africa and into the Arabian peninsula.[21] The archaic humans who moved into the Levant just before 100,000 years ago would originally have been associated with that industry. West of the Nile the North African Mousterian was in retreat in the face of the spread across the Sahara and North Africa of a newer Middle Stone Age tradition, Aterian, which some scholars derive from the Nubian complex. To the south all across the Congo Basin and in adjoining eastern areas of West Africa, the Lupemban complex was, and for many thousands of years had been, the prevailing Middle Stone Age tradition. Other Middle Stone Age traditions thrived farther west in West Africa. The Stillbay industry represents the Middle Stone Age of that period widely in southern Africa, while other Middle Stone Age industries predominated in eastern Africa and the Horn of Africa.

But after 70,000 BCE that picture slowly transformed, as our fully human ancestors brought into being the cultures of the Later Stone Age.

Eastern and southern Africa, 70,000–48,000 BCE

The evidence of human genetics places the emergence of the fully modern human ancestors of all of us today in the eastern side of Africa. Three deep sets of human genetic lineages exist. One can be found in people who belong to populations living in several areas from central East Africa to South Africa;

20 Stanley H. Ambrose and Karl Lorenz, "Social and ecological models for the MSA in southern Africa," in Paul Mellars (ed.), *The Emergence of Modern Humans* (Ithaca, NY: Cornell University Press, 1990), pp. 3–33.
21 Rose *et al.*, "The Nubian complex of Dhofar."

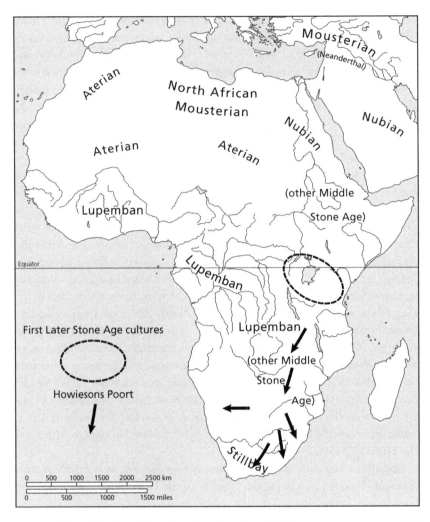

Map 14.1 The earliest Later Stone Age: the cultural world of the common ancestors of all modern humans, *c.* 68,000–61,000 BCE.

and a second, in the Batwa peoples – often called "Pygmies" (an inappropriate term that should have stayed in Greek mythology, and not been applied to real people) – who today reside in a scatter of communities all across Central Africa, from the western edge of East Africa as far west as southern Cameroon. The third set of deep lineages is typical of all the remainder of humankind.[22] The one world region in which all three deep lines of human descent anciently conjoined and overlapped was East Africa.

The findings of archaeology are consistent with placing the origin areas of our common fully human ancestors broadly in East Africa. These findings also confirm the expectation that fully modern behavior and technology would emerge not abruptly, but gradually or episodically over an extended span.

The period of this transition lies beyond the effective reach of radiocarbon dating. Methods suited to the time depth involved, such as thermoluminescence dating of sediments and electron spin resonance dating of teeth, have been applied in relatively few sites in East Africa so far. As a result, at several important sites the proposed dates of the early Later Stone Age rest on estimates of how long it would have taken to accumulate the Later Stone Age deposits that lie below the layers for which there are radiocarbon dates. Dates reached in this latter manner, although they do not command the same level of credence, fall closely in line, however, with the more reliable chronometric dates. Much further work on dating the East Africa finds is needed, but the evidence we do have is consistent in placing the transition to the Later Stone in the period between 68,000 and 48,000 BCE.

The earliest combinations of tools typical of the Later Stone Age cultural package gained prominence in the archaeological record first in East Africa and secondarily in several parts of southern Africa (see Map 14.1). A very early such item, appearing in sites in the Western Rift valley region along the western side of East Africa, was ground bone points. According to the most recent series of thermoluminescence determinations at the relevant sites, the dates for these finds cluster between 68,000 and 58,000 BCE.[23] A second feature of the Later Stone Age, the systematic and deliberate fashioning of quite small blades and small backed flakes and blades, may have originated in nearby areas of East Africa. The earliest occurrences yet known may be from the Mumba industry of northern Tanzania, estimated to date as early as 63,000 BCE.[24]

---

22 Sarah A. Tishkoff, Floyd A. Reed, Françoise R. Friedlaender, Christopher Ehret, Alessia Ranciaro, et al., "The genetic structure and history of Africans and African Americans," Science 324 (2009), 1,035–44.

23 J. K. Feathers and E. Migliorini, "Luminescence dating at Katanda – A reassessment," Quaternary Science Reviews 20 (2001), 961–6. These finds were originally dated to 82,000 ± 8,000 years ago.

24 Stanley H. Ambrose, "Chronology of the Later Stone Age and food production in East Africa," Journal of Archaeological Science 25 (1998), 377–92.

Farther south in southern Africa, blades and flake tools, alike in size and technique to those of the Mumba industry, along with bone tools (see Map 14.1),[25] make up what is called the Howiesons Poort culture. Dating to the period 63,000–58,000 BCE,[26] Howiesons Poort layers appear in sites in Kwazulu-Natal, the Free State, the two Cape provinces, Lesotho, Namibia, and Zimbabwe.[27] What is remarkable about the chronology of this incipient Later Stone Age industry is that, everywhere, it appears juxtaposed *between* strata with Middle Stone Age technology.

The findings have several historical implications. For one thing, the close resemblances of the Howiesons Poort with the Mumba toolkit – and the sharp distinctions between it and the Middle Stone Age industries that preceded and followed it in southern Africa – favor the conclusion that the makers of Howiesons Poort arrived as an intrusive population from East Africa. The South African archaeologist Hilary Deacon proposed that this tradition displays fully modern human behavior because it contains several characteristic features of the Later Stone Age, including the spatial organization of living sites around hearths and the exchange of formal blade-based backed tools made from stone imported sometimes from more

25 Lucinda Blackwell, Francesco d'Enrico, and Lyn Wadley, "Middle Stone Age bone tools from the Howiesons Poort layers, Sibudu Cave, South Africa," *Journal of Archaeological Science* 35 (2008), 1,566–80.
26 The solidly based dates for Howiesons Poort all fall within this time range. In a number of sites the manifestations of Howiesons Poort are undated, but in every instance these manifestations are preceded and followed by quite different, typical Middle Stone Age materials. See Zenobia A. Jacobs, Richard G. Roberts, Rex F. Galbraith, Hilary J. Deacon, Rainer Grün, Alex Mackay, Peter Mitchell, Ralf Vogelsang, *et al.*, "Ages for the Middle Stone Age of southern Africa: Implications for human behavior and dispersal," *Science* 322 (2008), 733–5.
27 Marlize Lombard, "Evidence of hunting and hafting during the Middle Stone Age at Sibudu Cave," *Journal of Human Evolution* 48 (2005), 279–300; Lyn Wadley, "What is cultural modernity: A general view and a South African perspective from Rose Cottage Cave," *Cambridge Archaeological Journal* 11 (2001), 201–21; J. C. Vogel, "Radiometric dates for the Middle Stone Age in South Africa," in Phillip V. Tobias, Michael A. Raath, Jacopo Moggi-Cecchi, and Gerald A. Doyle (eds.), *Humanity from African Naissance to Coming Millennia* (Florence: Firenze University Press), pp. 261–8; James K. Feathers, "Luminescence dating in less than ideal conditions: Case studies from Klasies River Main site and Duinefontein, South Africa," *Journal of Archaeological Science* 29 (2002), 177–94; Peter J. Mitchell, "Archaeological research in Lesotho: A review of 120 years," *African Archaeological Review* 10 (1992), 3–34; G. H. Miller, P. B. Beaumont, Hilary J. Deacon, A. S. Brooks, P. E. Hare, and A. J. T. Jull, "Earliest modern humans in southern Africa dated by isoleucine epimerization in ostrich eggshell," *Quaternary Science Reviews* 18 (1999), 1,537–48; C. K. Cooke, "Excavation in Zombepata Cave, Sipolilo District, Mashonaland, Rhodesia," *South African Archaeological Bulletin* 25 (1971), 104–27, and C. K. Cooke, "The Middle Stone Age in Rhodesia and South Africa," *Arnoldia* 6 (1973).

than 100 kilometers away.[28] But other archaeologists, among them Richard Klein and Stanley Ambrose, point out that the patterns of food resource exploitation at Howiesons Poort sites indicate that its makers were not yet as effective in their hunting and gathering as Later Stone Age peoples had become by 48,000 BCE.[29]

The capacities of the Howiesons Poort people for exploiting their environment, in any case, do not seem to have given them a significant advantage over toolmakers with Middle Stone Age technologies, because Middle Stone Age industries in southern Africa re-expanded and, by around 58,000 BCE, had replaced Howiesons Poort everywhere. That Howiesons Poort disappeared coincident with a shift to warmer conditions globally, at the beginning of Marine Isotope Stage 4, implicates climate change as a possible contributing factor. If so, this would be still another indicator that the Howiesons Poort people did not yet possess the full adaptive capacities in place by 48,000 BCE among our fully human ancestors.

In several parts of East Africa, however, sites dating as early as 60,000 BCE had begun to take on more and more of the characteristics of full Later Stone Age technology. In the Lemuta industry of northern Tanzania – dated to 60,000–57,000 BCE by electron spin resonance dating of associated teeth[30] – backed blades and geometric microliths typical of the mature Later Stone Age had become plentiful. At the Ntuka River site in southwestern Kenya, indirectly estimated to date possibly earlier than 58,000 BCE, narrow-backed microliths, blades, and small obsidian points are characteristic finds.[31] Farther north, in Ethiopia, the latest securely dated Middle Stone Age deposits belong to the period of 77,000–61,000 years ago,[32] so the emergence of fully

28 Hilary J. Deacon, "Southern Africa and modern human origins," *Philosophical Transactions of the Royal Society* 337B (1992), 177–83, and elsewhere, and Hilary J. Deacon and Sarah Wurz, "Middle Pleistocene populations of Southern Africa and the emergence of modern behaviour," in Lawrence Barham and Kate Robson-Brown (eds.), *Human Roots: Africa and Asia in the Middle Pleistocene* (Bristol: Western Academic and Specialist Press, 2001).

29 Richard G. Klein, "Why does skeletal part representation differ between smaller and larger bovids at Klasies River Mouth and other archaeological sites," *Journal of Archaeological Science* 6 (1989), 363–81; Ambrose and Lorenz, "Social and ecological models"; also Richard G. Klein, "Out of Africa and the evolution of human behavior," *Evolutionary Anthropology* 17 (2008), 267–81.

30 A. R. Skinner, R. I. Hay, F. Masao, and B. A. B. Blackwell, "Dating the Naisusu beds, Olduvai Gorge, by electron spin resonance," *Quaternary Science Reviews* 22 (2003), 1,361–6.

31 Ambrose, "Small things remembered."

32 J. Desmond Clark, Kenneth D. Williamson, Joseph W. Michels, and Curtis A. Marean, "A Middle Stone Age occupation at Porc Epic Cave, Diredawa," *African Archaeological*

Later Stone Age industries in the Horn of Africa may also have begun there not much later than 60,000 BCE. But that possibility remains to be adequately documented in the archaeology.

A final clinching advantage of the early fully modern humans came from their possession of a complex projectile technology, with either bows and arrows or spear-throwers and darts or with both, and thus the ability to disable or kill game at a distance. The earliest fully modern humans who moved from Africa into western Eurasia around 48,000 BCE, as John J. Shea and Matthew L. Sisk have shown, already possessed one version of this kind of technology, the spear-thrower, unknown previously outside the continent.[33] Earlier hominins may have had simple projectile weapons, that is to say, spears, but not bows and arrows or spear-throwers and darts.

Just how early Later Stone Age people in Africa began *regularly* to depend on this kind of weaponry is a historical issue very much in need of study. Some of the tool shapes employed by this technology go back earlier in Africa,[34] but the proliferation in early Later Stone Age sites of the kinds of smaller points essential for efficient weapons of this type indicates that the Later Stone Age was the period in which this technology became fully established. Archaeologists have proposed that the bow and arrow may have been present in the Howiesons Poort culture before 60,000 BCE.[35] But if so, the lack in those sites of the remains of animals of the kinds that would have been hunted with complex-projectile weaponry would seem to imply that the Howiesons Poort people had not yet mastered the full potential of this technology. By 48,000 BCE, however, complex-projectile technology seems well established in the cultural repertoire of fully modern humans.

The universality of the bow and arrow in Africa in later ages, and the lack everywhere in the African continent of spear-throwers and darts, suggests

Review 2 (1984), 37–71, and David Pleurdieu, "Le Middle Stone Age de la Grotte de Porc-Epic," *L'Anthropologie* 107 (2003), 15–48.

33 John J. Shea and Matthew L. Sisk, "Complex projective technology and Homo sapiens dispersal from Africa to Western Eurasia," *Paleoanthropology* (2010), 100–22.

34 John J. Shea and Matthew L. Sisk, "The African origin of complex projectile technology: An analysis using tip cross-sectional area and perimeter," *International Journal of Evolutionary Biology* (2011), Article ID 968012, www.hindawi.com/journals/ijeb/2011/968012/

35 Lucinda Blackwell *et al.*, "Middle Stone Age bone tools," and Marlize Lombard and Laurel Phillipson, "Evidence of bow and stone-tipped arrow use 64,000 years ago in KwaZulu-Natal, South Africa," *Antiquity* 84 (2010), 635–48.

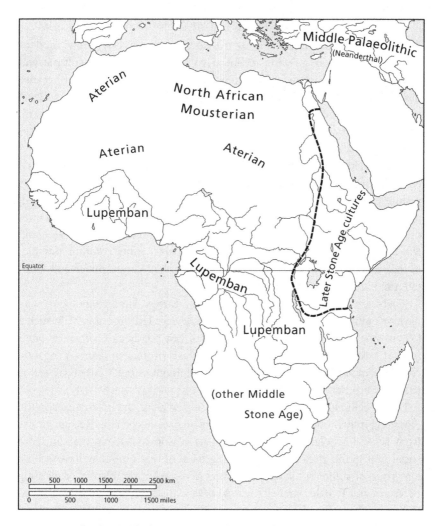

Map 14.2 At the threshold of human dispersal out of Africa: our common human ancestors of the Later Stone Age, *c.* 50,000–48,000 BCE.

that the bow and arrow was the original complex-projectile weapon of the early Later Stone Age, when all of our ancestors still lived in Africa. The spear-thrower and dart appear to have been an alternative invention brought into use by those modern human populations who moved out of north-eastern Africa by 48,000 BCE, into western Eurasia and also eastward along the Indian Ocean coasts to island South Asia and Sahul (Map 14.2).

Social relations among early fully modern humans

Perhaps even more important to the success of our early fully modern ancestors than their growing technical competence were the cultural and cooperative behaviors and institutions that they brought into being because of their command of the tools of syntactic language. They lived in larger local groups than all previous hominins, including their archaic human contemporaries in Africa, and they cooperated and exchanged goods with other communities over longer distances than ever before.

The development of systematic kinship reckoning was probably a crucial component in such relations. Locally, formal kin relations served to define people's positions and responsibilities in their community and to establish norms of behavior toward each other. Intermarriage between communities drew people into networks of formal affinal relationship; and people could also apply the metaphors of kinship to individuals in other communities and, in that way, cement peaceful relations among their communities and facilitate the exchange of valued goods.

There are a variety of indications that the earliest kin terminologies may have resembled a type that anthropologists have called "Iroquois."[36] In such a system one's parallel cousin – the child of one's father's brother or one's mother's sister – is called by the same term as a brother or sister. A separate cousin term applies to cross cousins – the children of one's father's sister or mother's brother.

Unilineal kin institutions, such as lineages and clans, did not yet exist in the emerging fully modern human societies of 70,000–48,000 BCE. Recent studies from several scholarly disciplines give us reason to believe that the core social unit in the gathering and hunting band of that time may have been a kin group of a different sort – a coalition of close female relatives, consisting of sisters and female parallel cousins, their daughters, and their daughters' children. These female kin groups would have been matrilocal; the local foraging band would have coalesced around them. The anthropologists Kristen Hawkes, James O'Connell, and Nicholas Blurton Jones observed just such female coalitions in operation in the Hadza gathering and hunting

---

36 Christopher Ehret, "Reconstructing ancient kinship in Africa," in Nicholas J. Allen, Hilary Callan, Robin Dunbar, and Wendy James (eds.), *Early Human Kinship: From Sex to Social Reproduction* (Oxford: Blackwell, 2008), pp. 200–31 and 259–69. "Iroquois" is used loosely here as a general cover term for Iroquois and Dravidian types of kin reckoning.

society of Tanzania in the 1980s and 1990s.[37] The historian Christine Saidi has shown that a similar institution, going back historically at least 1,500 and perhaps 3,000 years, existed among the early agricultural peoples of Central Africa.[38]

Coalitions of close female kin would have enhanced human survival in several basic ways. Older women helped with the gathering of food for younger women burdened with children not as yet weaned, and they also helped by taking care of weaned children. Cooperative multi-generation female kin groupings thus freed up time for women to go about the tasks of providing the majority of the food that sustained life in the band, while supporting the reproductive success of the group as a whole and enhancing the survival chances of their children. Among the Hadza, men gained access to marriage and reproduction with the women of these coalitions, and to the women's regular and ongoing subsistence productivity, through being able to provide – although in much more variable and intermittent fashion – meat from the hunt. Meat provides additional nutrients enhancing the health and survival of children, and thus good hunters would have been acceptable mates to the female kin group, which oversaw these matters. In the matrilineal farming societies of the past 2,000–3,000 years in southern Central Africa, studied by Christine Saidi, a man had similarly to prove his worthiness for marriage by undertaking a long stint of working for his future mother-in-law and her close female kin.

Religious belief and observance in the early Later Stone Age

What can we say about the inner life of the formative period in Africa of the Later Stone Age/Upper Palaeolithic cultural world of our earliest fully modern ancestors? How did the peoples of the period around 48,000 BCE understand their place in the universe?

A wide array of comparative ethnographic evidence, in conjunction with the evidence of rock art from around the world, strongly suggests that the

37 Kristen Hawkes, James F. O'Connell, and Nicholas G. Blurton Jones, "Hardworking Hadza grandmothers," in V. Standen and R. Foley (eds.), *Comparative Socioecology of Mammals and Man* (London: Blackwell, 1989), pp. 341–66, and Kristen Hawkes, James F. O'Connell, and Nicholas Blurton Jones, "Hadza women's time allocation, offspring provisioning, and the evolution of post-menopausal lifespans," *Current Anthropology* 38 (1997), 551–78.

38 Christine Saidi, *Women's Authority and Society in Early East-Central Africa* (Rochester: University of Rochester Press, 2010), pp. 77–9. In this region, a specific root word *-bumba designates this kind of female matrikin coalition. This word has been in use for at least 1,500 years and probably traces back to the still earlier proto-Savanna Bantu language of 3,000–4,000 years ago.

original religion of fully modern humans was shamanism. In this belief system existence is bimodal: it has two spheres – the concrete world of everyday experience and a parallel realm of Spirit. The surface of the earth forms the interface between the two realms. The shaman was the religious and medical practitioner, female or male, who tapped into the world of Spirit for the benefit (or sometimes the ill) of human beings. Shamans, as we discover from the operations of this religious system in more recent eras here and there around the world, were people able to put themselves into a state of trance. The trance experience, it was believed, transported them to the Spirit realm, allowing them to engage with Spirit power and bring it back into the everyday world in which their society lived.[39]

Rock art in southern Africa, dating to before 29,000 BCE at Apollo Cave in southern Namibia, as well as the European cave art of similar age, seem to have had the trance experiences of shamans as their principal subject.[40] In this art we discover fuller and more complex presentations of the images that inhabited the shamans' minds when they were in a state of trance. The specific spirit figures, animals, and other images of this art differed in different parts of the world because humans everywhere have been historical beings: over time they have developed different myths and associated images to convey their experience of the two realms.

But the shamanistic traditions also abounded in old shared structural features and specific imageries. For example, the rock surfaces on which early humans painted held special numinous significance as a boundary between the concrete world of everyday life and the realm of Spirit. In different parts of the world, we find cases where the painters depict an animal as emerging from or entering a crack in the rock, in other words, as a spirit animal passing from the one world into the other. More than just inherited human mental tendencies are involved here. Widely shared motifs, such as animals exiting or entering the rock surface, surely draw also on a more ancient heritage of ideas and imagery going back to our common ancestors in Africa.

The use of sheltered rock surfaces as canvasses of shamanist art all across the world, from farthest southern Africa to the most distant reaches of the

---

39 Among other sources, J. David Lewis-Williams, *Seeing and Believing: Symbolic Meanings in Southern San Rock Paintings* (London, New York: Academic Press, 1981).

40 W. E. Wendt, "'Art Mobilier' from the Apollo 11 Cave, South West Africa: Africa's oldest dated works of art," *South African Archaeological Bulletin* 31 (1976), 5–11, and Jean Clotte and David Lewis-Williams, *The Shamans of Prehistory: Trance and Magic in the Painted Caves* (New York: Harry N. Abrams, 1998).

Americas, suggests that this practice probably goes back, too, to the early Later Stone Age, before our common ancestors began to spread out of our home continent. Because in Africa and most of the world the artists painted in rock shelters or on open rock faces, works older than 10,000 years have probably nearly all been obliterated over time by wind and water. The cave art of the Upper Palaeolithic in Europe survived because the artists painted on rock surfaces deep under the earth. At Apollo Cave in Namibia, the painted surfaces were preserved by burial under other deposits.

Inside and outside Africa, to 48,000 BCE

From the available evidence, as scanty and uneven as it often is, it appears that the full development of Later Stone Age / Upper Palaeolithic technology and cultural behaviors took shape in the 20,000 years preceding 48,000 BCE. East Africa and possibly also the Horn of Africa were crucial regions of this transition. In all the other parts of Africa, archaic humans with Middle Stone Age industries still predominated. Our common human ancestors acquired the enabling evolutionary advance, the hardwiring for full syntactic language and a modern vocal tract, by around 70,000 BCE. Down to 48,000 BCE, they accumulated the knowledge and experience – the software – for taking full advantage of these new capacities. By 48,000 BCE, equipped with those capacities, modern human beings began to spread out of Africa and into other parts of the globe. At the same time, others of our common fully human ancestors began to spread their cultures and technologies southward and westward into other parts of the continent. In each of these expansions, they took with them also, it can be proposed, an understanding of the world and their existence in it that rested on shamanistic beliefs and practices and, very possibly already, an artistic tradition, one of the aspects of which would have been rock art expressive of that belief system.

Where were the staging grounds of the first movements of fully modern humans out of Africa and into Eurasia? The archaeology of the likely pivotal regions, from South Sudan and the Ethiopian highlands north to Egypt, remains almost unknown for the crucial era just before and around 48,000 BCE. In Egypt the latest securely dated Middle Stone Age finds belong to the period preceding 50,000 BCE,[41] in keeping with a history in which fully

---

41 Pierre M. Veermersch, Etienne Paulissen, Stephen Stokes, Célestin Charlier, Philip van Peer, Chris Stringer, and W. Lindsay, "A Middle Palaeolithic burial of a modern human at Taramsa Hill, Egypt," *Antiquity* 72 (1998), 475–84.

modern humans spread in the immediately succeeding era north out of Africa via the Red Sea hills and the Nile. Positive attestation of such a history does not yet exist, however. The current archaeological knowledge of Egypt and the Red Sea hills between around 50,000 and 42,000 BCE is pretty much a blank page; and even for the period from 42,000 down to 23,000 BCE, the known sites are few and scattered.

The finds from those later scattered sites, though, highlight just how important filling in the archaeological gap for this period in the Red Sea hills and Nile Valley is likely to be. In both regions the characteristic tools of the sites dating after 42,000 BCE have notable affinities with the Upper Palaeolithic tools that fully modern humans brought into the Levant at around 48,000 BCE. These features suggest that the African antecedents of the Upper Palaeolithic, as we call the Eurasian varieties of the Later Stone Age, may well have lain specifically in Egypt and the Horn of Africa.

A second set of our early fully modern human ancestors may have followed an alternative route, moving eastward more directly from the Horn of Africa, across the Bab-el-Mandab strait and southern Arabia, and then through southern Asia to island South Asia and Sahul.[42] Again, however, the archaeology of the crucial intermediate areas in South Sudan and the Horn of Africa in the period around and just before 48,000 BCE remains too poorly known for this proposed history to be adequately tested.

By around 50,000–48,000 BCE, then, the common African ancestors of us all inhabited a broad stretch of Africa, from East Africa at the south to the shores of the Red Sea at the north (see Map 14.2). They were poised at the threshold of a new era, in which some of them would migrate outward from the northeastern parts of Africa and across Eurasia into lands previously inhabited by more archaic hominins. Others would advance contemporaneously southward and westward from East Africa into other African regions still dominated by Middle Stone Age, archaic humans.

FURTHER READING

Allen, Nicholas J., Hilary Callan, Robin Dunbar, and Wendy James (eds.), *Early Human Kinship: From Sex to Social Reproduction*, Oxford: Blackwell, 2008.
Ambrose, Stanley H., "Late Pleistocene human population bottlenecks, volcanic winter, and the differentiation of modern humans," *Journal of Human Evolution* 34 (1998), 623–51.

42 Vincent Macaulay *et al.*, "Single, rapid coastal settlement of Asia revealed by analysis of complete mitochrondrial genomes," *Science* 308 (2005), 1,034–6.

Brooks, Alison. and Sally McBrearty, "The revolution that wasn't: A new interpretation of the origin of modern human behavior," *Journal of Human Evolution* 39 (2000), 453–563.

Hawkes, Kristen, James F. O'Connell, and Nicholas Blurton Jones, "Hadza women's time allocation, offspring provisioning, and the evolution of post-menopausal lifespans," *Current Anthropology* 38 (1997), 551–78.

Klein, Richard G., "Out of Africa and the evolution of human behavior," *Evolutionary Anthropology* 17 (2008), 267–81.

Lewis-Williams, J. David. *A Cosmos in Stone: Interpreting Religion and Society through Rock Art*, Walnut Creek, CA: AltaMira Press, 2002.

Lieberman, Philip. and Robert McCarthy, "Tracking the evolution of language and speech," *Expedition* 49 (2007), 15–20.

Mellars, Paul, Katie Boyle, Ofer Bar-Yosef, and Chris Stringer (eds), *Rethinking the Human Revolution: New Behavioural and Biological Perspectives on the Origin and Dispersal of Modern Humans*, Cambridge: McDonald Institute, 2007.

Phillipson, David W., *African Archaeology*, Cambridge: Cambridge University Press, 2005.

Tishkoff, Sarah A., Floyd A. Reed, Françoise R. Friedlaender, Christopher Ehret, Alessia Ranciaro, *et al.*, "The genetic structure and history of Africans and African Americans," *Science* 324 (2009), 1035–44.

Willoughby, Pamela R., *The Evolution of Modern Humans in Africa: A Comprehensive Guide*, Lanham, MD: AltaMira Press, 2007.

15

Africa from 48,000 to 9500 BCE

CHRISTOPHER EHRET

Fifty thousand years ago – in the broad span of centuries around 48,000 BCE – a new era in human history began. The fully modern human ancestors of all of us alive today, who had evolved in East Africa and secondarily in northeastern Africa, for the first time advanced outward from the continent. One line of their expansion passed into the Levant and then, in subsequent millennia, west to Europe and eastward toward East Asia. Others of our fully modern ancestors spread contemporaneously, most probably from the Horn of Africa, across the southern fringes of Asia, reaching Australia by or before 42,000 BCE. Still others among our common human forebears moved southward and westward from East Africa, into southern Africa and the Congo Basin.

Technology and economy in Africa, 48,000–22,000 BCE

SOUTHERN AFRICA, 48,000–22,000 BCE

In southern Africa in the period following 63,000 BCE, as we have already seen (in Chapter 14), makers of the incipient Later Stone Age Howiesons Poort culture had gained a foothold across many parts of southern Africa. But that cultural and technological intrusion from East Africa came to an end by around 58,000 BCE, and Middle Stone Age industries became once again universal across those regions.

Then, from around 46,000 BCE or possibly somewhat earlier, a new movement of fully modern humans south into southern Africa began (see Map 15.1). Possessing a developed Later Stone Age toolkit – with backed bladelets, crescents, backed points, becs, burins, awls, and drills – these communities established themselves first in northern Botswana. By 43,000 BCE these Later Stone Age communities had extended their lands another 1,600 kilometers to the south, as far as Elands Bay in the modern-day Western Cape Province of South Africa. Almost as early, and certainly before 37,000 BCE, still other Later

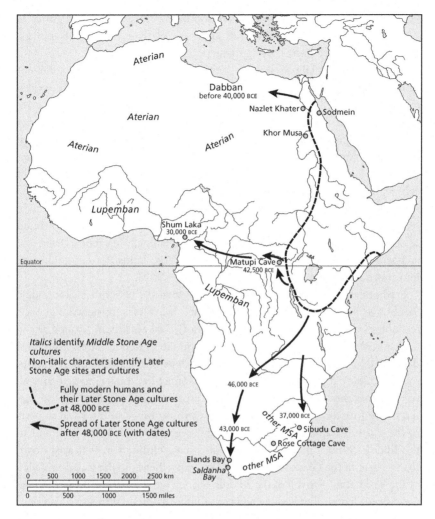

Map 15.1 Dispersals of fully modern humans with Later Stone Age technology across Africa, 48,000–30,000 BCE.

Stone Age communities spread to the eastern side of southern Africa, as far south as Swaziland and northeastern Kwazulu-Natal.[1] By no later than this

---

[1] Lawrence H. Robbins, Michael L. Murphy, George A. Brook, A. H. Ivester, Alec C. Campbell, Richard G. Klein, R. G. Milo, K. M. Stewart, W. S. Downey, and N. J. Stevens, "Archaeology, paleoenvironment, and chronology of the Tsodilo Hills White Paintings Rock Shelter, Northwest Kalahari Desert, Botswana," *Journal of Archaeological Science* 27 (2000), 1,085–113; John E. Parkington, "A view from the south: Southern Africa

period, the Later Stone Age peoples in southern Africa, and in East Africa as well, had begun to enhance the effectiveness of their hunting of animals, especially large herbivores, by applying poison to their arrows.[2]

The existing Middle Stone Age populations of southern Africa did not simply disappear, however. As in Europe and other parts of Eurasia, so also in southern Africa it is apparent that the earlier hominins – in this case, archaic humans – continued for thousands of years to persist in areas nearby to those occupied by the incoming fully modern humans. Through much of the Later Stone Age sequence from 43,000 down to 18,000 BCE at Elands Bay, for example, a very different Middle Stone Age industry, with a different subsistence focus, on shellfish, persisted only 50 kilometers away, at Saldanha Bay.[3] Two populations, it appears, one archaic human and one fully modern human, shared this region for up to 20,000 years. Only around 18,000 BCE did the Middle Stone Age tradition finally disappear from the archaeological record, with only Later Stone Age industries continuing on into more recent eras.

Farther east, often in the mountainous interior areas of South Africa, Middle Stone Age populations also maintained their ways of subsistence and their technology as late as the inception of the last Glacial Maximum, around 22,000 BCE. At Sibudu Cave in Kwazulu-Natal, the latest Middle Stone Age level dates to that time. In the Eastern Cape foothills of the Drakensberg escarpment, Middle Stone Age industries lasted somewhat longer, to 20,000 BCE, while across the Drakensburg range, in Lesotho, the final Middle Stone Age finds date to 19,000–18,000 BCE. In the Swartburg range in the western parts of the Eastern Cape, the Later Stone Age began around 20,000 BCE, and so the Middle Stone Age industry may also have endured in that area down to the onset of the Glacial Maximum. To the northeast, in the Caledon Valley of the Free State Province, the Middle Stone Age industry at Rose Cottage Cave prevailed until at least 26,000 BCE. Other materials at this site, dating to

before, during, and after the Last Glacial Maximum," in Clive Gamble and Olga Soffer (eds.), *The World at 18,000 BP* (London: Unwin Hyman, 1990), vol. II, pp. 214–28; and M. I. Bird, L. K. Fifield, G. M. Santos, P. B. Beaumont, Y. Zhou, M. I. di Tada, and P. A. Hausladen, "Radiocarbon dating from 40 to 60 ka BP at Border Cave, South Africa," *Quaternary Science Reviews* 2 (2003), 943–7.

2 Lawrence H. Robbins, Alec C. Campbell, George A. Brook, Michael L. Murphy, and Robert K. Hitchcock, "The antiquity of the bow and arrow in the Kalahari Desert: Bone points from White Paintings Rock Shelter, Botswana," *Journal of African Archaeology* 10 (2012), 7–20.

3 Deano D. Stynder, Jacopo Moggi-Cecchi, and Lee R. Berger, "Human mandibular incisors from the late Middle Pleistocene locality of Hoedjiespunt 1, South Africa," *Journal of Human Evolution* 41 (2001), 369–83.

around 19,000 BCE, provide an example of late Middle Stone Age populations adopting some of the tool-making techniques from contemporary Later Stone Age peoples and adding them to their otherwise Middle Stone Age technology.[4]

The establishment of Later Stone Age populations in northern Botswana by 46,000 BCE, and their extension southward to the Cape by 43,000 BCE, and to Swaziland almost as early, make it probable that the forebears of these peoples passed through Zimbabwe and eastern Zambia no later than 46,000 BCE on their way farther south. These two countries, after all, lay athwart the lines of cultural dispersal southward from the origin areas of the Later Stone Age in East Africa. The latest dates for the last Middle Stone Age industry in Zimbabwe, Bambata, are earlier than 40,000 BCE, in keeping with this expectation. Later Stone Age cultures certainly predominated across Zimbabwe and much of Zambia by the close of the period, 22,000–20,000 BCE, but the history of cultural and technological change of the intervening eras between 48,000 and 22,000 BCE remains poorly understood.[5]

Central and West Africa, 48,000–22,000 BCE

The spread of modern humans with Later Stone Age industries westward from East Africa probably began soon after 48,000 BCE as well. The earliest Later Stone Age level from Matupi Cave in the Ituri region of the

---

4 Lynn Wadley, "Preliminary report on excavations at Sibudu Cave, KwaZulu-Natal," *Southern African Humanities* 13 (2001), 1–17; Lynn Wadley, "The Pleistocene Later Stone Age south of the Limpopo River," *Journal of World Prehistory* 7 (1993), 243–96; Lynn Wadley, "Rose Cottage Cave: Archaeological work 1987–1997," *South African Journal of Science* 93 (1997), 439–44; Amelia M. B. Clark, "The final Middle Stone Age at Rose Cottage Cave: A distinct industry in the Basutolean ecotone," *Southern African Journal of Science* 93 (1997), 449–58; and J. C. Vogel, "Radiometric dates for the Middle Stone Age in South Africa," in Phillip V. Tobias, Michael A. Raath, Jacopo Moggi-Cecchi, and Gerald A. Doyle (eds.), *Humanity from African Naissance to Coming Millennia* (Florence: Firenze University Press), pp. 261–8.

5 Nigel J. Walker, "Later Stone Age research in the Matopos," *South African Archaeological Bulletin* 35 (1980), 19–24; C. K. Cooke, "Report on excavations at Pomongwe Cave, Matobo District, Zimbabwe," *South African Archaeological Bulletin* 18 (1963), 73–151; S. F. Miller, "The Natchikufan industries of the Later Stone Age in Zimbabwe," unpublished Ph.D. dissertation, University of California, Berkeley (1969); David W. Phillipson, *The Prehistory of Eastern Zambia* (Nairobi: British Institute in Eastern Africa, 1976); Janis Klimowicz and Gary Haynes, "The Stone Age archaeology of Hwange National Park, Zimbabwe," in Gilbert Pwiti and Robert Soper (eds.), *Aspects of African Archaeology* (Harare: University of Zimbabwe Publications, 1996), pp. 121–8; Nigel J. Walker, "Zimbabwe at 18,000 BP", in Gamble and Soffer (eds.), *World at 18,000 BP*, vol. II, pp. 206–13. A lot of the work took place thirty-five to fifty years ago and is now dated in its outlooks and in investigative techniques, and there has been little recent archaeological work relating to those time periods in those countries.

northeastern Congo Basin – characterized, among other things, by true microliths, small notched points for hafting, and burins – dates to before 42,500 BCE, although just how much earlier is uncertain.[6] By around 30,000 BCE, fully modern humans with a similar Later Stone Age technology had reached the other side of the Congo Basin. The earliest occurrence as yet identified from those areas is at Shum Laka rock shelter in western Cameroon (see Map 15.1).[7]

To the south of Cameroon, in the Congo Basin, just as in southern Africa, archaic humans with Middle Stone Age technologies did not simply disappear before the advance of fully human Later Stone Age people, but persisted for thousands of years. In southern Cameroon and Equatorial Guinea, for example, late versions of the Middle Stone Age Lupemban tradition survived down to the beginning of the Last Glacial Maximum. In those areas fully modern Later Stone Age people finally replaced them probably only as the climatic transformations of the Glacial Maximum took hold. In the eastern Congo Basin, as well, a late Lupemban population may have existed down even into the Glacial Maximum, perhaps exploiting different ecological niches than Later Stone Age modern humans, who themselves had been present in the region from before 40,000 BCE.[8]

But farther west in Africa, beyond the mountains that mark the western boundary of the modern-day country of Cameroon, the spread of Later Stone Age technology seemingly came entirely to a halt. West Africa from Nigeria to Mali and Senegal, for reasons not understood, remained a place solely of Middle Stone Age industries not just as late as 22,000 BCE, but down through the Last Glacial Maximum. The spread of Later Stone Age

---

6 Francis van Noten, "Excavations at Matupi Cave," *Antiquity* 51 (1977), 35–40. The dating of this site depended on radiocarbon methods, which reach their effective limit this far back in time. A date on charcoal from the relevant level gave an uncalibrated date of *earlier* than 40,700 years ago; hence the estimated calendar dating of earlier than 42,500 BCE.

7 Els Cornelissen, "On microlithic quartz industries at the end of the Pleistocene in central Africa: The evidence from Shum Laka," *African Archaeological Review* 20 (2003), 1–24; Jan Moeyersons, "Geomorphological processes and their palaeoenvironmental significance at the Shum Laka cave (Bamenda, western Cameroon)," *Palaeogeography, Palaeoclimatology, Palaeoecology* 133 (1997), 103–16.

8 Julio Mercador and Raquel Martí, "The Middle Stone Age occupation of Atlantic central Africa – New evidence from Equatorial Guinea and Cameroon," in Julio Mercador (ed.), *Under the Canopy: The Archaeology of Tropical Rainforests* (New Brunswick, NJ: Rutgers University Press, 2003), pp. 64–92; Els Cornelissen, "Human response to changing environments in Central Africa between 40,000 and 12,000 BP," *Journal of World Prehistory* 16 (2002), 197–235; and Julio Mercador and Alison Brooks, "Across forests and savannas: Later Stone Age assemblages from Ituri and Semliki, Democratic Republic of Congo," *Journal of Anthropological Research* 57 (2001), 197–217.

industries may have reached the mountains of western Cameroon by 30,000 BCE, but there the advance of fully modern humans halted for another 18,000 years.

Northern Africa, 48,000–22,000 bce

In North Africa at 48,000 BCE two different histories played out. The arrival of fully modern humans in Sinai and the adjacent Levant by 48,000 BCE suggests that, before spreading to Sinai, their immediate ancestors should already have reached Egypt by 50,000–48,000 BCE – a proposal, as we have seen, that the archaeology cannot yet confirm or disconfirm. West of Egypt, however, the Middle Stone Age industries remained unchallenged for several thousand years after 48,000 BCE. The Dabban culture, which finally replaced the Middle Stone Age in northern Libya no later than 40,000 BCE, possessed predominantly blade-and-burin toolkits, akin to the industries of the same period in nearby Egypt and the Red Sea hills and to those of the Upper Palaeolithic peoples in the adjacent regions of the Levant. The toolkit resemblances across this span of lands are not surprising. After all, the earliest fully modern human populations who moved out of Africa around 48,000 BCE, and brought the Upper Palaeolithic versions of the early Later Stone Age into the Levant, most probably emerged out of this corner of Africa.

The Dabban industry is the best-studied facies of this North African cultural complex (see Map 15.1). The arrival of the makers of this industry in Libya a bit before 40,000 BCE, brought an abrupt end to the last North African Mousterian industry, in existence previously for more than 100,000 years[9] and, presumably, the extinction of the archaic hominin makers of that earlier industry. For a Later Stone Age/Upper Palaeolithic culture, Dabban was especially long-lived, persisting down to around 19,000 BCE. Established first in the eastern parts of present-day Libya, it spread sometime after 40,000 BCE as far west as Jebel Nefusa in western Libya.[10]

The Egyptian facies of the wider cultural complex to which Dabban belonged are poorly known, and in fact the whole period in Egypt between 48,000 BCE and the inception of the Last Glacial Maximum is poorly served in the available archaeology. Nevertheless, the temporal and geographical spread of the few known sites – at Khor Musa, from around 42,000 to 36,000

9 Charles B. M. McBurney, *Haua Fteah (Cyrenaica) and the Stone Age of the Southeast Mediterranean* (Cambridge: Cambridge University Press, 1967).
10 Elena A. A. Garcea, "Crossing deserts and avoiding seas: Aterian North African–European Relations," *Journal of Anthropological Research* 60 (2004), 27–53.

BCE in southern Upper Egypt; at Nazlet Khater in Middle Egypt, dating to around 37,000 to 34,000 BCE; and at Sodmein Cave near the Red Sea, at around the same time or earlier[11] – show that industries similar to Dabban prevailed far south in Egypt in the same broad period and may have lasted in those areas down nearly to the Last Glacial Maximum (see Map 15.1).

The site at Nazlet Khater is solely Upper Palaeolithic in technology. The materials at Khor Musa are less clear in their historical implications. They prominently include burins and polished bone implements,[12] both features diagnostic of the presence of Upper Palaeolithic tool-making techniques in far southern Egypt by 42,000 BCE. But other tools, made with Middle Stone Age, prepared-core techniques, are also present in the Khor Musa sites. Two possibilities obtain here. Either the last Middle Stone Age peoples of far southern Egypt adopted new tool types from nearby Upper Palaeolithic humans, or an intrusion of Middle Stone Age implements into an overlying Upper Palaeolithic level took place, as happened with the Châtelperronian sites in Europe.[13] Either way, the presence of the Upper Palaeolithic tool types places the bearers of this technology in far southern Egypt no later than around 42,000 BCE.

In the Mahgreb west of Libya fully modern humans did not arrive until much later. The Middle Stone Age Aterian industry continued to prevail for another 15,000–20,000 years after 40,000 BCE. This industry had first spread out across much of the Sahara by 70,000 BCE, and possibly as early as 90,000 years ago. At its farthest south it reached to the southern edges of the Sahara,

---

11 Fred Wendorf, "Late Paleolithic sites in Egyptian Nubia," in Fred Wendorf (ed.), *The Prehistory of Nubia* (Dallas, TX: Southern Methodist University Press, 1968), pp. 945–95; Fred Wendorf and Romuald Schild, *Prehistory of the Nile Valley* (New York: Academy Press, 1976); Etienne Paulissen, Philip van Meer, and Pierre M. Vermeersch, "Palaeolithic chert exploitation in the limestone stretch of the Egyptian Nile Valley," *African Archaeological Review* 8 (1990), 77–102; and Célestin Charlier, W. Lindsay, Etienne Paulissen, Stephen Stokes, Chris Stringer, Philip van Peer, and Pierre M. Veermersch, "A Middle Palaeolithic burial of a modern human at Taramsa Hill, Egypt," *Antiquity* 72 (1998), 475–84.

12 Fred Wendorf, "Late Paleolithic sites"; Wendorf and Schild, *Prehistory of the Nile Valley*. The materials at the site of Khor Musa go back to the Middle Stone Age and before. Deposits immediately preceding Khormusan and its Later Stone Age toolkit were Middle Stone Age with Levallois techniques, and it seems probable to this writer that some intrusion of materials from the later era into the earlier one took place, causing confusion about where one left off and the other began, or whether a "transition" was involved.

13 Ofer Bar-Yosef, "The dispersal of modern humans in Eurasia: A cultural interpretation," in Paul Mellars, Katie Boyle, Ofer Bar-Yosef, and Chris Stringer (eds.), *Rethinking the Human Revolution: New Behavioural and Biological Perspectives on the Origin and Dispersal of Modern Humans* (Cambridge: McDonald Institute, 2007), pp. 207–18.

around 19 south latitude; its northern territories included the whole of the Maghreb. Increasingly arid conditions after about 30,000 BCE led to the abandonment of most of the Sahara, although there are indications that some Aterian populations may have lasted for several thousand years longer in parts of the Maghreb, possibly down to the onset of the Glacial Maximum.[14]

Overall, by 22,000 BCE fully modern human beings inhabited nearly all of eastern and northeastern Africa and large areas of southern and Central Africa. They pursued a variety of gathering and hunting strategies, adapted to the variety of environments they had mastered. Nevertheless, archaic humans with Middle Stone Age industries still found ways to subsist and survive alongside fully modern humans in several parts of southern and Central Africa, although probably in declining numbers. Interestingly, archaic humans apparently continued to be the sole inhabitants of West Africa.

An age of environmental challenge,
22,000–12,700 BCE

The onset of the peak conditions of the Last Glacial Maximum around 22,000–20,000 BCE both accelerated older trends of historical change and set in motion new directions of change. The climate across large parts of Africa, already trending drier over the previous several thousand years, became the driest it had been in tens of thousands of years. The Sahara became hyperarid, more arid than it is even today, and uninhabitable nearly everywhere. Its southern boundaries expanded several hundred kilometers south of their current locations. The rainforest belt immediately inland from the coast of West Africa broke up into several separate blocks of rainforest, surrounded by greatly expanded regions of open woodlands and savanna. The African equatorial rainforests also shrank greatly in extent, and savanna environments expanded across the heart of the Congo Basin.

The African climates became cooler as well, with year-round snow on the high Atlas peaks and with the glaciers of the high peaks of eastern Africa spreading far down the slopes of those mountains. As the advance of glaciers in the northern hemisphere locked up vast amounts of water, ocean levels fell, especially in southern Africa, uncovering large new areas of land for

---

14 Maxine R. Kleindienst, "What is the Aterian: The view from Dakhleh Oasis and the Western Desert, Egypt," in C. A. Marlow and Anthony J. Mills (eds.), *The Oasis Papers 1: The Proceedings of the First Conference of the Dakhleh Oasis Project* (Oxford: Oxbow Books, 2001), pp. 1–14.

human occupation. Unfortunately, we do not know what advantage human beings might have taken of this opportunity, because the re-expansion of the oceans since the end of the glacial age has submerged the potential evidence for that history.

Among the fully modern human communities of the continent, the climatic shifts of the Glacial Maximum led to new kinds of social formations and to new subsistence adaptations. In several parts of the continent our knowledge of the history of these developments is enhanced by a newly available kind of historical resource. From this period onward it becomes possible to propose the language affiliations of certain major cultural complexes and, from the linguistic evidence that has come down from those eras – the words of the ancient lexicons of culture – to add greatly to what the archaeology by itself can tell us. The speakers of any living language possess words for the full range of things they do, experience, know, and believe. To show, through the application of historical linguistic methods, that an ancient root word for a particular item of culture existed at a particular earlier period in language history is to show that the people who spoke the ancestral language of that period knew of the item or practice denoted by the word.[15]

For most of the remaining Middle Stone Age populations of Africa, the climate shift seems to have precipitated their final decline. In the southern, central, and northwestern regions of the continent, the onset of the Glacial Maximum nearly everywhere coincided with the disappearance of the last Middle Stone Age industries and populations. The climatic shifts may have caused just enough added stress on food resources to finally bring to an end the capacities of the archaic human populations to survive in face of the productive and social advantages of fully modern humans. Fully modern humans with Later Stone Age technology found ways, it appears, to cope; Middle Stone Age, archaic humans did not.

West Africa, 22,000–12,700 BCE

In West Africa, however, the makers of the Middle Stone Age technologies did not disappear. They abandoned the newly desert areas immediately south of the expanding Sahara, leaving them uninhabited. At the same time the resulting replacement of rainforest by savanna in parts of West Africa

---

15 Christopher Ehret, *History and the Testimony of Language* (Berkeley: University of California Press, 2011) provides an introduction to these methods and their applications to history.

nearer the Atlantic coast apparently opened up new favorable environments for the survival of the archaic humans and their technologies. In contrast to the outcome in most other parts of the continent, in West Africa the Middle Stone Age and its makers remained in sole possession for several thousand years longer, persisting as recently as 13,000–12,000 BCE all across the better-watered areas of savanna and residual rainforest, from Senegal in the west to southern Nigeria in the east.[16]

The one item of human skeletal evidence available from that era in West Africa, the skull from the Iwo Eleru archaeological site in Nigeria, dates to the very end of the period and reaffirms the late persistence of archaic humans in that part of Africa. In the words of the investigators, the Iwo Eleru skull "possesses neurocranial morphology intermediate in shape between archaic hominins (Neanderthals and *Homo erectus*) and modern humans. This morphology is *outside* the range of modern human variability" (emphasis added). They describe the Iwo Eleru skull as being most similar to the "anatomically modern" specimens from the Levant of around 100,000 years ago – and to specimens from other Middle Stone Age sites in Africa – and entirely distinct from the fully modern humans who have occupied West Africa since 12,000 BCE.[17]

The skull morphologies, in other words, of the "anatomically modern" makers of Middle Stone Age industries – from before 100,000 years ago down to the latest Middle Stone Age, as exemplified by the Iwo Eleru skull – were not actually modern. They indeed were closer related to us than Neanderthals, but they were *not* people just like us. They were archaic humans, and they lacked the full suite of capacities that characterize all humans today. Their capabilities were such that they sometimes coexisted for thousands of years with nearby fully modern human populations, before finally becoming extinct. They were also of close enough genetic relationship to us to have interbred in a few cases with fully modern humans in Africa, just as

16 Michel Rasse, Sylvain Soriano, Chantal Ribolo, Stephen Stokes, and Eric Huysecom, "La séquence pléistocène supérieur d'Ounjougou: Evolution géomorphologique, enregistrements sédimentaires et changements culturels," *Quaternaire* 15 (2004), 329–41; Philip Allsworth-Jones, "Middle Stone Age and Middle Palaeolithic: The evidence from Nigeria and Cameroun," in G. N. Bailey and Paul Callow (eds.), *Stone Age Prehistory* (Cambridge: Cambridge University Press, 1986), pp. 153–68; and Philip Allsworth-Jones, "The earliest human settlement in West Africa and the Sahara," *West African Journal of Archaeology* 17 (1987), 87–129.

17 Katerina Harvati, Chris Stringer, Rainer Grün, Maxime Aubert, and Philip Allsworth-Jones, "The Later Stone Age calvaria from Iwo Eleru, Nigeria: Morphology and chronology," *PLOS ONE* www.plosone.org/article/info%3Adoi%2F10.1371%2Fjournal.pone.0024024.

happened with Neanderthals and the early modern humans who moved out of Africa into Asia after 48,000 BCE.[18]

Central, eastern, and southern africa,
22,000–12,700 BCE

In eastern Africa, a new cultural complex, the Eastern African Microlithic – a Later Stone Age culture characterized especially, as this name implies, by very small stone blades and points – emerged in the aftermath of the Glacial Maximum.[19] Because the early regions of this complex lay in more arid parts of central and northern East Africa, its seems probable that the innovations in tool making and the eclectic foraging practices of the Eastern African Microlithic were an adaptation, and a particularly successful one, for dealing with the expansion of arid environments in that era (see Map 15.2).

The originators of the Eastern African Microlithic most probably spoke languages of the Khoesan language family. Two Khoesan languages, very distantly related to each other, Sandawe and Hadza, are spoken still today in the dry climes of central Tanzania, while other, now long-extinct languages of the family were formerly spoken in savanna, steppe, and desert areas of central and northern East Africa.[20] In keeping with the indications of the toolkit of the Eastern African Microlithic, the lexicon of culture in the earliest Khoesan languages included at least two verbs for hunting with a bow and arrows, along with nouns for two kinds of arrows and, most informatively, a noun for arrow poison, a substance that would have greatly increased the ability of hunters to take down larger animals. What is not self-evident from the archaeology, but is apparent from the ancient lexicon, is that honey collection was already an important subsistence activity for these peoples.[21] In addition, the reconstruction of the terminologies of kinship indicates that

---

18 Michael F. Hammer, August E. Woerner, Fernando L. Mendez, Joseph C. Watkins, and Jeffrey D. Wall, "Genetic evidence for archaic admixture in Africa," *Proceedings of the National Academy of Sciences* 108 (2011), 15,123–8.

19 Patrick J. Munson, "Africa's prehistoric past," in Patrick O'Meara (ed.), *Africa* (Bloomington: Indiana University Press, 1977), pp. 62–82.

20 Christopher Ehret, "The extinct Khoesan languages of East Africa," in Rainer Vossen (ed.), *The Khoesan Languages* (London, New York: Routledge, 2013), pp. 465–79, and Christopher Ehret, "Proposals on Khoisan reconstruction," *Sprache und Geschichte in Afrika* 7 (1986), 105–30.

21 These root words include *k'ade "arrow poison"; *ɣ'an "to shoot an arrow"; *//ue "to stalk an animal in order to kill it (with a bow and arrow)"; *ci "arrow"; *//ana "kind of arrow"; *kʷ'a "arrowshaft"; *taho "honey"; and *dani "honey, bee." The very unusual-looking consonant signs in some of the words indicate click consonants, especially characteristic of and rarely found outside the Khoesan language phylum.

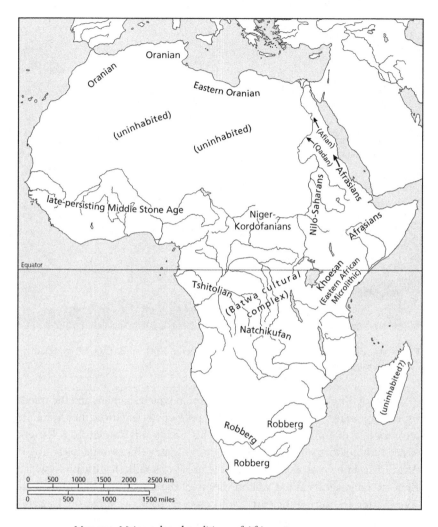

Map 15.2 Major cultural traditions of Africa, 16,000–15,000 BCE.

the early Khoesan peoples probably had an Iroquois system of cousin terminology. Interestingly, they appear to have called their mother's brothers by the same term as they used for grandfather, and their father's sister by the same term as they used for grandmother.[22]

---

22 Christopher Ehret, "Reconstructing ancient kinship in Africa," in Nicholas J. Allen, Hilary Callan, Robin Dunbar, and Wendy James (eds.), *Early Human Kinship: From Sex to Social Reproduction* (Oxford: Blackwell, 2008), pp. 200–31 and 259–69.

Figure 15.1 Elands, hunters, and spirit beings: Khoesan Rock art at Game Pass, South Africa (photograph by Christopher Ehret).

The early Khoesan held to a belief system in which shamans and the trance experience were central. Attesting to this religious orientation, they were the creators of a major rock art tradition. This tradition is known from Eastern African Microlithic sites and from the sites of later Khoesan peoples in East Africa. It is known as well all across the areas of southern Africa into which Khoesan languages and the Wilton variety of the Eastern African Microlithic spread later on, during the early Holocene era. Sandawe artists in Tanzania carried on this artistic tradition as late as the twentieth century.[23] Other examples of this tradition, painted during the last several thousand years, can be viewed in the magnificent representations of animals and spirit beings at such sites as Game Pass in Kwazulu-Natal in modern-day South Africa (see Figure 15.1).

23 Imogene L. Lim, "Archaeology, ethnography, and rock art: A modern-day study from Tanzania," in Geoffrey Blundell (ed.), *Seeing and Knowing: Understanding Rock Art with and without Ethnography* (Walnut Creek, CA: Left Coast Press, 2011), pp. 98–115 and 291–2.

Figure 15.2 Batwa Rock Art (photograph by Benjamin Smith).

In the vast Congo Basin of the western and central equatorial parts of Africa, another long-lived and distinctive cultural tradition emerged during the Last Glacial Maximum. As with the Eastern African Microlithic, a distinctive rock art tradition marks the presence of this "Batwa" cultural complex. The equatorial art tradition of the Batwa occurs all across the Congo Basin, as well as southward into modern-day Angola and parts of Zambia, and east into the African Great Lakes region (see Map 15.2). The most characteristic figures of this tradition are geometric (see Figure 15.2). Rock art scholars have shown that many of these figures were weather signs. This symbolism would have had practical implications for religious observances. In the woodland savanna areas of the southeastern Congo Basin, the rock art sites were places at which Batwa shamans probably carried out rain-making ritual. The latter-day non-Batwa inhabitants of those regions continue to use the sites for just that purpose down to the present.[24]

---

24 Benjamin Smith, *Zambia's Ancient Rock Art: The Paintings of Kasama* (Livingstone, Zambia: National Heritage Conservation Commission, 1997); Catherine Namono, "Rock art, myth and sacred landscapes: The case of a rock art site in Tororo district, Uganda," *Southern African Humanities* 20 (2008), 317–31; Catherine Namono, "Resolving the authorship of the geometric rock art of Uganda," *Journal of African Archaeology* 8 (2010), 239–57; and Catherine Namono, "Dumbbells and circles: Symbolism of Pygmy rock art of Uganda," *Journal of Social Archaeology* 12 (2012), 404–25.

Two Later Stone Age industries of the period following the Last Glacial Maximum can be suggested to correlate with different varieties of the Batwa tradition – Tshitolian in the western and southern Congo Basin and in Angola, and Natchikufan in the southern and southeastern Congo Basin. Because of the paucity of work on sites of this period in other areas where the Batwa artistic tradition flourished, its plausible archaeological connections elsewhere remain to be proposed. The tradition overall may go back before 18,000 BCE. The Later Stone Age communities dating to around 40,000 BCE at Matupi Cave in the northeastern Congo Basin, and the communities at Shum Laka of around 30,000 BCE, may well have been the direct cultural forebears of the Batwa of the past 20,000 years. This is a historical question of great interest and an important one for future archaeological investigation.

The peoples of the Batwa tradition since the Last Glacial Maximum have included populations of differing outward appearance. In the equatorial rainforest belt the Batwa of recent millennia have been people of particularly short stature. European outsiders in the nineteenth century, as already noted, gave them the highly inappropriate name "Pygmies," taken from Greek mythology. Other Batwa of recent times, residing in the southeastern Congo Basin, were not especially short, however, and it may well be that the shorter stature of rainforest Batwa was not an ancient physical characteristic, but something that developed over historical time.

In southern Africa the last Middle Stone Age cultures appear to have died out during the early stages of the Glacial Maximum, and the Later Stone Age cultures of fully modern humans like ourselves came finally to predominate everywhere. Across the southern parts of the Western Cape Province and in the Eastern Cape, a new Later Stone Age industry, the Robberg, occupies the archaeological record from early in the Glacial Maximum, around 18,000 BCE, down to the close of the Bølling-Allerød Interstadial in the eleventh millennium BCE. Microliths, including bladelets and backed blades and other pieces struck from bipolar and bladelet cores, were typical of the Robberg industry, along with worked bone pieces and ostrich eggshell beads. In the Eastern Cape and neighboring areas, the Robberg culture superseded and replaced the final manifestations in southern Africa of the Middle Stone Age.

Northeastern Africa, 22,000–12,700 BCE

Immediately north of East Africa lay another region of key significance for African history in the Last Glacial Maximum. The earliest speech territories of three major language families of Africa clustered in those areas:

Nilo-Saharan between the Nile and the western edges of the Ethiopian highlands; Afrasian (also called *Afroasiatic*)[25] in the highlands; and Niger-Kordofanian in modern-day South Sudan, probably in areas immediately west of the Nile (see Map 15.2). The southern Ethiopian highlands were even then a land of relatively high rainfall, and South Sudan possessed large areas with both permanently and seasonally available surface water, even with the lower flow rates of the Nile in those times. The archaeologist Steven Brandt has argued that, because of these environmental advantages, animal and plant food resources were more plentiful, and so these areas became population refugia during this arid period.[26] The peoples of this region stand off in one notable respect of their social histories from the Khoesan and from the Batwa. Unlike the societies farther south in Africa, the peoples in South Sudan and the Horn of Africa all seem to have developed unilineal descent systems during the span of the Last Glacial Maximum.

The archaeological evidence for the earliest Niger-Kordofanian and Nilo-Saharan peoples is as yet scant. Nothing is known of material culture during the Glacial Maximum in South Sudan and very little about the archaeology of adjacent areas immediately north of South Sudan and south of the expanded Sahara of that period. What little information exists suggests that fishing and the exploitation of other aquatic resources may have been important for both sets of peoples and that the hunting of large herbivores may have been significant in areas away from permanent streams.[27]

From the comparative ethnographic evidence it appears probable that the proto-Niger-Kordofanian society of that period had already added a new, deeper level of kin relationship – lineages and clans characterized by matrilineal descent rules. Membership in a lineage or clan is based on the claim of its members to descent from a common ancestor who lived, in the case of a lineage, several generations ago or, in the case of a clan, many generations ago. The likely earliest form of this institution among Niger-Kordofanian peoples would have been localized lineages of relatively shallow generational depth, rather than the clans common in later historical eras. In a matrilineal system one belongs to the lineage or clan of one's mother and not one's father. Shamanism surely remained the prevailing form of religious belief

---

25 A still earlier name for this family was "Hamito-Semitic"; but this is a term fraught with nineteenth-century, Old-Testament-based, racist conceptualizations of Africans and non-Africans and should *not* be used.
26 Steven A. Brandt, "The Upper Pleistocene and early Holocene prehistory of the Horn of Africa," *African Archaeological Review* 4 (1986), 41–82.
27 Munson, "Africa's prehistoric past."

and observance among the early Niger-Kordofanian communities in South Sudan, since it persisted as a living tradition down to recent times among peoples of the Kordofanian branch of the family.[28]

Among the early Nilo-Saharans, a similar religious orientation, with shamans as the spiritual mediators, continued to shape people's understanding of the world and their place in it.[29] The evidence of reconstructed ancient lexicon confirms, as well, that the proto-Nilo-Saharan society, which most probably dates to late parts of the Glacial Maximum, had begun to organize itself, too, around unilineal kin groups with matrilineal rules of descent and inheritance. There are indications in the derivations of ancient words relating to kinship that the Nilo-Saharan matrilineal clan institutions may have grown directly out of social relations that had previously revolved around coalitions of closely related women (see Chapter 14 for more on the early importance of this kind of institution). An extensive and systematic reconstruction of the kin nomenclatures of the Nilo-Saharan family, not yet possible for the Niger-Kordofanian family, shows that the proto-Nilo-Saharans had an Iroquois cousin terminology and indicates also that a preference for cross-cousin marriage was an ancient feature of their social relations.[30]

Interestingly, Nilo-Saharan and Niger-Kordofanian peoples anciently appear to have shared a particular idiom supportive of matriliny. Both among Nilo-Saharan peoples, such as the Uduk of Sudan, and among Niger-Kordofanian peoples, such as the Akan of Ghana, there has existed a belief – a probable shared inheritance going back to the South Sudan origins of both families during the Glacial Maximum – that one's blood comes from one's mother: that one is a literal "blood" descendant of one's mother but not of one's father. One may inherit other features from one's father, but not one's blood.

The Afrasian peoples of the Last Glacial Maximum operated out of a set of cultural perspectives and practices rather different from those of their Niger-Kordofanian and Nilo-Saharan contemporaries. To properly understand this

---

28 Siegfried F. Nadel, "A study of shamanism in the Nuba Mountains," *Journal of the Royal Anthropological Institute of Great Britain and Ireland* 76 (1946), 25–37.

29 The Uduk and other Koman peoples preserve a probable late version of this religion; see Wendy James, *The Listening Ebony: Moral Knowledge, Religion, and Power among the Uduk of Sudan* (Oxford: Clarendon Press, 1988).

30 Christopher Ehret, "Reconstructing ancient kinship: Practice and theory in an African case study," in Doug Jones and Bojka Milicic (eds.), *Kinship and Language: Per Hage and the Renaissance of Kinship Studies* (Salt Lake City: University of Utah Press, 2011), pp. 46–74, and Christopher Ehret, "Deep-time historical contexts of Crow and Omaha systems: Perspectives from Africa," in Thomas R. Trautmann and Peter M. Whiteley (eds.), *Crow-Omaha: New Light on a Classic Problem of Kinship Analysis* (Tucson: University of Arizona Press, 2012), pp. 173–202.

history, we need first to dispel two serious misconceptions about the origins of the Afrasian language family, both of which still sometimes turn up in the historical literature.

First and foremost, the Afrasian family did *not* originate in the Middle East. It originated in Africa and specifically in the Horn of Africa. The linguistic evidence is unequivocal. The first and most ancient divergence in the family gave rise to the Omotic branch and to a second branch, Erythraic ("Red Sea"), to which all the non-Omotic languages of the family belong. The languages of the first-diverging branch, Omotic, are entirely restricted to the southern Ethiopian highlands. At the second period in the history of the family, the Erythraic branch diverged into two sub-branches, Cushitic and North Erythraic. The languages of the Cushitic sub-branch extend through the rest of the Horn of Africa, along with one even more southerly outlier, the Southern Cushitic languages of Kenya and Tanzania. The divergence of the proto-North Erythraic language, the common ancestor language of the three northern subgroups of the family, Berber, ancient Egyptian, and Semitic – as well as the Chadic subgroup spoken to the west in West Africa – did not take place until the third and still later period of this history.[31]

The historical implications are clear: The homeland of the Afrasian family was in the Horn of Africa, most likely in the Ethiopian highlands, and the first two periods in the history of the family played out there. Only with the emergence of the North Erythraic sub-branch at the third era of early Afrasian history did a northward spread of Afrasian-speaking peoples out of that region take place. A recent linguistic study estimates that the first two divergences in the family fell in the rough time span of 22,000–15,000 BCE – coincident with the Last Glacial Maximum – and that the separation and expansion northward of the North Erythraic speakers took place in the immediately following era.[32]

31 Christopher Ehret, Shomarka O. Y. Keita, and Paul Newman, "The origins of Afroasiatic," *Science* 306 (2004), 1,680–1, sum up the issues involved. For more detailed arguments, see Harold C. Fleming, "Omotic as an Afroasiatic family," *Studies in African Linguistics*, Supplement 5 (1974), 81–94; Christopher Ehret, "Omotic and the subclassification of the Afroasiatic language family," in Robert L. Hess (ed.), *Proceedings of the Fifth International Conference on Ethiopian Studies, Session B* (Chicago: University of Illinois, 1980), pp. 51–62; and Christopher Ehret, *Reconstructing Proto-Afroasiatic (Proto-Afrasian)* (Berkeley: University of California Press, 1995), which lists the series of grammatical, lexical, and phonological innovations that define this succession of historical stages.
32 Christopher Ehret, Andrew Kitchen, Shiferaw Assefa, J. L. Gaston, and Tiffany Gleason, "Bayesian phylogenetic analysis of Afrasian identifies a Later Stone Age origin of Afrasian in the Horn of Africa," in preparation, and Andrew Kitchen,

The reconstruction of the ancient subsistence lexicon in the Afrasian family reveals a reliance of Afrasian peoples from the beginning on wild grains as a key food source: a goodly number of ancient root words for grains and the processing of grain go right back to the ancestral language of the family, proto-Afrasian. This evidence also reveals that, from an early period, they ground their grains into flour and made flat breads from it.[33] The ability to exploit grassland environments, which expanded greatly in the Ethiopian highlands during the Glacial Maximum, may have had a lot to do with growth and spread of the early Afrasian-speaking communities.

A second misconception is that the proto-Afrasians were farmers and/or herders. This idea, which has made its way into some recent archaeological literature,[34] is flatly counter-indicated by the linguistic evidence: there is no linguistic evidence of either the cultivation of crops or the raising of domestic animals by Afrasian peoples until the onset of the Holocene era. Lexicons of cultivation and herding did eventually develop among later Afrasian societies, but only separately and independently in each of the sub-branches of the family, long after the divergences and expansions that first spread Afrasian peoples from the Horn to northern Africa and the Levant.[35]

The earliest Afrasian peoples, besides differing from their Nilo-Saharan and Niger-Kordofanian contemporaries in being collectors of wild grains, differed also in their social organization and belief system. Already by the proto-Afrasian period, unilineal descent systems with clans, originally the

Christopher Ehret, Shiferaw Assefa, and Connie J. Mulligan, "Bayesian phylogenetic analysis of Semitic languages identifies an Early Bronze Age origin of Semitic in the Near East," *Proceedings of the Royal Society B: Biological Sciences* 276 (2009), 2,703–10.

33 Christopher Ehret, "Linguistic stratigraphies and Holocene history in northeastern Africa," in Marek Chlodnicki and Karla Kroeper (eds.), *Archaeology of Early Northeastern Africa* (Posnan: Posnan Archaeological Museum, 2006), pp. 1,019–55.

34 The source of this claim is Alexandr Militarev, "The prehistory of a dispersal: The Proto-Afrasian (Afroasiatic) farming lexicon," in Peter Bellwood and Colin Renfrew (eds.), *Examining the Farming/Language Dispersal Hypothesis* (Cambridge: McDonald Institute, 2003), pp. 135–50. Militarev rests his claim on a set of lexical reconstructions, none of which are actually diagnostic of food production, as is shown in Christopher Ehret, "Applying the comparative method in Afroasiatic (Afrasan, Afrasisch)," in Rainer Voigt (ed.), *From Beyond the Mediterranean: Akten des 7. internationalen Semitoha-mitistenkongresses (VII. ISHaK), Berlin 13. bis 15 September 2004* (Aachen: Shaker Verlag, 2007), pp. 43–70.

35 Christopher Ehret, "A linguistic history of cultivation and herding in northeastern Africa," in Ahmed G. Fahmy, Stefanie Kahlheber, and A. Catherine D'Andrea (eds.), *Windows on the African Past: Current Approaches to African Archaeobotany* (Frankfurt am Main: Africa Magna Verlag, 2011), pp. 185–208; Shiferaw Assefa, "Omotic peoples and the early history of agriculture in Southern Ethiopia," unpublished Ph.D. dissertation, University of California at Los Angeles (2011); and Christopher Ehret, "Linguistic stratigraphies."

organizing units of local communities, had become the rule among Afrasians. Whether the early Afrasian clans traced descent matrilineally or patrilineally is uncertain. Connected to these social developments, in the early Afrasian belief system each clan or alliance of related clans had its own particular deity to whom its members owed allegiance and to whom people sacrificed to seek good fortune for the individual or the community. Other gods existed, but they were the gods of clans or alliances of clans other than one's own and should not be paid homage to.

A belief system of this kind, in which people give allegiance either only or primarily to their community's or society's own god, even though they accept that other gods exist, is called *henotheism*. This conception of Spirit survived down to the twentieth century among peoples in southwestern Ethiopia who spoke languages of the Omotic branch of the Afrasian family.[36] It lies behind the pre-dynastic religion of the ancient Egyptians, each of whose nomes had its own god. Yahweh, the god of the ancient Hebrews, who spoke a language of the Semitic branch of Afroasiatic, was originally just such a god as well – he was the god of the allied clans (the "twelve tribes") of the ancient Israelites, but not of other, neighboring peoples. The wording of the first commandment in the Hebrew Old Testament – "Thou shalt have no other god before me" – takes for granted the existence of other gods. It does not say that there are no other gods, but rather that Yahweh/Elohim should be the only god recognized and worshipped by the Israelites. The ancient Afrasian root word for this kind of deity was *netl'-; the ancient Egyptian word for "god," *ntr*, derives from this old root word.

Northern Africa, 22,000–12,700 BCE

In northern parts of Africa, human adaptations to the conditions of the Glacial Maximum took a diversity of new forms. The archaeological information, despite great gaps in coverage, is on a far better footing than it is for either South Sudan or the Horn in this era. A succession of three historical periods, different in key features of economy and tool making, occupy this historical time span.

The first of these periods began with the appearance of a new archaeological complex in Egyptian sites from around 23,000–22,000 down to around

---

36 Gildas Nicolas, "The Dizzu of Southwest Ethiopia: An essay in cultural history based on religious interactions," unpublished Ph.D. dissertation, University of California at Los Angeles (1976), and Christopher Ehret, *The Civilizations of Africa: A History to 1800* (Charlottesville: University of Virginia Press, second edition, 2014), chap. 2.

19,000 BCE. In contrast to the emphasis in the long preceding age on blade-and-burin technology, the industries of this new period possessed abundant backed bladelets and introduced a new method for refining the cutting edges of tools, called Ouchtata retouch. The new industries were essentially microlithic, although they generally lacked geometric microliths. Around 21,500 the first phase of the new technocomplex, Fakhurian, gave way to the Halfan/Kubbaniyan culture of Lower Nubia and Upper Egypt. The inhabitants of the Halfan sites of this culture in Lower Nubia hunted such animals as antelope and wild cattle, as well as fished. The communities at Wadi Kubbaniya in Upper Egypt took up an additional subsistence strategy: they combined fishing with an extensive reliance on the tubers of sedge plants, grinding them into flour on grindstones.[37]

The developments of this first era, from the beginning of the Last Glacial Maximum down to 19,000 BCE, took place in areas along the Egyptian Nile. To the northwest the older Dabban tradition continued to predominate in Libya. Still farther west, in the Maghreb, human habitation may have been lacking entirely during this high period of the Glacial Maximum. The Middle Stone Age Aterian industry of those areas and its archaic human makers, in any case, had effectively disappeared from the North African archaeological record by that time.

With the easing, around 19,500–19,000 BCE, of the peak aridity of the Last Glacial Maximum, the second period began, with its effects felt much more widely across North Africa. This complex is represented by the Silsilian industry in Egypt and the Oranian and the Eastern Oranian industries farther west in North Africa. The shared, defining innovation of the new techno-complex was the microburin technique. The microburin, after which the technique is named, was not itself a tool, but instead a waste product, a small piece broken off in the fashioning of the actual tool.

The establishment of the Oranian (also called "Iberomaurusian") around 19,500–18,000 BCE in the Mediterranean vegetation zones of Morocco and Algeria marks the first certain appearance of fully modern humans in those regions.[38] Around the same time, the Eastern Oranian version of this

37 Anthony E. Marks, "The Khormusan and Halfan," in Wendorf (ed.), *The Prehistory of Nubia*, pp. 315–460, and H. N. Barakat, "Regional pathways to agriculture in northeast Africa," in Fekri Hassan (ed.), *Drought, Food, and Culture: Ecological Change and Food Security in Africa's Later Prehistory* (New York: Kluwer/Plenum, 2002), pp. 111–22.

38 As David W. Phillipson, *The Archaeology of Africa* (Cambridge: Cambridge University Press, 2005), p. 135, has noted: "In recent years the Oranian has been more generally referred to as 'Iberomaurusian.' This term does not follow the standard practice of naming an archaeological industry after a site at which it has been recognized and

technocomplex replaced the older Dabban tradition in Libya. Oranian was a bladelet-based industry characterized by bone points and often by very high frequencies of backed bladelets and microliths, including some geometrics in the later stages, and most notably, from the beginning, by the use of the microburin technique and by one of the products of this technique, La Mouillah points. Among other strategies, the Oranian communities hunted Barbary sheep and wild cattle, and they collected both land and water mollusks. The Oranian tradition persisted for around 9,000 years, although with modifications in tool inventories and with shifts in subsistence emphasis at times of climatic shift, down through the Bølling-Allerød Interstadial and the Younger Dryas, to the beginning of the Holocene.[39]

In Egypt, in contrast, this second era lasted for a shorter time, down to around 15,000 BCE. The last phase of the previous era, represented by the Halfan and Kubbiyan cultures, came to an end around 19,000 BCE, in keeping with a history in which the new technocomplex would have taken hold in Egypt about the same time as it did in the Maghreb. But because of a gap in the Egyptian archaeological record between about 19,000 and 17,000 BCE, direct supporting evidence for the new kind of tool industry is lacking until around 17,000, by that time the Egyptian counterpart of Oranian, the Silsilian, was well established in Upper Egypt. Silsilian like Oranian was characterized by various kinds of bladelets and, most notably, by abundant evidence, as for Oranian, of the new tool-making feature, the microburin technique.[40]

The origins of this technocomplex are uncertain, but in their high proportions of bladelets and microliths, both Silsilian and Oranian have more in

described, and it carries unwarranted implications concerning connexions between African and the Iberian peninsula." From the point of view of a historian, Iberomaurusian is, in addition to its misleading implication of a non-existent Iberian component, an unnecessary mouthful. Dates of 2,000–3,000 years earlier than 19,000 BCE have been obtained from some sites, but A. Bouzzougar, R. N. E. Barton, S. Blockley, C. Bronk-Ramsey, S. N. Collcutt, R. Gale, T. F. G. Higham, L. T. Humphrey, S. Parfitt, E. Turner and S. Ward, "Reevaluating the age of the Iberomaurusian in Morocco," *African Archaeological Review* 25 (2008), 3–19, argue that these rest on shaky ground or are otherwise suspect.

39 Angela E. Close, "The place of Haua Fteah in the late Palaeolithic of North Africa," in Bailey and Callow (eds.), *Stone Age Prehistory*, pp. 169–80; Angela E. Close and Fred Wendorf, "North Africa at 18000 BP," in Gamble and Soffer (eds.), *The World at 18000 BP*, vol. II, pp. 41–57.

40 Karl W. Butzer, "Late Quaternary problems of the Egyptian Nile: Stratigraphy, environments, prehistory," *Paléorient* 23 (1997), 151–73; P. E. L. Smith, "New investigations in the late Pleistocene archaeology of the Kom Ombo Plain, Upper Egypt," *Quaternaria* 9 (1967), 141–52; Wendorf and Schild, *Prehistory of the Nile Valley*; and Béatrix Midant-Reynes, *The Prehistory of Egypt from the First Egyptians to the First Pharaohs* (Oxford: Blackwell, 2000), chap. 4.

common with African Later Stone Age technologies farther south in the continent than with the pre-Glacial Maximum cultures of Egypt and Libya. The Oranian peoples practiced one custom of possible more southerly inspiration as well: they excised the incisor teeth. This trait is not known earlier in North Africa, nor was it found in the contemporary Silsilian in Egypt. But it was a very old custom among Nilo-Saharan peoples farther south in the middle and upper Nile regions.[41] Together these features suggest a possible history for future testing in the archaeology – that a new population element, following the Nile north from the Middle Nile Basin around 19,000 BCE, may have contributed to the origins of the new techno-complex of that period.

The third period in this sequence of historical eras began in Egypt around 15,000 BCE. Some elements of the technology of the previous age, notably the microburin technique, carried over into the new era. But two key developments of the new era represent a marked departure from the previous practices. Both are new and give the appearance of having originated elsewhere. Geometric microliths of a range of shapes, uncommon before in this region of Africa, but well represented in cultures farther south in the eastern side of the continent, now became prominent in the toolkit. And, most arresting for its economic implications, patterns of tool wear on the lunate microliths of these industries show that their makers practiced a kind of subsistence new to the region – the harvesting of wild grains for food.[42]

The farthest south representative of the new era was the Qadan industry of Lower Nubia and far southern Egypt. The Qadan culture lasted for more than 6,000 years, from 15,000 BCE down to the beginning of the Holocene era. It was primarily a microlithic flake industry. Its most typical tools were lunates, used for the harvesting of wild grain. Grindstones for grinding the harvested grains were also numerous in Qadan sites.

In Upper Egypt to the north of the Qadan culture, the Afian industry replaced Silsilian also around 15,000. Lasting down to around 13,000 BCE, the Afian toolkit had high percentages of backed bladelets and geometric microliths, including scalene triangles as well as lunates (see Map 15.2).

Between around 13,000 and 11,400 BCE, developments along the Egyptian Nile took new directions, with the emergence of numerous relatively large,

---

41 An ancient noun root specifically connoting this custom can be reconstructed back to an early period in the language family: Christopher Ehret, *A Historical-Comparative Reconstruction of Nilo-Saharan* (Cologne: Rüdiger Köppe Verlag, 2001), pp. 462–3.
42 Smith, "New investigations."

semi-sedentary sites of wild-grain-collecting people, notably in the Isnan culture of Middle Egypt. Around 15 percent of the retouched tools found in these sites show the sheen of grain harvesting. Endscrapers, denticulates, and notches were very common in their toolkits, as were grindstones, while bladelets became rare. As well, the microburin technique, innovated in the earlier period from 19,000 to 15,000 BCE, continued to be applied throughout this period.[43]

Industries belonging to this technocomplex apparently spread also to Lower Egypt, because the makers of another facies of this complex, the Mushabian, carried technological features, such as the microburin technique and La Mouillah points, north into Sinai and the Negev before 13,500 BCE. North of Sinai the microburin technique in particular spread via Mushabian to the Natufian culture of Israel and Palestine. Some scholars have recently claimed the Mushabian as an indigenous Levantine tradition without connections farther south in Africa, but their analyses do not take account of the fuller toolkit evidence connecting Mushabian to the other cultures of Egypt in that era and, more generally, to the key technological developments in northern Africa over the previous 6,000 years.[44]

There are strong reasons for viewing the conjoined cultural changeovers of the third era, beginning around 15,000 BCE, as the material signature of the arrival of Afrasian people, speakers of dialects of the proto-North Erythraic language, in the region. The shifts in technology and economy fall within the estimated time span, according to linguistic arguments, in which the spread of the ancestral North Erythraic people northward toward Egypt most likely took place. Geometric microliths have an earlier pedigree farther south in Africa. And the newly attested food resource of the period from

43 Butzer, "Late Quaternary problems."
44 Ofer Bar-Yosef, "Pleistocene connexions between Africa and Southwest Asia: An archaeological perspective," *The African Archaeological Review* 5 (1987), 29–38; Mina Weinstein-Evron, Reuven Yeshurun, Daniel Kaufman, Eileen Eckmeier, and Elisabetta Boaretto, "New 14C dates for Natufian of El-Wad Terrace, Mount Carmel, Israel," *Radiocarbon* 54 (2012), 813–22; D. I. Olszewski, "Issues in the Levantine Epipaleolithic: The Madamaghan, Nebekian and Qalkhan (Levant Epipaleolithic)," *Paléorient* 32 (2006), 19–26, argues that the microburin technique was separately present in areas east of the Jordan River from as much as 7,000 years earlier. But if so, it did not apparently have any immediate effect on tool making west of the Jordan, whereas the arrival of the Mushabian does seem to have had that kind of consequence. This work also does not take account of the fact that the microburin technique also occurred farther south in Upper Egypt already in the Silsilian culture of the period 17,000–15,000 BCE.

15,000 onward, wild grains, were an old feature specifically of the earliest Afrasian economies.

The Mushabian communities in particular seem the most likely people to have carried into the Levant the distant ancestor language of Semitic, the sole subgroup of the family found outside Africa today. No other population movement that might account for the presence of Semitic in Asia took place in later periods, and the earlier movements of human beings out of Africa were far too early in time.[45]

Attributing the developments of the third era to early Afrasian speakers accords with genetic findings as well. Y-chromosome evidence in particular places the movement of people from the Horn of Africa – from the early Afrasian-speaking regions – into Egypt during the same general time frame. Offshoots of this migration then spread from Egypt into the Levant and, in later times, westward across northern parts of Africa. The genetic markers of this succession of movements occur today in Egyptians as well as in Semitic-speaking peoples in the Levant and in the later Afrasian-speaking Berber peoples of North Africa.[46]

The genetic indications are also clear that wholesale population replacement did not take place. The incoming populations were a minority, although significant enough in numbers to leave a lasting genetic imprint, who settled among and intermarried with the existing populations. This blending of populations seems mirrored in the blending of old and new technological and economic features, in particular, combining the key innovation of the period before 15,000 BCE, the microburin technique, with new kinds of

45 The internal subgrouping of the Semitic branch locates proto-Semitic specifically in the Levant: see Robert Hetzron, "La division des langues sémitiques," in André Caquot and David Cohen (eds.), *Actes du Premier Congres Linguistique Semitique et Chamito-Semitique* (The Hague, Paris: Mouton, 1974), pp. 182–94 (*contra* claims of a homeland in the Horn of Africa in Grover Hudson, "Geolinguistic evidence for Ethiopian Semitic prehistory," *Abbay* 9 (1978), 71–85). Proto-Semitic was spoken at around 4000 BCE: Kitchen *et al.*, "Bayesian phylogenetic analysis of Semitic." One subgroup of very closely related Semitic languages is spoken today in the Horn, but it was brought in by an intrusive, first-millennium BCE settlement of people from South Arabia in regions previously inhabited entirely by speakers of the Cushitic languages: see Christopher Ehret, *History and the Testimony of Language*, chap. 7, for a detailed breakdown of the linguistic evidence.

46 Fulvio Cruciani, Roberta La Fratta, Pierro Santolamazza, Daniele Sellitto, Elaine Beraud Colomb, *et al.*, "Philogeographic analysis of haplogroup E3b (E-M215) Y chromosomes reveals multiple migratory events within and out of Africa," *American Journal of Human Genetics* 74 (2004), 1,014–22, and Shomarka O. Y. Keita, "History in the interpretation of the pattern of p49a,f TaqI RFLP Y-chromosome variation in Egypt: A consideration of multiple lines of evidence," *American Journal of Human Biology* 17 (2005), 559–67.

geometric microliths, and adding a productive new food source, wild grains, to the existing subsistence resources.

Out of these interactions, it can be proposed, new social allegiances would have emerged, accompanied by the adoption of the Afrasian language of the incoming people and, presumably, the Afrasian henotheistic religion, since this kind of religion persisted in later times in pre-dynastic Egypt. The ability of incoming groups to incorporate existing communities into new social formations often rests on whether or not the newcomers' ways of life give them a material or social advantage in their cross-cultural encounters with previous populations. A prime factor in this particular case may have been the introduction by the immigrants of a new suite of subsistence practices that would have added greatly to subsistence productivity – namely, wild-grain collecting. And because humans tend to interpret material success as an indicator of spiritual favor, the henotheistic religion of the incoming groups could have been seen as therefore efficacious and worthy of adoption.

The most direct route for the proposed spread of Afrasian speakers from the Horn of Africa to Egypt around 15,000 BCE would have followed the chain of mountains and hills connecting the two regions, along the African side of the Red Sea. From around 15,500 BCE an uneven trend toward warmer and somewhat wetter climate seems to have taken place at the northern end of the Red Sea and adjacent parts of the Levant and Arabia. Climate in the Red Sea hills zone has historically been more tied to these areas than to African areas to the west, making it possible that the effects of this rainfall increase extended to the Red Sea hills as well. If so, grassland areas, suited to wild-grain collection, would have expanded along that hilly and mountainous zone. The spread of grasslands would in turn have opened up an environmental pathway for the spread of Afrasian wild-grass collectors from Eritrea to Upper Egypt and for the establishment along the Nile, in the centuries around 15,000 BCE, of the new Afian and Qadan cultures, which practiced this kind of economy.

In a transitional age: Africa, 12,700–9500 BCE

Around 12,700 BCE another major global climatic shift, with repercussions in Africa, began – a period of climatic amelioration, the Bölling-Alleröd Interstadial, marked by the warming of global climates and by increased rainfall in many parts of the continent. For several centuries following the inception of the era, the Ethiopian highlands, which provide the majority of the water of the Nile River, went through a period of especially high rainfall, leading to disruptively high Nile flood levels in Egypt for several centuries. Except for a brief, partial hiatus midway through, this warming period lasted down to around 10,800 BCE. A thousand-year interlude of colder, drier climate, the Younger Dryas, then brought colder, drier climates back in Africa. Finally, around 9600–9500 BCE, warmer and wetter climate conditions returned again, marking the beginning of the Holocene era, in which all of us still live today.

Varieties of change, 12,700–9500 BCE

Nearly everywhere, the shift to wetter and warmer climates at the beginning of the interstadial seems to have stimulated significant change in culture as well as population movements and cultural replacement. In some cases the shifts in livelihood or culture were regional in their reach. In at least one case, the changes in population and culture spread trans-regionally into far-distant lands.

In East Africa a new culture, Eburran, adapted especially to the expanded montane forest-grassland ecotone areas of that time, took shape in the highland areas of modern-day Kenya. The subsistence strategies of this cultural tradition must have been highly efficient and adaptable, because the tradition in modified forms persisted, despite subsequent climatic changes and other historical challenges, down through the Holocene.[47]

In southern Africa, where the climatic effects were less marked, cultural continuity from the Glacial Maximum into the interstadial tended to be the general outcome. But the start of the Younger Dryas, around 10,800 BCE, changed all that. A new complex, the Oakhurst, fairly quickly replaced Robberg everywhere and lasted nearly 4,000 years, down to the arrival of Khoesan peoples with the Wilton variety of the Eastern African Microlithic tradition in the seventh millennium BCE.[48]

In the areas between the middle Nile and the Ethiopian highlands, the warmer temperatures and increased rainfall during the interstadial encouraged the movement of early Nilo-Saharan speakers outward into new environments. Three cultural groupings of Nilo-Saharan speakers had taken shape

---

47 Stanley H. Ambrose, "Archaeology and linguistic reconstructions of history in East Africa," in Christopher Ehret and Merrick Posnansky (eds.), *The Archaeological and Linguistic Reconstruction of African History* (Berkeley: University of California Press, 1982), pp. 104–57.

48 Christopher Ehret, "Sub-Saharan Africa: Linguistics," in Immanuel Ness and Peter Bellwood (eds.), *The Encyclopedia of Global Human Migration* (Malden, MA: Wiley-Blackwell, 2013), vol. I, chap. 12.

by this era. The earliest Koman peoples, judging from the linguistic evidence for their early locations, established themselves more widely in this era in several areas immediately along the eastern edges of the highlands and between there and the White Nile in South Sudan. The most probable locations of a second set of communities, the early Central Sudanians, would have been the riverine areas along and west of the Nile in South Sudan. A third set of communities, ancestral to the later Northern Sudanian peoples of the early Holocene, moved northward into areas newly reclaimed from desert by the climatic amelioration of that period.

Farther north along the Nile, extraordinarily high Nile flood levels accompanied the onset of the initial, Bølling phase of the Bølling-Allerød Interstadial and continued from around 12,700 to 11,800 BCE. The very high annual floods of this period washed away the evidence of human occupation close to the river, and they may also have discouraged people for several centuries from utilizing many of those environments. Archaeological evidence again becomes plentiful once this period is past, and it shows that several cultural shifts were underway by that time. By 11,000–10,000 BCE three broadly similar cultures – Shamarkian in Lower Nubia, Elkabian in Upper Egypt, and Qurunian in the Fayum – had replaced the Isnan and other cultures of the previous period. One striking change was a decrease in the size and relative number of sites. Cultural continuities nevertheless were many. Archbacked bladelets and geometric microliths were common in each of the new cultures, and wild-grain harvesting remained a key subsistence activity.[49]

In the Maghreb and in northern Libya, the Oranian tradition persisted through the climatic shifts, lasting down to at least the close of the Younger Dryas Stadial. Then, from around 8500 BCE, a new complex, the Capsian, took hold over large areas of North Africa. A new human population appears to have spread with this cultural replacement, mixing with the earlier populations who had made the Oranian. A newly important pursuit in the economy of the Capsian complex was the collection of wild grains, already long practiced along the Nile and anciently associated with peoples of the Afrasian language family.[50] This economic changeover suggests that a key factor in the establishment of the Capsian tradition was a westward spread of Afrasian speakers into Libya and the Maghreb. The Capsian communities, it can be proposed, most likely adopted languages belonging to the same branch of the Afrasian family as the more recent Berber languages of those

49 Butzer, "Late Quaternary problems."
50 Noura Rahmani, *Le Capsien typique et le Capsien supérieur* (Oxford: Archaeopress, 2003).

regions. This branch also includes the Chadic languages, which are spoken today on the other side of the Sahara, in Niger and in northern Nigeria, Cameroon, and Chad.[51]

West Africa, 12,700–9500 BCE: cultural and human replacement

On the other side of the continent, in West Africa, Middle Stone Age industries, using prepared-core techniques, and their archaic human makers still prevailed apparently everywhere down to the close of the Last Glacial Maximum, 13,000–12,000 BCE, from Senegal to Ghana and Nigeria. And then, in perhaps no more than 2,000 years, between around 13,000 and 11,000 BCE, the Middle Stone Age populations and their tools disappeared, replaced by different varieties of the fully Later Stone Age, West African Microlithic complex. The earliest currently known sites of the new complex occur from the Ivory Coast to Burkina Faso to southern Nigeria.[52] The Iwo Eleru skull, although representing an individual alive at time of the arrival of the new microlithic technology, was quite distinct from all subsequent West Africa modern humans and not ancestral to them. The intrusion of fully modern human communities brought the previous age to an end, and in a relatively short period they replaced the archaic human makers of the last Middle Stone Age cultures all across West Africa.

But where were these new people intrusive from? The languages of West Africa from 12,000 to 11,000 BCE onward belonged, as far as can be told, to the Western branch of the Niger-Kordofanian family. The limited extent of the other, equally complex primary branch of the family, Kordofanian, to areas just north of South Sudan today, indicates that the Western Niger-Kordofanian languages were carried to West Africa via a long-extended expansion of people westward from South Sudan. Virtually no archaeological work exists as yet for nearly all the crucial intervening regions – from western South Sudan, through the Central African Republic, to eastern Cameroon. Did this expansion proceed over extended stages westward

---

51 Ehret, Keita, and Newman, "The origins of Afroasiatic."
52 Allsworth-Jones, "The earliest human settlement"; Allsworth-Jones, "Middle Stone Age"; Signe E. Nygaard and Michael R. Talbot, "Stone Age archaeology and environment on the southern Accra Plains, Ghana," *Norwegian Archaeological Review* 17 (1984), 19–38; Robert Chenorkian, "Ivory Coast prehistory: Recent developments," *African Archaeological Review* 1 (1983), 127–42; Bassey W. Andah, "The Later Stone Age and Neolithic of Upper Volta reviewed in a West African context," *West African Journal of Archaeology* 9 (1979), 87–110; and Thurstan Shaw and A. G. H. Daniels, "Excavations at Iwo Eleru," *West African Journal of Archaeology* 14 (1984).

during the later parts of the Last Glacial Maximum, or was it a rapid dispersal at the onset of the Bølling-Allerød Interstadial, encouraged by the northward expansion of favorable savanna and woodland into those intervening lands? Those are questions we cannot yet answer.

Religious beliefs among the early Western Niger-Kordofanian societies, by the time of their movements into West Africa, may already have begun to evolve in a quite different direction from the belief systems of other regions of the continent, including among the related Kordofanian peoples of Sudan. It seems probable that the primary focus of religious observance around 9500 BCE in the proto-Niger-Congo daughter society of the early Western Niger-Kordofanians was the ancestral spirits of the clan or lineage community. In subsequent ages ancestor veneration was so primary a feature of religion all across the areas inhabited by Niger-Congo peoples that modern-day observers often think of these beliefs as typical of all Africans. They are not; they are specifically a feature of the Niger-Congo historical tradition. Territorial spirits of different localities may have been an equally early component of this belief system. The belief in a third, and highest, level of Spirit – in a single, transcendent Creator God – took hold early as well in Niger-Congo religion, although possibly not as early as 9500 BCE.[53]

From what little archaeology we have, the early Western Niger-Kordofanians in West Africa appear to have favored neither heavy rainforest nor dry savanna and steppe, but rather intermediate zones of woodland and well-watered savanna. This choice of environments may help to explain why one Western Niger-Kordofanian people embarked on a crucial leap forward in technology and subsistence sometime before 9500 BCE. The onset of the Younger Dryas around 10,800 BCE changed many of the areas settled by Western Kordofanians from relatively well-watered savanna into much drier savanna or steppe, forcing the inhabitants to either follow the retreating rainfall belts south or adopt new strategies for exploiting their now drier environments.

Facing that challenge, one particular group of Western Niger-Kordofanian communities, speakers of the proto-Niger-Congo language, adopted two mutually reinforcing innovations. They began to harvest several of the wild-grain species, such as fonio, that grew in abundance after the rains in the steppe grasslands and drier savannas. At the same time they independently invented

---

53 Ehret, *Civilizations of Africa*, chap. 3; also Christopher Ehret, *An African Classical Age* (Charlottesville: University Press of Virginia, 1998), chap. 5.

ceramic technology and applied the new technology in fashioning pots in which they cooked their grains whole.[54] When the Younger Dryas ended and the Holocene era began around 9600–9500 BCE, the belts of steppe and dry savanna advanced northward again toward the Sahara. And the proto-Niger-Congo people, it can be proposed, moved north following the spread of the environments that made their pursuits possible.

The earliest direct testimony yet available for this transformation comes from sites dating to before 9400 BCE, located along the Bandiagara escarpment in the modern-day country of Mali, in just the areas into which dry savanna and steppe environments spread around 9600–9500 BCE, at the end of the Younger Dryas.[55] By that time this economy and its technology already had a history. Its earlier stages would have taken place in the immediately preceding Young Dryas period; and because the lands around the Bandiagara escarpment appear to have been uninhabited desert during the Younger Dryas, these new developments must have come into being farther south.

The linguistic evidence suggests that still another innovative development – not self-evident in the archaeology – may have been underway among the Niger-Congo grain collectors as early as the later tenth and the ninth millennia BCE. Several verb roots for the deliberate tending and protecting of food plants can be provisionally reconstructed to the era in Niger-Congo linguistic history immediately following the proto-Niger-Congo period, and one such verb possibly back to proto-Niger-Congo itself. The early descendant societies of the proto-Niger-Congo people, this evidence indicates, were independently taking the first steps toward agriculture in the early Holocene, by engaging in pre-domestication cultivation.[56] On the other side of the continent, the first steps toward food production came as early as the ninth and eighth millennia BCE, when Nilo-Saharan peoples in the eastern Sahara initiated the earliest herding of cattle in world history. These same peoples probably not much later began also to engage in pre-domestication

---

54 Katharina Neumann, Ahmed Fahmy, Laurent Lespez, Aziz Ballouche, and Eric Huysecom, "The Early Holocene palaeoenvironment of Ounjougou (Mali): Phytoliths in a multiproxy context," *Palaeogeography, Palaeoclimatology, Palaeoecology* 276 (2009), 87–106.

55 Eric Huysecom, Michel Rasse, Laurent Lespez, Katharina Neumann, Ahmed Fahmy, Aziz Ballouche, Sylvain Ozainne, Marino Maggetti, Chantal Tribolo, and Sylvain Soriano, "The emergence of pottery in Africa during the tenth millennium cal BC: New evidence from Ounjougou (Mali)," *Antiquity* 83 (2009), 905–17.

56 Christopher Ehret, "Agricultural origins: What linguistic evidence reveals," in Graeme Barker and Candice Goucher (eds.), *A World with Agriculture* (Cambridge: Cambridge University Press, forthcoming).

cultivation – with probably gourds and melons and then grains as the early crops.[57]

In other words, Africa at the beginning of the Holocene was not a place apart. The same trajectories of human change were emerging in Africa as in several other parts of the world – toward agricultural ways of life and, much farther off in time, toward more complex and more unequal societies.

FURTHER READING

Allen, Nicholas J., Hilary Callan, Robin Dunbar, and Wendy James (eds.), *Early Human Kinship: From Sex to Social Reproduction*, Oxford: Blackwell, 2008.

Bar-Yosef, Ofer, "The dispersal of modern humans in Eurasia: A cultural interpretation," in Paul Mellars, Katie Boyle, Ofer Bar-Yosef, and Chris Stringer (eds.), *Rethinking the Human Revolution: New Behavioural and Biological Perspectives on the Origin and Dispersal of Modern Humans*, Cambridge: McDonald Institute, 2007, pp. 207–18.

"Pleistocene connexions between Africa and Southwest Asia: An archaeological perspective," *The African Archaeological Review* 5 (1987), 29–38.

Blundell, Geoffrey (ed.), *Seeing and Knowing: Understanding Rock Art with and without Ethnography*, Walnut Creek, CA: Left Coast Press, 2011.

Butzer, Karl W., "Late Quaternary problems of the Egyptian Nile: Stratigraphy, environments, prehistory," *Paléorient* 23 (1997), 151–73.

Cornelissen, Els, "Human response to changing environments in Central Africa between 40,000 and 12,000 BP," *Journal of World Prehistory* 16 (2002), 197–235.

Ehret, Christopher, *History and the Testimony of Language*, Berkeley: University of California Press, 2011.

Lewis-Williams, J. David, *A Cosmos in Stone: Interpreting Religion and Society through Rock Art*, Walnut Creek, CA: AltaMira Press, 2002.

Midant-Reynes, Béatrix, *The Prehistory of Egypt from the First Egyptians to the First Pharaohs*, Oxford: Blackwell, 2000.

Phillipson, David W., *African Archaeology*, Cambridge: Cambridge University Press, 2005.

Smith, Benjamin, *Zambia's Ancient Rock Art: The Paintings of Kasama*, Livingstone, Zambia: National Heritage Conservation Commission, 1997.

Willoughby, Pamela R., *The Evolution of Modern Humans in Africa: A Comprehensive Guide*, Lanham, MD: AltaMira Press, 2007.

57 Christopher Ehret, *History and the Testimony of Language*, chap. 6.

16

Migration and innovation in Palaeolithic Europe

JOHN F. HOFFECKER

The archaeological record is constituted of the fossilized results of human behavior, and it is the archaeologist's business to reconstitute that behavior as far as he can and so to recapture the thoughts that behavior expressed. In so far as he can do that, he becomes a historian.

V. Gordon Childe, *Piecing Together the Past*[1]

All history is the history of thought.

R. G. Collingwood, *The Idea of History*[2]

Human evolution and Europe

Human evolution may be divided into two phases. During the first phase, the earliest representatives of the human subfamily diverged from the African apes, roughly 6 million years ago. The divergence probably was triggered by a shift from quadrupedal to bipedal locomotion, which was likely tied to a change in foraging strategy. The extreme poverty of the fossil record for this time period obscures the earliest part of the human story. For more than 3 million years, humans remained small-brained 'bipedal apes' in the tropical zone of Africa.

During the second phase of human evolution, which began 2.5–2.0 million years ago, the larger-brained genus *Homo* appeared, along with stone tools and evidence for meat consumption. Roughly 2 million years ago, or shortly thereafter, representatives of *Homo* emigrated out of tropical Africa into the northern parts of the continent and also into Eurasia – as far as latitude 40° North. This was followed by several more migrations of various forms of

---

1 V. G. Childe, *Piecing Together the Past: The Interpretation of Archaeological Data* (London: Routledge and Kegan Paul, 1956), p. 1.
2 R. G. Collingwood, *The Idea of History* (Oxford: Oxford University Press, 1946), p. 215.

Homo out of Africa, culminating in the global dispersal of modern humans or *Homo sapiens*, beginning roughly 60,000 years ago.

The Ice-Age or Pleistocene prehistory of Europe nests within this wider pattern of human evolution. All of the human inhabitants of Europe past and present ultimately derive from Africa, although – in at least one case – an earlier form of human evolved some characteristic European traits. Many palaeoanthropologists have argued strenuously that this population (the Neanderthals) contributed in significant ways to the evolution of modern people, but the argument remains weak. It now appears that the Neanderthals made a modest contribution to the genetics of non-African populations that seems to have had little impact on their anatomy or behaviour.

Europe's role in human evolution has been determined largely by its geographic position in relation to Africa and Asia. By virtue of its location at the western end of Eurasia, Europe occupies a unique place in terms of climate and biota. Although most of the continent lies above $40°$ North, clockwise marine currents in the North Atlantic ensure a steady supply of warm, moist air from lower latitudes. As a result, Western Europe enjoys the mildest winters and the richest biota in all of northern Eurasia. The air becomes drier as it flows across Central and Eastern Europe, and the latter sees more continental climates and reduced biological productivity. The southeastern portion of Europe, north of the Black Sea, is especially dry and supports a steppe environment.

Europe is largely isolated from Africa and the Near East by the Mediterranean Sea, the Black Sea, and the Caspian Sea, and, to a lesser extent, by the Caucasus Mountains, which lie between the Black Sea and the Caspian Sea. Despite the fact that sea level has fallen dramatically during the past, when billions of gallons of water were locked up on land in the form of glaciers, the Strait of Gibraltar and the strait between Sicily and Tunisia (both more than 300 metres in depth) have been consistent barriers for people. Most movements of people into Europe during the Ice Age probably occurred at the comparatively shallow Bosporus (average depth of 55 metres) or via the Caucasus. Human populations in Europe tend to be at least partially isolated from those outside Europe, especially in Africa.

Despite its lesser role as a setting for the evolution of humankind, Europe was the birthplace of the natural sciences, including evolutionary biology and palaeoanthropology. A Swedish naturalist (Linnaeus) correctly identified the chimpanzee as the closest living relative of humans in 1751, while in 1858 English naturalists (Darwin and Wallace) offered an explanation of the process by which humans had evolved from earlier life forms. Equally important were the early geologists and palaeontologists (Lyell, Cuvier, and others), who established the principles of stratigraphy and constructed the geologic framework for the fossil record of evolution. The repeated discovery of human artefacts in buried stratigraphic context alongside the fossil remains of extinct animals such as mammoth, convinced nineteenth-century Europeans of the antiquity of humankind.

By the end of the nineteenth century, European scholars had uncovered the principal archaeological remains of the Ice Age and at least a few human fossils of the most recent phases of human evolution in Europe (that is, Cro-Magnon and Neanderthal). The archaeological remains, which mostly comprised stone artefacts, were organized within an interpretive framework that reflected a simple faith in progress. All Ice-Age archaeological remains were classified as 'Old Stone Age' or *Palaeolithic* (a term coined by Sir John Lubbock in 1865). The late or *Upper Palaeolithic*, which was subsequently divided into several successive industries, was eventually linked to modern humans or the Cro-Magnons. The preceding *Middle Palaeolithic* was associated with the extinct Neanderthals, and the early or *Lower Palaeolithic* with the pre-Neanderthal inhabitants of Europe.[3] Fossil remains of the latter did not surface until the early twentieth century and are still scarce.

Europe's seminal role in the emergence of evolutionary theory and archaeology may underlie the sometimes stubborn resistance to acceptance of its secondary place in human evolution, but the lengthy history of field research has yielded an unparalleled body of information on the human past. This is especially true with respect to the archaeological record of Ice-Age modern humans and their immediate predecessors in Europe. Although pertinent data now are being retrieved from Africa, the critical body of information regarding the emergence of the modern human mind still derives from Europe. It is the latter that documents the creative power of the mind in visual art, music, technology – and by implication syntactic language – with the appearance of modern humans.

Archaeologists have tended to emphasize the economic aspects of the prehistoric past, because questions about what people ate and how they made their tools are more tractable than those about what and how people thought before the advent of written records. It is the origin of the mind, however, that is the central issue in human evolution. It is not only the immense quantity of non-genetic information that modern humans collect and store, but it is also their capacity for creating novel structures or arrangements of that information that render them unique among living

---

3 The later *Middle Stone Age* of sub-Saharan Africa is associated with modern humans (*Homo sapiens*).

organisms. This evolution of this capacity – not the invention of writing – gave birth to the process of history, which R. G. Collingwood once defined as 'the history of thought'. And the archaeological record, as V. Gordon Childe observed, is a record of thought or the 'concrete embodiments of thoughts'.

Lower Palaeolithic: the initial peopling of Europe

The earliest prehistory of Europe also may be divided into two phases. The first phase took place before three-quarters of a million years ago, and is characterized by what appears to be limited and sporadic occupation of Southern Europe by several forms of earlier *Homo*. Their artefacts are confined to pebble and flake tools, similar to those of the earliest known Lower Palaeolithic artefacts in Africa. The second phase began after 600,000 years ago with the invasion of a large-brained later *Homo* (often referred to as *Homo heidelbergensis*), who made large bifacial tools or hand axes and left relatively substantial traces of settlement in Western and Central Europe, including as far as latitude 52° North in Britain.

Evidence for humans in Europe before 1 million years ago has only recently been confirmed with the dating of early *Homo* skeletal remains to 1.2–1.1 million years ago at the Sierra de Atapuerca in northern Spain (roughly 42° North).[4] The remains, which comprise a jaw bone and teeth, are associated with stone flakes and large mammal bones that exhibit traces of butchery (see Figure 16.1). The early *Homo* fossils at Atapuerca appear to represent the same general expansion out of Africa – which probably involved multiple migrations over some period of time – into the temperate zone of Eurasia that began after 2 million years ago.

Another recent discovery is a hand axe or large bifacial artefact dated to about 0.9 million years ago, which was recovered from Estrecho del Quípar in south-eastern Spain.[5] The hand axe was found together with other stone artefacts and two isolated human teeth. It may represent a later movement of early humans out of Africa that seems to have taken place about 1.4 million years ago. At that time, crude-looking hand axes – which were made as early as 1.76 million years ago in sub-Saharan Africa – appeared in the Levant.[6] The discovery in south-eastern Spain suggests that this migration also reached Europe.

---

4 Eudald Carbonell, et al., 'The first hominin of Europe', *Nature* 452 (2008), 465–9.
5 Gary R. Scott and Luis Gibert, 'The oldest hand-axes in Europe', *Nature* 461 (2009), 82–5.
6 Ofer Bar-Yosef and A. Belfer-Cohen, 'From Africa to Eurasia – Early dispersals', *Quaternary International* 75 (2001), 19–28.

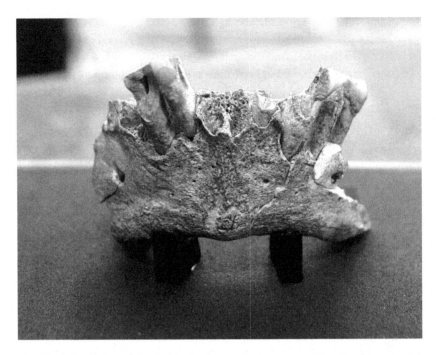

Figure 16.1 Jaw and teeth dated from 1.2 to 1.1 million years ago, found at Atapuerca in northern Spain (© Sani Otero/epa/Corbis).

Atapuerca has yielded somewhat younger human fossils (estimated at roughly 0.8 million years old) that are classified as a separate species (*Homo antecessor*) unique to Europe. Although no hand axes have been found in association with the fossils, this might be a sampling problem. In central Italy, at the site of Ceprano, a fossil skullcap is dated to between 1.0 and 0.7 million years ago. It may represent yet another expansion out of Africa, by a larger-brained form of *Homo* similar to *Homo erectus*.

The initial peopling of Europe seems to reflect a fundamental shift in human ecology and behaviour that took place in Africa after 2.5 million years ago, and permitted early *Homo* to occupy a much wider range of habitat and climate than its australopithecine predecessors. The shift entailed production of modified pebble and stone flake tools, which – although simple and essentially reductive in character – nevertheless lie outside the capacity of living apes. This development reflected the long-term consequences of bipedalism, which had led to increased forelimb specialization (that is, the evolution of the human hand) among the australopithecines. At least one of the functions of the tools was the killing and/or butchering of large mammals, reflecting the expanded role of meat in the human diet. The increased consumption of meat must have been a critical component of the changes in behaviour that facilitated the expansion into the temperate zone and into Europe.

Roughly three-quarters of a million years ago, a new large-brained form of *Homo* migrated out of Africa into western Eurasia. It is often referred to as *Homo heidelbergensis*, and represents the common ancestor of the Neanderthals and modern humans. Cranial volume averages more than 1,100 cubic centimetres and overlaps with that of living humans. In contrast to earlier forms of *Homo* – for which the evidence remains problematic – *Homo heidelbergensis* had mastered the control of fire. And in contrast to the earlier inhabitants of Europe, it manufactured a refined form of the hand axe or large bifacial tool. Production of the latter was not reductive, but rather required a preconceived design and several hierarchically organized steps. The steps included: (1) production of a very large flake from a stone cobble or core, (2) more or less complete flaking of both sides into an ovate shape in three dimensions; (3) careful trimming of the edges to yield a more finely shaped ovate form. The completed biface often was converted into a 'cleaver' by striking a tranchet blow across the pointed end.

Approximately 600,000 years ago, *Homo heidelbergensis* invaded Europe, most probably via the Bosporus, and its remains are well represented in a younger occupation at Atapuerca. The oldest hand axes in Italy date to about 600,000 years ago. Traces of *Homo heidelbergensis* are only slightly younger in southern Britain, where they are dated to a very warm interval roughly half a million years ago. A tibia or lower leg bone from Boxgrove, a Palaeolithic site in southern England, is rather massive and long, suggesting that the anatomical adaptations to cooler climates that eventually became typical of the Neanderthals had yet to evolve.

Boxgrove actually contains an entire 'landscape' of early human sites, and probably reveals more about the pre-Neanderthal inhabitants of Europe than any other site or group of sites known to date. Half a million years ago, Boxgrove was warmer than today, but otherwise similar – a low-lying coastal plain covered with grass. Small groups of *Homo heidelbergensis* moved across this landscape, killing and/or scavenging horses and other large mammals. At one location, they repeatedly gathered around what was probably a spring or waterhole, where hand axes often were discarded. At other locations, they sharpened their tools and used them to butcher a horse carcass.[7]

7 Matt I. Pope and Mark B. Roberts, 'Observations on the relationship between Palaeolithic individuals and artifact scatters at the Middle Pleistocene site of Boxgrove, UK', in

Another highly revealing site is Schöningen in northern Germany, which is dated to roughly 400,000 years ago. Climate conditions were somewhat cooler than at Boxgrove, and the habitat was a mixture of meadow and forest steppe. Horses were butchered here as well, but unlike Boxgrove, there are traces of hearths. Most unusual and a consequence of exceptional preservation conditions, Schöningen yielded wooden artefacts, including several long spears of pine or spruce. Detailed analysis of the multiple steps involved in their production demonstrated a surprisingly complex process. The pointed ends were carefully shaped and polished from the hardest wood, which occurs at the base of the tree.[8]

Middle Palaeolithic: the rise and fall of the Neanderthals

The Neanderthals (*Homo neanderthalensis*) appear to be the only true Europeans among the human family. This is because they evolved their characteristic features in Europe, reflecting both the effects of local environmental conditions, as well as the consequences of isolation and genetic drift. The Neanderthals evolved from the people who had colonized Europe roughly 600,000 years ago, that is, *Homo heidelbergensis*.[9] Although some of their characteristic traits are visible earlier, the evolved or 'classic' Neanderthals do not emerge from the fossil record until roughly a quarter of a million years ago.[10]

In terms of their physical appearance, the Neanderthals were stocky and barrel-chested with a powerful set of muscles. Their forearms and lower legs were shortened relative to humans of the tropical zone – an evolved form of cold-weather adaptation that mitigates heat loss in the extremities. Their

Clive Gamble and Martin Porr (eds.), *The Hominid Individual in Context* (London: Routledge, 2005), pp. 81–97.

8 Miram N. Haidle, 'How to think a simple spear', in Sophie A. de Beaune, Frederick L. Coolidge, and Thomas Wynn (eds.), *Cognitive Archaeology and Human Evolution* (New York: Cambridge University Press, 2009), pp. 57–73.

9 It now appears that at least two northern species of *Homo* evolved from *Homo heidelbergensis*, and that some cousins of the Neanderthals (the 'Denisovans') lived at roughly the same time in the Altai region and perhaps elsewhere in Northern Asia. Knowledge of the Denisovans is based on the analysis of ancient DNA extracted from a finger bone fragment from Denisova Cave. See David Reich, et al., 'Genetic history of an archaic hominin group from Denisova Cave in Siberia', *Nature* 468 (2010), 1,053–60.

10 Neanderthal skeletal traits are evident among the fossils from the Sima de los Huesos at Atapuerca (Spain) that have been dated to more than 500,000 years, but there is increasing doubt that these dates are accurate. See Chris Stringer, 'The status of *Homo heidelbergensis*', *Evolutionary Anthropology* 21 (2012), 101–7.

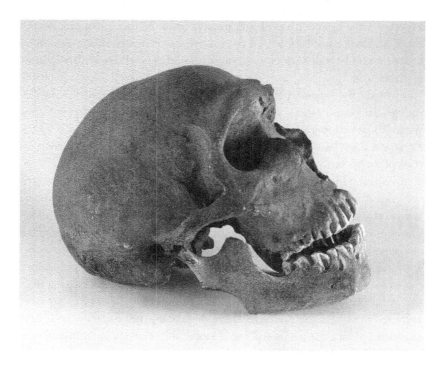

Figure 16.2 Neanderthal man skull (Homo sapiens neanderthalensis) (De Agostini Picture Library / A. Dagli Orti / Bridgeman Images).

heads were massive with a brain volume slightly larger than that of living humans, although the low, flat cranial vault and prominent brow ridge gave them a famously primitive appearance. The face protruded forward with a formidable nose and enlarged front teeth (see Figure 16.2). Despite some striking anatomical adaptations to cold climate, most of their characteristic features seem to have been a consequence of drift and isolation.[11]

Besides their peculiar physical appearance, how did the Neanderthals differ from their predecessors? The primary difference may lie in the improved ability of the Neanderthals to cope with glacial climates, and the distribution of their sites in both space and time is significant. While the earlier inhabitants of Europe are generally associated with the warm interglacial intervals, when climates in Europe were often as favourable as – or more than – those of today, traces of Neanderthal occupation are common during full glacial conditions.

11 Timothy D. Weaver, 'The meaning of Neandertal skeletal morphology', *Proceedings of the National Academy of Sciences* 106 (2009), 16,028–33.

Moreover, the Neanderthals appear to have been the first humans to inhabit the East European Plain, where the lowest winter temperatures are found today (in mid-latitude Europe). Although human skeletal remains are lacking, artefacts from Sukhaya Mechetka at Volgograd in southern Russia probably were made by Neanderthals. The occupation appears to date to the last interglacial period (about 125,000 years ago); today, the area experiences a mean January temperature below −6°C.[12] A comparison of ancient DNA from West and East European Neanderthal specimens suggests that the move east took place between 350,000 and 150,000 years ago.

A critical part of the adaptation to glacial climates must have been their special skill and success in hunting large mammals – including mammoth and woolly rhinoceros – which supplied them with a diet rich in protein and fat. Neanderthal sites often are filled with the bones and teeth of red deer, reindeer, bison, and other large mammals. The analysis of stable isotopes from Neanderthal bones indicates that most of their protein was obtained from meat. Newer techniques that permit identification of specific taxa from the stable isotope data reveal that mammoth and woolly rhinoceros were favoured prey.[13] At the site of La Cotte de la Saint-Brelade, on what is now the island of Jersey, mammoths and rhinoceros were apparently driven over a small cliff.[14] A harvest of mammoth and rhinoceros meat might have been essential to surviving the European winter.

Less critical, perhaps, to their ability to cope with the cold was Neanderthal technology, which seems to have lacked both sewn winter clothing and fire-making equipment. Eyed needles of bone and ivory are known only from the archaeological sites of modern humans, and, while the Neanderthals must have fashioned some sort of clothing and footwear, these presumably lacked the tight insulation of sewn clothing found among recent peoples of the Arctic. The only clues to Neanderthal clothing are characteristic traces of polish created by hide-working on some of their stone tools – and even here, the polish does not

12 Sukhaya Mechetka (originally known as the 'Stalingrad site') was excavated in 1952 and 1954 by S. N. Zamyatnin, who uncovered a large occupation floor. See S. N. Zamyatnin, 'Stalingradskaya paleoliticheskaya stoyanka', *Kratkie Soobshcheniya Instituta Arkheologii* 82 (1961), 5–36.

13 Hervé Bocherens, Dorothée G. Drucker, Daniel Billiou, Marylène Patou-Mathis, and Bernard Vandermeersch, 'Isotopic evidence for diet and subsistence pattern of the Saint-Cesaire I Neanderthal: Review and use of a multi-source mixing model', *Journal of Human Evolution* 49 (2005), 71–87.

14 Kate Scott, 'Mammoth bones modified by humans: Evidence from La Cotte de la St. Brelade, Jersey, Channel islands', in Robson Bonnichsen and Marcella H. Sorg (eds.), *Bone Modification* (Orono, ME: Center for the Study of the First Americans, 1989), pp. 335–46.

reflect the intense scraping often observed on the stone tools of modern humans used for hide preparation. As for the use of controlled fire, many sites occupied by Neanderthals contain hearths, but a recent study found their presence to be rather erratic, even during periods of extreme cold. The conclusion – the Neanderthals probably lacked the ability to make fire, and depended on capturing naturally generated fire in the landscape.[15]

The Neanderthals were, nevertheless, skilled technicians of stone. For the most part, their stone-working seems to have been comparable to that of modern humans. The size and shape of stone tool blanks often was controlled through the careful preparation of the core from which the blanks were struck (Levallois prepared-core technique). It is the appearance of prepared-core techniques in Europe, roughly 300,000 years ago, that marks the beginning of the Middle Palaeolithic. In the 1950s, the French Palaeolithic archaeologist François Bordes devised an intricate system of classification for stone artefacts to characterize the various forms into which the blanks were chipped (or 'retouched'). The Middle Palaeolithic contains a wide array of retouched stone blank forms (for example, point, transverse scraper). Microscopic traces of wear on tools indicate that they were used on soft and hard materials, including – as noted above – hide and especially wood. A few simple wooden artefacts have been recovered from Abric Romani in northern Spain, where unusual conditions acted to preserve the wood – extremely rare for a Palaeolithic site.[16]

The most impressive technical achievements of the Neanderthals have come to light only in recent years. These are the composite tools and weapons assembled from several parts, including various adhesives used to secure pointed or beveled-edge stone blanks into wooden shafts or handles. Indeed, the primary importance of the Levallois core technique may have been to ensure stone blanks of desired size and shape for these composite implements – an early version of interchangeable parts. Although not one example of a Neanderthal composite spear or scraping tool has been recovered, their presence is confirmed by traces of hafting wear on the stone blanks and of the adhesives, which include materials such as pine resin and bitumen.[17]

15 Dennis M. Sandgathe, et al., 'On the role of fire in Neandertal adaptations in Western Europe: Evidence from Pech de l'Aze and Roche Marsal, France', *PaleoAnthropology* (2011), 216–42.

16 E. Carbonell and Z. Castro-Curel, 'Palaeolithic wooden artifacts from the Abric Romani (Capellades, Barcelona, Spain)', *Journal of Archaeological Science* 19 (1992), 707–19.

17 Eric Boëda, Jacques Connan, Daniel Dessort, Sultan Muhesen, Norbert Mercier, Hélène Valladas, and Nadine Tisnérat, 'Bitumen as a hafting material on Middle Paleolithic artefacts', *Nature* 380 (1996), 336–8.

A heavy emphasis on Neanderthal diet and technology reflects not only the nature of the archaeological record, but also the outlook of many archaeologists, who have stressed the importance of economic issues in their research. A more interesting question is the Neanderthal mind and how it differed from our own. Did the Neanderthals have a language similar to ours? Did they differentiate themselves into local cultural or ethnic groups? Did they believe in an afterlife and worship some form of supernatural being? Did they have a sense of humour? The question of how similar or different the Neanderthals were to living humans is a controversial one in palaeoanthropology, and the range of answers and viewpoints is wide.

François Bordes was convinced that the Neanderthals who lived in France represented several 'tribes' or local ethnic groups on the basis of recurring assemblages of similar stone artefacts. In the 1960s, this was disputed by archaeologists who argued that the variations simply reflected the effects of sampling and functional differences among the sites.[18] The issue has never really been resolved. The British prehistorian Paul Mellars suggested that the variations in Middle Palaeolithic artefact assemblages in Western Europe could be explained at least in part by changes over time. Improved dating of key sites in recent years has provided support for this thesis.

An aspect of the archaeological record that is especially difficult to explain in purely functional terms is the burial of the dead. There is little doubt that the Neanderthals dug graves in their sites and intentionally buried the deceased (although probably without grave goods). Because burial of the dead among modern humans is invariably linked to a belief in the afterlife, the Neanderthal graves have been widely interpreted as reliable evidence of a religion or belief system. Here again, however, some archaeologists have argued that burial of corpses might simply reflect disposal of waste without ritual or belief in an afterlife. This question also remains unresolved.

Arguments for and against a Neanderthal language have raged for many years. There have been efforts to reconstruct the vocal tract and look for possible contrasts with modern humans. Thus far, these efforts have failed to demonstrate a significant difference between the two, and, in any case, it is not clear that major differences would preclude a Neanderthal language. More recently, the analysis of modern and ancient DNA has opened the possibility of identifying the presence or absence of genes implicated in speech or language in the Neanderthals. The identification of a gene among

18 Lewis R. Binford and Sally R. Binford, 'A preliminary analysis of functional variability in the Mousterian of Levallois facies', *American Anthropologist* 68 (1966), 238–95.

Figure 16.3 Head and shoulders of a sculpted model of a female Neanderthal, National Geographic Society, Washington, D.C. (© Mark Thiessen/National Geographic Society/Corbis).

modern humans (FOXP2) linked to speech function led to speculation that it might not be found among the Neanderthals. Recent publication of the draft genome for Neanderthals, however, revealed that FOXP2 was present.[19] And analysis of ancient DNA from a group of Neanderthals found in a Spanish cave (El Sidrón) revealed something else of great interest. The twelve individuals (six adults, three adolescents, two juveniles, and one infant) apparently died at more or less the same time and represent a social group. The three adult females each derive from a different maternal lineage, but the adult males all belong to the same lineage, suggesting a patrilocal mating pattern.[20]

The archaeological record of the Neanderthals may still offer important clues to their mind and their cognitive faculties, including language. In one fundamental respect, the Neanderthal record is starkly different from that of

19 Richard E. Green, et al., 'A draft sequence of the Neandertal genome', *Science* 328 (2010), 710–22.
20 Carles Lalueza-Fox, et al., 'Genetic evidence for patrilocal mating behavior among Neandertal groups', *Proceedings of the National Academy of Sciences* 108 (2011), 250–3.

modern humans in Europe. Despite the temporal changes in artefact assemblages observed by Mellars and the purported appearance of ornaments and bone tools in their youngest sites (see below), the Neanderthal archaeological record is essentially devoid of creativity and innovation. In their final millennia, they were still making the same sorts of artefacts that they had been producing 200,000 years earlier. Modern human language is inherently creative – living and recent humans generate novel sentences and narratives every day. Perhaps the lack of creativity in Neanderthal artefacts mirrors a similar lack of linguistic creativity.

Modern humans began to filter into Europe at some point after 50,000 years ago and the Neanderthals may have become extinct as early as 40,000 years ago (although later radiocarbon dates are reported from many Neanderthal sites, they may reflect contamination from younger carbon). Most palaeoanthropologists assume that the two events are related and that modern humans – through ecological competition or outright warfare, or perhaps some other factor such as disease – caused the extinction of the Neanderthals. Nevertheless, some argue that there is evidence for at least some degree of genetic or cultural mixture between the two taxa during the period that both were present in Europe.

Evidence for some genic exchange between Neanderthals and modern humans is reported in the recent publication of the draft genome of the former. The interbreeding is thought to have occurred before modern humans entered Europe – roughly 100,000 years ago in the Near East. At least one Neanderthal skeletal trait is said to be present in one of the oldest sets of modern human remains currently known in Europe – from a cave in Romania. But the primary source of evidence for interactions between the two taxa at the time that modern humans moved into Europe is the association of Neanderthal skeletal remains with archaeological remains otherwise associated with modern humans – ornaments and bone tools. These are known from several sites in southwest France in layers assigned to the 'Chatelperronian' industry. There is growing suspicion, however, that these layers represent a mixture of the remains of the youngest Neanderthals and earliest modern humans in the region.

Upper Palaeolithic: the coming of modern humans

Modern humans (*Homo sapiens*) evolved in Africa and subsequently migrated into Asia, Europe, Australia, and other parts of the earth. This conclusion is supported by the fossil record of modern humans as well as the genetics of living humans. The oldest fossils that may be assigned to *Homo sapiens* are found in sub-Saharan Africa, and their dating indicates that modern human anatomy is present there by roughly 200,000 years ago, if not earlier. Analysis of the genetics of living humans – specifically the non-recombining DNA of the mitochondrion and Y-chromosome – reveals that the present-day peoples of the world are either Africans or a subset of Africans. At some point after 60,000 years ago, modern humans expanded out of Africa and into southern Asia and Australia, as well as the Near East and northern Eurasia.

Modern humans seem to have invaded Europe in a series of migratory waves beginning possibly as early as 50,000 years ago. In the coming years, it seems likely that individual population waves into Europe will be identified in the form of genetic markers or haplogroups from ancient DNA extracted from the skeletal remains recovered from their sites. A series of haplogroups thought to represent the population movements into Europe already have been identified from the genetics of living people, but, to date, only a few modern human skeletal remains dating to more than 30,000 years ago have been analyzed for ancient DNA. At present, the migratory waves of *Homo sapiens* are represented primarily by archaeological proxies.

The archaeological record of Ice-Age modern humans in Europe is lumped into the Upper Palaeolithic – a classificatory term of the mid-nineteenth century that has become an anachronism. The archaeological remains of modern humans are fundamentally different from those of their predecessors, and reflect the unlimited creative powers of the modern mind: the capacity for generating a potentially infinite variety of informational or technological constructions. This capacity is illustrated by the presence of complex visual art – such as cave paintings and sculptures – in the early Upper Palaeolithic of Europe. It also is manifest in the dynamic character of the technology, which exhibits rapid change in time and space and constant innovation. The archaeological manifestations of creativity presumably reflect a parallel capacity in vocal communication – a fully syntactic language with phrase structure grammar and potentially infinite variety of sentences and narratives. Despite the fact that written language did not appear until several millennia after the end of the Ice Age, the process of history began with the advent of the modern mind.

It is the rapidly changing character of their archaeological record that permits the identification of migratory waves of modern humans into Europe after 50,000 years ago. Although ultimately derived from Africa, the immediate source of these population movements is the Near East, and despite the evidence from other parts of the world that modern humans already were creating watercraft, they seem to have moved into Europe by land across the Bosporus and through the Caucasus Mountains, as did humans during Lower Palaeolithic times. There is no evidence for movements across the Strait of Gibraltar or the strait between Sicily and Tunisia.

The earliest credible evidence for modern humans in Europe lies in a group of sites in Central and Southeast Europe that contain artefacts assigned to the 'Initial Upper Palaeolithic', but which are lacking skeletal remains that may be firmly attributed to *Homo sapiens*. More sites may exist in Eastern Europe. The artefacts are similar to those in contemporaneous sites of the Levant, where modern humans already were established. The Initial Upper Palaeolithic is comparatively simple – at least as currently revealed – and exhibits little of the technological innovation and creativity that emerges in subsequent phases of the Upper Palaeolithic. It is associated with an interval of significant and sustained warmth (corresponding to Greenland Interstadial 12 in the North Atlantic palaeoclimate record), and may indicate an unexpectedly important role for climate in the initial peopling of Europe by modern humans.

Technological innovation almost certainly played a critical role in the rapid expansion of modern humans out of Africa and into a wide range of habitats and climate zones, and it is strikingly evident in the next Upper Palaeolithic industry that appears in Europe. Widely termed the 'Proto-Aurignacian' because of similarities that it bears to the succeeding Aurignacian, this industry also bears a close resemblance to one found in the Levant ('Ahmarian'). It shows up in Southern and Eastern Europe roughly 42,000 years ago (possibly earlier in some places), and seems to represent population movements via the Bosporus and Caucasus Mountains. Like the Initial Upper Palaeolithic, associated skeletal remains are scarce, but in the case of the Proto-Aurignacian, the archaeological remains are so characteristic of the modern human mind that there is little if any doubt as to the identity of their makers.

Two significant technological innovations that appear with the Proto-Aurignacian intrusion into Europe are the eyed needle, which recently turned up in Mezmaiskaya Cave in the northwest Caucasus Mountains,[21] and indirect evidence for devices used to trap and/or snare small mammals. The harvesting of small mammals is indicated by concentrations of hare remains at Kostenki on the central plain of Eastern Europe. It is either accompanied, or shortly followed, by other novel technologies for harvesting

---

21 Liubov V. Golovanova, Vladimir B. Doronichev, Naomi E. Cleghorn, Marianna A. Kulkova, Tatiana V. Sapelko, and M. Steven Shackley, 'Significance of ecological factors in the Middle to Upper Paleolithic transition', *Current Anthropology* 51 (2010), 655–91.

birds and fish. The pattern reflects expansion of the human dietary niche relative to the Neanderthals – perhaps critical during cooler and drier intervals in Europe, when biological productivity declined. The most characteristic stone artefact of the Proto-Aurignacian – the backed bladelet – may have been used to produce a new type of composite weapon with razor-sharp blades inserted into lateral slots.

Evidence of visual art is still wanting in the Proto-Aurignacian (although a possible ivory figurine head is known from Russia), but personal ornaments – perhaps worn to symbolize social or ethnic identity – are common. Perforated shells and canine teeth are especially common, but stone pendants also are found.[22] Spectacular visual art has been dated to the younger Aurignacian industry (which seems to postdate 40,000 years ago) including imaginative sculptures from sites in southern Germany. Among them is the famous Löwenmensch ivory figurine from Hohlenstein-Stadel that depicts a half-human mythical creature. In Western Europe, the early Aurignacian is linked to an extremely cold interval (Heinrich Event 4) that may have finished off the last of the Neanderthals. Further east, this interval follows a massive volcanic eruption in southern Italy (Campanian Ignimbrite) that spread an immense cloud of ash across Southeastern Europe and the East European Plain, perhaps wiping out much of the human population.

A richer collection of human skeletal material from the interval between 40,000 and 30,000 years ago provides a glimpse of the physical appearance of the inhabitants of Europe at this time. Their anatomical proportions reflect adaptation to tropical climates (for example, elongated forelimbs), and offer a stark contrast to their Neanderthal predecessors. The pattern reflects the African origin of the European population. It also reflects the heavy reliance on novel and complex technology, which seems to have 'buffered' modern humans from the selective effects of cold climate, allowing them to retain their tropical anatomy for thousands of years at higher latitudes.

Major changes are evident in the European archaeological record by 30,000–25,000 years ago, both with respect to economy and art, and they underscore the historical character of the Upper Palaeolithic. In parts of Central and Eastern Europe, settlements of unprecedented size – probably occupied at least briefly by fifty or more persons – materialize.[23] This

22 Marian Vanhaeren and Francesco d'Errico, 'Aurignacian ethno-linguistic geography of Europe revealed by personal ornaments', *Journal of Archaeological Science* 33 (2006), 1,105–28.
23 Gravettian feature complexes on the central East European Plain at sites such as Kostenki, Avdeevo, and Zaraisk comprise a linear arrangement of hearths, surrounded by pits of varying size. They bear a resemblance to feature complexes in Late Dorset

presumably was a consequence of an increasingly efficient system of food procurement and storage, supported by various novel technologies. Among the latter were kilns used to fire ceramics at controlled temperatures of up to 800°C and refrigerated storage units. The period (Gravettian) is also characterized by particularly elaborate burial ritual, and widespread production of the famous 'Venus' figurines in ivory, clay, and other materials (see Figure 16.4).

The boom seems to have come to an end after 25,000 years ago with the onset of the Last Glacial Maximum. An immense ice sheet expanded over much of Northern Europe, and conditions of extreme cold and aridity prevailed for several millennia across a broad periglacial zone. Despite their impressive technological achievements, people apparently were forced to abandon many areas, and there is evidence of dietary stress among the refugees who continued to dwell in Southern Europe. Perhaps the retention of a tropical physique exposed people to higher risk of cold injury (that is, frostbite and hypothermia), while an absence of wood in the coldest and driest areas may have deprived them of adequate fuel.[24]

In any case, the later Upper Palaeolithic settlements of Europe (known as Magdalenian in Western Europe and Epi-Gravettian in Eastern Europe) reveal a successful reoccupation of the periglacial zone, as conditions ameliorated after 20,000 years ago. The final millennia of the Ice Age in Europe, which ended roughly 12,000 years ago, is characterized by increasingly large and semi-permanent-looking settlements in parts of Western and Eastern Europe. In the east, these included groups of oval houses constructed out of mammoth bone. Among the technological innovations are spear-throwers (that is, mechanical devices) and increasingly complex artificial memory systems. Outside Europe, in the Near East and southern China (where pottery vessels appear at this time), the pattern clearly anticipates the farming villages of the postglacial epoch.

sites of northern Canada, which are also thought to represent periodic and temporary aggregations of multiple families. See Robert McGhee, *Ancient People of the Arctic* (Vancouver: University of British Columbia, 1996).

24 Although Upper Palaeolithic people often used fresh bone as a substitute for wood fuel, experimental research reveals that bone must be supplemented with at least a modest quantity of wood in order to render it practical as a fuel, because very large quantities of the former are required to sustain a burning hearth without the latter. See Isabelle Théry-Parisot, Sadrine Costamagno, Jean-Philip Brugal, Philippe Fosse, and Raphaële Guilbert, 'The use of bone as fuel during the palaeolithic, experimental study of bone combustible properties', in J. Mulville and A. K. Outram (eds.), *The Zooarchaeology of Milk and Fats* (Oxford: Oxbow Books, 2005), pp. 50–9.

Figure 16.4 Venus of Dolni Vestonice, a small ceramic statue dating from 30,000 to 25,000 BCE, from a Gravettian era settlement in Moravia (© Walter Geiersperger/Corbis).

FURTHER READING

General

Bordes, François, *Typologie du Paleolithique Ancien et Moyen*, Bordeaux: Delmas, 1961.

Collingwood, Robin George, *The Idea of History*, Oxford: Oxford University Press, 1946.

Gamble, Clive, *The Palaeolithic Settlement of Europe*, Cambridge: Cambridge University Press, 1986.

The Palaeolithic Societies of Europe, Cambridge: Cambridge University Press, 1999.

Hoffecker, John F., *Desolate Landscapes: Ice-Age Settlement of Eastern Europe*, New Brunswick, NJ: Rutgers University Press, 2002.

Landscape of the Mind: Human Evolution and the Archaeology of Thought, New York: Columbia University Press, 2011.

Klein, Richard G., *The Human Career: Human Biological and Cultural Origins*, 3rd edn., Chicago: University of Chicago Press, 2009.

Mithen, Steven, *The Prehistory of the Mind: The Cognitive Origins of Art, Religion and Science*, London: Thames & Hudson, Ltd., 1996.

Svoboda, Jiri, Vojen Ložek, and Emanuel Vlček, *Hunters between East and West: The Paleolithic of Moravia*, New York: Plenum Press, 1996.

Trigger, Bruce G., *A History of Archaeological Thought*, Cambridge: Cambridge University Press, 1989.

Wells, Spencer, *Deep Ancestry: Inside the Genographic Project*, Washington, D.C.: National Geographic Society, 2007.

Wood, Bernard, *Human Evolution: A Very Short Introduction*, Oxford: Oxford University Press, 2005.

Lower Palaeolithic

Bar-Yosef, Ofer, and A. Belfer-Cohen, 'From Africa to Eurasia – Early dispersals', *Quaternary International* 75 (2001), 19–28.

Carbonell, Eudald, et al., 'The first hominin of Europe', *Nature* 452 (2008), 465–9.

Haidle, Miram N., 'How to think a simple spear', in Sophie A. de Beaune, Frederick L. Coolidge, and Thomas Wynn (eds.), *Cognitive Archaeology and Human Evolution*, New York: Cambridge University Press, 2009, pp. 57–73.

Pope, Matt I., and Mark B. Roberts, 'Observations on the relationship between Palaeolithic individuals and artifact scatters at the Middle Pleistocene site of Boxgrove, UK', in Clive Gamble and Martin Porr (eds.), *The Hominid Individual in Context*, London: Routledge, 2005, pp. 81–97.

Santonja, Manuel, and Paola Villa, 'The Acheulean of Western Europe', in Naama Goren-Inbar and Gonen Sharon (eds.), *Axe Age: Acheulian Tool-making from Quarry to Discard*, London: Equinox Publishing Ltd., 2006, pp. 429–78.

Scott, Gary R., and Luis Gibert, 'The oldest hand-axes in Europe', *Nature* 461 (2009), 82–5.

Stringer, Chris, 'The status of *Homo heidelbergensis*', *Evolutionary Anthropology* 21 (2012), 101–7.

Middle Palaeolithic and Neanderthals

Binford, Lewis R., and Sally R. Binford, 'A preliminary analysis of functional variability in the Mousterian of Levallois facies', *American Anthropologist* 68 (1966), 238–95.

Bocherens, Hervé, Dorothée G. Drucker, Daniel Billiou, Marylène Patou-Mathis, and Bernard Vandermeersch, 'Isotopic evidence for diet and subsistence pattern of the Saint-Cesaire I Neanderthal: Review and use of a multi-source mixing model', *Journal of Human Evolution* 49 (2005), 71–87.

Boëda, Eric, Jacques Connan, Daniel Dessort, Sultan Muhesen, Norbert Mercier, Hélène Valladas, and Nadine Tisnérat, 'Bitumen as a hafting material on Middle Paleolithic artefacts', *Nature* 380 (1996), 336–8.

Carbonell, Eudald, and Z. Castro-Curel, 'Palaeolithic wooden artifacts from the Abric Romani (Capellades, Barcelona, Spain)', *Journal of Archaeological Science* 19 (1992), 707–19.

Green, Richard E., et al., 'A draft sequence of the Neandertal genome', *Science* 328 (2010), 710–22.

Lalueza-Fox, Carles, et al., 'Genetic evidence for patrilocal mating behavior among Neandertal groups', *Proceedings of the National Academy of Sciences* 108 (2011), 250–3.

Mellars, Paul, *The Neanderthal Legacy: An Archaeological Perspective from Western Europe*, Princeton, NJ: Princeton University Press, 1996.

Sandgathe, Dennis M., et al., 'On the role of fire in Neandertal adaptations in Western Europe: Evidence from Pech de l'Aze and Roche Marsal, France', *PaleoAnthropology* (2011), 216–42.

Scott, Kate, 'Mammoth bones modified by humans: Evidence from La Cotte de la St. Brelade, Jersey, Channel islands', in Robson Bonnichsen and Marcella H. Sorg (eds.), *Bone Modification*, Orono, ME: Center for the Study of the First Americans, 1989, pp. 335–46.

Weaver, Timothy D., 'The meaning of Neandertal skeletal morphology', *Proceedings of the National Academy of Sciences* 106 (2009), 16,028–33.

Zamyatnin, S. N., 'Stalingradskaya paleoliticheskaya stoyanka', *Kratkie Soobshcheniya Instituta Arkheologii* 82 (1961), 5–36.

Upper Palaeolithic and modern humans

Anikovich, M. V., et al., 'Early Upper Paleolithic in eastern Europe and implications for the dispersal of modern humans', *Science* 315 (2007), 223–6.

Golovanova, Liubov V., Vladimir B. Doronichev, Naomi E. Cleghorn, Marianna A. Kulkova, Tatiana V.. Sapelko, and M. Steven Shackley, 'Significance of ecological factors in the Middle to Upper Paleolithic transition', *Current Anthropology* 51 (2010), 655–91.

Hoffecker, John F., 'Innovation and technological knowledge in the Upper Paleolithic of northern Eurasia', *Evolutionary Anthropology* 14 (2005), 186–98.

'The spread of modern humans in Europe', *Proceedings of the National Academy of Sciences* 106 (2009), 16,040–5.

Straus, Lawrence G., 'The Upper Paleolithic of Europe: an overview', *Evolutionary Anthropology* 4 (1995), 4–16.

Vanhaeren, Marian, and Francesco d'Errico, 'Aurignacian ethno-linguistic geography of Europe revealed by personal ornaments', *Journal of Archaeological Science* 33 (2006), 1,105–28.

17

Asian Palaeolithic dispersals

ROBIN DENNELL

Much of human prehistory is about movement. Sometimes these movements involved the colonisation of a new niche brought about by environmental change, or when our ancestors crossed a behavioural threshold that enabled them to inhabit new regions that were previously beyond their capabilities. Often, these movements were ones of contraction and expansion because of climatic changes that made a region either habitable or uninhabitable. At times, these movements brought groups into closer contact with each other; at other times, these movements resulted in their isolation. All these types of movements are seen in the Palaeolithic record of Asia, the largest of the continents settled by hominins (our own species, *Homo sapiens*, and its predecessors) in the last two million years or so.

Biogeographers define many different types of movement by animal and plant species.[1] Dispersals, or population expansions, refer to the extension of a species' range into new areas. Colonisation occurs if this leads to the establishment of a permanent population. Most dispersals involve no behavioural change, and result from either an expansion of a species' preferred habitat – as when, for example, a fall in sea level results in the expansion of the type of coastal plain already familiar to it – or (especially with birds), the ability to cross barriers such as mountains or the sea to reach favourable new habitats. Dispersals should be differentiated from migrations, which usually refer to seasonal movements within a defined annual range: many modern pastoral societies are examples of this type of seasonal movement between winter and summer pastures, as are modern hunting communities with distinct winter and summer territories, and many species of birds. This type of migration is distinct from emigration, which is the planned, and usually one-way movement of people from one region to another. Rapid dispersal

---

1 See Glen McDonald, *Biogeography: Space, Time and Life* (New York: John Wiley & Sons, Inc., 2003).

events (over a matter of decades or a few centuries) that are at the expense of indigenous communities (whether red squirrels or Australian aborigines) are sometimes termed invasions or irruptions; although there are numerous examples from historic contexts, these are unlikely during the Palaeolithic because population densities were so low. Dispersals by an immigrant species can sometimes be at the expense of an indigenous one and even result in its extinction (as may have happened to Neanderthals after the appearance of *Homo sapiens*), but this process may take several centuries or even millennia; here, 'population replacement' is a more appropriate term than 'invasion'.

Dispersals by humans and their ancestors are particularly interesting because they were often facilitated by anatomical, technological, or social changes. Examples might be an increase in brain size, the invention of stone-tipped projectiles, or the development of exchange networks that allowed groups to obtain resources such as high-quality stone that were not available locally. Dispersals can also occur if the colonising species is a predator that the indigenous fauna had never previously encountered. For example, the rapid dispersal of our species into and across Australia 40,000–50,000 years ago, and the Americas after 12,000–15,000 years ago may have been possible because the local fauna was 'naïve' with respect to the predatory nature of humans: the same process may also have occurred when *Homo erectus* first entered Asia over 1.8 million years ago.[2] In Palaeolithic Asia, human evolution is often discussed as the result of two, and possibly three major, continental-level dispersals. The first, known as Out of Africa 1, comprises the earliest expansion and subsequent colonisation of our own genus *Homo* from Africa into the Eurasian landmass.[3] The second, or Out of Africa 2, summarises a similar expansion of our species, *Homo sapiens*, from Africa across Eurasia and ultimately to Australia and the Americas.[4] Some researchers also recognise a third, which was the expansion of an African type of Acheulean, bifacial technology into Southwest Asia and perhaps India and

2 R. W. Dennell, "Hominin dispersals, environmental novelty and levels of group co-operation", In M. Petraglia, N. Boivin, and R. Crassard (eds.), *From Colonisation to Globalisation: Species Movements in Human History* (Cambridge: Cambridge University Press, in press).

3 See Ofer Bar-Yosef, "Early colonizations and cultural continuities in the Lower Palaeolithic of western Eurasia", in Ravi Korisettar and Michael D. Petraglia (eds.), *Early Human Behavior in Global Context: The Rise and Diversity of the Lower Palaeolithic Record* (London: Routledge, 1998), pp. 221–79 and Figure 1.

4 Paul Pettitt, "The rise of modern humans", in Chris Scarre (ed.), *The Human Past* (London: Thames & Hudson, Ltd., 2005), pp. 127–73 and Figure 2.

Europe *c.* 600,000–800,000 years ago.[5] As outlined below, some recent work in India and the Caucasus challenges this scenario.

Out of Africa 1

The timing of this process is defined by the earliest unambiguous record of hominins outside Africa. At present, this comes from the site of Dmanisi, Georgia, where a remarkable set of deposits 1.77–1.85 million years old were found under a medieval castle during restoration work. Excavations of only a small part of these deposits has so far produced four complete skulls of a very early form of *Homo erectus*, two mandibles, numerous post-cranial bones, hundreds of very simple stone tools, and a large number of animal remains.[6] Recently, the earliest stone tools from Dmanisi have been dated to 1.85 million years ago.[7] These hominins were small, with small brains less than half the modern size, and highly sexually dimorphic, with males considerably heavier than females. This may have implications on their social organisation: some researchers argue that a high degree of sexual dimorphism (as in gorillas, for example) implies a harem-type of social grouping, with a few males dominating several females. Although it is not yet clear whether the Dmanisi hominins hunted or scavenged, their stone tools would have been adequate for defleshing animals and smashing their limb-bones to extract marrow. A handful of sites across Eurasia mark the earliest recorded appearance of our genus outside Africa (see Map 17.1). In Java, the earliest finds of *Homo erectus* at Sangiran date from slightly before *c.* 1.5 million years ago; in

5 Naama Goren-Inbar, et al., "Pleistocene milestones on the Out-of-Africa corridor at Gesher Ya'aqov, Israel", *Science* 289 (2000), 944–7.

6 Leo Gabunia, et al., "Earliest Pleistocene hominid cranial remains from Dmanisi, Republic of Georgia: Taxonomy, geological setting, and age", *Science* 288 (200), 1,019–25; David Lordkipanidze, et al., "Postcranial evidence from early *Homo* from Dmanisi, Georgia", *Nature* 449 (2007), 305–10; Henry de Lumley, et al., "Les industries lithiques préoldowayennes du début du Pléistocène inférieur du site de Dmanissi en Géorgie", *L'Anthropologie* 109 (2005), 1–182; and G. Philip Rightmire, David Lordkipanidze, and Abesalom Vekua, "Anatomical descriptions, comparative studies and evolutionary significance of the hominin skulls from Dmanisi, Republic of Georgia", *Journal of Human Evolution* 50 (2006), 115–41. A. Mgeladze, et al., "Hominin occupations at the Dmanisi site, Georgia, Southern Caucasus: Raw materials and technical behaviours of Europe's first hominins", *Journal of Human Evolution* 6 (2011): 571–96; D. Lordkipanidze, et al., "A complete skull from Dmanisi, Georgia, and the evolutionary biology of early *Homo*", *Science* 342 (2013): 326–31.

7 Reid Ferring, Oriol Oms, Jordi Agusti, Francesco Berna, Medea Nioradze, Teona Shelia, Martha Tappen, Abesalom Vekua, David Zhvania, and David Lorkipandize, "Earliest human occupations at Dmanisi (Georgian Caucasus) dated to 1.85–1.78 Ma.", *Proceedings of the National Academy of Sciences USA* 108 (2011), 10,432–6.

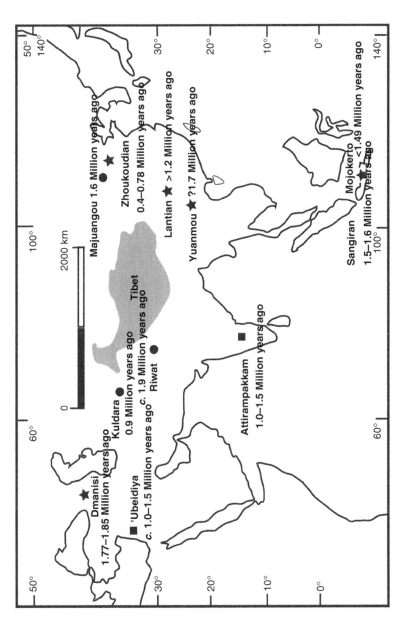

Map 17.1 Primary evidence for early *Homo erectus* in Asia. Stars denote sites with skeletal evidence of *Homo erectus*; circles denote sites with the earliest stone tool assemblages from different parts of Asia; and squares denote the earliest evidence for Acheulean assemblages. At present, there is little definite evidence of a hominin presence outside Africa before 1.85 million years ago, but the size of Asia and small number of observations should make us wary about excluding the possibility of an earlier presence. By 1 million years ago, hominins had colonised much of Asia as far as 40° N.

417

north China, the earliest artefacts from the Nihewan Basin currently date to *c.* 1.66 million and 1.6–1.7 million years ago, and the *Homo erectus* cranium from Lantian in Central China has recently been dated to 1.63 million years ago.[8] A mandible *c.* 1.3 million years old from Atapuerca in northern Spain and a tooth from Barranco Leon, Orce Basin, Spain that may be 1.4 million years old are currently the oldest evidence for our genus in Europe, and show that hominins were now distributed across the entire Eurasian land-mass south of 40° N.[9]

Three comments are worth making about the current evidence for our ancestors' first appearance outside Africa. First, the evidence is so slight that a chance discovery could easily transform our opinions of when they first left Africa: Dmanisi, for example, was a wholly unexpected discovery. Secondly, the dating of these very ancient sites is critically important, but not always as robust as one would like. Although dating techniques have improved hugely in recent years, dates (like share prices) can fall as well as rise, and some important finds have turned out to be much younger than first thought. Thirdly, we are almost certainly not dealing with a single dispersal event; instead, it is much more probable that the colonisation of Eurasia spanned scores of millennia and thousands of generations. With the very limited evidence at our disposal, we see only the cumulative end-result of what was likely a long, complex process, with many false starts and set-backs. Although the overall trend was from west to east, back-movements may have occurred at times, and perhaps (as has been suggested for the type of hominins evidenced at Dmanisi) even re-entered Africa.[10] What is likely is that sites even older than Dmanisi will eventually be found in Eurasia. One credible scenario is that our ancestors were able to expand their range and disperse into Asia shortly after they had mastered the repetitive and regular flaking of stone to produce sharp edges for cutting and scraping *c.* 2.6 million years ago. Because this innovation enabled hominins to deflesh carcasses rapidly, it must have conferred them with a considerable advantage over

8 Roy Larick, et al., "Early Pleistocene ^{40}Ar/^{39}Ar ages for Bapang Formation hominins, Central Jawa, Indonesia", *Proceedings of the National Academy of Sciences of the USA* 98 (2001), 4,866–71; and R. X. Zhu, et al., "New evidence on the earliest human presence at high northern latitudes in northeast Asia", *Nature* 431 (2004), 559–62; H. Ao, et al., "New evidence for early presence of hominids in North China", *Nature Scientific Reports* 3 (2013) 2,403; Zhu Zhao-Yu et al., "New dating of the *Homo erectus* cranium from Lantian (Gongwangling), China, *Journal of Human Evolution* 98 (2013), 144–57.
9 Eudald Carbonell, et al., "The first hominin of Europe", *Nature* 452 (2008), 465–9; I. Toro-Moyano, et al., "The oldest human fossil in Europe, from Orce (Spain)", *Journal of Human Evolution* 65 (2013), 1–9.
10 Rightmire, Lordkipanidze, and Vekua, "Anatomical descriptions".

their competitors by allowing them to delay consumption until after they had procured their food.[11]

Expansion of Acheulean assemblages

One major dispersal – or more likely, sets of dispersals – from Africa into Asia involved the expansion of Acheulean assemblages.[12] Acheulean assemblages are typically characterised by bifacially flaked handaxes, large cutting tools, and often cleavers: all heavy-duty items that could be used for splitting and shaping wood, smashing bone (to extract its marrow), or digging (for example, to obtain edible tubers). The earliest in Africa date back to c. 1.7 million years ago but are not found at Dmanisi.[13] In Asia, the earliest are from the site of 'Ubeidiya, Israel, and date from c. 1.0 to 1.4 million years ago. Recent work in India has shown that the earliest bifaces at Attirampakkam in South India are 1.0–1.5 million years old – considerably older than previously thought for South Asia.[14] Likewise in Armenia, it now appears that Acheulean bifaces in the Caucasus may be over 1 million years old; again, much earlier than previously reckoned.[15] Together, this evidence may indicate that the use of this technology was diffused between groups – or dispersed by incoming groups – across Southwest and South Asia before 1 million years ago. Unfortunately, there is no skeletal data to indicate what type of hominin(s) made them. A second set of dispersals – again unsupported by hominin skeletal evidence – may be indicated at another Israeli site, Gesher Benot Ya'aqob, where African types of handaxes and cleavers date from c. 700,000 to 800,000 years ago.[16] If this denotes another dispersal event, it appears to have been confined to the Levant as it is not found elsewhere. For reasons not yet understood, Acheulean assemblages do not appear in Europe until 500,000–600,000 years ago; here,

11 Robin W. Dennell and Wil Roebroeks, "An Asian perspective on early human dispersal from Africa", *Nature* 438 (2005), 1,099–104.

12 The term "Acheulean" is derived from St. Acheul, near Paris, where these types of tools were first recognised in the 1850s.

13 Christopher J. Lepre, Hélène Roche, Dennis V. Kent, Sonia Harmand, Rhonda L. Quinn, Jean-Philippe Brugal, Pierre-Jean Texier, Arnaud Lenoble, and Craig S. Feibel, "An earlier origin for the Acheulian", *Nature* 44 (2011), 82–5.

14 Shanti Pappu, Yanni Gunnell, Kumar Aklilesh, Régis Braucher, Maurice Taieb, François Demory, and Nicolas Thouveny, "Early Pleistocene presence of Acheulian homi-nins in South India", *Science* 331 (2011), 1,596–9.

15 Sergey L. Presnyakov, Elena V. Belyaeva, V. P. Lyubin, N. V. Rodionov, A. V. Antonov, A. K. Saltykova, Natalia G. Berezhnaya, and S. A. Sergeev, "Age of the earliest Paleolithic sites in the northern part of the Armenian Highland by SHRIMP-II U–Pb geochronology of zircons from volcanic ashes", *Gondwana Research* 21 (2012), 928–38.

16 Naama Goren-Inbar, *et al.*, "Pleistocene milestones".

they are usually associated with *Homo heidelbergensis*, which was likely an immigrant into Europe from Southwest Asia.[17]

Out of Africa 2

Out of Africa 2 is the name given to the expansion of our species, *Homo sapiens*, from Africa. Many researchers argue that the oldest evidence of our species in Africa is *c.* 190,000 years old from the Awash Valley, Ethiopia.[18] Outside Africa, the earliest skeletal evidence of our species dates from the last interglacial, *c.* 70,000–125,000 years ago, from the caves of Skhul and Qafzeh in Israel.[19] It appears to have been confined to the Levant, and *c.* 70,000 years ago was displaced by Neanderthals who may have been forced southwards by the increasingly harsh conditions of MIS 4.[20] After being present in the Levant for *c.* 50,000–60,000 years ago, these early populations of *Homo sapiens* became extinct, possibly because they were not as socially and cognitively advanced as later populations of *Homo sapiens*.[21] After an assumed increase of populations in Africa, *Homo sapiens* is thought to have expanded across southern Asia between 40,000 and 60,000 years ago (see Map 17.2).[22] Genetic studies of modern populations indicate that the modern inhabitants

17 Katharine McDonald, María Martinón-Torres, Robin W. Dennell, and José María Bermudez de Castro, "Discontinuity in the record for hominin occupation in south-western Europe: Implications for occupation of the middle latitudes of Europe", *Quaternary International* 271 (2012), 1–14.

18 Tim D. White, et al., "Pleistocene *Homo sapiens* from Middle Awash, Ethiopia", *Nature* 423 (2003), 742–7.

19 F. McDermott, et al., "Mass spectrometric dates for Israeli Neanderthal/early modern sites", *Nature* 363 (1993), 252–5.

20 John J. Shea, "Transitions or turnovers? Climatically-forced extinctions of *Homo sapiens* and Neanderthals in the East Mediterranean Levant", *Quaternary Science Reviews* 27 (2008), 2,253–70. MIS stands for Marine Isotope Stage. Ocean floor sediments comprise an incomparably detailed and continuous record of climate change extending back in places many millions of years. The main palaeo-climatic indicator is the isotopic composition of the shells of minute marine organisms called foraminifera. Put briefly, these record variations in two types of oxygen in sea-water, and this reflects the prevailing salinity and hence the amount of ice and snow on land: in cold periods, an enormous amount of water is locked up on land as snow and ice sheets, and because these are formed of fresh water, the salinity of the ocean increases slightly. Analysis of cores of ocean floor sediment can reveal these minute changes in salinity, and are divided into marine isotope stages (=MIS). Even-numbered ones denote cold periods, and odd-numbered ones, warm periods when ice sheets melted and retreated. We are currently living in MIS 1; the severest part of the last ice age was MIS 2.

21 Paul Mellars, "Going east: New genetic and archaeological perspectives on the modern human colonization of Eurasia", *Science* 313 (2005), 796–800.

22 Richard G. Klein, "Out of Africa and the evolution of modern behaviour", *Evolutionary Anthropology* 17 (2008), 267–81.

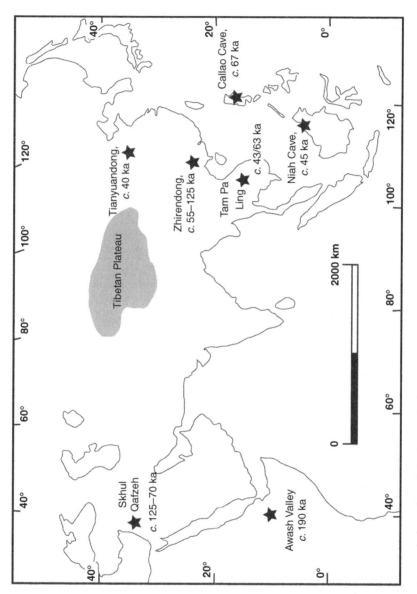

Map 17.2 Sites with the earliest skeletal evidence for *Homo sapiens* in Asia and northeast Africa. Note the absence of any relevant skeletal evidence for *Homo sapiens* between Arabia and Southeast Asia; ka = thousand years ago.

of South and East Asia probably arose from communities that arrived *c.* 50,000–60,000 years ago, and this estimate is consistent with the earliest dates for the arrival of our species in New Guinea and Australia, which would have been conjoined into a giant landmass (along with Tasmania) during the last glaciation when sea levels were lower than today.[23] In Israel, the earliest communities of *Homo sapiens* used a Middle Palaeolithic type of toolkit (that is, one in which cores were shaped by flaking prior to the detachment of the required type of flakes) similar to that used by Neanderthals, and only much later – after perhaps 45,000 years ago – developed an Upper Palaeolithic technology that utilised a large number of blades. In India, it is probable that the earliest immigrant communities of our species used a Middle Stone Age toolkit (roughly equivalent in Africa and India to the Middle Palaeolithic of Europe and Southwest Asia), although so far human skeletal remains have not been found.[24] Southeast Asia presents a very different picture, as the populations that are evidenced there after 40,000–50,000 years ago used a very simple stone technology that nevertheless appears to have been successful in enabling humans to utilise tropical rainforests for the first time.[25]

As with Out of Africa 1, a number of health warnings are necessary over Out of Africa 2. The first is that there is almost no human skeletal evidence from Southwest Asia between 190,000 (when modern humans first appeared in East Africa) and 125,000–70,000 years ago, when they first appear in the Levant, and therefore, *Homo sapiens* may have left Africa before 125,000 years ago. Secondly, there is no human skeletal evidence between the Levant, *c.* 70,000 years ago, and Tam Pa Ling, Laos, *c.* 45,000 years ago and therefore we can only guess when our species first appeared in Arabia and India.[26]

---

23 Vincent McCaulay, et al., "Single, rapid coastal settlement of Asia revealed by analysis of complete mitochondrial genomes", *Science* 308 (2005), 1,034–6; Glenn R. Summerhayes, et al., "Human adaptation and plant use in Highland New Guinea 49,000 to 44,000 years ago", *Science* 330 (2010), 78–81; and Richard G. Roberts, "The human colonisation of Australia: Optical dates of 53,000 and 60,000 years bracket human arrival at Deaf Adder Gorge, Northern Territory", *Quaternary Geochronology (Quaternary Science Reviews)* 13 (1994), 575–83.

24 Michael D. Petraglia, et al., "Middle Paleolithic assemblages from the Indian Subcontinent before and after the Toba Super-eruption", *Science* 317 (2007), 114–16.

25 See Graeme Barker, et al., "The 'human revolution' in lowland tropical Southeast Asia: The antiquity and behavior of anatomically modern humans at Niah Cave (Sarawak, Borneo)", *Journal of Human Evolution* 52 (2007), 243–61.

26 Fabrice Demeter, Laura L. Shackelford, Anne-Marie Bacon, Philippe Duringer, Kira Westaway, Thongsa Sayavongkhamdy, José Braga, Phonephanh Sichanthongtip, Phimmasaeng Khamdalavong, Jean-Luc Ponche, Hong Wang, Craig Lundstrom, Elise Patole-Edoumba, and Anne-Marie Karpoff, "'Anatomically modern human in Southeast Asia (Laos) by 46 ka", *Proceedings of the National Academy of Sciences USA* 109 (2012), 14,375–80.

Thirdly, because those communities of *Homo sapiens* that inhabited the Levant *c.* 125,000 years ago have left no genetic signature in modern populations, it follows that modern humans in South and Southeast Asia may have a deeper antiquity than indicated by genetic studies of modern populations. The greatest impediment to understanding when our species left Africa is the lack of skeletal evidence between the Levant and Southeast Asia before 45,000 years ago, and from Southwest Asia before 125,000 years ago. We may yet discover that our species left Africa before 125,000 years ago, and dispersed across southern Asia before 60,000 years ago.[27]

Dispersals and climatic change

The hominin populations that have inhabited Asia in the past 1.75 million years would have had to respond to numerous cyclical climatic changes that occurred throughout the Pleistocene. These changes occurred primarily because of variations in the earth's orbit, and are often known as Milankovic cycles, after their discoverer. As is now well known, the Early Pleistocene (2.5–0.8 million years ago) was characterised by frequent and usually minor fluctuations in precipitation and temperature, on an average cycle of one every 40,000 years. In the Middle Pleistocene, these fluctuations were much greater, and the last 600,000 years have been dominated by four lengthy and major periods of reduced temperature and precipitation, each lasting up to 100,000 years, and separated by relatively short interglacials that were warmer and moister (see Figure 17.1). In Europe, these cold periods are termed glaciations, and were dominated by the southwards advance of ice caps over Scandinavia and northern Britain. In Asia, ice sheets were never as extensive, and the equivalent of glaciations were periods when the summer monsoon over South, Southeast, and East Asia was severely weakened, leading to major reductions in rainfall. Because the winter monsoon (which drives cold, dry air southwards across these regions) was stronger, temperatures were also considerably cooler than today.

These climatic shifts had profound effects on plant and animal communities, including hominins. In warm, moist periods, hominins and their

---

27 Robin W. Dennell and Michael D. Petraglia, "The dispersal of *Homo sapiens* across southern Asia: How early, how often, how complex?", *Quaternary Sciences Reviews* 47 (2012), 15–22; Robin W. Dennell, "Smoke and mirrors: The fossil record for *Homo sapiens* between Arabia and Australia", in R. W. Dennell and M. Porr (eds.), *Southern Asia, Australia and the Search for Human Origins* (Cambridge: Cambridge University Press. 2014), pp. 33–50.

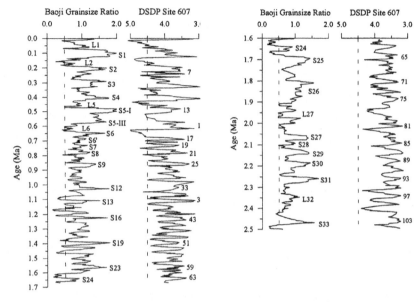

Figure 17.1 The climatic pulse of the Pleistocene. This shows the loess (dust) record from Baoji, central China, and the isotopic record of a sediment core from DSDP (deep-sea drilling program) site 607. Without going into the technical details of each, both show a remarkably similar record of climate change, with numerous low-amplitude changes before 600,000 years ago, and a few major, high-amplitude changes thereafter. The odd numbers on the right of the DSDP record denote periods when the climate was warm and moist, like the present. In the Chinese record, "S" (for example, S16) denotes periods of soil formation, when rainfall was higher, and "L" (for example, L1) denotes dry, cold, and windy periods when the type of wind-blown soil known as loess accumulated. Our ancestors had to cope with a climate that was frequently highly unstable. Source: Tungsheng Liu, Zhonglli Ding, and Nat Rutter, "Comparison of Milankovitch periods between continental loess and deep sea records over the last 2.5 Ma.", *Quaternary Science Reviews* 18 (1999), 1,205–12.

resources could expand northwards and often longitudinally from source populations, and dispersals into neighbouring regions were often feasible: when these happened, populations could interbreed. Because conditions were favourable, population levels and densities could rise.[28] In cold, dry periods, populations had to retreat or become locally extinct, and surviving ones were confined to refugia. These fluctuations therefore shape the

---

28 Robin W. Dennell, María Martinón-Torres, and José María Bermudez de Castro, "Hominin variability, climatic instability and population demography in Middle Pleistocene Europe", *Quaternary Science Reviews* 30 (2011), 1,511–24.

Palaeolithic settlement of Asia: 'The early hominin settlement of Asia is. . .a repeated theme of regional expansion and contraction, colonisation and abandonment, integration and isolation as rainfall increased or decreased. When viewed in closer detail. . .much of the Asian Early Palaeolithic record is likely to comprise regional discontinuities and local extinctions, rather than long-term continuity and permanent residence.'[29] Figure 17.2 provides a simple summary of these types of population dynamics.

This type of climatically driven dispersal is best evidenced at the northern limits of the hominin range across the Eurasian landmass, from western Europe to northern China. One excellent example comes from Tajikistan in Central Asia, which has a long sequence of Palaeolithic sites from the last 900,000 years. Investigations showed that Palaeolithic occupation occurred only during warm, moist periods when soils could develop; in cold, dry periods, when dust storms were common and enormous deposits of loess (wind-blown dust) accumulated, hominins either retreated southwards or became extinct (see Figure 17.3).[30] A similar pattern of expansion and contraction is evident in Britain and western Europe, and likely also in north China. This type of movement is not surprising as hominins are climatically sensitive, especially to lengthy sub-freezing winters.[31]

In addition to Milankovic cycles of glacial–interglacial conditions (or their equivalent in monsoon-dominated regions), there were also shorter periods of abrupt climatic change, the reasons for which remain poorly known. In glacial periods, the most important are known as Heinrich events, when conditions suddenly became considerably colder for a few centuries or millennia. These must have had profound effects on hominin populations, but because most Palaeolithic sites >50,000 years old cannot be dated to within a margin of error of less than 5,000 or even 10,000 years, they cannot be correlated to these short-term events. However, it is sometimes possible to see the effects of short term climatic change on populations from the last 30,000 years. One excellent example is late glacial western Europe. Here,

29 Robin W. Dennell, *The Palaeolithic Settlement of Asia* (Cambridge: Cambridge University Press, 2009).
30 Vadim A. Ranov, "The 'Loessic Palaeolithic' in South Tajikistan, Central Asia: Its industries, chronology and correlation", *Quaternary Science Reviews* 14 (1995), 731–45.
31 Dennell, Martinón-Torres, and Bermudez de Castro, "Hominin variability"; Robin W. Dennell, "The Nihewan Basin of North China in the Early Pleistocene – Continuous and flourishing, or discontinuous, infrequent and ephemeral occupation?", *Quaternary International* 295 (2012), 223–36; and S. A. G. Leroy, K. Arpe, and U. Mikolaiewicz, "Vegetation context and climatic limits of the Early Pleistocene hominin dispersal in Europe", *Quaternary Science Reviews* 30 (2011), 1,448–63.

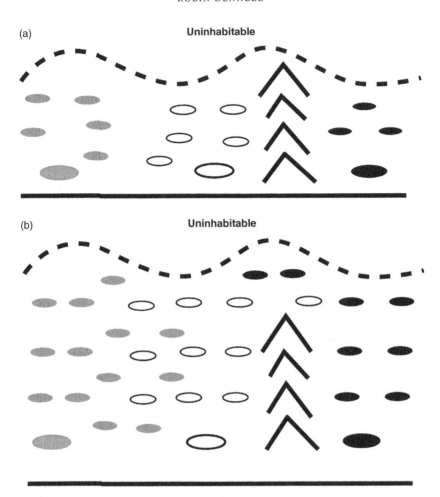

Figure 17.2 Summary model of population dynamics under the climatic shifts of the Pleistocene in continental Asia. This simple model envisages three populations, one of which is separated from the others by a mountain range. In (a), populations are confined to a small number of refugia during the equivalent of a glacial maximum, when conditions were much colder and drier than today. During these periods, populations are likely to have been at their lowest levels, and isolated from each other. In (b), populations are able to disperse northwards during the equivalent of an interglacial, when the climate was similar to today's. Under such conditions, they are also likely to have overlapped in parts of their range, thereby allowing exchange of mates, ideas, and techniques; and even in this case, some exchange between populations formerly isolated by a mountain range. The Tajik record (see Figure 17.3) provides a good example of this type of "regional expansion and contraction, colonisation and abandonment, integration and isolation as rainfall increased or decreased" (Dennell, *The Palaeolithic Settlement of Asia*, Cambridge: Cambridge University Press, 2009) in Central Asia.

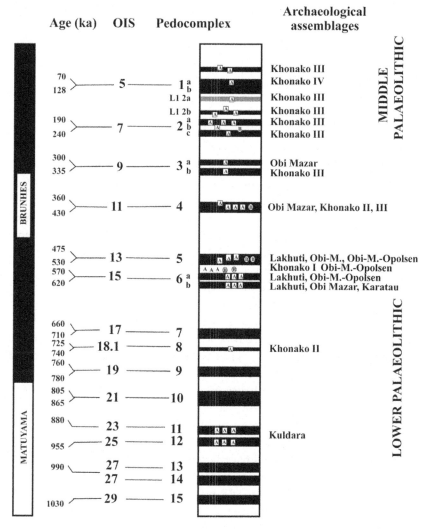

Figure 17.3 The Tajik loess and palaeosol record (reprinted from *Quaternary Science Reviews*, 18 (10–11), Tungsheng Liu, Zhongli Ding, and Rutter, N., 'Comparison of Milankovitch periods between continental loess and deep sea records over the last 2.5 Ma.', pp. 1205–12, copyright 1999, with permission from Elsevier). Black bars denote interglacials, when soils formed; intervening white parts denote colder and drier periods when loess (wind-blown) dust was deposited. As is clear, hominins were present only during periods of soil formation. It was likely that this part of Central Asia was depopulated in cold, dry periods.

humans moved rapidly northwards from their refugia in southern Europe when the ice sheets began to contract after *c.* 15,000 years ago. Following a sudden re-advance of the ice sheets *c.* 12,000 years ago, populations once again retreated southwards, and the re-colonisation of northern Europe was delayed for two millennia.[32]

Dispersals, evolutionary change, and innovation

Hominins differ from other mammals in the extent of their anatomical changes, and also in their capacity for cultural change. The most obvious evolutionary change in the hominin lineage is the increase in brain size over the last 2 million years, from *c.* 600–750 cc. at Dmanisi to 1,200–1,500 cc. in Neanderthals and *Homo sapiens*. This increase in brain size was accompanied by a shortening of the gut, and was probably caused by the way hominins shifted towards carnivory and the regular intake of high-quality protein: this reduced the need for a long digestive tract suitable for processing low-quality plant foods, and under-pinned the expansion of energetically expensive brain tissue.[33] As noted above, stone tools would have given hominins an edge over their competitors in enabling them to deflesh carcasses and extract marrow; these skills in turn also depend upon a large brain. In this instance, carnivory and tool-making may have been the impetus behind the earliest dispersals of our genus from Africa.

As hominin brains became larger, so the amount of information that they could store and process increased. Brain size in primates is correlated with group size, as large social groups involve greater skills of communication (including language) and negotiation. As group size increased, the social landscapes of hominins would have become larger and more complex, and included factors such as mapping the location of scarce resources (such as high-quality stone), and the developing exchange networks. In short, the development of a 'social brain' would have widened the potential scope for hominins to disperse into new types of environments, or to utilise them more effectively.[34]

---

32 Clive Gamble, et al., "Climate change and evolving human diversity in Europe during the last glacial", *Philosophical Transactions of the Royal Society, London* 359 (2004), 243–54.

33 Leslie C. Aiello and Peter Wheeler, "The expensive tissue hypothesis", *Current Anthropology* 36 (1995), 199–222.

34 Andrei E. Dodonov and L. L. Baiguzina, "Loess stratigraphy of Central Asia: Palaeoclimatic and palaeoenvironmental aspects", *Quaternary Science Reviews* 14 (1995), 707–20; and Robin I. M. Dunbar, "The social brain: Mind, language, and society in evolutionary perspective", *Annual Review of Anthropology* 32 (2003), 163–81.

The ability to disperse into new types of environments in Asia is most pronounced for *Homo sapiens* in the last 50,000 years. For over a million years, the hominin range did not increase significantly. However, in the last 50,000–60,000 years, several new type of environments were colonised for the first time. The most striking in continental Asia is the colonisation of Siberia, which probably began *c.* 40,000–50,000 years ago, and which brought humans to the Arctic Ocean and ultimately to North America via the Bering landbridge *c.* 15,000 years ago.[35] As major an event was the colonisation of the Australian landmass in the last 50,000–60,000 years, which would have required the use of boats or rafts with paddles and sails, as well as some navigational abilities. The development of navigational skills also led to the colonisation of Japan *c.* 40,000 years ago and outlying islands such as Okinawa (30,000 years ago) and the Solomon Islands (30,000 years ago). It is also probable that the tropical rainforests of Southeast Asia were colonised in the last 40,000–50,000 years.[36] And finally, at the end of the Pleistocene, the Tibetan Plateau, with an average altitude of 5,000 m above sea level, was also settled by humans.[37]

The Palaeolithic history of Asia (and the Eurasian landmass generally) has been shaped by different types of dispersals, operating at different spatial and temporal scales and in a wide variety of environments. Rather than studying the Stone Age settlement of Asia in terms of different types of artefact assemblages, it is probably more fruitful to study how its inhabitants dispersed in response to different opportunities and challenges at different levels of physical and mental ability over the last 1.8 million years.

FURTHER READING

Aiello, Leslie C., and Peter Wheeler, 'The expensive tissue hypothesis', *Current Anthropology* 36 (1995), 199–222.
Bar-Yosef, Ofer, 'Early colonizations and cultural continuities in the Lower Palaeolithic of western Eurasia', in Ravi Korisettar and Michael Petraglia (eds.), *Early Human*

---

35 Ted Goebell, "Pleistocene human colonization of Siberia and peopling of the Americas: An ecological approach", *Evolutionary Anthropology* 8 (1999), 208–27. An alternative hypothesis is that North America was colonised from western Europe by groups that lived along the margins of the Atlantic sea ice. Dennis J. Stanford and Bruce A. Bradley, *Across Atlantic Ice: The Origins of America's Clovis Culture* (Berkeley: University of California Press, 2012).
36 Barker, *et al.*, "'Human revolution' in lowland tropical Southeast Asia".
37 P. Jeffrey Brantingham, et al., "A short chronology for the peopling of the Tibetan Plateau", *Developments in Quaternary Sciences* 9 (2007), 129–50.

Behavior in Global Context: The Rise and Diversity of the Lower Palaeolithic Record, London: Routledge, 1998, pp. 221–79.

Barker, Graeme, et al., 'The "human revolution" in lowland tropical Southeast Asia: The antiquity and behavior of anatomically modern humans at Niah Cave (Sarawak, Borneo)', *Journal of Human Evolution* 52 (2007), 243–61.

Brantingham, P. Jeffrey, et al., 'A short chronology for the peopling of the Tibetan Plateau', *Developments in Quaternary Sciences* 9 (2007), 129–50.

Carbonell, Eudald, et al., 'The first hominin of Europe', *Nature* 452 (2008), 465–9.

Demeter, Fabrice, Laura L. Shackelford, Anne-Marie Bacon, Philippe Duringer, Kira Westaway, Thongsa Sayavongkhamdy, José Braga, Phonephanh Sichanthongtip, Phimmasaeng Khamdalavong, Jean-Luc Ponche, Hong Wang, Craig Lundstrom, Elise Patole-Edoumba, and Anne-Marie Karpoff, 'Anatomically modern human in Southeast Asia (Laos) by 46 ka', *Proceedings of the National Academy of Sciences USA* 109 (2012), 14,375–80.

Dennell, Robin W., 'The Nihewan Basin of North China in the Early Pleistocene – Continuous and flourishing, or discontinuous, infrequent and ephemeral occupation?', *Quaternary International* 295 (2012), 223–36.

The Palaeolithic Settlement of Asia, Cambridge: Cambridge University Press, 2009.

Dennell, Robin W., and Michael D. Petraglia, 'The dispersal of *Homo sapiens* across southern Asia: How early, how often, how complex?', *Quaternary Sciences Reviews* 47 (2012), 15–22.

Dennell, Robin W., and M. Porr (eds.), *Southern Asia, Australia and the Search for Human Origins*, Cambridge: Cambridge University Press, 2014.

Dennell, Robin W., and Wil Roebroeks, 'An Asian perspective on early human dispersal from Africa', *Nature* 438 (2005), 1,099–104.

Dennell, Robin W., María Martinón-Torres, and José María Bermudez de Castro, 'Hominin variability, climatic instability and population demography in Middle Pleistocene Europe', *Quaternary Science Reviews* 30 (2011), 1,511–24.

Dodonov, Andrei E., *Quaternary of Middle Asia: Stratigraphy, Correlation and Paleogeography*, Moscow: Geos, 2002.

Dodonov, Andrei E., and L. L. Baiguzina, 'Loess stratigraphy of Central Asia: Palaeoclimatic and palaeoenvironmental aspects', *Quaternary Science Reviews* 14 (1995), 707–20.

Dunbar, Robin I. M., 'The social brain: Mind, language, and society in evolutionary perspective', *Annual Review of Anthropology* 32 (2003), 163–81.

Ferring, Reid, Oriol Oms, Jordi Agusti, Francesco Berna, Medea Nioradze, Teona Shelia, Martha Tappen, Abesalom Vekua, David Zhvania, and David Lorkipanidze, 'Earliest human occupations at Dmanisi (Georgian Caucasus) dated to 1.85–1.78 Ma.', *Proceedings of the National Academy of Sciences USA* 108 (2011), 10,432–6.

Gabunia, Leo, et al., 'Earliest Pleistocene hominid cranial remains from Dmanisi, Republic of Georgia: Taxonomy, geological setting, and age', *Science* 288 (2000), 1,019–25.

Gamble, Clive, et al., 'Climate change and evolving human diversity in Europe during the last glacial', *Philosophical Transactions of the Royal Society, London* 359 (2004), 243–54.

Goebell, Ted, 'Pleistocene human colonization of Siberia and peopling of the Americas: An ecological approach', *Evolutionary Anthropology* 8 (1999), 208–27.

Goren-Inbar, Naama, et al., 'Pleistocene milestones on the Out-of-Africa corridor at Gesher Ya'aqov, Israel', *Science* 289 (2000), 944–7.

Klein, Richard G., 'Out of Africa and the evolution of modern behaviour', *Evolutionary Anthropology* 17 (2008), 267–81.

Larick, Roy, et al., 'Early Pleistocene ^{40}Ar/^{39}Ar ages for Bapang Formation hominins, Central Jawa, Indonesia', *Proceedings of the National Academy of Sciences of the USA* 98 (2001), 4,866–71.

Lepre, Christopher J., Hélène Roche, Dennis V. Kent, Sonia Harmand, Rhonda L. Quinn, Jean-Philippe Brugal, Pierre-Jean Texier, Arnaud Lenoble, and Craig S. Feibel, 'An earlier origin for the Acheulian', *Nature* 44 (2011), 82–5.

Leroy, S. A. G., K. Arpe, and U. Mikolaiewicz, 'Vegetation context and climatic limits of the Early Pleistocene hominin dispersal in Europe', *Quaternary Science Reviews* 30 (2011), 1,448–63.

Liu, Tungsheng, Zhonglli Ding, and Nat Rutter, 'Comparison of Milankovitch periods between continental loess and deep sea records over the last 2.5 Ma.', *Quaternary Science Reviews* 18 (1999), 1,205–12.

Lordkipanidze, David, et al., 'Postcranial evidence from early *Homo* from Dmanisi, Georgia', *Nature* 449 (2007), 305–10.

Lumley, Henry de, et al., 'Les industries lithiques préoldowayennes du début du Pléisto-cène inférieur du site de Dmanissi en Géorgie', *L'Anthropologie* 109 (2005), 1–182.

McCaulay, Vincent, et al., 'Single, rapid coastal settlement of Asia revealed by analysis of complete mitochondrial genomes', *Science* 308 (2005), 1,034–6.

McDermott, F., et al., 'Mass spectrometric dates for Israeli Neanderthal/early modern sites', *Nature* 363 (1993), 252–5.

McDonald, Glen, *Biogeography: Space, Time and Life*, New York: John Wiley & Sons, Inc., 2003.

McDonald, Katharine, María Martinón-Torres, Robin W. Dennell, and José María Bermu-dez de Castro, 'Discontinuity in the record for hominin occupation in south-western Europe: Implications for occupation of the middle latitudes of Europe', *Quaternary International* 271 (2012), 1–14.

Mellars, Paul, 'Going east: New genetic and archaeological perspectives on the modern human colonization of Eurasia', *Science* 313 (2005), 796–800.

Pappu, Shanti, Yanni Gunnell, Kumar Aklilesh, Régis Braucher, Maurice Taieb, François Demory, and Nicolas Thouveny, 'Early Pleistocene presence of Acheulian hominins in South India', *Science* 331 (2011), 1,596–99.

Petraglia, Michael D., et al., 'Middle Paleolithic assemblages from the Indian Subcontinent before and after the Toba Super-eruption', *Science* 317 (2007), 114–16.

Pettitt, Paul, 'The rise of modern humans', in Chris Scarre (ed.), *The Human Past*, London: Thames & Hudson, Ltd., 2005, pp. 127–73.

Presnyakov, Sergey L., Elena V. Belyaeva, V. P. Lyubin, N. V. Rodionov, A. V. Antonov, A. K. Saltykova, Natalia G. Berezhnaya, and S. A. Sergeev, 'Age of the earliest Paleolithic sites in the northern part of the Armenian Highland by SHRIMP-II U–Pb geochronology of zircons from volcanic ashes', *Gondwana Research* 21 (2012), 928–38.

Ranov, Vadim A., 'The "Loessic Palaeolithic" in South Tadjikistan, Central Asia: Its industries, chronology and correlation', *Quaternary Science Reviews* 14 (1995), 731–45.

Ranov, Vadim A., and Andrei E. Dodonov, 'Small instruments of the Lower Palaeolithic site Kuldara and their geoarchaeological meaning', in J. M. Burdukiewicz and

A. Ronen (eds.), *Lower Palaeolithic Small Tools in Europe and Asia*, Oxford: British Archaeological Reports (International Series) 1,115, 2003, pp. 133–47.

Rightmire, G. Philip, David Lordkipanidze, and Abesalom Vekua, 'Anatomical descriptions, comparative studies and evolutionary significance of the hominin skulls from Dmanisi, Republic of Georgia', *Journal of Human Evolution* 50 (2006), 115–41.

Roberts, Richard G., et al., 'The human colonisation of Australia: Optical dates of 53,000 and 60,000 years bracket human arrival at Deaf Adder Gorge, Northern Territory', *Quaternary Geochronology (Quaternary Science Reviews)* 13 (1994), 575–83.

Shea, John J., 'Transitions or turnovers? Climatically-forced extinctions of *Homo sapiens* and Neanderthals in the East Mediterranean Levant', *Quaternary Science Reviews* 27 (2008), 2,253–70.

Stanford, Dennis J., and Bruce A. Bradley, *Across Atlantic Ice: The Origins of America's Clovis Culture*, Berkeley: University of California Press, 2012.

Summerhayes, Glenn R., et al., 'Human adaptation and plant use in Highland New Guinea 49,000 to 44,000 years ago', *Science* 330 (2010), 78–81.

White, Tim D., et al., 'Pleistocene *Homo sapiens* from Middle Awash, Ethiopia', *Nature* 423 (2003), 742–7.

Zhu, R. X., et al., 'New evidence on the earliest human presence at high northern latitudes in northeast Asia', *Nature* 431 (2004), 559–62.

18

The Pleistocene colonization and occupation of Australasia

PETER HISCOCK

The ice-age discovery and settlement of Australasia was one of the remarkable stories in the global dispersion of modern humans. Genetic, archaeological and environmental evidence combine to yield an image of the arrival more than 50,000 years ago of migrating groups who had moved out of Africa and through southern or central Asia. Subsequent physical, social and economic adjustments of human groups over time in the varied environments of Australasia resulted in cultural diversification. Tracing the colonization and cultural radiation of humans in Australasia provides unique insights into the earliest human history in this region of the world.

The arrival: 75,000–50,000 years ago

Australasia was colonized by groups of *Homo sapiens* whose ancestors had migrated out of Africa many millennia earlier. The pathways taken by migrating human groups throughout this journey, and the motives driving successive generations to expand over such immense space, have been difficult to establish, but questions about the dispersal process are clarified by the Australian evidence. At the time of colonization cooler global temperatures resulted in substantial quantities of water being locked in glaciers in the Northern Hemisphere and the consequent lower sea levels exposed now submerged land, linking mainland Australia with the large islands of Tasmania to the south and New Guinea to the north. This palaeo-continent is called Sahul, and it was always separated from the palaeo-landmass of peninsula southeast Asia, called Sunda, by a series of deep water passages. The rate of migration across these barriers, and the social and economic systems that facilitated the spread of people from Africa, have been much debated.

Map 18.1 Pleistocene continent of Australia.

Much of the archaeological evidence for the entrance of people into the Australasian region has reflected chronological models developed from genetic analyses. Two models of the migration to Australia have been grounded in genetic patterns: one proposing a 'late dispersal' while the second suggests a relatively 'early dispersal'. Until recently the late dispersal proposition was dominant, positing that humans had exited Africa little more than 60,000–65,000 years ago, based on the estimated time from the common ancestor of the MtDNA haplogroups L3 (found in Africa) and the descendant M/N groups (found outside Africa). Archaeologists and geneticists alike have used this age estimate to constrain the departure of modern humans, and consequently many interpretations have been built on this relatively late date for the initiation of the global dispersion of humans from Africa.[1]

1 Paul Mellars, 'Going east: New genetic and archaeological perspectives on the modern human colonization of Eurasia', *Science* 313 (2006), 796–800; and Pedro Soares, Farida Alshamali, Joana B. Pereira, Verónica Fernandes, Nuno M. Silva, Carla Alfonso, Marta D. Costa, Eliska Musilová, Vincent Macaulay, Martin B. Richards, Viktor Černý and

That 'late dispersal' model had several implications for reconstructions of the passage of *Homo sapiens* to Australia. For example, it obliged its proponents to hypothesize that groups of *Homo sapiens* had moved out of Africa on multiple occasions between 120,000 and 70,000 years ago.[2] Since skeletons of modern humans were present in the Middle East substantially before 90,000 years BP a much later genetic estimate for the movement out of Africa of groups whose descendants are represented in living non-African populations required that archaeologists view those skeletons as a false start: a small excursion beyond Africa of humans who then became extinct or retreated back into Africa.

Most importantly, a late dispersion chronology required that human populations had spread from Africa to Australia in a remarkably short amount of time. A rapid migration has commonly been explained by positing three characteristics of the geographic expansion. First, it has been common to think of populations moving from Africa to Sahul in a direct fashion, along the Southern Arc of Dispersal: the southern coast of south Asia and southeast Asia and straight into northwestern portions of Sahul. Second, archaeologists have argued that populations expanding on that arc had economies that were narrowly focused on marine resources and that this facilitated rapid move-ments.[3] For instance O'Connell and Allen hypothesized that migrating groups focused on resources such as molluscs that were readily depleted but supported large population sizes, thereby committing people to continue their migration in search of unexploited food supplies.[4] Such a process might have driven fast colonization of coastlines all the way to Sahul. Third, O'Connell and Allen reject dates for many Australian and New Guinean sites that are claimed to be older than 45,000 years and advocate a relatively late colonization, thereby providing slightly more time for the dispersal process.[5] Together these propositions provide a coherent hypothesis

Luísa Pereira, 'The expansion of mtDNA haplogroup L3 within and out of Africa', *Molecular Biology and Evolution* 29 (2011), 915–27.

2 Rainer Grün, C. Stringer, F. McDermott, R. Nathan, N. Porat, S. Robertson, L. Taylor, G. Mortimer, Stephen Eggins and M. Mcculloch, 'U-series and ESR analyses of bones and teeth relating to the human burials from Skhul', *Journal of Human Evolution* 49 (2005), 316–34; and Jeffrey I. Rose, Vitaly I. Usik, Anthony E. Marks, Yamandu H. Hilbert, Christopher S. Galletti, *et al.*, 'The Nubian Complex of Dhofar, Oman: An African Middle Stone Age industry in Southern Arabia', *PLoS ONE* 6 (2011).

3 Mellars, 'Going east'.

4 James F. O'Connell and Jim Allen, 'The Restaurant at the End of the Universe: Modelling the colonization of Sahul', *Australian Archaeology* 74 (2012), 5–17.

5 James F. O'Connell and Jim Allen, 'Dating the colonization of Sahul (Pleistocene Australia – New Guinea): A review of recent research', *Journal of Archaeological Science* 31 (2004), 835–53.

depicting the timing and mechanism of a rapid dispersal from Africa to Australia, a movement propelled and given direction by the structure of coastal geography and early foraging focus on specific marine foods. However, mounting archaeological and genetic evidence indicates the human passage to Australasia was slower and far more complex than is allowed in such rapid dispersal models.

The plausibility of the emerging alternative, an 'early dispersal' model, has been increased by the demonstration that the human mutation rates had been significantly overstated and that consequently the antiquity of the movement of *Homo sapiens* out of Africa has been significantly under-estimated.[6] Calculating time using twenty-five years as the typical generational span, the revised mutation rate indicates that the separation of Africans and non-Africans, and by implication the geographical separation created by migration from Africa, began about 120,000 years ago. This far earlier estimate means that early sapiens skeletons outside Africa are most likely not anomalous and mark the passage of dispersing humans rather than failed excursions. Genetic evidence also indicates that the people who colonized Australia, the ancestors of Australian Aboriginal people, were part of an early dispersal of *Homo sapiens* across south and eastern Asia.[7]

Ancestral Australasian populations split from ancestral Eurasian populations, probably more than 75,000 years ago, as a result of both adaptations / drift and through hybridization with archaic hominids that had left Africa previously.[8] In modern Australian Aboriginal people there are a substantial number of genes from Denisovan hominids, a sister group of hominids who were distantly related to Neandertals and evolved from a common ancestor (perhaps *Homo heidelbergensis*) who had left Africa more than 500,000–600,000 years ago. These genes reveal inter-breeding between dispersing humans and Denisovans. While the Denisovans are known only from northeast-central Asia, Stewart and Stringer hypothesize a southwards depression of their range during the colder periods, which brought them in contact with colonizing *Homo sapiens* populations.[9] Nevertheless there is no reason to think the Denisovan distribution extended across Asia, and so there is every

6 Aylwyn Scally and Richard Durbin, 'Revising the human mutation rate: Implications for understanding human evolution', *Nature Reviews Genetics* 13 (2012), 745–53.

7 Morten Rasmussen, Xiaosen Guo, *et al.*, 'An Aboriginal Australian genome reveals separate human dispersals into Asia', *Science* 334 (2011), 94–8.

8 Svante Sankararaman, Nick Patterson, Heng Li, Svante Paabo and David Reich, 'The date of interbreeding between Neandertals and modern humans', *PLoS Genetics* 8 (2012).

9 J. R. Stewart and C. B. Stringer, 'Human evolution out of Africa: The role of refugia and climate change', *Science* 335 (2012), 1,317–21.

likelihood that dispersing humans whose descendants reached Australasia: (1) spread far from the southern coastline of Asia and therefore were not dependent on only marine foods, and (2) moved slowly and indirectly towards Australia, expanding across territories already occupied by culture-bearing hominids. Furthermore, since those genes are absent from modern East Asian populations it seems that after the original expansions of hybridized human population into southeast Asia and Sahul, and subsequent to the extinction of Denisovans, later waves of *Homo sapiens* moved into the Asia region. And because the same lineages are found in ancient and modern DNA within Australia we know that no population replacement occurred there (see below). Hence the genetic evidence indicates that colonization of Australia was carried out by some of the initial populations dispersing eastwards across the Old World.

Archaeological evidence dates the arrival of humans in Australia at between 50,000 and 60,000 years ago, an antiquity that is readily accounted for through an 'early dispersal' model in which ancestral groups left Africa more than forty millennia earlier. The appearance of humans in the landscape of northern Australia is documented in the rock shelters of western Arnhem Land. At the Malakunanja II shelter the lowest artefacts were in sands estimated, by luminescence analysis of associated sand grains, to be 50,000 and 60,000 years old. At Nauwalabila, the lowest artefacts were estimated to be between 53,500 and 67,000 years old.[10] Critiques of these associations, and suggestions that all of the lowest artefacts have moved down vertically through the deposit, overlook stratigraphic evidence in Malakunanja II for a small pit dug more than 40,000 years ago, and this cannot have been vertically displaced.[11] Humans were occupying these sites more than 45,000–50,000 years ago, and this represents a minimum date for the occupation of Sahul.[12] Sites with a similar antiquity are found around Sahul, confirming the widespread presence of people across the continent at or not long after 50,000 years ago and suggesting that the movement of people into different niches was rapid. For instance, in central Australia open sites such as Parnkupirti and cave sites such as Puritjarra were occupied in excess of 40,000–45,000 years ago; in the southwest the Devil's Lair cave

10 Richard G. Roberts, Rhys Jones and M. A. Smith, 'Optical dating at Deaf Adder Gorge, Northern Territory, indicates human occupation between 53,000 and 60,000 years ago', *Australian Archaeology* 37 (1993), 58–9.
11 O'Connell and Allen, 'Dating the colonization of Sahul'.
12 Peter Hiscock, *Archaeology of Ancient Australia* (London: Routledge, 2008).

was occupied about 46,000–47,000 years ago, and in southeastern Australia debris from human occupation was present at Lake Mungo at least 45,000–50,000 years ago.[13] It may have taken some time for population levels to grow to a point where material indicators of human activity became sufficiently common that they can still be found by archaeologists today, and hence humans may have been present in landscapes for a prolonged period before they become archaeologically visible at about 50,000 years ago. However, archaeologists currently have no reliable indications of an earlier human presence and it is the sites dating from the period 45,000–55,000 years ago that appear to record the expansion of people across the continent.

Dispersion and growth of regionality: 50,000–35,000 years ago

Our record of the physical form of people who dispersed across Sahul comes principally from the skeletons that have been recovered from the southeast. Human skeletons dating back about 43,000 years have been preserved at Lake Mungo. These remains are the visible indication of the early and widespread settlement of the continent soon after colonization. They also provide a remarkable insight into physical characteristics of the people dispersing into the new environments. A key example is the body of the individual labelled WLH3. We cannot tell if this was a male or female, but they were an older adult with osteoarthritis in the vertebrae and right arm, and teeth worn down so much that the pulp cavities were exposed. The head of WLH3 was spherically shaped, with a high forehead and moderately thin cranial bones; the face was relatively flat and above the eye sockets there was only a slight thickening of bone along the supraorbital ridge, giving it a

---

13 Peter Veth, Michael Smith and James M. Bowler, et al., 'Excavations at Parnkupirti, Lake Gregory, Great Sandy Desert: OSL ages for occupation before the Last Glacial Maximum', *Australian Archaeology* 69 (2009), 1–10; Mike A. Smith, Michael I. Bird, Charles S. M. Turney, L. Keith Fifield, G. M. Santos, P. A. Hausladen and M. L. di Tada, 'New ABOX AMS-14C ages remove dating anomalies at Puritjarra rock shelter', *Australian Archaeology* 53 (2001), 45–7; Charles S. M. Turney, Michael I. Bird, L. Keith Fifield, Richard G. Roberts, Mike Smith and Charles E. Dortch, et al., 'Early human occupation at Devil's Lair, southwestern Australia, 50,000 years ago', *Quaternary Research* 55 (2001), 3–13; and James M. Bowler, Harvey Johnston, Jon Olley, John Prescott, Richard G. Roberts, Wilfred Shawcross and Nigel A. Spooner, 'New ages for human occupation and climatic change at Lake Mungo, Australia', *Nature* 421 (2003), 837–40.

modern appearance.[14] Ancient mtDNA has been extracted from this skeleton, and although there have been some concerns about the extent of post-mortem destruction of the DNA and the chance of contamination, the results offer clear evidence that WLH3 was from a distinctive ancient Aboriginal lineage.[15] This individual was an ancestor of modern Australian Aboriginals. The mtDNA sequences of WLH3 are still known in living people, showing that those ancient lineages still exist. This demonstrates that after the colonization there were no substantial later migrations into Australia during prehistory, and certainly the founding populations were never replaced by later incoming populations.[16] This outcome reflects the extent to which the colonizing population grew in size as it progressively occupied each part of the continent, until the overall population was very large; small groups who subsequently arrived would not have had much impact on the gene pool across the continent.[17] The Sahul mtDNA evidence is consistent with a single colonization event followed by a long period of genetic isolation. Physical and cultural variation evident in the Australian archaeological, historical and biological records emerged largely from adaptations to social and physical environments within the continent.

WLH3 was buried at Lake Mungo in southern Australia after his/her ancestors had gradually spread from landing points along the northern coast. The dispersion of humans across Australia probably began shortly after humans arrived on the shores of the continent. Even acknowledging the ambiguity created by uncertainties in radiometric dating techniques the minimum antiquity for sites in many portions of Australia is little different. As described above, the earliest sites in Arnhem Land show evidence for

14 S. G. Webb, *The Willandra Lakes Hominids* (Canberra: Department of Prehistory, Australian National University, 1989); and David W. Cameron and Colin P. Groves, *Bones, Stones and Molecules: 'Out of Africa' and Human Origins* (Sydney: Academic Press, 2004).

15 Gregory Adcock, Elizabeth Dennis, Simon Easteal, et al., 'Mitochondrial DNA sequences in ancient Australians: Implications for modern human origins', *Proceedings of the National Academy of Science* 98 (2001), 537–42; and Peter Brown, *Peter Brown's Australian and Asian Palaeoanthropology*, accessed 20 February 2013, www personal.une. edu.au/~pbrown3/palaeo.html.

16 A. Cooper, A. Rambaut, V. Macaulay, E. Willerslev, J. Hansen and C. Stringer, 'Human origins and ancient human DNA', *Science* 292 (2001), 1,655–6; Gabriel Gutiérrez, Diego Sanchez and Antonio Marin, 'A reanalysis of the ancient mitochondrial DNA sequences recovered from Neandertal bones', *Molecular Biological Evolution* 19 (2002), 1,359–66; and Georgi Hudjashov, Toomas Kivisild, Peter A. Underhill, et al., 'Revealing the prehistoric settlement of Australia by Y chromosome and mtDNA analysis', *Proceedings of the National Academy of Sciences* 104 (2007), 8,726–30.

17 Colin Pardoe, 'Becoming Australian: Evolutionary processes and biological variation from ancient to modern times', *Before Farming* 1 (2006), article 4.

occupation about 50,000–60,000 years ago and archaeological sites further south across mainland Australia and to the northeast in New Guinea have evidence of initial occupation dating to more than 45,000 years ago. This evidence documents human settlement of many ecosystems: in sandy deserts (Puritjarra), rocky deserts (Allen's Cave), semi-arid grasslands (Cuddie Springs), tropical savannah (Malakunanja), tropical woodland (Ngarrabull-gan), tropical coasts (Mandu Mandu Creek), and southern alpine uplands (Parmerpar Meethaner).[18] *Homo sapiens* dispersed across the accessible portions of the continent, settling multiple different environments, but did not penetrate locations surrounded by substantial geographical barriers such as Bass Strait. From before 50,000 years ago the colonizing population was not restricted to any specific environment, or to the coastal margins. Settlers entering each environment had flexible and adjustable economic systems and this, combined with expanding populations, created the capacity to occupy the diversity of environments within the Sahul landmass. Economic strategies may have been transformed early in the colonizing process following humanly induced changes to the environment of Sahul.

The expansion of people across all of these different environments is likely to have been facilitated by population increase. While genetic studies suggest early population growth this has been difficult to see in the archaeological record. The abundance of radiocarbon age-estimates has been used as a measure of demographic trends, on the presumption that dated charcoal comes from hearths and that there is some fixed relationship between hearths and number of people. The demographic curve proposed implied minimal growth until recent millennia, a pattern that is not congruent with genetic evidence.[19] It is likely, however, that few early hearths were preserved, so the carbon record has decayed, and is therefore insensitive to the demographic processes that may have underpinned the dispersion and settlement of people across Australia.

A much debated, but largely unresolved, question about this initial period of settlement is whether the appearance of human hunters had a significant impact on Australasian environments. One focus of research into this question is whether the humans dispersing across Australia were an agent causing the extinction of animal species. Fossil bones show that a suite of very large animals had lived in Australia at some time prior to the arrival of humans:

---

18 See Hiscock, *Archaeology of Ancient Australia*.
19 Alan. N. Williams, 'A new population curve for prehistoric Australia', *Proceedings of the Royal Society B* 280 (2013), 20130486.

giant kangaroos (such as *Macropus rufus* and *Macropus giganteus titan*) and giant wombat (*Phascolonus gigas*), tall flightless birds (*Genyornis sp.*), four-legged marsupial browsers and grazers the same size as some species of hippopotamus and rhinoceros (such as *Diprotodon optatum*, *Zygomaturus sp.*, *Palorchestes sp.*). In island landscapes such as New Zealand there is a repeated pattern of human hunters entering the environment for the first time, targeting and over-exploiting large animals to such an extent that human predation was a significant contributor to the extinction of species. Since in Australia some studies found a broad coincidence between the time at which species of large marsupials disappeared and the time that humans arrived, it seems likely that the human colonization of Australia might have triggered a trophic collapse in which particular kinds of animals were driven to extinction.[20] If the early dispersal model is correct, as is likely, and *Homo sapiens* has spread from Africa across Eurasia exploiting a great diversity of animal resources in varied niches, then the humans who arrived in Sahul were the descendants of many generations of accomplished and adaptable hunters. As skilful predators whose hunting behaviours were unfamiliar to marsupial prey the dispersing humans no doubt had the capacity to reduce the viability of vulnerable species, especially if hunters targeted the young of animals that reproduced slowly and/or if the prey species were limited in distribution and predictable in movement such as being tethered to rare resources.[21]

However, archaeologists in Australia have never found killing sites where large extinct animals were killed and their bodies butchered in preparation for transport of the meat back to campsites. This is curious because in other lands, most notably the Americas and New Zealand, kill sites have been found in abundance during periods in which hunters targeted large game. Perhaps there is a minimal archaeological signature of early hunting because the extinction process occurred very quickly and because it was long ago, diminishing the chance of bones being preserved, and yet it seems unlikely that if hunting of now extinct animals was intensive no butchered animal

---

20 Richard G. Roberts, Timothy F. Flannery, Linda K. Ayliffe, Hiroyuki Yoshida, Jon M. Olley, Gavin J. Prideaux, et al., 'New ages for the last Australian megafauna: Continent-wide extinction about 46,000 years ago', *Science* 292 (2001), 1,888–92; and Gifford H. Miller, John W. Magee, Beverly J. Johnson, Marilyn L. Fogel, Nigel A. Spooner, Malcom T. McCulloch and Linda K. Ayliffe, 'Pleistocene extinction of Genyornis newtoni: Human impact on Australian megafauna', *Science* 283 (1999), 205–8.

21 Barry W. Brook and David M. Dowman, 'Explaining the Pleistocene megafaunal extinctions: Models, chronologies, and assumptions', *Proceedings of the National Academy of Science* 99 (2002), 624–7; and Barry W. Brook and David M. Dowman, 'The uncertain blitzkrieg of Pleistocene megafauna', *Journal of Biogeography* 31 (2004), 517–23.

bones would have been identified even in the few archaeological sites with favourable preservation.[22] There are few archaeological sites older than 35,000–40,000 years BP with bones well-preserved, but those that have been found show a hunting focus on small rather than large game.

One site that might have evidence for butchery of naturally trapped animals, though not for hunting, is Cuddie Springs, which has stone artefacts and bones of extinct animals together in levels 33,000–40,000 years old.[23] Evidence of humans still butchering the extinct species as late as 33,000 years ago, perhaps 15,000 years after people occupied the region, is not consistent with the notion that early hunting targeted species with large body mass to such an extent that those species were rapidly exterminated.[24] For this reason the reality of the apparent association between artefacts and fossil bones at this site is critical, and has been persistently challenged, with indications that dating and stratigraphic associations are complex and that extinctions might have occurred earlier, near the initiation of human occupation.[25] If Cuddie Springs is eliminated from consideration on that basis there is little or no archaeological evidence that bears upon the question of large mammal extinctions.

A variety of environmental signatures consistently point to the reduction in range and density of large animals, if not their final extinction, between 40,000 and 50,000 years ago, and so the correspondence between the spread of humans and the stress on faunal populations suggests that the appearance of human hunters in the landscape is implicated in the extinction process.[26] The timing of population reductions in these animals coincides with

22 Tim F. Flannery, 'Pleistocene faunal loss: Implications of the aftershock for Australia's past and future', *Archaeology in Oceania* 25 (1990), 45–67.

23 Clive N. G. Trueman, Judith H. Field, Joe Dortch, Bethan Charles and Stephen Wroe, 'Prolonged coexistence of humans and megafauna in Pleistocene Australia', *Proceedings of the National Academy of Science* 102 (2005), 8,381–5.

24 Stephen Wroe and Judith H. Field, 'A review of the evidence for a human role in the extinction of Australian megafauna and an alternative interpretation', *Quaternary Science Reviews* 25 (2006), 2,692–703.

25 Rainer Grün, Stephen Eggins, Maxime Aubert, Nigel Spooner, Alistair W. G. Pike and Wolfgang Müller, 'ESR and U-series analyses of faunal material from Cuddie Springs, NSW, Australia: implications for the timing of the extinction of the Australian megafauna', *Quaternary Science Reviews* 29 (2010), 596–610; and Richard G. Roberts and Barry W. Brook, 'And then there were none?', *Science* 327 (2010), 420–2.

26 Miller, Magee, Johnson, Fogel, Spooner, McCulloch and Ayliffe, 'Pleistocene extinction of Genyornis newtoni'; Bowler, Johnston, Olley, Prescott, Roberts, Shawcross and Spooner, *et al.*, 'New ages for the last Australian megafauna'; and Susan Rule, Barry W. Brook, Simon G. Haberle, Chris S. M. Turney, A. Peter Kershaw and Christopher N. Johnson, 'The aftermath of megafaunal extinction: Ecosystem transformation in Pleistocene Australia', *Science* 335 (2012), 1,483–6.

intensification of long-term continental drying, reductions in resource levels and restructuring of the environment, and so even low levels of predation by the new human hunters may have tipped some species into terminal declines, or accelerated declines already underway.[27] Most likely it was not intensive or exclusive hunting of these large animals that reduced their populations perilously but merely the addition of a new social carnivore to stressful ecological circumstances. While the extinctions themselves have captured the imagination of researchers it is the removal of those animals from the Australian landscape that shaped subsequent human occupation, as Flannery observed.[28]

The consequences of a reduction in the number of large marsupials, and subsequently their extinction, would have been dramatic. Removing large browsers and grazers from the ecosystem means they are not actively consuming vegetation, potentially resulting in reduced openness within forests, reduced ecosystem patchiness and increased fuel load, which might facilitate altered fire regimes and subsequently nutrient cycles. Evidence of this chain of ecological transformation is recorded from several places, but most notably from Lynch's Crater, a swamp in northeast Australia. Cores drilled into the deep sediments of this swamp provided a record of pollen, charcoal and spores of the fungus *Sporormiella*, which is passed through the bowel of large herbivores and can be used as a proxy for their presence in a landscape.[29] Counts of *Sporormiella* spores, and by implication the abundance of large herbivores, declined markedly about 41,000 years ago. Immediately afterwards, charcoal fragments in the sediments, and by implication fire frequency/intensity, increased in response to increased fuel. The sequence from Lynch's Crater is consistent with charcoal pulses in many sedimentary sequences across Australia dating to between approximately 40,000 and 50,000 years ago.[30] Although these charcoal signals have often been discussed as possible signals of the arrival of humans it is more likely, given the earlier dates now available for occupation, that altered burning regimes mark the

---

27 See Judith H. Field and Stephen Wroe, 'Aridity, faunal adaptations and Australian Late Pleistocene extinctions', *World Archaeology* 44 (2012), 56–74.

28 Flannery, 'Pleistocene faunal loss'.

29 Robert S. Feranec, Norton G. Miller, Jonathan C. Lothrop and Russell W. Graham, 'The *Sporormiella* proxy and end-Pleistocene megafaunal extinction: A perspective', *Quaternary International* 245 (2011), 333–8.

30 Peter Kershaw, Sander van der Kaars, Patrick Moss, Bradley Opdyke, François Guillard, Sue Rule and Chris S. M. Turney, 'Environmental change and the arrival of people in the Australian region', *Before Farming* 1 (2006), article 2.

point at which new ecological relationships emerge in a land now largely devoid of very large herbivores.

Settlement of new territories across the continent may have been assisted by the exploitation of substantial meat packages represented by the large herbivores, but that prey would have been found in small numbers, geographically variable in abundance and for only a limited period, and consequently early foraging practices would have been reasonably diverse. Certainly the early archaeological assemblages of animal bones are a consequence of flexible foraging strategies focused on hunting a wide range of small- to medium-sized game. The prey composition in each locality reflected a selection of animals from the suite of game locally available. For example, early desert economies, at least in the period 35,000–45,000 years ago were often based on the exploitation of large, permanent desert lakes as reliable resource-rich zones. Sites of this kind, such as Lake Mungo, contain the remains of marsupial species, reptiles, as well as fish and mussels. Fishing was accomplished with a range of technologies, including spears, nets and hook and line; while terrestrial hunting used spears and perhaps traps and thrown artefacts such as sticks or perhaps even boomerangs (though these are not reliably dated before 10,000–15,000 years ago). It is likely that plant foods such as yams and seeds would have supplemented meat in the deserts, and that these would have varied between environments, though the archaeological evidence for this foraging is rare. Regional differences in economic strategies, probably combined with disparate demographic histories, most likely underpinned regional differences in cultural practices that emerged as each landscape was settled and groups adapted their social life to the specific circumstance they encountered.

Regional traditions of behaviour are clear in this period, and especially visible in technology and symbols. Geographical difference in technology is revealed in the stone artefact assemblages, which have preserved extremely well.[31] Most obvious is the manufacture and use of hafted edge-ground axes in northern Australia but not in southern Australia.[32] Additionally the technology for making tools through flaking differed across the continent in response to raw material characteristics and the economic incentives to produce expedient or maintained, and large or small tools. Such

---

31 See Hiscock, *Archaeology of Ancient Australia*.
32 Jean-Michel Geneste, Bruno David and Hugues Plisson, et al., 'Earliest evidence for ground-edge axes: 35,400±410 cal BP from Jawoyn country, Arnhem Land', *Australian Archaeology* 71 (2010), 66–9.

technological variations are not simply adaptations to local stone materials; they also indicate the transmission of local conventions of tool manufacture and tool use. This is substantiated by the regional-scale difference in public signalling through symbols 40,000–50,000 years ago. In this period jewellery, probably in the form of necklaces or bracelets, made of perforated shells or bones with mastic and ochre, was made only in the northwestern portion of the continent. Its absence in the east and south is not a consequence of poor preservation since in some localities, especially the Tasmanian uplands, there are well-preserved faunal assemblages but no beads. At the very least this indicates regional traditions in the way ornamentation was produced, with only perishable plant materials being used for jewellery in the southeast, and it may well indicate the absence of ornamentation across a substantial portion of the continent in the millennia following settlement. A similar pattern of regional difference exists in the residues of painted art production. Small ochre fragments have often been recovered from the sediments of occupied caves, often the only visible evidence of art on the walls that disappeared long ago, and the changing abundance of ochre in different levels of the deposit may indicate changing intensities of rock painting. This phenomenon is most pronounced in the northern and western portions of the continent and has rarely been reported in the southeast. Furthermore, ochre pallets with ground facets are typical of northern Australia and it may be that paint was prepared in a different way in the south. Ochre was used in the southeast, such as in the burial of WLH3, where it was scattered around the interred body before the grave was closed, so we know these regional differences were not the presence/absence of symbol use or ritual, but different expressions of those activities. Hence a range of archaeological indicators reveal different symbolic expressions between north/northwestern regions and south/southeastern ones, and perhaps more local traditions that have not yet been defined.

These cultural differences emerged as human groups settled different environments, most likely in part through a process of drift and also as they adjusted their social and cultural systems to historically contingent situations confronting them. Even during the early millennia of settlement it was geographical diversity and cultural adaptation rather than pan-continental uniformity and cultural stability that were the features of human occupation of Sahul.

The great drying: 35,000–25,000 years ago

Following the widespread settlement of landscapes throughout Sahul the climate shifted, gradually but persistently towards cooler, drier conditions.

The amount and reliability of rainfall gradually diminished, evaporation increased and, in many areas, there was a decline in the availability of permanent surface water, resulting in a progressively more arid interior and the expansion of desert areas. The trend to cooler, drier climates began 45,000 years ago but the last glacial cycle intensified rapidly with the onset of a particularly cold, dry period approximately 30,000–35,000 years ago. At that time moisture became locked up as ice or snow at high latitudes and ocean levels lowered dramatically, revealing the continental shelf to a depth of almost 150 metres below the present sea level.[33] The extensive exposure of the continental shelf greatly increased the landmass available to humans and changed environments in which they lived. Reduced effective precipitation led to decreasing trees/shrubs in many regions and an increased distribution of grasslands.[34] Many inland areas were then located even further from the sea than they had been, creating increasingly dry, continental situations that compounded the effects of drying climates after 30,000–35,000 years BP. For instance, monsoonal rain was much reduced and consequently Lake Eyre, which had been more frequently filled prior to 35,000 years ago than it is today, dried and remained so until around 10,000 years ago.[35] At Lake Mungo and nearby lakes there were lower, fluctuating water levels and dune-building processes were activated.[36] Reduction and disappearance of lakes was a widespread pattern, though timing of drying varied geographically. Environmental reconfigurations during this period, specifically the reduced surface water and expanded deserts and grasslands, have been discussed as triggers of economic and social innovation.

An example of the impact of these drying climatic trends was the development of economic and social systems suited to the extreme dry and cold

33 Kurt Lambeck, Yusuke Yokoyama and Tony Purcell, 'Into and out of the Last Glacial Maximum: Sea-level change during Oxygen Isotope Stages 3 and 2', *Quaternary Science Reviews* 21 (2002), 343–60.

34 See review in Peter Hiscock and Lynley A. Wallis, 'Pleistocene settlement of deserts from an Australian perspective', in Peter Veth, Mike Smith and Peter Hiscock (eds.), *Desert Peoples: Archaeological Perspectives* (Oxford: Blackwell, 2005), pp. 34–57.

35 Gifford H. Miller, John W. Magee and A. J. T. Jull, 'Low-latitude cooling in the Southern Hemisphere from amino-acid racemization in emu eggshells', *Nature* 385 (1997), 241–4; John W. Magee and Gifford H. Miller, 'Lake Eyre palaeohydrology from 60 ka to the present: Beach ridges and glacial maximum aridity', *Palaeogeography, Palaeoclimatology, Palaeoecology* 144 (1998), 307–29; and B. J. Johnson, Gifford H. Miller, M. L. Fogel, John W. Magee, M. K. Gagan and A. R. Chivas, '65,000 years of vegetation change in Central Australia and the Australian summer monsoon', *Science* 284 (1999), 1,150–2.

36 James M. Bowler, 'Willandra Lakes revisited: Environmental framework for human occupation', *Archaeology in Oceania* 33 (1998), 120–55.

conditions that emerged. It has been argued that the initial dispersion of people across inland Australia when conditions were comparatively good, especially rainfall and surface water availability, provided a fortuitous context in which economic and social systems could be adapted to inland resources.[37] Subsequent climatic shifts towards colder, drier landscapes were gradual and progressive, again providing a context that might facilitate human groups developing practices that suited the emerging conditions. There were multiple changes to cultural systems during this period, including amplification of the use of grinding technology, the development of more ecologically dedicated economic strategies and the strengthening of trade network systems.

In arid and semi-arid landscapes in southeastern Australia the archaeological record documents the gradual expansion of the variety of grindstones and the increasing emphasis on grinding technologies during this period of drying and enlargement of grasslands. This shift towards the use of plants such as grass seed and related processing technology that were labour intensive and expensive relative to nutritional returns has been thought to be a response to ecological stress and resource declines.[38] Although energy gains were low, processing seeds offered reliable returns that might have provided a buffer against deteriorating conditions.

As more extreme environmental conditions developed, specific foraging and social strategies were able to be modified, partly because groups resident in each environment were modifying economic practices based on an established, detailed knowledge of their local environment. For instance, in the increasingly severe desert landscapes created after 35,000 years ago resident foraging groups living in regions with no large water bodies employed dispersed patterns of settlement based on flexible but unspecific terrestrial economies, developing more desert-dedicated economic strategies. Another example is the creation and gradual intensification of a dedicated economic system in the increasingly cold, alpine heath land of the Tasmanian uplands. Between 35,000 and 25,000 years ago Pleistocene hunters resident in those uplands targeted, almost exclusively, young and older Bennett's Wallaby, which were tethered to grassland patches, thereby exploiting a predictable meat resource. Hunters travelled to grassland patches, located and killed wallabies that they butchered or transported whole back to the limestone caves that have preserved archaeological traces of their activities.

---

37 Hiscock and Wallis, 'Pleistocene settlement of deserts'.
38 Richard Fullagar and Judith H. Field, 'Pleistocene seed grinding implements from the Australian arid zone', *Antiquity* 71 (1997), 300–7.

A different economic and social strategy that becomes visible at this time is long-distance trade of objects. Since the objects moved were typically small and of little or no practical use as food or tools, it is likely that the reason for transporting such things over many hundreds of kilometres was in order to maintain social relationships, as a token of connections rather than as a functional item. Some of the clearest examples of long-distance linkages signified by such imported objects are from the northwestern, Kimberley region. There objects such as crustacean carapace and marine shells, neither of which had dietary value, were transported/traded hundreds of kilometres to receiving groups far from the coast. Such specific trade goods, like marine shells, may have been sought after because they had value as symbols, perhaps particularly because as exotic items they were rare and costly. Additionally or alternatively the reciprocal relationships that underpin long-distance trade may have been maintained through or facilitated by public displays or gifts of ornaments that carry social meaning about the reciprocal commitment. This evidence indicates that broad inter-group political and economic networks were probably growing during this phase of climatic deterioration.

The construction and maintenance of inter-group political relationships may have been elaborated in particular ways during this period in response to relatively persistent climate change. Widespread reductions of water availability and temperature, with accompanying decreases in environmental productivity, continued for millennia, and had the cumulative effect of destabilizing economic systems. One response to the changing resource base was the modification/expansion of resource use, as indicated by the greater emphasis on seed processing indicated by grindstones during this period. Invention, or greater employment of, technologies to exploit more marginal resources may have been, in some regions, an effective and successful economic strategy. However there were also some regions in which small shifts in processing technology and reconfiguration of foraging practices appear to have been inadequate in creating viable economies within the evolving, drying landscapes. In some instances the archaeological evidence indicates failure of the economic system and consequently human abandonment of local areas or even entire regions. For instance, human groups abandoned the long Cape Range Peninsula on the west coast, documented in the cultural hiatus in sites such as Mandu Mandu Creek, Jansz, and C99.[39]

39 Kate Morse, 'Coastwatch: Pleistocene resource use on the Cape Range Peninsula', in Jay Hall and Ian McNiven (eds.), *Australian Coastal Archaeology* (Canberra: Australian National University, 1999), pp. 73–8; and Kathryn Przywolnik, 'Long-term transitions in

Local withdrawal from resource-poor or high-risk localities appears to have been the initial response to economic difficulties, and in instances where that did not produce viable economic conditions the entire region was abandoned. Geographic territorial contractions and abandonments became more frequent over time in this period, as climate change proceeded. While the loss of economic capacity was undoubtedly greater in the subsequent Last Glacial Maximum (see below), the onset of processes of substantial economic change, and of the struggle of economic systems to formulate viable foraging strategies, is evident more than 30,000 years ago. In this context the elaboration of inter-group social networks through the formalization of exchange patterns, signified in the exchange of rare/exotic items, reveals another response to changes in landscapes, one that perhaps exploits the advantages of maintaining relationships with adjoining groups in the expectation that access to neighbouring territory would help buffer resource fluctuations.

Surviving the Glacial Maximum: 25,000–18,000 years ago

Cooling conditions that had long been developing since humans arrived in Australia suddenly and significantly intensified after 25,000 years BP to create what is recognized as the Last Glacial Maximum (LGM). Lasting from approximately 25,000 until 18,000 years ago this period offered some of the cruellest and most confronting climate conditions to the occupants of Australia, and it is possible that the human responses to these extreme circumstances helped shape the subsequent cultural evolution of the ancestors of Aboriginal people.

Mid-way through the LGM the oceans surrounding Australia reached their lowest, and coldest, levels. Sometime before 22,000 years ago the oceans dropped to a low-point of 125 metres below their present level.[40] At approximately the same time sea-surface temperatures reached their lowest values

hunter-gatherers of coastal northwestern Australia', in Veth, Smith and Hiscock (eds.), *Desert Peoples*, pp. 177–205.

40 Yusuke Yokoyama, Patrick De Deckker, Kurt Lambeck, Paul Johnston and L. Keith Fifield, 'Sea-level at the Last Glacial Maximum: Evidence from northwestern Australia to constrain ice volumes for oxygen isotope stage 2', *Palaeogeography, Palaeoclimatology, Palaeoecology* 165 (2001), 281–97; and T. J. J. Hanebuth, K. Stattegger and A. Bojanowski, 'Termination of the Last Glacial Maximum sea-level lowstand: The Sunda-Shelf data revisited', *Global and Planetary Change* 66 (2009), 76–84.

and on land it became exceptionally cold and dry.[41] These conditions were the peak of a long-term trend that altered the physical environment in which human occupants operated. Evaporation and windiness were greater than today, a combination that reduced surface water availability.[42] Consequently, in the LGM, landscapes surrounding the arid core of Australia dried to such an extent that they too became deserts, expanding the arid interior. Rainfall was about half the amount received today, although water availability varied seasonally in some regions.[43] Glaciers formed in high-altitude areas, and many upland areas became extremely cold, dry and treeless.[44] The land surface of Sahul reached its maximum extent at this period, producing more continental climatic regimes and reducing rainfall from monsoons and cyclones. Because of the flattened topography of the now submerged continental shelf, islands close to the coastline would have been scarce. In summary environmental conditions rapidly became more severe than any encountered since humans had arrived in Australia.

The consequences of these extreme conditions for people should not be under-estimated. Reduced vegetation cover triggered major sediment erosion. For instance, a significant phase of dune-building in the interior was initiated and aeolian dust storms were intense.[45] The drying of lakes and

---

41 Timothy T. Barrows, John O. Stone, L. Keith Fifield and Richard G. Cresswell, 'The timing of the last glacial maximum in Australia', *Quaternary Science Reviews* 21 (2002), 159–73.

42 John Chappell, 'Late Quaternary environmental changes in eastern and central Australia: Their climatic interpretation', *Quaternary Science Reviews* 10 (1991), 377–90; N. N. Hubbard, 'In search of regional palaeoclimates: Australia, 18,000 yr BP', *Palaeogeography, Palaeoclimatology, Palaeoecology* 116 (1995), 167–88; and Magee and Miller, 'Lake Eyre palaeohydrology'.

43 G. Singh and Elizabeth A. Geissler, 'Late Cainozoic history of vegetation, fire, lake levels and climate, at Lake George', *Philosophical Transactions of the Royal Society of London B* 311 (1985), 379–447; J. R. Dodson and R. V. S. Wright, 'Humid to arid to subhumid vegetation shift on Pilliga Sandstone, Ulungra Springs, New South Wales', *Quaternary Research* 32 (1989), 182–92; and Hubbard, 'In search of regional palaeoclimates'.

44 Barrows, Stone, Fifield and Cresswell, 'The timing of the last glacial maximum'; Timothy T. Barrows, John O. Stone and L. Keith Fifield, 'Exposure ages for Pleistocene periglacial deposits in Australia', *Quaternary Science Reviews* 23 (2004), 697–708; and Susan Sweller, 'Vegetational and climatic changes during the last 40,000 years at Burraga Swamp, Barrington Tops, NSW', unpublished BA (Hons) thesis, University of New South Wales (2001).

45 J. E. Ash and R. J. Wasson, 'Vegetation and sand mobility in the Australian desert dunefield', *Zeitschrift für Geomorphologie NF Supplementbande* 45 (1983), 7–25; James M. Bowler and R. J. Wasson, 'Glacial age environments of inland Australia', in J. C. Vogel (ed.), *Late Cainozoic Paleoclimates of the Southern Hemisphere* (Rotterdam: Balkema, 1984), pp. 183–208; James M. Bowler, 'Quaternary landform evolution', in D. N. Jeans (ed.), *The Natural Environment – A Geography of Australia* (Sydney: University of Sydney

reduced surface water was often linked to lowered water tables and the formation of salt crusts.[46] Some of these environmental changes created massive, sometimes irreversible, alterations to landscapes and to plant and animal resources found within them. Foods sometimes disappeared, as was the case when water levels in Lake Mungo and its neighbouring lakes reached a low level and/or became brackish. Rainfall was highly variable compared to earlier periods, and most likely this made it harder for foragers to predict when rainfall would fill water sources, as good rains occurred less often and more irregularly.[47] The nature of extreme conditions varied geographically during the LGM, but across the continent it was generally a far more difficult environmental context for people. Archaeological research has yielded evidence of the dramatic impact of these climatic conditions on humans attempting to live in drying landscapes.

The most obvious archaeological signature of the severity of these conditions for human groups is the increased frequency with which people abandoned their lands. This is revealed when the multiple archaeological deposits display no cultural material during the LGM, even though artefacts and food debris show humans had been resident prior to the LGM. The absence of cultural materials, revealing abandonment of the local area, was widespread across Australia at this time. Examples of abandoned localities include the Lake Eyre Basin and Strzelecki Desert, Nullarbor Plain near Allen's Cave, Central Australian Ranges near Kulpi Mara and Sandy Desert regions.[48] It is difficult to quantify the extent of abandoned territory since

Press, 1986), pp. 117–47; Paul P. Hesse and Grant H. McTainsh, 'Last Glacial Maximum to Early Holocene wind strength in the mid-latitudes of the Southern Hemisphere from aeolian dust in the Tasman Sea', *Quaternary Research* 52 (1999), 343–9; and G. C. Nanson, D. M. Price and S. A. Short, 'Wetting and drying of Australia over the past 300ka', *Geology* 20 (1992), 791–4.

46 John W. Magee, James M. Bowler, Gifford H. Miller and D. L. G. Williams, 'Stratigraphy, sedimentology, chronology and palaeohydrology of Quaternary lacustrine deposits at Madigan Gulf, Lake Eyre, South Australia', *Palaeogeography, Palaeoclimatology, Palaeoecology* 113 (1995), 3–42.

47 Lambeck, Yokoyama and Purcell, 'Into and out of the Last Glacial Maximum'.

48 Ronald J. Lampert and Philip J. Hughes, 'The Flinders Ranges: A Pleistocene outpost in the arid zone?', *Records of the South Australian Museum* 20 (1987), 29–34; Peter Hiscock, 'Prehistoric settlement patterns and artifact manufacture at Lawn Hill, Northwest Queensland', unpublished Ph.D. thesis, University of Queensland (1988); Peter B. Thorley, 'Pleistocene settlement in the Australian arid zone: Occupation of an inland riverine landscape in the central Australian ranges', *Antiquity* 72 (1998), 34–45; Peter Veth, 'Islands in the interior: A model for the colonization of Australia's arid zone', *Archaeology in Oceania* 24 (1989), 81–92; and S. O'Connor, *30,000 Years of Aboriginal Occupation: Kimberley, North West Australia* (Canberra: Australian National University, 1999).

evidence for abandonment of an entire region is equivocal where only one or two sites have been excavated, and only parts of those regions may have been unused during the LGM. Nevertheless the mounting evidence indicates that large tracts of land became unoccupied.

When regions were completely deserted it is likely that this was not a sudden, single event. In most instances it would have been the final outcome of a gradual succession of local abandonments as people retreated from risky landscapes. We observe this process in a number of places where a well-watered core portion of their territory, an oasis, allowed occupation to persist long enough to leave a record of the gradual abandonment of peripheral territory. The outstanding example of this process comes from the gorge systems inland from the Gulf of Carpentaria, particularly the gorges of the Lawn Hill River and its tributaries. These gorges are cut deep into limestone strata and today the rivers that flow through them, fed by the vast aquifer contained in the rock, do not rely on local rainfall and do not vary in discharge. Even during the LGM Lawn Hill River continued unabated, supporting a variety of aquatic fauna (fish, turtle, mussels, crocodiles) and fringing forests containing edible and useful plants. These gorge sites, such as Colless Creek Cave, record regular and relatively intense occupation during the LGM, as shown by the large numbers of artefacts, bones and shells left behind. This signature of intensive occupation reflects the contraction of life to the oases found within the gorges. Before and after the LGM people living in such sites were exploiting a wide range of adjacent environments, documented in the animal bones and artefacts that were brought some distance to the cave. However, during the LGM virtually all food came from animals living in the gorge, and the stone artefacts were made from nearby rocks; no food or artefacts were brought from areas away from the gorges. At that time people constricted their foraging range, avoided high-risk environments away from the oases, and concentrated on exploiting relatively reliable resources. This strategy made it possible for small groups of people to reside in the gorges, at least periodically until resources were exhausted, at which point they moved to other well-favoured gorge systems. Without a refuge, the humans living along Lawn Hill River may not have survived the hyper-arid conditions of the LGM.

Within the expanded arid zone human groups persisted in some localities and vanished in others. This mosaic of adaptation or abandonment was conditioned by a variety of factors. A single oasis or well-provided core area was often insufficient, as food would soon be exhausted in a foraging radius around permanent water, and foragers would have required a series of such patches to make territorial contraction a viable strategy over months or years. Additionally, the ability to occupy any region depended on more than simply the ability to capture sufficient food year round. To maintain a population over the long-term any group would need to be able to occasionally meet adjacent groups, to exchange marriage partners and information, and so the viability of neighbouring groups was also a potential limiting factor. Some inland areas contained enough geographical diversity to allow groups to continue their occupation through the more desertic conditions of the LGM. Lawn Hill River, for instance, was one of several large aquifer-fed rivers running through gorges in the region and providing a chain of reliable resource-rich locations that would have enabled people to move to and from surviving neighbours. Another well-provided location was the MacDonald Ranges of central Australia where foragers could move between springs, gorges and major seasonal rivers to exploit resources and facilitate genetic and cultural contacts.[49]

Across Australia territorial contraction and abandonment, population reductions, reconfiguration of territory and altered inter-group interactions would have been accompanied by transformations of social practices and even of human biology. The biological evidence for adaptation to the ice-age conditions comes principally from southeast Australia, specifically from areas along the Murray River, where skeletons have been excavated at sites such as Kow Swamp and dated to between 22,000 to 9,000 years ago.[50] These skeletons present an image of people who have evolved in response to the ice-age cold, through natural selection that favoured larger, more robust builds. In the cold conditions during and immediately after the LGM human bodies in southern Australia were 10–20 per cent bigger than more recent Aboriginal people. Skeletons from this period have skulls that are larger, with thicker bones and broader teeth than their descendants, an expected pattern because increased body size and skeletal robustness in cold environments is often observed in animals.[51] The greater body size was more evident in males, leading to a more pronounced difference in size and robustness between the sexes. Such biological adaptations were exaggerated by cultural modifications of the body. For instance, some groups, such as the people at Kow Swamp, marked their identity through artificial cranial deformation of

---

49 Thorley, 'Pleistocene settlement in the Australian arid zone'.
50 Tim Stone and Matthew L. Cupper, 'Last Glacial Maximum ages for robust humans at Kow Swamp, southern Australia', *Journal of Human Evolution* 45 (2003), 99–111.
51 Peter Brown, 'Pleistocene homogeneity and Holocene size reduction: The Australian human skeletal evidence', *Archaeology in Oceania* 22 (1987), 41–67.

the still-plastic skulls of young children, giving adults exotic long heads with sloping foreheads that would have been instantly recognizable to any observer. Signalling a distinct identity in this way may have reflected local ideologies that had emerged during the LGM as inter-group contact reduced and social characteristics diversified, and/or it may have been designed to provide a benefit in inter-group negotiations. Certainly the practice of artificial cranial deformation was not practised in Australia in more recent millennia; it was a cultural convention that probably emerged during the LGM and subsequently gave way to other forms of social signalling.

Post-glacial adaptations: 18,000–10,000 years ago

The climatic cooling trend that had led to the LGM peaked around 22,000 years BP, and after that time global warming and consequent sea-level rise gradually began. Sea-level rise accelerated dramatically in the millennium between 19,000 and 18,000 years ago, with a rise of more that 15 metres in ocean levels (>1–2 cm p.a.), as millions of cubic kilometres of ice in the Northern Hemisphere were released into the oceans. From a maximum point of 125 metres below the current sea level, oceans rose to *c.* 100 metres below current level by 18,000 BP and thereafter steady rises brought seas to within 20 metres of their modern levels by 10,000 years BP. While these sea-level changes reflect temperature increases that would have been significant for plant growth and enhanced availability of plant and animal resources, the sea rises themselves had a direct and visible impact on human land use along the coasts.

In the north coastlines retreated southwards more than 1,000 kilometres as the gently sloping continental shelf was inundated. The diverse habitats that existed on the exposed shelf, including the huge brackish Lake Carpentaria, vanished as the oceans flowed onto the shelf and flooded the region.[52] Although the loss of land elsewhere around Sahul was not as great, it was often still substantial. Whole territories were drowned, forcing people into the lands already occupied by other groups, and demanding territorial restructuring and re-conceptualization. The result was not only a landmass almost one-third smaller but a transformed coastline. Rapid sea-level rise prevented the formation of stable inshore ecosystems in many localities, reducing the supply of food resources accessible along the shore. For

---

52 T. Torgersen, M. R. Jones, A. W. Stephens, D. E. Searle and W. J. Ullman, 'Late Quaternary hydrological changes in the Gulf of Carpentaria', *Nature* 313 (1985), 785–7.

example, in northeastern Australia it was not until sea level began to stabilize about 3,000–4,000 years ago that ecosystems rich in mangroves as well as sandy shores formed and abundant shoreline foods such as molluscs and crustaceans became available. This created post-LGM some coastal economies that were configured to target a relatively narrow set of resources.

One example of developing coastal economies is the island-creation in the Whitsunday region on the northeast coast. There sea-level rise flooded low-lying areas of the continental shelf to leave a long peninsula of high ground, and then as the ocean continued to rise the peninsula was progressively cut into a series of islands. Throughout this process constant changes in sea level prevented the development of fringing mangroves and shoreline foods, and at the same time the diversity and abundance of terrestrial fauna reduced as land was broken into small islands, leaving the islands themselves as limited sources of food. Archaeological deposits preserved in large rockshelters on some islands document that the foragers in this landscape were frequently fishing, often in deep water, and at least occasionally capturing large marine mammals such as dugong and turtles. Hunting and fishing on the open seas provided significant supplements to the diet that could be obtained through terrestrial foraging, and required a specific and reliable toolkit. Sound water-craft are demonstrated not only by the capture of large marine mammals that rarely or never come ashore but also by the regular and large-scale transportation of stone artefacts between islands at the end of this period.[53] People made large, regularly shaped artefacts with sharp edges and blunt backs and transported these widely within the islands – possibly as a technological device to help them explore and exploit the region at a time of resource uncertainty and change.[54]

At the southern extremity of Sahul sea-level rise inundated the Bassian Plain, creating the 200-kilometre-wide Bass Strait about 14,000 years ago and isolating humans in the newly created Island of Tasmania. A number of subsequent shifts in economic practices, social life and demography have

53 Bryce Barker, 'Coastal occupation in the Holocene: Environment, resource use and resource continuity', in Hall and McNiven (eds.), *Australian Coastal Archaeology*, pp. 119–27; Bryce Barker, 'Nara Inlet 1: Coastal resource use and the Holocene marine transgression in the Whitsunday Islands, central Queensland', *Archaeology in Oceania* 26 (1991), 102–9; and Bryce Barker, *The Sea People: Late Holocene Maritime Specialisation in the Whitsunday Islands, Central Queensland* (Canberra: Australian National University, 2004).
54 Lara Lamb, 'Rock of ages: Use of the South Molle Island Quarry, Whitsunday Islands, and the implications for Holocene technological change in Australia', unpublished Ph.D. thesis, Australian National University (2005).

been inferred and often interpreted as long-term consequences of the physical isolation of Tasmania. Such responses can be seen as yet another example of cultural diversification, a process that has operated throughout the human history of Australasia.

FURTHER READING

Adcock, Gregory, Elizabeth Dennis and Simon Easteal, et al., 'Mitochondrial DNA sequences in ancient Australians: Implications for modern human origins', *Proceedings of the National Academy of Science* 98 (2001), 537–42.

Ash, J. E., and R. J. Wasson, 'Vegetation and sand mobility in the Australian desert dunefield', *Zeitschrift für Geomorphologie NF Supplementbande* 45 (1983), 7–25.

Barker, Bryce, 'Coastal occupation in the Holocene: Environment, resource use and resource continuity', in Jay Hall and Ian McNiven (eds.), *Australian Coastal Archaeology*, Canberra: Australian National University, 1999, pp. 119–27.

'Nara Inlet 1: Coastal resource use and the Holocene marine transgression in the Whitsunday Islands, central Queensland', *Archaeology in Oceania* 26 (1991), 102–9.

The Sea People: Late Holocene Maritime Specialisation in the Whitsunday Islands, Central Queensland, Canberra: Australian National University, 2004.

Barrows, Timothy T., John O. Stone and L. Keith Fifield, 'Exposure ages for Pleistocene periglacial deposits in Australia', *Quaternary Science Reviews* 23 (2004), 697–708.

Barrows, Timothy T., John O. Stone, L. Keith Fifield and Richard G. Cresswell, 'The timing of the last glacial maximum in Australia', *Quaternary Science Reviews* 21 (2002), 159–73.

Bowler, James M., 'Quaternary landform evolution', in D. N. Jeans (ed.), *The Natural Environment – A geography of Australia*, Sydney: University of Sydney Press, 1986, pp. 117–47.

'Willandra Lakes revisited: Environmental framework for human occupation', *Archaeology in Oceania* 33 (1998), 120–55.

Bowler, James M., and R. J. Wasson, 'Glacial age environments of inland Australia', in J. C. Vogel (ed.), *Late Cainozoic Paleoclimates of the Southern Hemisphere*, Rotterdam: Balkema, 1984, pp. 183–208.

Bowler, James M., Harvey Johnston, Jon Olley, John Prescott, Richard G. Roberts, Wilfred Shawcross and Nigel A. Spooner, 'New ages for human occupation and climatic change at Lake Mungo, Australia', *Nature* 421 (2003), 837–40.

Brook, Barry W., and David M. Dowman, 'Explaining the Pleistocene megafaunal extinctions: Models, chronologies, and assumptions', *Proceedings of the National Academy of Science* 99 (2002), 624–7.

'The uncertain blitzkrieg of Pleistocene megafauna', *Journal of Biogeography* 31 (2004), 517–23.

Brown, Peter, *Peter Brown's Australian and Asian Palaeoanthropology*, accessed 20 February 2013, www-personal.une.edu.au/~pbrown3/palaeo.html.

'Pleistocene homogeneity and Holocene size reduction: The Australian human skeletal evidence', *Archaeology in Oceania* 22 (1987), 41–67.

Cameron, David W., and Colin P. Groves, *Bones, Stones and Molecules: 'Out of Africa' and Human origins*, Sydney: Academic Press, 2004.

Chappell, John, 'Late Quaternary environmental changes in eastern and central Australia: Their climatic interpretation', *Quaternary Science Reviews* 10 (1991), 377–90.

Cooper, A., A. Rambaut, V. Macaulay, E. Willerslev, J. Hansen and C. Stringer, 'Human origins and ancient human DNA', *Science* 292 (2001), 1,655–6.

Cosgrove, Richard, 'Forty-two degrees south: The archaeology of late Pleistocene Tasmania', *Journal of World Prehistory* 13 (1999), 357–402.

Dodson, J. R., and R. V. S. Wright, 'Humid to arid to subhumid vegetation shift on Pilliga Sandstone, Ulungra Springs, New South Wales', *Quaternary Research* 32 (1989), 182–92.

Feranec, Robert, Norton G. Miller, Jonathan C. Lothrop and Russell W. Graham, 'The *Sporormiella* proxy and end-Pleistocene megafaunal extinction: A perspective', *Quaternary International* 245 (2011), 333–8.

Field, Judith H., and Stephen Wroe, 'Aridity, faunal adaptations and Australian Late Pleistocene extinctions', *World Archaeology* 44 (2012), 56–74.

Flannery, Tim F., 'Pleistocene faunal loss: Implications of the aftershock for Australia's past and future', *Archaeology in Oceania* 25 (1990), 45–67.

Fullagar, Richard, and Judith H. Field, 'Pleistocene seed grinding implements from the Australian arid zone', *Antiquity* 71 (1997), 300–7.

Geneste, Jean-Michel, Bruno David and Hugues Plisson, et al., 'Earliest evidence for ground-edge axes: 35,400±410 cal BP from Jawoyn country, Arnhem Land', *Australian Archaeology* 71 (2010), 66–9.

Grün, Rainer, Stephen Eggins, Maxime Aubert, Nigel Spooner, Alistair W. G. Pike and Wolfgang Müller, 'ESR and U-series analyses of faunal material from Cuddie Springs, NSW, Australia: Implications for the timing of the extinction of the Australian megafauna', *Quaternary Science Reviews* 29 (2010), 596–610.

Grün, Rainer, C. Stringer, F. McDermott, R. Nathan, N. Porat, S. Robertson, L. Taylor, G. Mortimer, S. Eggins and M. Mcculloch, 'U-series and ESR analyses of bones and teeth relating to the human burials from Skhul', *Journal of Human Evolution* 49 (2005), 316–34.

Gutiérrez, Gabriel, Diego Sanchez and Antonio Marin, 'A reanalysis of the ancient mitochondrial DNA sequences recovered from Neandertal bones', *Molecular Biological Evolution* 19 (2002), 1,359–66.

Hanebuth, T. J. J., K. Stattegger and A. Bojanowski, 'Termination of the Last Glacial Maximum sea-level lowstand: The Sunda-Shelf data revisited', *Global and Planetary Change* 66 (2009), 76–84.

Hesse, P. P., and G. H. McTainsh, 'Last Glacial Maximum to Early Holocene wind strength in the mid-latitudes of the Southern Hemisphere from aeolian dust in the Tasman Sea', *Quaternary Research* 52 (1999), 343–9.

Hiscock, Peter, *Archaeology of Ancient Australia*, London: Routledge, 2008.

   'Prehistoric settlement patterns and artefact manufacture at Lawn Hill, Northwest Queensland', unpublished Ph.D. thesis, University of Queensland (1988).

Hiscock, Peter, and Lynley Wallis, 'Pleistocene settlement of deserts from an Australian perspective', in Peter Veth, Mike Smith and Peter Hiscock (eds.), *Desert Peoples: Archaeological Perspectives*, Oxford: Blackwell, 2005, pp. 34–57.

Hubbard, N. N., 'In search of regional palaeoclimates: Australia, 18,000 yr BP', *Palaeogeography, Palaeoclimatology, Palaeoecology* 116 (1995), 167–88.

Hudjashov, Georgi, Toomas Kivisild and Peter A. Underhill, et al., 'Revealing the prehistoric settlement of Australia by Y chromosome and mtDNA analysis', *Proceedings of the National Academy of Sciences* 104 (2007), 8,726–30.

Johnson, B. J., Gifford H. Miller, M. L. Fogel, John W. Magee, M. K. Gagan and A. R. Chivas, '65,000 years of vegetation change in Central Australia and the Australian summer monsoon', *Science* 284 (1999), 1,150–2.

Kershaw, Peter, Sander van der Kaars, Patrick Moss, Bradley Opdyke, François Guillard, Sue Rule and Chris S. M. Turney, 'Environmental change and the arrival of people in the Australian region', *Before Farming* 1 (2006), article 2.

Lamb, Lara, *'Rock of ages: Use of the South Molle Island Quarry, Whitsunday Islands, and the implications for Holocene technological change in Australia'*, unpublished Ph.D. thesis, Australian National University (2005).

Lambeck, Kurt, Yusuke Yokoyama and Tony Purcell, 'Into and out of the Last Glacial Maximum: Sea-level change during Oxygen Isotope Stages 3 and 2', *Quaternary Science Reviews* 21 (2002), 343–60.

Lampert, Ronald J., and Philip J. Hughes, 'The Flinders Ranges: A Pleistocene outpost in the arid zone?', *Records of the South Australian Museum* 20 (1987), 29–34.

Magee, John. W., James M. Bowler, Gifford H. Miller and D. L. G. Williams, 'Stratigraphy, sedimentology, chronology and palaeohydrology of Quaternary lacustrine deposits at Madigan Gulf, Lake Eyre, South Australia', *Palaeogeography, Palaeoclimatology, Palaeoecology* 113 (1995), 3–42.

Magee, John. W., and Gifford H. Miller, 'Lake Eyre palaeohydrology from 60 ka to the present: Beach ridges and glacial maximum aridity', *Palaeogeography, Palaeoclimatology, Palaeoecology* 144 (1998), 307–29.

Mellars, Paul, 'Going east: New genetic and archaeological perspectives on the modern human colonization of Eurasia', *Science* 313 (2006), 796–800.

Mijares, Armond Salvador, Florent Détroit, Philip Piper, Rainer Grün, Peter Bellwood, Maxime Aubert, Guillaume Champion, Nida Cuevas, Alexandra de Leon and Eusebio Dizon, 'New evidence for a 67,000-year-old human presence at Callao Cave, Luzon, Philippines', *Journal of Human Evolution* 59 (2010), 123–32.

Miller, Gifford H., John W. Magee and A. J. T. Jull, 'Low-latitude cooling in the Southern Hemisphere from amino-acid racemization in emu eggshells', *Nature* 385 (1997), 241–4.

Miller, Gifford H., John W. Magee, Beverly J. Johnson, Marilyn L. Fogel, Nigel A. Spooner, Malcom T. McCulloch and Linda K. Ayliffe, 'Pleistocene extinction of Genyornis newtoni: Human impact on Australian megafauna', *Science* 283 (1999), 205–8.

Morse, Kate, 'Coastwatch: Pleistocene resource use on the Cape Range Peninsula', in Jay Hall and Ian McNiven (eds.), *Australian Coastal Archaeology*, Canberra: Australian National University, 1999, pp. 73–8.

Nanson, G. C., D. M. Price and S. A. Short, 'Wetting and drying of Australia over the past 300ka', *Geology* 20 (1992), 791–4.

O'Connell, James F., and Jim Allen, 'Dating the colonization of Sahul (Pleistocene Australia – New Guinea): A review of recent research', *Journal of Archaeological Science* 31 (2004), 835–53.

'The Restaurant at the End of the Universe: Modelling the colonisation of Sahul', *Australian Archaeology* 74 (2012), 5–17.

O'Connor, Sue, *30,000 Years of Aboriginal Occupation: Kimberley, North West Australia*, Canberra: Australian National University, 1999.

Pardoe, Colin, 'Becoming Australian: Evolutionary processes and biological variation from ancient to modern times', *Before Farming* 1 (2006), article 4.

Przywolnik, Kathryn, 'Long-term transitions in hunter-gatherers of coastal northwestern Australia', in Peter Veth, Mike Smith and Peter Hiscock (eds.), *Desert Peoples: Archaeological Perspectives*, Oxford: Blackwell, 2005, pp. 177–205.

Rasmussen, Morten, and Xiaosen Guo, et al., 'An Aboriginal Australian genome reveals separate human dispersals into Asia', *Science* 334 (2011), 94–8.

Reich, David, Nick Patterson, Martin Kircher, Frederick Delfin, Madhusudan R. Nandineni, Irina Pugach, Albert Min-Shan Ko, Ying-Chin Ko, Timothy A. Jinam, Maude E. Phipps, Naruya Saitou, Andreas Wollstein, Manfred Kayser, Svante Pääbo and Mark Stoneking, 'Denisova admixture and the first modern human dispersals into Southeast Asia and Oceania', *American Journal of Human Genetics* 89 (2011), 516–28.

Roberts, Richard G., and Barry W. Brook, 'And then there were none?', *Science* 327 (2010), 420–2.

Roberts, Richard G., Rhys Jones and M. A. Smith, 'Optical dating at Deaf Adder Gorge, Northern Territory, indicates human occupation between 53,000 and 60,000 years ago', *Australian Archaeology* 37 (1993), 58–9.

Roberts, Richard G., Timothy F. Flannery, Linda K. Ayliffe, Hiroyuki Yoshida, Jon M. Olley and Gavin J. Prideaux, et al., 'New ages for the last Australian megafauna: Continent-wide extinction about 46,000 years ago', *Science* 292 (2001), 1,888–92.

Rose, Jeffrey I., Vitaly I. Usik, Anthony E. Marks, Yamandu H. Hilbert and Christopher S. Galletti, et al., 'The Nubian Complex of Dhofar, Oman: An African Middle Stone Age industry in Southern Arabia', *PLoS ONE* 6 (2011).

Rule, Susan, Barry W. Brook, Simon G. Haberle, Chris S. M. Turney, A. Peter Kershaw and Christopher N. Johnson, 'The aftermath of megafaunal extinction: Ecosystem transformation in Pleistocene Australia', *Science* 335 (2012), 1,483–6.

Sankararaman, Svante, Nick Patterson, Heng Li, Svante Paabo and David Reich, 'The date of interbreeding between Neandertals and modern humans', *PLoS Genetics* 8 (2012).

Scally, Aylwyn, and Richard Durbin, 'Revising the human mutation rate: Implications for understanding human evolution', *Nature Reviews Genetics* 13 (2012), 745–53.

Singh, G., and Elizabeth A. Geissler, 'Late Cainozoic history of vegetation, fire, lake levels and climate, at Lake George', *Philosophical Transactions of the Royal Society of London* B 311 (1985), 379–447.

Smith, Mike A., Michael I. Bird, Charles S. M. Turney, L. Keith Fifield, G. M. Santos, P. A. Hausladen and M. L. di Tada, 'New ABOX AMS-14C ages remove dating anomalies at Puritjarra rock shelter', *Australian Archaeology* 53 (2001), 45–7.

Soares, Pedro, Farida Alshamali, Joana B. Pereira, Verónica Fernandes, Nuno M. Silva, Carla Afonso, Marta D. Costa, Eliska Musilová, Vincent Macaulay, Martin B. Richards, Viktor Černý and Luísa Pereira, 'The expansion of mtDNA haplogroup L3 within and out of Africa', *Molecular Biology and Evolution* 29 (2011), 915–27.

Stewart, John R., and Chris B. Stringer, 'Human evolution out of Africa: The role of refugia and climate change', *Science* 335 (2012), 1,317–21.

Stone, Tim, and Matthew L. Cupper, 'Last Glacial Maximum ages for robust humans at Kow Swamp, southern Australia', *Journal of Human Evolution* 45 (2003), 99–111.

Sweller, Susan, *'Vegetational and climatic changes during the last 40,000 years at Burraga Swamp, Barrington Tops, NSW'*, unpublished BA (Hons) thesis, University of New South Wales (2001).

Thorley, Peter B., 'Pleistocene settlement in the Australian arid zone: Occupation of an inland riverine landscape in the central Australian ranges', *Antiquity* 72 (1998), 34–45.

Torgersen, T., M. R. Jones, A. W. Stephens, D. E. Searle and W. J. Ullman, 'Late Quaternary hydrological changes in the Gulf of Carpentaria', *Nature* 313 (1985), 785–7.

Trueman, Clive N. G., Judith H. Field, Joe Dortch, Bethan Charles and Stephen Wroe, 'Prolonged coexistence of humans and megafauna in Pleistocene Australia', *Proceedings of the National Academy of Science* 102 (2005), 8,381–5.

Turney, Charles S. M., Michael I. Bird, L. Keith Fifield, Richard G. Roberts, Mike Smith and Charles E. Dortch, et al., 'Early human occupation at Devil's Lair, southwestern Australia, 50,000 years ago', *Quaternary Research* 55 (2001), 3–13.

Veth, Peter, 'Islands in the interior: A model for the colonization of Australia's arid zone', *Archaeology in Oceania* 24 (1989), 81–92.

Veth, Peter, Michael Smith and James M. Bowler, et al., 'Excavations at Parnkupirti, Lake Gregory, Great Sandy Desert: OSL ages for occupation before the Last Glacial Maximum', *Australian Archaeology* 69 (2009), 1–10.

Webb, S. G., *The Willandra Lakes Hominids*, Canberra: Department of Prehistory, Australian National University, 1989.

Williams, Alan N. 'A new population curve for prehistoric Australia', *Proceedings of the Royal Society B* 280 (2013), 20130486.

Wroe, Stephen, and Judith H. Field, 'A review of the evidence for a human role in the extinction of Australian megafauna and an alternative interpretation', *Quaternary Science Reviews* 25 (2006), 2,692–703.

Yokoyama, Yusuke, Patrick de Deckker, Kurt Lambeck, Paul Johnston and L. Keith Fifield, 'Sea-level at the Last Glacial Maximum: Evidence from northwestern Australia to constrain ice volumes for oxygen isotope stage 2', *Palaeogeography, Palaeoclimatology, Palaeoecology* 165 (2001), 281–97.

19

The Pleistocene colonization and occupation of the Americas

NICOLE M. WAGUESPACK

The first migration of humans into the Americas initiated a peopling process that eventually covered over 42 million square kilometers of human occupation spanning high latitude arctic to equatorial environments. As a large-scale demographic and ecological event, the archaeological record provides the only direct evidence of when and how this process unfolded. As reviewed below, key issues concern the timing of paleoclimatic conditions that impacted possible human entry and migratory routes, the location and age of early archaeological sites, and the lifestyle attributes of the colonizing population as interpreted from artifacts. Emphasis is placed on reviewing the Clovis archaeological record as the iconic cultural group widely accepted as evidence of a permanent human presence on the continent. What may have preceded Clovis and the general attributes of immediately subsequent populations are also discussed. Current evidence implies early colonizers quickly established a growing and geographically expanding population with unique technological attributes well-suited to exploring and occupying a vast and changing landscape.

It was not until the Late Pleistocene that the Americas, the last of the major land masses to experience human colonization, were first occupied by Paleolithic humans. The initial migrants encountered a landscape dominated by continental ice sheets in the north, altered coastlines, and environments supporting a menagerie of now extinct Pleistocene megafauna. Glaciation during the Pleistocene, the geologic epoch spanning approximately 2.5 million to 13,000 years ago, resulted in lowered sea levels and exposed continental shelves as terrestrial ice accumulated in massive sheets and glaciers. The landscape was continuously reconfigured as climate oscillated between glacial and interglacial events; during glacial periods when colder temperatures led to ice accumulation, a strip of land called Beringia was exposed across what is now the Bering Sea that connected Eurasia to North America. Beringia, or the Bering land bridge, provided the hunting and gathering populations of northeastern Eurasia a direct overland route into the Americas at various times throughout the Pleistocene.

The archaeological record suggests that it was not until approximately 14,500 YBP (Years Before Present) however, just prior to the end of the Pleistocene, that a small but viable human population traversed Beringia and established a permanent presence. Entering the Americas through Alaska, these migrants eventually colonized both North and South America, the last large-scale colonization event accomplished by Paleolithic foragers. By the Late Pleistocene only Antarctica and a variety of small islands remained uninhabited by humans. In other parts of the world, hunter-gatherers living in long-occupied landscapes began the process of domesticating plants and animals and aggregating themselves into settled villages. Africa, Europe, Eurasia, and Australia had experienced tens of thousands of years of human occupation before foragers of northern Eurasia set foot in North America and chose to move onward into unfamiliar lands. Subsequent, post-Pleistocene migrations occurred, but this initial colonizing population fundamentally contributed to the cultural, biological, and ecological diversity of the Americas.

Many aspects of the initial colonization event remain speculative, poorly evidenced, and heatedly debated among archaeologists. The Americas' first inhabitants were likely small highly dispersed populations living a nomadic lifestyle. These behavioral characteristics can produce an archaeological record that is both sparse and spatially dispersed compared to the larger settled populations of the more recent past. Early sites are more likely to be deeply buried and subjected to taphonomic processes that further exacerbate their rarity and integrity. Sites and deposits that pre-date 14,000 YBP are subject to heavy scrutiny and few have gained widespread acceptance among archaeologists. Colonization events are complex processes that involve the dispersal and growth of a population that unfolds across space and time; in the Americas this space is both vast and environmentally diverse extending from the arctic to the tropics. Migration into new lands involves multiple "firsts": the first people, the first site created, the first dated material, and the first artifact deposited are ideally required in each new region colonists entered to fully understand the spatiotemporal dynamics of the process. The scale of resolution provided by the archaeological record and radiocarbon dating makes true "firsts" extremely difficult to find and identify. It must also be considered that multiple human groups may have ventured into North America during the Pleistocene leaving sites and artifacts but without establishing a permanent presence, creating a record of first explorations but perhaps revealing little about the eventual colonizers.

The archaeological record documenting the colonization process contains comparatively few sites and the earliest evidence of human occupation from North, Meso-, and South America differs both temporally and in artifact typology. With small samples, the earliest dates, sites, and recovered artifacts provide no clear spatiotemporal trends indicating the exact timing or dispersal patterns of the initial colonizers. Consequently, understanding of the colonization process remains coarse-grained, because the evidence needed to derive specifics regarding the timing of human arrival and subsequent migration routes and settlement patterns remains scarce. Based on the earliest accepted evidence, as opposed to the "first" occurrence of a behavior, and the inferences made from the stone artifacts and associated materials a general overview of the timing and lifestyle of the initial colonists can be constructed from the archaeological record.

Beginning in the late 1920s American archaeologists excavated a series of sites in the western United States that provided unequivocal evidence of artifacts in association with extinct Pleistocene fauna. Prior to these discoveries it was speculated that non-European human occupation of the Americas was either an extremely recent event or had deep antiquity on the scale of hundreds of thousands of years on par with the prehistory of Europe. Projectile points and extinct *Bison antiquus* remains reported at the Folsom site in 1927, followed five years later by the discovery of artifacts associated with mammoth remains at the Dent site (Map 19.1), established the Pleistocene-aged presence of humans in the Americas.[1] A series of sites throughout North and South America repeated the pattern of stone tools found among the remains of Pleistocene mammals and with the advent of radiocarbon dating solidified the antiquity of human occupation to the Late Pleistocene. A uniquely American early cultural phenomenon was identified, now referred to as Paleoindian. The Paleoindian time period extends into the Early Holocene when it transitions into the Archaic at different times in different regions. The Archaic is marked by significant changes in projectile point typologies, reduced mobility, and a more diverse use of food resources and associated procurement technologies. Encompassing a suite of cultural traditions defined by the temporal and geographic distribution of projectile point types, the earliest Paleoindian material is associated with human colonization. Paleoindian populations, although coeval with the archaeologically defined Neolithic time period on other continents, were mobile hunter-gatherers known for their flintknapping skill and hunting proficiency.

---

1 David J. Meltzer, "The seventy-year itch: Controversies over human antiquity and their resolution", *Journal of Archaeological Science* 61 (2005), 433–68.

1. Nenana Valley
2. Wenatchee
3. Paisley Cave
4. Simon
5. Anzick
6. Colby
7. Dent
8. Murray Springs, Naco, Lehner
9. Blackwater Draw
10. Aubrey, Gault, Buttermilk Creek
11. Meadowcroft
12. Topper
13. Taima Taima
14. Pedra Farada and Toca da Tira Peia
15. QuebradaJaguay
16. Monte Verde

Map 19.1 Location of Late Pleistocene sites mentioned in text from the Americas.

Durable architecture and ceramics are not evident in Paleoindian sites and ground stone, bone needles, human skeletal material, plant-based technologies, and art/decorative objects are rare. Paleoindian material culture was likely designed to be highly portable and certainly contained perishable implements of leather, wood, plant fibers, and other materials that are not preserved.

Entry into the continent via Beringia was possible at various times throughout the Pleistocene and the settlement of the Americas likely represents a larger dispersal and expansion of human populations into northeastern Eurasia that pushed ever eastward until turning south into the Americas.[2] Providing a corridor linking the Old and New Worlds various mammalian species are known to have crossed back and forth, but it was not

2 John F. Hoffecker, *A Prehistory of the North: Human Settlement of the Higher Latitude* (New Brunswick. NJ. Rutgers University Press, 2005).

until after approximately 18,000 YBP during the Last Glacial Maximum (LGM) that a stable human presence was established in Siberia providing a population for eventual dispersal into North America.[3] During the LGM glacial conditions likely prohibited stable populations from occupying the high latitudes adjacent to Beringia and few sites are known from the area. On the eastern side of Beringia, two large ice masses, the Laurentide and Cordilleran, coalesced during the LGM covering much of present-day Alaska and Canada, effectively blocking access to unglaciated land further south. After the LGM, glacial conditions ameliorated and the ice masses diverged, creating an ice-free corridor located in the Yukon and McKenzie River Valleys of North America (Map 19.1). At the terminus of Beringia colonists were free to move southward either through the ice-free corridor or along the Pacific coastline. As the ice receded new territories became habitable and Pleistocene coastlines were eventually inundated. Consequently, climatic events imposed geographic barriers to possible human migration routes, the timing of entry, and directly impacted the archaeological visibility of early coastline sites.

The Clovis archaeological record

The earliest archaeologically distinct Paleoindian culture identified in the Americas is Clovis, named after a unique style of projectile point found at the Blackwater Draw site near the town of Clovis, New Mexico (Map 19.1).[4] Often found in association with the skeletal remains of mammoths and other megafauna, Clovis points have been found from Canada to Mexico. Clovis sites date to approximately 13,500 YBP and typically consist of stone tools, debris from stone tool manufacturing activities, and the faunal remains of their prey. Diagnostic Clovis points have unique manufacturing and mor-phological attributes that distinguish them from previous and contempor-aneous Upper Paleolithic technologies of Eurasia and from subsequent projectile point types found in the Americas. Made from cryptocrystalline raw materials (glass-like stone with fine-grained crystalline structures) Clovis points are commonly 10 centimeters in length, bifacially worked (flaked on both surfaces), lanceolate in shape, and have distinct flakes removed from

---

3 Ted Goebel, Michael R. Waters, and Dennis H. O'Rourke, "The Late Pleistocene dispersal of modern humans in the Americas," *Science* 319 (2008), 1,497–502.
4 James J. Hester, *Blackwater Locality No. 1: A Stratified Early Man Site in Eastern New Mexico* (Taos: Fort Burgwin Research Center, 1972).

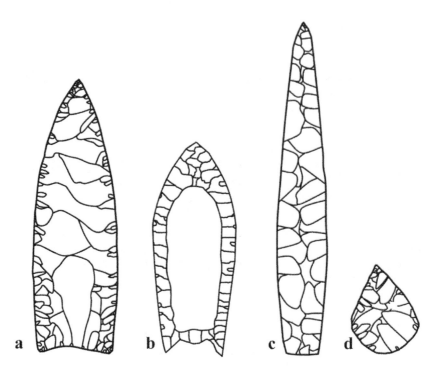

Figure 19.1 A sample of Early Paleoindian projectile point types: (a) Clovis, (b) Folsom, (c) tapered-base point from South America, (d) Chindadn.

their bases referred to as "flutes" (Figure 19.1). Clovis, and the Folsom culture that followed it, are the only two populations known in human prehistory to have manufactured fluted projectile points. Flutes may serve a functional purpose, as controlling the thickness of point bases facilitating hafting, but must also be considered stylistic attributes unique to Early Paleoindians. Lithic raw materials were selected carefully and considerable flintknapping skill is evident in the manufacture of Clovis points.[5] Hafted to spear shafts and delivered via atlatl, Clovis points were utilized as hunting weapons and secondarily as cutting implements.

A unique bifacial manufacturing technique known as outré passé flaking was used to produce points and other bifaces, a characteristic Clovis shares with the Upper Paleolithic Solutrean culture of Europe. Some archaeologists

5 Bruce A. Bradley, Michael B. Collins, and Andrew Hemmings, *Clovis Technology* (Ann Arbor, MI: International Monographs in Prehistory, 2010).

posit that this similarity reflects an ancestral relationship between Clovis and Solutrean populations, but the shared use of outré passé flaking more likely represents a shared adaptive reliance on bifacial tool production.[6] Regionally distinct variants and gradients of Clovis point morphology are also known. Early Paleoindian projectile points from the Northeast, Southeast, and Great Basin of the United States have distinctive forms that are contemporary with or slightly younger than Clovis. In South America, the earliest projectile points are bifacial and lanceolate but lack flutes and exhibit fish-tail and tapered base morphologies (Figure 19.1). Such variation in the Early Paleoindian record may reflect regional differentiation among Clovis peoples as they established themselves in new environments and / or gradational changes in point morphology as populations dispersed through time.[7] However, the Clovis point and its associated toolkit undeniably provide the first widespread, technologically consistent, material culture record present in unglaciated regions of the Americas.

With the exception of isolated projectile point finds, which include over 4,000 specimens, the Clovis archaeological record is dominated by open air kill sites and a smaller number of caches.[8] Kill sites (for example, Colby, Dent, Naco, Lehner, and Blackwater Draw, Map 19.1), containing projectile points and other stone tools likely utilized for butchery tasks found among the skeletal remains of prey animals, are occasionally found in association with adjacent residential campsites (for example, Murray Springs and Gault, Map 19.1). Clovis kill sites provide the clearest and richest source of evidence documenting human predation of extinct proboscideans (that is, mammoths) known from the global archaeological record. The assemblages of residential camps typically contain a more diverse array of artifacts including functionally varied stone tools, implements made of bone / antler / ivory, and the lithic debris resulting from tool manufacture and refurbishing activities. Clovis artifact assemblages typically contain bifaces and finely retouched flake tools functioning as scrapers, gravers, and knives. Non-bifacial tools are made on

---

6 Dennis J. Stanford and Bruce A. Bradley, *Across Atlantic Ice: The Origin of America's Clovis Culture* (Berkeley. University of California Press, 2012).

7 Marcus J. Hamilton and Briggs Buchanan, "Spatial gradients in Clovis-age radiocarbon dates across North America suggest rapid colonization from the north," *Proceedings of the National Academy of Science* 104 (2007), 15,625–30; and Juliet E. Morrow and Toby A. Morrow, "Geographic variation in fluted projectile points: A hemispheric perspective," *American Antiquity* 64 (1999), 215–31.

8 David G. Anderson, D. Shane Miller, Derek T. Anderson, Stephen J. Yerka, J. Christopher Gillam, Erik N. Johanson, and Ashley Smallwood, "2010: Current status and Findings: Archaeology of Eastern North America," *PIDBA (Paleoindian Database of the Americas)* 38 (2010), 63–90.

flakes struck from tabular cores and, particularly in the Southern Plains region of the United States, on large prismatic blades derived from conical blade cores.[9] While consisting of standard prehistoric hunter-gatherer tool types and forms, Clovis lithic technology is often lauded as the quintessential toolkit for a highly mobile foraging population due to the functional flexibility of working edges and the high degree of skill exhibited in their manufacture and design. Non-lithic tools include osseous bone rods that are cylindrical in shape and beveled on one or both ends; the function of these artifacts remains unknown. Discrete aggregations of Clovis artifacts known as caches have also been found in the United States (for example, Wenatchee, Simon, and Anzick, Map 19.1). Caches often contain extremely large bifaces with shaped Clovis points upward of 20 centimeters long and are generally interpreted as collections of stone tools and tool blanks intentionally cached for later retrieval and use.[10] Cached assemblages may also represent ritual offerings and/or burials as the exaggerated size of some specimens may imply they were manufactured and deposited for non-economic functions. Clovis lithic technology bears some superficial resemblance to the coeval and earlier lithic industries of Western Beringia but presents a distinct suite of manufacturing and morphological attributes only found in the Americas.

Known almost exclusively from the stones and bones of their tools and meals, the Clovis archaeological record is consistent with a highly mobile hunter-gatherer population. Small grinding stones, charred plant materials, and incised stones are rare but have occasionally been found in Clovis deposits. The absence of large grinding stones and features, nearly ubiquitous artifacts in Holocene-aged archaeological sites, implies that certain plant resources such as small nuts and seeds were not frequently utilized by Clovis foragers. Consequently, interpretations of Clovis lifeways are predominately focused on technology and subsistence behaviors that can be empirically addressed. Radiocarbon dates consistently place Clovis sites within a 600-year time span, implying a dispersed and possibly fast-growing population.[11] With stone tools frequently made on lithic raw materials deposited hundreds of kilometers from their source locations, Clovis peoples are interpreted to have been highly nomadic populations that established only temporary occupation sites near necessary resources and animal kill sites. Traditionally construed as

9 Michael B. Collins, *Clovis Blade Technology* (Austin. University of Texas Press, 1999).

10 J. David Kilby, "An investigation of Clovis caches: Content, function, and technological organization," unpublished Ph.D. Dissertation, University of New Mexico (2008).

11 Michael R. Waters and Thomas W. Stafford, Jr., "Redefining the age of Clovis: Implications for the peopling of the Americas," *Science* 315 (2007), 1,122–6.

having a hunting-based subsistence economy that focused on the predation of Pleistocene megafauna, a lifestyle facilitated through high mobility and sophisticated weaponry, Clovis is seen as a unique foraging adaptation to a largely unpopulated Pleistocene landscape. Hunter-gatherers with predominately hunting-based subsistence economies are known from the ethnographic record to move frequently in order to maintain access to sufficient prey populations. Quickly moving, fast growing, and reliant upon prey species with vast distributions across the continent, Clovis exhibits behavioral characteristics consistent with a rapid pan-American colonization event.[12]

By the end of the Pleistocene epoch, approximately 13,000 YBP, the Americas were undergoing rapid climatic, environmental, and biogeographic changes. As the ice melted over thirty genera of large-bodied Pleistocene animals were, or were rapidly becoming, extinct while human populations continued their spread across the continent. For many archaeologists and paleontologists the arrival and dispersal of humans onto the landscape directly contributed to the Pleistocene extinction event. Following a global pattern of mammalian extinctions preceded by human migration into other continents, Clovis hunting of megafauna may have fueled colonization while driving their preferred prey to extinction.[13] Megafauna are especially susceptible to the negative demographic effects of predation and Clovis points have been shown to effectively penetrate proboscidean hide.[14] However, the significance of Pleistocene megafauna to the Clovis diet remains contested. The ubiquitous presence of mammoth remains in Clovis faunal assemblages could result from biases in the archaeological record that tend to favor the discovery/study of large-bodied skeletal material over that of smaller animals.[15] It is argued that Clovis megafauna sites are exceptionally visible components of the record but that species such as mammoth and mastodon made little caloric contribution to the everyday diet of Clovis peoples.[16]

12 Robert L. Kelly and Lawrence C. Todd, "Coming into the country: Early Paleoindian hunting and mobility," *American Antiquity* 53 (1988), 23–4.
13 David A. Burney and Timothy F. Flannery, "Fifty millennia of catastrophic extinctions after human contact," *Trends in Ecology and Evolution* 20 (2005), 395–401.
14 William J. Ripple and Blaire van Valkenburgh, "Linking top-down forces to the Pleistocene megafaunal extinctions," *BioScience* 60 (2010), 516–26; and George C. Frison, "Experimental use of Clovis weaponry and tools on African elephants," *American Antiquity* 54 (1989), 766–84.
15 Donald K. Grayson and David J. Meltzer, "Clovis hunting and large mammal extinction: A critical review of the evidence," *Journal of World Prehistory* 16 (2002), 313–59.
16 Donald K. Grayson and David J. Meltzer, "North American overkill continued?", *Journal of Archaeological Science* 31 (2004), 133–6.

Others favor an interpretation of Clovis peoples as specialized hunters of Pleistocene prey[17] whose efforts likely contributed to megafauna extinction and established the hunting-based subsistence patterns of subsequent Paleoindians. The subsistence debate largely concerns what is theoretically expected of the faunal record produced under different Paleoindian hunting strategies as opposed to the general composition of the data. It is clear that Clovis populations killed and butchered Pleistocene megafauna and also utilized smaller-bodied prey species. The relative degree to which they preferentially sought and pursued large- versus small-bodied prey is the issue debated. If Clovis foragers only rarely or occasionally targeted now extinct megafauna, and in the absence of any evidence of significant human modification to the environment (for example, the intentional setting of wildfires or other forms of habitat modification) or the introduction of a novel pathogen, their role in the extinction event becomes tenuous. Favoring interpretations of Clovis subsistence behavior that includes a more diverse mix of plant and small game resources and more regionally differentiated diets, the extinction of Pleistocene fauna is attributed to rapid climate change.[18] A brief period of rapid cooling known as the Younger Dryas coincides with both the onset of extinction and the transition from Clovis to Folsom in the archaeological record. It remains a contentious point of debate whether Early Paleoindians of the Americas contributed to or simply witnessed the demise of the mammoths, mastodon, ground sloths, and other megafauna. After Clovis, Paleoindians focused their hunting efforts on the remaining large-boned species as American fauna evolved into their contemporary range of species diversity and habitats known from the Holocene.

Continuously traversing into new landscapes and encountering new subsistence and raw material resources, Clovis peoples may have rapidly hunted and gathered their way from Beringia to Tierra del Fuego, populating the Americas and acquiring regional adaptations along the way. This "Clovis first" model, initially developed in the 1930s and largely accepted by the 1960s, interpreted Clovis populations as terrestrial mammal hunters who traveled through the ice-free corridor and quickly expanded southward in pursuit of prey. While it remains a plausible and supported option today, many archaeologists have begun to question the fundamental components of

---

17 Nicole M. Waguespack and Todd A. Surovell, "Clovis hunting strategies, or how to make out on plentiful resources," *American Antiquity* 68 (2003), 333–52.

18 Tom D. Dillehey, *The Settlement of the Americas: A New Prehistory* (New York. Basic Books, 2000).

this scenario. Clovis undoubtedly represents the first continuous occupation of many North American regions but it remains unclear if Clovis represents the development and spread of an *in situ* cultural development by an existing North American population(s) or if Clovis peoples were truly the first to colonize the continent. Some archaeologists also favor a coastal route through the Americas over the ice free-corridor.[19] Suggesting that colonists could maintain a degree of habitat consistency and reliable resource access by preferentially occupying the coastline, Clovis is then cast as a later inland development of an earlier colonization event by coastally oriented foragers.[20] Rising sea levels at the end of the Pleistocene have submerged any sites that may have been left on or in the immediate vicinity of the coast. Some coastal sites, such as Quebrada Jaguay in Peru (Map 19.1), do indicate the use of marine resources during the Late Pleistocene.

The lack of spatiotemporal trends in the Early Paleoindian record remains problematic and lends credence to the probability that the time range of Clovis will be pushed further back in time with new discoveries and / or that evidence of a pre-Clovis culture will be found. No clearly discernible patterns in the dates of Early Paleoindian sites indicating the entry route and dispersal trajectory are currently evident. Dated cultural deposits from within the ice-free corridor and near-coast localities are exceedingly rare and post-date the earliest Clovis sites. Analyses of Early Paleoindian artifact morphology also produce equivocal results. Notably, the earliest artifact assemblages from Alaska, where colonists would necessarily enter from Beringia, present no clear cultural affinities to Clovis. Isolated fluted points have been found in the region, but the oldest reliably dated artifacts from excavated deposits are of the Nenana complex.[21] Characterized as a predominately flake and blade industry, Nenana complex assemblages contain large bifacial knives, retouched blade tools, endscrapers, pieces esquilles, and diagnostic teardrop to triangular-shaped projectile points (that is, Chindadn points). Nenana may

19 E. James Dixon, *Bones, Boats and Bison: Archeology and the First Colonization of Western North America* (Albuquerque. University of New Mexico Press, 1999).

20 David G. Anderson and J. Christopher Gillam, "Paleoindian colonization of the Americas: Implications from an examination of physiography, demography, and artifact distribution," *American Antiquity* 65 (2000), 43–66; and Jon M. Erlandson, Torben C. Rick, Todd J. Braje, Molly Casperson, Brendan Culleton, Brian Fulfrost, Tracy Garcia, Daniel A. Guthrie, Nicholas Jew, Douglas J. Kennett, Madonna L. Moss, Leslie Reeder, Craig Skinner, Jack Watts, and Lauren Willis, "Paleoindian seafaring, maritime technologies, and coastal foraging on California's Channel Islands," *Science* 331 (2011), 1,181–5.

21 Michael R. Bever, "An overview of Alaskan Late Pleistocene archaeology: Historical themes and current perspectives," *Journal of World Prehistory* 15 (2001), 125–91.

date to as early as 13,400–13,900 YBP but most sites are coeval if not slightly younger than Clovis.

Blade tools are common components of Upper Paleolithic technologies of Siberia and some Clovis assemblages. Broadly similar morphological attributes shared between Nenana and Clovis in the manufacture and style of flake and blade tools can also be construed as reflecting an ancestral cultural relationship to populations in Western Beringia.[22] If Nenana is an extension of Late Pleistocene lithic industries of northeastern Eurasia and the progenitor of Clovis, then a general trend of increasing reliance on bifacial technology occurred as colonists moved south, perhaps culminating in an established tradition of fluting projectile points. Linking similarities in material culture to genetic ancestry is not straightforward and the temporal and demographic relationship between Clovis and Nenana remains unclear. Genetic and/or skeletal analyses can potentially clarify the relationship among Early Pleistocene technologies but too few biological samples have yet been found. An extremely small sample (fewer than ten individuals) of human skeletal material is reliably dated to the Late Pleistocene and/or associated with Early Paleoindian artifacts. The paucity of early human remains is typical of mobile foraging populations and may indicate that Paleoindian funerary practices did not involve burial. The skeletal sample exhibits little morphological similarity among specimens and few resemblances to any single contemporary population.[23] Genetic studies of contemporary native populations from throughout the Americas have also produced disparate results regarding the timing and route of the initial migration but do consistently identify Siberia as the likely source of origin.[24] In addition to these evidentiary gaps in the archaeological record a growing body of sites pre-dating Clovis is reported from both North and South America.

22 Thomas D. Hamilton and Ted Goebel, "The Late Pleistocene peopling of Alaska," in Robson Bonnichsen and Karen L. Turnmire (eds.), *Ice Age Peoples of North America: Environments, Origins, and Adaptations of the First Americans* (Orono. Center for the Study of the First Americans, 1999), pp. 156–99.

23 C. Loring Brace, *et al.*, "Peopling of the New World," in C. Michael Barton, Geoffrey A. Clark, David R. Yesner, and Georges A. Pearson (eds.), *The Settlement of the American Continents: A Multidisciplinary Approach to Human Biogeography* (Tucson. University of Arizona Press, 2004).

24 Bonnie Pitblado, "A tale of two migrations: Reconciling recent biological and archaeological evidence for the Pleistocene peopling of the Americas," *Journal of Archaeological Research* 19 (2011), 327–75.

The pre-Clovis archaeological record

Sites purportedly pre-dating Clovis are received skeptically and subject to considerable, perhaps inordinate, validation criteria. Numerous pre-Clovis sites have emerged as contenders but few Paleoindian archaeologists agree as to which sites and artifacts they accept as definitive evidence of a pre-Clovis colonization event. Currently, a human coprolite from the Paisley Cave site (Map 19.1) is widely accepted as the earliest evidence of human occupation. Dated to approximately 14,000 YBP it is not associated with diagnostic artifacts, so it could be representative of Clovis or an earlier population of migrants or non-colonizing explorers. Since Clovis was identified and defined, claims of pre-Clovis aged sites became ubiquitous throughout North and South America. Often lacking chronological control, found in disturbed contexts, and containing equivocal artifacts most of these sites have struggled to gain widespread professional acceptance. With the reporting of excavations at the Monte Verde site in Chile in the 1990s, claims for pre-Clovis occupation gained considerable support if not outright acceptance by many archaeologists.[25] Cultural deposits dated to between 14,650 and 15,600 YBP remain controversial, but Monte Verde, located over 1,500 kilometers from Beringia, provided the first pre-Clovis aged site with a distinctly non-Clovis artifact assemblage to challenge the Clovis-first model.

Sites in North America such as Meadowcroft, Buttermilk Creek, and Topper all contain potentially pre-Clovis aged artifacts (Map 19.1).[26] Meadowcroft, a multicomponent rockshelter in Pennsylvania, is a long-standing contender for evidence of a pre-Clovis occupation. Artifacts in its lowest levels pre-date 14,000 YBP and if verified provide a second instance of early cave use. The Buttermilk Creek site in Texas (Map 19.1) contains a lithic assemblage below diagnostic Clovis artifacts. The pre-Clovis level contains a mix of blade, flake, and bifacial tools from deposits potentially dated to 15,000 YBP. The Topper site in Georgia produced an assemblage of over 1,000 small flakes and microblades. Like Buttermilk Creek, the early material was found

25 Tom D. Dillehay, *Monte Verde: A Late Pleistocene Settlement in Chile* (Washington, D.C.: Smithsonian Institution Press, 1997).
26 J. M. Adovasio, J. Donahue, D. R. Pedler, and R. Stuckenrath, "Two decades of debate on Meadowcroft Rockshelter," *North American Archaeology* 19 (1998), 317–41; Michael R. Waters, Steven L. Forman, Thomas A. Jennings, Lee C. Nordt, Steven G. Driese, Joshua M. Feinberg, Joshua L. Keene, Jessi Halligan, Anna Lindquist, James Pierson, Charles T. Hallmark, Michael B. Collins, and James E. Wiederhold, "The Buttermilk Creek complex and the origins of Clovis at the Debra L. Friedkin Site, Texas," *Science* 331 (2011), 1,599–603; and Albert C. Goodyear, "Results of the 1999 Allendale Paleoindian Expedition," *Legacy* 4 (1999), 8–13.

below a Clovis occupation level and may exceed 15,000 YBP. Concerns about stratigraphic disturbance and inaccurate dates have plagued interpretation of these sites.

In addition to Monte Verde, possible South American pre-Clovis aged sites include Taima-Taima in Venezuela and Pedra Furada in Brazil. Both of these sites have lithic artifacts derived from deposits dated in excess of 15,000 YBP, but like North American sites have been accused of lacking stratigraphic integrity resulting in erroneous dates and artifact identifications. The Toca da Tira Peia in Brazil has produced a small assemblage of quartzite cobble and flake tools that reportedly date to 20,000 YBP.[27] Unfortunately, or tellingly, pre-Clovis deposits often lack material suitable for radiocarbon dating and researchers rely instead on optically stimulated luminescence dates, a less preferred dating method for Late Pleistocene aged materials. Which, if any, of these sites provide indisputable evidence of a distinct pre-Clovis population of colonizers remains unresolved.[28] Many archaeologists accept one or more of these sites as evidence of a pre-Clovis presence in the Americas but it is unclear at what point in the colonization process human populations obtained a sufficient size or duration of occupation to attain archaeological visibility.

Early Paleoindian occupation of the Americas

In North America, Folsom is the most widespread and technologically distinct Paleoindian population following Clovis. Found throughout the Rocky Mountain and Great Plains region of North America, Folsom technology is world renowned for a unique style of projectile point. Similar to Clovis, Folsom projectile points are fluted, but with flake scar channels that extend almost the entire length of the point (Figure 19.1). Removing such long flutes is notoriously difficult and channel flakes are considered diagnostic artifacts of the period. Associated artifacts include extremely thin bifaces, an array of unifacially retouched flake tools, morphologically distinct spurred endscrapers, and delicate tools for engraving dated from approximately 12,800 to 11,900 YBP.[29] In regions beyond the grassland-dominated region of

---

27 Christelle Lahaye, et al., "Human occupation in South America by 20,000 BC: The Toca da Tira Peia site, Piauí, Brazil," *Journal of Archaeological Science* 40/6 (2013), 2,840–7.

28 Tom D. Dillehay, "The Late Pleistocene cultures of South America," *Evolutionary Anthropology* 7 (1999), 206–16.

29 Daniel S. Amick (ed.), *Folsom Lithic Technology: Explorations in Structure and Variation* (Ann Arbor, MI. International Monographs in Prehistory, 1999).

Folsom sites, a variety of regional Paleoindian point forms appear. Folsom and contemporaneous peoples are interpreted to have led highly nomadic lives, continuing the general high mobility hunting-based foraging lifestyle of Clovis in post-Pleistocene America.

The Early Paleoindian archaeological record of the Americas documents a hunting and gathering way of life in an environment with no modern parallels. Clovis, and perhaps earlier populations, migrated into the unfamiliar landscapes of a continent rapidly undergoing environmental change as the Pleistocene came to a close. As new sites are discovered and the chronology refined, the route of entry, dispersal pattern, and growth rate of the colonizing groups will become clearer. No single site, artifact, or radiocarbon date can explain the cultural and demographic process of colonization, and the pre-Clovis archaeological record currently consists of a wide variety of far-flung site locations, disparate artifact assemblages, and dates that lack clear indications of when and how the migration process proceeded.[30] Clovis remains the most consistent and widespread cultural phenomenon identified in the Americas. Clovis is likely older than current dates reveal and may be derived from a population with a wholly distinct technological culture; it remains, however, the prototypical founding population of the American archaeological record.

FURTHER READING

Adovasio, J. M., J. Donahue, D. R. Pedler, and R. Stuckenrath, "Two decades of debate on Meadowcroft Rockshelter," *North American Archaeology* 19 (1998), 317–41.

Amick, Daniel S. (ed.), *Folsom Lithic Technology: Explorations in Structure and Variation*, Ann Arbor, MI: International Monographs in Prehistory, 1999.

Anderson, David G., and J. Christopher Gillam, "Paleoindian colonization of the Americas: Implications from an examination of physiography, demography, and artifact distribution," *American Antiquity* 65 (2000), 43–66.

Anderson, David G., D. Shane Miller, Derek T. Anderson, Stephen J. Yerka, J. Christopher Gillam, Erik N. Johanson, and Ashley Smallwood, "2010: Current status and findings: Archaeology of Eastern North America," *PIDBA (Paleoindian Database of the Americas)* 38 (2010), 63–90.

Barton, C. Michael, Geoffrey A. Clark, David R. Yesner, and Georges A. Pearson (eds.), *The Settlement of the American Continents: A Multidisciplinary Approach to Human Biogeography*, Tucson: University of Arizona Press, 2004.

Bever, Michael R., "An overview of Alaskan Late Pleistocene archaeology: Historical themes and current perspectives," *Journal of World Prehistory* 15 (2001), 125–91.

30 Nicole M. Waguespack, "Why we're still arguing about the Pleistocene occupation of the Americas," *Evolutionary Anthropology* 16 (2007), 63–74.

Brace, C. Loring. *et al.*, "Peopling of the New World," in C. Michael Barton, Geoffrey A. Clark, David R. Yesner, and Georges A. Pearson (eds.), *The Settlement of the American Continents*, Tucson: University of Arizona Press, 2004.

Bradley, Bruce A., Michael B. Collins, and Andrew Hemmings, *Clovis Technology*, Ann Arbor, MI: International Monographs in Prehistory, 2010.

Burney, David A., and Timothy F. Flannery, "Fifty millennia of catastrophic extinctions after human contact," *Trends in Ecology and Evolution* 20 (2005), 395–401.

Collins, Michael B., *Clovis Blade Technology*, Austin: University of Texas Press, 1999.

Dillehay, Tom D., "The Late Pleistocene cultures of South America," *Evolutionary Anthropology* 7 (1999), 206–16.

Monte Verde: A Late Pleistocene Settlement in Chile, Washington, D.C.: Smithsonian Institution Press, 1997.

The Settlement of the Americas: A New Prehistory, New York. Basic Books, 2000.

Erlandson, Jon M., Torben C. Rick, Todd J. Braje, Molly Casperson, Brendan Culleton, Brian Fulfrost, Tracy Garcia, Daniel A. Guthrie, Nicholas Jew, Douglas J. Kennett, Madonna L. Moss, Leslie Reeder, Craig Skinner, Jack Watts, and Lauren Willis, "Paleoindian seafaring, maritime technologies, and coastal foraging on California's Channel Islands," *Science* 331 (2011), 1,181–5.

Frison, George C., "Experimental use of Clovis weaponry and tools on African elephants," *American Antiquity* 54 (1989), 766–84.

Goebel, Ted, Michael R. Waters, and Dennis H. O'Rourke, "The Late Pleistocene dispersal of modern humans in the Americas," *Science* 319 (2008), 1,497–502.

Goodyear, Albert C., "Results of the 1999 Allendale Paleoindian Expedition," *Legacy* 4 (1999), 8–13.

Graf, Kelly E., and Dave N. Schmidt (eds.), *Paleoindian or Paleoarchaic? Great Basin Human Ecology at the Pleistocene–Holocene Transition*, Salt Lake: University of Utah Press, 2010.

Grayson, Donald K., and David J. Meltzer, "Clovis hunting and large mammal extinction: A critical review of the evidence," *Journal of World Prehistory* 16 (2002), 313–59.

"North American overkill continued?", *Journal of Archaeological Science* 31 (2004), 133–6.

Hamilton, Marcus J., and Briggs Buchanan, "Spatial gradients in Clovis-age radiocarbon dates across North America suggest rapid colonization from the North," *Proceedings of the National Academy of Science* 104 (2007), 15,625–30.

Hamilton, Thomas D., and Ted Goebel, "The Late Pleistocene peopling of Alaska," in Robson Bonnichsen and Karen L. Turnmire (eds.), *Ice Age Peoples of North America: Environments, Origins, and Adaptations of the First Americans*, Orono: Center for the Study of the First Americans, 1999, pp. 156–99.

Haynes, C. Vance, Jr., and Bruce B. Huckell (eds.), *Murray Springs: A Clovis Site with Multiple Activity Areas in the San Pedro Valley, Arizona*, Tucson: University of Arizona Press, 2007.

Hester, James J., *Blackwater Locality No. 1: A Stratified Early Man Site in Eastern New Mexico*, Taos: Fort Burgwin Research Center, 1972.

Hoffecker, John. F., *A Prehistory of the North: Human Settlement of the Higher Latitude*, New Brunswick, NJ. Rutgers University Press, 2005.

Kelly, Robert L., and Lawrence C. Todd, "Coming into the country: Early Paleoindian hunting and mobility," *American Antiquity* 53 (1988), 23–4.

Kilby, J. David, "*An investigation of Clovis caches: Content, function, and technological organization,*" unpublished Ph.D. dissertation, University of New Mexico (2008).

Meltzer, David J., *First Peoples in a New World: Colonizing Ice Age America*, Berkeley. University of California Press, 2009.

Folsom: New Archaeological Investigations of a Classic Paleoindian Bison Kill, Berkeley. University of California Press, 2006.

"The seventy-year itch: Controversies over human antiquity and their resolution," *Journal of Archaeological Science* 61(2005), 433–68.

Morrow, Juliet E., and Toby A. Morrow, "Geographic variation in fluted projectile points: A hemispheric perspective," *American Antiquity* 64 (1999), 215–31.

Pitblado, Bonnie, "A tale of two migrations: Reconciling recent biological and archaeological evidence for the Pleistocene peopling of the Americas," *Journal of Archaeological Research* 19 (2011), 327–75.

Ripple, William J., and Blaire van Valkenburgh, "Linking top-down forces to the Pleistocene megafaunal extinctions," *BioScience* 60 (2010), 516–26.

Stanford, Dennis J., and Bruce A. Bradley, *Across Atlantic Ice: The Origin of America's Clovis Culture*, Berkeley: University of California Press, 2012.

Thomas, M., P. Gilbert, Dennis L. Jenkins, Anders Götherstrom, Nuria Naveran, Juan J. Sanchez, Michael Hofreiter, Philip Francis Thomsen, Jonas Binladen, Thomas F. G. Higham, Robert. M. Yohe II, Robert Parr, Linda Scott Cummings, and Eske Willerslev, "DNA from pre-Clovis human coprolites in Oregon, North America," *Science* 320 (2008), 786–9.

Waguespack, Nicole M., "The organization of male and female labor in foraging societies: Implications for Early Paleoindian archaeology," *American Anthropologist* 107 (2005), 666–76.

"Why we're still arguing about the Pleistocene occupation of the Americas," *Evolutionary Anthropology* 16 (2007), 63–74.

Waguespack, Nicole M., and Todd A. Surovell, "Clovis hunting strategies, or how to make out on plentiful resources," *American Antiquity* 68 (2003), 333–52.

Waters, Michael R., and Thomas W. Stafford, "Redefining the age of Clovis: Implications for the peopling of the Americas," *Science* 315 (2007), 1,122–6.

Waters, Michael R., Steven L. Forman, Thomas A. Jennings, Lee C. Nordt, Steven G. Driese, Joshua M. Feinberg, Joshua L. Keene, Jessi Halligan, Anna Lindquist, James Pierson, Charles T. Hallmark, Michael B. Collins, and James E. Wiederhold, "The Buttermilk Creek complex and the origins of Clovis at the Debra L. Friedkin Site, Texas," *Science* 331 (2011), 1,599–603.

Index

Figures, tables, and maps are denoted in bold typeface

Index

Made in the USA
Coppell, TX
24 March 2021